An Ordinary Nun

Copyright © 2002
Linda Roy M. Cross

Library of Congress Card Number: 2002092350

ISBN 0-9718824-0-1

First printing April 2002

Copies may be ordered:
5777 N. Via Amable
Tucson, Arizona 85750-1213

Printed in the U.S.A by
Morris Publishing
3212 East Highway 30,
Kearney, NE 68847
1-800-650-7888

An Ordinary Nun

The Life and Letters of
Sister Veronica Mary
(Ila Mae) Roy, CSJ

LINDA ROY M. CROSS

An Ordinary Nun
The Life and Letters of Sister Veronica (Ila Mae) Roy CSJ

Cover design by Chip Cole
Production by Mike Camp and Chip Cole

Cataloging-in-Publication Data

Cross, Linda L. Roy Monarchi, 1945-
    An ordinary nun; the life and letters of Sister Veronica Mary Roy, CSJ, (Member of Sisters of St. Joseph, Concordia, Kansas.) Tucson, Arizona, March 2002.
    497 pg. Photos. Includes index and endnotes

    1. Roy, Sister Veronica Mary, CSJ, Ila Mae, 1939-1995 — Biography. 2. Sisters of Saint Joseph (Concordia, KS) — Biographies. 3. French Canadians in Kansas. 4. Kansas (Rooks County). 5. Women in Kansas. 6. Roy (John and Olive) Family. I. Title.

Dedicated to:

My husband Randy Cross.
And my sons David Monarchi and Christopher Cross.
They have endured with me many years of
preoccupation with this work of love.

The retired Sisters of St. Joseph at Concordia, Kansas.
They will be the beneficiaries of any profits from the sale of this book.

ACKNOWLEDGMENTS

I am deeply indebted to my brother, Father Duane Roy, OSB. Over the years, from start to finish, he provided continuing support. A major contributor with his own personal anecdotes, he reviewed the manuscript and offered invaluable clarifications and insights into the world of the religious life with his steady stream of e-mails from Brazil and Kansas. He also shared his substantial collection of personal letters and photographs.

A special thank you to my sister, Cheryl Roy Calvin, who also provided letters and was always available to rehash tedious details. Additionally, I thank my siblings Kenneth, Allan (deceased), Roger and Rodney Roy and Joan Rader, and their families, for their contributions.

Many thanks go to Shirley Morin Riney for helping to calm the tone, and to a Martha and two Marys: Martha Kessler, who encouraged me beyond the rough stages, and helped me see my way to the finish; Mary Rowley for her invaluable grammatical editing; and Mary Feisley for her wisdom. I thank CSJ Sisters Patricia McLennon and Christine Doman for their gentle reviews and Sisters Diane Brin and Ginger Pearl, CSJ, for their heart felt contributions.

My thanks for additional contributions from the parishioners of St. John's Parish in Logan; St. Joseph parishioners in New Almelo; and Christ the King parishioners in WaKeeney, Kansas: Gertrude McNeive, Geneva Long, Betty Otter, Bernadine Diederich, Rosalia Stephens, Verna Flax, Marie Billinger, Rosann Felder, Marion Parke, Elaine Newcomer, Rosemary Bollig, and Mary Aschenbrenner. My gratitude to relatives and friends: Bill and Jeanette Hinz, Paul and Zella Rickard, Mel and Marguerite Desmarteau, Eunice Berland, Mareida Newell, RoseLee Benoit, Vula Roy, Irene Morin, Eleanor Bellerive, Valerie VanLoenen, Arlene Gosselin, Marjorie Biery and Merle Grover (both deceased), Jean Grover Lindsey, Lorabell Arbogast, Glenn and Gwen Mitchum, Wendy Shelquist and Clara Chamberlain. My thanks for the contributions from CSJ Sisters Vera Meis, Carm Thibault, Esther Pineda, Frederic Eilert, Anna Marie Broxterman, Rosalyn Juenemann, Helen Hake, Joseph Ellen Divel, Rosemary Farrell, Mary Kevin Walker, Margaret Schreck, and Marilyn Diane Carpenter, OSB, and to Fathers Dan Sheetz, C.K. McCarren and Gilbert Wolters, OSB. I thank Allen Cunningham of Mi Nidito Children-to-Children, for his insight into children's grief issues.

I also wish to thank those supporters, who never knew my sister and, nevertheless, cheered me on never doubting I would finish the manuscript. I especially thank Lina Gavino, who provided untold hours of respite childcare during 1993-1996, and Chriss Rainey, a northern Virginia neighbor who first urged me on. I owe a large measure of gratitude to Chip Cole and Mike Camp for their technical expertise with the electronic layout of this book.

This book could not have come into light without Sister Veronica's own attention to detail. Furthermore, her two genealogical books, *Our Saindon Cousins* and *Ma Famille* provided the gist of the chapters on our ancestors, and is a constant resource.

As an important side note, I did not first set out to write a book after the tragic death of my sister. Rather, it was a therapeutic way of working through grief. I accumulated information in the early stages, not always citing sources in a scholarly fashion. My apologies to those whose names I have inadvertently omitted.

The judgments and opinions expressed, in this book, are entirely the author's own. I have tried not to be deliberately disruptive, defamatory, disparaging or offensive in any way to any group, or to any single person.

Foreword

Sister Veronica Roy, CSJ, was a dedicated servant of the Lord in her prayerful presence in many parishes throughout the Diocese of Salina as she touched the lives of many people.

Her ministry as a Sister of St. Joseph brought her into contact with people in the reality of their living. In education and pastoral ministry, in service to the poor and needy, and in many other ways she was able to bring the presence of Christ into the challenges of life.

I have been involved in significant events in the Roy family. I was present at the funeral Mass of Olive Roy, the mother of Sister Veronica. I was also present at the silver jubilee mass of Fr. Duane Roy, OSB. In 1995 I was present for Sister Veronica's funeral Mass.

As you read and meditate upon these pages depicting the life of an "ordinary nun" you will come to know Jesus Christ and His love for all of us. Her example and witness to Christ gave her the strength to have an impact on the lives of many people in their journey of faith.

Let us continued to pray for more such vocations to the priesthood and religious life.

+George K. Fitzsimons
Sincerely yours in Christ,

Most Rev. George K. Fitzsimons
Bishop of Salina

Preface

*"Throughout the centuries great stories have been written
about ordinary people who become extraordinary by dealing well
with what they could not perfect."*
—Sister Joan Chittister, OSB. *There is a Season*

To explain the title of this book, *An Ordinary Nun*, Sister Veronica was canonically a Sister, and not a Nun. However, I use these two terms interchangeably, as Religious Women themselves do.

For the sake of clarification, the title "Sister" is capitalized in this book, when referring to a Religious Woman actively involved in apostolic works in the church and society, just as is Nun — one living the cloistered life with little or no contact with society. I also capitalize Bishop, Priest and Monk, as well as the Habit — the distinctive long black garb Sister Veronica once wore. Order, meaning the religious group to which they belong, is also capitalized, as is the religious Congregation of Sisters of St. Joseph Community (CSJ), to distinguish it from a neighborhood community.

To those who are not familiar with the Roman Catholic faith, I repeatedly mention in this book the Second Vatican Council, which took place in Rome from 1962 to 1965, the outcome of which created massive changes for Catholics. When I refer to pre-Vatican II, that is the time before changes occurred.

This biography of a Sister is written through the eyes and language of a laywoman. I am the biological sister of Sister Veronica Roy, CSJ and a Benedictine Monk, Father Duane Roy OSB — Ila Mae and Gary, as I refer to them in childhood. I have other siblings, too — Kenneth, (Ronald and Allan, both deceased), Joan, Roger, Cheryl and Rodney. People often ask me, "What is it like to be from a family of ten? And to have two siblings in the religious life?" Both are wonderful experiences — fascinating and humbling.

After Sister Veronica's death, I wanted to know more about Religious Life for women. I found books written by women who had left the convent — some disgruntled and biased. Those did not hold an accurate portrayal of my sister's life. I delved into the four hundred or more letters she wrote to my siblings and me. She helped me reconstruct her story. I reread those family remembrances that she wrote, contributing significantly to a collection of childhood stories to present to our Mother, as well as her additional personal recollections to Mother's biography, both of which I authored.

In my task, I found that she left another source of rich information. Sister Veronica wrote her own Life Review for the 1883-1983 Centenary of the Sisters of St. Joseph in Kansas. However, a Sister living the "hidden life" does not write her own life story in intimate detail. Perhaps that is why, in her premonition of death, she neatly arranged a tidy package, which, in her mystical way, she bequeathed to me. She also gave me power of attorney.

Through a meticulous and organized assortment of treasures in a box of her saved letters, photographs, calendars and clippings, she continued to reveal to me her complex life, her true self — not the idealized one — as she persisted to walk this holy path. As my writings developed into a full-blown manuscript, I relived many of her distressful moments. It began to feel like an invasion of privacy. It is important to remember these were not private journals I had tapped. She was telling her life story to us, in bits and pieces, as she lived it. I merely "connected the dots."

I began to understand as she repeatedly said, "People don't understand us Religious. They try to put us on a pedestal." She did not want this "romanticized portrayal."

Nathaniel Hawthorne purposely destroyed love letters his wife wrote when she was his fiancée. Their idealized image of each other prompted the burning. Like Hawthorne, in those earlier days grieving my sister's sudden death, I, too, wanted to guard her idealized saint-like image, as did the rest of our large family.

At least one person who had put Sister Veronica on a pedestal said, "I don't think she would have wanted all this published." On the other hand, an elderly, crone-like Sister told me, "Yes! Put it all in. It shows that she, and we, too, are merely human with frailties and weakness." Another CSJ, relating to her own difficult experiences said, "These occurrences she had were 'rock polishers' rubbing off the rough edges, which make each of us smooth and gentle."

This written account documents the life of a "white martyr" — one ordinary woman who wanted to be a Catholic Religious Sister, and was all her adult life. Ila Mae/Sister Veronica was six years older than I. Telling her story after her death, I came to understand her more. I perceived her day-to-day struggles, as she adhered to her vows, lived to the fullest the Maxims of Perfection and came to embody the CSJ charisms. I came to honor my cherished sister, not as a saint, but as an ordinary woman as she wished to be viewed. I am sure she tried to live a saintly life, and in so doing became extraordinary. Her work was noble; her life sometimes incomprehensible, if not misunderstood. Many may wonder, "Why?"

In contrast to Hawthorne, I remove the rose-colored glasses to reveal the realistic account of her individual story, through my own interpretation of facts, events and motives. I do this, however, not without hesitation, not without emotional pain and not without deep personal anguish.

Sister Veronica's human drama is marked with loss and life-long anxiety. Hearing impairment, introversion and difficulties with relationships hindered her. She responded early in life to a call to religious life. She possessed a championing and pioneer spirit, completely dedicated to her religious vows, her CSJ Community, her family and its history.

While she was not famous, the lifestyle she chose is noteworthy. With the onset of the new millennium, the number of Sisters appears to be dwindling into extinction. That apostolic way of life seems to be phasing out and may all but disappear in the next few decades. Or who knows, it may flourish again.

I have neither meant to exploit Sister Veronica's life, nor the lives of other Sisters in any way. Rather I continue the storytelling she set out to do, which she found healing. In her forewarning of imminent death, she mystically laid the groundwork, in her compassionate ways.

Readers may respond with admiration to her saintly qualities; others with dismay and disdain at her human frailty. However, it is comforting to know she was not afraid to brave the truth in accepting her weaknesses and faults.

Some parts of her story are painful: "an unreal life for a Nun," as she once said. Where there is pain and hurt, forgiveness heals. This story is one of forgiveness. It may offer an opportunity for understanding and forgiveness for us who transgressed against her in our humanness, and allow her to forgive us also. To insist that she remain on a pedestal, however, would be wrong.

Most importantly, this story is grounded in the consoling truth of the resurrection, and recognizes her devotion and love for Jesus Christ. It tries to show how she unwaveringly witnessed this. Her life was unique and different, but perhaps there is a common thread, with surprising similarities, which weaves throughout the lives of other Women of Faith.

May this one ordinary woman rest in the peace of the Risen Lord. Amen.

Linda Roy Monarchi Cross
Tucson, Arizona
March 19, 2002
The Feast of St. Joseph

CONTENTS

PART I: BACKGROUND HISTORY

PART II: 1949-1958 ILA MAE'S YOUTHFUL SEARCH

PART III: 1959-1968 WEARING THE HABIT

PART IV: 1968-1980 BELVIDERE YEARS — TRANSITIONS

PART V: 1981-1995 THE WAY OF A PIONEER

Chapter One

"Who is this valiant woman, this woman of prayer, this Martha and Mary, intertwined in balance?" Sister Ginger Pearl eulogized her friend of over thirty years. *"Who is this woman, this blend of quiet presence with informed action? Who is this rock of faith and gentle love; this salt of the earth and yeast for bread; this earthen vessel, freely molded; this generous heart and gem of goodness giving, 'The More?'"*

On the Wednesday night of November 15, 1995 the telephone jolted me from sleep in northern Virginia. I had a foreboding sense of doom.

My brother Kenneth Roy, "K.R." as he is known in law enforcement nationwide, was trained to be calm and factual. "Sister Veronica was killed around 8:30 tonight," he had to repeat several times.

It seemed he went on nonstop: "She was driving back to the Concordia Motherhouse from Salina a 1980 Pontiac tried to pass two semis it came into her lane and hit her nearly direct head-on she was pronounced dead at the scene it was a cold night not snowing visibility was good three teenagers just got in a hurry going to a bar in Salina."[1]

Within minutes, Ottawa County EMT rescue units were on the scene checking for vital signs.[2] Sister Veronica was visible in the driver's seat, still strapped with seat belts. Extrication was required. Kansas troopers Goodness and Knopp took the investigative fatality report, assisted by Caldwell and Cates, who helped gather the contents scattered, from her Corsica, along the darkened highway. Reports from the truckers and other witnesses were taken, too. Her wristwatch was later found among the wreckage. The crystal was smashed as the hands pointed to 8:37.

In the daylight at the Baccus towing station near Minneapolis, Kansas, gruesome photographs were snapped of the two mangled cars, as insurance adjustors require. Once again another traffic accident, on the treacherous stretch of U.S. 81 northbound from Salina, claimed two more victims. One loss was my sister.

The next days were a blur, but the question Sister Ginger delivered at the funeral vigil continued to haunt me during the months and years ahead. "Who, indeed, was Sister Veronica? Who was this dear woman? My sister. My glue. Who was Ila Mae, as some schoolmates from childhood continued to call her.

In my grief I wanted to know more. It was clear to me she was different and complex. She publicly professed lifetime vows of poverty, chastity and obedience. Her life style was simple. Her clothes were plain; house and furnishings were common. There were her birth order, childhood responsibilities and teenage years to consider. Her hearing loss and anxieties complicated things, too.

Furthermore, after ten years in religious life a changing world made its impact. She opted for institutional living, entering the religious life in the "Confident Church." Gradually, she moved into non-institutional living, and spent the remaining twenty-six years in the "Confusing Church," as sociologist Father Andrew Greeley calls it, making a distinction between the pre- and post-Vatican II eras.

"I always thought when the next move comes along I would start using the name Sister Ila Mae," she wrote. "Not sure I could handle it as my identity, however. I still relate strongly to Veronica. I was always afraid I would not come across strong enough as a Sister, to those who knew me before as Ila Mae, and they would think I left religious life." However in 1990, the logical time when she moved to a different town to take another position, she did not make the name change.

She was the fourth of ten children, born to John and Olive Morin Roy, on December 28, 1939. "My earliest childhood memory was when I took the baby bottle from Gary, my little brother, and hid with it behind our wood-burning stove. Sometimes I took the bottle from the infant, Joan, too."

With only thirteen months separating the younger births of Gary and Joan, both required bottle-feeding for a while. This added to the workload of our busy mother, not to mention the never-ending cloth diapers, which needed to be washed and hung outside to dry.

"My second earliest childhood memory was when I was barely four and a half," Ila Mae said. "I have always believed I recall the day [my second oldest brother] Ronald gave me a 'horsey-back' ride. The eight-year-old carried me around and around the living room, from sofa to chair, from chair to chair, as his smiling face, sprinkled with freckles, beamed from ear to ear. During all this fun, he crawled upon the sofa, and hung on the wall a picture of the Assumption of Mary — the one with the angels around her. I was told Ronald died a few days after that."

Is it possible for Ila Mae to have reversed her first and second earliest childhood memories? A grieving child needs comforting and often regresses to infant-like behavior, crying for the bottle again. A young child has no ability to sense time and space in dealing with severe loss. Ila Mae carried her grief for years, never giving it full expression. Throughout life she never felt able to express her depth of feeling. Perhaps it was her openness to mystery and awe in her approach to life that sustained her.

Well meaning, and solid in her religious belief, most likely the extent Mother talked about the incident was, "Ronald was taken to Heaven," which added to Ila Mae's expressed fear, and feeling of abandonment by her favorite brother playmate. Perhaps Mother pointed to the picture on the wall and said that is where Ronald is now.

> *"Rejoice with the Mother of God,*
> *With angels and saints,*
> *And celebrate this great feast:*
> *The Assumption of the Virgin Mary."*

Childhood memories help form a person spiritually, and it is interesting that even at so young an age she took note of a piece of art associated with this traumatic time. It was probably "The Assumption" (of the Blessed Virgin) by the Flemish painter, Peter Paul Rubens (1577-1640). Six years after Ronald's death, Pope Pius XII declared the Assumption a doctrine of faith, in 1950, to bring humanity back to the people following the horrors of World War I and II.

August 15, the date of the Feast of the Assumption, and a holy day of obligation since the fifth century, has been a significant one for this family. Our parents first met on this date in 1930; ten years later, in 1940, it was possibly the conception date of Gary/Father Duane. It was the birth date of their granddaughter, Denise Rader Mooney in 1965, and in 1992 it was the start of Ila Mae/Sister Veronica's second genealogy book that she authored, *Ma Famille*.

Kenneth, the eldest of ten siblings, and nineteen months older then Ronald, remembered him as a big kid, size-wise. Both he and Allan recalled their brother as, "all boy, knowing no fear and full of mischief." He was mechanical, too. Allan added, "Both Ronald and I got into trouble with Dad for taking the carburetor apart on his DeSoto."

This lively child added a lot of psychic energy to the family with his happy demeanor, wide grin, sturdy frame and red hair. Ronald probably would have grown to look a lot like Grandpa Roy. With her ginger-colored freckles, Ila Mae was pleased to resemble them both. She even captured a reddish tint to her hair in her final months of life.

Ronald drowned in the summer of 1944 while crossing the swollen Sand Creek, just south of home. The pain of loss for our parents was immense. It was not until thirty-seven years later that Mother could bring herself to share the details with her children and even then, she still couldn't talk about the tragedy without shedding tears. She said, "On that terrible day, it was hot, and the boys wanted to wade in the creek. Kenneth warned his younger brother to be careful." Ronald, a carefree and daring child, did not listen.

The day was a typical Kansas scorcher, just right for a late harvest. On the Thursday afternoon of July 20, our brothers, Kenneth, 10; Ronald, 8; and Allan, 6; walked through the field the short distance to the nearby creek. This was a favorite spot to cool off, play and pick wild chokecherries for Mother.

Knowing that the children often played there, Josie McEwen, a neighbor to the east, came by the day before to warn the family that a heavy rain, from a few days earlier, overflowed the creek bed and created deep washed-out holes. The family was visiting in Damar with relatives and were not home to get the news. These were before the days of cellphones and answering machines.

Kenneth recalled, "I noticed the water was getting deeper. I told the boys to not go any further. Suddenly Ronald disappeared." Kenneth, who had not yet learned to swim, yelled for help.

A neighbor, Marjorie Biery, and her daughter, Juanita, came running across the field from the south, but they could not help, nor could they swim. They ran to get Raymond Biery working in a nearby field. He could not swim either. Frantically, they drove to where our dad was on his tractor working an adjacent field. "The hardest thing I ever did was get John to rescue his son," said Marjorie Biery.

As a youngster, Dad learned to swim, both in a water hole near his home, and in the Solomon River near Damar. "My dad was the one who dived in and retrieved Ronald's lifeless body," Kenneth recalled.

The Rooks County Record, a local newspaper, reported the tragic event: "Ronald Roy, and his two brothers, had gone after chokecherries and were crossing Sand Creek near its mouth. It is usually shallow at this place, but recent rains had evidently washed a deep hole, into which Ronald slipped. This hole was about eight feet deep, and Ronald couldn't swim.

"Mr. [John] Roy dived into the hole and brought out his son's body just a few minutes before help arrived from Stockton. Evan 'Pop' Simpson, and Lester Balderston immediately started artificial respiration, and with the help of Wayne McCaslin and Oria Grover, who arrived later, continued until 4:30 p.m. Dr. H.C. Brown arrived at that time and pronounced the boy dead. It was estimated that the body had been in the water around twenty minutes before it was recovered."

Our mother, Olive Roy, was a mother of many, but each one precious. Marjorie Biery recalled, "She was so brave when we told her what happened. Even then Olive was a woman of faith."

Thirty-six years later, in a letter to her children Mother wrote, "The greatest lesson of all is faith in God. Even in times of grief, I have never lost this feeling that God [holds] all of us in His hands giving us great joy, as well as many challenges. I have often felt that if God were to take away all His material blessings, and leave me but one gift, I would ask for faith."

The next day Dad sent a telegram from the closest wire office, in Damar, to Mother's sister, Sister Rose Irma Morin, at St. Mary's Hospital in Manhattan, Kansas where she was in charge of the kitchen facilities: *"July 21, 1944. 1:00 p.m. Ronald drowned last night. Funeral Saturday morning. John Roy."*

Sister Rose Irma replied at once by mail. "My dear Olive and John. Friday the sad message was received at 3:30 p.m. Really I feel so bad about our dear little nephew's death. It came so sudden and especially for the dear parents. My heart goes out in sympathy for you Olive and Johnnie. I cannot find words to express my grief in your sad hour that is now before you.

"Yes in a case like this one, all what we can say and do is God's Will be done. Our faith is our greatest consolation in trials like yours. And I do know you will find your cross heavy to bear.

"But is it not light, when we think of the one that our Divine Lord carried for us. I know it is easier said than done. But after all, we do all have to leave this world sooner or later. Just think you have a little Angel in Heaven to await your own coming. No doubt God took him from this world to spare him from man's trials and crosses in their trying world. So don't grieve too much over the loss of your dear little one. But resign everything into God's hands. He always knows best for all of us. Be good and carry your cross bravely like our Blessed Mother did when she too saw her dying Son on the cross of death.

"I hope and pray that you won't feel bad being I didn't get to go for the funeral. The message came too late. I simply couldn't make any train connections for tomorrow — Saturday. If the telegram could of reached me a few hours sooner. It looks as if I had to make this sacrifice by not going. I am in spirit with all of you. Being I do know the Sorrows you have to go through.

"We Sisters are having a Mass said for our dear little nephew tomorrow. And we will pray for the dear parents that our Lord will give them grace and strength to carry on their cross bravely. So I place myself with you, Olive and Johnnie at the foot of the cross near our Mother of Sorrows. Yours in Prayers."

Meanwhile, Dad's brother, Phil Roy, was serving with Dursion Artillery, in New Guinea, during World War II. Upon hearing the disheartening news of the death of his young nephew, he spoke with Father Shannon, the military chaplain, who wrote a letter of condolence to offer comfort to the grieving parents.

Even though most of the Belmont Township neighbors were not Catholic, together they joined in an expression of sympathy by having two Masses said at St. Thomas Catholic Church in Stockton, by Father Bernard H. Dickman, for the repose of the soul of their little neighbor boy.[3]

Ronald Warren Roy is buried at St. Joseph Cemetery, in Damar. Our parents are buried beside him.

Among parents of drowned children, research shows the divorce rate is 80 to 90 percent. It is devastating for a family to lose a child, but drowning has an added measure to it. There is guilt to be assumed, or blame to be laid. Mother, of course blamed herself. But there was also culpability directed at her by a few insensitive people. Our parents grieved deeply for this child, but they continued to love each other, and bear four more children.

After that tragedy Mother was terrified at the sight of water, but over the years she made sure each child took swimming lessons when public pools, with lifeguards, were built in the nearby towns of Hays, Plainville and Stockton. It wasn't until many years later that she took lessons herself, along with her youngest children, although she often panicked and could never relax enough to pass the swim test.

Dad neither spoke to his children about this profound loss, nor did we ask. He valued each child and no doubt, as he kneeled by his bed to pray each night, he thanked God for their safety. Normally calm and unflinching, in later years, Dad was horribly shaken when there were three potentially life threatening farm equipment accidents to his younger sons, Roger and Rodney.

As a young boy, Kenneth was also deeply influenced by the accidental drowning of his brother. Furthermore, the Stockton sheriff, "Pop" Simpson, who came to the farm in an attempt to resuscitate the young Ronald, left a lasting impression. Six or so years later, during Kenneth's high school years, Sheriff Simpson, as summer softball coach, took him and a few other boys to ball games in the police car. Unknowingly the sheriff became a role model.

As an adult, Kenneth also chose a career in law enforcement, a role dedicated to helping others. He rose to become a respected leader and was elected as president of the National Association of Chief of Police in 1987-1988, as well as serving on International Association committees. In 1996, after serving as Chief of Police, Kenny, or K.R., as he was locally known, retired with twenty-nine years in the department at WaKeeney, Kansas.

There was always a sense of responsibility that Kenneth carried as first-born. Ila Mae carried that burden, too, as the oldest daughter. Birth order is a strong factor in the development of the Self.

Many years later she recalled this early heartbreaking memory, in an attempt to deal with the loss. Sister Veronica wrote in 1980, "I am certain I remember the day Ronald drowned. I was standing on the bank of the creek next to my mother, but I don't remember seeing anything. Afterward, his body was laid in the front bedroom downstairs. The viewing, and the wake, was held at our home. I crawled up on a chair to see him, but I don't think I understood the meaning of what happened."

As a four-year-old child, it is most likely Ila Mae did not understand the meaning of what happened, but she intuitively knew it was dreadful. For some time this tragedy took the joy of living from our parents, and two older siblings, and no doubt, their grief spilled onto her.

Children experience unnamed emotions, and have not yet developed the verbal skills necessary to successfully put together their inner world with their outer experience. The world of feelings can sometimes be confusing; they do not have grown-up words to express their loss. It is possible this event was the primary source of her lifelong anxiety, which is characterized as a sensation one gets when feeling helpless about the unknown, or when experiencing a vague, fearful feeling not associated with anything in particular.

Ronald's death was not discussed among the family, making the disappearance of her beloved brother even more troublesome to young Ila Mae's mind, which probably added to her fear and apprehension. Spiritual issues and concerns often accompany the death of a family member. Losing him affected her deeply. Perhaps, as the Catholic French novelist Georges Bernanos says, "Faith begins on the other side of despair."

Chapter Two

Sister Veronica wrote in her Life Review, "My mother said on Christmas Eve, several days before I was born, she had an unbearable earache. I'm told that Dad drove her into nearby Plainville to see Doctor Peterson at his upstairs office. Dad assisted the physician by holding the sedating ether over Mother, as the doctor lanced Mother's eardrum. Dad got a whiff of the anesthetic, and when he stepped outside to clear his head, he fell down the long flight of steps from the second floor office. He was accused, by a passerby, of being drunk." Anyone who knew our Dad would have known that could not have been further from the truth.

On display at the Rooks County Kansas Historical Society is Doc H.C. Brown's medical journal. Entry number 1283 reads: "Baby girl born to John and Olive Roy." A plump baby, she weighed nearly eight pounds at birth. The rural physician attended the home delivery at the two-bedroom house, which Dad rented from his father. Located on a hill, in the otherwise flat terrain, about four miles east of Damar, Mother called this their "little house on the prairie." Two of our brothers, Ronald and Allan, were also born here.

"My parents affirmed that I brought only joy into our home. I was very mild mannered, and often heard that my dad was especially pleased with me — his first long-awaited daughter. Mother told me that Dad gave me my first bath, and that I was loved and welcomed into the family," recalled the beloved fourth-born, and first-born daughter.

Ila Mae knew deep down she was not only Dad's favorite, but Mother's as well. Mother confirmed, "Our first little girl was very dear to us — a special little Christmas gift. The boys thought so, too."

Dad cooked for his sons, ages five and a half, four, and two, and took care of his wife and the new baby for the first several days. A few days later her oldest niece, Rita Brin (Newell) — her sister, Mary's, daughter — came to help for another week or so, until Mother was out of bed.

"During that era, there was an old wives' tale that new mothers could die if they didn't stay in bed for ten full days after a delivery," said Mother. "It was quite a chore with the three little ones crawling on my bed saying, 'What are we going to eat? Where's this? Where's that?' It would have been a lot easier to get up and get something for them. Since they were normal little boys, but still too cold for them to go outdoors, I'm sure they were bored with nothing to do."

"I'm told that my next older brother Allan had a miserable infancy due to malnourishment and illness," wrote Sister Veronica. "Even as a toddler, he cried all the time. Consequently, Mother feared my birth. From the womb, I believe I intuitively knew I had to be good."

At birth, Sister Veronica was given the name Ila Mae Jean Roy, in part, after grandmother Laura May Roy. Siblings affectionately called her "Mae." Jean, her middle name, is a French derivative of John, her father's name. This also held ancestral significance since both maternal, and paternal great-great-grandparents' were named Jean-Baptiste Roy and Jean-Baptiste Morin, as well as carrying the name of great grandfathers Jean Leon Hebert and Jean Archille Saindon.

The inspiration for the formal sounding Hungarian name, Ila, is uncertain. It is interesting to note that in 1938, the year before Ila Mae's birth, a Romanian princess with a similar name, Ileana, inherited a 16th century fortress from her mother. Perhaps this news reached the Kansas plains.

Occasionally the name, Ila, springs up among those from Nebraska. Perhaps Dad heard the name when he worked as a migrant laborer, in that neighboring state, in the early 1930s. His younger sister-in-law, Vula, has a sister by the name of Ila Dell. Another possibility is Dad may have been influenced by a similar name: Ida (Roberts) Martell, an orphaned teenage cousin his own age, lived with his parents for three years.

Another speculation is that Dad saw the name in a newsreel, or in the newspapers, which covered the San Francisco Golden Gate Bridge opening in May 1937. Many of the bridge workers were members of the International Longshoreman's Association (I.L.A.) and the initials were painted on sides of buildings to solicit support for labor union workers responsible for the construction.

The lively musical movie classic, *The Wizard of Oz*, about the fantasy adventures of Dorothy Gale, a rural Kansas schoolgirl in a gingham pinafore and ruby slippers, was released the year Ila Mae was born. Unlike Dorothy, she had neither ruby slippers, nor a dog named Toto, although she did have her own fantasies; and many of her dreams came true. Like Dorothy and her friends, she had a brain, a heart and courage.

In 1933, six years before her birth, our parents listened to accounts on the radio as Hitler assumed control of Germany.[1] Up until 1939 Franklin D. Roosevelt, the thirty-first United States president, appealed to Hitler and Mussolini for a peaceful settlement, while moving to make the United States the "arsenal of democracy." The next year FDR broke tradition by accepting the nomination for third term (1933-1945) under the campaign slogan, "Mr. Roosevelt must be re-elected if we are to escape national tragedy."

Ila Mae was born at the end of 1939; just two months after the Nazis invaded Poland. There were still only forty-eight states, and a mere nine U.S. cities had populations over one million. Damar, Kansas, the home of our immigrant grandparents, was a simple village, and the majority of those living there were farmers, of French Canadian descent, and devout Catholics.

FDR declared, "One-third of a nation is ill-housed, ill-clad and ill-nourished." He could have been describing the lives of our family, as well as neighbors and relatives. Our parents were lucky enough to have a few cupboards for their meager belongings, but they had no indoor plumbing. Water was drawn from an outdoor cistern with a bucket and rope. Mother was not a complainer. "I don't remember being poor, or unhappy. I guess there was just too much work, like chopping wood to cook a meal, instead of turning a knob on the stove."

Since Mother and Dad met and married during the Depression years, goods were not plentiful, and in the beginning their wealth didn't amount to much. Although, with a little good luck, sheer hard work and a lot of determination, they eventually amassed substantial property and rose to middle-class status. At the time of their deaths they left a considerable estate, but around the time of Ila Mae's birth, they were struggling. A person's environment greatly affects one's outlook on life.

Implemented in Europe years before, Social Security did not reach the United States until 1935, as part of Roosevelt's New Deal Program. The first Social Security checks were distributed in 1937. Roosevelt's political commitment was to the common man and downtrodden, just as Sister Veronica/Ila Mae's commitment throughout her life would be. He dramatically attacked the Great Depression by speaking out against greed and aggression. A little over two decades later, in taking religious vows, Sister Veronica also took a formal and lifelong stand against greed and aggression.

In 1935, while living near Damar, Dad worked to help build the sixty-four acre county lake south of Stockton and earned top dollar, a little over four dollars a day for four hours work, because he provided his own team of horses, Dick and Diamond.

Before and after Ila Mae's birth, FDR's Works Projects Administration, (W.P.A.) from 1935 to 1943, provided jobs like this to many unemployed men on relief across the country. One local example was the Rooks County Fairground buildings made of native limestone that later become a place of significance for Ila Mae, and the entire Roy family, because of 4-H activities held there. Another project was the highway north of Bogue, which Dad also helped build.

Dad did the best he could for his family, doing whatever it took to put food on the table. He and Mother even picked wild sand plums and sold them for two dollars a bushel during these difficult times. "John was a good provider. If there was nothing else to eat, he'd go out and shoot a cottontail, or some pigeons," Mother said in her biography. "I honestly think we would have starved during these years, had we not received commodities from the W.P.A. We had to go to the

Rooks County Courthouse [another W.P.A. construction project] to apply for these benefits. We received beans, rice, canned meat, dried prunes, flour and cornmeal.[2]

"By the time Ila Mae came along, the little boys' clothes were pretty much worn out." A few weeks after her birth, the W.P.A. also provided "a lovely white layette with gowns and diapers."[3]

When Father Thomas L. Aumais baptized the nine-day-old Ila Mae Jean Roy, on January 6, 1940, Uncle Dona and Aunt Nathalie Asselin Roy were godparents. The baptism took place in the stunningly beautiful and majestic St. Joseph's Catholic Church, which both grandfathers helped build on the isolated Plains.[4]

Damar is a French Canadian colony formed from older Cloud County, Kansas settlements from Clyde and Concordia, Kansas, and also from those around Kankakee, Illinois. According to Sister M. Evangeline Thomas, in *Footprints on the Frontier*, "Like a typical European village, with the church large and impressive around which the few buildings make up the town cluster, Damar was described [at the time of Dad's birth, in 1910] as having a thrifty population of about 300; it has two general stores, a lumber yard, a bank, two grain elevators, a [Sisters of St. Joseph] convent, and a Catholic church."

St. Joseph's Church was the site of many family sacramental celebrations, and where our parents were married a little more than seven years earlier. Dad was baptized there in 1910, Mother in 1914, as were their sons, Ronald, Allan, and Gary in 1935, 1937 and 1941, respectively. In 1959, Allan and Geraldine Desair, a Palco native, were also married there, and most recently, in 2001, their newborn grandson, Mitchell Roy Davis was baptized there, surrounded by twenty-seven family members.[5]

At age fifty, and after achieving professional success in life, Sister Veronica was sorely disappointed not to be welcomed back to Damar, in 1990, as native daughter, to serve as parish minister at St. Joseph's Church. By then it was a mission parish and served by a visiting Priest, rather then having its own resident pastor. The local parish council did not accept her job application as parish administrator. Like Jesus in the gospel, she was a prophet not welcomed back to her own village. This rejection was an important event, and a turning point in her life, which is addressed in a later chapter.

In the meantime, Dad's brother, Omer Roy, and his wife, Olive Roberts, rented a large stone house in 1937, west of Stockton; reminiscent of the house the bridegroom lived in before his marriage. The next year, during her third pregnancy, our aunt, Olive, tragically died, at age twenty-eight, of toxemia/uremia poisoning.

Not long after, our twenty-nine-year-old widower-uncle Omer, along with his two young children, moved back for six years to live with his parents, P.H. and Laura Roy, on their rural farm. The grandparents helped care for the three-year-old, Joe Mac; and one-year-old, Alice; until Omer's re-marriage to Vula Felderman, seventeen years his junior. The rental house, owned by the Farmland Mortgage Holding Company of Jackson County, Missouri, now stood empty.

After Ila Mae's birth, it was evident the tiny two-bedroom house was too small. It became increasingly important for Mother to have a larger, more comfortable home for her rapidly expanding family, which was certain to grow, since the rhythm method was not successful. Moreover, as a devout Catholic, Mother did not believe in artificial birth control.

Dad contacted the rental agent of the vacant house and in March 1940, three months after Ila Mae's birth, the family of six moved into the eleven-room stone house situated on a dusty county road one-half mile south of "old" Highway U.S. 24, eight miles west of town. Kenneth, the oldest child, thought it was a mansion.

Stockton, located in Rooks County in northwestern Kansas, in the valley of the South Fork of the Solomon River at the junction of U.S Highway 24 and 183, was incorporated in 1880. At the end of the railroad line, and primarily a livestock region, Longhorn cattle were driven up from Texas and west to be shipped out. According to Rooks County historian, Leo E. Olivia, founders believed the area was primarily suited to ranching, and they hoped their town would become the market center for a large stock growing area. Myrtle Feisler, another local writer, added that the early settlers, being largely stockmen, first named the town Stockmen.[6]

Well over sixty years before Dad acquired this land (which, at the time of this printing, continues to be family-owned), a government patent, authorizing the grant of 320 acres of public land, was conveyed to Eli Sherman (b.1821-d.1896) in 1883. The fifty-seven-year-old Sherman was among a wave of immigrants when he moved to Rooks County four years after the grasshopper plague and severe nationwide drought of 1874. Originally from New York State, perhaps he left Oneida County because of its association with the peculiar religious society of Perfectionists.

While lack of timber on the treeless Kansas plains forced many pioneers to live in sod houses, Sherman built his home of locally quarried limestone, around 1885, taking advantage of the Homestead Act of 1862. He was also allotted more acreage by participating in the Timber Act (1871-1891). He planted cottonwood and elm trees, which still stand, along the nearby winding Sand Creek.

The exterior of Sherman's house was a simple, yet dignified design with subtle detailing. The finished stone structure was whitewashed, and stood like a proud jewel on the plains. This must have been the envy of neighboring homesteaders, many of whom were still living in dugouts and sod houses well into the 1890s. A root cellar, which Mother used for storing canned goods in the 1950s, still exists and may have served as Sherman's dugout, his temporary homestead living quarters.

While he may have had the vision of building a grand house, his was not as flamboyant as some built nearly eighty miles to the south, in Ellis County around Victoria, which had plentiful outcroppings of post rock limestone. Still Sherman's well-constructed two-story house, with a full-length dirt floor basement, was considered a showy dwelling for its time and fitted his prominent position in town. He was elected to the Board of County Commissioners, representing the county in the legislature. His obituary mentions, "He filled his office with credit to the county." In 1896, he died in this stone house, at the age of seventy-five.

The stone house, which our family would eventually come to own, continued to have a history of prominent owners, including city commissioner and Stockton Mayor John Collins (J.C.) Edwards. However, after his death, and due to the stock market crash of 1929, back taxes on the Edwards home and land were not paid in 1934, according to the abstract of title. The mortgage company foreclosed upon the Edwards estate, which was not uncommon during the time of the Great Depression (1929-1941). In one Kansas county alone, seventy-five percent of taxes were unpaid during this era.

Two years after the foreclosure, Farmland Mortgage acquired the house and 320 acres, for a little more than $8,000 at a Sheriff's Sale for back taxes. Uncle Omer said, "I paid rent to Vigil Smith, [the Farmland Mortgage agent], as did later on, my brother, John. This agent for the bank was an unmarried man, living in Missouri, who drove a car called a Terraplane that had an electric shift and a cork clutch; its nickname was 'the Terrible Pain,'" he recalled with a chuckle.

In 1941, Kurt Von Mayrhauser acquired the Kansas rural farmhouse and land from Farmland Mortgage Holding Company of Jackson County, Missouri. An Austrian immigrant, he settled in this county, not far from Kansas City, and held a prominent seat on the Board of Trade, according to Uncle Paul Rickard.

Our eldest brother, Kenneth, remembers the man occasionally coming to the house to collect rent from Dad. "He had snow white hair, even though he was a young man. I recall hearing stories that Von Mayrhauser escaped Hitler's regime just in time, a few years earlier, with enough jewels to create a new beginning in America."

Von Mayrhauser also bought other bank-owned, Farmland Mortgage property throughout Kansas, including some in neighboring Graham County; however, this was his only land in Rooks County. From 1865 to 1900, about fifteen million sheep were driven from the mountains east into the Great Plains of Kansas.[7] In the 1940s, sheep raising continued to be a strong livelihood throughout this county. Adjacent to the property was land owned by the Watkins Woolen Mill located in Holt, Missouri, the next county over from his residence. Speculation is that he purchased the land as an investment, with the intent of renting out the grazing land, or raising sheep, and selling the wool.

In 1990 Sister Veronica/Ila Mae wrote pages full of cherished memories of living in the native stone house, where she spent her entire childhood and youth. On the other hand, Mother said in her own biography, "I could have cried when I first saw the condition of the house. Standing empty for some time, it had a bad odor throughout." While Mother appreciated the roominess for her growing family, she said the house first looked abandoned, was filled with cobwebs and dust, and needed lots of work to make it livable. "The rough wooden floors were splintery, and I wondered how my three little boys would be able to play in there. And the new baby, Ila Mae, would soon be crawling."

Mother was a reasonable but tidy housekeeper, who wanted her new home to be presentable. "[Mr. Von Mayrhauser] the landlord told us that if we would do the repairs, he would pay for the supplies. After John had already worked a full day in the fields, he wallpapered at night, by the light of a coal-oil lantern. It took a long time to complete all eleven rooms. [Before the days of wallpaper adhesive] I mixed up batches of flour and water into a paste."

Seventeen months after Ila Mae's birth, the fourth son and fifth child, Gary Lee Jerome Roy/Father Duane, was born on Mother's Day 1941. Mother said, "My dear sister, Mary [Brin] was the midwife. I was unaware that she was pregnant herself, as she was prone to being heavyset." Mary's eleventh and youngest child, Diane, was born on May 16, five days later. Sister Diane Brin CSJ went on to take religious vows six months after Ila Mae.

While Mother and all her sisters, and sisters-in law, willingly accepted all the children they were blessed with, it was not unusual, even years following the straitlaced Victorian era, not to discuss their pregnancies. Babies just mysteriously appeared. An older cousin, Marieda Newell, explained, "They were embarrassed. It became obvious they were having intimate relations with their husbands, even after age forty, or older."

On December 8, 1941, when Ila Mae was almost two years old, the United States declared war on Japan, following an attack on Pearl Harbor the previous day. Within a few days the Germans declared war on the United States. That same month a new Selective Service Act was passed, making men between the ages of eighteen and forty-five eligible for military service. All men between eighteen and sixty-five were required to register. As the need for men in the armed services increased, deferments for essential employment and for family dependents were steadily cut, but Dad was never called up.

Dad was exempt from the selective service, as were other men who had large families to look after. At age thirty-one, Dad had six dependents, and another on the way. His unmarried brother, Emile, entered the service, as did his brother, Phil, who was married with one child. Mother's brother Joseph (Joe), married with three children, also served as did their unmarried brother, Levi and brother-in-law Oliver Brin.

By now Mother had her hands full, raising five children under the age of eight "with rarely a dull moment," as she was prone to say. "In 1942 we hired my brother Alphonse, and his bachelor son, Omer Morin, to make repairs and remodel our stone house, adding a kitchen wing and porch. One afternoon I took Ila Mae and the two older boys into town. Gary, a toddler, was asleep outdoors in the playpen. When he awoke and started to cry, Alphonse took him out. When they weren't watching, Gary found the bucket of tar they were using to coat the north side of the house. When I got home, I found 'a little tar baby' that needed to be scrubbed."

In February 1942, President Roosevelt signed an executive order giving the military authority to relocate and intern Japanese-Americans, which was fictionalized in the Pen/Faulkner award winning book, *Snow Fallings on Cedars*. But there were no Japanese living in Rooks County at the time, or any foreigners for that matter. However, Catholics were held in almost as much contempt.[8]

During wartime there were many restrictions and inconveniences. A scrap rubber drive, throughout the nation, was implemented to keep the war effort rolling. Tires, gasoline, meat, and sugar were rationed, among other goods. Prior to this time, our parents did not drink coffee, but once it was rationed, it became a desirable commodity. Due to the war, Americans were also issued coupons and limited to three pairs of leather shoes per year, which clearly exceeded the number of shoes in Mother's meager closet. There were also fabric limitations. Black and white photographs show Mother's dresses were like those of many others; hemlines were higher to save fabric, which was on the drab side. Men no longer wore vests, and there were no cuffs on trousers.

Believing that sacrifice is important, the 1943 nationwide slogan, "Save everything. Use it up, wear it out, make it do, or do without," continued to be a lifetime motto of our parents, and for Sister Veronica, in particular.

Chapter Three

Maternal grandparents Stanislas and Rosanna Hebert Morin died long before Ila Mae was born. In the last decade of her life, she played a major role in piecing together the story of their lives, as well as those of the paternal grandparents and other ancestors.

Our paternal grandfather Philisime Roy (pronounced Physim), or P.H. as he came to be known, and Stanislas Morin did not know each other when they first arrived in Kansas, as unmarried men looking for cheap land, following the Homestead Act of 1862. They were French Canadian Catholics, and had similar temperaments, too — strict and stable, strong and hardworking. Each grandfather married, in his thirties, to much younger women. There is hearsay that men married later in life, during that generation, as a form of birth control, although this was not an effective method for them. As flourishing farmers they were also successful at "planting children." Our Roy grandparents had eleven children; our Morin grandparents had thirteen.

Grandfather Stanislas Morin, one of fifteen children, traveled by way of Illinois, from his home in St. Theodore d'Acton, Province of Quebec, to homestead in Graham County, Kansas, in 1880.

Grandmother Rosanna Hebert Morin's parents, our great-grandparents Jean-Leon and Louise Hebert, were born near Montreal. Around 1856 they moved near Beaverville, Illinois where Rosanna was born in Sainte Marie. They produced fourteen children, but only nine reached adulthood. When Grandmother Rosanna was about ten years old, the family moved to Kansas.

Stanislas was smitten with Rosanna Hebert, the olive-skinned, young dark-eyed beauty, thirteen years his junior. In 1894, when she turned eighteen, and he was thirty-one, they married in Zurich, Kansas, lived four miles southwest of Damar, and began their large family two years later.[1]

Pope Leo XIII, one of seven children himself, was at the helm then (1878-1903). He instituted the feast of the Holy Family, and issued a notable encyclical on Christian marriage.

In 1914 their eleventh child, our mother Olive was born, and named after her French Canadian paternal grandmother, Olive Morin, who allegedly married, with dispensation, a Morin cousin — which was not encouraged, but also not uncommon for those times around 1840.

Not yet forty-two years old, Grandmother Rosanna Morin had already given birth to twelve babies, not including several pregnancies that ended in miscarriages. Grandmother was unattended by a physician, like her other home deliveries. As far back as biblical times, and well described in the book, *The Red Tent* by Anita Diamant, it was typical for unlicensed midwives, female friends and relatives to preside over the "social childbirth."

Even though of hardy stock, Grandmother was like the countless other pioneer women, and women throughout the ages, who died during childbirth due to blood loss, unsanitary conditions, infections, complications, and lack of modern medical knowledge. It was dreadful. Stretched out on the kitchen table, Grandmother bled to death from a blocked breech delivery. Before she lost consciousness her screams could be heard a half-mile away.[2]

While in ancient pre-Hispanic cultures death in childbirth was a great honor, and these women were often deified, Stanislas Morin was in shock over the loss. She was the love of his life. Compounding the heartbreak, this day was their twenty-third wedding anniversary. He never remarried. The wake was at home. The organ, located in the parlor, and mirrors were all draped with sheets, which was standard for that era. In September 1917, the mother and unnamed baby daughter were buried together in the church cemetery, in the country, south of Damar.

Following this tragedy, there was a sadness about the fifty-four-year-old widower, and he oftentimes seemed stern: his mood morose and joyless. He was strict, but kind, and the children adored their father as he gathered up the two youngest ones, Olive, age three, and the one-year-old baby, Levi, to his lap on the rocking chair. Stanislas often sung a plaintive French melody reverting back, during these times, to his native dialect.

In later years Mother struggled in vain to recall memories of the dark-haired woman, with an upswept Gibson hairstyle. When she held the sienna-colored photograph of her mother, she noticed the brown, intense, yet gentle eyes, full sensual lips and an exquisitely tailored dark-colored dress.

Mother often held in her hand the same lapel watch seen in the photo, a gift that her father had given her own mother. After Rosanna's death, he saved the heirloom, stamped Geo. W. Messier, Holyoke, Mass., for Olive, his youngest daughter. The lapel watch has since been passed from youngest granddaughter, Cheryl Roy Calvin, to its fourth owner, Laurielle Calvin, Cheryl's youngest daughter.

Stanislas's daughter, Mary, married in 1920, and within the year her siblings Anna, Alphonse and Rosa also married. Angele, who took the name Sister Rose Irma, also left home in 1920 to join the convent. Stanislas raised his five younger children remaining at home the best he knew how during the four years following his wife's death. But when his oldest daughters married and the child-raising support now gone, Stanislas Morin realized his youngest daughter, Olive, needed a mother figure.

In 1921, when she was seven years old, Olive moved to town, to live with her newly married sister, the twenty-five-year-old Anna Desmarteau. Olive also worked for, and lived with another married sister, Mary Brin. At eleven years old, she returned to help on the farm with household chores. She mended, cleaned, and shopped for her father and brothers Edward (Ed), Phillip, Joseph (Joe) and Levi. "My father taught me how to cook, and he fried almost everything, using lots of salt pork."

According to census records Stanislas was a successful farmer, owning 480 acres planted in winter wheat (probably Turkey Red, and other Russian strands), corn and Sudan grass. He did not own a tractor, but he had mules, horses, cattle and a cream separator. He was also a carpenter and helped build the magnificent St. Joseph's Catholic Church, in Damar.

During the summer of 1929, when Olive was fourteen, and Levi, the youngest, was thirteen, their father collapsed while milking cows. The two teenagers found Stanislas unconsciousness in the barn with "sweats of blood pouring from his face." While Levi stayed with his father, Olive rushed to the house to use the crank wall telephone to contact the operator, who put her through to Doc Peterson from Palco. Stanislas was taken to the hospital.

Three days later the long-awaited marriage of Uncle Edward (Ed) Morin and Irene Roberts took place as planned. Shortly after the newlyweds arrived, by a horse-drawn surrey, at the Hays hospital, his father Stanislas Morin died of kidney failure — possibly Bright's disease.

Our mother, Olive, and her siblings became orphans. Their father died intestate, that is, without a Will. Phillip and Joseph, the older unmarried boys, continued to live on the farm. Young Levi went to live with their oldest married brother, Alphonse, who was appointed legal guardian of the minor children.

The first Kansas Catholic high school, in what was then known as the Concordia diocese, was in Manhattan, at the corner of Juliette Avenue and Pierre Street. The Sacred Heart Academy was known to be a "select boarding school for young lady students."[3]

The next month, Alphonse arranged for Olive, a budding and energetic girl in the bloom of her youth, to travel, by eastbound train, to the Academy, which served as a grammar and high school and provided a home for the teaching Sisters. Olive's sister, Sister Rose Irma Morin, who was thirty-one years old, had been assigned, from 1923 to 1936, to the Academy, a job that included meal preparation and house cleaning.[4]

When Olive got the chance to see her sister, it was to work in the kitchen to help pay off room and board debt. Olive would try to engage her sister in conversation; instead, the busy cook would gently nod at the teenage prattle. Olive soon came to dread the elaborate Sunday meals, and especially the seven-course dinners, for the sacred feast days of the other teacher-Sisters, (which were celebrated instead of their birthdays). "It would take me all afternoon to wash the crystal, china and silver," recalled our mother of her early life.

It was standard protocol, during that era, to wear black clothing for one full year (or at least a black arm band), even for grieving children. Olive carried on board the train a cardboard suitcase filled with her new clothes. There were five black and white print dresses, and one black dress for Sundays, black shoes, and long black cotton stockings, too. A seamstress, Alice Roberts, Uncle Ed's new mother-in-law, was paid to sew the appropriate wardrobe.

It started off as a lonesome school year for Olive, having just turned fifteen the month before. Most of the other girls lived nearby, and did not board on the weekends. Often alone, she was kept busy cleaning the basement, and three-story house on Saturdays and Sundays, when not doing homework, because her sister knew that manual labor was a way of avoiding a bigger problem for teenagers. "An idle mind is the devil's workshop," was Sister Rose Irma's response when her youngest sister started to complain. Olive also adhered to this adage during her child-rearing years.

The death of a parent can have profound psychological repercussions, as there may be guilt and remorse in addition to sorrow and anger. Social support is crucial so that children can have a measure of resiliency and the capacity to mourn and live. The grieving process includes learning how to go on with one's life.[5]

Children should not have to face loss alone and so, while still mourning the death of her father just months before, Olive was surrounded with newfound friends and her spunky attitude began to return. Her peers provided much needed support. The teenage Olive Morin was popular at school. Full of chatter, she made friends easily, a trait that lasted a lifetime. Unfortunately, this ease was not transferred to her oldest daughter, Sister Veronica.

By now the Charleston had been the dance craze for several years. The flapper look was in vogue, and Olive began to wear her hair bobbed, as did her schoolgirl classmates, Leona Bagley, Josephine Hoover and Catherine Martin. She missed her brothers and sisters, back home in rural Damar, but toward the end of the school year she actually looked forward to returning for the fall semester to begin nurses' training at the Academy High School in the big town of Manhattan, Kansas. But it was not meant to be.

"My brother and legal guardian, Alphonse, discouraged me from nurses training," Mother said. "'You don't want to do someone else's dirty work, do you?' he said. 'Emptying bedpans and all?'" Several decades earlier the nursing profession was not held in high esteem, as it is today. Handling and seeing the unclothed body was thought to coarsen females, and was falsely associated with prostitution, in the minds of many.

On Black Thursday, four months after Mother was orphaned, stock market prices plummeted, and collapsed a few days later on Black Monday October 29, 1929. The stock market panic, and the Great Depression affected this family deeply, as it did many others, who found it hopeless to pay off debts, as mounting interest payments continued to accrue. The months ahead were desperate, and many family farms were lost to banks.

"At the end of the school year, in May 1930, Alphonse said the boarding school cost too much. So, I returned to Damar on the westbound train." As a fifteen-year-old, it is most likely she did not have a clear understanding of exactly how much of a financial drain her schooling and support had become on the estate. The next year the economic situation throughout rural Kansas, and most of the country, was frantic. In many towns banks and businesses closed, and jobs were lost. To add to the disaster, droughts took their toll on farms, and rock bottom prices were offered for grain and beef.

Olive was faced with yet another tragedy two months after she returned home. In July 1930, a week before her sixteenth birthday, her doting twenty-three-year-old brother, Phillip, died of injuries a few hours after an oncoming train struck his Model T Ford.[6]

Upon her return to Damar, and until her marriage two years later, once again Olive took turns living with her married sisters, Anna and Mary. "I loved them dearly, and they were good to me." Between the two families there were lots of new babies and young children to care for: Victor, Evon, Cecilia, Melvin, and JoAnn Desmarteau, and Rita, Clarence, Marieda, Levi, Francis, and Barbara Brin, not to mention the nieces and nephews who were born after Olive's marriage. "I also helped with the cooking, cleaning and laundry."

Off and on, between 1930 and 1932, Olive also worked for her maternal grandmother, an elderly widow in her late eighties. She rented out two rooms of her house in Damar. "She'd pay me two dollars a week to cook and clean," recalled our mother. Other grandchildren worked for their grandmother Louise Frigon Hebert by hauling coal, some of whom recalled the house smelled of onions.

"Grandmother had beautiful wavy hair, like my mother's, I was told, worn up in a bun," said Mother. Photographs show Great-Grandmother Hebert as a very pretty young woman at one time, with red hair, blue eyes, beautiful, clear fine skin and no freckles. She was petite, and known to be neat and modestly clad in dark dresses, of high necklines and long sleeves. She taught her daughter (our grandmother Rosanna) how to sew — a talent passed down through the generations: to Mother, Ila Mae, and her other three daughters.

"By time I knew her, Grandmother Hebert was a stern woman, stooped, thin, and frail looking, and walked with a stiff-legged limp as a result of a broken hip," our mother said. As a teenager, Olive learned not to speak about her late father to her grandmother who viciously blamed him, her son-in-law, Stanislas Morin, for her daughter's death, "by giving her one too many babies."

According to second cousin Rosalie Hebert, "Grandmother Hebert refused to speak English and spoke only French. Neither grandparent was ever inside a school, nor did their children have much education. The Hebert family were neither book readers, nor storytellers. I was in the homes of all the aunts and uncles, and saw schoolbooks and prayer books, but no Bibles, and grew up thinking these were only for Priests."[7]

Louise Frigon Hebert died in 1933, the year after Mother married. Aunt Irene Morin recalled, "We went to church on Sunday and heard that she was already buried, but nobody bothered telling [the grandchildren]."

Mother regretted that she was never given a treasure from the estate. "I remember seeing beautiful crystal and china, in a corner cabinet. But as a newlywed [in 1932] I did not receive a pretty dish, or anything from grandmother Hebert's fine china collection, or even after she died the next year." Ila Mae recalled that Mother especially wondered what happened to the statue of the Feast of the Assumption of Mary with the angels at her feet, and other impressive religious articles.[8]

According to Sister Veronica's research, paternal grandmother Laura Saindon Roy's parents, Jean-Archille "Archie" Saindon and Henriette Caron, immigrated to Kansas in 1884, from Cacouna, Rimiski County, Canada. After traveling for three weeks by railroad boxcar, they arrived in Cloud County, near Concordia, where many other French Canadians were living. They continued to travel further west to Zurich, Rooks County, taking a claim in Logan Township on a creek bank. Their shelter, from the searing hot summer sun and the icy blast during winter months, was a house of native turf grass sods, called a soddy. The inside walls were plastered with clay.

In 1901 great-grandfather Saindon, built a house of lumber, which was still standing one hundred years later. He owned 960 acres of land. The Saindons had the largest family, at that time, in Rooks County. Grandmother Laura May Saindon, the ninth of sixteen children, was their first child born in Kansas.

Grandpa P.H. Roy was born in 1871, one of twenty-one children of Jean-Baptiste Roy. With his second wife, Rosalie Lanoue, it is recorded they had twelve children. Grandpa grew up on a farm located three miles south of the St. Sebastien Church, Iberville, Province of Quebec, in the Richelieu River Valley, sixty miles south of Montreal, about halfway to the U.S.-Canadian border, in what is now known as the ice wine region.

In 1899, when the average U.S. annual income was $375, Grandpa Roy immigrated to Kansas, at age twenty-eight, nineteen years after maternal grandpa Stanislas Morin arrived. P.H. Roy joined the ranks as farm laborer — the most common job of the era — and soon after homesteaded in Damar, Graham County, where he, like Grandpa Morin, built a sod house.

In sharp contrast to his great-great grandchildren (who in 2002 travel world wide by jet, surf the Internet, and watch television, movies and major league sports), the popular leisure activities at the turn of the twentieth century were bicycling, playing baseball, singing along with a player piano, and visiting saloons (for men only).

As we came to know him, Grandpa was kind enough, but to younger grandchildren he rarely smiled and seemed to have a stern demeanor. A tall, barrel-chested man with a full head of snow-white hair, he had freckles head to toe. Ila Mae resembled him most with her ruddy complexion.

Five years after he arrived in Kansas, P.H. Roy married Laura Saindon on Valentines Day 1904, at St. Ann's Catholic Church in Zurich. He was thirty-two years old. She was eighteen. The first two of their eleven children (Dona and Edmond) were born in a sod house northeast of Damar. Not long after, they built a two-story frame house, where John (our Dad), and four other siblings were born (Omer, Oscar, RoseLee and Philip/Phil). Next, they moved to a large stone house slightly further northeast, where the last three children were born (Zella, Emile and Jeannette).

Hospitals were mostly for the homeless and the poor. Grandmother became an unlicensed nurse-midwife (meaning with woman), and helped with home births throughout the neighboring Rooks and Graham counties, often staying with the women in delivery for many hours. Grandmother was holistic in her approach. She employed the human touch long before it became fashionable, and before technology took away most of the common sense of health care. Although not pioneered until the mid-1960s, had Grandmother known of the pain-relief benefits of a gentle underwater delivery method, which lessens the trauma of a normal birth, no doubt she would have assisted.

Grandmother's talent was not all spent on outsiders. She cared for her family, as well. According to Kathy Kalina's *Midwife for Souls: Spiritual Care for the Dying*, concern for the dying has traditionally been a function of the family, with generous community support.[9] Before the notion of Hospice care, family nursing duties were a woman's responsibility. Currently, only 1.4% of men care for the sick and aged, while 13% of female family members do. According to Aunt Zella, Grandmother and her younger sister, Celina, cared for their mother, Henriette Saindon, until she died, in 1934, at the P.H. Roy farm home — much like Sister Veronica did while caring for Mother in her final months.

Their stone house continued to be lived in by their son Omer and Vula Roy. Grandpa commuted to farm this land near Damar. After settling into the house on Cedar Street, in Stockton in 1944, Grandmother spent many afternoons at the card table with the neighboring ladies playing Canasta or Pitch. She adapted well to town life. With evening card parties our grandparents entertained nearby neighbors — the Coolbaughs, Millers, and Judge Skinner. They enjoyed company and whomever they invited, "to stay and have a bite to eat" were often treated to fresh turnips, from grandmother's garden, and sandwiches of thickly sliced bologna. As a child, Ila Mae took note of their generous hospitality.

Their one-story, compact, gingerbread-style house, with only three bedrooms, seemed tiny compared to our own family's two-story, eleven-room farmhouse "mansion." Nevertheless, our grandparents continued hosting the annual New Year's Day feasts into the late 1950s, which were started years earlier by Grandmother Roy's parents, Jean-Archille and Henriette Saindon.

Driving in from Colorado, Nebraska, Missouri, Illinois, Iowa and Texas the families of our aunts and uncles, and those living in the neighboring counties, showed up for the holiday. When a cousin appeared at the gathering with a boyfriend or girlfriend that was a sign there would be a marriage within the year.

Mother told us that while Christmas was a holiday for children, it was a French Canadian custom for New Year's Day to be celebrated by adults. Aunt Jeannette added, "It's also a French custom to kiss everyone you see on New Year's Day, including your husband," she added with a twinkle.

Unlike Mother and Dad, our grandparents spoke with a hint of French Canadian dialect, and often mixed French and English. The older aunts and uncles also spoke with a lingering accent, and the noise level on these occasions took on an exotic tone.

For many years Mother was in charge of preparing the largest turkey she could find, which she placed in a low temperature oven at midnight. The family awoke to a tantalizing aroma the next morning. No nibbling was allowed, and the tempting main course was dropped off intact, at grandmother's house in town, on the way to New Year's Day Mass — the feast of Mary, Mother of God, a holy day of obligation.

Grandmother made potatoes and gravy. Aunts contributed salads and cakes and pies made from scratch with enough to feed the hungry horde. Every room of the congested house was filled to capacity for the festive noontime potluck dinner. A long table for twelve was set up for adults, in the cramped living room, everyone taking turns, or eating with a plate on their lap in the oversized sitting room, or adjoining master bedroom that was scattered with card tables set up for eating, and later for games of Pinochle and Pitch.

A dozen or more women were crammed in the tiny kitchen exchanging family gossip, or comparing who was "P.G." Often two or more of the aunts, or older married cousins, were visibly pregnant, in their tent-like two-piece maternity dresses, and stories of child rearing were freely exchanged over the washing and drying of dishes.

The younger children romped on the spare guest bed, or ran in and out of the house, since it was not unusual for Kansas weather to be mild on this day. Teenage cousins lingered for a while, and then borrowed a car to drag the nearly deserted Main Street. But not Ila Mae. She hung around with the adults to help with clean-up.

Grandpa passed around glasses of Kosher Mogan David Concord wine, which he kept stored in the outdoors cellar. Some years he made his own from fermented grape juice. The sweet wine was served in everyday glasses as an aperitif to "whet the appetite," as Mother would say. Another glassful, or two, may have been taken after dinner, or during card games. The festive holiday air rang with joy and laughter, sometimes from a relative who had a wee bit too much. Although these must have been happy times, for no mention has been made of a disagreement or fight breaking out.

The Eighteenth Amendment prohibited the manufacture and sale of alcoholic beverages. Later in 1933, the year after our parents marriage, and with the repeal of prohibition long past, as a result of the Twenty-First Amendment, the family was comfortable with drinking beer, wine, and whiskey, although none were known to drink in excess. Hard liquor was on hand in a cupboard above the range, but only taken down on social occasions, or during evening card parties with friends. During summer months there was Hamm's beer in the refrigerator for Dad, after coming home, hot and sweaty, from the dusty wheat fields. Mother occasionally shared a glass with him at the kitchen table. Children were allowed to have a small sip, but no more.

From 1921 until 1924, our grandparents were appointed guardians of their niece, Ida Roberts (Martell), after grandmother's sister, Amelia Saindon Roberts, died. Then, from 1938 to 1944, they were called upon, in middle age, to help care for their two young grandchildren, Joe Mac and Alice, when Omer was left a widower. In 1950, on Christmas Day, a daughter-in-law, Alma Newell Roy, died of cancer and, barely a year later her husband and their son, Edmond, died of viral pneumonia at age forty-four, leaving their six children orphaned. By then Uncle Edmond and Aunt Alma's oldest children, Gilbert and Rita, each had married. Geraldine and Karen went to live with Rita. Aunt Zella raised Annette, and Germaine lived with the Roy grandparents for three years until she completed high school in Stockton.

Helping to raise several grandchildren may be, in large part, the reason the grandparents did not make a fuss over other grandchildren. Another obvious answer is the sheer number vying for attention. In 1954, when Ila Mae was fifteen years old, they already had forty-eight grandchildren and twelve great-grandchildren. Still she, and Gary/Father Duane, held a special place in their hearts.

When our grandparents celebrated their fiftieth wedding anniversary, Ila Mae, along with her cousins, made party favors of flowers from facial tissue for more than two hundred guests. Father Louis Dupont celebrated the Anniversary Mass. He was a nephew to P.H. Roy and son of great aunt, Hormisdas/Hortence Roy Dupont. Grandfather Roy died six years later, in 1960, at the age of eighty-nine, from hardening of the arteries (arteriosclerosis), heart disease, and pneumonia.

Grandmother lived alone, in Stockton, for another seven years. A petite woman, she was gracious, and had a ready smile for her grandchildren. Prim and proper, she was the epitome of a lady, with her hair stylishly rolled in the fashion of the day. The seams of her nylon stockings were always straight, and even with her everyday dresses, she wore a bit of jewelry.

She moved to Damar, in 1967, and lived next to the church, which her husband helped build more than a half-century earlier. She lived there only a short time, before her health began to fail, and was moved, by her children, to the Solomon Valley Manor nursing facility south of Stockton where she continued to live nearly four more years.

While Grandmother was much loved, and well cared for, Mother saw how distressed she was living in the nursing home. Mother made her wishes clear, and often prayed that as she grew elderly she would continue to live out her final years, and die, in her own home, which she did.

During the week, and after church on Sundays, our parents visited grandmother. Dad was her last visitor when she died, at age eighty-six, of pneumonia, in 1971. Both grandparents are buried in St. Joseph's Cemetery, south of Damar. Not inheriting any token remembrances from maternal Hebert great-grandparents, or Morin grandparent's estates, Sister Veronica was especially pleased to receive a small pair of crystal salt and peppershakers when Grandmother's possessions were distributed.

Our dad, John Felix Roy, was the fourth of eleven children born, in 1910, to P.H. and Laura Roy. A few years later during World War I, the family, along with the rest of the country, experienced meatless Tuesdays and wheatless Wednesdays to conserve and economize. This, and other harsh elements, created difficult times. Dad was raised by a strict code of hard work, and performed man's work at an early age. While his dad was the disciplinarian in the family, his mother was the tender caregiver who doted on him as much as she could with all the other children in tow.

Dad used both spellings, "Johnnie" and "Johnny," when he attended Hillside, a county school in district 88, located five and a half miles southwest of the town of "old" Webster. In those days a grade school education was thought of as high school is today. Consequently, it was not unusual for many rural children to not attend the higher grades, and college was only for the privileged. It was with great pride that he saw his beloved daughter, Sister Veronica, graduate from college in 1963.

There is an unresolved difference of opinion of exactly how long Dad attended school. Mother said, "An injury to the chest from a horse kept him from going beyond sixth grade." This coupled with an injury to his back, made it difficult for him to sit for long periods in the classroom, and plagued him throughout life. However, his eldest brother, Dona, said Dad completed the seventh grade, while Omer said his brother completed the eighth grade. Even though Dad had a limited education, his practical ability with math amazed his children, as he added long columns of numbers in his farm journal.

During the 1920s, fortunate children in the cities played with colorful and elaborate electric Lionel toy trains. None of these expensive toys were in this remote farmhouse. Dad and other rural children made up games, and created their own amusements, such as Blackman, crack the whip, ante-over, and a boy's game, shinney. "We'd go ice-skating in the winter, and swimming in the summer at the South Solomon River, which ran near the farm where I was born and grew up," he said.[10]

"There wasn't much in the way of childhood entertainment during this decade. Most of our travel was on horseback, or we would walk, which tended to keep us near home and made for a close-knit family. I believe those days were far better, as far as pleasure was concerned, than they are today," he said. "There was always a friend's house to visit, where we would dance, and just have fun." He and his siblings spoke of enjoyable times together as youngsters, and they continued to stay in touch throughout their lifetimes.

When Dad was ten years old his childhood hero, Babe Ruth, hit fifty-four home runs. Baseball was a game Dad played in his youth, and later rarely missed watching his sons and daughters play at school games.

When Dad was eleven years old he went to live and work, for three years, for his maternal grandparents, who lived nearby. Perhaps this was to provide more sleeping room in the house after his parents took in an orphaned cousin his same age.[11] He enjoyed living with the Saindons, a kind, loving, and happy couple. Dad returned to live with his parents when he was fourteen.

Dad and his brothers were hard workers, helping their father around the farm. Uncle Omer said, "We didn't have a tractor. Instead we used as many as twenty mules for most of the 1,200-farmed acres, firmly commanding them 'gee' and 'haw,' to the left or right. The work got fairly strenuous."

Uncle Dona agreed, "Our dad, P.H. Roy liked mules, which he raised and sold. It wasn't unusual to get kicked by one of these stubborn animals." Dad added, "At corn picking and wheat harvest time extra farmhands were hired, to ensure our crops got in on time. We also raised quite a bit of feed, since we had to winter several head of cattle." The brothers found other work where they could. Uncle Omer said, "My first paying job, at age fifteen, was shelling corn for fifty cents a day, for Val Schneider, a widower."

Dad was shy and reserved. Making friends did not come easy, but he had close relationships with his cousins. One of them, Arlene Gosselin, remembered, "Around 1925, during the 'good old days,' when John was old enough to drive, he asked to use the family car, a black Model T. Cousins piled in, and he drove us to old Webster. [This was long before the reservoir flooded the town.] Along Main Street he pointed out the bank, grocery store, and hotel, and would tell us who lived where. It was cheap fun, and everyone enjoyed the day."

The Roaring Twenties, as the decade came to be known, was an age of thrill seekers. Dad was the first generation of "teenagers," since the word was coined during this decade. When we begged him, he would tell us about his mischievous years. "My brothers and I took the family car to the railroad track, let air out of the tires, and drove on the track," but he warned his children to never try that stunt. During this time a federal highway system was organized, and the number of automobiles nearly tripled.

Two weeks after she turned sixteen, Mother met the love of her life. Their romance was blessed from the beginning: a story with a happy ending. Their love and marriage lasted a lifetime, "until death us do part." In her biography Mother said, "I first met Johnny at the annual church picnic and carnival, in Damar, on August 15, 1930. We both attended St. Joseph's, but we didn't know each other. Those church activities were the main social events for young people.[12]

"I knew from the beginning he was the special person with whom I wanted to share my life. Had I stayed at the Academy in Manhattan for nurses training, I never would have met him. I never regretted not finishing my education. While living and working for my married sisters, Johnny had to drive from house to house, looking for me on Saturday nights, when we were dating. I never knew myself, from week to week, where I'd be living."

The orphaned teenager received lots of attention from her brothers and sisters, but it was no substitute for parental love, for which she grieved. Reflecting on the untimely death of her own mother, she spoke of feeling deprived of maternal love during her childhood. She was also still reeling from the death of her beloved twenty-three-year-old brother, Phillip, a month earlier.

Mother and her youngest brother were close, even though living apart. The fifteen-year-old Levi was protective of his sister. "One Sunday afternoon Olive was visiting our brother Alphonse's house, where I lived. A man, whom I didn't know, arrived to call for my sister. I asked my brother about him. 'He is from a very nice family. His name is John Roy,' Alphonse told me." Several months later, the sixteen-year-old Olive asked her brother, Levi, to be Best Man for their wedding, because she had already made up her mind to marry the twenty-year-old. Over the years Sister Veronica was impressed that throughout their lifetimes these two siblings continued exchanging birthday cards.

In later years, on the subject of marriage, Mother emphasized, "Watch how a man talks about his mother. This is an indication of whether he will treat you with kindness. I dated a few other boys, but they didn't suit me. When I met Johnny Roy he treated me with such respect, and I knew he was the one for me."

As a teenager, Mother was animated and lively. Perhaps she was a little dramatic, with an optimistic view of life, balancing her pride with a positive outlook. Mother preferred a simple style of dress, with few ruffles or frills even then, but her feminine nature did not go unnoticed by our dad, who kept her heart overflowing with admiration. Not willing to settle for "just any ol' beau," she fell for Dad's gentle flattery, good manners and masculine appeal. In turn he knew this orphan girl was out of the ordinary. Although his means were limited, he did his best to be properly attired to keep her attention. He also whistled a lot in the early years, before he was fitted for dentures.

On one of their dates, three days after Christmas on December 28, 1930 at Webster, Kansas, Mother asked Dad to sign her ever-present autograph book. Ila Mae Jean, their beloved and saintly first daughter, was born nine years later on the same date.

Six months after they met Mother attended a silent religious retreat, in February 1931, held at what was then called Marymount Academy in Salina, Kansas. It would later become Marymount College for women — Ila Mae's alma mater. Sponsored by the Daughters of Mary Sodality this retreat, for unmarried teenage girls, was a withdrawal from everyday routine, and meant to foster social, education and spiritual growth. Instead, during the week, the gregarious Olive Morin, and her newfound friends, broke the mandatory silence of the retreat with giggles, whispers and notes, as they took turns writing in Mother's autograph book. Perhaps it was Sister Rose Irma who recommended the retreat for purpose of assessing a religious vocation for her sister. It was too late; the teenage girl had already fallen in love.[13]

Dad and Mother dated for exactly two years. Three weeks after her birthday, and after the marriage banns were announced on three successive Sundays according to church law, John Roy and Olive Morin were married on August 23, 1932 in St. Joseph's Church in Damar, by Father Romanus (Raymond) Mattingly.[14] The parish Priest gave the new bride this advice, "Always get up and fix your husband's breakfast to keep a marriage happy." Like her own mother, Rosanna Morin, Olive was just eighteen.

"August was a good time for weddings in rural areas, since by then the harvesting was over. Marriages could not take place in the spring during Lent," pointed out Father Gilbert Wolters OSB, a retired sociologist. "Weddings were always in the morning. Mid-week ceremonies were usual during that era. Typically there were only two witnesses, unlike some lavish wedding parties in later decades. Usually the ceremony was a low Mass with no singing, although sometimes a soloist sang the *Ave Maria* [Hail Mary].[15] When the newly wed couple exited the church there was rice — the symbol of fertility — rather then the often-used birdseed, or confetti used today. There are more regulations now, such as seeing the Pastor four to six months before the intended wedding, and the young couple must endure a series of three or four instructions."

In her wedding day memento Mother noted, "John wore a navy blue suit, with an artificial boutonniere on his lapel. My bridal veil was borrowed from our parish Sodality of Mary, and I carried a bouquet of plastic flowers." In those days, many brides wore a suit for the ceremony, and then wore it for travel on their honeymoon — as did her sister-in-law Ona Robicheaux Morin — but Mother wore a tea-length white satin dress instead. There was no honeymoon. The newlyweds had only twelve dollars between the two of them, although they received several cash gifts of two dollars each.

"The morning following the wedding, we were expected to awaken early and be hard at work in the fields," Mother said. They started married life living with his parents, working side-by-side during corn-shucking season. Ten years later, in 1942, they took a three-day trip to Colorado, which she considered their long awaited honeymoon.

Mother never received an engagement ring; her single wedding band was a linked heart design. She was not materialistic, and throughout their marriage she never asked for a lot, although she was sentimental, and appreciated simple tokens of affection. "When we were dating he gave me a wrist watch. That must have been my engagement gift. He traveled to Nebraska as a migrant farm worker shucking corn for four cents a bushel to earn the money. He also gave me a watch for our twenty-fifth anniversary. Both were gifts of love. He was so kind and generous."

After living a few months with his parents, the young newlyweds were invited to stay with their cousins, Oliver and Lillie Gosselin. Here Mother helped with the housework and cared for the family. Years earlier before he married, Dad worked as their farm hand.

Five years earlier, in 1927, the radio carried the news of Charles Lindbergh's historic first nonstop, solo, trans-Atlantic flight, just as it carried the news of the kidnapping of the Lindbergh baby in 1932, the year of Mother and Dad's marriage. Mother rarely spoke of news events from her past, but she told of suffering in anguish upon hearing the tragic news, just as the entire nation did when the baby was found dead, the same year Franklin Delano Roosevelt was elected president.

There was already talk of war in the early 1930s. In the larger cities there were unemployment lines and soup kitchens. Many of these out-of-work Americans left the cities to return to the land. The migrant farm worker became a symbol of the Great Depression; Dad got his start in life this way. These tough times, during the thirties, were also known as the bartering years, and it was common for people to be unable to pay their bills. To Dad, his honor and integrity depended upon staying free of debt. Never waiting for work to find him, he was one to always find employment at odd jobs of any sort. While he was never considered a rich man, he was never truly broke either. He also shucked corn for widower Frank Brin, and Mother's sister, Rosa, and her husband, Frank Balthazor.

There was little money to be made locally in northwest Kansas, aside from

Dad helping his cousin as a farm laborer; so not long after their marriage they went out west to earn a living. He and his eager young bride made the three-hundred-mile trip in the difficult-to-shift Model T Ford coupe.

At first they lived in a cleaned-out and whitewashed brooder house intended for chickens, while Dad worked in the sugar beet fields, of northeastern Colorado, near Brush. After the growing season was over, Dad became a ranch hand for the Leroy Painter family. Nearby was the town of Gary, a thriving sugar beet community in the 1930s, but now a ghost town. Gary is the name they chose for their fourth son.

Kenneth Eugene, their first child, was born in Colorado and carries the middle name of Dad's brother, Oscar Eugene, who served as witness at their wedding eighteen months earlier.[16] Together P.H. Roy, and Dad's brother, Edmond, drove Grandmother Roy to Colorado where she stayed for two weeks to help care for the baby. By now, Grandmother already had seven other grandchildren: Viola, Eugene, Gilbert, Orville, Clifford, Rita, and LaVerne.

Although an experienced midwife, Grandmother Roy did not assist with her daughter-in-law's delivery. After piecing together stories of how her own mother died, Mother was insistent on not having a country doctor. Since hospital doctors, in those days, usually only attended women of means, who could afford the higher fees, Dad managed to save enough money to pay the physician in cash to come to the house.

Kenneth was baptized at St. Mary's Catholic Church, in Brush. Grandmother served as godmother, and Grandpa Roy was named godfather, by proxy. A few days later, John drove his mother to Genoa, a burg seventy miles to the south of Brush, to catch the eastbound night train back to Damar, Kansas.

Not much later our mother, as a nineteen-year-old, admitted to being overwhelmed, when both she and her new baby contracted whooping cough at the same time. Pertussis, as it is also called, makes it difficult to eat, drink and breath. Mother recalled, "I was exhausted caring for my first baby. Kenneth would start to choke, and turn blue every fifteen minutes, and then made a whooping sound after a bout of coughing. I'd turn him upside down so he could catch his breath."

About seventy-five percent of American children in the 1920s and 1930s contracted the contagious disease. Before the Pertussis vaccine was introduced in the 1950s, the disease killed more children annually in the United States than all other infectious diseases combined. Because of this country's current and aggressive childhood immunization program many diseases that used to be commonplace are now rare. (The vaccination for *rubella*, German measles, was not available until 1969. It is very possible that Ila Mae/Sister Veronica and several of the other siblings developed hearing losses as very young children, because the measles, mumps and rubella vaccinations were not yet obtainable.)

In 1934, when Kenneth was two months old, the family of three returned to live in Kansas. It took them three days to travel due to the Model T breaking down. Kind strangers, near Colby on old highway 24, allowed them to stay in their cleaned-out chicken house for several days, until the car could be repaired.

Upon the arrival of her first child, Olive Roy began a lifelong career as a dedicated and devoted mother. Losing her own parents at a tender age most likely conditioned her to want a secure family life. The babies came regularly, one every year or so, just as they did in the families of her sisters (Anna, Mary and Rosa), Morin sisters-in-law (Rosalie, Irene, Lucille and Ona), and Roy sisters-in-law (Nathalie, Alma, Olive, Vula, Alice, RoseLee, Evelyn and Leona). There were sixty-four maternal first cousins and almost as many on the paternal side. Nearly everyone had large families from the predominately Catholic French Canadian families in the Damar area.

Mother was strong, conceived easily, and had five more babies at home with the assistance of midwives during twenty-two of her childbearing years, up until the time of menopause. For the most part her pregnancies, and subsequent seven births of Ronald, Allan, Ila Mae, Gary, Joan, Linda and Roger were trouble free.

By 1938, childbirth norms began moving out of the home, and into the hospital, for nearly half of all women in the United States. Changes were slow to reach rural areas. Although, by 1954, the year the ninth child, Cheryl, was born, ninety-five percent of women had their bags packed, and rushed to the hospital, when labor started, to be attended by male doctors, who introduced drugs, and the "flat on your back" type childbirth.

Mother considered herself fortunate to be in a hospital, and assisted by doctors, for her last two deliveries. "My most difficult was Cheryl, who came breech, weighing nearly ten pounds, and not taken by Caesarean section." By now Mother was forty years old — about the same age as her own mother, who died as a result of a failed breech delivery. While there has been a re-introduction of home births, attended by trained midwives, who encourage a return to a natural squatting position for childbirth, Mother welcomed hospital stays, as much-needed vacations, and powerful, pain-control medications. She was not one of those women who would later complain about the "medicalization" of childbirth.

Conservative religious moral values did not allow Mother to practice birth control long before the church's position on contraception was spelled out in July 1968 by Pope Paul VI's *Humanae Vitae*, an encyclical prompted in part by the new availability of birth control pills. The Vatican, then and today, does not approve of the Pill, or other birth-control methods for that matter, except for the rhythm method, as it states that every marital act must remain open to creation.

Mother never seriously considered artificial birth control, since "go forth and propagate" is a teaching of the Church. The new European abortion pill RU486, or Mifeprex as it is called in the U.S., would have been especially unthinkable. Our parents lovingly accepted all the children God gave to them, although Mother was almost embarrassed to tell Dad she was pregnant once more. Their tenth and last child, Rodney, (Sister Veronica's godchild), was born just days short of Mother's forty-second birthday.

Mother did everything she could to not gain weight since the complicated delivery had frightened her a year or so earlier. Being victims of the tobacco industry themselves, even doctors did not understand the harmful effects to the fetus and approved of her smoking for a short time, to curb her appetite.

She also suffered terribly from morning sickness during this pregnancy. It is fortunate the notorious drug thalidomide, mistakenly prescribed for morning sickness, would not yet be available for another year. Within that short time many babies were born with hideous birth deformities, including missing arms and legs, before the drug was taken off the market.

Her role as a day-to-day mother lasted for more than forty-five years, from 1934 to 1980. Not long before Rodney, the youngest child, was to leave home for college, she agreed to take in Carlos Eduardo Bezerra, a high school foreign exchange student from Recife, Brazil. Another couple from Stockton agreed to host the boy, but after discovering he was Catholic, and they were not, they asked our parents to take him in for the rest of the school year.

In 1934, after our parents returned from living in Colorado to northwestern Kansas, Dad rented land near Damar from his father, and started farming on his own. In full swing was the New Deal, an expression from FDR's nomination, which described laws designed to combat the economic depression, and to address long-range social and economic reforms.

Wheat crops were sparse, damaged by the combination of a thin layer of topsoil, little rain, and high winds typically above twenty mph. Many farmers began to lose their land due to dust storms and drought, which gripped the entire Midwest. Contributing to the crisis was the over-zealous plowing of huge tracts of fragile, virgin prairie grasslands, combined with corner-to-corner planting of winter wheat to get as much profit out of the land during the short term. Our parents endured the dustbowl years (1934-1937) by sheer determination.

The skies darkened as dust, from dry farm fields and unpaved roads, swept through the area. The general population was at risk for respiratory infections, cardiac disease, bronchitis and asthma due to poor air quality. Sinuses were clogged and lungs inflamed. There were at least two recorded deaths in the Damar area from dust pneumonia.

After their second child, Ronald, was born in September 1935, during the worst of the "Dustbowl Dirty Thirties," Mother stuffed wet rags around windows and doors, to keep the dust out. She covered the infant's bassinet with a wet sheet, to prevent baby Ronald from choking on the powdery dirt that seeped through cracks of their prairie home.

In Mother's biography she told of many times, during the three-year period, when dust billowed up into the sky, and blotted out the sun. She had to light a coal oil lantern, due to the blackened sky, and feared her husband would not be able to find his way home, after taking his horses to work for the day at the Stockton Lake.

Our parents, Mother more than Dad, passed on accounts like these. Some versions weren't shared until our adult years. Even more stories unraveled after their deaths, many of which Sister Veronica researched and documented in the two family history books.[17]

Mother was well into her third pregnancy, in July 1937, when our parents heard on the radio that Amelia Earhart, the "angel of the air" and one of the best-known women worldwide, (and born at her grandparents' home, in Atchison, Kansas within blocks from Benedictine College) disappeared while attempting to fly around the world. Incidentally, it would be thirty more years before Mother took her first commercial flight.

The worst of the dust storms throughout the Midwest were nearly over, but as a result prairie grass was scarce, and cows had nothing to graze on, except for wild Russian thistles. Allan Everett Joseph Roy was born that year in November. "Cow's milk was foul tasting and didn't agree with the new baby," recalled Mother. It is most likely Allan suffered an intolerance of cows' milk resulting in croup, allergies, headaches, failure to gain weight, and failure to thrive. People told her, "That baby won't live to see his first birthday."

"In those days we didn't have special milk formula, or prepared baby food in jars to buy at the store," Mother said. "If a family was lucky they had an icebox for refrigeration, but we didn't. The Doctor suggested we get a goat. When the baby needed to be fed in the middle of the night, my husband got up to milk the goat."

Gary/Father Duane commented, "Mother had a notion that breast feeding violated Christian modesty. This view, common during the time of 1934 to 1951, was also typical thinking of her sisters, sisters-in-laws, and neighboring friends. Perhaps more importantly, around the 1930s, the medical profession 'sold out' to the milk industry [especially canned milk products], with the help of modern advertising, suggesting that breast feeding was old-fashioned, out of style, and not healthy for mother or child." On the contrary, today's studies show that breast-feeding is physically, emotionally and economically advantageous for an infant, especially in the first six months.

It is notable, in the last years of Sister Veronica's life, that she overcame Mother's puritanical beliefs and was instrumental, during her rural pastoral ministry, as an advocate of breast-feeding, especially through LaLeche League and WIC programs in Rooks and Phillips Counties.

Breast-feeding is among one of the many basics taught through *Pastoral da Criança*, Pastoral of the Child, a Brazilian program sponsored by the Brazilian Catholic Bishops, intending to prevent infant mortality. This program was a nominee for the 2001 Nobel Peace Prize. A center, housing this facility in Mineiros, Goiâs, Brazil, where Father Duane lived for nearly thirty years, was financed by the friends and family of Sister Veronica Roy, and dedicated in her memory in March 2000.

Allan survived a rough beginning, and he, along with his older brothers Kenneth and Ronald often romped barefoot through the plowed fields in overalls and homemade shirts of printed flour-sacks. There was time for play, but Kenneth, being the oldest, was relied upon to help with chores.

Children born into hard times learn early the cruelty and rewards of nature. As they grew older, responsibilities were assumed. Boys worked alongside Dad and girls, in the house, with Mother. Each became aware of the importance of being productive, since manpower was needed on the farm. There were opportunities to learn, and responsibilities accepted, to make a real contribution to the welfare of others, a legacy Sister Veronica, especially, took to heart.

✝

Chapter Four

During Ila Mae's childhood in this rural area of Kansas, heritage was still honored. Old Glory was briskly raised at the beginning of the school day, and ceremoniously lowered at the end. When the "Star Spangled Banner" was heard, students and parents stood, placed their right hand over their hearts, and looked toward the American flag. There were neither debates about free speech, nor vicious disputes about church and state. It was a time of honest innocence. A note was sent home with rowdy children and they returned to school, the next day, minding their manners, and showing respect to their teachers.

"Ila Mae was a good student," recalled Jean Grover Lindsey, a neighbor and five years older. "She was a quiet, pleasant little girl, and always a willing helper, whether it was cleaning erasers or helping first graders with their lessons."

"Do you remember the thrill of starting a new Big Chief tablet?" Ila Mae asked. One of her first letters, written from Fairview School, shows excellent penmanship for a child of five, going on six. "Dear Mother, I can spell. I can read. I have seven more pages to go. I can count to 200. I know my ABC's. I know a piece for Christmas."

From the first day of school she developed a love of learning. "Those early days were the beginning of my desire to be a teacher." Perhaps her role model was Dorothy Sprick, an older girl, who also lived in our Belmont Township. After leaving the area and earning a teaching certificate, she returned to be Ila Mae's first teacher.

Only four years old when she started first grade, Ila Mae attended two years at the one-room country school. "I loved school, and brought books home every day, until Wayne Grover, the neighbor boy, hit me on the head with them." He was a typical 1940s boy. Our brother, Gary, also started school, at age four, to be a classmate with his playmate, Wayne, who was a year older.

"I walked through our neighbor's pasture with my brothers to the Fairview School, district 99, one-half mile northwest of our house on old Highway 24," Ila Mae said. "Often during recess, or after school, we played in the surrounding chalk hills, between school and north of home, with pretend guns and arrows shaped by Kenneth."

Jean Grover Lindsey added, "This shortcut probably took longer as we stopped to play 'Hide and Seek' or 'Cowboys and Indians' in the hills, or wade in the creek, before we parted for the day. We three older students [Kenneth and Allan Roy, and Jean] probably made life rough for the younger ones, but Ila Mae, Gary and Wayne all turned out to be good Christian citizens [a Nun, a

Priest, and a Veterinarian] who worked to make this world a better place.

"Our families were good friends, and our fathers helped each other with farm work. In both of our homes there was lots of love, a time for work, play, worship, and plenty to eat. What more did we need? I found a photograph of the school, but not one with the children who attended," said Jean. "We probably couldn't afford to buy film, but we never felt poor."

The Roy and Grover children were the only ones to attend the last two years of the country school. After Fairview permanently closed, in 1947, they were bussed to the Webster school, dedicated in 1914, and located in the nearby town of old Webster.

In Ila Mae's combined seventh and eighth grade class there were only fourteen students.[1] She started her record of academic excellence early in life, and as a twelve-year-old, she was nearly a straight A student, as witnessed by the superintendent, Charles Garrison, as well as Pansy Coolbaugh, her teacher, school principal and a fine Christian woman.

Separation of church and state was not purely adhered to in the 1950s, as evidenced by presence of the Women's Christian Temperance Union, which Mrs. Coolbaugh invited into the classroom monthly for a while. The prayer meeting, during school hours, required school-age girls to take a pledge against having alcoholic beverages in their home. Our family was exempt from the W.C.T.U. prayers. Prior to the Second Vatican Council, Catholics could participate only in their own church prayers.

Moreover, neither divine, nor natural, law forbade the use of alcohol in moderation. The Catholic Church generally opposed extreme measures, and believed that reform must come from within. Many strong-minded Methodists in this community held a different view.

Just under the surface was an undercurrent of general unrest going on in Rooks County for at least two decades; the moderate use of alcohol was but one of several issues including oil, water, land, religion and education. Furthermore, the construction of the Webster Reservoir muddied relationships and provoked consequences for the school and other social systems for many years.

According to newspaper accounts much credit for building the Webster Dam, or blame depending on whom you ask, goes to Mrs. Curtis Fry, a general store owner. Known as the "Mother of the Bureau of Reclamation Webster Dam Project," Mrs. Fry initiated the plan twenty years earlier in 1932 during the Great Depression, with a letter to the Kansas governor, Harry H. Woodring, (1931-1933), requesting a dam be built to utilize the Solomon River in Rooks County.

While the U.S. Bureau of Reclamation has been around since 1902, it wasn't until after the droughts of the late 1920s and early 1930s that interest in reclamation really took hold. At which time, this agency began working alongside the U.S. Army Corps of Engineers to build dams for management and sale of power and water. The Flood Control Act of 1944 broadened the federal authority and, in most instances, the Bureau of Reclamation not only constructed dams, but also controlled sites. This was possible because all land ultimately belongs to the state under the power of Eminent Domain, by which land may be transferred by condemnation proceedings.

The government began purchasing land in the 1950s throughout Belmont, Rush and Richland Townships for the purpose of constructing the Webster Reservoir. Even a cemetery had to be moved. Harry Griffin relocated two hundred coffins to the Webster addition of the Stockton cemetery. The remaining twenty-nine were moved to other parts of the state, according to Carl R. Brown, Rooks County historian.

The end result was those 3,740 acres of land, where the town and school of old Webster once stood, were bought up and ultimately covered in water. After serving as an elementary and high school for thirty-eight years, the redbrick, three-story Webster school was dismantled.

The foundation for the Webster Dam was completed in 1953. The government employed our brother, Kenneth, after high school graduation to drive a water truck.[2] The dedication of the Webster Dam took place in June 1956 and was well attended by dignitaries, as well as many locals.

One historical account in the hometown *Rooks County Record* newspaper reported, "[After receiving payment from the government] there were many families who had to give up their homes and move to other locations."[3]

While our family only lost 1.8 acres by right of Eminent Domain for easement purposes along new Highway 24, there were bitter disputes between citizens forced to move off their homeland, and those whose home sites were not affected. Losing choice land, on which crude oil may have been drilled, seemed to be a primary bone of contention after the fact. It soon came to be informally known as "The Damn Dam." Cries of injustice came from both sides.

Albert and Friona Richardson, one family forced to move, were among the first to settle at the new Webster town site, which had been previously voted into existence. They established a country market, which came to be known as "Arkie's Store," where locals could buy gas and fish bait. The store closed on Friday at sundown, as they were Seventh Day Adventists. Dad stopped his school bus here for five minutes or so after each school day to allow children to buy bubble gum, penny candy, or other treats. Sometimes, he bought Popsicles for every child on the bus. It was here that Dad bought his favorite, thick, hand-sliced bologna, rather then in town.

The *Hays Daily News* stated, "Webster is the town that was moved lock, stock and barrel from its original location in order to build a huge dam on the site it once occupied. There was considerable unhappiness over the move, for there were those who did not favor the location chosen for the new town [and the new school]."[4]

The multi-layered story went much deeper. Jealousy, political and religious beliefs were also among the many facets. Father Duane recalled, "A few Methodist families moved their church building to the south side, on the Richardson's property. Together on a few acres the new school, the Methodist church and the store, along with four or five residences, became 'new' Webster.

"Our family was among the three Catholic families (Veverkas and Bedores) in this predominately Methodist rural township. The Catholics were neither vocal, nor insistent enough, and their vote did not hold much weight in the selection of the most logical site of the new school, which our Dad believed was on the north side, near the newly constructed Highway 24."

There were not even the required one hundred students enrolled in the new Webster consolidated elementary and high school. Some schoolchildren, who previously attended Webster, no longer did because of the geographical location. No new families moved into the area, and the school-age population declined. What was once an emotionally packed episode of this town's history soon proved that an ill-fated choice had been made. Dad's logic proved correct. The high school closed nine years later, in 1963, with a graduating class of three.[5] The elementary school closed a few years later, and children were bussed eight miles or more into Stockton.

In this normally laid back, sleepy little community, the hostilities were out of proportion, and there was great public divide over building the Webster Dam, the site of the new town and school. Often tempers flared, while voices and fists were raised in anger. "John and I decided that we would maintain a neutral stance," said Mother who, along with Dad, was non-confrontational. "To show no partiality, we decided the younger children would attend the lower grades at the newly completed Webster school, and Allan and Ila Mae, the two oldest, would attend high school in town."

Father Duane speculates, "While Ila Mae was told her attendance at the Stockton school was a way the family could remain neutral, I think it was a decision made in protest of the school's location. What is strange to me now is why did she have to go to Stockton, and I didn't? It could have been that I was a classmate of Wayne Grover since first grade, and Dad and Mom didn't have the heart to separate us."

This was most likely true. The Roy family tried very hard to mend the one-time rift with the neighborly Grovers. As staunch, teetotaler Methodists, they were highly offended that alcohol was served at a wedding reception in the school gymnasium, even though the school board granted permission as the building was about to be torn down.

Allan preferred the larger Stockton school and continued there until his graduation, and subsequently joined the U.S. Army. Ila Mae, who preferred

Webster, was dissatisfied with the change. "I attended both the old and the newly built Webster schools from grades three through twelve, with exception of my freshman year in Stockton." It wasn't until three years later when, as a senior at Webster High, Mother explained to Ila Mae why she first sent her to Stockton. "I never knew which school I would attend until the first day of classes."

As a big sister, Ila Mae seemed taller than five feet, six inches. Throughout high school she remained a thin size six. Strong, yet trim, she moaned that she was "too skinny, and not built like some of the other girls in town." A Stockton yearbook photo shows Ila Mae, a fresh scrubbed freshman, wearing a jewel-necked sweater, dark-rimmed eyeglasses, and short wavy hair. With a lovely smile and scattered freckles, she was attractive, in a wholesome sort of way. She confided of a longing to be told she was pretty. "The freshman year I attended Stockton, I was the only teenage girl there not wearing make-up. I thought Mother would tell me when I could."

There is no doubt the girls in our family were sheltered. Mother only wore a little lipstick herself that barely defined her lips, as if put on without a mirror. She believed it cheap for high school girls to wear make-up, a belief that did not change over the next fifteen years. In 1970, the youngest daughter received a light pink lipstick and cheek blush for her sixteenth birthday from high school girlfriends, who were already wearing light make up. "It was so mild compared to what teenage girls are doing today, but when Mother found out, all hell broke loose," Cheryl said.

Undoubtedly, Ila Mae's classmates thought of the country girl as different. As a shy teenager, she thought she did not fit in with the town kids. However, at Stockton High she outrivaled her classmates, as usual, and that spring she won the 1955 Betty Crocker Homemaker Award. Nevertheless, and much to her delight, she returned to the small rural Webster school her sophomore year.

According to the *Hays Daily News*, "The budget to build the new school came from the $108,000 payment for the old Webster school building. In addition, the government supplied a generous, but undisclosed amount. The State of Kansas was broadening its rural education program at the time with consolidated schools."[6]

In a sense the yellow brick new school, located one mile south of the Webster Dam and not far from our farmhouse, remained only several steps removed from one-room country schools of yesteryear. Teachers taught combined grades in the same room: first and second grades were pooled, as were third, fourth and fifth, and sixth through eighth grades. High school classes were grouped, as well.

Another article in the *Hays Daily News* touted the new Webster school, "Probably one of the finest rural high schools in western Kansas..." For this reason, it attracted dedicated teachers who were willing to travel to this farming community. As pivotal role models, in separate years, Ila Mae excelled under the guidance of Caroline Carlley, and later Mrs. Robert Brin, her home economics teachers, who also served as librarians. In the autumn of 1955, the small school library received $1,000 to purchase additional books to add to its nine hundred volumes. Ila Mae was studious and valued books, even though they were rare at home.

With direction from the combined industrial arts and math teacher, Leland Balthazor, she took algebra and geometry, and had dreams of becoming a mathematics teacher like he was. Hubert Dillon, the school superintendent, doubled as drivers education instructor and taught her how to maneuver a car.

All able-bodied students were required to participate in sports activities. The pride of the community was the school gymnasium. Here the rule of "no street shoes on the gym floor" was strictly adhered to, unlike the old Webster gymnasium where Gary's eighth grade graduation ceremony was held in May 1954. Not only did he play plenty of basketball, but roller skating parties were held there, too.

The twenty-nine year old Glenn "Mitch" Mitchum taught history, health, bookkeeping, and typing. He later served as school principal, until the high school closed. Most importantly, he was the sports coach who encouraged Ila Mae to use her talents on the basketball court, which helped boost her confidence. She gave a lot of credit to her coach, and it is likely he was one of the ten most influential people in her life. What she learned, under his guidance, served her well. She was glad to have the opportunity to compete, which she believed made a positive difference in her life. Throughout the years, coach Mitchum, and his wife Gwen, stayed in touch with his former student, and when their daughter, Susan, was married, Sister Veronica served as Lector at the wedding.

The night after Sister Veronica's death, Mitchum described her as, "Aggressive on the basketball court. She might elbow someone and say she was sorry, but only after making the basket," he chuckled.

Before Title IX, the federal law regulating equity in the treatment of the sexes in sports, there were six-person teams in girls' high school basketball. Three played offense, three on defense. Farm girls had plenty of stamina, but the half-court rule was a restriction we accepted without question, not knowing about human and civil rights issues during this time. All we knew was that we had fun, and enjoyed the hard work, practice, and discipline of teamwork. "I ate and slept basketball in the winter season," Ila Mae said.

Our sister, Joan, one of Ila Mae's teammates, also loved sports. "At the beginning of the school year, we were required to clean the tumbleweeds and summer overgrowth, from the wire fence behind the catcher's box, before beginning softball practice."

When Mickey Mantle was a national childhood hero, Coach Mitchum arranged for a television to be set up in the school cafeteria so the entire school could watch the World Series.

Many school activities centered on sports, and our parents attended all afternoon and evening games. Being farmers, they didn't punch a time clock. They were never too busy to watch us participate in sports, music events, school activities, or 4-H programs. Mother said, "It seemed there was always some activity." Track meets, and practice in the spring kept us busy, too, with high jumps, broad jump, fifty-yard dashes, and relay races.

Letter jacket pins were awarded for all kinds of sports, as well as band, chorus, woodworking, reading, and other activities. Ila Mae was also an enthusiastic cheerleader for the small team, for four years, which she continued into her freshman year at college.

According to the *Hays Daily Newspaper*, "Webster School, standing like a monument on the prairie [eight] miles west and perhaps a half mile south of Stockton, offers to its seventy-two pupils an education including...a musical program so exceptional it is probably not equaled by any other school in the state...The music teacher is especially proud of the well-balanced representation of instruments including an oboe, bassoon and two pianos. The superintendent, Charles Garrison, believes music to be a universal language, which will always be useful.

"A forty-two piece band is supported entirely by the school. Musical instruments, and the finest gorgeous blue, white and gold uniforms, are furnished free of charge. In full uniform, the well-known Webster marching band often performs throughout Kansas. They appeared in Salina, Fort Hays State University Parents Day, the State Fair in Hutchinson, and for sporting events at Bogue and Zurich."[7]

"We also paraded the streets of Stockton [on October 5 and 6, 1956] when the Webster Dam was inaugurated," Ila Mae added. Fourteen Kansas towns banded together and sponsored a dedication ceremony, a parade and free barbecue. A dedication speech from Assistant U.S. Secretary of Interior, Fred G. Aandahl kicked off the festivities.[8]

Middle and high school students were required to take part in chorus and band. As music teacher, Paul Darnell inspired his charges, as in the movie, *Mr. Holland's Opus*. Under Darnell's discipline and direction, Ila Mae learned to play the clarinet and saxophone, which she continued during her first year at college, before entering the convent.

"P.T.A. meetings, a family affair, were expected to be attended by at least one parent," said Ila Mae. "Both upper and lower grade school children showed up as well, since they provided the musical or theatric entertainment for the evening. In surroundings like these, we learned to appear before an audience, and make use of our talents."

Dale Arbogast and Jack Becker were her classmates. As the *Webster Eagle* yearbook editor for two years running she wrote, "We, the Seniors of Webster High School, class of 1957, do hereby dedicate our Annual to you, our parents: Mr. and Mrs. O.J. Arbogast, Mr. and Mrs. Raymond Becker, and Mr. and Mrs. John Roy. It is with the deepest respect and appreciation that we do so. Without your constant guidance and understanding, it would have been impossible for us to attain our goal. Our yearbook is one of the most important achievements in our school life and we would like to share it with you."

In the Class Will she wrote, "I, Ila Roy, will my ability to write shorthand notes, with Marilyn Lowry, to boys who wish to decipher them; my natural curly hair to anyone who complains about theirs being straight; and my 4-H awards to younger members so they won't get discouraged."

"These years were opportunities to learn at individual paces, and to participate in everything available, as the school was quite small," she said later on. That is an understatement, which underplays her class valedictorian status. Nevertheless, she rightfully earned many scholastic honors and athletic and music awards, including serving as student council president. "All of the high school activities gave me numerous skills and confidence for whatever lay ahead."

Perhaps those who knew of her shyness would never think Ila Mae would enjoy having a leading role in nearly all high school plays. Even thirty years later, on a paper and pencil test of her interests, she showed a high, yet unfulfilled interest in dramatics.

She was a nice, quiet, well-behaved girl, unsophisticated yet prim, with a genuine smile for everyone. Like other teenagers, Ila Mae had a need to feel special, and was pleased to receive praise from grown-ups. Task-oriented, she saw a strong relationship between a job well done and getting recognition, and throughout high school she excelled at everything she tried.

In perfect penmanship she addressed envelopes to each Uncle and Aunt. Enclosed was an announcement of the senior class of Webster High School commencement exercises to be held on May 22nd, 1957 at eight p.m. A three-cent Liberty stamp was neatly affixed.

Good study habits continued throughout college. Aspiring to her dream of becoming a teacher, she was happy to help her siblings with homework. She was bright and intellectually curious, disciplined, and never rushed through projects haphazardly. She was a person who could stay focused on the task at hand, whether it was her studies, or a 4-H project of sewing, steer raising, or record keeping.

Her environment formed her, and Ila Mae's parents and teachers sheltered her from any rural bickering. She felt safe and secure, and admitted to receiving a good foundation for learning, which served her well throughout life.

✝

Chapter Five

The 4-H motto "Learn by Doing" never changed throughout the years, and provided a guiding light, developing character and determination in the Roy children. Operated by the Extension Services of the U.S. Department of Agriculture, 4-H clubs are organizations for boys and girls living in rural communities. This educational program, initiated in 1914, was designed to improve methods of agriculture and home economics, promote high ideals of civic responsibility, and provide training for community leadership.

At each monthly meeting members of the club recite the oath:
> *I pledge —*
> *My Head to clearer thinking*
> *My Heart to greater loyalty*
> *My Hands to larger service*
> *My Health to better living for*
> *My Club, My Community, and My Country.*

Ila Mae valued the practical side of the organization saying with pride, "I belonged to the 4-W 4-H club (Webster's Willing Workers) from age eight to eighteen. Our family owes a lot to the club, and much of the credit goes to the 4-H leaders who encouraged us (Helen Lindsey, Charlotte Riffe, and Beluah Kellogg.) They expected us to complete whatever we set out to do."

Father Duane added, "Some of the most important figures in my life were those local adult male leaders[1] including Dad, who served as conservation leader for several years, and Mother, as health leader."

When she was only twelve years old, Ila Mae was considered a champion in her particular field of cooking and sewing; a perfectionist even in her youth. She was one of the honorees at an Achievement Banquet, sponsored by the Farm Bureau Association, Stockton Chamber of Commerce, and the Rooks County 4-H Council. The *Rooks County Record*, the hometown newspaper featured the event.

Good at detail and organization she had a gentle leadership style, leading by example. As an introvert, she balanced shyness with courage, and managed to stand in front of a crowd and demonstrate the proper way to perform a task. "These years [1947-1957] gave me many opportunities to be creative, responsible and a visible leader in the community. I used my recognized talent for improving farm and community life. It also tied in with the betterment of the school."

The 4-H club also provided an outlet for recreation, and helped develop social skills, too. On the square dance team, Ila Mae participated in competitions and performed on live television on Channel 2, the Great Bend station.

She, and others in the family, held various offices in the club. "By the time I left for college, I had served as president and secretary/reporter and was presented the 'Who's Whoot' 4-H Award." Ila Mae earned an all-expenses paid American Royal trip to Kansas City for her accomplishments, and won Junior Leadership awards through her service on county councils, county fair judgings, and music and dance festivals.

The Rooks County Free Fair was recognized as one of the finest in the state and rewarded 4-H members, making it possible for many to excel. Her projects were formally registered on the first day of Fair Week. The five-day event, the "Fair of Champions" as it boasts, first began in 1879. It was held just before the start of the school year, oftentimes around August 15, the feast of the Assumption, a holy day.

At the county fair, grandstand entertainment included tractor pulling contests, stock car races, demolition derbies, motorcycle races, horse races, and big name music attractions. For the youngsters there was a greased pig-catching contest, a hilarious sight. While the trashy midway carnival, with its sideshows, rigged games and stomach-churning rides, held an attraction for most of the youth, Ila Mae was content to visit the educational booths, and exhibits of domestic arts, grains, and livestock.

St. Thomas Catholic Church and the 4-H clubs erected and operated food stands on the fair grounds each year. Ila Mae was pleased to be a part of these fund-raising operations. Our sister-in-law, Jacalyn Roy, described her own experience working with the food stand in 2001: "We were busy, and with no air-conditioning. I was a greasy, sweaty mess when I got out at 11 p.m., although it was fun and I enjoyed watching the kids wait on the customers. I was in charge of the hot dogs, polish sausage, sloppy Joes, Frito pies and nachos. It is amazing how much stuff comes out of one little area. There was also the hamburger, barbequed beef area, and the pie, ice cream and malt area." The menu and conditions have not changed since Ila Mae volunteered there forty-five years ago.

As an eleven-year-old, in 1951, Ila Mae won blue-ribbon cooking awards for yeast breads, which Mother taught her to make, and for cherry pies made from the fresh fruit that our family handpicked, then preserved. Her membership in the 4-H club helped to develop her talent in nutrition, a springboard for a career in dietetics. However, it is interesting to note that while cooking, or directing it, was what she did for the bulk of her adult life, Ila Mae talked very little about it from an adolescent view, because it was a field not of her choosing.

Home conservation projects included sewing, and in the 1940s and 1950s Mother sewed all the girls' school and church dresses, pajamas, and even underwear, from thoroughly washed cotton flour sacks of printed fabric. In her own biography Mother said, "It was rewarding to see all the children accomplish so much through 4-H. We took great pride in their work, and I learned right along with my girls. My oldest daughter was the one who taught me how to use a dress pattern. Before that I never used one, because they were too costly."

In the eighth grade, Ila Mae sewed a simple half-apron, from a small-floral print fabric, with "rick-rack" trim. Even though this required only basic skills, her apron was sewn to perfection. The next year she tackled a more difficult project, a dress with contrasting Peter-pan collar, placket inset, and cap sleeves.

Ila Mae admired the older girls in the 4-H club. Some were sewing garments that are more complicated: suits and dresses. One of girls was Jean Grover Lindsey, a longtime neighbor and friend: "When I was in high school I helped younger members at the cooking and clothing project meetings. Ila Mae was quiet, pleasant and conscientious. She always had a smile on her face."

"I worked for hours, to place and pin the pattern on the fabric just so, before I ever cut any fabric," Ila Mae said. "One time I spent all afternoon cutting out a tailored cotton slip, but I don't think I even wore it after that." She demanded much of herself and adhered to the philosophy, "If it's worth doing, it's worth doing right." Aunt Jeanette recalled that when they were living not far from each other in Illinois, Sister Veronica/Ila Mae often went to visit her in the 1970s. She was welcomed to use the sewing machine, and continued to adhere to high standards, matching plaid or patterned fabric to come out just so.

"Dad never seemed to mind how much I sewed but once he asked me, 'How much does a store-bought dress cost?' I only remember owning two in my youth; one was plaid, and the other, a mousy-colored brown." Joan recalled that her first purchased dress, for her Confirmation ceremony, was at age nine; for this writer, it was an eighth-grade graduation dress.

"We got our new electric Singer sewing machine about the time I moved away from home, but it seemed too fast for me," said Ila Mae. "I learned to sew on an old manual machine, which I preferred." She rhythmically rocked her foot back and forth on the treadle, while guiding the fabric in straight even stitches.

Throughout the ten years of her participation in 4-H, she won numerous medals and awards with entries in Room Improvement, Sewing, Foods and Bread Making, Home and Grounds Beautification, and Livestock. One of the highlights of Fair week, for locals, was the Best Groomed Boy contest and clothing Style Review for girls. "I worked hard on contest entries and, for several years, was eligible to represent our county at the Kansas State Fair in Hutchinson," said Ila Mae. She won the Reserve Champion award in Style

Review, for a dress she fashioned out of boucle wool.

"Several 4-H experiences boosted my personal self-esteem," added Gary/Father Duane. "Around 1957 Mom purchased for me a tweed winter suit, and encouraged me to sign up for the boy's contest, which accompanied the Style Review at the Rooks County Fair. On the night of this competition, all contestants lined up on stage before a full grandstand. A brief judging took place, and soon the official results were announced through the loudspeakers: 'Gary Roy. Sixteen years old. Grand Champion winner. Best Groomed Boy of Rooks County.' My photo appeared in the *Rooks County Record* newspaper. I won a $12.00 cash prize, and eligibility to compete at the State Fair. Just imagine — a farm boy walking off with that honor! My stylish double-breasted suit, with freshly shined shoes, was a sharp contrast to normal everyday attire, of dungarees and plaid work shirt. I went to school in bib overalls, and later on in western denim jeans, even before they came into style. The Roy family was well known throughout Rooks County from these activities."

Without the fancy label of visualization, a trendy term in the 1980s, she had used this technique twenty-five years earlier. "As the County Fair approached in mid-August, I'd often walk along the cow path in the pasture, imagining being on stage, and modeling the garments that I sewed for the event."

For her junior year high school banquet, she sewed a mid-calf length, strapless dress from pink tulle over taffeta. Since the enrollment of Webster High was too small to have a prom, this sit-down dinner, at a restaurant in town, was a compromise. No doubt, she also wore this dress to one of the formal dances during her first year at Marymount College, where she caught the eye of Bernard Scholl.

The next year, as a senior in high school, she won the Grand Champion prize for a fully lined, two-piece khaki green, wool jumper and jacket that she sewed. She finished off the ensemble with a long-sleeved beige blouse, and matching beige accessories typical of the fifties: purse, hat, gloves and pumps. One of the few professional-looking garments she owned, most likely she wore this tailored and modest outfit for her first interview with Mother Superior.

Like Mother, Ila Mae was not a clotheshorse. Garments did not mean much to her, unless she had the satisfaction of sewing them herself. One of the few exceptions was an exquisite ready-made dress of silvery, powder blue *mousseline de soie*. When she was sixteen years old, Ila Mae was a bridesmaid for her cousin's wedding when Melvin Desmarteau married Marguerite Holmes, an Ellis native. This dress, with cap sleeves and demur bodice, was the most elegant creation Ila Mae would ever wear. She also wore this special outfit for her senior high school photo. She added Mother's costume jewelry of silver earrings and matching necklace, encrusted with square-cut rhinestones — quite a sophisticated look for a farm girl who normally wore jeans everyday.

"In the eighth grade Dad let me own, groom and care for a lightweight Hereford steer, which also won champion ribbons from livestock judgings," said Ila Mae. A newspaper clipping and photo, dated 1952, shows her wearing a sleeveless white cotton blouse, denim jeans triple rolled at the cuff, bobby sox and penny loafers. Dad and brothers Gary and Allan surrounded her. Joan also raised a steer that she named "Tony," after the popular movie star Tony Curtis, no doubt.

Another photograph captured Ila Mae, as a senior in high school, taking center stage holding the reins of her prized heifer. At that time, her 4-H project would have sold for nearly thirty-two cents a pound. Currently the animal, on hoof, would bring barely twice that much, while other goods and services have increased in price ten times, or more. In her last years of life, she became involved with rural farm life and sustainable agriculture issues. She fully understood that farmers' and ranchers' lifelong dreams and occupations are up against an economic pinch.

Another benefit of 4-H membership was attending, for five days each summer, the statewide Rock Springs Ranch co-ed camp near Junction City, along with nearly two hundred other teenagers. The International Farm Youth Exchange program (IFYE), which began in 1948, was incorporated into this camp. This was the first time many rural teenagers met others from foreign countries, their same age, and often later corresponded with their new pen pals.

For many rural youths, like Ila Mae, this was also the first and long-awaited opportunity of being away from home on their own. There were numerous activities to keep the youths busy — rotating KP duties, swimming, crafts, horseback riding, and dancing. The terrain was hilly, there were many steps to climb, and at the end of each full day their youthful energy was nearly spent. There were eight to ten girls (or boys) and two leaders to each tent. Beds had to be made each day. Postcards and stamps were provided, as they were encouraged to write home. Later, as a junior in high school, she was selected as a camp counselor.

Ila Mae and Gary also attended a specialized weeklong Conservation Camp for teenagers. Afterward, they jointly submitted several articles for the local newspaper, and presented numerous talks and demonstrations at 4-H meetings, including one on measures for rat control to preserve stored grains. Both she and Gary enjoyed outdoor work, and learned about soil conservation techniques from Dad, who planted corn, wheat, milo, hay, and clover, in rotation over the years, to avoid depleting nutrients from the earth. Adhering to lessons learned from dust bowl days, Dad also built terraces to prevent soil erosion.

Home and Grounds Beautification was another 4-H project. Prior to the mid-1950s, there was no grass around the farmhouse, just lots of loose and blowing dirt. "Mother drove us to the pasture where we dug patches of native buffalo grass, which we transplanted to keep soil in the yard from washing away. This dramatically improved the appearance of the area around our farm house," said Ila Mae. "I also helped build a fence around the yard to keep chickens out. Cement cylinders were placed around the edges as an additional barrier. The fence also acted as a backdrop for zinnias, and other varieties of annual and perennial flowers.

"Cherry, apricot, and various shade trees, and small evergreen shrubberies, were also planted nearby. In the 1950s, a windbreak [of Chinese elm and black walnut trees], which continued to thrive [for nearly five decades], was planted on three sides of the farm. Branches were regularly trimmed for neater growth."

In the mid-1950s, Oria Grover, our neighbor and long-time soil conservation leader, organized a tree-planting weekend for the members of our club. Ila Mae was among the youth group, of fifteen or so, who worked tirelessly to dig holes and plant hundreds of saplings on the east and west sides of the Webster Reservoir. These are now mature cedar trees, a native to Kansas.

"Planting a tree…is symbolic of what each of us should do separately to help restore and preserve our landscapes," Grover wrote for the ceremony. "Future generations will enjoy the fruits of our labor, just as we enjoy the trees planted, and cared for by our forefathers. It is our privilege to leave the world more beautiful than we found it."

In the early 1990s, a tornado damaged many trees on the grounds of the Motherhouse Convent in Concordia. Our brother, Roger, and his wife, Jacalyn, purchased a tree in Sister Veronica's memory. "The Starburst Honey Locust tree was planted near the pagoda, south of the grotto, and within sight of the Cemetery, where Sister Veronica is buried," said the CSJ president Sister Christine Doman. "Those [of the remaining 250 Sisters] living at or nearby the convent on May 1, 1996, attended the ceremony and prayer service. That day is the Feast of St. Joseph the Worker, an appropriate day to celebrate. The opening and closing song of the ceremony was 'Touch the Earth.' We prayed, 'Unless a seed falls to the ground and dies, it remains just a seed; but if it dies, it produces much fruit.'"[2]

Like the 4-H pledge she recited in her youth, Sister Veronica moved through life using her head, heart, hands and health in clear thinking, loyalty and service. She planted seeds and ideas — spiritual and otherwise. The fruits of her labor that she first began during her youth in 4-H culminated in much good during her lifetime. To paraphrase her one time soil conservation leader, Sister Veronica left the world more beautiful then she found it.

Chapter Six

Remember, of these parents you were born; what can you give them for all they gave you?

— Sirach 7:28

Mother was talkative, charismatic almost, dominating conversations yet drawing friends near. Ila Mae admired Mother's outgoing nature, but it was Dad's gentleness, and quiet leadership through example that she cherished the most.

A farmer like his father before him, owning land and livestock, Dad had a genuine smile for friends and strangers alike. Our six brothers, the other significant men in Ila Mae's life, were a reflection of Dad's calm and easy-going manner. Our parents loved watching things grow, especially their children.

Just after World War II ended, the six-year old Ila Mae already had five remaining siblings. The war years, for our family, were years of growth through frugality. There is a saying, "Security is not measured by the things you have, but rather by the things you can do without." Life on the farm, during the 1940s and 1950s, taught her self-reliance, optimism, patience, resilience, determination, and not to be down for long. "Making sacrifices, making do," was a motto that marked her early formation.

Growing up in the heartland of immigrants created a sense of being rooted, and was a sanctuary for Ila Mae, even though she was born during a time when this family had no electricity, no indoor plumbing, not even a tractor for farming the land. All extra income was put back into farm equipment, and needed for basic survival.

According to generational values author Morris Massey, the way we work, when we work, how we work, and whether we work is all keyed into value systems.[1] While honoring one of St. Benedict's principles, which suggests that idleness is the enemy of the soul, our family also adhered to the pre-Vatican II church law that forbade servile work on Sunday — no washing clothes or sewing, no construction work, plowing, or digging on this day. Work that is necessary for survival, like harvesting a crop, was allowed.

Our dad was a kind man, but on a rare occasion it was not beyond him to call someone a lazy bum if he deserved it. He was a good judge of character. It was important to be industrious and constantly busy, a trait that describes each of the siblings to this day. Cultivating the land and watching over animals affect the way one approaches all life-and-death matters. The physical work of living on a farm makes a person sleep well at night.

Mother and Dad's goal was to raise children as decent people. Perhaps as farmers in rural America, our parents' own contentedness prevented them from dreaming grander dreams for their children. Instead, they focused on simple pleasures, causing them to overlook the need to nurture talents in the arts, or other hidden ambitions. The children were not groomed for anything but to find one's way in life. It mattered little what career choices each made, although Dad discouraged a granddaughter from becoming an airline flight attendant. "Glorified waitresses," he called them. And he preferred that his daughters remain at home during their child-raising years.

Our working-class home life could not have been any more different from F. Scott Fitzgerald's classic tale, *The Great Gatsby*, of a lavish lifestyle of money and greed. None of our relatives or friends were doctors or tycoons. Instead, they were farmers, teachers or small business owners. Not one of the uncles and aunts ever became so rich as to warrant the envy of other family members, and none aspired to great wealth — only to have enough to provide a safe and comfortable life for their families. Ila Mae and her siblings felt they had everything they needed. For those who married, it was into families within a similar social-economic class with basically comparable values.

Dad wore bib overalls nearly every day of the week, except to church on Sundays, or for social outings. Trim throughout life, in the younger days photographs of him show ill-fitting clothes hanging from his gaunt, angular frame. Nevertheless, he was a handsome man, in a shy sort of way. Just under six feet, he seemed taller because of his proud bearing and excellent posture. His kind and gentle nature attracted the young Olive Morin, and perhaps as well, the good qualities often associated with mothers — fair and generous, soft spoken and reserved. Especially he was honest, and his handshake and word were good. Not boastful, he kept his pride to himself. An exceptional father, he was a strong, silent role model for his children. Ila Mae, who was a lot like Dad, learned early from his example to be a virtuous person.

Free of arrogance, he was a true Christian man in all ways, and his sons followed in his footsteps. He appeared to be introverted, but his oldest son Kenneth recalls, "Dad could talk to anyone. I admired him because he could walk right up to someone, and start a conversation."

A successful farmer, he loved his land. For him, farming was not just a means of making money; it was something he loved to do — an avocation. Yet it was hard work, not just an eight-to-five job, and a gamble at that. Farmers must not only be determined to succeed, but they must also be lucky, which Dad was, but he created some of his own luck. There were times he would have to take side jobs, other then farming, to meet expenses.

With the exploration of oil in Rooks County during the early 1950s, Dad took on a job in Belmont Township as oil well operator for his own wells, and those of his neighbors. Occasionally, he worked as a county road patrol operator — a road grader. Utilizing his own pasture, he also rented land in a cattle feeder operation. When the school bus driver retired in the mid 1950s, to supplement the family income, Dad took over the position, which he held for nearly twenty years. In 1955, he worked on a new bridge on county road 258, a half-mile south of the family home. During this construction, a boomer from a crane hit him on the side of the head, breaking his jaw and dentures, and nearly cutting off his ear.

"He helped build the new Catholic Church in Stockton. An active member of church committees, he was a Fourth Degree Knights of Columbus, and a member of the men's Holy Name Association in the parish," said Sister Veronica. "He blossomed in his later years to being very interested in others, to which he credited *How to Win Friends and Influence People*, a Dale Carnegie public speaking course based on a book by the same title, which he took in the early 1960s."

John Roy had a profound influence on many people — young and old alike. He was competent, and admired for his subtle and considerate leadership style. When Walter Lowry, a Webster High School board member, died unexpectedly, Dad was asked to fill the clerk position. "I didn't want the job, but the committee insisted I take it. It seemed like those of us on the Board were married to that job." His reluctance may have been a lack of formal education past eighth grade, but with his strong sense of practical judgment, he proved to be wiser, and more successful, than many of those more highly educated. "Dad did much toward bettering the school, its facilities, amenities and faculty," said Sister Veronica. "At school events, especially sports and other activities involving his children, he and Mother were always present."

Pheasant and quail hunting, and walleye, crappie and bass fishing, are main attractions to the area, although Dad fished very rarely, and hunted even less. Even though he butchered calves as needed for meat, when his car rammed into a deer at dusk and the sheriff was called to put the deer out of its misery, and the sheriff offered the meat to Dad, he refused. He could never eat venison after that.

In the face of adversity, Dad got on with life. He was not a complainer, but like Henry Ford II, neither was he an explainer. If there was a job to do, he did it. Gifted with common sense, and being a matter-of-fact man of few words, he was a no-nonsense type with plenty of guts and gumption.

On several occasions, when snakes got trapped in the water well near the barn, his children thought him especially brave as he lowered himself down a narrow ten-foot deep dirt and brick pit. His sister, Jeannette, and his youngest daughter, Cheryl, stood by as he yelled out, "stand back," as snakes came flying out.

Mother grew vegetables and baked bread, buying only what was necessary. She was self-sufficient, out of necessity and belief. On the other hand, it was fun to go grocery shopping with Dad, the permissive parent. He bought the extra things that Mother would not, such as grape soda pop, bon-bon candies, and cashew nuts, although we did not like the horehound cough-drop tasting candies he bought for himself.

The natural-born farmer and his homemaker wife were a happy couple. They said it wasn't all hard work on the farm; they also enjoyed life. Life was simple then, and fun was what you made of it. Mother credits the hard times she and Dad went through to making their accomplishments, their home life more meaningful. She was like the late cowgirl Dale Evans, who was often quoted as saying, "Roy (Rogers) and I have known the hard times and the good, and we appreciate what we've got."

As a young woman Mother was outgoing, and enjoyed attending barn dance parties and other neighborly events, such as charivaris (a surprise serenade to newlyweds in the country, which were popular in the 1930s and 1940s.) Mother and Dad began entertaining more in the late 1940s. The spacious rooms of their much-loved large stone house accommodated 4-H square dance practices, school parties and 4-H meetings for thirty or more.

Years later our parents hosted their own 35th wedding anniversary party after moving into their new ranch-style house. They often hosted large family gatherings around the holidays for out-of-state visitors, who knew they were welcome to spend the week.

An unpretentious duo, what they enjoyed most was the company of their siblings, neighbors and fellow church members. Mother was charming, gracious and always a lady. Known for her hospitality, she was a grand hostess to the many guests who unexpectedly dropped by. She offered them "a bite to eat," along with iced tea or coffee, and many times cooked a full meal for them, too. As a friend, Mother was loyal and sociable, and continued to receive many visitors at home up until a few days before her death.

Having the stronger personality, Mother appeared confident and self-assured. She demanded respect and ruled the household, however, she was not strong-willed with her husband. Rather than have words or a disagreement with Dad, she would step outside to cool off, and come back counting her blessings. While Dad was the silent rock, Mother was the guiding force who camouflaged her dominance in a retiring sort of way. Throughout her marriage and child-raising years, she made it clear to her children, "Dad is the boss." It was not until adulthood that some of her children realized that it was she who was often the clever decision maker.

Ila Mae and her Midwest-raised sisters carried the "steel magnolia" element, too: soft and feminine on the outside, tough and capable on the inside. The married sisters wanted their partners to be strong, practical and competent, too, like Dad. Once each one of her children married, Mother stopped directing their lives. "You've made your bed, now you've got to lie in it," a quip she repeated over the years. Holding great respect for the sacrament of marriage and its call for faithfulness and commitment, it caused great disappointment for Mother when her three married daughters each divorced.

Mother and Dad avoided that which destroys a family. Neither tried to upstage the other; theirs was a harmonious marriage. They avoided indecent words, and were wise to know that even when foul language is used without ill intent, it can cause harm to those who hear it.

In addition to no profanity, screaming, or name-calling, there was also no jealousy or hatred, no rivalry or selfishness, no personal ambition, no materialism, no false teaching. Especially, before the Second Vatican Council, there were to be no marriages outside the Catholic Church, as they followed the biblical teaching that marriage is not allowed between a believer and a non-believer.

The Nurture Assumption, by Judith Rich Harris, is based on the theory that parents do not have much influence over the basic personality and temperament traits of their children. Instead, the book speculates that peers have a much greater impact. Mother and Dad made certain their children were not exposed to undesirable elements. "You are known by the company you keep," was another adage this family lived by.

In the small farming communities of Webster, Stockton and Damar, everyone seemed to know what everyone else was doing. On a regular basis, townspeople buzzed with gossip. Mother and Dad kept an ear out for what was important for their childrens' benefit.

Each child was unassuming. Restraint was a trait that began at home, keeping feelings to themselves, especially anger. Laughter and joking did not come easy, and we kept the noise level down in the house. "We were a quiet family, and not commotion-causing," the siblings agreed. Tragically, when Ronald died, the family also lost a free spirit, full of joy and mischief.

Mother often remarked that her first real home was when she married our Dad, because she was so young and she had to stay in different places after her mother died. "Perhaps after growing up without a mother, moving from house to house to live with her sisters, and the vigor of the depression era, Mother learned to keep her own emotions in tight check, which likewise contributed to developing the subdued personalities of her own children," suggests Father Duane.

There was little physical display of warmth, but in hindsight each of us knew intuitively we were loved. There was no hovering during sickness, or gushing or pampering with mushy sentiments. Aunt Irene Morin reflected that it was not uncommon, during this era, for the job of making a living to overshadow taking care of the human needs of the family, such as showing affection. While our parents did not provide individual, focused attention on the older children, they were nearby, in the field or barn, kitchen or garden, to provide a guiding eye.

While Ila Mae respected our self-sufficient Mother, in many ways she was quite different. A master at monologue — a one-sided conversation — Mother adhered to the Victorian philosophy, "Children are to be seen, but not heard." It is clear throughout her life that Ila Mae never felt comfortable with small talk. Several other family members are introverted, too, but she was the most extreme in her desire for silence and solitude.

Everyone else listened while Mother chatted on about everyday happenings. There were few exchanges of ideas, or opinions, between mother and child. Times changed, however, in our family in the mid-1960s, when only the two youngest were at home, and there was more two-way conversation. Perhaps by the time Cheryl was a teenager, Mother was passed the irritable moods of menopause, and her life became calmer, with fewer children to care for.

Cheryl, the chattiest in the family, recalled, "As a typical teenager, I pouted and was moody, which Mother didn't like. She got frustrated because I talked all the time. Full of questions, I wanted to argue with her, but that wasn't allowed. She took it as an insult for one of us to be assertive. It was almost like the doctor-patient relationship common in those days. The doctor says to do something, and the patient obeys without questioning, which was another of her beliefs."

Mother did enjoy taking a few leisurely moments on the rocking chair, or the covered porch swinging with the youngest child. She did not have a great voice, but that did not stop her from singing the refrains of the 1940 classics "Red River Valley," or "You Are My Sunshine." But the bulk of the time it was big sister, Ila Mae, who showered her attention on the younger ones.

To her credit, Olive Roy was a good wife and mother with high family values. Each child was protected from neglect, abuse, abandonment and cruelty. Each knew the subtle difference between "Don't cry," and "Hush up," and each phrase was used appropriately. Mother never said, "Shut Up!"

Mother's maternal role models were her sisters, especially Mary and Anna, with whom she lived, and from whom she learned a practical and no-nonsense approach to parenting. She also had occasions to practice parenting skills on her young nieces and nephews, before she married and became a mother herself.

Her firm beliefs about child-rearing included early discipline and toddler training, "while still in the high chair." She strongly believed, "If you wait until they're teenagers, it's too late. You have to say 'No!' and let them know you mean it." Mother did not tolerate disrespect to her parental authority. She was like other typical mothers of fifty years ago, as a current conservative child psychologist and columnist John Rosemond admiringly describes: "The mothers of that period were very formidable women who intimidated their children. She was not their servant, but rather there to teach them to stand on their own two feet. If one of her children talked back, that child regretted it. She had no reservation about saying to them things like: 'I don't have time for you right now, so run along. If you can't find something to do, I'll find something for you to do.'"

Mother did not shy away from a task, and did not ask permission. It was not a democracy, as in many permissive homes today. She did not ask for agreement, consensus or take votes. She never read self-help books, and it is doubtful she read the writings of Emily Post, which defined modern good manners and conduct. Nevertheless, Mother ran a tight ship, demanded order, and chaos was not allowed. She did not worry about catering to our self-esteem; that would come later with accomplishments.

A natural born leader and capable in crisis, she conducted her family as if she was the General and "her kids," as she called us, were the troops. She had the guts to be an in-charge parent. Laying down uncompromising guidelines, there was no walking over the line. Mother's strictness was a part of caring. Discipline was fair in our house, but as in all families, some children required more than others. Mother said, "Neither John nor I had to lay a hand on Gary."

A wise woman, her discipline was immediate. She never used the tactic, "Wait until your father comes home." If we were caught misbehaving, we were made to stand in the corner. For more serious offenses, we were spanked on the spot. She parented "in the moment" rather than waiting for a more convenient time to get her message across. If it involved a sibling disagreement, we were made to kiss and make up. Fighting or teasing among siblings was not tolerated and, consequently, we grew up to be friends, without the typical sibling rivalries. No child was ever allowed to make fun of another in destructive ways.

She made sure it was the child, and not she, who endured the punishment of a tantrum. If one of her children misbehaved in church, for instance, she didn't sit there tolerating it; she took him or her out and gave a spanking, or at least a warning of one. It was understood that if you got in trouble in school, you would be in equal trouble upon returning home. Both parents were well acquainted with the teachers. Mother visited the classrooms and was always home when the school bus arrived.

The architect I.M. Pei said, "You have to draw from the past to move forward. If the roots are very much on the surface, one windstorm and everything is gone." This principle applies to raising a family as well. Our parents fostered deep roots, strong family connections, and enduring values, which they taught long before it was politically correct to do so.

All I Ever Knew I Learned in Kindergarten, a best seller in the late 1990s, repeats the common sense rules of our household: "Honor thy Father and thy Mother. No talking back to one's parents. Be good. No fighting. No yelling. Keep your word. Work hard. Don't waste (especially food)." Fairness was firmly ingrained. The creed "share and share alike," was believed so strongly by our parents that it was written into their Last Will and Testament.

Mother did not gossip behind peoples' back. She also avoided offending others by refusing to discuss religion, as well as sex. Furthermore, political affairs were not discussed in the home. Unaffected by the outside world, national news didn't hold much interest for the family, although Kenneth recalls when Bob Dole, from Russell, traveled through Stockton, and other small Kansas towns, handing out cans of Dole brand pineapple juice during his successful campaign for Senator.

The children did wear "I Like Ike" buttons during the 1952 presidential campaign, and it was families like ours who helped put a General in the White House. (Our eldest brother Kenneth, a Chief of Police in WaKeeney, Kansas until his retirement, served as a security guard at Eisenhower's burial in Abilene, Kansas in 1969.)

The Nineteenth Amendment gave women the vote in 1920, the year Mother turned six. This implication impressed upon Mother her civic duty to vote, which both she and Dad did in all elections, and she was often asked to serve at elections as a poll watcher. She did not hide the fact she was one of the few Democrats in the township and never considered changing her political views to go along with the crowd. Eisenhower was the exception however, as he was Kansas born.

After Ronald drowned, there were some in the farming community who felt Mother was to blame for failing to accompany the youngsters to the creek that tragic day. She understood grief, and knew what it was like to be lonely and shut out. A generous woman, Mother often sought out people who needed some cheering up with her fancy breads, jams or other homemade gifts. Her life revolved around being a devoted wife and mother, but much later in life and faced with an empty nest, she quickly volunteered at the local nursing home as a Gray Lady, and donated her time to the American Red Cross and church activities. In her retirement years, Mother took up a multitude of handicrafts especially sewing quilts tops, decoupage, ceramics, rope wheat-weaving, oil and water painting and making greeting cards. She also corresponded on a regular basis with her children sending hand-written letters to each — a time-consuming task.

Sixteen months after Ronald drowned, this writer, the seventh child, Linda Leona, was the first to be born outside the family home at the Harwood Nursing Home, a birthing center in town. It was the end of November 1945, and World War II had been over for three months. Uncles Levi and Joe Morin, Oliver Brin and Phil Roy returned home safely after serving their county in the war, as did numerous cousins. Dad's brother Emile Roy, a paratrooper, returned from China. He married my namesake, Leona Kriley, on the day of my birth, and the newlyweds served as godparents.

Eighteen months later, during her eighth pregnancy, Mother miscarried following a mishap while lighting the kitchen gas oven. Church and state law forbade abortion, then called intentional miscarriages, and even though Mother suffered a spontaneous miscarriage, there was gossip. Some relatives, and a few of whom she considered friends, criticized her for being responsible for the accident, which added to the anguish of the loss.

After the string of events, including Ronald's drowning in 1944, my birth in 1945, and Mother's miscarriage in 1947, in her biography she recalls telling her oldest daughter, "I don't know what I would do without you. You are the happiness of my life."

Ila Mae added, "After Mother's miscarriage, my younger sister Linda was turned over to me to care for, when she was two years old and I was eight. Joan and I shared a big bed, but Linda always managed to crawl out of her little bed and in between us pleading, 'Tell me a story,' which went far into the night. Then I'd cry myself to sleep because she wouldn't go to sleep. In the mornings, if I had been called too many times for breakfast, and someone had to be sent upstairs to awaken me, I'd fall to the floor on my knees, in prayer, as to get out of any further trouble." Ila Mae's hearing loss also accounted for her failure to awaken some mornings.

As this writer reflects on a wholesome childhood, and having been partially raised by big sister "Mae," it was she who provided the glue one needs to get through adversity — she cemented the sense of well-being to last a lifetime. I received nurturing from two mothers who loved me, but it was Ila Mae, as surrogate mother, who was always there just for me. Given the overwhelming responsibility of watching over and entertaining the younger children, she anguished for days, over what might have happened, after I lost my balance and fell off our horse, Trigger, as we rode double one day, merrily galloping over terraced fields.

The eighth child was born in March 1949, during a severe snowstorm. The nearest plowed road was some distance from the house, yet our practical Dad thought ahead to park the car on the highway the day before, when Mother sensed her due day was near. When the time came she and Dad bundled up, climbed on the tractor, drove to the awaiting car, and onto the Harwood Nursing Home, in Stockton. The siblings were responsible for naming the new baby. Kenneth, Allan, and Gary, and Ila Mae, too, all insisted on the name Roger, since they had seen a Roy Rogers movie the week before.

Mother said in her biography, "The older boys helped with the dishes and other housework, too, until Ila Mae was old enough. They also took care of the younger children — Kenneth until he left home to marry, and Allan as a high school student, before he enlisted with the U.S. Army." But it was the nine-year-old Ila Mae, who was charged with the care of the newborn, Roger, an event that seemingly gave direction to her life. When she could not hear her baby brother cry, this was yet another recognizable clue of hearing impairment and she began to understand she was different from others.

Ila Mae demanded much of herself, and even as a teenager carried more than her share of the workload. Mother said, "I relied on her so much. When she left home for the convent, I didn't know what I would do, but by the grace of God, I managed."

Our parents rarely drove the eight miles to town for the children to be treated by the doctor. During Mother's eighth grade school year, at the Sacred Heart Academy in Manhattan, Kansas, she expressed the desire to continue her education, and become a trained nurse — a dream not to be. Years later, she often remarked of the plenty of practical experience she got nursing her sick children back to health.

Among her home remedies were poultices made of milk, bread, egg and sugar. She also used a non-prescription herbal drawing agent held in place by a loose bandage. These were applied to infections from stickers, or embedded barn wood. Before the advent of antibiotics, (and except for painkillers) Mother probably managed as well as most doctors. However in later years, without question, she obediently took any medication prescribed for her.

Living on a farm one is exposed to a variety of germs, dust and dirt. Recent studies suggest that people in rural areas are less likely to develop allergies, or asthma, than those living in cities. A separate study shows that excessive cleanliness leaves the body's immune system underemployed, and begins to overreact to ordinarily harmless substances. Mother neither knew this, nor insisted her family wash hands at meal times upon coming in from work, or outside play. It is remarkable the family was very healthy with few cases of colds, flu, or allergies, supporting the theory that greater exposure to livestock, and a farm environment, can be protective.

On the other hand, farming can be a dangerous profession because of heavy equipment usage. Our brothers often helped Dad with machinery repair, and there were several farm accidents that could have been fatal. Rodney's neck was caught in the combine belts, nearly cutting his windpipe; a combine heavily loaded with wheat ran over Roger's back, but by the grace of God the soil was soft and muddy; and there was another incident when barbed wire twisted around the pre-teen Roger's torso while riding on a small tractor in a spin.

In light of these incidents — in addition to the accidental drowning of our eight-year-old brother Ronald, the death of uncle Joe Morin from being pinned under an overturned tractor, and Dad's jaw having been broken on a bridge building accident — it is little wonder that Mother taught us to pray to our Guardian Angel both morning and night for protection and guidance, and to remember October 2nd, the feast day of Holy Guardian Angels. A regular churchgoer, she was a believer in the power of prayer.

Chapter Seven

In 1937, during shale oil exploration throughout Kansas, Farmland Mortgage gave S.T. Jocelyn (later Gulf Oil Corporation, and then Tide Water Associated Oil) an assignment of oil and gas leases. In 1950, several years after Dad bought this land, these leases were conveyed to him. A few months later Richard Findess, a businessman in Stockton, approached Dad about assigning his oil, gas and mineral rights to a drilling company, which began to provide a steady income for the family. In February 1952, "B and D Drilling, Inc. completed drilling a successful oil well on the John Roy land," according to the register of deeds.

Ila Mae remarked on the family's good fortune, "An oil well was drilled and crude oil was struck south of our house when I was about thirteen. Our parents often spoke of returning a portion of this found money back to God — to the Church." In times of thick or thin, our parents were generous in offering a tithe of one-tenth. "I understood early in life that they never failed to give, even when there was little, and something would turn up during the week in return."

From the proceeds of their first oil check, Mother purchased twelve place settings of china (a Homer Laughlin rosebud pattern) and stainless flatware with a rosebud design. These arrived in time to set a lovely table for a wedding party brunch at our home. Ruth Ann Jackson, a Methodist, who converted to Catholicism, joined Kenneth in marriage at St. Thomas Church in Stockton in April 1953.

In 1995 Rooks County was the fourth highest in Kansas oil production in barrels. In the years before this, several more oil wells were drilled on the land, but our share continued to be a small fraction of the net revenue. Consequently, we never became rich, even though some locals thought so. Our good luck, and the little extra income that did come our way, was not bragged about, and it never affected the way our parents related to their friends. Still, a few families were jealous, when oil continued to be randomly struck on some land in Belmont, and other surrounding townships, but not on theirs.

Furthermore, community tension mounted when people were forced to move, by power of Eminent Domain, making way for the Webster Dam, a federal watershed construction project. Residents were given a governmental cash settlement. Anger stemmed from the logic that, had these families not been required to move, oil might have been discovered on their land, which by now was covered with water.

Mother had her own taste of injustice much earlier, in 1933, when she and her siblings were shut out of rightfully inheriting their deceased mother's share from their grandmother, Louise Hebert's estate. The court division orders of the Hebert estate indicate that the children of the deceased Rosanna Morin were to be included in the inheritance. Instead, the estate was divided among grandmother's seven siblings (Henry Hebert, Nalda St. Peter, Joseph Hebert, Exilda Senesac, Fred Hebert, Rosaelda St. Peter, Rosalie Frigon) who, according to court records, "drew up an equal division of the household goods of the estate, rather than force the sale of property at a public auction." Consequently, Mother, and her siblings, (Anna Desmarteau, Alphonse Morin, Sister Rose Irma Morin, Mary Brin, Rosa Balthazor, Edward (Ed), Joseph (Joe) and Levi Morin) did not receive their mother's share of the inheritance.

Joseph Hebert, Mother's bachelor uncle, continued to live on the homeplace and inherited the bulk of the land. He died intestate in May 1939. A court petition was made to sell the property of 1,440 acres through a sheriff's sale. There was an encounter in the Hill City courtroom when someone, (most likely Alphonse, as the former guardian for Levi and Olive), stood up to challenge, "What about Rosanna Morin, our mother's share?" From this outcome our mother, Olive, and her siblings each inherited $372. This amount sounds small by today's standards, but it was an amount that would later enable our parents to make annual mortgage payments for nearly four years.

Grandfather Stanislas Morin also died intestate, ten years earlier in 1929, and it is unknown why Mother did not receive her share of that inheritance, either, until seventeen years later. In 1946 Mother was awarded $1,640, making it possible to purchase a new postwar Chevy for the growing family. World War II was just over, and the next year the movie, *It's a Wonderful Life*, starring James Stewart, was nominated for three Academy Awards. The family would have agreed with the movie title because that same year he made a down payment, and took out a $5,000 loan to buy the surrounding land and large stone house they had been renting since 1940. Mortgage payments of $100 were paid annually, and Dad paid off the fifteen-year debt in only four years.

With pride Mother said, "We also made loan payments on our first combine and tractor, which made farming easier for John." This economic windfall created new hope because he was still farming with horses. This set them on the path of independence and economic stability. It was a dream come true.

As an impressionable twelve-year-old, Kenneth remembers the first tractor, "an International Farmall tricycle wheel. Dad also bought an eight-foot one-way for plowing, and a six-foot blade combine for cutting wheat. That first year Dad almost paid off the remaining loan, cutting 400 to 500 acres of wheat for all the neighbors, including Oria Grover, who did not yet have his own machinery." In turn, Oria helped Dad with his fieldwork until his sons were old enough.

While a practical man, Dad was also caught up with the rest of the population in a time of heady optimism. The giddy years of postwar prosperity enabled him to purchase a 1948 GMC one and a half-ton truck. "It was a dependable companion into the 1970s," Father Duane noted. "With newer and larger machinery, in the autumns of the early 1950s, Dad was a custom cutter harvesting milo as far west as the Royal Gorge in southern Colorado. "He kept the combine in good shape, every year tending to a few repairs. The weeks preceding harvest he parked the combine under a shade tree, checking and replacing parts. One summer when the combine broke down, during the peak of a full harvest, as it was known to do, a son overheard him mutter, 'A guy could lose his religion over a machine like this!' That was as strong a statement as Dad ever made when faced with adversity.

"During 1953-1954, Dad made the transition to even larger, more costly equipment, so the Farmer's State Bank, in the nearby burg of Bogue, was again called upon to extend credit. He bought a new International W-9 tractor, 12-foot one-way, and wheat drill. Those turned out to be the bleak years that left Dad indebted to the bank," continued Father Duane. "Bad harvests, several years in succession, due to hail, floods, and droughts, made it seem next to impossible to pay back the loans." But one thing was certain; there were never bill collectors pursuing John Roy. He managed, with the income from his other jobs, to pull through the bad times. No doubt St. Isidore, the patron saint of farmers, was watching over him.

"Dad paid off his debt and recouped his health from those 'ulcer years,'" said Father Duane. "After that he wasn't one to 'count his chickens before they hatched.' Dad was to say, 'If we can get a decent harvest every four years, we can make it.' His tenacity was his key to success."

Although a wise money manager, Dad did not discuss money with his children even when times were tough. The topic also seemed to be considered taboo among the Donna Reed-type families on television. Thinking of ourselves as neither rich, nor poor, we simply felt well fed, and provided for. While Mother had free rein with the checkbook, the children learned from example how to live frugally and within a budget, and picked up another of Dad's values: "Always pay your debts. Or better yet, don't go into debt." Each of his children acquired his lifetime discipline of honoring outstanding balances in a timely manner, and each are proud homeowners themselves.

Well known and respected around the community as a business-like farmer, Dad was approached and given the option to farm land, as it became available, on a sharecrop basis in Belmont Township. He also farmed U.S. Bureau of Reclamation government land, used as a wildlife reserve, around the nearby Webster Reservoir. Gradually, more land, of several soil types of silt and sandy loam, was acquired. For nine years, between 1956 and 1965, Dad farmed more than nine hundred acres, with nearly four hundred of it planted in basic strands of Pawnee and Kiowa winter wheat, and later the hybrid, Tam. Kansas is one of the nation's leading producers of wheat.[1]

While the livelihood came primarily from harvesting this golden grain, the land was also used for growing alfalfa, hay, clover, and corn, while the infertile land pastured cattle. There were fields planted in milo, also called sorghum, derived from Old World tropical grasses similar to Indian corn. It is extremely resistant to drought and ideal for growing in the hot Kansas summers.

Forty acres were wasteland, and not farmed due to three-hundred-million-year-old outcroppings from the Cretaceous era (meaning chalk). Even some of the fertile land had these deposits. Roger recalled that Dad occasionally expressed his disgust when smaller chunks of chalk, spread throughout the fields, dulled farm equipment, especially the one-way blades used for turning soil before planting.

While Ila Mae was a major housework helper, she also picked up on farming principles. She understood that all Dad wanted was a plot of land to call his own. He modernized his operation, adopting low-till methods using even larger machinery, selected seeds and fertilizers. With his green thumb, he managed to get the proverbial "silk purse out of a sow's ear," provided the weather cooperated. He could read the skies and its effects on a crop. Ripe wheat will not wait. He knew the right time to move into action for a quick and efficient harvest. Mother was not often superstitious, but when the boys killed snakes and put them on the barbed wire fence she yelled at them, "Take them off. They'll bring on bad weather."

A hailstorm or a heavy rain, just before harvest time, could destroy an entire years profit. The weather segment, on the radio or television, was more important then the news, since income was a direct outcome of its nature. The rain gauge was checked each morning after summer showers.

Other elements could ruin a crop, too. Allan told of blowing dirt accumulate as high as fence lines, in the early fifties. Another time he saw the barn blown down, while cattle were still inside, during a severe windstorm. He recalled seeing our parents hold rugs and blankets to the window, and under the kitchen door on the west side of the house, to keep out blowing dust. Still those dust storms, which smothered crops in the 1940s and 1950s, were not as severe as those in the "Dirty Thirties," which brought farming to a standstill.

We grew up to expect spring rains, and summer heat, to bring on cycles of growth and abundant harvests. "These years were both good and bad; plenty of rain followed by drought. But somehow, something would always come though," said Mother. "God seemed to have blessed our crops for many years," Sister Veronica agreed. "We put palms, from Palm Sunday, in our wheat fields."

Dad enlarged the dairy herd, jokingly or not, "to keep the boys at home." Before and after school there was hay to put up, newborn calves to nurse, and special feed to prepare for hogs and cattle that were later sold or butchered. The production, gathering and preparing of food (growing, canning, or freezing fruits and vegetables, gathering eggs, herding and milking cows and separating cream) were simply a part of everyday life. The boys performed outside chores in the barn and fields, and never ventured inside to perform women's work. However, the girls were capable and hardworking, especially Ila Mae, and did some of the work the boys performed, when strong enough and able.

On warm, Indian summer days we played in the fields, and stocks of dried corn plants were pitched "tee-pee" style. Knowing hard physical labor builds strong bodies, Dad sometimes made mundane chores into games after school, when even the girls tossed heavy bales of hay onto the flatbed Ford. Like the word "ain't," "can't" was not allowed in our vocabulary. Eager to ride on farm equipment, the girls also knew how to wield a hammer and other tools.

During the early 1950s artificial insemination was used, for genetic improvement, to increase productivity of the cattle. Even though Ila Mae and Joan owned and cared for Herefords, as 4-H projects, Dad drew the line, and didn't allow his daughters to see this, the birthing of animals, or the castration of steers. On the other hand, when he brought fresh "Rocky Mountain oysters" into the kitchen, we knew what they were, showed our disgust and then helped Mother cook them anyway.

The cows were milked by hand for many years, and then machines were installed in the mid 1950s. One of Ila Mae's jobs was to operate the milk separator and clean it, too. Milk and cream was sold in town for a while, until legislation required modern hygienic conditions. In 1956, Dad gave up that operation, because of the strict standards, but kept a cow, or two, to put milk on our table.

During harvest time, when Dad needed extra hands, the girls were called upon to take over milking cows. Joan recalled one late afternoon when she and Ila Mae were herding ten Holstein cows into the barn for milking. "Whitey, the lead cow, got spooked and bolted back to the pasture, with the other cows following." Fighting through the sunflowers, sage, yucca, prairie cactus and dense tall grasses wasn't easy, all the while dodging gopher holes. Devil's claws, with the deceivingly pretty lavender and yellow orchid-like flowers, grabbed onto pant legs, and often caused one to loose a step. "The struggle to round up the cows through all this was enough to cause Mae to swear — something she was very seldom known to do." Nevertheless, it speaks of her humanness. For all her goodness, even as a teenager, Ila Mae experienced frustration, as well. While not a saint, she strived to live a virtuous life.

✝

Chapter Eight

In 1950, when Rural Electrification Administration (R.E.A.) came along, farms across America had access to inexpensive electric power and light. A neighbor, Merle Grover said, "That was a great day for farmers." Mother added, "Electricity, indoor plumbing, and running water all seemed like a gift from heaven." This made it possible for a bathroom to be plumbed in the space previously used as a huge walk-in pantry. After enduring an outdoor privy, and previously having no indoor bathing facilities, the new conveniences were a luxury.

"Before this, wind-charged, propeller-like blades, on the chicken house roof, powered a generator to a row of batteries in the cellar. Drinking water came from a well fifty yards from the house. In the kitchen was a cistern pump, needing to be primed, which stored rainwater caught by eave troughs, and then channeled by a downspout," said our brother, Kenneth.

Water for washing clothes was pumped from an outdoor cistern fed by rain run-off, and filtered charcoal softened it. When there was no available rainwater, a supply was hauled by bucketfuls at some distance, from a well near the barn. It took many pails to fill the copper boiler. This heavy and tiresome job often fell to Ila Mae. There were many loads to wash, even though clothing was always worn more than once, and bath towels were shared and reused until the weekly washday.

Clothes were first scrubbed on a corrugated washboard, boiled, then removed with a sawed-off broomstick. More cold water was pumped from the cistern for the rinse tub, and laundry was wrung out by hand, before mechanical wringers came along. Liquid bluing was added to the white clothes. Dress clothing, mostly Sunday white shirts, were held until last, and dipped in a diluted powdered starch.

Up until the mid-1960s, Mother and her neighbor, Merle Grover, made their own laundry soap outdoors, in a black iron kettle, from tallow, scraps of pork fat and grease, and lye. Ila Mae suffered from an occasional bout of red, itchy eczema, perhaps as a result of these harsh products, or perhaps from house detergents, gardening and poison ivy — all of which she was exposed to.

Although a gas-powered Maytag wringer washer was an improvement, it is difficult to imagine how much work was involved washing clothes. Moreover, the small outdoor washhouse had no heat in the winter, and was stifling hot in the summer.

An automatic clothes dryer was not owned until the early 1960s, and so before this laundry was hung outside to dry year-round. In the winter clothes, sheets, and towels were frozen stiff. But with each new baby, the cloth diapers always came out smelling fresh and pristine white. When Mother was near her due date, or away having another baby, routine household chores fell to her daughters, but mostly Ila Mae. Another day was devoted just to ironing the mountain of clothes.

Since washday was an all-day affair, early each Monday morning Mother began to simmer homemade navy bean soup, with ham hocks, for the noontime meal. Even as an adult, this was one of Sister Veronica's favorites. A frugal shopper, she bought ten or so packages of various beans, mixed them up, and repackaged into a thoughtful homespun gift, topped with a colorful bow.

Sister Veronica reminisced of other favorite foods that "make me think of home. There was always something good to eat — chicken and dumplings made from scratch, a goulash of elbow macaroni, canned tomatoes and ground beef, boiled potatoes with Polish ring sausage, and jellyrolls.

"Each morning there were stacks of pancakes with 'lace' from a hot, greasy griddle. We always warned each other, 'You're going to get sugar diabetes,' from the quantity of pancake syrup consumed, not really knowing what the disease was. There were Friday night grilled-cheese sandwiches, but Mother prepared a special stew of canned oysters and fresh milk for Dad. Waffles made Sunday nights special. For an extraordinary treat she prepared homemade doughnuts and holes.

"Without fail, Mother had fresh hot dinner rolls, loaf bread, or sticky cinnamon rolls at the Saturday noon dinner when we returned home from Catechism." Ila Mae learned from Mother how to make these and other yeast breads, which were 4-H prizewinners.

Sliced Wonder bread came on the market in 1930, but Mother only began to buy it at the grocers in town in the 1960s, after most of the children left home. Cake mixes were available on grocer shelves as early as 1949, but she did not use these conveniences either, until years later, because of the cost. And then, our family complained of the "cardboard" taste of these products, after being spoiled with the homemade variety.

Much of our food was directly grown, or raised on the farm. We had cattle and pigs. Fried chicken, our favorite meal, was freshly butchered several times a week, except for winter time when we drew from the stock on hand in the deep-freezer. Other times there was food on our table not available in the markets, such as Rocky Mountain oysters, chicken feet, and blood pudding. As children we watched headcheese being made, "a French delicacy," we were told. The head, feet, tongue and heart of a pig were first boiled, chopped up, seasoned and pressed into a big jellied mass. This special treat was left for our parents and adult relatives to enjoy. Other specialties at our kitchen table were fresh chicken livers, hearts and gizzards. Nothing edible was wasted.

Laying hens provided the dozen or so fresh eggs whites for homemade angel food cake. Ila Mae baked and topped the airy sponge cake with a white, sticky, seven-minute cooked frosting — a typical birthday treat. We looked forward to this delicious delight, and unlike other times, when everyone got the same size serving, the birthday child got the largest piece.

In the early years Mother churned homemade butter from fresh cream. Later when oleomargarine was available in stores, and we saw our friends eating it, that's what we wanted, too. Farm-fresh cream was also the magic ingredient that went into making the caramel topping for sweet rolls, popcorn balls and homemade ice cream — the *piece de'resistance*. Sister Veronica, like the rest of the family, associated ice cream and popcorn as comfort foods, bringing to mind sweet childhood memories. "There were times in the early years, when ice cream was made from snow. During wintertime we sat around the kitchen table, or placed our feet close to the propane heat stove to keep warm, while eating the frozen delight. On Tuesdays and Saturdays Mother sold the oversupply of eggs and cream, we could not use, to the local creamery in town, which provided money to pay for extra groceries."

Ila Mae learned to cook at a young age on a gas Roper kitchen range, having two ovens side by side, and a broiler underneath. Even though Mother cooked most all the meals, the girls assisted, and helped with everything else, too — the housework, laundry, flower and vegetable gardening.

During her child-raising years, Mother did not have time for hobbies. Instead, she found it relaxing to dig in her garden. Between the rows of vegetables she planted zinnias, which thrived in the hot Kansas sun. These grew into hot crayon colors of pink, red, yellow and orange. She taught her daughters to hoe straight rows outlined with a string, and plant, seed-by-seed, an abundant garden of lettuce, green beans, tomatoes, onions, carrots, and cucumbers. She picked only the ripest, and what was needed daily. She knew not to refrigerate these; otherwise, the farm-fresh flavor would be lost. Although we never heard of the term "organic" we knew our food was fresh, safe and tasty, unlike that bought in the market in town.

We ate our fill of sweet corn from the field, which ripened each August. Ila Mae helped par-boil the roasting ears, cut the kernels, and then freeze it up for wintertime meals. In some years, watermelon and cantaloupe — we called it muskmelon — grew in the sandy soil near the creek.

During the summer, the entire family pitched in to pick sour cherries, eating the unwashed fruit while perched on the flatbed GMC truck backed underneath higher branches. Friends from town, neighbors and relatives were invited to pick their fill, as well. A few days' delay and the birds would have stolen the ripened crop from the easy to grow, attractive landscape trees with the beautiful bark. The girls helped Mother pit tubs of these tart cherries with hairpins. These were frozen, which Ila Mae later turned into award-winning pies.

"There were several years, in the 1950s, when Dad traveled to Grand

Junction, or Fruita, Colorado (once with Mother, and another time with his brother, Omer.) Each time they brought home a pickup truck load of fresh Red Delicious apples, which were stored in the underground storm shelter, used primarily as a food storage cellar for home canned goods. In general food was conserved, not wasted, and used in moderation," Sister Veronica recalled.

Few people telephoned ahead to announce a visit, as was the custom in rural areas. Mother was always prepared to offer guests something to eat with items she pulled from the cellar, refrigerator or full-size deep freezer. Her bountiful table was loaded with food, company or not, holiday or every day, perhaps a result of having so little to eat during the Great Depression.

Once we got a television, Mother forbade eating in front of it, or even having the volume turned on during mealtimes; a rule she adhered to over the years. Our family looked forward to eating together in our typical 1950s kitchen boasting a new table of chrome and gray Formica. A four-foot strip of linoleum, stamped to look like gray tiles, covered the kitchen wall to where a gray and green trellis and flower wallpaper design took over.

In rural communities, it was typical for meals to be taken at home around the kitchen table. Aunt Vula suggested that, before the late 1950s in the Midwest, eating in restaurants was considered low-class, and was only for truck drivers and hobos (a term coined in 1889 describing homeless and migratory workers who were usually penniless vagabonds.) Perhaps this early thinking was the reason Dad did not consider waitressing an admirable job.

While dessert was presented after nearly every dinner or supper, Mother often did not partake perhaps as a way of watching her weight. Mostly likely she sacrificed her portion so there would be more for the others. However, she lingered at the kitchen table with Ila Mae, after everyone else left the room and the children hurried outside to play.

Later on, Sister Veronica emphasized in her Life Review, "Surely none of the siblings realized how frustrated I was, as a teenager, when everyone left the table. I felt totally responsible for cleanup duty. Often I'd try a confrontation: 'Look, if you don't help, then I'll have to do it all myself!' Actually there wasn't much to store away for another meal, because Mother and I sat back down to finish the leftover meat, potatoes and salad." Perhaps this was her first identification with the biblical Martha.[1]

Chapter Nine

Ila Mae and her siblings were shy, backward children who didn't ask for much. Once in a while Bob and Lorene Miller, family friends who came to visit, or Ken Pauley, the gas man, brought treats such as Juicy Fruit chewing gum. Uncle Omer would often bring Cherry Mash candy bars. When children don't have a lot, small pleasures like these are memorable. Each child received one gift for Christmas and birthday, which frequently was something to wear.

During one abundant crop season, on a rainy day when it was too wet to work in the fields, Dad took the two oldest, Kenneth and Allan, to the Western Auto Store in town and said, "Boys, go pick out your new red motor-scooter." Dad was a loving parent, and generous, too, when he could be. "That was one of the happiest days of my childhood," Allan recalled.

The Ig Gross family, who attended our church, owned the local Western Auto Store. Each holiday season this businessman hosted a random drawing of Christmas toys. One year our brother, Roger, won a Lionel train set; another year, as a teenager, this writer won a portable stereo record player. Seeing how little we had on the farm, perhaps this kind-hearted storeowner played Santa by pre-arranging for us to be prize winners.

Many times, after the Saturday noontime meal, the family went into town: Mother to shop, the children to a matinee. Dad went to the pool hall, where he found camaraderie over a red beer (mixed with tomato juice), but we never saw him intoxicated. He played pool and snooker, or card games of pitch, pinochle or poker with other local men. Only the boys in our family were allowed to go beyond the swinging doors of the bar into the gaming room. Decorum dictated this was not a place for a proper lady. Girls only went into the outer portion of the pool hall to quickly tell the bartender, who was to inform Dad, we were ready to go home and that Mother was waiting in the car.

In the mid-1950s, as the older children outgrew the youthful fun of playing in the fields and wide-open spaces, and were eager for a variety of entertainment, Dad purchased a secondhand regulation-size snooker table. It took four men to carry each of the three heavy thick slates upstairs to the spacious spare room. Here there was adequate space to maneuver cue sticks. There were so many visitors, coming to try their hand at the game, that later the pool table was moved to the home's dirt floor basement with an outside entrance.

Pool playing became a favorite summer pastime for the entire family, in the coolness of this musty darkened place illuminated with only a single bare light bulb. Ila Mae could easily handle a pool cue, as could Gary who, during seminary recreation, was a constant winner at the game.

Our first vacation, several years after Ila Mae left for college, was to see Dad's brother, Phil, in Iowa. Another year the family crammed in the car to visit Uncle Emile Roy, in Colorado. In 1970 our parents took their first airplane trip together, along with the two youngest, to Disneyland and to visit Joan, who had married and moved to California. Before this, Ila Mae was the trusted babysitter while Dad and Mother took short vacations by themselves.

The older siblings took turns babysitting the younger ones on Saturday nights, while our parents went square dancing. The other siblings were just down a block or so on Main Street, at the Nova movie theater, reminiscent of the one in the movie, *The Last Picture Show.*[1]

The Legion of Decency censored movies like *Johnny Belinda* featuring Jane Wyman, and each month Mother carefully scanned the Catholic diocesan newspaper to insure the upcoming movie attractions were not forbidden. Instead, Mother made certain we watched wholesome movies, which changed about every two weeks, like *Ma and Pa Kettle*, or *Francis, the talking mule* series. Other favorites were westerns starring Gene Autry, Gary Cooper, John Wayne or Lassie. We hummed along with the familiar songs on the radio, "Tumbling Tumbleweeds," "Cool Water," and "Happy Trails," since the actor/singer Roy Rogers, the King of the Cowboys; his palomino, Trigger; and Dale Evans, Queen of the Cowgirls; and her horse, Buttermilk, were family favorites, too, along with their musical group, The Sons of the Pioneers. Favorite movies included *My Pal Trigger, Apache Rose,* and *Don't Fence Me In.* The popularity of these B Westerns may have faded in other parts of the country, but in the early 1950s in rural Kansas they were big hits.

Ila Mae wasn't interested in the current sex-symbol movie stars, such as Ava Gardner, Lana Turner or Marilyn Monroe, like other girls her age. Instead, she admired Esther Williams, the water ballet star, and tried to imitate her graceful moves during 4-H swim outings, at a swimming pool forty miles away, in Hays. Later on she would swim in the convent pool.

While our parents respected teachers, and the education each child received at the Webster schools, they were poorly educated themselves. Children were not read to and there were few books in our house, as our parents probably assumed that what was needed could be brought home from the school library, although comic books were purchased at the Five-and-Dime.

The well-stocked, old Carnegie public library, built in 1916, was rarely visited, even during summer vacation months when we went to town more often. It is remarkable that several family members later became avid readers. Father Duane admitted he discovered the joy of reading only later in life. "I was in high school already when I first devoured the *Peter Rabbit* series from the library." He went on to earn a master's degree in library science.

When Cheryl was a teenager she brought home a Harlequin-type romance novel. Mother took one look at the subject matter on the cover, and took it away. Mother also considered movie star magazines, such as *Silver Screen*, cheap, trashy, low-class publications. These were not allowed in the house, and were not to be read at someone else's house, either.

Orders, from a Catholic book club for teenage girls, arrived in the mailbox for a short time. The biographies of St. Joan of Arc, St. Thérèse of the Little Flower, or Our Lady of Fatima were fervently read before the week ended. These mail orders soon stopped, however, as these and other books were considered expensive. However, Dad purchased, from a traveling salesman, *The Columbia Encyclopedia*, a massive book of more than 2,000 pages and it was treasured for its wealth of information.

The *Capper's Weekly*, a rural Kansas tradition out of Topeka, as well as the local weekly newspaper, *The Rooks County Record*, arrived by mail, and provided light reading. After church on Sundays, Dad picked up a newspaper at the local Rexall drugstore, alternating between the *Denver Post* and *Wichita Eagle-Beacon*, but the children read only the comics — the funny papers.

There were regular subscriptions to five Catholic magazines, including *The Catholic Digest*, and the Diocesan periodical, and usually a pamphlet or two on the writings of Archbishop Fulton J. Sheen, who had a popular Sunday night television program. Other religious booklets were picked up in church on Sundays, and the children's *Catholic Messenger* was available.

There was a Bible in the home, although before the Second Vatican Council, reading this sacred scripture was mostly a Protestant practice, and Catholics were not encouraged, for fear of misinterpretation.

What was encouraged was for children to play outside. There were very few days considered too cold. During winter blizzards, when snowdrifts were as tall as the fifteen-foot-high chicken house, Ila Mae climbed with her siblings to the rooftops, and each jumped into fresh powdered snow. She showed how to make snowmen, or angels in the snow. Neither cautioned of frostbite — nor sunburn during the summer months — we threw snowballs without mittens, long past when fingers were red and stinging. Then we came inside to warm ourselves, in front of the propane heat stove in the cozy kitchen, and play on the linoleum floor.

Our big sister kept us entertained. "We played store by cutting out paper money, and arranging canned goods on the kitchen table. Other times, I delighted in crawling into cupboards, taking everything out, washing shelves, then arranging everything so neatly," she said.

During winter storms, when fierce blizzards knocked out the electrical power for days at a time, by nightfall our parents were forced to ease up on their work, and play cards with us by the low light of kerosene lanterns. "We played Pitch and Pinochle. The younger children especially enjoyed Crazy-Eight,

Hearts, Kings in the Corner and Old Maid," recalled Ila Mae.

Before the arrival of television, warm summer evenings were spent playing outside, long after the sun went down. Stargazing in a rural setting — where the inky blue-black sky, neither obscured by tall buildings or trees, nor made faint by bright city lights — is an experience every person, young and old, should have. On the farm, it was ours to enjoy as often as we wanted. Catching fireflies at twilight even brought our parents outside.

Love of the outdoors is second nature to farm children, who were encouraged to "run wild," and just be kids. The youngest made mud pies while, for hours, the older ones played games of Red Rover, throwing balls over the washhouse, and a hide-and-seek game calling out a truce, "oly, oly, oxen free."

During the June harvest, when fresh-cut wheat was stored in the barn, siblings jumped from the rafters into piles of golden grain, while Dad used the auger to dry out the wheat. Mother raised baby chicks, and when the brooder house was no longer in use for the season the girls swept it out and decorated it as a playhouse.

On summer evenings, or after Sunday Mass, there were picnics at the nearby Webster Dam, and water skiing behind the boat belonging to Kenneth, who was married by then. These activities brought the family together, as did bowling, a popular family entertainment throughout the mid-west during the 1960s.

The older children participated in track. "We had foot races, and Dad built a high-jump and broad-jump sand pit," Ila Mae reminisced. "We spent hours there, as well as practicing basketball free throws in the barn."

There were no Schwinns on the farm; those were for kids in town who had sidewalks and streets, but we had a gentle horse, Trigger, named after Roy Roger's horse. Billie, a black and white collie, appears in numerous family photos. No pets were allowed inside the house until the late 1960s, when Mother found, took in, and fell in love with a stray Pomeranian, which later had pups. When the feminine and charming reddish miniature, with the fox-like face, pointy ears and long, fluffy hair disappeared, Mother was heartbroken. The petite Suzette, as Mother named her, was most likely a coyote's prey.

In the 1920s, electrification brought radios into homes across America. Even later rural families crowded around their vacuum-tube-operated Philcos to listen to newscasts, comedies, children's shows, variety hours and presidential speeches — this family included.

Even though electrical power lines were laid in 1950, it was more than half way through that decade when, unannounced, Dad surprised us with our first television. The family was mesmerized, for hours at a time, amidst the snowy static. Mother was dismayed at the latest distraction, in seeing its comatose effect on her family. And domestic life, as she knew it, would forever be changed.

There was no need for "v chips" in those days. Television shows did not have to be censored by parents, since networks already did that. The shows like *Roller*

Derby, Sky King, Hopalong Cassidy, Lawrence Welk, Perry Como, Dinah Shore and *Your Hit Parade* were clean entertainment. Typically, Catholic families watched the *Bishop Fulton J. Sheen Hour*, instead of *Milton Berle*, which was billed at the same time.

In late 1954, Cheryl was the first in the family to be born in a hospital. The last child, Rodney was born in mid-1956, eighteen months later, and four days before Mother's forty-second birthday.

Older brothers and forty-six-year-old Dad, all sporting crew cuts, were in sharp contrast to Elvis Presley, who appeared, from the waist up, on *The Ed Sullivan Show* in 1956. The dark long-haired, rockabilly star did not make a favorable impression on Ila Mae, however. No doubt, like many adults, she thought of him as vulgar, even though at live performances his swiveling hips dazzled thousands of teenage girls, causing them to swoon.

During her last year at home, Ila Mae sat together with the family in front of the television, to eat popcorn, which Mother was a good sport to make soon after the evening meal. With Ila Mae's hearing loss, however, television did not have much appeal. She did not spend much time listening to the radio either, even though she was aware of Bill Halley's, "Rock around the Clock," and the Platters,' "Only You."

Rock and Roll music like Chuck Berry's, "Maybellene," and the Everly Brother's, "Bye Bye Love," was just beginning to come into the farming community through dance programs on television, but Ila Mae preferred square dancing instead. Dick Clark's *American Bandstand*, premiering in 1957, didn't interest her either, even though it was an after-school favorite of almost every teenager. As a senior in high school, she lived through most of her teen years without television. She was developing her religious identity and interests, and was deeply involved with God, family and community. When the Beatles later hit the music scene, she could not have cared less.

By now there were seven unmarried children living at home. Long before the days of mini-vans and SUVs, our family had only one car, but Dad's pick-up truck was often used, too. Drivers education, taught in high school, emphasized safety and courtesy. We learned, on country roads, how not to endanger the lives of others.

As an adult, driving became a source of relaxation and entertainment for Sister Veronica. Since she and the other Sisters considered air travel terribly expensive, she was often called upon to shuttle them to meetings, and was the designated driver when they went on vacations together. After she moved to Illinois, she voluntarily took a Defensive Driving Course in 1978.

Gary/Father Duane said, "I was a confident kid with the family car. There was never a hassle to use it. We did not abuse privileges. Driving was a task to do, a responsibility assumed." On summer afternoons we walked the half-mile to the mailbox and later, as teenagers, we drove the short distance.

The farm was a happy place to grow up; no one complained of boredom. "That was because we didn't know the concept of boring," joked Father Duane. "In reality, putting the romance of childhood memories aside, life on the farm was drab."

It is argued that many young people involved in juvenile delinquency, or more serious crimes, do not have enough to keep them busy. Consequently, it would have been a mistake for the Roy children to complain, "There's nothing to do around here." A task would have been found in short order, like washing the kitchen floor, cleaning the family car, shoveling out the barn, or plowing a field. There was always something to do: a place to walk and hide and dream, and always somebody to do it with.

Children in the early part of the twenty-first century are overextended with soccer, Little League, piano, swim team, karate, and countless other activities that force parents to be mere taxi drivers. Mother did little of this. As a result, this "creative absence" made each child responsible for finding his or her own entertainment.

Between the house and Sand Creek to the south, there is a broad expanse of land with elm trees in the distance, following the snaking creek bed. In the pasture east of the house and near the creek, enormous cottonwood trees stand surrounded by an unplowed and often muddy field of flowering pale pink bouncing bets. Mother proudly put these stinky wildflowers that we picked for her into our only flower vase, and placed them on a 1940s buffet in the living room.

An abundance of prairie flowers dot the plains; purple bull thistles, white soap weed, orange wallflower and yellow sunflowers. Yet all the lovely colors pale when compared to the magnificent Kansas sky at sunset, which fostered a connection with the universe, and a feeling that all is right with the world.

Rich in history from the Cretaceous Era, when Kansas was a great shallow sea, the bluffs on the farmland property surround Sand Creek. The pasturelands offered adventure and exploration, too. Allan, a loner as a child, admitted to spending a lot of time in the pasture and chalk hills, in quiet solitude.

Roger was proudly convinced he found enough Indian arrowheads in these hills, to fill a gunnysack, which he emptied next to the barn, only to have Dad remark, "What are these fossil rocks doing here?"

Rodney, the youngest, said, "When I was about seven years old, Mom packed a lunch of fried chicken, potato chips and Kool-Aid, and I was ready to go exploring for the afternoon all by myself with backpack and canteen." Cheryl was a bold adventurer, as well. "I climbed up the rocks, stood as close as possible to the bluff edge, and looked down the sheer drop-off." Unlike Cheryl and Rodney, with their daring tales of risky adventure, Ila Mae confessed, "Actually the hills caused some dread in me."

The south-facing house looked out to white chalk bluffs spread over many acres — a veritable playground. In general, the creek bed and chalk hills were safe places to play. However, Gary recalled it was an understood taboo to not go on the east side of Sand Creek where Ronald drowned. Instead, he rode Trigger elsewhere.

Ila Mae had been warned, too. "Sometimes Joan, Linda, and I would walk up to [the hills on the west side], but I felt a little uptight, and somehow responsible, if others were along. There was also a fear of the unknown. Is this where mountain lions and tigers lived? Snakes, too? I had some trepidation about falling off a cliff, stepping into a hole, or breaking a leg. Then I'd have to crawl home."

Some of her fears were not unreasonable since gopher and prairie dog holes, left by small burrowing rodents that forage on roots and tubers, are abundant in the pasture. In the camouflage of gray and brown knee-high grasses, it is difficult to see burrow holes, which could leave an unsuspecting horse, milk cow, farmer, or his children with a twisted ankle, or worse.

"Mostly, the hills were just a place to go herd cows at milking time," Ila Mae said. "But as the Rooks County Fair approached each August, I often walked along cow paths and imagined myself modeling garments, which I sewed, and would soon be showing at the final night of 4-H Dress Revue.

"I went through my teenage crisis years there on those cow paths. 'What did others talk about?' I wondered. 'What kind of things would I talk about? And why wasn't I shaped like the girls at school?' I moaned that I was too skinny to be beautiful like others. It was on my trips there, and back, that I did my childhood daydreaming. I'd hum a song I heard from Mother — the Doris Day tune that was popular then, '*Que Sera Sera*, whatever will be, will be... the future's not ours to see.' During many of these days, walking along cow paths, I pondered 'When would I be a Sister? After high school? After college?'"

As a youth, she became grounded in wisdom beyond her years. Because of her high standards, she valued rare moments of free time without responsibilities, restrictions or expectations. "With all that hesitation, the only nice thing I remember about the pasture and hills were the black current bushes, and the view of home in the distance. Yet somehow this place beckoned me often."

Many years later Sister Veronica said, "I've unsuccessfully browsed through family photographs trying to find views of these chalk hills in the background. We must have not thought them worthy of photographs, taking them for granted until 1980, when Alvin Morin's wife Velda said, 'You have such beautiful hills.' On this occasion, even Mother expressed how she had never really noticed them before, but agreed they were quite a fine-looking sight." As adults, siblings traipse the farmland acreage, along with their children and grandchildren, in awe of the serenity of a childhood playground.

✝

Chapter Ten

Sister Veronica recalled from childhood, "My household duties included cleaning windows with vinegar water and newspaper. I especially liked the beauty of the deep window ledges, where Mother usually kept flowerpots, and were wide enough to sit on." No doubt the teenaged Ila Mae spent many solitary hours there, perched on ledges, daydreaming of her future.

This house was where her dreams were born. She lived in the old rock house from infancy until college age. In future years, when the Roy clan gathered, she was in the middle of retelling stories of this childhood home. While there are ongoing folk tales of ghosts and aliens, the house held an attraction for the siblings in almost a mystical sense. Father Duane eulogized this house in a poem, (found at the end of this book), which reveals much of our family personality and values.

Mother assigned many household tasks, giving responsibility according to each child's ability. She wasn't one to insist on doing things only her way, or up to her speed. After each noonday meal one daughter swept the gray linoleum kitchen floor, while two older girls washed, dried and put away the dishes. We were never ashamed to invite friends over to visit. Mother made sure the house was kept clean, but she wasn't obsessive about it. Nevertheless, "Cleanliness is next to Godliness," was another of her favorite sayings, and could have been on her long list of epitaphs.

Mother attached terrycloth towels to the sofa armrests and seat cushions to prevent excessive wear. In the early years, there was linoleum throughout, since carpet would have soon been ruined with soiled shoes tracking in from the barnyard, or fields. This home was modestly furnished, and geared for children.

Before the Webster Dam was constructed, the town was relocated and the State of Kansas sold what could be salvaged from the contents of the old brick 1914 Webster school building, before it was demolished. When Ila Mae was about thirteen years old, Dad purchased part of the school gymnasium floor. He removed the linoleum in the living room and master bedroom, and installed the hardwood, which became the pride of our home and was cared for meticulously.

"Every other Saturday morning Ila Mae and I cleaned our new floor by dancing, whirling, sliding and pulling each other around on mats and rags," said Joan who most liked to clean. "We used old socks as polishing cloths, after applying Johnson's Paste Wax. Everyone admired our work and said how nice it looked."

The sparse decorations in each bedroom were mostly of a religious nature:

a crucifix, and braided palms from Palm Sunday. Even though there were few windows, leaving a lot of wall space, the only picture in the living room was of "The Last Supper."[1] Hanging in the kitchen was an inexpensively framed copy of "The Gleaners," an everyday field scene painted by Millet, a Frenchman, himself who worked in the fields. Our family could relate to this subject matter, which portrayed rustic lives of laborers.

The south-facing bay window in the parlor was a distinguishing architectural feature, and was noticeable to visitors as they approached. Ila Mae recalled, "The parlor (eventually turned into the master bedroom) was the most elegant of rooms, and reserved for special occasions. It was bare of furniture, and only had two little four-inch-high cameo type figurines hung on the wall." We danced in this room. Among the meager collection of 78 rpm records were, "The Yellow Rose of Texas," "Tennessee Waltz," "Anniversary Waltz," and "Abbadabba Honeymoon." Tchaikovsky's "Sleeping Beauty Waltz" was a favorite among the younger girls, as each pretended to dance with the charming prince after being awakened by his kiss.

Looking out from inside the parlor bay window was a view of the trees that were planted alongside Sand Creek, as a result of the Timber Culture Act, in the late 1880s by the homesteader, Eli Sherman. Along with the changing seasons came a variety of color. The light from the low winter sun flooded the room and created a welcomed warmth.

"The original master bedroom was the tiniest room of the house, barely 8 by 8 feet, with room for only a double bed," recalled Ila Mae. "There was no central heat in the house." Propane gas heated the kitchen and living room only. "Our parent's northern exposure bedroom, where ice sometime formed on the interior walls, could only be described as ice cold in the winter." Both Gary and Joan were born during summer months in this room.

Mother sometimes placed her cherished autograph book, scrapbooks, and treasured photo albums in the master clothes closet. Otherwise they were found in her cedar chest, a generous wedding gift from her sister Mary Brin, as payment for her pre-marriage years when she provided loving care for Mary's children. Here, handmade heavy winter quilts were also stored. The closet and cedar chest both provided good snooping ground for wrapped birthday and Christmas presents. With more than one hundred nieces and nephews, there were many weddings to attend, and Mother always had gifts on hand, which were mostly sheet and towel sets.

We girls were proud to show our bedroom to friends, even though our dressing table was made of two orange crates standing on end, with a board joining the two. Ila Mae cleverly covered these with yards of yellow dotted Swiss, made into ruffled skirts to conceal our childish treasures. A small, upright and mirrored *chiffonier* wardrobe was shared for our meager four or five dresses each.

In the summer months this upstairs room, with a southern orientation, was uncomfortably hot for sleeping. In this rural, crime-free area the girls occasionally slept downstairs, in front of an open screen door, to catch a rare breeze. It was only after the November 15, 1959 murder of the Herbert W. Clutter family, wealthy Kansas farmers, little more than two hours away, and written about in Truman Capote's *In Cold Blood*, that doors were locked for the first time. But that fear did not last. There was a later time when our family came home to find two strange teenage boys in our house using the telephone and claiming to have run out of gas. Our Dad's calm manner defused the issue, along with Mother's silent prayer.

There were ongoing efforts to maintain and remodel the house, making it as livable and attractive as possible. Upstairs there were large, separate wings for boys and girls. As the girls got older, their wing was remodeled and made into two bedrooms. The downstairs parlor was converted into a master suite. The kitchen and entrance were enlarged. The exterior was patched and whitewashed. A torn porch screen removed, and a porch swing added.

Over time Mother became increasingly dissatisfied with the house, as it required constant maintenance. She didn't want a lot of money spent fixing it. "Someday we will have a new home, and I will never miss this creaky old house," she often repeated.

The stone house, built sometime around 1885, was almost seventy-five years old when Ila Mae went away to college. With fondness she said, "There was something unique about that house. I could never understand why Mother was always speaking of a new one someday."

Since problems were never discussed with children, perhaps Ila Mae did not know the house seeped water through cracks in the porous limestone, where snakes had been seen crawling. Each of the eleven rooms was frequently wallpapered — some on an annual basis — to camouflage the weather-damaged walls. In 1960, when the house was torn down, at least seventeen wallpaper layers were counted in the living room, in a wide variety of styles and colors. Mother insisted that her newly constructed ranch-style frame house would not have wallpaper — only painted walls.

Mother captured everyday events through the lens of her Agfa box camera, preserving precious memories of family members, and of that house. While she had grumbled in the past about the creaky house, she later admitted, "I had mixed emotions when it was torn down. In fact I shed tears because I knew how much it meant to the older children. I have beautiful memories of the house where Joan and Gary were born. Everyone pitched in to help make it lovely. Lots of time, work, love and prayers went into it." It was a sad day for all when this cherished childhood home was demolished.

Kenneth was in the last class of old Webster High and upon his graduation

Dad rewarded his eldest son with a car. Several years later, the wheat production yields were larger than normal. These financially good "bumper crop" years of 1957-1960 allowed Dad, in 1958, to also buy a car for Allan, following his honorable discharge from the U.S. Army, having been stationed at White Sands (N.M.) Missile Range and Proving Grounds. "Dad purchased a John Deere diesel tractor that year, as well," said Father Duane. When it came turn for Ila Mae, Gary and Joan, they each chose to forfeit a car in exchange for college tuition.

"These bumper crop years were also a turn of fate that helped Mother's dream of a new house come true," recalled Father Duane. "It seemed the right time to build. The size of the family was rapidly diminishing: Kenneth and Allan had already married; Ila Mae and I were in the religious life; and Joan was off to college. That left only the four youngest at home: Linda, Roger, Cheryl and Rodney."

The day after their twenty-eighth wedding anniversary, in 1960, Dad obtained a $10,000 mortgage to build a four-bedroom, two-bath, ranch style house, complete with a finished basement. Ten years later, the mortgage was paid in full. "Mother's nephew, Alvin Morin, a locally well-known building contractor, was consulted and a blueprint agreed upon. Her primary requirement was a large living room with a picture window facing south toward Sand Creek," said Father Duane.

"By Divine Providence, our parents were able to build a new house positioned a few yards to the east," Sister Veronica said. "The home was torn down, after living there for twenty years. There were improvements inside and out, especially the last six years. In 4-H, I started a Home and Grounds Beautification project for the old house, and the family continued improvements with the new house by transplanting native buffalo grass, and filling in the yard with zoysa grass seed, building a yard fence, pouring a sidewalk and planting a row of lilac bushes."

The new "rec-room" basement floor, inlaid with tile in a shuffleboard court design, was a source of pride, and a draw for friends. A ping-pong table was set up at the other end of the oversized room. When someone initiated various games, there was space. Outdoors there were playground equipment and swings for the two youngest children.

The contents of a house reflect a family's values. High school graduation studio portrait photographs, framed exactly alike, were precisely lined up on a living room wall. Candid photos competed on flat surfaces, and every knick-knack gift, given to Mother, was on display, creating a cluttered effect.

Habits established in the old house continued here. All meals were taken at the kitchen table, and the television was shut off during mealtimes. Following meals, the boys and Dad retired to the living room to watch television, while girls finished cleaning up the kitchen.

Behind the new house a retaining wall was built, from leftover limestone remaining after the old house was dismantled — a symbolic, yet practical gesture.

After Ila Mae left home for the convent, she told Mother about an Outdoor Marian Shrine as seen in the *Sunday Visitor* Catholic newspaper.[2] In a grotto of elm trees our brother, Roger, and Mother built a shrine from more limestone left behind. Two milk separator stainless steel tanks, no longer in use, were turned into flower planters and placed on either side of a concrete kneeling pad. In their childhood innocence, playmates often asked if someone was buried at the site.

Following Mother's death, the house was sold to the Rick Lowry family, and the statue of Our Lady of Fatima was removed, and presented to Joyce, the eldest granddaughter. The new owners of the house — non-Catholics — dismantled the shrine, and in its place a gazebo was constructed in the late 1990s as a retreat for bird watching and quiet meditation, in keeping with the original intent as a place of tranquility.

Sister Veronica never lived in the new house, and was not as emotionally attached to it, but she enjoyed visiting family, and picking cherries from the orchard of fruit-bearing trees. In the late 1980s and early 1990s the Lowry family invited her to return as often as she wished. One time she picked enough to make a cherry cordial concoction to share with her family when they came for a holiday visit.

Living on a farm shelters children from some learning experiences. On the other hand, it also shields them from many hard knocks plaguing city kids. Ila Mae's childhood was unsophisticated, unblemished and naïve, unlike those in the twenty-first century where ten-year-old children, and even younger, are exposed to the dangers of drugs, pornography, crime, and the least of which is the damaging violence shown on television and video games and the addiction of the Internet.

While the vast farmland provided space, and a sense of wonder, Ila Mae was focused and forward-looking, and too responsible to be carefree. It wasn't until later in life that she captured the adventurous spirit with her colleagues. Her friend, Sister Ginger Pearl, eulogized Sister Veronica, "On one occasion we went to Estes Park, Colorado to go backpacking with two other women. She had energy for the long hike. It was a week we will never forget." Walking in the mountains and camping allowed her to return to nature and the fresh open air of her youth. One item in her car trunk, at the time of her death, was a sleeping bag.

In 1954 President Dwight D. "Ike" Eisenhower, who spent his boyhood years in Abilene, Kansas, signed a proclamation, as petitioned by the Knights of Columbus and, by an act of Congress, added the words, "One Nation under God" to the Pledge of Allegiance, which is recited each morning by school children everywhere. He said that it symbolizes our strength as a nation, and recognizes the need for moral character. The pledge suddenly became a patriotic oath and a public prayer.

Various other events influenced the person Ila Mae became as an adult — WWII and rationing, Catholicism under Pope Pius XII, economic struggles and the W.P.A. There were other factors like the necessity to be frugal, her birth order and assumed responsibility.

"Mae," as her siblings affectionately called her, was a product of rural America. She was the outcome of wheat fields and homegrown foods, running barefoot, handmade and hand-me-down clothing, cisterns, weekly baths with reused water, one towel a week for the entire family, cold bedrooms and heavy patchwork quilts, and living with the smell of abundance from barnyards and fresh crude oil from wells within eyesight of the front yard. And Sunday Mass.

The lived concepts of family values, commitment, morality, a two-parent household, and religion have become more rare in the last decade, but they were at the very core of how Ila Mae was raised. If there were any scandals, they were not discussed in the presence of children. Instead, the family kneeled together to pray for those in trouble. She cherished her home: a symbol of security and stability.

"Under the beautiful fresh skies, with melancholy in my heart, I pondered as a young child, how terrible someday to die and not relish such beauty around me again, nor enjoy the warmth of my family," she said.

Ila Mae had a lot of acquaintances through 4-H, school and church activities, but it is difficult to assess whom she considered her best friend. She had siblings, and first cousins as playmates, but no intimate girlfriends, with whom she could laugh and giggle and share childish secrets. Uncovering the stories of Ila Mae's youth reveals that she didn't have a perfect childhood. But, all in all, it was as close as it probably comes.

Faith in God gave her a strong foundation, as shown by our parents, who tolerated blinding blizzards, blistering sun and dust bowl winds. They didn't complain. They felt justly compensated by watching their children develop, and the farm crops grow.

Later in life their oldest daughter willingly returned to rural Kansas, and became actively involved in rural life issues during her last fifteen years. Sister Veronica understood long before the Kentucky-raised Tucson author, Barbara Kingsolver, longingly reminisced in a televised interview, "A childhood in the country is a privilege."

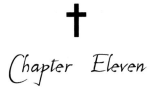

Chapter Eleven

"These commandments that I give you today are to be upon your hearts. Impress them on your children."
— Deuteronomy 6:6-7

Ila Mae felt blessed to have come from a large family, which Sacred Scripture and the Church's traditional practice see as a sign of God's blessing. As far back as she could remember she felt special and set apart. Signs indicate her vocation began early in life; perhaps while still in the womb, since it is believed the soul is created, and infused with grace, at the moment of conception. Vocation (*vocare*) means, "to call," and she might have argued that every Christian has a calling — an invitation to have a personal connection with God.

Grandpa Morin had a sibling, Sister St. Emmanuel Morin, who entered the Order of Sisters of Presentation of Mary, at St. Hyacinthe, Quebec, in 1887. His daughter, Sister Rose Irma, was named after our great-aunt, as both their baptismal names were Angele. Once Sister Rose Irma made a decision to join the convent, her father, Stanislas, wanted her to enter the same as Sister St. Emmanuel, but Sister Rose Irma wanted, "to be nearer her people in Kansas."

On the other side of the family was Grandpa P.H. Roy and his seventeen to twenty-one siblings (from two mothers), among whom was our great-aunt, Sister Evangeline Roy, a cloistered Nun in Montreal.

"When P.H. Roy was a young man, still living in Canada, there was a girl whom he wanted to marry. She entered the convent instead, and wanted him to become a Priest," as the story goes according to Aunt Vula Roy. Priests were the patriarchs of French Canadian life in those days.

Like ninety percent of French Canadians, our immigrant grandparents were Catholic. Our great-grandparents lived near the church, as was typical, and parishioners stopped to pray upon hearing the bells toll. The old French Canadian tradition was to give the first fruits to religious life. As the first daughter, perhaps Ila Mae was groomed for religious life, like other relatives before her.

"In March of 1940 the John and Olive Morin Roy family, with four children, moved to the Stockton parish of St. Thomas when I was three months old," said Ila Mae/Sister Veronica in her Life Review. "Six more children came along, and we were noticeably the largest family in the Stockton and Webster communities."

"Protestants predominated the population in Rooks County," Father Duane added. "At first, after moving into the area, our parents experienced prejudice. Some town folk would have rather crossed the street than meet up with a Catholic. In the midst of Protestant neighbors and classmates, who sometimes manifested prejudices against 'Papists,' we were taught, as children, to be just and humble, not to fight, and remain firm in religious practices and convictions. Living among non-Catholic neighbors, Mother and Dad were ecumenical in their attitudes, but truly faithful to their religious ties. They imparted in us principles of religious identity and fidelity."

"From a child's eyes, belonging to the Church meant doing lots of activities besides attending Mass in our best clothes. It also meant we had a certain identity about our home and ourselves," Sister Veronica said.

Being Catholic defined one's culture and distinctiveness, especially during the pre-Vatican II era prior to 1962. Mother and Dad loved their Church, followed the teachings faithfully, accepted the dogma without argument, and lived with the faith that Jesus dwells in our hearts.

The spirit of God was expressed daily by our farmer-parents, who lived close to the earth, and knew that life is cyclical. Tilling, planting, fertilizing and nurturing yielded bountiful harvests, some of which were held back, and provided seed for the future. Wheat gave new life, nourished our family, and provided a financial reward in return.

Throughout her years, Ila Mae prayed to be more like Mother and Dad, and also to be able to express herself in charitable ways. "One experience, which surely prepared me for the encounter with God, was the spirit of generosity I learned from my dad," which she wrote in her Life Review and was echoed in her eulogy. "None of us children got an allowance. Instead, we just asked for what was needed. If I needed a tablet for school, and asked for ten cents, Dad would give me fifteen. If I wanted fifteen cents to buy candy on a Saturday afternoon, he would give me a quarter. I always received more than I asked for, and usually, things for which I didn't have the sense to ask. I wanted to be generous like that, too, if and when possible. I came to expect the Heavenly Maker to be like that, and found it was true. My relationship with God was a freeing one. As soon as we learned to talk, we were taught to pray."

We were trained to genuflect in church by bending the right knee, signifying humility, penitence and instant prayer. Mother believed that prayer is a weapon against the devil, which lives in the shadows of one's life.

Even when very young we could make the Sign of the Cross, a sacramental gesture signifying the redemption of mankind by our Lord's death on the cross. Without fail, Grace before Meals, a communal family prayer, was recited at the supper meal in a rote manner with no ad-libbing. *Bless us O Lord, and these thy gifts, which we are about to receive, through Your bounty and Christ, Our Lord. Amen*. While kneeling bedside, morning and evening prayers were recited —

the Act of Contrition, Apostle's Creed, Lord's Prayer, Hail Mary and the Glory
Be to the Father.

A bedtime favorite was to Our Guardian Angel: *Angel of God, My guardian
dear, to whom His love commits me here; ever this night (or day) be at my side,
to light and guard, to rule and guide. Amen.* The concept of angels was a
household belief, in our family, long before it sprang to popularity in the 1980s
and 1990s.

We invoked saints, too. Meaning holy, "saint" is a special term for those in
heaven who lived as servants of God, united by faith and baptism, and whose
achievement of holiness is a model of true Christian life. Catholics do not pray
to saints, but ask for their intercession on one's behalf. Devotion, or veneration
of the saints, can be traced to the second century as a form of worship to God
who made them holy.

The role model saints we knew from childhood were the serene, classically
beautiful people on prayer cards. While the martyred saints were portrayed as
either stoic, or in a state of ecstasy, few statues or paintings showed sorrowful,
tortured souls, heads bent as if in supplication, or resignation. It was only in
adulthood when we realized saints were only people, with their all-too-human
frailties, doing ordinary deeds in extraordinary ways.

Mother made certain we knew about the tried-and-true saints, and the
causes to which they are commonly associated: St. Francis of Assisi, the patron
saint of animals; St. Vincent de Paul, of charities; St. Nicholas, of children; St.
Valentine, of lovers; St. Luke, of physicians, and St. Monica, for the conversion
of adult children.

Mother gave a prayer card to our chief of police brother, Kenneth, to keep in
his wallet as St. Michael the Archangel is the one saint Holy Scripture describes
as having led heavenly forces to triumph over the powers of evil. A statue of St.
Christopher, patron saint of travelers, adorned the dashboard of our family car.
Mother often prayed Novenas, a devotion repeated daily for nine days, for some
special intention — especially to St. Jude, the patron of hopeless and desperate
causes. After Sister Veronica's death, many family members and friends have
adopted Sister Veronica as their own personal patron saint upon making
important decisions, and who rivals St. Anthony in helping to find lost articles.

In 1999 the Vatican's Observation Service for the Internet announced that
St. Isidore, the patron saint of farmers, would also be the patron saint of
computer and cyberspace pioneers. During the years she was collecting
genealogy, Sister Veronica could have used his help with her introduction to the
utilization of computers.

Religious education was primarily instilled at home, since we did not attend
Catholic elementary or high schools due to distance. The closest parochial
schools were at Damar and Plainville, not even in our parish, and fifteen and

twenty-five miles each way, respectively.

"Each Saturday morning the Sisters of St. Joseph came from Plainville for our weekly catechism lessons, [now called Catechetical Christian Doctrine/CCD], which we attended during the school year," said Ila Mae. The Sisters were a positive influence and awe-inspiring, too. The immaculate, large white bib over the heavy black serge garments, with oversized rosaries hanging at their sides, made them seem intimidating, yet holy; otherworldly, almost.

"We spaced ourselves around in church, by age group, for catechism classes. I recall the joy of opening a brand new Baltimore I or II Catechism [a statement of Catholic doctrine], and helping the younger siblings with their lessons." The Catechism taught us that we were made to know, love and serve the Lord so that we may be happy with God in this world, and in the next. "My favorite part of religious education class were the contests where those with correct answers remained standing until all, but a winner, were eliminated. Gold stars were awarded for memorizing prayers, and attending daily Mass before class. After age sixteen, we attended CYO [Catholic Youth Organization]."

The Sisters also came for two straight weeks each summer to teach. The Religious Vacation School movement, started in 1921, enabled over ninety percent of those in the Catholic Church to receive religious instruction.[1]

"Mrs. Sidie Reed was the Altar Society president throughout my youth, and at the helm of all these religious education activities," said Ila Mae. "With her son, Raymond, they provided hospitality to the Sisters during summer vacation school, and I suppose to visiting Priests."

Mother was also a gracious and generous host to at least one visiting Sister. In 1963, coinciding with the summer this writer moved away from home, which freed up a bedroom, Mother offered to let Sister Cortona stay at our home for the duration of summer vacation school.[2] After she departed, there was a prompt thank-you note. "J.M.J. My dear Mrs. Roy, Words are inadequate to express to you my thanks for all the deeds of kindness and hospitality you have shown me during the ten days of my stay in your beautiful home. May God's Angels always hover over it and keep you, your family and others in it from harm. You shall be in my prayers when I especially pray for my benefactors. Yours in Christ."

"The Religious Vacation Schools were wonderful," Ila Mae recalled. She eagerly awaited the chats with Sister Mary Jeanette Jansen, CSJ, her teacher in 1954, and the next year with Sister Agnes Joseph Goyette, CSJ. "There were upper and lower grades, and perhaps middle grades, too, if a third Sister came."

An Eastern philosophy states there are seven key figures in one's life, who influence and play a crucial role in an individual's formation. For Ila Mae, Mother and Dad would be at the top of the list. Her high school basketball coach, Glenn Mitchum, would have been in that category, as well as our aunt, Sister

Rose Irma Morin, and our pastor, Monsignor Bernard Dickman (1906-1974).

While some of our public schoolteachers' names have long been forgotten, the names of the Nuns are fondly remembered. Some stories abound about mean-spirited Nuns, but nobody in our family ever came in contact with one. Although, Cheryl relays that one of Father Dickman's sisters, Sister Mary Martha Dickman, came down very strict for not saying the 'Hail Mary' correctly. "She also pulled the hair on top of my head to illustrate how to sing the high notes during children's choir practice. She was stern and strict, but not mean."

Even though some adult Catholics still complain of bad childhood experiences, one would have been comforted with religious education classes under the direction of saintly Sister Regina Marie, another sister of Father Dickman.[3] She taught advanced catechism and choir to the older students. "*Glo...oor...oor...oor...oria in Excelsis Deo*. Now pronounce it *in-egg-shell-sis-day-o*," she would enunciate. The Sisters handed out holy cards and medals as rewards for learning lessons, singing hymns, and memorizing the *Confiteor* (a general confession in Latin, pleading *Mea Culpa*, meaning through my fault). We learned about Holy Days, and heard stories about virgin saints.

Cheryl's favorite teacher was Sister Thomas Ann Pearl, who after the Second Vatican Council, returned to her given name of Sister Virginia, and is now affectionately called Sister Ginger, or Ginny. She and Ila Mae entered the convent together, and became lifelong friends.

"In the 1950s we picked up the children of the Richard Bedore family for religion summer school, but they didn't live there for long. Later the Joseph and Eleanor Bellerive family moved four miles north of us, and their children matched the younger Roy children in age.

"For recess all classes played softball together," Ila Mae recalled. Other times boys scrambled to climb mulberry trees, while the girls pulled the loaded branches lower to pluck, and eat the sweet, juicy blue-black morsels. Those big old trees are gone now, cut down to make room for the rectory.[4]

These times created lasting memories of bright June mornings, when the air was thick with God's love, and the sweet fragrance of purplish lilac bushes weighted down with blooms. If one ever doubted the innocence of children, a more glorious beginning cannot be imagined for a First Holy Communion.

During these two summer weeks, the visiting Sisters showed the group of seven- and eight-year-olds, who were preparing to make their first Holy Communion, how to kneel at the communion rail. They demonstrated how the Priest would place the wafer on their tongue, while the altar server boy held the gold circular paten under each chin to make certain that no sacred host, or particle of one, fell to the ground.

Ila Mae recalled the joyful occasion. "I received my First Holy Communion, in 1947, at the old St. Thomas Church, in Stockton. Three younger children were flower girls." The group of second-grade boys, each with slicked back hair, looked like little angels in starched white shirts, ties, and dark trousers. The girls in white organza dresses and veils, ruffled socks and shiny, new white shoes, looked like young brides of Christ.

"First Communicants were especially watched, by parents and older siblings, to not break the midnight fast." Canon law dictated in 1957 that water would no longer break the fast, but it did when Ila Mae was young. Then neither food nor water could be taken after midnight before receiving Communion the next morning. "On Saturday nights and Sunday mornings, a towel was placed over the water pump in our kitchen, to remind us not to drink from it. To break our fast, during summer religion school, Mother packed hard-fried egg sandwiches, which we ate on the church steps outdoors, after daily Mass."

The age of reason, signifying the time when a child can distinguish between right and wrong, is an important stage for young Catholic children. Before receiving the sacrament of First Communion, the child makes his or her First Confession, now called the sacrament of Penance, or Reconciliation. On Saturday afternoons going to confession meant standing in line, and slowly edging closer toward the booth-like cubicle.

Three separate compartments served as the confessional and each opening was covered by a heavy velvet curtain, which muffled voices. The middle cubicle, for the Priest, had two opaque and mesh-covered screens on either side, just large enough to speak through. The penitent's identity was unknown. Each sliding screen was alternately closed, before hearing confession on the opposite side, while the other penitents were examining their conscience — asking themselves about right intentions; willingness to live their faith; praying for God's direction; not taking the Lord's name in vain; keeping Sundays and feast days holy; avoiding false gods, including money; sharing possessions with those less fortunate; loving one's neighbors; and being faithful to parents, children and spouses. The Priest's role was as conduit between private conscience and God. Venial sins would be remembered from previous confessions.[5]

Directly after the assigned penances, of however many Hail Mary, Our Father, or Glory Be prayers, the penitent recited another memorized prayer, the Act of Contrition: *Oh my God, I am heartily sorry for having offended You. I detest all my sins because they offend You, My God, who are all good and deserving of all my love. I firmly resolve, with the help of Your grace, to sin no more, and to avoid the near occasion of sin. Amen*.

"I first learned to deal with deafness in the confessional," Ila Mae explained. "There I watched for the Priest's hand making the shadow of the closing Sign of the Cross on the screen." Because of her hearing loss, she admitted to not wanting to appear stupid. "I assigned my own penances."

Cheryl, who also has a hearing impairment, agreed it was difficult to use the confessional in the 1950s and 1960s, especially when one has trained herself to read lips. Following the changes with the Second Vatican Council, the sacrament of reconciliation may now be taken face-to-face, but an anonymous confession is still available for those who prefer this method. Unlike years ago, many specially designed confessionals are now equipped with hearing devices.

"I recall confronting the Lord during sermons, at Sunday Mass, as a child," Ila Mae said. "'Look, if I am supposed to know something, if it is expected that I should learn anything, the Lord had better teach me, or let me know what it is.'

"When it was my turn to babysit on occasional Sunday mornings, and after the rest of the family went to church, I'd line up the chairs in the kitchen and make my younger siblings sit there," she continued. "We practiced genuflection, recited at least part of the Rosary, and other known prayers, and closed with eating flattened bread or crackers. Sometimes I'd have them read from the [Missal] prayer book for Mass. Surely the Lord was delighted in the children trying to be good, and in their attempt at Latin.

"As Gary left for the Seminary, he revealed he never had to babysit on Sundays, as he always got to be a server at Mass. Each of our brothers served as altar boys, over the course of twenty-five years from 1940 on." Consequently, we always arrived early for Mass. During summer religious school our brothers were trained, from fourth grade on, to assist the Priest at Holy Mass. Before Vatican II only boys were allowed to be altar servers. Never girls.[6]

When Father Duane celebrated his first Mass, in 1967, in front of the Our Lady of Guadalupe altar, in the crypt at St. Benedict's Abbey, our brother, Rodney, and a cousin, Monte Morin, had the privilege of being his altar server.

Another practice we learned was tithing, or giving a tenth part to the Church. It became an instilled value, as was the Eucharistic fast. Our parents believed tithing was a way to show gratitude for all we received, through the generosity of the Heavenly Father. Money was meaningless to them, beyond being able to meet basic needs. They felt luxuries could easily be done without.

Ila Mae emphasized, "By regularly contributing to the Sunday collection, we tried to do our part in compliance with the exhortations of the National Catholic Rural Life 'to work and pray for shared abundance.'" In today's world, it is evident that donations of time are equally important, and the value of volunteerism, among Catholics, is immeasurable. We learned to be generous in the spirit typical for most Catholics of that era. Sister M. Evangeline Thomas explained in *Footprints on the Frontier* when money was needed to build Marymount College, "Catholics will provide the money because they have been educated to give and have learned that it is a privilege, rather than a burden."[7]

Our family observed all church laws diligently. Before the Second Vatican Council meatless meals, such as fish, grilled cheese sandwiches, and potato soup were taken every Friday without fail. During Lent, Mother made it a point to encourage the children to give up candy and cut down on desserts. Our life in 1959 was completely different from the weaknesses shown during Lent in Joanne Harris' 1999 novel and subsequent movie, *Chocolat* which was set in the same time period.

"We knew it was our fault that schools served fish every Friday," said Ila Mae. "Being a Catholic also meant maybe we'd be a tad late to the PTA meetings, school plays, music programs, ball games, or to 4-H activities, if we dallied about while our family kneeled in the living room to recite the Rosary."

October, like the month of May, is dedicated to the Blessed Virgin Mary. Not only did our parents pray for us, they prayed with us in a comfortable manner. There was no embarrassment, or awkwardness, in praying together during these times, or kneeling at bedside to say morning and evening prayers. It was a natural part of our existence. "The family that prays together, stays together," was practiced and preached by Mother.

In the 1940s and 1950s, newspapers in the north carried denunciations of Roman Catholics and infidels who were trying to exclude the King James Bible from the classroom. "As our earliest teacher, Mother took a serious and active role in our spiritual formation," Ila Mae remembered. "She gave us instructions to refuse to take part in Scripture memorization, and bible handout, or WCTU pledges at school." Our parents were hardly the couch potato variety of Catholics, who simply go through the motions. Instead, they put faith into action, which involved each child. Mother, humble and submissiveness to the Divine Plan, was especially instrumental in instilling faith.

Ila Mae/Sister Veronica often prayed to be more like our parents. One could not ask for a more devout mother than ours. Evelyn Bassoff, the Boulder, Colorado clinical psychologist, who is also a columnist for *Parents Magazine* suggests, "A daughter looks to her mother as a mirror where she wants to see her own goodness reflected."

"We drove eight miles to church for all holydays[8] and were probably late for school on those days, too," Ila Mae continued. "During athletic competitions I'd deliberately flip out my scapular medal in religious pride. My heart skipped a beat when I saw other Catholic youth from neighboring small communities with religious medals on, too."[9]

"Even though we were the only Catholic family at the Webster Schools (until the Veverka family started in 1950), we were proud to be identified with our faith. Both of our dads served on the school boards at the new Webster school. Partly through Dad's influence, several Catholic teachers successfully taught in our public school for a few years.

"Our pastor, Monsignor Dickman, was invited to give the Baccalaureate address for Gary's graduation in 1958. The year before, my class of three students (Jack Becker, Dale Arbogast and myself) invited Father John Moeder to give our Baccalaureate address," said Ila Mae. "The Priest commented in later years that at the time he wondered, 'What good would come from Webster?' Later I smirked, knowing that two Religious coming from there was a blessing." The rural area of Webster might be compared to Galilee, also known as a hick town, and there were those from biblical days who wondered, "What good would come from there?"

"When our new house was completed, Father Dickman was invited to drive out to the farm to bless it, and all therein. We had holy things in every room," said Ila Mae. "Pieces of palm [blessed from Palm Sunday] were planted in every corner of our fields. We brought crop seed to be blessed, and attended Holy Mass on Rogation Days [the three days preceding Ascension Thursday and observed by the Church as days of supplication for God's blessings, especially for the harvests]. After praying for good crops and rains, we were usually blessed with a plentiful harvest. We always tried to remember to give thanks to God, from whom all abundance comes, and to recognize our dependence on the Lord."

As a child of the land, and the daughter of farmers, Ila Mae learned from our parents that like seeds for crops, seeds of faith, and of God's word, must be planted to grow in the human soul. Rain, symbolizing God's grace, softens the soil and nourishes the seed, and His word takes root and sprouts.

"I have very little memory of the original St. Thomas Church except being in the balcony for catechism," said Ila Mae. This is where she made her First Communion. "Dad had a part in demolishing the old church made of native limestone, which was historically the oldest church in Rooks County (1878-1951). The church was later reconstructed in the center of the Catholic cemetery, as a replica of the original.

During the 1950s Bishop Frank Thill's busy schedule did not allow him to travel annually throughout the diocese of his jurisdiction to small, rural communities for the sacrament of Confirmation, which only Bishops confer. When he went to Stockton, on October 18, 1951, for the dedication of the newly built St. Thomas Catholic Church, the trip coincided with confirming those who were eligible. Ila Mae and four other siblings, (Kenneth, Allan, Gary and Joan — one of the youngest at age nine), were among the sixty-one confirmed that day. In the midst of the largest class in this parish were thirteen converts to the Catholic faith. "The example of Christian living, exhibited by our parents, inspired many people to become converts, including our schoolteacher, Glenn Mitchum and his wife Gwen," said Ila Mae.

Our cousins, Geraldine (Roy Molina) and Dorothy Roy, were also confirmed at this time, the latter sponsored by Mother. Our parents were repeatedly asked to be godparents at baptisms, and confirmation sponsors for relatives and parishioners alike. "By the time our parents were in their fifties, it became more evident they were parish ambassadors, and were endeared by the more than one hundred parish families, especially the newcomers," Father Duane noted.

Ila Mae took St. Mary Goretti as her patron saint. Goretti, a teen martyred in 1902, was canonized the previous year, in 1950. For her sponsor she chose our aunt, Vula (Mrs. Omer) Roy, herself an earlier convert, who gave her a statue of Our Lady of Grace.

Even though this was a special day in her life, Ila Mae recalled very little. "I remember only where I sat, and what I wore. There is neither memory of preparation, nor a moment of grace." Yet the gift of courage, which the Holy Spirit promises on the day of Confirmation, grew deeper and more persistent in every facet of her life. As an adult she drew from that spiritual courage to face hard decisions and bear many crosses in her journey toward eternal life.

Dad served on the church board of directors, and was installed as vice-president of the Holy Name Society, which held meetings once a month after Mass. He was also a member of the Knights of Columbus and by advancement to Fourth Degree Knighthood he was expected to live a dignified lifestyle of devotion, service and fraternity. This society, of American Catholic men, actively engage in many charitable and educational works, and provides a wide variety of opportunities for family involvement through picnics, dances, parties, Communion breakfasts and family church attendance.

"Once a month, on Thursday afternoons, Mother faithfully attended Altar Society meetings. Those, and the activities of Christian Mothers and [Mount of Olives] Daughters of Isabella [a women's auxiliary of the Knights of Columbus], seemed to be her main daytime social event. We could see the many useful things these ladies did for our church," Sister Veronica/Ila Mae said. "Since there was no church custodian, Mother, along with several other parish ladies, also volunteered on a rotating basis to clean the church on Saturday afternoons [and her daughters often helped]."

As children we learned how to get along and work with others, through a willingness to perform dull, routine, and even unpleasant tasks without thought of personal gain. "As we got old enough, we participated in school, church and community activities. It was a privilege to help at the Rooks County Fair hot food stand, sponsored by our church. I felt a certain pride, being identified as a Catholic. Beforehand we cleaned up the area, erected the food stand, contributed supplies and several hours of work.

"The other big money raiser for the parish was the annual church bazaar dinner and carnival [held each November.] There were fishpond prizes for the children, cakewalks, bingo, needlework and handicrafts for sale, and a big item raffle. Not only were the women involved, but men worked all day, too, hauling, peeling, cooking, setting up, and finally undoing it all, long into the night."

Ila Mae's childhood was stable and sure, embracing what was then called the "True Church," containing all the world's truths. The family prayed for the unbaptized and non-believers. At that time Catholicism, handed down as a birthright, was instilled as the only right way to live. The ecumenical posture of the Second Vatican Council, which recognized and valued other faiths and non-Catholic Christian traditions, were still a few years away.

For the children, going to Mass was an obligation having great appeal, since it was also a social outing. Mother believed that dressing up for the occasion was a reflection on the dignity of the Mass. Unlike in the 1990s, and beyond — when many parishioners began to attend Mass casually dressed in jeans and t-shirts with beer slogans, or shorts and halter-tops, attire that is not even acceptable for serving on jury duty today — during the bygone era of the 1950s a woman's head was covered when entering the church. Mothers and daughters wore hats, and later *mantillas*.

"Without fail we attended Sunday Mass and sat together. When, as a group, our 4-H club attended another denomination's church, our family first attended Mass at our own church," said Ila Mae.

We stayed seated during Protestant services and did not sing their Christian hymns, which were accompanied by a piano. To us the Protestant songs seemed common, in contrast to the heavenly organ music and Latin, the mysterious language of the Roman Catholic Church.

Mother's friend, Eleanor Bellerive, said, "As her [other] children got older Olive prayed they would not lose their faith." Mother's steadfast prayer was for her children to find salvation, knowing there is no guaranteed cause of faith, or its loss. She fervently believed in active participation, the power of prayer and the will of God.

Studies show that only fifty percent of baby boomers are still practicing Catholics. It is not unusual for young adults to leave the Church for a while, and live a churchless way of life, but Mother did not have to worry about her oldest daughter. Being in touch with her spiritual side from an early age, Ila Mae found the Holy Sacrifice of the Mass, divided into various parts, to be spiritually forgiving, healing and satisfying to her soul.

At Mass in pre-Vatican II days, the Priest's back was toward the congregation, as he prayed at the altar, in Latin. As in drama, there are many parts of the Mass. The *Introit* introduced the spirit of the feast. In the *Confiteor* sins were asked to be forgiven; the *Kyrie eleison* pleaded for mercy; the *Collects* were prayers for intentions of the community. From the pulpit the Priest delivered the Epistle, Gospel and sermon in English. Following the *Credo*, the public act of faith, the Priest lifted the paten with the bread, and the chalice, holding water and wine, symbolizing the divine offering of Christ to God.

During the subsequent Eucharistic Prayer came the *Sanctus*, a song of praise, and the Consecration, the moment of sacrifice and proclaiming His death and resurrection. The Faithful Departed were remembered to God, and there were prayers for the whole Church. In reciting the Our Father, we prepared for Holy Communion where bread is broken and shared, in the Jewish custom of friendship, and the sacrificial banquet begins. After the Priest prayed *"Dominus vobiscum,"* even children knew to respond, *"Et cum spiritu tuo."*[10]

While kneeling at the altar rail, with head bowed and hands clasped, Holy Communion was a sharing of deep friendship between God and man, and was served only on the tongue, and only from Priests, no matter how long the line of communicants. The boy servers at the altar represented the faithful.

After washing the chalice and the Priest's fingers, a final blessing bestowed His message with us into daily life. Before leaving the altar, however, the Priest would read silently the prologue of the Gospel of St. John.

Benediction, during which the Holy Eucharist was exposed for public adoration, was another common devotion. It sometimes would follow the celebration of High Mass, or be a separate rite in itself. Many times it would be a late afternoon or evening event. The impressive ceremony included veneration of the Blessed Sacrament in the monstrance, and singing of Latin hymns by the congregation, while incense, burning in a censer or thurible, reminded parishioners of the ascent of prayer to God.

Upon entering and leaving a Catholic church, the faithful do a genuflection, a bending of the knee of the right leg, to acknowledge the presence of the Blessed Sacrament in the Tabernacle, mindful that "the Word was made flesh."

Our parish Priest had a strong and manly voice. His erect posture and a slight tilt of his head, caused by a football injury to his neck as a star player in the 1940s at St. Benedict's College in Atchison, gave him an even more dignified and mysterious air, perhaps aloof and ethereal at the same time.

Our family sat close to the front of the church to make it easier for the children to pay attention and listen intently to his sermons, which Mother often said were beautiful. As our beloved pastor for twenty-eight years, from 1939 to 1967, Father Bernard Dickman was spoken about highly as were the other parish Priests throughout the years, even though some were better liked than others. In 1952 his Bishop honored Dickman with the title, Monsignor, probably in recognition of his leadership in constructing churches in Zurich, Stockton and Hill City. In 1960 many parishioners attended his Silver Jubilee celebration at the City Hall, in Stockton.

Our Canadian-born second cousin, Father Louis Dupont assisted Father Dickman for several years, in the 1950s, during construction of the new church in Stockton. Dupont served St. Catherine's parish in Dubuque, Kansas from 1948 until at least 1953. "With vigor he continued the expansion work of the church started earlier, as well as planting more than one hundred black locust and Russian olive trees," states a fifty-year celebration document.

Father Dickman lived at Zurich until the first Stockton parish rectory, patterned after an English country house, was completed in 1960, and in which Dad was involved in planning.

Much like our Roy and Morin grandparents, who helped construct St. Joseph's Church in Damar, Dad helped build the new church in Stockton, at 727 Main Street. Made of Kansas-quarried Benton Limestone, in a modern Gothic design, it was completed in 1951. Family members Kenneth, Roger and Cheryl were married there. The baptisms of Cheryl and Rodney, and nieces and nephews Joyce, Amanda, Joshua and Christopher took place here, too, as did the funeral Masses for Mother, Dad, and infant niece Janice.

Sister Veronica was one of only three Nuns from the parish, the other two considerably older.[11] While her Silver Jubilee was celebrated at Christ the King parish, in WaKeeney, where she was working at the time, her Stockton home parish of St. Thomas also held a celebration Mass.

Father Duane offered his first Mass there, in 1967. In 1992, he celebrated his 25th Silver Jubilee Mass there, too, and is the only Priest to have come from this parish.

"Living in a rural area, we children didn't know the Catholics in town, with a few exceptions. Ignatius [Ig] and Lydia Gross came to our rescue many Christmases with their Western Auto hardware and toy store," recalled Sister Veronica. "The brothers George and Charles Ostmeyer were at their farm implement store when we were sent into town on errands for machinery parts, and they were also visible and prominent leaders of our grand Rooks County Free Fair. Robert and Lorene Miller, who were next-door neighbors to our Roy grandparents, in Stockton, often visited our parents at the farm to play pitch and pinochle. Our closest Catholic rural neighbors were Mrs. Addie Reed and her son, Freddie."

Throughout her lifetime, Sister Veronica led by example, something she learned by watching our model parents. They led pious lives, and loved each child equally. Yet it is easy to see how, with subtlety, they favored their eldest daughter with her saint-like qualities. It's been said that God falls in love with certain people, and it seems Ila Mae Jean Roy was one of God's special chosen children.

While humans look at the external, theologians say God looks at the whole. St. John of the Cross wrote of the involuntary pleasure that comes about when God caresses the soul, and how it overflows into the senses. Perhaps this was how she felt in trying to explain a spiritual encounter as a child, which almost defies description — an inwardness; an intensely personal experience; a longing to escape from the world and worldliness — in her effort to find God. She was engaging and transforming in her faith, possessing a unique feeling experienced by people truly touched by Christ, and baptized in his Spirit, the source of her strength.

"My years at home were secure yearrs," she said. "I loved anything that had to do with religion: summer vacation religion school, going to church, the mystery of the creator in nature, and all that went with being a good child. I was confident in my abilities. I felt like a special person, marked in God's eyes, and surrounded in the mystery of eternal life. As a young girl standing on a hill under a beautiful sky, I felt that at the end of life, I'd never enjoy that sight again."

She intuitively recognized and appreciated the awesome beauty of nature. The scientist and theologian Father Teilhard de Chardin wrote of the contemplation of nature, the wonder at nature, communion with nature, and communion with what is beyond nature. But it would be many years before the young farm girl discovered his lofty writings for the sophisticated mind.

In response to "Whom shall I send? Here I am Lord; send me," surely was her plead.[12] Even during her early years, she was anxious to serve. On a holy mission into adulthood, and known for her thoroughness and persistence, she wanted a leadership role only to better bring the Gospel, God's word, to others. She attempted to reason correctly and understand the nature of the universe through the strength of God's will. Resigned to the Divine plan, she tried to recognize the necessity of events, as part of the Divine order of the universe. Somehow she knew there was more to life than what others were experiencing.

Undoubtedly, she was a mystic, even at a young age, and unable to express her feelings, which were probably overwhelming, bewildering and distressing. She tried to explain her youthful experiences. "While sitting in church, I would have the feeling that I would never have the closeness of my family, or to hear music again after the end of my life. These were such dreadful thoughts that would seize me, unexpectedly, until I wanted to run from them before I fainted. These same feelings followed me into my religious life until approximately age thirty-five, when I no longer feared death."

As she matured, she breathed virtue and right living, and continued her spiritual ascent. She developed an understanding of the soul's yearning for God, which released her from the dreadful thoughts of death she'd had as a child upon losing her brother, Ronald. When the human personality is dissolved, or dies to oneself, and is absorbed into the unity of God, this supernatural prayer is at its highest peak. The surrender to death causes no fear in one who has surrendered first to God. In the opera *Chronicles of the Carmelites* this is aptly portrayed as the to-be-martyred Nuns marched onward to the guillotine singing the *Salve Regina* during the French Revolution's Reign of Terror.

"There were several religious experiences I had that prepared me for knowing I wanted to belong to God. One of these was a tremendous sense of eternity." This intuitive anxiety of a timeless oneness is immediate, invisible, and inaccessible. This concept — beyond time — is hard to grasp. And mysticism cannot be acquired by thought — only by love. Mystical writings are often incommunicable and beyond comprehension. Mystics are often portrayed as lonely and isolated figures wrestling with their vision of God and their developing understanding of God's ways. Some theologians argue that fear and desire are the first signs of a vocation; the first contact with God is disturbing, and the calling is heard only in the heart.

Her friend, Sister Ginger Pearl CSJ, and our cousin, Sister Diane Brin CSJ, both agree on other signs of a vocation. "It was something I needed to do. It is not something that one decides for oneself. It is being chosen, a strong conviction and a mystery even to those who are called," said Sister Diane. "Even when one fights hard against choosing the religious life, there is an overwhelming feeling that the only way to really know is to try it and see," agreed Sister Ginger. When Gary/Father Duane indicated that he wanted to study for the Priesthood, Ila Mae was supportive, "The only way you know is to try it."

An event that was significant enough for her to write about happened when Ila Mae was about ten years old. It may have affected many decisions she later made. "In a sense, I just knew someday I'd be a Sister, but I didn't dare say anything. One evening, when I was about in fifth grade, I was babysitting Roger, and the rest of the kids. As the night grew on, I began to panic that I wouldn't be able to hear the baby cry, so I sat up next to the crib, waiting for the folks to come home, instead of going upstairs to sleep myself. I was so humbled that I could never make a responsible parent that then I said, 'Yes, I would be a Sister.' After that it was merely a matter of knowing when, how, and where," she wrote in 1980.

It might appear that her concern, and seemingly feeling incapable of being a good enough mother due to her hearing loss, led her to consider this life, as she prayed earnestly for God to show her a way. Even though these are Ila Mae's quoted words, her close friend, Sister Ginger, was emphatic that the convent would not have accepted Ila Mae into religious life if it appeared she was running away out of fear from a married life with children.

One might wonder whether the movie classic, *The Bells of St. Mary's*, played a small part in her decision. In 1945 Bing Crosby co-starred with the stunning Ingrid Bergman, who played Sister Benedict, a young strong-willed Nun who believed that prayer solved all problems. It is suggested in Bergman's biography, "her performance influenced many impressionable young girls to enter the closed confines of a convent."[13]

On the other hand, in reading the biographies of famous Religious Women, such as Mother Cabrini and Sister Mary Frances Clarke, it becomes evident they also knew of their vocation to the religious life early on. Sister St. Joan Willert, former CEO of Carondelet Health Network in Tucson, Arizona, said that in her junior year of high school she acknowledged the calling to religious life, which she had considered, off and on, since fourth grade. Like Ila Mae, she never gave up her childhood dream, and always knew she would be a Nun someday.

While Sister Veronica was in college, our parents were presented the Kansas Rural Catholic Farm Family of the Year award, in 1960, by the SCCN National Rural Life Committee, due in part to her outstanding documentation and extensive six-page application. As a teenager in 4-H, she learned to be a consummate record keeper, which served her well in later years. An article in the Salina Diocese Catholic newspaper, the *Sunday Register* read, "The couple [John and Olive Roy] have been an outstanding example of Catholic farm life, including participation in civic and religious group betterment action over a period of years."

In her last weeks of life, Mother told Father Duane that when she was in Salina, for a women's retreat, she spent some time in front of the Blessed Sacrament and offered this prayer, "Lord, I don't know why you have blessed me with many sons and daughters. I am very grateful. I want to offer to you one to be a Priest." As years went by she saw this prayer, and more, come true to her immense joy.

Mother lived her faith and was pious, without being long-suffering about it. Even after losing eight-year-old Ronald to a drowning accident, for which outsiders unfairly blamed her, she offered her children to God. "You have given them to me, Lord. Take one to do your work," she said. When two entered the religious life, she considered herself doubly blessed.

Mother's influence on Ila Mae's vocation cannot be denied. In her own biography Mother said, "Since I had four daughters, I prayed for one of them to become a Nun. One day, I clipped a prayer [for vocations] from the *Our Sunday Visitor* Catholic newspaper. I taped it on the wall going up the stairway, where it could be seen by the girls [and boys] on their way to bed. I hoped one of them would notice it."

The message in the clipping deeply touched Ila Mae. "I noticed the Prayer, 'To Know My Vocation.' Now why did Mother do that? I wasn't going to let on that I even noticed it, but I'd look at it out of the corner of my eye as I went by, or I'd dillydally there to shut off the light at night, and slowly I learned it by heart. Every Sunday after Mass, I'd take the *Sunday Visitor* and read the Victory Noll, or Maryknoll Missionary Sisters ad, but I didn't want anyone to catch me looking at it.[14]

"I still didn't know where, or when I was to become a Nun. All during high school I tried to reason, 'When? Should I finish college, and work long enough to pay back the folks first? Would I lose my vocation by waiting too long?'" If the ad didn't plant the seed then, certainly, it fed and germinated what was already there.

Had Ila Mae asked for a brochure from the American Missionary order, the convent surely would have mailed her information about their work and prayer life. Instead, she still did not want anyone to know of her vocation, and since Mother was the first to scan the incoming mail, Ila Mae knew she would have been quizzed. As a result, the teenager had no literature to hold and ponder, except for the advertisement. "It was always the same simple ad, and I think it is still hasn't changed after twenty-five years."

The well-written promotion ad would have caught the interest of a thinker like Ila Mae. In the 1950s, when not many women had college degrees, Sisters were typically intellectually very capable, and overwhelmingly better educated than housewives, or even lay teachers for that matter. A graduate of Smith, a highly regarded women's college, Mother Mary Joseph Rogers (1882-1955) founded the Maryknoll (later Mary Rogers) College, and a motherhouse at Maryknoll, New York.

Notwithstanding the Maryknoll Missionary Order ad, it is easy to see why Ila Mae leaned toward the familiar Congregation of Sisters of St. Joseph (CSJ), having heard of them since childhood, and with whom our family had a long history. Our aunt, Sister Rose Irma Morin, entered the congregation in 1920, after being influenced by the Sisters who taught grade school in Damar since 1904. No doubt she, in turn, influenced Mother who, as an orphaned teenager, lived with her sister at the convent and Sacred Heart Academy boarding school during the 1929-1930 school year.

In 1940, the year after Ila Mae's birth, Aunt Jeannette Roy joined the CSJ of LaGrange, Illinois. Later, three maternal cousins entered the convent in the 1950s after attending Damar High School, which had CSJ Sister-Teachers up until 1977. Other role models were the Sisters of St. Joseph, who traveled from Plainville and Concordia, to teach weekly Saturday morning catechism classes and vacation summer school.

Many people carry from their school days, into adulthood, grudges of an outdated image of strict Nuns. The childhood reminders of stern women, who taught them years earlier in parochial schools, set them off. Catherine Whitney wrote of this experience in *The Calling: A Year in the Life of an Order of Nuns*. Before she became a wiser soul she was a Catholic rebel, and dismissed her childhood teachers as archaic and out of touch with reality.

On the flip side, Ila Mae's childhood experiences with Nuns were positive, as she received encouraging words from the ones who nurtured her desire. She could combine her dreams of becoming a Teacher and a Nun, since this CSJ Order valued education, and their charism leaned toward the fields of teaching and nursing.

In *Virgin Time: In Search of The Contemplative Life*, the author Patricia Hampl explained the charism of a religious order as the *espirit*, or the heart by which it interprets its "Rule," a formal document to which the Sisters adhere.

The charism is further explained in a revised 1994 recruitment brochure: "The Sisters [of St. Joseph] minister in, and with, the Church in a variety of works, which respond to people's needs for God and reconciling love. Through their personal and communal prayer, they share the 'state of their heart' and are led into the mystery of God's action in their lives. Together they witness to unity. Whether they live alone or with others, they are responsible to each other for the way they live their communal life." This was the spirit of the Order and the lifestyle that first attracted Ila Mae.

The Sisters of St. Joseph, of Concordia, are located in Cloud County, Kansas. This county, settled in 1860, has a strong French Canadian Catholic history. The town name itself, Concordia, has been used as a synonym for our ancestral city of Montreal, (Mount Royal), the motto of which is *Concordia salus*, or *"le salut par la concorde*," which means, "well-being (or health) through harmony."[15]

Just like Ila Mae's bloodline ancestors, this order of Sisters had their roots in France. The Holy Spirit led them in many directions, and the Sisters quickly branched throughout the United States and Canada. Mother Superior Stanislaus Leary first traveled by stagecoach from St. Louis/Carondelet, Missouri, in 1883, and became the foundress of the apostolic religious community and congregation in Concordia. By 1888 Cloud County had nine railroad lines, which made it a practical sight for the Motherhouse.[16]

The mother institute at Rochester, New York first launched into the nursing field when the CSJ of Concordia became a nursing order in 1903, when the St. Joseph Hospital in that town was opened. More than sixty years later, during 1964-1968, Sister Veronica spent four years at this same hospital, as assistant dietitian, and later head of that dietary department.

Before that, the general purpose of the congregation was managing hospitals, charitable institutions, homes for the aged and schools for the deaf.[17] Being hearing impaired herself, it is unknown whether she was influenced by their affiliation in working with the deaf in Missouri. Instructing the youth was another of their works of charity. Later the CSJ opened orphanages, and were charged with opening a parochial school in almost every parish in Kansas, according to *Footprints on the Frontier*, which follows the CSJ order historically up to 1948.

Not all, but many of the Concordia CSJ members are from rural areas. The innocence and purity that comes from life in the country cannot be denied. In its serenity — where one can hear birds sing, rather than neighbors shouting, horns honking, or airplanes roaring; smell fresh-turned soil, rather than automobile exhaust from busy commuters; taste home-cooked meals, rather than fast foods; see wide open spaces of undeveloped land, rather than concrete and tall buildings — it is easier to see God's hand at work.

As a humble woman, and farm girl at heart, Ila Mae was unaffected by worldliness. Her simple unsophisticated style never changed over the years, and she continued to be natural, decent and kind, calling on her inner strength to see her through difficult situations, in her walk with the Lord.

Father Duane pointed out, "In biblical days women accompanied Jesus in his ministry, ministering to Him and with Him to others.[18] In the Acts of the Apostles, there are ample references to women as leaders in the early church communities, no longer connected to Synagogue, but in the homes of the faithful. During the fourth century monastic movement in Rome, St. Jerome encouraged women of the nobility to the monastic way of life. When Pacomius began coenobitic monasticism in Egypt, his sister wanted to be part of it. He told her to start her own, which she did. In the sixth century, again in Rome, the twins, Benedict of Nursia and Scholastica, became notable re-organizers of monasticism for men and women. In subsequent times many monasteries where founded for the daughters of nobility. There were also places that received poor widows, shelters for abused women, and places of refuge for female prostitutes.[19] These monastic groups remained the norm until the Era of the Mendicants (11th Century). The famous Saint Clare, friend and follower of St. Francis of Assisi, made the consecrated life possible for women of all classes. It was, however, only in the 17th century, with groups like the Sisters of St. Joseph, that there was a flourishing of the missionary type of consecrated life for women, ministering to the impoverished of war, pestilence and class struggle," Father Duane concluded.[20]

Sue Evans, an assistant professor of educational psychology, points out that there are Buddhist Nuns, just as in the Catholic faith. Evans offers two prime reasons why a woman would choose the path of dedicating her life to serving a higher power. "One reason is that it is an inbred, inborn response, and a drive to know more. This calling becomes a priority." Evans says that another reason for becoming a Nun is, "the result of a triggering event over the loss of a loved one. In that shock, or surprise, the individual wants something more permanent in life; something that can be relied upon. This is not a sudden shifting of priorities. Instead, it comes about when one begins to reflect on God more, and less on the world at hand."[21]

When Ila Mae entered the Convent in the fall of 1958, Catholics were experiencing the height of Pope Pius XII's era. His stance framed a rigid code of behavior instructing Catholic minds across the world, and little was left to their own conscience. These "cradle-Catholics" were able to recite *The Catechism* by rote, yet unable to defend their faith through clear thinking. The message of this Pope greatly affected the childhood of Ila Mae Roy, leaving an indelible mark on her adolescence, as it did for many other Catholics born before the Second Vatican Council, many of whom still mourn for the "Latin" church.

Pope Pius XII's point was that every Christian is bound to attempt to reach that sacred pinnacle, but it is the religious man or woman who proceeds on a path, which is entirely his or her own, and relies upon help of a higher nature: the religious life has a special purpose in the Church, namely, to lead all people to the side of holiness. From the time of his coronation in 1939, until his death, he had come to be almost worshiped by millions of Catholics, and many regarded him as a saint.

During the 1940s and 1950s the CSJs of Concordia numbered over 600 members. It is significant to observe that following his death, in the fall of 1958, vocations soon dramatically declined. Sister Veronica's band was the last large group to enter the convent in the late 1950s. At the time of her death in 1995, the number had dwindled to 250, and she was among the youngest. A recent nationwide survey shows that of the 70,303 women religious, 77 percent are older then age 70, leaving only 23 percent which are younger.

Ila Mae was born, reared and educated in the pre-Vatican II church, in post-war prosperity America, of parents who lived through the struggle of two world wars, a depression and the dust bowl years. Using terminology coined by sociologist Father Andrew Greeley, Father Duane wrote, "Veronica entered the religious life, and was formed a Religious Woman, in a Confident Church. She matured and ministered in the Confusing Church. She lived the best and the worst of the two."

✝

Chapter Twelve

Ila Mae was a neat, quiet, and cooperative high school student possessing qualities expected of girls during this era, although she wasn't embarrassed to show her intelligence and answer questions. She may have been shy, although she liked raising her hand with the right answer. Having high academic goals, she paid attention, worked hard, dutifully turned in her homework, and was never accused of goofing off in class.

As a general rule, girls typically perform better in school than do boys. Unfortunately girls' math scores tend to drop during the middle school years, when they discover boys and become more concerned with make-up and clothes — all which did not influence Ila Mae.

Prior to 1976, when Congress passed the Title IX Education Amendment, a mandate against discrimination in education few schoolgirls were encouraged to take higher-level math and science classes. Even though trigonometry, calculus and physics were not offered at Webster high school, Ila Mae had the aptitude and, given the opportunity, could have chosen a high-paying job in accounting, engineering, or computer science, each as possible careers.

Nevertheless, Dad encouraged his oldest college-bound daughter to follow a stereotypical, and traditional field for women, an education more fitting for someone he thought would one day be a wife and mother. He, as well as the rest of rural America, had never heard of "gender equity." Dad took the sensible approach to life. Ila Mae respected his opinion. "I thought perhaps I'd like to teach math, but my dad, being so practical, encouraged me to go into something like home economics, which I also enjoyed. So, that became my goal."

With the arrival of the new millennium, it is evident there is a shortage of qualified math teachers because most of them go outside of teaching and on to higher paying jobs into business. If Dad had encouraged her in math, had she not entered the convent, and had she grown up fifty years later, or even twenty-five for that matter, her life might have been dramatically different.

In her last decade of life, she was eager to learn more about computers. Having an introverted personality, she would have been a natural "techie." She was known to be one of the more computer-literate Sisters within the CSJ community. Sister Ginger Pearl speculates that Sister Veronica's analytical and math aptitude were assets in developing her computer skills, which made it easier for her to compile two extensive family genealogy books.

In 1930, when Mother was sixteen years old, she attended a silent religious retreat with other girls her age at what was then called Marymount Academy.

When the eldest daughter expressed her desire to attend Marymount College, our parents were pleased with Ila Mae's choice of the all-female Catholic school.

Before the Second Vatican Council, Catholic educators were not in favor of coeducation in secondary schools. According to a pre-Vatican II Catholic dictionary, Pope Pius XI pointed out that coeducation is founded on naturalism, a denial of original sin, or a confusion of the real relationship of the two sexes.[1]

Studies show those who attend all female schools have an added advantage over women in co-ed schools because they are given more opportunities for leadership skills to emerge. A separate study agrees that girls who are shy, meek and mild begin to assume positions as school leaders in an all-female environment, as there are fewer discipline problems and better academic results. Here students are trained to develop not only an independent intellect, but a graceful, confident style, as well. Three recent First Ladies attended women's colleges: Nancy Reagan and Barbara Bush, at Smith, and Hillary Rodham Clinton, at Wellesley. However, Laura Welch Bush, a Texan born and bred, attended Texas colleges.

A detrimental effect of co-ed high schools and colleges, in the 1950s, was that typically young women deferred to males during classroom participation, a practice still too often occurring today. In larger and more crowded classrooms, there is a tendency for teachers to call on boys more than girls. Instead, at the Webster rural school, which Ila Mae attended and where enrollment was low and several class levels were grouped together, she received a lot of attention.

Women's History Month, in March, brings to mind that it wasn't until 1918 that all people had the vote, "except the insane, idiots, imbeciles, [foreign] aliens...and women." Furthermore, women were not allowed to serve on juries until 1954, a mere three years before Ila Mae entered college.

She was the first in the immediate family to attend college, as well as one of the few, out of more than one hundred first cousins, who went on to earn a master's degree. In contrast, in the Ed and Irene Morin family alone, there are three who earned master's degrees, and one earned a jurisprudence/law degree.

Our parents were proud to provide this opportunity of higher education to their daughter. Several times that first year they made the 130 mile drive to visit and have a meal with her in the main dining hall, where she worked to pay towards the cost of her tuition.

In 1963, the year of her college graduation, two siblings also graduated; this writer Linda from high school, and Roger from elementary school. With only three children remaining at home, Mother returned to the women's college, that summer, for another silent religious retreat to reflect on her many blessings.

Salina, the seat of Saline County in central Kansas, is near the confluence of the Saline and Smokey Hill Rivers. At the time of Ila Mae's entrance into college, the town, located about 170 miles west of Kansas City, was an important commercial center for livestock and grain. As one of the leading centers of the hard-winter-wheat-belt, Salina was the site for the movie *Picnic* starring Kim Novak. Ila Mae pointed out that local grain elevators figured in a significant scene in the movie.

Compared to farm life in northwestern Kansas, this small college town seemed large and exciting. Home of Kansas Wesleyan (Methodist) University and St. John's (Episcopalian) Military School, Salina was also the location of a Strategic Air Command (SAC) U.S. Air Force base. There were occasional social events between the young women at Marymount College and the men stationed at the Air Force Base.

Early in the semester, at one of the first dances, Ila Mae met Bernard L. Scholl, a young enlisted man stationed there, who fell head-over-heels in love with the shy farm girl with the pretty smile. On their weekend dates, Bernard took her to a pizzeria, a new concept of restaurants in college towns, with booths and red-checkered vinyl tablecloths.

When she returned home for the Thanksgiving holiday, our sister never shared the news about dating. Instead Ila Mae told us of the "pizza pie" that she found delicious. Our family had never heard of this new food, and we were astounded to hear how much it cost, thinking that much was paid for "a piece of pie." As the oldest daughter, she was the one to first educate this family to big town ways.

During that same holiday visit, in the fall of 1957, she brought home a foreign exchange student, a classmate from Formosa (now Taiwan). Knowing that it would be okay with our kind-hearted mother, who was keen on hospitality, Ila Mae noted, "Otherwise she would have spent the week alone in the dormitory." When this freshman student was later diagnosed with infectious tuberculosis, and confined to a TB Sanatorium at Norton for a six-month antibiotic treatment, Ila Mae urged her siblings to write letters to this lonely person, "so far away from family."

At home Ila Mae was delighted to see her godson again, our toddler brother, Rodney, and cherubic, three-year-old sister, Cheryl, with her wavy hair a mass of Shirley Temple-like finger curls. Our oldest niece, Joyce, was born just months before, and was still a babe in arms. Because they were so young when she left home, Sister Veronica continued to hold dear to her heart these three, and their children, throughout the years.

The next month, at the end of her first semester, our big sister turned eighteen. Her early days at Marymount were the first contact she had with a world that had, so far, remained entirely unknown to her. For the first time she attended a ballet, the magical *Swan Lake*, and was exposed to the cultural arts of opera, stage plays, musicals and concerts — including the Fred Waring orchestra the same year his group played at the White House for Queen Elizabeth and Khrushchev.

"I chose Marymount College, in Salina, simply because it was a Catholic college," said Ila Mae, who matriculated on September 11, 1957.

Fifty years earlier, in 1907, Mother Marie Joseph Butler, of the Congregation of the Sacred Heart of Mary, opened Marymount School in Tarrytown, New York, which by 1919 developed into a college for Catholic women. Other Marymount schools were later established to spread the work of the original school, including those in Palos Verdes Estates, California, New York City, Paris, and Rome.

Built of Pennsylvania crystal brick, with Bedford stone trim, the first four-year college for women in Kansas was opened in 1922, and operated by the Sisters of St. Joseph. Mother Antoinette Cuff, who served as CSJ Superior from 1899-1922 came up with the concept for a Midwest college. "It was her deep conviction of the importance of educating Sisters, and other women for service in teaching and nursing — needs which were crying to be met in the early decades of the twentieth century in Kansas. The steady growth of the Sisterhood convinced authorities, in Concordia, of the need for a school which would, in the summertime, minister to the educational needs of the Sisters," according to the 1983 Centenary CSJ newspaper.

In *Footprints in the Frontier*, Sister M. Evangeline Thomas quotes Mother Antoinette: "The College stands as a beacon light on the plains and is a symbol of education in the heart of America. The location is one of the most beautiful I have ever seen."[2] The Sisters were pleased with the sweeping view of the winding Smokey Hill River and the valleys that surround it.

Later in the century, from 1953 to 1965, Mother Mary Helena Robben served two six-year terms as Mother Superior of the Congregation. During her administration she completed or initiated many extensive building projects at Marymount College, including dormitories and a new fine arts building.[3]

Ila Mae's first year at Marymount was full and happy. She had fond memories of the college and spoke of its closing with deep regret. After serving for sixty-seven years, her alma mater was sold, in 1989, for one dollar to the Diocese of Salina, due to a two million-dollar debt. Later it was sold to a private family and no longer served as a college.

This was not the only small Catholic college in trouble nationwide. Father Duane's alma mater was in danger of closing, too, and at its darkest hour, in 1988, just the year before. In June 2000, an article in *USA TODAY* addressed its salvation: "Benedictine College would wrestle for the rest of the century with rising debt, declining enrollment and a diminishing Catholic identity. As they let go of those Priests and nuns…who ran the institution and taught the classes for no pay…they had to do something to keep this place going." Successful retired alumni returned to the college to teach and accepted entry-level wages. This success story of resurrection was due to their devotion to their alma mater in the spirituality of giving back. "The only reason I was successful in business is because of what I learned here, the value system, the resilience," said Joe Brickner, an alumnus of St. Benedict's. Carol Shomin, another graduate, said that one of the lessons of the good Sisters stuck in her head. 'Somebody helps you, you turn around and help someone else.'"[4]

Sister Etta Louise Knaup was the Dean at Marymount the year Ila Mae matriculated. As a significant woman to many of the CSJs, Sister Etta Louise was described as having a "spirit of hiddenness and embodied the spirit of the Congregation over the past century. While a leader, she served with zeal and acceptance of others, without setting herself up for distinction."[5] No doubt, she also served as a role model to the students.

Ila Mae noted in her Life Review, "The second stage of my spiritual journey was the first year at Marymount as a lay student. This was a chance to let grace work, as I attended daily Mass, and went to the chapel gallery for private night prayers. It was here I learned who Jesus was. I was confused until then about the connection between the person in the crib, and the person on the cross. I took on a devotion to the Suffering Christ and the Stations of the Cross, and began to inquire who the Spirit was. I began to learn that religion has to have some social action also."

This message stayed with her throughout life, having many opportunities to reflect on this theme. "The Cross is God's gift of redeeming love. This serves as motive and model for our willingness to apostolic service. The Resurrection and Gift of the Spirit, foundation of the Catholic Faith, not only are proofs of Christ's divinity, but promise of victory over sin and death," Gary/Father Duane explains.

"After the Student's Fall Retreat, during my freshman year, six of us women went to see the [Priest who served as] retreat master, and told him we wanted to enter religious life. I didn't think I could wait any longer." He hit a chord with these young women in speaking to their needs. The Jesuit probably emphasized the concept of being special. A vocation to the religious life is something precious, and linked with family pride.

The CSJ of Concordia promotional brochure, from the 1980s, was basically the same as the one from the 1950s. During this period of adjustment, the candidate lives with a small group of Sisters as part of a family, sharing prayer, meals, and household responsibilities. However, one noticeable difference now is the greater number of months required in the Postulancy. No doubt, Ila Mae was given a promotional brochure describing the CSJ community. Now, four decades later, religious communities don't limit themselves to handing out brochures. There are well over two hundred Internet pages for women's vocations, among them a website for the CSJ of Concordia.[6]

Following the student's retreat she didn't waste time. No doubt she read and re-read the promotional brochure, and had it committed to memory. After being in college barely a month and a half, on October 21, 1957 she wrote to our parents. "Retreat just ended yesterday morning. It started Wednesday at 8 p.m. We had five conferences a day each for an hour long. They were about Beatific Vision, Vocations, Sins, Sacraments, etc. I don't know what the first three were about; I didn't have enough sense to sit closer. The others were quite interesting. I learned more than I did in [high school] Catechism class. We read most of the time we didn't have conferences. I read quite a bit of *My Way of Life* and *The Family That Overtook Christ*. It was really easy to keep still, except at meal times. Every noise and action became very funny.

"The Freshmen beat the Juniors in volleyball last night 48 to 19. I didn't play because I don't have time to practice. But I am one of the cheerleaders. All we do is lead yells." Her friend, Sister Ginger Pearl explained, "Ila Mae also worked in the dining room to serve the other students, taking time away from practice. In addition, daily Mass and private prayers were a part of her day."

"What would you say if I decided to enter the convent?" Ila Mae's letter continued nonchalantly. "This may come as a surprise, but don't think that I want to just because of the retreat. I have been considering it for the last four years [since age thirteen, and as a freshman in high school.] Perhaps you remember that as soon as I started elementary school I wanted to be a teacher. That desire has stayed. I am sure that planning to be a Nun, for the past four or more years, could not be a mistake. I want to receive the Habit on St. Joseph's feast day, so that's another year and one-half off, but I want to enter next fall. Okay?"

The day Mother received the letter in the rural mailbox. She sat down at the kitchen table and openly wept tears of happiness and joy, as she repeated the surprising news to our family.

"Pat McLennon[7] and Faye Huelsmann were freshman at Marymount, like Ila, who also went to see the retreat master," said Sister Ginger Pearl. "A fourth woman, Elaine Meyer, also entered the religious life, but later returned to lay life, in the 1960s, as a teacher in parish schools."

"We made an appointment with Mother Helena [Robben] to visit her at the Motherhouse in Concordia," said Ila Mae. The position of Mother Superior was an elected one. To be eligible to accept leadership positions, Sisters had to be at least thirty-five years old, and have professed vows at least ten years earlier. During her tenure, this woman shouldered more accountability than many corporate directors, in her wide range of administrative duties, while serving primarily as spiritual leader.

During the pre-admission interview, the imposing Mother Superior, covered in heavy black serge robes like all the other Sisters, posed questions to Ila Mae and the other students. Sister Ginger noted, "The kind of questions asked in a typical interview were: Are you freely choosing this life style? Is anyone forcing you to seek entrance into religious life? (As in marriage, it would not be a valid union if force were being used.) Do you desire to enter the religious life out of some fear? What attracts you to the Sisters of St. Joseph of Concordia? Are you in good health? Do you have any serious impediments? Or anything such as a disease, debts, or responsibilities that would need to be taken care of?"

Our parents were not aware of Ila Mae's plans to enter the convent when they asked her to be the newborn, Rodney's godmother. Also unknown to our parents was that, as her godson, he became the legal and sole beneficiary of her patrimony estate, instead of the convent, until he turned twenty-one years old. This was an obligation addressed by the Motherhouse.

Recognizing a true vocation is not scientific. No doubt her motives were pure, but perhaps some were subconscious. Although, Sister Ginger is quick to explain the intricacies of distinguishing a true calling from a decision made in fear: "I know the Church would not have accepted Ila Mae, as a Religious Woman, if she had come out of fear that she would not make a good mother because of her hearing loss. During her additional calls from God, possibly the one during the retreat at Marymount, Ila Mae would have had to process this fear, into a freedom of giving the gift of life back to God, which includes conceiving a child within her personal womb, bearing a child and caring for that child."

Ila Mae held fast to her convictions. She did not enter to please her parents, or teachers or a parish Priest. She entered the convent for higher reasons: to serve and give herself wholeheartedly to God. Like an anxious bride for her bridegroom, Ila Mae was certain she wanted to be faithful in her love relationship with Christ.

At this same time it would have been made clear to Ila Mae that her high regard, of aunts Sister Laura Annette and Sister Rose Irma, and cousins Sister Marie Rene and Sister St. Theresa, was not a reason to enter the convent. While admiration of her relatives may have helped guide her, it was not the source of her longing. This calling, this beckoning was not an audible one. Instead it was a strong inclination to devote one's life to God's service.

Mother Superior was looking for women with a spirit of generosity, common sense, reasonable health, stability and a desire to give themselves utterly and unconditionally to God. She also assessed the physical, intellectual, and moral aptitude the young women had for religious life. The ability to get along with others was also essential, and did not pose a problem for Ila Mae; living among a large family guides one into a state of cooperation.

Following the retreat Ila Mae contacted her hometown Priest, Monsignor Bernard Dickman, in Stockton. She requested a written recommendation from him, as her pastor and confessor. He confirmed in a letter that she was his parishioner, that she was a good candidate, and that she was not running away from anything to join the Order. And in addition, he stated that for some time he believed that she had a true vocation.

Ila Mae was also required to provide a recent medical certificate, or submit to a physical examination. As a result, Mother Superior Helena said her hearing loss would not be a handicap, even though it was important that the entrant not be incumbered by any impediment.

Even after the interview, Ila Mae was fun loving. "In the meantime, I was dating Bernard from the Air Base just because I liked him. One of my friends tried to tell me, 'If you're going to be a Nun, you should leave him alone,' but I insisted he wasn't serious about me and that I was okay; I wouldn't give myself a chance to love him. Every time before we went out together I'd stop by the chapel gallery, and pray my heart out that I wouldn't change my mind."[8]

She could have married, but God's urging was stronger. It was not that she wasn't attractive or wasn't wanted; Bernard's proposal proved that. It wasn't a question of not wanting children either, as most Sisters love children. Many have, in later years, confirmed that the maternal tug, the internal clock, ticks for Nuns, too, in their private hours — Sister Veronica included.

According to the web page of the CSJ of Tipton, Indiana, "Just as some women choose single life or marriage, a religious vocation is a life choice. As Sisters of St. Joseph, women have a chance to make a difference in the world, as well as to experience a lifetime of joy, and spiritual fulfillment."

Just after Christmas, on her eighteenth birthday, Ila Mae received a greeting card from her beau. The following month she said, "We had a dance here last night, and [the Marymount girls] were invited to the Air Base next Friday night. I never danced so much in my life as I do here." The enlisted man was enamored with the shy farm girl. He was smitten, continued to court her, and sent a Valentine's card a month later.

"Sure enough, Bernard did ask me to marry him, and I had to tell him my secret plans of being a 'Bride of Christ.' He said he knew something was up, but he wanted to wait, in case I changed my mind." For the next year he kept open his proposal of marriage.

"[After I entered the convent] a bus load of us Postulants, from the Motherhouse in Concordia, went back to Marymount in Salina for a 'special day' to see the performance of *The Sound of Music*. Bernard must have found out we were coming because he was there to meet the bus. He said, 'I took one look and I knew you hadn't changed your mind.'"

Following the Second Vatican Council there were retreats, workshops and discussions, for both Priests and Sisters, on an entirely new theology of sexuality. Friendship was valued. Human love is essential. As an example, new interpretations of the *Song of Songs* stress the importance of one's capacity to love. In 1980 Sister Veronica wrote, "I know the power that comes from loving, and being loved by a particular person. I know what it feels like to be set free, for my love to be freed into motion because of this interpersonal love. So it truly is possible for celibates to love one another."

At the top of each of her letters was JMJ, an abbreviated version of Jesus, Mary and Joseph, pray for us. At the beginning of February 1958 she wrote. "Dear Dad and Mother, Have you received my report cards yet? I know I got four Bs. One teacher said I would have gotten an A in three of these college courses if I had tried a little harder at the first of the semester. The funny thing is that I tried my head off at first, and didn't do anything at the end."

The total of three students in her senior high graduating class were a sharp contrast to the ninety-five in her first year of college. Ila Mae's first semester grades were good, considering that previously she had individual attention in the small high school. She received Bs in English, Fundamental Theology, Home Economics, Logic, Art Appreciation and Inorganic Chemistry, while receiving an A in both major sports, and choir, for enthusiasm no doubt, since she claimed to be tone deaf.

The following semesters her grades were even better, earning mostly As, with the exception of Cs in Dogma, Organic Chemistry and General Bacteriology Lab. The last two classes were a stretch, since chemistry was not offered in high school. Throughout her education, she was an excellent student, and determined to succeed at whatever she undertook.

During her first semester, half of the instructors were laywomen — Moloe, Bush, Bohem, and Young. The other half were Religious — Sisters Mary Giles St. John, Sister Redempta Eilert, and Sister Gabriella Halbleib. Another teacher, Sister Eloise Johannes taught sociology. The elderly woman died three years after Sister Veronica, and remembered her former student as "being very quiet." Sister Ginger described Sister Eloise Johannes as a "rock" to those who knew her. "In her final months she could not see, hear, or walk, but she declared, "Other than that, I am fine." On the day of her own death, Sister Veronica went to visit the elderly Sisters at St. Mary's Convent in Concordia, as she did several times each week. During an earlier visit that week she gently and lovingly told the ninety-two-year-old Sister Eloise, "Years ago you were in charge of me. Things are reversed, and one of the missions that I oversee is St. Mary's. Now I am in charge of you," she grinned.

Her college friends like Mary Ann Landoll, who had a Priest-Uncle, were other Catholic girls like herself with relatives in religious life. Another friend, Donice Meylor recalled, "Ila Mae was a shy Marymount student who later blossomed into a confident, capable woman using her talents for the Lord." Her friend, Jodi [last name unknown] from Lincoln, Nebraska signed her college photograph, "Dear Ila, Happy essay writing now and forever, especially when you're water skiing."

The summer before she entered the convent, Ila Mae spent many evenings water skiing into dusk, and Sunday afternoons, behind our brother, Kenneth's boat, at Webster Reservoir one-half mile from our farmhouse. Mother often packed a picnic supper of fried chicken, potato salad, grape Kool-Aid and watermelon, which the family enjoyed at the water's edge.

During the day, she helped Mother with the laundry, or in the kitchen. Otherwise, she quietly prayed for her vocation, while the younger children played outside for hours with the hoola hoop, the latest fad across America.

In shared recollections with her siblings in 1980, she wrote of her ultimate choice to enter the convent in the fall of 1958, and her correspondence with the Motherhouse. Still she was quiet about the decision. "I felt rather odd about doing this, and still didn't particularly want people to know my plans. I don't remember talking with the family about it."

Maybe she didn't want us to view this step as a great offer she was about to make. "How could having a deeper relationship with God be a sacrifice?" she must have thought. Surely she prayed her secret path would lead to God's garden. Whether "Mae" knew it or not, we siblings viewed our sister as different. She had always behaved as a holy person. After the initial surprise of hearing about her decision, it seemed a natural thing for her to do.

Perhaps had she told our family, we would have had the opportunity to understand her decision, and she would have enjoyed even more respect and admiration. But for some reason she did not want it known. Did she think someone might talk her out of it, just as Dad had talked her out of majoring in math?

Finally she received the long awaited acceptance letter from the Motherhouse, and prepared for entrance into the convent. "I received a CCD [Catechetic of Christian Doctrine] Diploma from Marymount College, so I asked Monsignor Dickman if I could teach the Catechism summer school in Stockton, and he hired me. Being the first lay teacher there, sure enough, those kids had me figured out. 'Are you going to be a Sister?' they asked."

Chapter Thirteen

"And everyone who has given up home or brothers or sisters or father or mother or children or lands for the sake of my name will receive a hundred times more, and will inherit eternal life."
— Matthew 19:29

On September 8, 1958, the feast of the birth of the Virgin Mary, Ila Mae Jean Roy became a Postulant with the Congregation of Sisters of St. Joseph for a six-month period. Surely the eighteen-year-old did not sleep well the night before, from either excitement or trepidation.

She had heard or read about the need to detach from one's family to enter fully into religious formation. "On that morning, I remember telling my brother Roger, and sisters Joan and Linda 'Goodbye,' as they left for school, and as if I'd never see them again. It seemed so cold and cruel."

The entrants were requested to arrive before 4 p.m., so they departed after Ila Mae and Mother finished the noon meal dishes. "Dad, Mother, Gary and I rode off in the car; Cheryl and Rodney, ages three and one, also went along."

The 130-mile drive from the stone farmhouse to her new residence in Concordia was not a long drive, a little over two hours. About mid-way, and to break up the drive and delay the inevitable, Dad tried to indulge his dearly loved daughter with a childhood treat — a lifelong weakness. "On the way, we stopped at the Dairy Queen in Beloit for ice cream, but I was so nauseated that I didn't want any," she recalled.

"Then Dad turned to me and said, 'When you ring the doorbell, and they ask what do you want, what are you going to say?' That summed it all up. What in the world did I want? None of it seemed really what I wanted, but was part of a plan developing for me, and I wanted to give a generous 'Yes' to the Loving Father." Dad was a wise man with his simple questions.

A bell rang in the Nazareth Motherhouse Convent. Moving slowly, it seemed the final act of parting was all too quick. There was neither time for last minute clutching, nor sentimentality, which did not seem proper. This was before the Second Vatican Council.

Families of the Postulants reluctantly exited, through the solid wood doors of the grand front entrance, and down the long flight of steps. Walking to the car parked on the spacious convent grounds, Mother did not take note of the glorious blue-sky day, or the pleasant touch of fall in the air, with oak and maple leaves just beginning to turn color. Instead, she dug into her pocketbook for a clean white handkerchief.

At home, raising her brood, she was too busy to be emotional, but tears flowed easily in church — and at all things sacred. No doubt, Dad disguised his own lump in the throat by fiddling with his fedora, and turning away to light an unfiltered Camel on this holy ground.

"Gary was driven on to Atchison later that same day for his first year at St. Benedict's [now called Benedictine College], a place where he gave grace the chance to work at daily Mass," Sister Veronica later recalled.

"It was a long, sad journey coming home after leaving those two behind," Mother said. "We made sure the little ones never forgot Ila Mae. The first Sunday of each month, when we were allowed to visit, we'd make the trip together."

Our cousin Diane Brin, the daughter of Mother's sister, Mary, entered the convent six months later. She, with her parents, left Damar, and drove east for more then two hours on desolate country roads, amidst endless plowed fields of wheat stubble and through, or nearby, mundane small towns along Highway 24, following the road Dad had traveled earlier: Stockton, Woodston, Alton, Bloomington, Osborne, Downs, Cawker City, Glen Elder, Beloit, Glasco and Asherville before heading north to Highway 81.

Upon the approach to Concordia, and suddenly seeing the majestic red brick mansion of the Motherhouse sitting on higher ground, Diane started to cry. "My beloved Papa [Oliver Brin] asked if I wanted to go back home. 'No, I'll be all right,' I said. It seemed so final, even after being near the surroundings for the previous four years. My parents never pressured me one way or the other. It was always my idea to enter the convent."

Four years earlier, from 1954 to 1959, Diane Brin was one of the first to attend the Aspirant/Apostolic boarding high school run by the Sisters of St. Joseph. Here she lived what she called the "half-life" of a Nun. "During my freshman year in school I was lonely for my boyfriend, girlfriends, and family back home. Then when I returned home, to Damar, for the summer, I was lonely for my friends at the Aspirant school. By the time I was a senior in high school, I couldn't not go back. It was a part of me. The way of life was ingrained so strongly at that time, and it's something I truly wanted to do. I felt a compelling need to go without any further thought. I have no regrets. Even before all the changes of the Second Vatican Council, it was not all that bad. My band, of the nine 'Junior Angelicas,' knew each other all through high school. We were a youthful and rowdy bunch, an intimate and tight group."

According to the CSJ centenary newspaper, Mother Mary Helena Robben established the high school for Aspirants, at the Motherhouse, to assure that many young women would receive a good education, as well as an orientation to possible vocations. The school flourished for over a decade.

Some families could not otherwise afford to educate their daughters in an exclusive boarding school setting, and chose to send them here. It became increasingly expensive, and eventually the Apostolic school became more strict in weeding out those young women who were there for the fun of being away from home, or merely there to receive a secular education, since the ultimate goal was to assess religious vocations.

"The Church gained great wisdom over the ages," noted Sister Ginger Pearl. "There may have been a time in France, a century ago, when an education could not be otherwise attained, the family was too poor to feed another mouth, or was looking to place a young daughter with someone who would give her a roof over her head. Today our vows would not be valid if that were the case."

Later the CSJ Aspirant school closed, and that avenue for recruitment was no longer in favor. Instead, a woman wishing to make religious vows today must be an adult having seen some of the world, perhaps already with a career, and knowing about commitment.

Nevertheless, Sister Diane recalled her youthful calling as, "a knowing. There were subtle clues. It was like following a vision. It was somewhat of a mystery. More like an internal call. When I was in eighth grade, I felt something moving me."

A group of women accepted into the convent on the same day is called a "band." Since applicants were numerous the year Ila Mae entered, the Postulants were spaced into two groups with different entrance dates. Ila Mae was among the sixteen who entered in March, and Diane Brin was one of nine who entered six months later in August.[1] Ila Mae's band elected to call themselves the "Sixteen Prophets," being the same number as the prophets of the Old Testament since they, too, were called by God.[2]

In the Bible a prophet was chosen and received a call, subject entirely to divine will, to be God's spokesperson. Modern prophets continue to instruct and witness, mediating God's wisdom to His people. For this, they need to form their own minds, by academic and spiritual preparation. These sixteen women-prophets, and other Sisters, chose to follow a high road of spiritual excellence. Ila Mae completed the six-month Postulant stage of her religious formation, and moved on to the yearlong Novice phase the month after our cousin's entrance date.

Having completed only one year of college, the eighteen-year-old Ila Mae, was one of the youngest Postulants in her band, unlike Madonna Ready/Sister Mary Antoinette who was nearly fifty years old upon entrance. Even though Bernadine Divel/Sister Joseph Ellen was nearly thirty years old when she entered, she had not graduated from high school. "But Ila/Veronica always made me feel equal to those in our band who had gone to college. Later on when I got my high school equivalency certificate, and then received my Nurse's Aide Certification, she congratulated me and expressed her great joy in my accomplishment. That made me so happy. When we all lived together, during our first six months as Postulants, Ila/Veronica set my hair every Saturday and did a beautiful job. That was such a gift because I wasn't good at it, and she made me look nice for the week ahead. She continued to show great virtue in every aspect of her life, and was a wonderful example, to me, of what a Sister of St. Joseph should be."

Virginia Pearl, or Sister Ginger, as she is now fondly called, is a fellow Kansan from an Irish and Native American/Potawatomi Catholic family. From that day on she and Sister Veronica began a lifelong friendship, drawn together not only by their deep faith of God, but also by sharing a rural heritage and love for the land.

Sister Ginger vividly recalls her own vocation. "I was called by God as a sophomore in high school. I tried to shake it, as I was very active, and not the subdued type. I prayed that God would call my sister, Molly (Maureen) instead of me. God continued to pursue me — taking the initiative — always. God revealed the plan a second time, as a student at Marymount. Then a third time, when I was teaching in Topeka, after graduating from college. So I entered, not because it was my idea, but because it was God's plan. I could not imagine that I would have the inner stability and holiness I thought it would take. I truly felt that I would not be accepted. I thought I would have done my part, and then I could be 'scott-free' to go about my plans."

As Sister Ginger clearly demonstrates, no one chooses this path of one's own accord. The poet, author and Benedictine oblate, Kathleen Norris confirms in *Cloister Walk*, "You are chosen, you resist, you resort to rage and bitterness, and finally you succumb to the God who has given you your identity in the first place."

The author Gregg Levoy in *Callings: Finding and Following an Authentic Life* writes, "The true calls tend to keep coming back over years, and sometimes decades. And they come back through a lot of different channels: your body, your dreams, intuitions and synchronicities. Callings keep surfacing until we deal with them. These callings tend to start out kind of quiet and polite, and they tend to increase in voltage, and volume, the more we ignore them. If one ignores their true call, they court disaster."

Similarly, the Tucson, Arizona untrained artist Daniel Martin Diaz, who creates passionate portraits of the martyrs and others who suffered for the faith, emphasizes, "It's beyond my control," he said of his artistic gift and calling. "It chose me; I didn't choose it."

Sister Ginger continued, "As I walked up those long front steps of the Motherhouse, my heart was heavy with mystery. I didn't think I'd see my family for a long time. I remember every detail of that day. Ila Mae was stately and very thin. She seemed to be able to obey the rules easily. It was not that easy for most of us."

Perhaps where the Motherhouse is located, the name Concordia, a derivative of the word concordant, meaning in agreement, harmonious and consistent, was symbolic for Ila Mae's new way of life — the hidden life, which the Sisters embody.

After the new Postulants arrived, and their parents departed, the heavy, yellow pine doors closed for the day on what would be their new home. Mother Superior Helena Robben spoke to the eager entrants. She delivered a loving and welcoming message about what lay ahead.

The period as a Postulant would take six months. The next twelve-month period, as a Novice, offered the individual the opportunity to focus on prayer, solitude, study, reflection, and limited involvement in ministry, without much exposure to the outside world. It later became a two-year period. After this time, the candidate pronounces temporary vows for a period not less than three years. It is only after this three-to-nine year period of temporary vows that the candidates can make the lifetime commitment of final vows.

A promotional brochure, from the 1980s, expounded the same basic information that guided the Sisters the previous twenty years: "The formation of a Sister of St. Joseph is a lifelong process of 'growing up in every way into Christ who is the head.' (Eph. 4:15)." The following key points are listed in the brochure.

"Apostolic: The zeal of the Sister of St. Joseph finds its origin in her call and her mission. Her call is heard in the depth of her heart and leads her to a profound desire to incarnate the love of God in our world in service to the neighbor.

"Celibate Life Style: The vows of chastity, poverty and obedience, lived in community, allow for a single-hearted commitment to God. Day by day, the Sister of St. Joseph responds to the transforming love of God as she enters into the ordinariness of life doing ordinary things in an extraordinary way.

"Ministry: The ministry of the Sister of St. Joseph is her presence to the neighbor in whatever ways her particular gifts and talents best enable her to make visible the love of God in her midst.

"Prayer: The prayer of the Sister of St. Joseph, like her ministry, is apostolic. It is, above all, a constant loving and peaceful attention to the presence of God. From this source, compassion is born in her and moves her to apostolic action."

The kindly Postulant mistress, Sister Therese Marie Stafford, explained in practical terms what their new life and new surroundings would demand of them. It would be broken into structured and distinct routines: domestic chores, classroom, and prayer throughout the seventeen-hour days beginning at five o'clock.[3]

In the book, *Wild Swans: Three Daughters of China*, author Jung Chang writes of her mother's experience as a new Communist. "As the platform slipped out of sight, my father tried to comfort her. He told her that she must be strong, and that, as a young student joining the revolution, she needed to go through the five mountain passes, which meant adopting a completely new attitude to family, profession, love, lifestyle, and manual labor, through embracing hardship and trauma."

While not suggesting that formation in the convent was anything like formation into the Chinese Communist party, what is evident is that both directions took discipline, on a young person's part, to one's dedicated cause.

That evening the Postulants were shown to their sleeping quarters, on the top floor of the five-story building. The pristine dormitory, with large, tall windows, held rows of alcoves, each containing a twin size bed, a chair and simple dresser. In this antiseptic all-white room, each cubicle section was surrounded by heavily starched canvas-type cotton curtains tied back around posts when quarters where not in use. The curtains were closed when sleeping or dressing. The beds were not sat upon. In the morning a crucifix lay on the pillow of the neatly made bed, and at night, it was placed on the dresser.

Sister Ginger said, "Everyone was so excited to be there that the small size of each cubicle did not matter. Through the heavy canvas we could hear each other snore throughout the night. Someone would start giggling, it was contagious, and before long, the whole floor was giggling.

"Each Postulant had two black skirts (one for Sunday, and one for everyday), three blouses, a short cape, cap and stockings." White cuffs were pinned at the wrists of the blouse, and a small white linen detachable collar was affixed in place. The thick-heeled and laced black shoes were the sensible type, like those Grandmother Roy was also wearing in the 1950s. (In the mid 1990s, these "granny" shoes became the height of teen-age fashion.)

Sister Christine Doman (CSJ president 1995-1999) added, "Before entrance day, a dressmaker's pattern was sent to each Postulant. Each brought the home-sewn separates with her, otherwise there were some left by previous Postulants, and available for use."

There would be nothing to remind the Postulants of their sexuality — no feminine frills, pastels, and lace; no delicately scented hand lotion or soap. Everything was plain. If gifts were received outside this parameter, they were locked away as gifts for benefactors. The next month, when our family visited, Mother brought along her Agfa box camera and captured her beloved daughter, on black and white film, posed in the grotto gardens smiling proudly, in her new garb.

It wasn't long before Ila Mae learned to talk like a Sister. The new Postulant spoke in moderated tones, which wasn't really new, since she was never boisterous to begin with. She began to walk like one, too, although secretly she had practiced for years, and even before this she carried herself like a lady — an image she learned from Mother.

Both as a Postulant and a Novice, rising before dawn was standard, just as was pausing to pray seven times a day. During formation Ila Mae learned about the canonical hours divided into eight parts. The Daily Office is recited corresponding to the division of the day, as observed among the early Christian monastic orders.

Everyone arose at 5 a.m. to the ring of a hand-bell. Shortly after, the Postulants entered the chapel for *Matins* — very early morning prayers and meditations pertaining to their spiritual growth. There were three Psalms, and three readings; lessons from Scripture, from the lives of the saints, or from papal writings. These were alternated three times.

Since *Matins* and *Lauds* were often said together, Ila Mae opened her Daily Office prayer book to follow the second of the canonical services chanted or sung in the choir at dawn, in praise of God, the Light of the World. "He who sings, prays twice over," the words of St. Augustine remind us.

Prime, at 6 a.m., and known as one of the four Little Hours, is a prayer of consecration to God, and a petition for spiritual and material assistance. Following Mass, breakfast was also a time of silence for the Postulants, as they listened to more spiritual readings.

Alternating chores followed: cleaning the kitchen, sweeping the refectory, dusting the chapel, polishing the dormitory and scouring bathrooms. Scrubbing floors, on hands and knees, did not seem harsh to Ila Mae, as it might have to some of the other Postulants; she learned to clean at home this way, as taught by Mother.

At 9 a.m., the second of the canonical hours, came *Terce*, remembering the hour when the Holy Spirit descended on the Apostles at the Pentecost. Study hall followed, where the Postulants had classes in religious life, scripture, liturgy, or practiced choir.

Sext, the fourth of the seven canonical hours, falling just before or at noon, was the time to ponder passages of Scripture. *None* was also recited before noon. In times past, it was said at three o'clock, the ninth hour, and marked the moment when Christ died, a time for silent meditation.

Spiritual table readings took place during noontime dinner. Only when the superior intoned the *Benedicamus Domino*, a Latin phrase meaning, "Let us bless the Lord,'" talking at the meal would be permitted.

All meals were taken in the refectory, where the Postulants were expected to take at least a tablespoon serving of everything, just as Ila Mae had been trained at home. Here she learned convent table etiquette. Each Postulant had her own silverware and was responsible for cleaning it, before rolling it up in a cloth napkin, for the next meal. This was a different experience from home where there were no napkins on the table, not even paper ones. The first cloth napkins in our home were those she later sewed as a gift for Mother.

Life as a Postulant was not all silence and solitude. A half-hour period of recreation, or games, followed the noon meal. However, these free times were painful, when she could think of nothing to say to the other Postulants, an issue she continued to face for the rest of her life. After supper, another period of recreation was held, in the gathering room, with her fellow band members. They were urged not to be idle even during this period of relaxation, which could be used for darning, crocheting, needlework or other types of hand sewing. There were indoor and outdoor games, too, or walks in the grotto and gardens, purposely alternating this experience with a different band member each time.

Vespers, the evening hours of praise, took place between four and six, with the setting of the sun. *Compline*, at eight o'clock, another period of intimate worship and the official night prayers at the seventh of the canonical hours, was the last service of the day.

No talking was allowed after nine p.m. The "Grand Silence" was not to be broken, except for the gravest of emergencies, until after breakfast the next morning. As the community timekeeper, the campanile bell rang three times, calling to mind the Holy Trinity. Under the vow of obedience, this was a time to examine one's conscience and failings of the day, learning to overcome faults of pride and self-will.

She continued, in the months and years ahead, to understand that silence is a virtue to be used to recharge one's spiritual batteries. Even as a child, she liked to spend part of the day alone — in the house, or outdoors. It seemed, during these times, she was able to develop a sense of purpose and ultimately, holiness.

Located on expansive acreage at 13th and Washington Street, the large building was completed, in 1903, under the direction of Mother Stanislaus Leary. It served as a boarding school for girls from ages five to eighteen. "Not a finishing school, but a place where a girl could get a practical Catholic education, while learning to live among other girls," said tour director Sister Margaret Schreck. The number of boarders varied from eighty in 1914, to a low of forty in 1922, at which time it was converted into a Novitiate for the Sisters. This coincided with the opening of Marymount College and Academy High School in Salina.

Resembling a Gothic mansion, the Motherhouse convent rises from the otherwise flat plains of this farming community. "Our Community is centered in the heartland among fields of wheat and the quiet of open spaces," invites the current CSJ web page.[4] Awesome and massive, enticing yet forbidding, the five-story ornamental red brick structure, with accents of cut limestone, can be seen from a long distance. It is a most impressive sight, as one approaches the town at a curve in the road, driving north on Highway 81. With corner minarets and a central tower reaching 125 feet high, there is no doubt to visitors, upon arrival and departure, that this is "Holy Ground."

Our immediate family was only allowed to see Ila Mae one day a month during these trips in the late 1950s. Sister Christine Doman noted, "However, if there were good reasons for other visits, these were probably granted."

Dad was a chain smoker and the absence of ashtrays, in the dark and formal parlors for visiting, created a problem for him. Weather permitting, Ila Mae took the family outside for a breath of fresh air, and a stroll, where Dad was allowed to smoke as he wished.

A favorite place to gather, on the convent grounds, was Our Lady of Lourdes Park, which is a reproduction of a typical European cloister garden. A shrine, to the Congregation's patron saint, St. Joseph the Worker, was added when the garden was enlarged in the 1950s. At the back of the park is an exceptional 40-by 55-foot Lourdes Grotto, where a statue of the Virgin Mary, made of Carrara marble, stands above the central altar. Nearby there are benches, and a gazebo, called The Summerhouse.

"The family was always good about coming on visiting Sundays," Ila Mae/Sister Veronica wrote in her Life Review. "I suppose that is why it seems my youngest sister and brother never forgot me. Cheryl and Rodney captured the hearts of the other Sisters, as well, and they continue to ask about them."

During these periodic trips to the Motherhouse, the family noted the abundance of religious statues. We were exposed to their many images, unlike our non-Catholic playmates. On the well-kept grounds is a life-size seated sculpture. When the younger siblings were two and four years old, they climbed onto St. Francis of Assisi's stone lap. On the day of Sister Veronica's funeral, several elderly Sisters remembered with glee the antics of Cheryl and Rodney, as little children, scampering around the grounds.

Flowerbeds and abundant produce gardens, well tended by the Sisters, take up part of the acreage. Rows of trees have been neatly trimmed to provide the growing number of elderly Sisters, confined to their rooms, a view of Mount Calvary Cemetery. It is wheelchair-accessible and located at the far south end of the grounds; laid out and consecrated in 1905. This is where all CSJ members, including Sister Rose Irma and Sister Veronica Mary, are buried. Their nicely spaced graves are marked by identical, close-to-the-ground gray stones, which have been simply and minimally engraved.

The interior, of the Motherhouse convent, is just as impressive as the outside. It is grand and glorious, with high towering ceilings and massive stairways, and like nothing this family had ever seen in the late 1950s. It was also quiet, serene and dignified, just like Ila Mae. Her new home fit her.

Realizing that the Sisters of St. Joseph heritage was of notable interest, and something to be publicly shared, a civic relationship was developed with the city of Concordia in recent years. The Motherhouse building was renovated, placed on the National Register of Historical Places in 1973, and is now available for tours. "Even though the massive, yellow pine doors are heavy, they slide so easily that it takes just one hand to move them," Sister Margaret Schreck demonstrated for a visitor.

Before this, for many years, the Motherhouse convent was minimally maintained. Sister Margaret explained that, during the restoration, several Sisters volunteered their efforts. They asked day-laboring men to move two pews at a time to an area where they could strip the darkly stained pews to a lighter color. The total cost of expenditures, for the entire pew maintenance project was only $230 in supplies.

In 1991 Beth Woods of Valiant Products, an interior design firm from Denver completed the restoration to the late Victorian style of 1903, the year it was built. Upholstery on furniture and window coverings, on the first and main floors, was changed. Ten years later, after a long delay, much needed renovations began in the kitchen and dining room.

For many years there have been beautiful, and potentially valuable religious paintings hanging on the walls in each of the public rooms, hallways, and dining room of the convent. These are a feast for the eyes, which elevate the mind and spirit. It was like a first-time visit to a fine art gallery for Ila Mae and her family.

While there were rumors that one of the outstanding paintings in the parlor was done by Elisabetta Sirani (circa 1663), an art dealer and appraiser from Sotheby's declared it could not have been. Nevertheless, there were several talented Sister-artists who did many of the paintings; among them were Sisters Thomas Halle, Elizabeth Belisle, Leonida Loch, and Florence Sullivan. Most prolific was Sister Norbertine Echterling who began painting many of the works, now on display, when she was eighteen.[5]

As Sister Margaret Schreck noted, "Sister Norbertine painted the faces with eyes so expressive and full of emotion. She painted for only five years before she died of an illness."

Ila Mae did not have much exposure aside from one art appreciation class in college, although later in life she became interested in, and valued the presence of these beautiful pieces for their uplifting and spiritual quality. In Aristotle's words, "Art releases unconscious tensions and purges the soul." One of her last photographs was taken in front of the painting of the Sirani-like angels in the Motherhouse parlor.

"A round fifteen-foot, rose-patterned, stained glass window, visible from the front, outside the convent, was part of the original plan of the chapel and was to be situated toward the vestibule of the church," continued Sister Margaret. "The chapel was to be much bigger. Instead, plans changed. For many years the room, where this window is located, was used for storing linens.

High shelving obstructed the stained glass window from being seen inside."

Most recently, the large room, with a twenty-foot high ceiling, is used as a television, exercise and sewing room. Recognizing that only resident and visiting Religious Women are allowed on this upper floor, and are the only ones who can see the splendor of the magnificent window with the outside light illuminating its beauty, Sister Veronica captured its glory just months before her death, and the framed photograph hangs near the current entry of the Motherhouse interior.

Also hanging at the Motherhouse is a framed verse Father Marius Nepper S.J. translated from the French, the Maxims of the CSJ founder, Father Jean-Pierre Médaille, S.J. *To Be A Sister of St. Joseph...What Does That Mean.*

> *A woman with eyes open on a world*
> *Both miserable and sinful*
> *But a world worked on by the Holy Spirit,*
> *Ears attentive to the sufferings of the world*
> *Like St. Paul to the plea of the Macedonia*
> *Spirit alert never settled down,*
> *Always in holy disquietude*
> *Search to divine what God and the dear neighbor*
> *Await from her today,*
> *Now, for the body and for the soul.*
> *Sleeves rolled up for ministry without excluding*
>   *the more humble,*
> *The less pleasing, the less noticeable;*
> *Finally, in her face reflection of the virtue proper*
>   *to our Congregation,*
> *Continued joy of spirit.*

In the 1950s, incoming and outgoing letters were first read, on a regular basis, by the Postulant Mistress, whose job it was to censor the mail. The new Sisters were her responsibility, and she taught them the ways of Religious Life.

There was a letter, either destroyed or held back, holding objectionable communication, of the death by questionable means of one of Sister Veronica's high school classmates. In the pre-Vatican II days, of little leniency, if a death was by suicide this was viewed as a mortal sin, an infringement of God's right. The formation period was a time of sheltering the Postulant from moral decay, rather then discussing the tortured causes of the darker side of life.

Sister Ginger noted, "Censorship did occur, and the ones withholding personal letters felt duty bound by rules. But like the Old Testament, when

Jesus came along and enhanced the rules to become invitations, so it was with Religious Life. Vatican II opened the windows and doors of our 'withins,' freed the hard and fast rules, and transformed them into invitations to love. A lot of the strict rules were adapted to be meaningful. After we had a General Chapter election, in 1969 under the direction of Sister Therese Marie Stafford, [by now the Mother Superior] she and her council didn't take the time to check incoming or outgoing mail because they trusted us. It is important, in the CSJ Community, to not reflect on negative attitudes that simply were not present," she added.

As in the secular business world, much satisfaction within the convent depends on its leadership. This applies to past and current histories, and may explain why biographies of some women, who have since left convents, tend to take on a tone of negativity, which she did not experience.

"After Vatican II most of the strict rules were withdrawn," agreed Sister Christine Doman. "All along Sisters could write letters once a month. Throughout the years Veronica dutifully wrote to her parents, grandparents, and siblings." However, these early letters did not speak of her inner feelings. Furthermore, more frequent correspondence through the mail was discouraged. With few exceptions, talking on the telephone was also not permitted, and regular social visits, merely to drop in and see one another, were not encouraged, either.

Within four months after Ila Mae entered the convent, Gary began seminary studies, at the age of seventeen, at St. Benedict's Abbey, located on a high and shrubby bluff, overlooking the Missouri River Valley. The Benedictine Monks arrived in Kansas in 1856 and established a priory in Atchison.

In mid January 1959, he wrote to our parents from his dorm room in the administration building. "I am glad you called the other night so I could tell you, and not have to write it out. I guess I should have told you I was going to come up here during Christmas vacation, but I wasn't sure I could get in this semester. I moved up to 'The Hill' yesterday morning, about eleven o'clock. There were about five or six guys from Freshman Hall, who helped me. There are twenty-three boys up here now. I was the only one who moved in this semester. My roommates are Larry Gahr, a farmer from Nebraska, and Mike Keenan, from Oklahoma City.

"About all of our prayers and vespers are in Latin, and I don't know any Latin at all. Father Matthias [Schmidt] said not to worry about it because there are boys who have been up here for two years, and still don't know their prayers.[7]

"Right now I am planning to study for the Diocese. That is, study to be a parish Priest. Most of the boys are planning to study for the House. That is, being a teacher or something like that. I don't think it will be very hard because we get a lot of help. Love, Gary." He later chose to become a Monk and live together "in Community," unlike parish Priests who lived alone in a rectory.

Undoubtedly, Mother made a rare telephone call to the convent to share the news with Ila Mae. In response to our brother's decision to study at the monastery, and in part to reassure our parents of her own intentions, she wrote to them that same Sunday evening as the phone call: "There is only one way to find out if you like anything, and that is to try it...After a while everything becomes really clear, and you know that there's a purpose in what you're doing. One has only to resign himself to the Will of God.

"Am I in earnest? I surely hope I didn't cause you to think otherwise. There is nothing so important to me as to do what God wants of me. I believe that is to return His love for me in the religious life. I know I have been here just a short time, but this seems the only life I have known. Everything else is foggy and uninteresting, for once one has tasted of the goodness and presence of the Lord, one lives each moment as if it were the last. Our Beloved is so good to us in beginning our early new way of life — everything is like springtime, and His Presence is so sweet. But after the spring comes summer, so we have to prepare ourselves very hard for moments when we begin to wonder when we don't see our efforts in their fruition.

"Oh, of course, my secular life means so much to me. That I have, and I am. How can I even thank God for such wonderful parents who glorify God by sacrifices and deeds for others? As one is in his early life, so will he very probably be later; and as one lives, so will he die.

"I guess I never did say, 'Yes, I want to receive the Habit.' But I do! Only I am not accepted yet. Remember how I waited for my letter of acceptance to the Postulancy until about the middle of August? Whatever they say, I firmly believe in the Lord's Will; so pray that they may be guided by the Holy Spirit. Love and Prayers." Signed, "Ila."

In her Life Review she recalled, "One of my fondest memories happened the first Christmas in the Convent, which was my second year away from home. I received no cards in the mail during Advent, but I never thought anything about it because of being one of over sixty cousins on the Morin side [and one of over fifty on the Roy side]. Surely there would be one coming from the folks and the siblings, with their own names signed. Christmas came closer and still nothing. Not even a box!

"Well, maybe it will all be one package with the after holiday/birthday doings, I thought. It never dawned on me that no one else had gotten anything either. Christmas Day, we were not allowed into the Postulancy room until after Mass. There before our eyes, everyone had piles of cards tied with bows, and boxes, too. Of the sixteen piles [for the sixteen prophets], I was the one with the most cards of all, from aunts and uncles and Grandma Roy, and a big box of course from home. What a thrill that was."

Grandmother spoke both French and English, but her writing ability was limited. Nevertheless, the cherished letters she wrote to Ila Mae in the convent were preserved in her granddaughter's small box of choice treasures.

As mentioned before, the beloved Sister Therese Marie Stafford was elected as the CSJ President, after she served as Ila Mae's Postulant mistress and responsible, in part, for religious formation. The six-month period as a Postulant, under her direction, was a time of preparation for a final break with the past. For it to be total and lasting, it had to be severe. This was to be a clean break.

As required, Ila Mae began the effort to detach from family, and all things that evoked any special feeling from her former life. Controlling her emotions would take diligence. If she shed tears, she saved them for private moments. She was encouraged to neither talk of, nor dwell on the past, nor discuss what went on behind convent walls. What seemed mysterious to non-Catholics was a sacred mystery to her family, as well.

Each Religious Order has its own Papal-approved constitution including its aims, restrictions and regulations. The Sisters of St. Joseph have adopted to live by the teachings, and beautiful spiritual directives, of their founder, Father Médaille, S.J. The Jesuit wrote the *Maxims of Perfection for Souls Aspiring to Great Virtue Based on Pauline Principles*. This rule book lists exercises for emptying the self, putting on Christ Jesus, and imitating Him in His hidden and public life, in the form of prayers and conversations with the Savior. Only by discerning the search of a sublime vocation, and by meditating and following the Maxims can one hope to attain perfection. It is recommended to look inward, and practice deep humility and charity; examine the Paschal Mystery, and build a relationship with God, neighbor and self, in the spirit of "The More," and the better, day-by-day.

Sister Ginger said, "The Rules of the Order were in a very small thin book — a Formulary. We each had to memorize this to be able to hold 'The Sacred Rule' close to our hearts."

The words in *Maxims of Perfection*, by which Ila Mae would live the rest of her life, inspired her every action from the day of acceptance into the convent. Each Maxim gave her direction on the concepts of humility, purity of intention, patience, obedience and fidelity to grace, and to superior persons, gentleness and peace of heart, charity toward the neighbor, love of God, indifference, abandonment and conformity before the will of God, zeal, hope, and the good use of time all the while serving in the spirit of St. Joseph.

A modest and pious person, Ila Mae came to live the simplicity, gentleness and moderation of the Gospel with an innocent purity of heart. The seriousness of the Vows was becoming clear-cut, as she grew more comfortable with the language and customs of convent life. Formation was an excursion into self-discovery, both to test her faith and to give her Superiors a chance to test her suitability to wear the Habit.

Conforming to the model of obedience, she learned to practice the Holy Rule minute-by-minute. She examined her conscience daily and accused herself of wrongdoings. She learned about detachment. She learned to bear her crosses. She learned the spirit of her congregation. In accordance with the fifth Maxim of Patience, she willingly gave up her Self and died to things of this world.

In Father Médaille's, *Maxim of Perfection*, 5:6 was one of her favorite readings: "'I belong to my Beloved, and my Beloved belongs to me.' The *Canticles* also captured my heart." The sensuous imagery of the *Song of Songs*, considered part of biblical wisdom literature, fed her yearning for divine beauty.[8] In these readings are references to the virtue of celibacy, and she eagerly prepared for the day she would be a bride of Christ, "The Divine Lover" in a symbolic marriage.[9]

Sister Ginger also recalls daily life, during early formation, to be likened to "the delight of responding to a lover," much like in the *Song of Songs*. "Even though I was not anxious to follow the call, I chose to come to Religious Life to try it until I got dismissed. [During this time] I really felt a deep, interior, mystical love drawing me closer and closer to His Sacred Heart.

"The Postulancy was a 'vacation with Jesus' — learning who Jesus really was for us, and whom we were beginning to get a glimpse to serve. It was like being engaged [to be married] and I couldn't do enough for the One whom I had fallen in love with — the One who had first called and fallen in love with me. I can't say for sure, but I feel that Ila/Veronica felt much the same way. It was like a dance. Prayer and work were delightful. The dread feelings that others might describe seem heavy, and out of place for my Postulant year of formation."

The first stage of Ila Mae's religious journey was as a child in awe of eternity. The second stage was during a retreat at Marymount. "My third stage was the Spiritual Journey that occurred in the early formation years. My favorite readings were about the divine indwelling and the divine lover." The belief that the Holy Spirit is the heart of Christian Life is the core of the "indwelling" she wrote about — this thick darkness where God dwells. The soul moves from darkness to light following a spiritual ascent. Catholics believe the growth of the spiritual life is aided through the Sacraments, the liturgical expression of the mystical Body of Christ.

Ila Mae did not attend college during this six-month period, or for the twelve months of her Novice year either. Instead, formation of the total person was an endless round of prayer, penance, and work, as well as a time of receiving spiritual direction from the convent Chaplain. Sister Ginger went on to emphasize, "Before we could take first vows, we had to be cleared. Our Chaplain, Father Weber, spent several days, individually, with each Postulant, prior to the eight-day retreat, asking questions to assess our readiness for the upcoming journey. He interviewed us at length to make sure there was no force, or that we were not here to avoid marriage."

Canon law directs all Religious Orders to have periodic retreats. And so in the years ahead, she would regularly attend many more to regain the inner silence, and be filled with courage and calm. The purpose, of the temporary withdrawal from everyday life during the six-month Postulancy, was to draw closer to God by prayer and meditation. Now it was time to ponder the essay questions set before her. It is a time to contemplate the meaning of life. Ila Mae began the weeklong retreat marking the end of this stage and the beginning of another. She reflected on the tremendous commitment she was about to make.

✝

Chapter Fourteen

The count down began. In her meticulous handwriting, Ila Mae addressed envelopes, to relatives and guests, for the formal invitation: *The Sisters of Saint Joseph request the honor of your presence at the Ceremony of the Investiture of the Religious Habit at ten o'clock, Saturday, March 19, 1959, Sacred Heart Chapel, Nazareth Motherhouse and Novitiate, Concordia, Kansas.*

The night before the ceremony, for one last time, the teenager slept on pin-curled hair like she had done many times before. The next morning, like an eager bride wanting to look her finest, she excitedly styled her hair the way she had always worn it.

One can imagine the sixteen Postulants giggling and chattering, while getting dressed in their splendid new dresses. Ila Mae's size six, pristine white bridal gown fit her to perfection. She went with Mother to select it at Weisner's department store in Hays, seven months earlier, the month prior to her entrance. No doubt, the sales clerk was puzzled when neither a groom's name was mentioned, nor the wish to be included in the bridal registry.

The pre-Vatican II style Sacred Heart chapel, in the Nazareth Motherhouse convent, was dedicated in 1908. Romanesque in design, it featured magnificent pilasters and cornices. Having a capacity of 250, that day the chapel was filled to overflowing with many large families.

Our sister, Cheryl, only four, and two-year-old Rodney dragged their little fingers in fascination along the end of each pew, tracing the rounded detail, which looked like the bottom curve of an egg representing life. The other sharply spaded, shovel-like pattern, represented death.

On this glorious morning, the day before the vernal equinox, the spring sun shone brightly through the stained glass windows. Standing 8 by 7 feet, and created by the Munich Studio of Chicago, Illinois, each are still full of detail, rich and vibrant in color to this day. After many years, during a period of restoration, workers removed small sections of glass, for re-glazing and re-leading, without breaking a single piece. Counted among the many miracles here are the fourteen windows that have survived the harsh Kansas weather, exposed to elements and high windstorms with no outside covering.

At ten o'clock sharp, the single file of women floated down the aisle, like a vision, to the strains of *Veni Sancte Spiritus, Veni Sponsa Christi Joseph Fili David* (Come Holy Spirit, Come Spouse of Christ, the Son of Joseph and David).

Music from the, at that time, thirty-five-year-old pipe organ, built in 1924, stirred a variety of emotions. Neither a crisp handkerchief, nor the back of a hand, could stop the flow of tears shed on that beautiful, yet poignant and bittersweet occasion.

The nineteen-year-old Ila Mae made a radiant virgin bride. While she was enraptured and dry-eyed, some family members grieved she would never have the chance to become a loving wife, or caring mother. It wasn't until nearly thirty years later that she gave voice to the momentary regret herself. "Perhaps I was crying [while tending Mother and Dad's grave sites] that my own family history stops with me." She would bear no descendent by personal option.

The Postulants, in their bridal gowns and veils of various lengths, symbolized purity and chastity. For each "Bride of Christ" was an accompanying flower girl, also dressed in white, carrying a ten-pound bundle of heavy black wool down the aisle. The young flower girls (purposely not relatives), were from a local school, and had recently made their First Holy Communion.[1] At the altar rail, each handed her assigned Bride-Postulant the folded black Habit.

Years later, the symbolism of being a Bride of Christ was dispensed and eliminated. It became unacceptable to the modern Sisterhood, with its male imagery. The representation of discipleship became the model, for male and female, all called to be followers of the Lord. In 1959, however, the outcome of the Second Vatican Council was still several years away.

Following the Gospel, at the Solemn High Mass, Bishop F. W. Freking, of the Salina Diocese, repeated to each of the Postulants, "What do you ask of the Sisters of St. Joseph, my daughter?" Each responded the classical words requesting to be invested with the religious Habit and be received into the Congregation of the Sisters of St. Joseph, Concordia.

After the metaphorical marriage ceremony, and before the Mass resumed, Ila Mae, and the other women, eagerly hurried back to their dressing rooms for another symbolic gesture. A rapid and choppy haircut was another example of their willingness "to die to the world."

Our aunt, Sister Rose Irma Morin, came, from her assignment in Manhattan, Kansas, to celebrate and assist Ila Mae in quickly donning the custom-fitted long black Habit. The distinctive white bib-like guimpe attached at the neck, with a crucifix hanging beneath. The chaplette, a long black rosary, hung from the left side of her waist.

Months before, each Postulant was measured and expert Sister-seamstresses, in the convent sewing room, turned thick French serge into heavy pleated garments. Ila Mae did not see this dark fabric, which now enclosed her body, as depersonalizing. Rather, she embraced it as part of renouncing the past and her commitment to a new lifestyle.

The color symbolized dying to the world, and the style of the garment held historical significance. When the Sisterhood was formed in LePuy, France during the mid-1600s, the garb resembled that which a typical widow wore — a long black garment and headdress covering the forehead and neck, hence, "widow's garb." Personal safety was an issue, as women had few if any rights, in the seventeenth century. These unmarried women wanted to go unnoticed, as they first started the religious community, and chose to disguise themselves, so they could safely reach out to orphanages, and others in need, without harassment.

The use of a similar long garb has been traced to the sixth century. It is much like the dark robe known as an *abaya*, a garment worn by Muslim women in Middle Eastern countries, such as Saudi Arabia.[2]

While the color black might seem unbearably uncomfortable in the hot Kansas summers, Sister Margaret Schreck suggests that the heavy wool might have actually acted as a heat retardant. "Perhaps the most uncomfortable was the non-fabric piece, worn at the forehead, which caused skin eruptions for some of the Sisters."

Sister Rose Irma also helped adjust the headdress for Ila Mae. Her hair was first covered with a coif and bandeau of tight bands of white linen, topped off with a black veil to declare her consecration to Christ.

Years later our cousin, Sister Diane Brin, commented, "The peaks on the headdress had to be pinned equally high on each side, otherwise it looked peculiar. Veronica could never seem to get [the positioning just] right and it often seemed to fall flat, which was frustrating for her. She asked me one time, 'How do you get the peaks to stand up? Your veil is always hanging back just right.' For this reason alone the elimination of the Habit, and particularity the headdress [in the late 1960s] was a blessing for Veronica, because she never did get the hang of the folds."

No more than fifteen minutes later, dressed and reassembled, the women reentered the chapel, in a solemn procession, wearing the veil and Habit of the Sisters of St. Joseph.

"Another aspect of this rite of Investiture, with the religious Habit, was in receiving a new name. Ila Mae would henceforth be called Sister Veronica Mary. It speaks to the new identity assumed in the religious life, following a divine call. The name is also a patron that will be invoked and imitated," explained Father Duane/Gary.

"Afterward, when I exited the chapel, Cheryl and Rodney immediately greeted me with my new name. I will always remember their tiny voices calling me Sister Veronica Mary for the very first time, instead of 'Mae.'"

You shall be called by a new name, pronounced by the mouth of the Lord.
                                                                 — Isaiah 62:2.

She wrote to our parents a few days following the ceremony, "Like

Veronica, who wiped the holy face of Jesus on the Way of the Cross to Calvary, I wish to comfort Him who is suffering in our neighbor, in little, hidden ways... I am sending this small pamphlet about the sixth Station of the Cross, and pray you come to love my new name as I do."

In "Everyman's Way of the Cross," a pamphlet used on Good Friday, at the sixth station Christ speaks: "Can you be brave enough, my other self, to wipe my bloody face? 'Where is my face?' you ask. At home whenever eyes fill up with tears, at work when tensions rise, on playgrounds, in the slums, the courts, the hospitals, the jails—wherever suffering exists—my face is there. And there I look for you to wipe away my blood and tears."

Weeks before the ceremony Ila Mae was asked to provide three possible names, from which Mother Superior, and her council, would chose one for her. This would be her new identity, whereby she would be listed in the CSJ Name Book. Some of the other band members, like Sister John Michael (Sister Patricia McLennon, the current CSJ president at the time of this writing), took back her given name) and Sister Joseph Ellen Divel, took male biblical names. Sister Thomas Ann, (Sister Ginger Pearl) explained that Thomas is a family name, and her mother had a life-long devotion to St. Ann.

The name Rose Veronica was Ila Mae's first choice, rather than Veronica Mary. Her third choice is unknown. The name Rose held great family significance for her. It was a symbolic identity carrying the names of maternal aunts Sister Rose Irma Morin, and Rosa Morin Balthazor, and grandmother, Rosanna Hebert Morin. Later in life, while conducting research for *Ma Famille*, (a genealogical book she authored), she discovered that LaRose was an ancestral title on the Hebert side. Furthermore, when Mother attended the Sacred Heart Academy boarding school as a teenager, the rose was listed as her favorite flower, and remained so throughout her lifetime. The name is carried on the paternal side as well, by Aunt RoseLee Roy Benoit, as well as the name of Great-Grandmother, Rosalie Lanoue Roy.

However, on that day a fellow Postulant, Rosemary Farrell, was assigned the name, Sister Rose Gabriel. She later took back her baptismal name, and is now affectionately known as Sister Rosie.

There were also a large number of CSJ Sisters, still alive in the 1950s, who carried the name Rose: Sisters Rose Claire Brunette, Rose Catherine Brungardt, Rose Theresa Caspar, Rose Deatric Dreiling, Rose Grennan, Rose Irene Gibbs, Rose Ann Karis, Rose Anthony Moos, Rose Alma Newell, Rose Etta Richard, Rose Margaret Stegemen, Rose Cecelia Stegeman, Rose Vaughan and Rose Estelle Vering, among others.

In later years, following the Second Vatican Council, Sister Veronica Mary was given the option of returning to her baptismal name. She especially liked the idea of using, "Sister Mae." However, concerned that some may think she had returned to lay life, she kept the name assigned to her. There is only one other CSJ of Concordia woman with this similar name — Sister Veronica Ann Baxa.

A new name is a figurative expression for a new state of happiness. Veronica, a graceful sounding name, was a symbol of her new life, and a sign of that which lay ahead. It is unknown whether the name is formed from the Greek, *Berenike* (bearing victory), or if the distinguishing epithet, *Vera icon* (true image), as applied to Christ's image on the sacred veil, is the basis for the tradition surrounding the name.[3]

Father Duane suggests, "It could be Luke's character description of the 'true disciple' — she who manifested solidarity with the rejected Jesus, recognizing Him as the true Lord." Veronica is a name that fit her, or perhaps she conformed to fit the image of the name.

Following the sacred ceremony there was a reception for the new Novices in the convent auditorium. (At this same place, many more family and friends gathered thirty-six years later for her funeral vigil service.) Since the large room of the auditorium had to be shared with other families, who traveled to celebrate the joyous occasion, relatives gathered chairs in a circle around the newly invested Religious, to chat, while obedient small children played quietly nearby.

Sister Veronica received many letters and cards on that day, but the gifts were not hers to own. They became property of the Motherhouse as all belongings were held in common. The Superior decided what material goods one would have. Now she would experience the vow of Poverty.

Each Sister was required to give up earthly belongings to identify more closely with those who possessed little. Since Christ is the supreme model of poverty, the virtue helped her detach from worldly possessions, in preference to higher goals and enrichment far beyond material goods. Money received went into her patrimony fund. The Religious Community held this in trust.

Mother was not one to focus on riches and material wealth either: she put the love of her family first. For Sister Veronica this vow would not be difficult. She had already overcome a desire for worldly possessions — a few to help attain her supernatural end were all she was allowed.

The Community provided for all of the Novices needs: food, shelter, clothes, and transportation. They were bound to renounce personal belongings such as money, jewelry, automobiles, books, houses, stocks, and more, based on the conviction that materialistic concerns are one of the more harmful elements of secular life.

Sister Veronica didn't mind what she ate or wore, an aspect remaining throughout life. Even twenty years later she called it, being frugal. "It feels good to get rid of stuff that ties us down, and clutters life. We have been set free; nothing need stand in the way between the Father and us. Jesus is risen, and we have much choice about the newness of our life," she wrote.

The formation of those in religious life is built on the three vows of Poverty, Chastity and Obedience — turning a vocation into a state of perfection. The vow of Obedience called for giving up the right to pursue one's own path in life, and to be available for God to use, as He wants. Growing up as an obedient child, this would not be new for her.

The vow of Chastity, the celibate state, is defended, "for the sake of the Kingdom," and required abstinence from actions and feelings, maintaining a sensible modesty in all things. As a chaste and modest teenager, she was bound to God. She saw chastity as a grace, not a penance: a virtue, not a sacrifice.

Under the direction of Sister Macrina Kiernary, the mistress of Novices, Sister Veronica and the others in her band studied only theology, sacred music, and the Rules of the Order in the Community room twice a day, over the next twelve cloistered months. Prior to the outcome and changes of Vatican II, canonical Novices were cloistered, that is cut off from the outside world for one year. No doubt, Mother Superior Robben conducted regular conferences each Sunday, for the Novices on the religious life, just as her predecessor Mother Superior Antoinette Cuff did long ago in 1914.[4]

There are some religious communities that permanently remain within their convent confines, devoting their lives to silence, prayer and contemplation. An excellent photo study of cloistered life is, "The Convent Series" by Canadian photographer Clara Gutsche. She captured typical everyday life inside several convents around Montreal. These cloistered women are properly referred to as Nuns. The Sisters of St. Joseph, on the other hand, are apostolic, which means reaching to the outside world in mission work, and these women are properly called Sisters. However, this writer has used the terms Sisters and Nuns interchangeably, as do Sisters themselves.

Just as during the Postulancy, and in addition to their studies, the Novices were responsible for household duties including kitchen clean-up. Perhaps Sister Veronica recalled the stories Mother told about her days at the Academy in Manhattan when, as a fifteen-year-old, she hand washed and dried the endless amount of dishes, for Sister Rose Irma, on Sundays and Feast Days, in the school convent, to help offset her boarding school costs.

Soon Sister Veronica came to walk like a Nun, as she noiselessly floated along in her floor-sweeping garment. After seeing her this way, the youngest siblings wondered about private matters that only a child could dream up and thought up many personal questions you don't ask a holy person. "Did she have to cut her hair as short as a man's? What did she wear in the convent swimming pool? Did she have to bathe wearing undergarments? Did she sleep in "shorty" pajamas like at home?"

Sister Ginger answered other questions that came up, too. "Time was allotted each Saturday to change our clothing linens. This meant we made up a new headdress for the coming week, but if we were working outdoors, we changed our headdress twice a week. While self-discipline was stressed, there were bathing privileges as needed; and given the option of showers with unscented soap, and hair washing everyday. Adjoining our sleeping rooms were bathrooms, with built-in sinks, although in the early 1950s there was only a bowl of water available for washing, [just as it was for many rural family homes during that time, which had no running water]."

Mother and Dad were extremely proud of their daughter, and supportive of her decision to enter the convent. Sister Veronica acquired an antique framed copy of the following poem, which belonged to Sister Regina Marie Dickman, her childhood religious education teacher, after she gave the eulogy at Sister Regina's funeral, only months before her own death.

I'M THE MOTHER OF A NUN
Sure my daughter has been vested,
And my job I cannot hide;
For I've watched her from the cradle
With a mother's honest pride.

But the morn she left me early
I was feeling mighty blue;
Just a-thinking how I'd miss her,
And the things she used to do.

But now, somehow, it's different,
With each rising of the sun
And my heart is ever singing
"I'm the mother of a nun."

Since to err is only human,
There's a whole lot on the slate,
That I'll have to make account for,
When I reach the golden gate.

But then I'm not a-worrying
About the deeds that I have done,
I'll just whisper to St. Peter;
I am the mother of a nun."

"The day Ila Mae received the Habit was a beautiful one, but full of mixed emotions. After that day, she couldn't come home for five years [1959-1963]," said Mother as she lamented the three empty chairs around the kitchen table.

As a newly invested and cloistered Novice, Sister Veronica did not attend college for three semesters, and was not free to travel at will either. She was also to be cut off from family, and not to receive visitors, but because our parents each had a sister, who was a CSJ member [Sister Laura Annette and Sister Rose Irma], Mother Superior Helena Robben took these infrequent visits and strict regulations in stride.

Sister Ginger clarifies, "We could go for walks, or leave the Motherhouse for many things. For example, we went to town for shoes, or for visits to the doctor, hospitals, nursing homes, and other necessary trips. However, Canon Law guides the Novice during the Novitiate years, and events such as family weddings were not usually attended during this time."

Therefore, Sister Veronica was not permitted, that same year, to go to the June wedding of our brother, Allan, who married Geraldine Desair at St. Joseph's Church, in Damar, Kansas. Nevertheless, she was there in spirit, as she sewed the flower girl dress for four-year-old sister, Cheryl, whom the groom delighted in calling, "Suzy." Otherwise, the rest of the family was present at the wedding: Joan, as bridesmaid, while Gary served as usher.

Several days later Tony Kreller, a traveling salesman and friend of the family offered, since he was going in that direction, to drive Gary to Conception, Missouri, a Benedictine Seminary, where Gary spent most of the summer. The time he spent at the seminary was not a requirement, but he felt in need of an intense Latin course, of eight college credits, which later provided an excellent foundation.

"I never did have much difficultly with further studies," he said. "It was a good introduction into seminary and Benedictine Monk life. It was my first exposure to the devotional talks, exercises and readings in this more rigorous regime, and I participated in the liturgies almost daily. There I met Priests who hold a lasting influence on my life, by their edifying lives and words. It was also a happy summer. There was swimming, and I was a good ballplayer, not to mention this is where I perfected my pool playing.

"Daily I wore the black cassock, which was gladly loaned to me by the Stockton pastor, Monsignor Dickman. One afternoon, I was called in to the office of Father Rafael, Director of the Seminary. He wanted to know who I was, and for what reason was I there, since I wasn't a candidate to their Abbey. I just showed up without prior approval of any Bishop. I told him that I didn't know if I was going to be affiliated with the Diocese of Salina, or with St. Benedict's Abbey. I simply wanted the necessary Latin credits, and he allowed me to stay in the program," recalled Father Duane of his youthful exuberance.

"After the two-month course I hitchhiked my way back, arriving at our Roy Grandparents' home in town on a Saturday evening. Here I had to tolerate the hugs and kisses from aunts Nathalie, Vula, RoseLee, and Leona who, along with their families, had gathered to visit."

Unlike the shortages experienced in the 1990s and beyond, there were many who felt they were "chosen by God" for religious life in the 1950s. In those days, every large Catholic home was expected to give a son or a daughter to God. Our family was doubly blessed to have two in religious life. Sister Veronica and Father Duane were good about keeping in touch with each other, and corresponded frequently throughout the years.

Sister Veronica wrote in her 1959 Christmas letter to our parents, "May these final moments of preparation bring you to wait with Mary for Jesus...I will always be grateful for your love. May this little card say, Thank You." She included one of her many handmade greetings, created over the years, exhibiting frugality and creativity, coupled with devotion and love. On this card she wrote: "My Christmas Gifts to You: Holy Masses, 35; Visits 140; Rosaries 35; Holy Communions 35; Litanies 105; Ejaculations 1550."[5]

And to her younger siblings she added, "The Novices got to set up the ten-foot-high Christmas crib scene outdoors. It really looks nice with the lights on at night. It can be seen from the highway [U.S. 81] to the east of the [Motherhouse] entrance road. We have been practicing for the Mass choir, and all the usual Christmas songs. Every once in a while someone sings with a moan, 'I'm not getting anything cause I have been nothing but bad.' Of course, Santa is coming here, too. We Novices also have the special privilege of getting up forty-five minutes earlier Christmas Morn to sing to the other Sisters still in bed. We get to visit the sick Sisters in the [St. Joseph's] hospital [in Concordia] on Christmas Day. There surely aren't any Scrooges in the convent."

Her letter to the family continued, "I can well imagine the excitement there. I hope you don't have too much of a problem keeping the Christmas tree in place, but surely the two little ones [Cheryl and Rodney] know it's just to look at."

Ila Mae, as she had been known up to this time, began to bloom as a young woman in her senior year in high school, and as a freshman in college. Before entering the convent, she had a clear-cut idea of who she was. Good grades boosted her self-esteem and confidence. She was a leader. Then during religious formation something happened to change all that; she became reclusive and introspective nearly all the time. In many ways, 1959 was a painful year for her.

"The one and a half years, of my Postulancy and Novitiate, were grace-filled times," Sister Veronica wrote in her Life Review. "However, I believe my ideals were set much higher then they needed to be. These years were a time when I felt my personality changed drastically. I seemed to become 'a nobody.' I painfully accepted that, but I tried so hard to break through the pain to reach out and touch someone. I could not understand why all my leadership abilities, as a youth, seemed to dissipate.

"We were sixteen Postulants. Then when nine more joined us [Sister Diane Brin's band], for the last six months of Novitiate, I was noticeably the quietest of twenty-five people. I worked hard at trying to have something to say during recreation time, and *Benedicamus* at meals. I occasionally wrote prose, those early years, trying to express myself. I recall writing a booklet of stories, and jokes, and daily happenings to carry in my huge pocket."

Sister Diane said, "Yes, we Sisters found the big pockets to come in handy; you could even carry your lunch in them." She admitted that ten years later the full, flowing Habit concealed her own weight gain. "Even the collar could be expanded, using safety pins looped together."

Sister Veronica said that she practiced these stories and jokes that she kept stored in her pockets, "but somehow I never got the opportunity to jump in and say anything. I felt scared in the presence of the other younger members, most of whom tried so hard to help me." Not adept at repartee, she was not a storyteller, in the oral sense, as others were. When Sister Veronica tried to entertain, her collection of stories fell flat.

Sister Diane agreed. "I consider myself introverted, but Sister Veronica was at the height of introversion. You could tell she was trying to think of something to say, to give voice to her thoughts, but it was hard for her to get it out. I was as uncomfortable as she. It was almost painful to watch her."

Examining her conscience, Sister Veronica wondered about her detachment from social graces, which seemed so important and natural to others. But this, too, she offered up as a cross. What mattered most to her were small gestures of kindness and she understood the truthfulness of the biblical passage, "An anxious heart weighs a person down, but a kind word cheers one up."[6]

"She was deeply spiritual and prayerful. In meditation she was almost transparent in her spiritually, as if you could see through [to her soul]," said Sister Diane. Perhaps Sister Veronica could be compared to St. Anthony, and recognized as someone whose heart had achieved total transparency to others.

In living according to these principles, she tried not to set herself apart. Instead, she focused on the needs of those around her, a quality she learned as a child. She continued to memorize the words of *The Maxims of Perfection*, the guide by which CSJ Sisters live. Chapter ten in the little book of *Maxims* refers to indifference, abandonment and conformity before the will of God.

During this time of religious formation, it was essential to shake loose the confines and comforts of one's biological family, and so Sister Veronica's family did not know she was going through a painful transformation. She used her letters to paint a cheerful façade, while keeping her emotions tightly in check. Many years later, when [an unnamed person] said something hurtful that made her eyes well up with tears, that person snapped, "What's that about? You have no right to cry!"

Later in the mid-1980s, she confided in private of being publicly humiliated by a Priest, at which time she pasted an enormous smile on her face. After the incident someone questioned what she was smiling about. "I knew if I didn't smile, I would have cried."

"During formation Religious Women were encouraged to be very strong, brave and stoic," Sister Diane said. After all, these women were held in high esteem — if not feared. She called it, "sticking it out, or being an example of heroism, of extreme courage."

One of the requirements for canonization is heroic virtue. New Novices, in the pre-Vatican II era, were striving for sainthood early on. As the Catholic French novelist Georges Bernanos said, "The Church does not need more reformers, it needs more saints." But this was before the Second Vatican Council, with the outcome of which now declares, "a saint is a servant of God, an ordinary person doing ordinary deeds in an extraordinary manner."

Convents, in general, before the Second Vatican Council, were not known to be nurturing, or places of emotional warmth. Daily recreation was taken in pairs and a different companion was chosen each time Novices went for walks together. Sister Diane recalls, "This was supposed to promote love for all. These general friendships were not mentioned as a way of preventing close personal relationships, but looking back, that's what it seemed to be alluding to." They were instructed to keep their hands to themselves during formation, yet both Sister Ginger Pearl and Sister Ellen Divel recollect, "We did put up each others' hair, and would often touch one another."

Cautioned to be prudent, it was not hard for Sister Veronica to avoid brushing up against others, since she did not grow up with a lot of maternal hugs or kisses at home, or intimate shared conversations, for that matter, which would have revealed her feelings. Even laughter was restrained. Only a few in the family learned to cultivate a sense of humor; remarkably Father Duane has the best, and the others are developing, in their later years.

In the late 1960s and early 1970s, following the outcome of the Second Vatican Council, positive changes were made, regarding the importance of developing honest-to-goodness friendships with both males and females. Yet when these rules were relaxed, and even though surrounded by her family, Sister Veronica's display of physical affection was often stiff and awkward, try as she might. And she did try.

She never quite overcame the combination of a sterile upbringing, and the strictness of religious training. It took years to form her, and no overnight decree could dictate a sudden change. It didn't come natural for her body to express itself with a simple embrace. But in her last few years one could tell she was making progress, as she enjoyed the warm greeting of a hug, giggling like a schoolgirl, and beaming with joy.

Chapter Fifteen

"Come then, my love: my darling, come with me."
— *Song of Songs 2:13*

After one year as a cloistered Novice, Sister Veronica made first profession vows on March 19, 1960. Prior to the event, she wrote to Mother and Dad. "With deepest gratitude and love, I share my First Profession Day with you. '*Omnipotent everlasting God, I, Sister Veronica Mary, most desirous of living for Thee alone, and in complete dependence on Thy grace, pronounced to Thy divine Majesty, the temporary vows binding for three years of obedience, chastity, and poverty.*'"

The above is the formula she would use in the rite of profession. Then, she would hear the following words from the officiating Bishop as he presented to her the traditional cross the Sisters use: "Receive my dear daughter, the cross of Our Lord Jesus Christ, to which you are attached with Him by the three vows by as many nails so that as you will have lived and died, like Jesus Christ, in the love of the Cross, you may with Him also triumph in glory." She ended the letter by her promise to pray for them a novena, "Fifteen Saturdays of prayer in honor of Our Virgin Mother."

Entering the convent in 1958, she had high ideals and expectations that never wavered. Later in life, she admitted her principles were unrealistically high. Others viewed her as close to a picture of perfection as many have ever seen. In the words of St. John of the Cross, "This was an all or nothing approach." She did not take lightly to keeping her vows and professing her faith. She was highly motivated and formed in spirituality prominent of the Sister of St. Joseph for over three centuries, summed up in these words of their founder:

Stimulated by the Holy Spirit of Love and receptive to His inspirations, the Sisters of Saint Joseph move always toward profound love of God and love of the neighbor without distinction from whom she does not separate herself and for whom, in the following of Christ, she works in order to achieve unity both of neighbor with neighbor and neighbor with God directly in this apostolate and indirectly through works of charity/ In humility — the spirit of the Incarnate Word/ In sincere charity — the manner of St. Joseph whose name she bears/ In a unique climate of striving after excellence but always in a spirit of gentleness, peace and joy. Jean Pierre Médaille, SJ.

This same year, Sister Veronica returned to academic life at Marymount College. She was to find the world different, moving into the 1960s, which demanded a response. She continued her big sister role through letter writing. "If only more people realized that charity toward one's neighbor is the proof of love of God, there would be more peace in the world. Even just to say, 'May I help you?' Or to do something kind for someone who is not so kind to us. These little ways can be our way to fight on the battle front lines against Communism."

During the Cold War, there was fear of internal subversion, and as youngsters, her siblings watched the television program, *Comrades*, as Communists unsuccessfully plodded to overthrow the U.S. government.

According to the writings of Pope Pius XI, the fundamental remedy for Communism was a "sincere renewal of private and public life according to the principles of the Gospel." Basically, the Church's dispute with Communism was not over economics; it was about human rights. Following Vatican II, an agenda called Renew was emphasized to address these needs, and Sister Veronica became increasingly active in the program in the 1980s and '90s.

In the 1960s, fifteen years after the end of World War II, there were still human rights violations, and the evilness of Hitler's exterminations and the Nazi regime was still fresh in the memory of the nation, where not only those of the Jewish faith lost their lives during Hitler's regime, but many Catholics, including Priests and Nuns did as well.

In later years, there would continue to be those martyred over human rights issues, including three American Nuns and a social worker, killed by the Salvadoran military in 1980. There were hundreds, even thousands more martyred Nuns and Priests, such as El Salvador's Archbishop Oscar Romero and Polish Solidarity chaplain, Father Jerzy Popieluszko. The definition of modern martyrs suddenly became more real, and not just pious faces on holy cards.

The year before Khrushchev became leader of the communist world, John F. Kennedy was elected the first Roman Catholic President, in 1960, and naturally, our family rallied behind his election. This was the year of the "Harvest of Shame," an exposure of migrant farm workers' poverty.[1] It was also the year of the flower-child, love-ins, dopers and draft-dodgers. Yet Sister Veronica, and our family, could not have been any more out of touch with those extreme liberal political values. "Busy days are happy days; no wonder we are so happy here. For the past week we have been housecleaning, which will take another week, or so. This is a really big place, but it is very inspiring to see everyone's cheerful spirit and helpfulness."

Her letters continued to instruct this writer's teenage mind. "Yes, college is a little hard, but anything worthwhile is hard. You have to study or you might as well not be here; one would just be wasting time and money. I really don't think I ever did study until I was a freshman here. True, I got mostly A's in high school, I did my assignments, but in the strict sense of the word, I didn't study. I know when I start teaching it will be hard to get it into anyone's head that they should study. At the high school age, it just seems like there are more important things, doesn't it?"

In her Life Review she said, "As a lay student, the [college career] counselor recommended I go into Dietetics based on my aptitude testing." There were several Catholic hospitals run by the Sisters of St. Joseph that needed professional dietitians. However, she put aside that recommendation, and even as late as August 1960 Sister Veronica continued to believe she would be a teacher. She believed that dream was within reach and perhaps the only role she could imagine possible for herself. "Then the Motherhouse Council asked me to pursue this area of study, of which I didn't know anything about, except that I didn't like it. This change caused many extra courses and about 180 credit hours before I ever got out of Marymount, in May 1963."

Since Sister Veronica did not have basic high school courses in the study of organic chemistry, which would have given her a background from which to draw, she attended at least two summer school sessions. "The Sisters will soon be coming back to Summer School," she wrote. "This year a different schedule will be experimented with to allow for 'depth in learning.' We are having two, three, six, and eight-week sessions with one course in each. I will be carrying History of Europe, Educational Psychology and Dietetics. Sounds like fun."

It wasn't all studies. "We played the professed Sisters in volleyball, and won. Tuesday night we got out the softball equipment, and had a game."

She was allowed to finish her bachelor's degree before being sent on a mission, unlike the teaching-Sisters who received only two years of college, then were required to complete the remaining credits during the summer months. What was a privilege seemed a burden to her.

"All of the other Sisters in my band were allowed to leave the Juniorate [a three year period of temporary vows] to teach *Catechism*." Normally, summers were spent going to parishes throughout the state to teach, but I was kept at Marymount [to study over the summer], not even given a CCD assignment until my last year there. This alienated me further with a threat to my self-worth. Then one day I understood what was happening. I wasn't going to be a teacher. I had to sever the thin thread of my childhood dream."

Before the Second Vatican Council, a Sister was not someone who had wishes and desires of her own. She had to reckon with that disappointing blow. She had thought of nothing else for years. She offered up this loss to God, as a cross she must bear. Her entire life would be colored by the burden of introversion and the hearing loss. It is difficult to assess which one affected her more, and which took away her dream.

During early formation, her weaknesses were magnified and her self-image diminished. Perhaps her hearing disability might have hampered her ability to control a classroom of unruly teenagers. And rather than ruling with a heavy fist, she had a soft voice and gentle touch.

No doubt Mother Superior Helena, and the Motherhouse Council felt they were doing the right thing. Even a national study, forty years later, reveals that even though new teachers were eager and enthusiastic, sixty percent believed they entered the profession without enough experience managing a classroom, maintaining discipline, and reaching problem students.[2]

She yielded to the direction of her Superior. Steered away from her dream, she was positioned on a different career path not of her choosing. Following the Maxim of obedience and fidelity to grace, she did not question the arrangement.

St. Francis de Sales teaches that whenever one encounters pain and suffering in this life there is a positive side. God affords us the opportunity to unite our trials with that of Christ, who never abandons us in times of great pain and suffering, including the emotional kind.

Sister Veronica committed to heart the Maxims 18, 19 and 20: "Apply yourself seriously and totally to perform with perfection the present will of God. Make so perfect a sacrifice of self, and of will, that you are empty of self from this time on and thus you will no longer be able to choose deliberately anything except that God's will be completely and perfectly accomplished in you...Recognize and cherish tenderly this very loving will in all that happens in your life, whatever this may be, and in all the orders of your superiors, unless something manifestly sinful is commanded."

And so, it was not in the model of the biblical Mary — of educating, teaching, and helping others learn — that she heeded the call. Rather, she adopted the biblical Martha, and was resigned to minister in the kitchen, "in the mystery of yeast and salt."

Her desire to be a teacher did not diminish, however, and twenty years later she began to combine the Martha and Mary roles. Blending her talents, in rural ministry, she found an outlet through teaching CCD, giving lectures in the health and nutrition field, and writing articles and press releases.

Our sister, Joan, left home for Atchison, Kansas during the autumn of 1960. Here she attended Mount St. Scholastica College, founded in 1856. At this sister college to St. Benedict's, she hoped to be near our brother, and see him periodically. "When he came across town to say daily Mass, I could see him at the altar, but could not speak with him," she said. Father Duane recalled that even though they were close [within a mile, or so] in proximity, "we were worlds apart due to my religious life mentality at that time." He regrets he did not visit her once during that year.

Lonesome and homesick, she transferred to Marymount College, her sophomore year, to be near Sister Veronica. That wasn't the answer either, as Sister Veronica was extremely busy with difficult studies, and the rigors of a new vocation. It seemed to Joan that good grades came easily to both our sister and Father Duane and discouraged after the second year, she left college, moved to Denver, and began working.

Some studies were easy for Sister Veronica; others were not. Nevertheless, she had the determination to do well in any undertaking. Long before the days of computers, she turned in well-written papers, adhering to the vow of obedience, because it was also necessary to strive for perfection in her studies. Religious life did not, in itself, demand that perfection be already attained, but obligated one, under the pain of sin, to work daily to attain it. A Religious who did not want to become perfect neglected her principal duty.

Sister Veronica committed to memory Maxim 10, "Speak neither well, nor ill of yourself, without necessity, have no esteem of yourself, nor of what you do, since what you are and can do is nothing before God."

In keeping with this Rule, she revealed little of her inner feelings. Instead, she wrote of lighthearted, cheerful and inspirational events, or in generalities, such as this letter dated Easter's Tide, 1962. House of Studies. Marymount College: "Twenty-nine children had special reason to rejoice Easter Morning. They received their First Holy Communion at the [SAC military] Base Chapel. Cherubs indeed! If they didn't inspire their parents with a deeper love for their religion, I don't know who will."

That same year Americans were in space. Sister Veronica gave no indication whether she knew, or even cared. Her family, at home in rural Kansas, had a choice of only two television channels, in Hays and Great Bend, for keeping abreast of current events. Even though Dad picked up the *Wichita Eagle-Beacon*, or the *Denver Post*, from the pharmacy in town after Mass on Sundays, the family did not subscribe to a daily newspaper featuring national or international affairs. The *Rooks County Record*, our hometown weekly newspaper, focused only on local stories.

It is important to remember that during the pre-Vatican II era all communication from the Sisters was to be approached as an occasion to educate, enlighten and entertain others. The year before, in 1961, the Bay of Pigs Invasion ended in disaster, and the Green Berets were off to Vietnam. Sister Veronica was aware of the Cuban Missile Crisis, which she mentions in a letter dated November 8, 1962. "Dear Linda. Did you figure out the shorthand message of last month? 'All things work for the good of those who love God.' Does that look like it? I think that statement applies to the world now faced with the Cuban crisis.

"The day after the major scare, the Chapel was filled with students. But now that things have quieted down, too many are content to stay in bed at the redemptive hour of Holy Mass."

In a similar tone, thirty-nine years later, the week following the September 11, 2001 terrorist attacks on the World Trade Center and U.S. Pentagon, clergy reported vastly increased attendance at religious services. "At our masses on

September 15 and 16, there were faces I had never seen before. Something has happened that brought these people to their knees, and they've felt the need for God in their life. I think it's a real phenomenon here and all over the world," said Monsignor Robert Fuller.[3]

Sister Veronica's letter to this writer continued, "For the first time, I think Latin Americans are beginning to recognize Soviet influence in Cuba. I am in favor of our President's steps, as he says, 'The worst thing to do would be to do nothing.' We must trust in God that some good will eventually merge from this tense and troublesome world." Nearly forty years into the future, these same words ring true.

In the same letter she inquired, "How did the Day of Recollection go?" Targeted at high school students, this is a series of spiritual exercises similar to a retreat, except that it is completed in a single day. The St. Thérèse Vocation Society was formed to foster and encourage vocations to the Priesthood and religious life, as well as to pray for, support, and affirm those already committed to this life.

During her academics at Marymount, Sister Veronica received a letter from Mother Superior Helena Robben. "I am happy to let you know that you have been accepted as a candidate for Final Profession of Vows on March 19, 1963. I congratulate you, and I pray that you will always be a worthy and true Sister of Saint Joseph.

"Sister Etta Louise [Knaup, the President and Superior of Marymount] has been advised to allow you to come to the Motherhouse for this important event in your religious life. We wish you to come on March 17 so that you participate in a Day of Recollection on the 18th. This will be conducted by Father Carl Kruger, S. J. of St. Mary's.

In case you are prevented from coming to the Motherhouse, I have appointed Sister Etta Louise, as my delegate, to receive your act of profession on March 19. We are sending you invitations, in a day or so. Be sure you invite your Chaplain, and the Pastor of your home parish. You and Sister Mary Antoinette [Ready] may sign your names on the same invitation for Father Blake [their Chaplain]."

Sister Ginger Pearl explained, "They were the only two temporary professed in college, at Marymount, during this time. It was important to invite the Chaplain to something so beautiful."

Mother Superior's letter continued, "We are praying for favorable weather as we are anxious to have all the Sisters here who are making final professions. May God bless you always and grant you an abiding desire to grow daily in His holy love. Devotedly in Saint Joseph."

Our family, as well as relatives and close friends, attended the ceremony, of which there were now less then the original Sixteen Prophets, as in their discernment, a few women did not renew their vows and made other life choices outside the convent.

Bishop F. W. Freking individually blessed the solemn profession rings of those remaining Sisters to signify their betrothal to Christ and their final vows, in a symbolic and mystical union. Sister Veronica continued to wear the silver band, on her left hand, throughout her lifetime.

Following the gathering she wrote to our parents, "I hope you got home all right after my big day here at the Nazareth Motherhouse. Thank you so much for everything that made possible my happiness. There were so many with us, and it seemed like the afternoon passed so fast that I hope I didn't slight anyone.

"I really do appreciate the briefcase you gave me, and I know it will certainly be useful. Thanks again from the bottom of my heart for everything! May Our Lord reward you with graciousness matching your own. Lovingly in Christ."

Sister Veronica graduated two months later with a Bachelor of Science degree in Nutrition. There were a total of three graduates in the family that year. Father Duane earned a Bachelor of Arts degree, in Philosophy, at St. Benedict's College, and this writer, Linda, concluded high school in the last graduating class of rural Webster High School, as it closed that same year.

At twenty-three years old, Sister Veronica was about to embark on a professional career. She made a home visit, the last week of June 1963, the first time in five years. The opening of the Second Vatican Council had taken place in October 1962, but outcomes had yet to trickle down. There were restrictions; trips were still chaperoned, and Sisters were required to travel "two-by-two." Sister Veronica asked permission for Sister Ginger (then known as Sister Thomas Ann) to be her traveling companion.

Sister Ginger explained the logical choice. "Veronica had met my aunt, May Thomas, who lived in nearby Woodston, twelve miles east of Stockton. When my uncle, George, was in St. Joseph's Hospital in Concordia, I had the wonderful opportunity of visiting him there every day, and sometimes Veronica visited him with me, too. He died, in January 1959, while we were still Postulants." She added, "Then my father died when we were Novices. I had a Professed Sister, Sister Francis Eileen [Healy], who took me under her wing, and was a part of our family for those sacred days."

After this first visit home Sister Veronica wrote a follow-up note to our parents: "Happiness in a home reaches far and wide. It will surely follow all the days of my life, especially in reflecting on the wonderful days and years in our home."

Sister Ginger continued to be her chaperone for several more home visits. "On one of these visits her youngest brothers, Roger and Rodney, took us on their motorcycle." She hiked up her long heavy Habit to straddle the two-wheeler. "Veronica's veil flew in the wind, and she loved it."

Chapter Sixteen

In July 1963, after graduating from Marymount College, Sister Veronica began a one-year internship of graduate study in dietetics at Good Samaritan Hospital in Cincinnati, which is affiliated with the General Hospital Food Clinic and Taft Sanitary Engineering Center. Her fellow interns were four other Sisters and twelve laywomen.[1] During this stint she was eligible to become part of the American Dietetic Association (ADA) and Registered Dietitians (RD), two memberships she maintained for life.

In the years ahead she would see many changes, not only in the church of her youth, but also in the secular world. However, she neither commented when Dr. Martin Luther King, Jr. gave his "I Have a Dream" speech, nor wrote about the indelible mark on the memory of the nation when President John F. Kennedy was assassinated later that year, on November 22. Instead, a few days later she sent a postcard. "This is our city; across the [Ohio] River is Covington, Kentucky.

The garb for the hospital Sisters on staff, when she first started, was a heavily starched white apron attached to the black wool Habit. "Those [Nuns] in dietetics changed that year to a white polyester Habit, which was lighter in weight, and much cooler, too." She received many compliments from acquaintances and patients on the new look.

"Give us today our daily bread." "I am the bread of life." "Bread that sustains His heart." With these scriptural passages she integrated the symbolism of bread, and began to identify with the biblical Martha. "I am gaining Purchasing experience now. Fabulous. Sixty loaves of bread a day. Whew!"

Another scriptural verse, "Man does not live by bread alone," seemed to fit this stage in her life. "I was proud to be a CSJ. Yet, I wrestled with the vows I had just perpetually professed that spring. This was a traumatic and long year away from my CSJ Community and immediate family. I reached for all kinds of help, but mostly becoming more and more afraid, unloving and unfree. Still, I remained a hardworking, and very quiet Nun."

Part of the wrestling with her vows may have been from "raging hormones." She was twenty-four years old, and dealing with the demands of celibacy. Kathleen Norris explains in the book, *The Cloister Walk*, that younger celibates are often more edgy, as they struggle with their desire for intimacy within the confines of this state. Sometimes it is not until later years that the unmarried life, and the vow of chastity, is viewed as a freedom, which allows for a greater sense of hospitality. As Norris suggests, a sense of openness then develops, which attracts people of all ages. Likewise, even many married women tend to come into their own after the childbearing years. When the outer beauty fades oftentimes the inner beauty shines forth in these females; they become more genuine, more open and albeit, oftentimes more outspoken.

Growing up in the 1950s, when virtuous chastity, modesty and wholesomeness was still valued, and when personal identity was closely linked to being a wife and mother, turning sexual energies into a passion for doing God's work could be viewed as a freeing experience.

While she was not exposed to the "free love" sexual revolution of the 1960s, what Sister Veronica was undertaking was also an overwhelming mission. To argue that celibacy can elevate the true self — the soul — may bring on blank expressions. A mystery to many, it means more than mere abstinence; it is a transparency of the heart, as well as purity of body.

Understanding that celibacy is more than self-denial can be challenging in this day of declining values. The vow of chastity is difficult for many to comprehend in this current age where virginity is mocked in the entertainment world. This virtue also brings out the animosity and insecurity of some men, who have their own agenda.

This was still the era when Sisters had only general friendships — rather then close friends. Being lonely and alone in her new professional experience and new surroundings may have triggered feelings of inadequacy. Perhaps in her moments of black doubt she encountered the dark night of the soul, just as have other followers of Christ. No one's faith is so strong that they never falter or question their beliefs. But faith moves in mysterious and strange ways, like the cycles of life.

Having no one with whom she could confide her doubts deepened the aloneness and torn by uncertainty, she experienced a spiritual exhaustion in her search for answers and identity. Being a perfectionist, she might have thought, "What if I am unable to meet the challenge? What if I fail?"

Father Duane explained, "She was searching her manner to serve, and adapting to religious community life and professional services. Her 'self-worth' was in doing or being something."

Our cousin Sister Diane Brin offered another possibility for the wrestling with vows. "Veronica loved the CSJ Community and was committed to her permanent vows, but part of the wrestling may have come from not being fully accepted for her hearing loss."

Furthermore, she was living amidst the many changes of the Second Vatican Council. "If the years from 1962 on were a time of turmoil, they were also a time of deeper understanding for apostolic Religious Women of their role in the church world."[2]

Within a few years following the end of the Vatican II, pronouncements from Rome abolished many Latin prayers. The entire liturgy of the Church began celebrating in the vernacular — the local language of the people. The elimination of the liturgical language of Latin, as a result of modernizing the church, was a dramatic adjustment, one of which more than a few Catholics still mourn today.

These changes also allowed Priests to face the congregation as they celebrate the Mass, which required Catholic churches around the world to be remodeled with the altar moved forward and turned. The communion rails were removed, in some churches, as that was part of the artistic and liturgical renewal going on at the time, which interestingly, is still finding resistance. Removal of the rails was an "opening" of the sanctuary, or a "democraticalization," as Father Duane calls it.

Amidst the turmoil was a complete reorientation of Catholic devotion. An extensive system of novenas, Stations of the Cross, Forty Hours devotion, miraculous medals, parish missions and other usages were pushed aside in some parishes. Instead, partial replacement was found in Bible study groups, directed retreats, and liturgical workshops. Never before in the recent history of Catholicism has such a radical adjustment of attitude been required. These numerous and sudden changes were implemented, often without adequate explanation to the laity.

Stoically, Sister Veronica hid her anxiety from our family and continued to write upbeat letters, as if she was full of self assurance, like this one on Mother's Day 1964: "This is filled with grateful prayer for all you have done for us...The nursing students had May Crowning last evening. Two hundred and fifty nurses in white, each with a pink carnation for our Lady [the Blessed Virgin Mary], certainly were an inspirational sight.

"Do you remember the story told at our Baccalaureate last May [at Marymount] about the wheat field and the neighbors tramping it down looking for a little child? For our speech class, I told that story and they voted me the best speaker of the day — Ho Hum — I think they were just surprised that I could talk for one minute. I am somewhat anxious to be finished here around the first week of July."

She seldom mentioned in her letters what was going on in the world, although it's unlikely she would have noticed the lava lamp, and all things psychedelic, which began to crop up among the youth, so unlike herself. The Beatles hit American soil in February, the same year the Civil Rights Act went into effect.

That summer our brother, Allan, and Geraldine, his wife of five years, adopted their first child, Duane John, and named him after the baby's uncle Father Duane and grandfather John. This couple were heroes, in the eyes of our family, for opening their hearts and home to this child. In the following years, the young couple adopted Teresa Mae and Michael Frank.

Sister Veronica's extended family continued to expand with the births of nieces Michelle and Denise Rader, in 1964 and 1965 respectively. As a proud aunt, Sister Veronica began a long life habit of dragging out photos of her loved ones at any opportunity, and of the ones who came along later (David Monarchi, Jr., Jackie Lowenthal, Laurie and John Calvin, Jason, Kellie and Joshua Roy).

In July, Allan and his wife traveled to Atchison, taking the newborn Duane, to celebrate when Father Duane/Gary took solemn vows. At twenty-three years old he became spiritually, and legally, a full member into the Religious Order of St. Benedict. The rest of the family, and many relatives were there, too, as was Sister Veronica, having just completed the internship in Cincinnati.

She was also there three years later when Father Duane was ordained in Atchison, in June 1967, as well as at the home parish in Stockton, where he celebrated his first Mass a few days later. The Sisters of St. Joseph sent a good-sized delegation, including our cousins Sister Mary de Lellis (Diane Brin), Sister Marie Rene (Shirley Morin) and Sister St. Theresa (Juanita Morin).

Merle Grover, a longtime friend, neighbor and devout Methodist, who watched Father Duane grow into adulthood, was overcome with humility and pride at being invited to his first Mass and reception. "Anyone who wished to come forward could do so. When I knelt and his hands laid on my head bestowing God's blessing…Oh! How blessed I was. And to think that my little neighbor boy was such a blessing to me, and to countless others."

A maternal second cousin, Mark Berland, (grandson of Mother's sister, Rosa Balthazor) was ordained several years later in 1974. Mother confided in a loving manner to his mother, "Isn't it a burden to be the mother of a Priest," as she gave her niece, Eunice Berland, a comforting hug. Then Mother added, "Actually, I've always felt at ease in the presence of Priests, maybe because I have one as a son, too."

Sister Veronica's band was one of the last sent on mission, where each was most needed. In keeping with the vow of obedience, these moves were assignments without choice. She spent the next four years [1964-1968] at St. Joseph's Hospital, 1100 Highland Drive, in Concordia, Kansas.[3] This was a 49-bed hospital, with 175 employees, founded by the Sisters of St. Joseph in 1903. The first two years here, she was assistant to dietitian Sister Donata Bissett; the last two as head of the department, where she served as general hospital administrative and therapeutic dietitian.

During this time she closely followed the Holy Rule echoed in Maxim 45: "Always be serious when you are with others, but let it be a joyful seriousness, courteous and full of a gentle and reserved simplicity."

In her early management days, she also followed the advice of many schoolteachers to not smile during work hours. Perhaps she was told terrible stories about Sisters who lost control of their classroom because they weren't strict enough.

Even Dr. James Dobson writes in *The Strong Willed Child*, "Respect for authority must precede the acceptance of love. Those teachers who try to spread love in September, then discipline next January, are destined for trouble. It won't work. It is my recommendation that teachers don't smile until Thanksgiving."[4]

It becomes apparent she carried this principle to extreme. "During my first four years in dietetics at Concordia, I had no self-confidence and dared not smile at anyone, less they run away with the department." This continued and she confided to Sister Diane that if she smiled, employees wouldn't do as she requested. If new teachers shouldn't smile for six months, surely she thought this was the way for a kitchen dietitian to handle her staff, too. This also reinforced in Sister Veronica what she called her "unloving nature."

While all Sisters worked hard they were also allowed to take vacations, and it was a common practice to travel with other members of one's band. During the summer of 1966 she sent a postcard postmarked Marty, South Dakota. "Saw the [Black Hills] Passion Play, twice in Spearfish, and have really seen a lot in the past seven days."

At the end of that year on New Year's Eve, she was unable to get off work to travel to Golden, Colorado, for this writer's marriage to David Monarchi. Instead, she wired a telegram to the reception with her good wishes, and mailed a *della Robbia*-style wall plaque that she hand-molded from plaster of Paris, and then painted.

In the meantime Madelyn Murray O'Hair, the self-described "America's most hated woman," made an appearance in Sister Veronica's hometown of Stockton. She made history, and a raft of enemies, with her successful 1963 lawsuit to ban prayer in public schools. O'Hair's creed was "Religion is the enemy." This was against all Sister Veronica, her family, and hometown believed in and worked for. Outspoken, middle-aged and one of the best-known atheists at that time, O'Hair and her representatives went into Rooks County, in the mid-1960s, with the intention of looking to buy a large parcel of cheap land, from a local sympathizer and supporter, on which to build an atheist-based center.

O'Hair was viewed as a poisonous weed, and weeds are not welcome in this grain-producing county. Before the land could be purchased (these were before the days of anti-discrimination real estate laws), local churches, and townspeople alike, banded together to let O'Hair and her group know they were not welcome.[5]

While Sister Veronica was only one of three Nuns (and Father Duane is the only Priest) from this rural area that O'Hair tried to infiltrate, Rooks County was then, and still is, a family-oriented community populated primarily with churchgoers holding Midwest-hometown values, and having no patience for outsiders with ideas contrary to God, Home and Country.

In the meantime, Mother was busy at home still raising children. She received an award for helping her two youngest in elementary school maintain an outstanding attendance record. As Cheryl and Rodney grew older, Mother had more free time. "She developed her missionary side, seeing the direction Sister Veronica and I were taking," said Father Duane. "She got involved, traveled, read, followed charismatic renewal, and participated in marriage encounters."

At the close of Vatican II, and following directives from Rome, there were significant changes taking place in religious life. Religious Women were called to review their spirituality, and mission by returning to their origins. They searched the initial charism of their founders. As a whole, the next ten years, from 1965 to 1975, were spent in a quest for identity, new lifestyles and alternate ministries. More contact with the outside world was allowed — even encouraged. They began to look to fellow CSJ community members as mentors, guides and peer counselors as advocates at the Motherhouse, in case problems arose in their day-to-day lives.

Before it became democratic, as it is today, the leader of the Community was called the Superior General/Mother Superior. Her council, a group of six Sisters called Home Superiors, assisted in the administration.

Then, religious congregations began holding special general chapters every four years, instead of six as in the past, for the purpose of electing a President, Vice President, Treasurer and three regional coordinators/councilors and where the specifics of community renewal and reform were legislated. Together they were called the Leadership Team (to which Sister Veronica was elected in 1995.)

Currently, the President of the Congregation is simply called Sister — with no maternalistic title to distinguish herself from the others. Sister Therese Marie Stafford, who was Sister Veronica's Postulant Mistress in 1958, was elected as CSJ president in 1965.[6] She took the lead, set the pace, and guided her charges with good sense and compassion, while inspiring confidence at a time when many worried about the future of the Congregation.

The year before, in September 1964, following a recommendation from Rome, the concept of a simplified Habit was introduced. Once they had the liberty to modify their traditional garb, as a progressive Community the Sisters of St. Joseph followed the trend to modernization. But it would not be until a few more years when all the details were ironed out.

The years 1967 and 1968 were turbulent ones throughout the nation. The Sisters in Concordia were also in a state of unrest, and split over many issues. One of their hottest controversies had to do with shortening the skirt of the religious Habit. Sister Therese Marie was among the first in her Community to adopt the modified look. In contrast to the miniskirt, which many lay women around the world seemed to be wearing, her perfectly tailored Habit was two inches below the knee. Her exposed legs were covered in black hose.

There was also a period of experimentation with a cap and shortened veil clipped, leaving a little patch of hair showing in front. The Sisters went on to debate, among themselves, whether they could remove their veils in public, and wear makeup, panty hose and fashionable shoes.

Many of the older Nuns were attached to the idea of the traditional Habit and elected not to change. To our aunt, Sister Rose Irma, who entered the convent in 1920, these modifications must have seemed monumental, but she, too, changed with the times. At the time of her golden jubilee, she was wearing a shorter veil with front hair revealed. Father Duane, who by now was doing graduate work at Emporia State, visited her in Manhattan often for the two years he had weekend chaplain duty, at nearby Fort Riley, during the Vietnam War. Sister Rose Irma continued working there at St. Mary's Hospital until 1970, when she moved to Concordia to retire after fifty years of service.

"The changes in Vatican II were experienced throughout our Community my last years [1967-1968 while working at the Concordia hospital]," Sister Veronica said. She took time from her busy schedule, as dietitian, to attend regular workshops, and CSJ discussions, spreading over weeks and months. "I participated in committee work on changing from the Habit, and began work with several other Sisters to prepare a home for small group living outside the hospital, but I was transferred [in August 1968] the week the new home was to be entered." It was disappointing for her to not be there to see the fruits of her labor, but she took it in stride as living in "hidden ways."

Within months of having been given the option to modify their Habits, or wear ordinary clothing, in February 1968 our cousin, Sister Diane Brin, was sent to work as Director of Nursing at St. Joseph's Hospital in Belvidere, Illinois. She was the first Sister of her CSJ Order who went directly from the full Habit, into secular, street clothes, bypassing the transitional stage. For many months she was the only one, among the twenty-five Sisters working at the hospital, not wearing at least a modified Habit. It was traumatic for her. "People would stare at me," she said. "Employees heard through the grapevine that I was a Sister, but I didn't look like one."

Since Sisters do not complain, in their charism of "hiddenness," it is doubtful that anyone will ever fully know the numerous problems Sister Diane, Sister Veronica, and all the others encountered in adjusting to the new post-Vatican II world. Certainly they remembered the day of the pristine wedding dress, the day of the symbolic haircut, the day of investiture and dressing in black. Now, what did it all mean?

"The changing of the Habit wasn't circumstantial," said Father Duane. "Sister Veronica was part of a profound change — a renewal — while maintaining her initial dream, conviction and allegiance. There were many who didn't. What gave Veronica the tenacity? Was she afraid to turn back and opt for another lifestyle? Did she have a good formation to see clearly the advantages of the changes? Did she have the good friends, companions, and spiritual directors who could give the needed support? Did she feel pressure from family and friends not to abandon the religious commitment?

"Looking back over these past fifty years, the 1950s were, from a critical point of view, the height of the 'institutional church,'" continued Father Duane. "Indeed, reform was needed, which came during the 1960s, with a lot of resistance. Sister Veronica entered, embraced and was formed in one model of 'church' with all its spirituality. Within a short time she was forced to make an option for another. Not one to get on the bandwagon of all the changes, she would have to observe, think and consider them though," he said. Regardless of the way she felt, she dealt with these changes the Second Vatican Council thrust upon religious life in her own way.

By Easter 1968, when she traveled with Mother and Dad to Golden, Colorado to visit her latest infant nephew, David Monarchi, Jr., and this writer, Sister Veronica had made the transition to an experimental modified Habit.

Then she made another leap later that year. But just before this change, her high school teacher and basketball coach, Glenn Mitchum, jokingly asked her when she was going to start wearing ordinary clothes. She replied, "Never. I'll never give up my Habit." Several months later, when Mitchum and his wife, Gwen, saw her she had on a simple blouse and skirt below the knees. She openly smiled, "Well, Nuns can change their minds, too."

She quickly reclaimed her flair for sewing, developed in her youthful 4-H days, and made a fully lined suit of blue wool, with a rounded Peter-Pan collar, three-quarter-length sleeves, and matching fabric-covered buttons. The only outward symbol to distinguish herself, as a Religious, was a crucifix, received on the day of professed vows, and worn around her neck on a black cord outside her clothes. She continued to sew sporadically throughout the years and almost as a symbolic reminder, of her talent and a life interrupted, was a half-sewn garment hanging in her closet at the time of her death.

Since consecrated Religious Women take vows of poverty, chastity and obedience, they abandon most of the things that differentiate one person from another — possessions, a spouse and unimpeded free will. The new change in clothing styles was one way of bringing out their uniqueness. On the other hand, for some Sisters, abandoning the Habit was an emotional experience. This long dark garment singled them out as walking in Christ's footsteps.

There are those who question whether there will be a trend of Sisters going back to the practice of wearing the Habit. If so, the belief is it will come from new members who need distinct symbols to identify themselves as members of a religious community.

With the dawning of the new millennium, it became more unusual to see Sisters in public wearing Habits. In 1999 when my seven-year-old son, Christopher, saw two Sisters so attired in a supermarket he innocently asked, "Are they pilgrims?"

†

Chapter Seventeen

Belvidere, Illinois, in the Diocese of Rockford, was a laid-back community in 1968. It is located in Boone County, the county seat, in an important agricultural section of the state.

When Sister Veronica was sent there, on mission, to work at St. Joseph's Hospital she never mentioned in her letters the media events other people were talking about. Both Martin Luther King and Robert F. Kennedy were assassinated that year. Charles Manson, a smaller-scale version of Hitler, was spewing his message of hate.

The hippie "invasion" flaunted marijuana being smoked openly. This was labeled the "summer of love," in contrast to nationwide unrest. The counterculture, a generalized protest against scattered ideas of cultural authority, was officially born this year, amid campus upheavals and street demonstrations.

Only 78 miles from Belvidere, close, yet far away in politics, Chicago was a hot seat of civil unrest. Hundreds of thousands of anti-war demonstrators and the police riot at the Chicago Democratic Convention sparked controversy. It seemed the entire country was ready to destroy itself showing a whole new political face, complete with obscenities, radicals, violence and Vietnam.

Not only was the nation in trouble, ecclesial authority also suffered heavy blows. The Catholic Church was having internal problems of its own following Pope Paul VI's encyclical *Humanae Vitae*, on "human life and love," the document that officially denounced use of birth control.

The name Belvidere, *Belvédère* in French, means viewpoint. Sister Veronica developed some views and opinions, as well as deep-rooted friendships. In later years, she referred to these times as "mountaintop experiences." Yet, these were difficult times to sort out one's life.

There had been much confusion during the period immediately following the Second Vatican Council (1962-1965) and after the turmoil droves of Sisters and Priests were leaving their Religious Orders nationwide. A few women left the Sisters of St. Joseph of Concordia while Sister Therese Marie Stafford served as President (1965-1969). Our cousin, Sister Diane Brin noted, "It was not a reflection on her; rather just a sign of the times."

According to the CSJ newspaper, "Sister Therese Marie guided the entire congregation through the pivotal Senate of 1969, a series of deliberations which set a new course for all facets of religious life."[1] Many of the members of the Congregation considered her an angel. They saw better times ahead, not only in the change in dress and lifestyle, but helping to heal the psyches.

Suffering from cancer, Sister Therese Marie died her last year in office. Stafford Hall, for the aged Sisters at the Motherhouse, is named in her memory.

Following her death, Sister Christella Buser served as CSJ President (1969-1973), and there were even more departures. Furthermore, after eleven women were ordained Priests in the Episcopal Church, no doubt some of the remaining Sisters wondered — Sister Veronica included — "Could the ordination of Catholic women be far behind?"

Many Sisters now began to live alone, or in small groups outside the larger convent community. The rules of everyday life seemed to change monthly. In more than a few cases, these modern innovations provoked some Religious to leave — some who might otherwise have stayed, especially many of the younger Sisters below the age of thirty-five. Their expectations of the Vatican Council were not fulfilled and some felt that either Rome, or their Congregation, was hindering progress.

Perhaps others left, now that there was a slight lifting of the stigma of leaving the convent, seeing others leave, and having tasted a freedom of choice.

Even though we Americans descend from numerous nationalities, many of our foreign customs — many of which affect family life — do not seem to fit in with the American way of life. For example, still today in Japanese culture the oldest son is expected to care for his elderly parents. Another unfamiliar custom, which may seem peculiar, is that in the Catholic French Canadian culture, during the first half of the twentieth century, "first fruits" were to be given back to God. It was expected that at least one child, in each good Catholic family, was destined for the religious life. With few exceptions, many families felt truly blessed when one of their children heeded the "calling from God."

Having French Canadian roots ourselves, several in our extended family became Nuns, and some later left their Orders. At one time there were four maternal first cousins in the convent, three of whom were taught by the Sisters of St. Joseph at the Catholic school in Damar.

Our cousin, Diane Brin, having attended all four years at the Nazareth Motherhouse Apostolic High School, pronounced temporary and final vows in 1960 and 1963 respectively, and received the name Sister Mary deLellis. She remained in religious life although, she returned to her baptismal name, Diane, in 1967, as allowed by the Second Vatican Council.[2]

Another cousin, Shirley Morin, made vows in 1954, and received the name, Sister Marie Rene. Juanita Morin, another first cousin, entered in 1955, pronounced final vows in 1959, and received the name Sister St. Theresa. Shirley and Juanita both returned to lay life in 1969 — the same year an American flag was placed on the moon, in the greatest technological feat of that age.

Both cousins later married: Shirley in 1972; and Juanita in 1979, and again in 1993. In lay life, Shirley continued to teach elementary school, and was later employed by Iowa State University, until her retirement. Juanita, who previously taught in the elementary grades, joined the Peace Corps and lived in Chad, Africa for seven years after returning to lay life, and went on to teach with the Job Corps in Oregon and Arkansas. As a widow, she continues to help Oregon students obtain their GED.

In the 1930s and 1940s, it was a common practice at home and abroad to enlist young girls for the convent life. Sister Mary Kevin Walker, an older friend of Sister Veronica, verified that with a similar story about her early life. "After my father died, I cleaned rooms of a hotel in Dublin and worked in its kitchen, too. One day some American Nuns were visiting, and asked if I would consider a religious life, and move to America some day. I rushed home on the bus to tell my mother, lest I lose heart. Mother said, 'If I say no, I might be interfering with God's work, and never forgive myself. If I say yes, I will lose my child [to America], and my heart will be broken.'"[3]

Typically, girls from rural areas were recruited for the convent, and parents were reassured their daughters would receive a superior education. In the 1940s, this was the assigned job of our distant cousin, Sister Wilfred Desmarteau, and she recruited Dad's youngest sister. As a sixteen-year-old, our aunt Jeannette entered the Order of the Sisters of St. Joseph in LaGrange Park, Illinois.

Our aunt took the name Sister Laura Annette — Laura being her mother's name. She received a fine education, as promised. The most highly educated of her siblings, she became an elementary and special education teacher, an elementary school principal in the Archdiocese of Chicago, and later a department head.

Dad was fond of his youngest sister, and he taught her how to drive a car, on Kansas's country roads, when she was still a very young Nun. On another of her visits, Dad took her into town teaching her to parallel park on the streets of Stockton. This brought stares from the local townsfolk, as this petite woman, with the enchanting smile, peered over the steering wheel wearing the distinctive black Habit.

At age forty-four, and after twenty-eight years as a Sister, our aunt left the religious life. Many of the Religious, both Priests and Nuns, discovered that it was difficult to cope with too much newfound freedom, which had suddenly been thrust upon them. She was among others who struggled with the Second Vatican Council changes and felt the pressure of modifications in attire and living styles. She knew of Sisters living alone in apartments and, like others, she wondered what the difference was now, between the inside and the outside of the convent. The former clearly defined lifestyles were now blurred.

Among the most positive and notable internal differences following the Second Vatican Council was the way Sisters were treated with tact and respect upon leaving the religious life. Today, the CSJ Motherhouse of Concordia even host reunions of former members and aspirants.

Granted dispensation from their vows, they were allowed to say proper goodbyes. This is hardly the picture painted nine years earlier in the last scene of the 1959 movie, *The Nun's Story*, when Audrey Hepburn, playing the role of Sister Luke, was required to depart, in the dark of night, as she left the convent forever.

Every religious community has the obligation to provide for the spiritual, moral and social, as well as temporal well being of its members, while they retain their membership in the Congregation. This commitment also extends itself somewhat to those, under certain conditions, who leave the religious life under the principles of equity, justice and social responsibility.

Sister Diane noted, "Sister Mary Savoie [president 1973-1977] indicated there was a sliding scale of funds available, for those leaving the convent, based on the number of years in the religious community." Sister Christine Doman [president 1995-1999] agreed, "Sisters, who leave, are given an amount according to their particular needs to reestablish themselves. Church regulation requires this to be done in the name of charity. Patrimony money [such as an inheritance and special gifts] is returned to her if a Sister leaves the CSJ Community, which only uses the [accrued financial] interest during her lifetime."

Perhaps it was an oversight that Aunt Jeannette was not included in the Last Will, while she was still a Sister, and therefore was excluded from inheriting from her parent's estate. Dad and other members of the family shared a small portion of their inheritance when she left the convent.

Perhaps due to the heightened awareness, our parents, who believed in charitable works, included both the CSJ of Concordia and St. Benedict's Abbey, as equal partners, along with their children, in their Last Will and Testament.

Our aunt took back her given name and, after leaving the convent, she visited our dad. It is unknown whether it was an attempt to make his sister feel more comfortable when Dad confided that he would not be surprised if, in time, Sister Veronica would also leave the convent and "that would be all right." Most likely Dad would have never said this if Mother were in the room. After all, Mother prayed for vocations to the religious life and the changes, with Vatican II, were not going to stop her heavenly plea. Even the day before Mother died she requested the Mass, at her bedside, be offered for religious vocations.

It took courage for our aunt to reenter public life, even as spirited as she was. Many of the relatives did not know she had requested a dispensation, and returned to lay life. The new Aunt Jeannette made an appearance, at a family reunion in Kansas. When she dared to wear a dress above the knees there were shocked looks. Even though it was 1968, and mini skirts had already been in fashion for two years. Furthermore, relatives did not know what to call her. Some nieces and nephews never knew she had another name besides Sister Laura Annette.

In 1970 she married Bill Hinz, a tall, handsome man, ten years her junior, a former Priest from Chicago. She, and her husband of over thirty years, are generously active in their parish in Bartlett, where he serves as Eucharistic Minister. They serve in parish ministry through adult education, including Bible study classes. Jeannette, in her seventies, remains attractively spunky, and is adored by her extended family.

Sister Veronica was affected by the turbulent times of religious life, in the 1960s and 1970s, and its radical changes in prayer style, ministries and government. She tried to break with old traditions, and work through the many conflicts stemming from rapid changes in her environment. She was cautious about the impression made in her style of dress. Even much later, in 1989, when she briefly considered taking back her given name Ila Mae (especially Sister Mae), she considered how it might be perceived, and decided against it, as others might think she had opted out of the religious life.

Perhaps some Sisters remained in religious life because they were fearful of the future following these changes, as they had grown accustomed to the "institutional church," the Habit, schedules, authority and privileges. One might wonder whether these women allowed themselves to bemoan the simplicity of the past, saddened by the loss of traditional practices which, although confining and repressive, afforded them definition, protection and respect.

Many of the Sisters who stayed in their religious communities after Vatican II began making feelings and wishes known. Some wanted to discard what they saw as out-of-touch and old-fashioned in religious life.

One thing was certain: Vatican II jolted religious life, and the question of identity rocked many Congregations and Orders. Even among these gentle women, sides were taken and tempers came close to fraying.

As a result of fewer vocations, combined with the thousands of Sisters and Priests across the nation who asked to return to lay life, the once flourishing schools, such as the Aspirant school in Concordia, Damar High School, Marymount College, St. Benedict's College, and even other Catholic institutions, such as St. Joseph's Hospital in Belvidere, began to experience a decline in Sisters and Priests available for service. The end result was a death knell, which meant coming close to, or even closing the doors in financial ruin for many institutions.

In the world at large there continued to be chaos during these trying years. National Guardsmen shot and killed four students during the dissent over the American invasion of Cambodia in a 1970 incident at Kent State University, in Ohio. Students continued to protest the violence in Vietnam, and the next year, the play *Jesus Christ Superstar* left Christians wondering if this musical was a blasphemy, or a true commentary on the life of Christ. During this decade new legislation, Supreme Court rulings, and increasing pressure from women's organizations, such as N.O.W., brought about tremendous changes in women's roles and expectations in American society. Women were burning their bras, and marching for equality and the Equal Rights Amendment (ERA).

During her visit home, for a family reunion in 1973, Sister Veronica observed her three grown sisters wearing hot pants, the new fashion rage, and dresses so indecently short that one could hardly bend over. However, she never once voiced her displeasure; she was not one to criticize. Although she did pray at length, this same year, when abortion became legally available, with the outcome of Roe v. Wade.

When the occupation by the Lakota Sioux Indians of Wounded Knee, South Dakota resulted in a bloody standoff, she empathized with her friend, Sister Ginger Pearl, whose own Potawatomi ancestors followed the 1838 Trail of Tears. In 1974, Richard M. Nixon resigned, as President, following the Watergate scandal. The next year saw the fall of Saigon.

Closer to home Sister Veronica had her hands full running a department, and volunteering in parish and local community activities. Yet when Mother asked her if our sister, Cheryl, could stay, for a short time, in the convent quarters of the hospital, Sister Veronica felt obligated to take on the responsibility.

During the summer following her senior year in high school our youngest sister had a hometown boyfriend who frequently got speeding tickets. Dad openly called the guy a "bum," believing he was a bad influence. For the first time our little sister saw another side of gentle Dad, as he heatedly predicted this boy would not go far in life.

Sister Veronica made the long drive from Illinois, to pick up our sister, and immediately put her to work at the hospital for minimum wage. For three weeks, Cheryl drudged from 8 a.m. until 3 p.m., in the scullery, loading the large industrial dishwasher, cleaning tables and putting food away. Sister Veronica showed her how to properly set the long tables. All the while Mother prayed. The tactic worked. Soon little sis forgot about the unsavory boyfriend, and she successfully went off to college in Colby that fall.

Cheryl actually enjoyed this retreat. "The convent quarters were compact, with separate bedrooms on the top floor of the hospital, and there was usually an extra bedroom or two for female guests. On this floor was a small community kitchen for making coffee and snacks, such as popcorn. The Sisters were outgoing, energetic, and fun to be with, and it was great to see our cousin, Sister Diane, again, too.

"Here I first met Sister Kevin Walker, an especially warm and friendly Irish woman with a delightful brogue," our youngest sister said. More than twenty-five years later, in 1999, Cheryl Calvin visited with the retired and elderly Sister living at the Motherhouse. "Sister Veronica's dear friend is so gentle, and full of kindness. She reminds me of our late aunt, Sister Rose Irma. I hugged her so much, and it was hard to say goodbye."

In his book, *How We Got Here*, the author David Frum suggests that the 1960s got the bum rap for what really took place in the 1970s: promiscuity, cheap drugs, women's lib and the breakdown in the American family. Frum blames several factors in the '60s and '70s that led to these changes: a breakdown in trust in government, the changing status of women and the attempt to feminize men, the abandonment of reason in favor of emotion, the obsession with rights, and a rebellion against duty to family and nation, among other issues.

When one of our sisters was experiencing difficultly in her marriage, she asked Sister Veronica if she could come with her young daughter to stay in the convent apartments at St. Joseph's Hospital for a while, just to sort things out. Sister Veronica didn't think it was a good idea. While it was difficult for her to turn down a request, she didn't want to show support, or give the impression of lending a sympathetic ear to a failing marriage.

It is a sobering fact that during the 1970s couples were divorcing at the drop of a hat. By 1975, the divorce rate doubled from the decade before. Ultimately, every state had some form of no-fault divorce, and the first marriages of each of Sister Veronica's three sisters failed in 1975, 1976 and 1977. On the other hand, Sister Veronica took her religious vows seriously. Like a marriage, she made a commitment and was determined to "get through this" and "keep in there," even though times were tough for her, too.

Before the Second Vatican Council, the Sisters would emotionally isolate themselves from others, although Sister Veronica, herself, was embraced as a professional, with a career in dietetics and nutrition. It was believed that by formality, they could better serve all of mankind. Suddenly, with the Vatican II program of Renewal, Sisters were encouraged to develop interpersonal skills, not only as professionals, but also as friends. Aloofness, detachment and indifference were no longer seen as a virtue.

It was slow going for Sister Veronica, and she often seemed hesitant. Yet, in her Life Review, she noted, "I developed strong friendships in Belvidere, particularity with [Sister Francis Alma Royer], an older Sister, who helped me verbalize much of the spiritual growth that was occurring." According to Sister Diane, "Sister Francis Alma Royer was Sister Veronica's closest friend during this time, and the two of them often ate lunch and shopped together. They prayed together, and were both in the Charismatic group. Sister Jean Befort and Sister Kevin Walker were also very supportive of her."

In 1974 our cousin, Sister Diane, left the hospital in Belvidere as director of nursing to return to graduate school, and the bond of kinship was not rekindled with Sister Veronica for many years, due to distance.[4] Father Duane explained, "In the early years of religious life relatives didn't get special treatment or consideration." But fourteen years later, on a return visit to Kansas, Sister Diane spent a weekend visiting her cousin. After that, they sought out each other's company as often as possible.

Much earlier in 1959 the pastoral letter of the recently elected Pope John XXIII, *Princeps Pastorum* (on the Missions), called religious men and women to develop mission activities in Third World Countries. Four years later in 1963, the year Sister Veronica graduated from college, the Sisters of St. Joseph of Concordia opened a mission in Teresina, Piauí, Brazil, as a direct link to deepened concern for the poor and oppressed. Five CSJs of Concordia served for many years in northeast Brazil: Sister Donna Otter, a band member with Sister Veronica; and Sisters Patricia Neihouse; Rosa Maria Dwyer; Patricia Vaughan, and Margarida Boucher.

The Monks of Atchison, Kansas also answered the pontiff's call, in 1961, when they established a Benedictine foundation in Mineiros, Goiás, Brazil. (A new monastery is called a foundation, in the process of being established.)

After Father Duane's ordination in 1967, he pursued graduate studies at Emporia (Kansas) State College, earning a master's degree in library science. In the summer of 1970, he was awarded a grant to study data processing applied to library science at the University of Southern California, in Los Angeles. The following summer, however, he traveled to Houston, Texas to apply for a permanent visa for Brazil. After thirteen weeks of Cultural Studies and Portuguese, the language of Brazil, he joined five other American Benedictines at the budding priory, Mosteiro São José, in the central interior of Brazil.[5]

During that summer of 1971 Sister Veronica made the twelve-hour drive to Kansas along with our sister, Joan, and her two young daughters, who lived in Glenview, Illinois, to bid Father Duane farewell, as did other siblings.

Years after Father Duane moved to Brazil, Pope John Paul II, elected in 1978, declared that religious life, as a whole, was in a state of crisis, not only in the lack of vocations, but also because many were leaving the religious life and Priesthood, with or without dispensations of their vows. All the while two U.S. Priests, the Berrigan brothers, Daniel and Philip, became heroes to some people for their celebrated anti-war activities. Some of the Church's religious leaders, while forbidden to hold office, were beginning to make political statements, even though at the time there was a Vatican order that Priests should stay out of politics.

Sister Veronica wrote to Father Duane in Brazil on a regular basis. In her volumes of letters it becomes clear that she greatly admired him, and sought out our brother to assist her in more fully integrating the Maxims of her Congregation, including 13:5, which states, "In order to walk more securely on the spiritual way, choose a wise director; be candid in revealing to him the deepest part of you; follow his guidance and his advice, and do nothing of importance without his direction."

✝

Chapter Eighteen

Sister Diane Brin, R.N. was assigned as Director of Nursing for the hospital in Belvidere in February 1968, and Sister Veronica was assigned Clinical Dietitian in August later that same year.

A promotional piece boasted that St. Joseph's General Hospital at 1005 Julien was completely air-conditioned, and had a television and telephone in each room. According to *Footprints on the Frontier*, the hospital is located in a healthful part of Illinois, with extensive and beautiful grounds, and that thirty years prior, there were twenty Sisters administering to the needs of approximately 2,000 patients.

The two cousins were among the last Sisters of St. Joseph to be sent on mission without a choice of their own. It would be another three years before Sisters were no longer assigned a move, and each would decide on their own where they wanted to live and work. Sister Veronica said, "There were twenty-five Sisters here when I first started. Now there are eighteen." Some retired but, "everybody stayed, and two new ones came to work here, which is amazing considering we can work where we want to now. Just means, I guess, that all like it here. Actually, it is very exciting since there is so much in the newspaper this month that Belvidere doesn't need two hospitals."

The same year the two cousins started working at this hospital, a tornado damaged the competing Highlands Hospital on the other side of town, rendering it out of commission for over a year. As a result, the 100-bed Catholic hospital was often filled to overflowing. Sister Diane remembers it well: "Beds were placed in alcoves, and even a young brother and sister shared the same bed to save space. We worked morning to night." Consequently, Sister Diane doesn't recall much about her cousin during this time. "If we saw each other at recreation time, it was almost a miracle. Any relationship I had with Veronica was work oriented. It was an unusual life in that we were extremely busy. We both worked very hard."

It was rare for the two of them to spend much time together, but on one occasion they drove to the naval base in Glenview to visit our sister, Joan, and her family. Another time they drove to Naperville to visit Aunt Jeannette, a former Nun, who lent a sympathetic ear to their busy lives.

Their heavy workload did not lessen over the years. When Uncle Joe Morin tragically died from injuries of an overturned tractor, on the old homestead near Damar in August 1973, his two nieces were regrettably unable to attend the funeral because the hospital was short staffed.

Two years after Sister Veronica's arrival, the *Belvidere Daily Republican* newspaper featured a story about the local St. Joseph Hospital. "This kitchen is big business...Sister Veronica Roy and Mrs. Edna Johnson supervise a staff of 24 people in the preparation of...40,000 meals prepared annually."

Several years later in 1974 the same newspaper carried another story. "Sister Veronica Roy...is the only dietician at her hospital and has been working in dietetics for ten years. Her interests, developed through 4-H, led into dietetics. Her work at St. Joseph Hospital includes both administrative and therapeutic work, a combination she finds interesting and challenging. She sees the popularity of snack foods both good and bad...Some snacks have good food value in them and may be useful, provided they are eaten in moderation...The brain functions on glucose that comes from carbohydrates...dieters refusing breads, potatoes and cereals may find themselves feeling sluggish...Noting that this Nutrition Week's theme is Nutrition Saves, Sister Veronica emphasized that eating wisely can save your health, and your money. 'The better a person eats, the less he has to spend on medication,' she was quoted."

Another article appeared that same year, "What does a Nun do for recreation? Would you believe challenge thirty medical students to a four-mile run?" In March she challenged the Shappert Community Health Center medical students to a race at the Belvidere High School track, in observance of National Nutrition Week. The theme for the week was "Set the Pace."

She confided in a letter, "All winter I have been running about two miles in the hospital basement, three to four times a week. I secretly hoped there would be no takers, as my only motive was to shake up some of those out-of-shape students of being challenged by an old Nun. I suspected they would ignore it, but the response kept growing to fifteen 24-to-30 year-old medical students, and two Doctors. My time was 40 minutes, 30 seconds; next to last. I called it a 'Fun Run,' but they called it the 'Nun Run.'

"I hoped to create an awareness that good nutrition combined with an exercise one enjoys is a winning combination. People are more concerned with nutrition, and that interest is tied to concern for physical fitness, as typified by the growing popularity of jogging. It was good for them to set an example of healthy fitness. It helped public relations, yet the Administrator complains of not enough medical news coverage around here." Sister Veronica was actively committed to community relations and public awareness.

For a July 4th celebration in 1979, she signed up for a 6.2-mile run (10K). "I have been running 3 to 3.5 miles, so if I can comfortably work up to five miles, I'll probably be in it primarily for the good example expected of one in health care, especially a nutritionist, who of all people should keep in shape. I'll just register as Veronica Roy, in case I don't finish. I am 39 ½, but I would sure rather run in the 40-and-over age division, than in the 30-

to-39 group, as it would give me more of a chance."

She was on the cutting edge of physical fitness, and her enthusiasm for the sport greatly impressed others. "She was so involved. Who ever heard of a Nun jogging before the spring of 1974?" said Aunt Jeannette.

Dr. Kenneth H. Cooper published *Aerobics*, in 1968, calling attention to disease prevention through aerobics. During the 1970s, millions of Americans took up jogging as fitness swept the country. Later that decade, sneaker sales soared to fifty percent of all shoe sales. One person in nine ran daily. By the end of the decade, more than 25 million Americans were on the road.

Sister Veronica knew this popular activity was a good way to lose weight, exercise the heart, and promote general physical conditioning. She understood the natural healing energy of the body, enjoyed both walking and jogging, and took physical exercise seriously to keep up her health and stamina. Although, being a Nun, she was not inclined to focus much on herself. Increasingly, over the years, she developed a habit of taking on more work and obligations, rarely had time for herself, and began to begrudge the time it took to exercise. Having to choose priorities, exercise began to take a back seat. She was not alone in this phenomenon.

It is not uncommon for women to use their natural healing energy to heal others, but not themselves. Furthermore, on an emotional level, women often don't give themselves the permission they need, or set aside the time it takes. Sometimes it is difficult to learn to care for oneself joyfully, and without guilt. It would take Sister Veronica a long time to relearn this.

I will set a feast for them...
— Isaiah 6

Within a year or so after starting her job, Sister Veronica began hosting International Feast buffets for the hospital employees, which became annual events.

In 1974 the Belvidere newspaper featured yet another article about her. "A change of pace to please the palate and up lift the spirit...Sister Veronica Roy hosted her fifth special buffet...serving 140 people. Over the past five years she has [researched and] prepared Mexican, Oriental, Italian and Polish dinners. This year's Brazilian buffet featured twenty different dishes. When asked why the chief dietitian, who is normally busy with preparing the many different meals needed for patients would tackle such a project, she said, 'It's just the delight of pleasing the employees. They always seem to be quite appreciative.'"

"Veronica often wrote her own press releases," said Sister Diane. The tone she used for the news article suggests she was reaching out to embrace and serve where her talents lay. These were prophetic words, as "a change of pace" is what she needed most at the time.

When she visited our parents two year later, in the spring of 1976, our hometown newspaper, the *Rooks County Record*, reported, "While at home on vacation Sister Veronica Roy, CSJ, prepared the foods for a Brazilian feast including marinated chicken, potato-shrimp balls, pickled perch, black beans, fresh fruit salad and coffee pudding. The menu had been pre-tested by employees of St. Joseph's Hospital, where she is an administrative therapeutic dietician. [She recently prepared] a Bicentennial buffet with a Southern flair."

"She delighted in serving others and was at her happiest, her best, and her peak when planning a party for the hospital staff," said Sister Diane. "Holidays were a special time for her, and she couldn't be outdone."

She spent long hours in preparation for these annual events. Yet, among colleagues, there were always some who did not appreciate novel recipes. Sister Veronica would not allow trivial complaints to dampen her spirits. No doubt she kept handy the prayer card of the patron of dietitians and dietary services, *"Dear Saint Martha, who so often prepared meals for Jesus Christ, and served this Divine Guest and His friends in your home in Bethany, help me to fulfill my duties as dietitian with a spirit of supernatural charity and graciousness so that all that I do for my neighbor may be done for Christ, in Christ, and with Christ. Amen."*

When the Sisters gathered for mealtimes at the hospital convent refectory, they sat at a long table in order of rank and age. The house Superior sat at the head. The oldest Sister sat next to her. As in biblical times, the seating order placed Sister Veronica and Sister Diane, as the two youngest and least number of professed years, at the end of the table. In the early years, silence at breakfast was still a practice for meditation.

"When I first went to Belvidere," said Sister Veronica, "that convent was a retirement home for many of our Sisters. Shortly thereafter, many of them were recalled to other community retirement centers [including Médaille Center in Salina].

"In these early years (1968-1973), new styles of community leadership were expected to emerge. As one of the youngest Sisters, I became the local house coordinator for too many years, and often felt caught between the pull of the old and the new thinking. My desire for unity was so strong that I was hesitant about leaving that convent [location] until mission accomplished. I wanted to move [faster] but felt sensitive to the pace desired by the others."

Chapter Nineteen

"If today you hear his voice, harden not your heart."

— Ps 95

Reflecting back to many years earlier when, at the age of twenty-nine, Sister Veronica began working as a department head, she was not unlike many managers during that era, or even of today for that matter. "I first ran the department according to my theory that basically people are lazy and need to be watched in order to produce. I operated on the XYZ principle that everybody will get away with the least amount of effort, unless I spell out what they need to get done.

"My 6 a.m. to 8 p.m. work for the Lord left me cold and harsh." During religious formation she was drilled to have a stiff upper lip, to be stoic and unemotional. Sister Veronica's hardness was a protective shield and one she learned along the way. "I know my twenties and thirties were my hard-hearted years." She was a complex person, easily misunderstood and continued to adhere to the principle that persons in authority should not smile.

There were a series of meetings, for the Sisters, where a facilitator conducted Communication Workshops. "During this time we were encouraged to use the model of Transactional Analysis (T.A.) framing differing opinions in the 'I' statement, rather than 'you,'" said Sister Diane Brin. "If we had a disagreement with someone, we might say for example, 'I feel hurt that you didn't let me complete my sentence before walking away, rather than, 'Why did you walk away from me?'" But Sister Veronica said, "I tried so hard at communication that it came out artificial."

The first several years appeared to go smoothly because, in 1971 she wrote, "We all like it here." But the same year that Sister Diane returned to college Sister Veronica said, "After six years of this [1968-1974], I was miserable in both my professional and spiritual life, and was continually confronting the Lord, my Spouse. I disliked reading. I doubt that I even read at all during these previous five years."

It is evident Sister Veronica became gravely concerned that her "prayer life had soured," as she put it. "I began to sleep more during time of prayer." The strict regiment of assigned time for prayers was relaxed, and Sisters were allowed to awaken naturally without a bell summoning them. Morning prayers could be made up during the day.

There are many ways of trying to experience God. In the 1960s the drug

LSD became popular, among the college set, to achieve an awakening of the soul. Sister Veronica chose a safer route.

She went on an eight-day spiritual retreat in 1975 at the Manna House of Prayer in Clyde, Kansas which was directed by a Jesuit. Since their founder was a Jesuit, they often would seek out Priests of that Order to conduct their spiritual retreats. "I told the [retreat] director I was there because I needed a love relationship with Jesus.

"The fourth stage in my spiritual journey followed this retreat. Afterward, I really was smitten, and my life has not been the same. I began taking a leisurely approach to the morning and found what God's mercy was. I was terribly hungry for spiritual literature, and spent long hours into the night reading and enjoying the quiet presence of God again. At age thirty-five, I no longer feared death.

"My management style immediately changed. I began to love the employees and understood what they had been trying to tell me all along by their cooperation and generous gifts. I experienced reciprocal love and felt transformed. I was freed of my fear of smiling at people and being vulnerable to them."

The burden began to lift. These were what she called her "growth years." Before this she thought she was not well liked by her staff. She was mistaken; her staff liked and respected her, as well. There was a certain camaraderie among the workers. When Father Duane telephoned her at work one day from Brazil, she replied to him in a letter, "It was a delight. All my kitchen ladies were about as excited as I was, as we were all together in the kitchen when you called."

Several of them continued to correspond with her, including an older employee, Clara Chamberlain. "I worked in the hospital kitchen for ten years, then I quit to care for my aged mother," she said. "After my mother went to a nursing home Sister Veronica asked me to come back." Mrs. Chamberlain worked for another eight years before a layoff of all the older employees forced her retirement.

"Sister Veronica was in Illinois on business the month prior to her own death. [Almost as a premonition] she made it a point to return to visit the hospital where she once worked. Many of her previous staff came to gather for a special luncheon hosted in her honor," said the elderly Mrs. Chamberlain. Any tense relationships Sister Veronica may have had with upper management were forgiven years ago. While there, she enjoyed a tour of the facilities guided by Sister Mary Luke.

In Sister Veronica's small box of lifetime treasures was a note from some of the young kitchen helpers. "Because of your kindness and help to the kitchen staff, we wish to express our gratitude with these pies. Signed, 'The night girls of the kitchen.' P.S. The cherry pie had a little accident, but it is still edible." Sister Veronica penciled a note below, "Four pies, and a bread, made by four of the high school girls themselves." Small tokens of appreciation, or "generous gifts," as she called them, did not go unnoticed.

One of the young employees was Wendy Tripp Shelquist, who began working in the hospital kitchen dietary department in 1973, right out of high school. "I was impressed that [as a Nun] Sister Veronica was wearing street clothes. She was my first boss, but she was more than that. I continue to use her abbreviations for supplies and things in the kitchen; chix for chicken; sc for sauce; pla for pineapple. I even write the time 10oo instead of 10:00. That's how she did it.

"In 1976, my best friend, Beth Worrell, and I invited Sister Veronica to an outdoor Christian concert in Rockford twelve miles away. She loved it." Sister Veronica noted in one of her many letters: "I went to a folk music festival last week, and a festival of the arts today, instead of taking a day of prayer this month. I will have plenty of time for that [when I go on an extended retreat.]"

Shelquist continued, "I quit working at the hospital during my last year in college, and we both had tears in our eyes when I gave notice. She and Sister Kevin Walker came to my college graduation party, which meant a lot to me.

"Years later, when my husband threw a surprise party for me, he asked all my friends and relatives to write a letter, which he put in a book. Sister Veronica wrote a very special letter reminiscing about our times together. We corresponded at Christmas for twenty-one years, until her death.

"I was raised Presbyterian, and did not know much about Catholics, or Nuns in general. When I made my *Cursillo*[1] (it was Ecumenical in Peoria where I lived at the time), I learned to appreciate even more about what Catholics believe."

The practice of Ecumenicism grew out of the Second Vatican Council after which common ground was sought in dealings with those of other faiths. Orthodox, Protestant, and other churches, even those who are not Christian, were invited to send official delegate-observers to the 1962 and 1963 sessions. Gradually there was intense study, discussion and experimentation regarding the reverence for the traditions of other Christian churches.

"I went to the [Catholic] hospital chapel one day and discovered something I had never known about — The Stations of the Cross," Shelquist went on. "I felt I had been cheated out of this, and was overcome with emotion. I think we Protestants need to learn about these, too.

"We also talked about her name. For the first time, I learned that in the Bible, Veronica was the woman who wiped Jesus' brow on His way to Golgotha. I thought a lot more about Sister Veronica after that," said Shelquist. "She was one of a kind, very down to earth, and nice to everyone. I asked her if she was charismatic and she said, 'Oh yes, and I have been for sometime now.'"

In her Life Review, Sister Veronica wrote, "I was part of a charismatic prayer group that reshaped itself many ways the nine years I was associated." Following

Vatican II there was a decline, in many parishes, of devotional expressions, and these were replaced with more personalized retreats and other charismatic movements, which supplied new insights, fresh fervor and creative action.

Sister Veronica and her co-worker friend, Sister Francis Alma Royer, participated in the Charismatic Catholic Renewal, which became strong in the United States beginning in 1971. A spiritual experience of repentance and purification, the movement is rooted in a deep love and desire to serve the Kingdom of Christ. It sparked a re-founded love for the Scriptures, a discovery of the power of praise and evoked a giving of self to the influence of the Spirit.

Surely, Sister Veronica began to see all things anew with a foretaste of Heaven, giving her glimpses of divine love and echoing the words of St. Catherine of Siena, "All the way to Heaven, is Heaven."

In the meantime, in 1973, Sister Veronica reclaimed her dream, in a teacher-role, when she was certified and commissioned as a Religious Educator in the Diocese of Rockford.

In 1974 Elizabeth Ann Seton, (a widow, who converted, then later became a Nun) was beatified the first U.S. born saint. That same year Sister Veronica was formally commissioned to administer the Sacrament of the Holy Eucharist in the church of St. James, Belvidere. This was a high point in her life. "I felt very good about myself between the years 1974-1980 [when she was 33 to 39 years old]. I served the parish, and the hospital as an extraordinary communion minister." Her appointment by Bishop Arthur J. O'Neill, Diocese of Rockford, was renewed each year she lived in Illinois.

A year or so after, on her feast day she remarked, "I baked a small, whole-wheat Eucharistic bread for the Mass. I also gave the homily about who shall see the face of God and live: 'Sometimes the veil between us is transparent, sometimes opaque, but He is always there.' Only the Priest said anything. Such is life! If I could lower my expectations, I won't have to be so hurt, or [feel] criticized. His love and His grace are enough reward."

The National Conference of Catholic Bishops was formed after Vatican II, and in 1974 laywomen were allowed to be active in the Eucharistic Service — in some dioceses. Although then, and still today Religious Women are considered no more then the laity, with no more privileges then a layperson.

✝

Chapter Twenty

By the mid-1970s many women had left the ranks of religious life, and difficult decisions had to be made, as vocations were at low ebb. With a renewed sense of prayer as ministry, a variety of retreats were made available to each Sister. Included in these was one lasting for thirty days, and based on the teachings of the founder of the Jesuit Order, St. Ignatius of Loyola (whom our mother considered her own patron saint, sharing the same birth date.) In the summer of 1976 Sister Veronica chose to make a thirty-day retreat.

"Not every Sister makes a thirty-day retreat, although Sisters are free to request one at any time " said Sister Christine Doman. "However, this is usually done when one is taking a new step in life, for example, when making final vows, moving into a new ministry, or entering into a new stage. It is a once-in-a-lifetime experience, and strictly voluntary."

Within the practice of an extended retreat lies the idea of the desert, symbolizing the setting in which the traveler, stripped of non-essentials, comes face-to-face with God. Tribal cultures required members to spend time alone in the wilderness for spiritual purposes, especially self-discovery.

The season of Lent, the forty days between Ash Wednesday and Easter, remind many people of the need for "a desert experience." The purpose is to dispel illusion, set aside distraction, and cut away the superficial. It may even symbolize a place of spiritual combat, where the powers of evil are likely to be discovered from outside and within.

Religious retreats consist of silence, reflection and prayer. Solitude is used as a vehicle for prayer or meditation. It leads retreatants to develop a loving trust in God. During the process each attendee is reminded of various forms of prayer. Coming into vogue was the concept of Centering Prayer, a contemporary name for an ancient form of contemplative prayer that goes beyond words, thoughts, images and concepts; beyond the superficial psychological self of the senses, to the deep inner self that St. Paul refers to as the "inward person." It is sometimes called the "Prayer of the Heart."

Other prayer techniques, such as the Scriptural rosary, or *lectio divina*, may also be used. The latter is a four-fold process — receiving the word of God, allowing the word to be present, giving rise to prayer, and resting in God's presence.

"Those making such a retreat usually ate and prayed together in common," Sister Christine continued. "Although, there was no visiting, except with the Sister's spiritual director, and Veronica would have requested direction, asking her spiritual director to pray with her. There were exceptions [regarding silence] made during the thirty days, including an occasional outing and conversation."

According to *Lives of the Saints*, the St. Ignatius retreat instructs that the Spiritual Exercises require a month, as it is a systematic extensive searching from within. The first week of the retreat is given to the consideration of sin and its consequences; the second week, to our Lord's earthly life; the third week, to His Passion; and the fourth week, to His Resurrection.

Sister Veronica was instructed to bring to mind all her sins, looking at her life year by year, or period by period. She was given a self-reflective guide. "Look at the place and house where I have lived. Look at the dealings I have had with others; at the calling in which I have lived. Weigh the sins. See who I am in comparison to all mankind, to Angels and Saints, and the creation in comparison to God. With a cry of wonder, with a flood of emotion, question how the Angels have guarded me, and the Saints have interceded, and prayed for me."

During the second week the written guide urged, "Ask for what I want. See all the persons of the earth. Consider the three Divine Persons on the throne, and how they regard the whole face of the earth. See Our Lady, and gather fruit from the sight. Ask grace of Our Lord that I be not deaf to His call." In the following weeks she was further instructed, "See how I stand before God."[1]

The objective was to induce such a state of inner calm that one can thereafter make a choice, either as to some particular crisis, or as to the general course of one's life. The choice would be unbiased by any excessive like or dislike, and guided solely by why one was created — to consider the glory of God, and the perfection of one's own soul.

Over the course of days Sister Veronica read, wrote and meditated on these topics. It is most likely during this time that she began to write drafts of her Life Review. After Sister Rose Irma Morin died in 1988, Sister Veronica acquired a small notebook that became especially meaningful to her, in which our aunt penned her own retreat notes.

Years later Sister Veronica was tempted to attend another thirty-day retreat, but did not. "That one time was a spiritual oasis," she said. This was a powerful experience and perhaps one of her more blissful months in life.

Bill Moyers, quoting Joseph Campbell's work on the power of myths, suggests that bliss is when you put aside terror, temptation and the requirements of life...Follow your bliss...where your body and soul want to go, and stay with it." With each look inward she became more charismatic, more of a mystic.

At the same time Sister Vera Meis, a co-worker, also made the thirty-day retreat at the Sacred Heart School of Theology in Hales Corners, Wisconsin. "Veronica expressed a profound feeling of God's Presence in her life during the retreat. It's hard to put into words such an intense experience." "The retreat is deeply spiritual," Sister Christine Doman agreed.

Sister Veronica never detailed what burst upon her as Truth. One can surmise that through ways that are inaccessible to the senses or reason, she sought to renew her thirst for union with God in contemplative ways. It is not easy to comprehend. She experienced God in a freeing and trusting manner and herself as one precious in His sight. Once again she was in love with the Holy Spirit — a feeling that was similar to when she took her first vows.

The year before, the hospital Sisters filled three cars for a day trip. Often they drove to the Wisconsin Dells, and returned by nightfall. Other times they visited the National Shrine of Our Lady of the Snows, in Belleville, Illinois, near St. Louis, one of more than 120 pilgrimage shrine sites in the United States. The vacations she and other Sisters took were of this nature.

Following the thirty-day retreat, she and nine other Sisters spent six days together, first driving Interstate 44 from St. Louis to Springfield, heading south to the Ozarks, a popular southwest Missouri tourist area, near Branson. They rented two connected cabins. Occasionally, summers there can be scorching, but Sister Veronica was not one to complain of the weather. "We used our Christmas gift money from people around here to take this vacation, which was the first time we have ever gone together like that for more than one day." They saw the outdoor presentation of "*Shepherd of the Hills.*" "I never realized the hills were so beautiful.

"I just returned home from [one week at the Ozarks and] five weeks of Ignatian Spiritual Exercises," she wrote to Father Duane summarizing her uplifting experience. "It is hard to have so much to say, but who wants to hear more after the first greeting. I knew it would be this way. This is the final day of my six-week vacation, and honestly I don't know where it has gone. For once I am not ready to get back into the grind.

"We were thirty-five Sisters at my retreat, with ten directors. We wouldn't have needed that many, but they were quite a team — five CSJ Sisters, four Jesuits, and one Sacred Heart Priest, Father Frank [Witlouck], who was my director.[2] I met with him fifteen to forty-five minutes, nearly every day, to discern which passages to pray next.

"*The Imitation of Christ* was recommended reading. Even with their fantastic library, I didn't read a thing, except Scripture. I even brought some oil paints, but didn't touch them. It was a rather gentle time in recognizing that God communicates, most intimately, in our [emotional] consciousness. As I moved through Scripture, and recognized feelings of loneliness, joy, fear, brokenness, love, longing and more, I trust He was there. It seemed like whole days would be spent on these themes, although they were actual graces, and I see them now as holding me accountable to sharing deeply with the hopes, and joys, and fears of others — of Jesus touching our lives.

"The retreat could be a parallel to the story of the potter, and the process of turning clay into pottery,"[3] a theme she would return to five years later. "The first week was on creatureliness and sin. First all the air has to be 'whacked' from us. Then we have to be centered on the wheel. As we keep getting off center, it is only when we are back on center that God can do much with us. Of course, there has to be a lot of 'sloppy wetness' all the time. After a good foundation, then He can shape us as He chooses, but not if we don't yield to the shaping. It is after the firing that you get to be decorated. Then more firing. If you like the symbolism, you can try to fit it to your own life," she wrote to Father Duane, her own lifetime spiritual director. "But then one doesn't always know where they are in life either, or whether one has a good foundation and centered, or yielding to His movements.

"The hardest part for me was the desire to keep my eyes on Him, but always swinging around to how I felt about that: living, suffering, and finding new life in Him. I kept coming face-to-face with Self when seeking Him. It did bring me to realize I have to trust myself to follow Him before I can trust Him to lead.

"Another thing I came to realize was that in always looking for the deeper meaning, 'The More' (of our CSJ spirituality), I miss the subtle touches. I spent two days trying to bury Him, to let go, then blurted out how afraid I was He wouldn't be there for the Resurrection. It was such a real fear. (No fair peeking ahead to what we know.) Then after all day of a dry praying of the Resurrection, I spent the most peaceful sleepless night. It was rather late that I recognized He was there in a friend, a consoler; His subtle appearance when I expected more.

"Of the two methods we were supposed to attempt (meditation and contemplation), I found I was probably just ruminating, like an old cow savoring a little bit for a long time, chewing it over during free time when the feeling came out about the prayer periods. So I was sort of confused with yesterday's feelings, and today's prayer. A slow reactor, I wanted Him to hurry up. The way we are with others is the way God deals with us."

She continued, "During my retreat the song 'Earthen Vessels' from the St. Louis Jesuits' cassette tape of the same name grabbed me. 'Seek the Lord' really haunted me, too. As I consider my resistance to His spirited indwelling, the only way I know of doing things is the way I know, which is but a small measure of what could be."

A strong warning is issued in doing the Spiritual Exercises, as outlined in *Lives of Saints*: "When God has appointed a way we must faithfully follow it, and never think of another under pretense that it is easier and safer. The most certain way to perfection is to endure many and grievous afflictions for the love of Christ."[4]

She said of a co-worker friend, "I dearly wait for Sister Francis Alma to come home, from her [short] retreat, so we can share deeply." The next July after Sister Francis Alma Royer made the thirty-day retreat Sister Veronica said, "We are making a forty-day shared prayer this Lent, following the Ignatian exercises."

When Father Duane came to the United States to spend one summer, Sister Veronica counseled him, "I hope you enjoyed your [Franciscan] retreat experience, [at Steubenville, Ohio] and can use many of the insights you gained this summer. Don't be afraid to share them. People's interest is not always measured by their initiating questions.

"No, I don't think you need to think about it, if it hasn't grabbed you yet," she told him after he asked whether she thought he needed to consider a thirty-day retreat. "Probably once in a lifetime is enough for anybody, but if you would like to take in a few days, or visit during a thirty-day retreat in Hales Corners, I know they took [Religious] transients last year for a few days at a time. You would also do well with Emmaus House in Des Moines. Our Sisters are using the Ursaline Motherhouse, Paola, Kansas for a June retreat, also a retreat house in Clyde, Kansas. There is the Oshkosh, Wisconsin retreat house and another in Barrington, Illinois, but I haven't been to either."

In 1977 Sister Veronica, and nine others from the hospital in Belvidere, went to the Franciscan Friary in Lake Geneva, Wisconsin for a day of recollection. It was an easy drive, not far across the state border. "These are beautiful grounds, but I can't get settled to pray until I get this note, and a Mother's Day card, in the mail," she wrote to Father Duane. "I want you to see this place right on the Lake. Lovely, yet simple. My spiritual director was Father Bill [Runde], SJ, of Rockhurst College, Kansas City, Missouri."

Another time she made a retreat conducted by a team of three: "The Motherhouse Chaplain, a Jesuit, and a CSJ Sister." In the late 1970s, the Sisters began participating in small group sharing, and even female directors were called upon, one of which was Sister Jeanette Broxterman, CSJ.

"I suspect it may be difficult to go through the usual Death/Resurrection theme of a directed retreat, during Easter week, if I have truly arrived at Easter this Lenten period," Sister Veronica said. "But then last year's retreat didn't follow any pattern and maybe I'm just supposed to be heightening the Resurrection theme. I am not really concerned. The Lord always has such neat things in store for me.

"It dawned on me I never made a retreat resolution. This is the organizational month in goal setting for convent living. I agree with our CSJ Community's concern that Christ be at the root of our lives, and being so dependent on the Father that all things are seen and treated in a new light.

"I would like to share with you some directed retreat experiences. A real conscious way I've grown since retreat (actually it came out of my Lenten penance) is to allow my fellow Sisters to barge in on my 'Holy Leisure.' It is such an effort not to be giving off signs for them to bug off when I'd rather they leave me be. That is the Romanticism danger, the fantasy of loving people without the people. Religious, of all people, should be the most loving, and that colors everything."

In the spring of 1978 she said, "We are taking Ash Wednesday as our common day of prayer and discernment over our ministry and community living for this year. We had a mini-workshop last Saturday on a simpler, responsible lifestyle. We have two more workshops this year on the spirit of Poverty." Perhaps they used the theme of Gandhi, "Live simply, so that others may simply live."

"I hear so strongly that we already know what to do, which is an automatic barrier to discernment. Right now I feel a lot of freedom to respond, but also a fear I won't hear God correctly. God truly does speak to us just as we are [even though we are] maybe a little deaf and slow reacting, but also adventurous! It has been difficult, for us as a group, to value any such time given to discovering our response to God's will."

Later, she wrote, "Fifteen of our Sisters are at Hales Corners making their thirty-day retreat, where I made mine two years ago. Two of our Sisters are helping with the cooking. I told them that if they needed help to let me know." Later she said, "They called me in mid-July, and I helped for the next three days, as well as sharing their liturgy. It was very relaxing, just being in the special atmosphere.

"I got a call from the director of our Manna House of Prayer, in Concordia, asking if I would consider being on their staff. Strangely, two different people asked me if I had considered retreat work [within the CSJ community]. I would have to hear that from more people. I had hoped to at one time, but the time just doesn't seem right. I really need to pray over this. I'm in no hurry, [although the Belvidere hospital-convent] is such an 'old house.'" She had few people there her own age to talk with.

In July 1979, following an annual retreat in Concordia, she wrote to Father Duane, "I had a wise old Jesuit for my directed retreat. Many of the Sisters, at the Motherhouse, use him for spiritual direction during the year. It was an especially privileged time, as he is also the director for my own director, with whom I communicate by letters monthly. He is retired so he has been traveling to Concordia monthly, but will alternate months since not that much happens to a person in one month's time.

"The retreat director was top notch. But at first I didn't understand [the direction he was taking] and was so annoyed with all his repetitious questions like, 'How did you feel about that?' It made me feel I was doing something wrong, and that he wasn't listening. I prayed more during this time than the whole year, but it was uncomfortable. The Retreat was stifled by my ignorance, and I didn't realize there was a difference [between] Direction, Counseling, and

Faith-Sharing. I can appreciate the process now, and can't believe I didn't know the difference then."

Four years later, the wise old Jesuit, Father Bill Diebold, caught up with her from reading a news article about her twenty-fifth jubilee year. "The snapshot I have of your lovely cake for the Chaplain Farewell is always before me, as is the wonderful experience of getting to know you during the retreat at the Motherhouse," he wrote. "It is really invigorating for this old man of skin and bones to meet you again. The thought of you gives me a renewed lease on living. I love you for being yourself and being attentive to me. Of course, I remember you in my Masses. And I beg you to send an occasional Hail Mary my way."

Her letter to Father Duane continued, "What I learned was twofold: the freedom to go ahead and blush, or be radiant, at being loved, and let it be evident that I am joyful in my religious life. And secondly, desire unity among all my associates, knowing [that as an introvert] I have to work harder than an extrovert at keeping my focus on Jesus, instead of on myself. I had to relearn, or experience freedom, in making conscious choices. It is okay to say 'no.' Always saying 'yes' to people, being unfreely generous or wanting them to be happy, is not being free.

"These have been great years for me, and the Lord Jesus is so good in sharing His companionship. (Phil 4:4). I feel it is the companions, along the way, who really teach all what it is to love Jesus, and to be loved by Him. And yet, no matter what the friendship, we only come to meet Jesus alone."

✝

Chapter Twenty-one

With the experience of another retreat behind her, and back to her routine Sister Veronica said, "I never got caught up from my four weeks off duty, in August 1977, when I went to Kansas to celebrate our parent's forty-fifth anniversary." In reflection, she was glad to have spent the time with them. On an earlier wedding anniversary she wrote: "Over the years, you will probably think back that all has worked out for the best, just like in the Gospel, 'For those who love God, all things work together for a good.'"

There is an adage reminding parents, "The greatest gift a father can give his children is to love their mother." Solid and healthy marriages have a foundation of trust, commitment and respect. Our parents had all that, and more. Dad was a caring husband and father, and a good son, too.

After his father P.H. Roy died, in 1960, Dad heeded the biblical words of Timothy: "Give proper recognition to those widows who are really in need. But if a widow had children or grandchildren, these should learn first to put their religion into practice by caring for their own family, and so repaying their parents and grandparents, for this is pleasing to God." Mother was considered a fine daughter-in-law and together she and Dad often visited his mother in the Solomon Valley Manor nursing home south of Stockton, before Grandmother Roy died, in 1971.

"A son's a son 'till he takes him a wife, but a daughter's a daughter for the rest of her life," goes the proverb, but this did not ring true for Dad, or his sons. Even after marriage, father and sons remained emotionally close to their parents, but none were ever "mama's boys." Furthermore, as a mother-in-law, Mother was not meddlesome and adhered to the adage, "Once you've made your bed, you lie in it."

Our parents attended a Marriage Encounter Weekend that, as Mother was quick to point out, "was not for troubled marriages." As part of the structured program, they composed love letters to the other. "Dear Johnnie my love," Mother wrote, "The reason I was attracted to you many years ago was because of your kindness and thoughtfulness. You made me a better person. I wouldn't change you in any way because growing old is just another phase of life — and who wants to be young again. We've had our share of happiness, joy and sorrow. That goes with life. There have been good times and hard times, but I really think that's what made us grow so strong — like two old oak trees."

"I think the secret to our happy marriage was praying together," Mother wrote later in life. "Each night we kneeled together beside our bed, even when

John was home between hospital visits and so sick."

A wonderfully steady man, he lived the gospel, and set a fine example in his speech and deeds. "My dad was an extremely patient man, and so gentle," said Sister Veronica. "He was most at peace riding the tractor in the fields, surely one with the Creator."

It seemed that Dad was blessed with an intuitive nature from an early age, along with a keen sense of practical judgment, although his sensitive and nervous stomach never eased up. He never bothered others with his troubles, stoically keeping them inside. He battled several cases of gastric ulcers treating them with a concoction he called "kickapoo juice," of squeezed cabbage and carrots.

While he was also burdened with low blood pressure, cigarettes were ultimately the death of him. Having smoked since age twelve, when cigarettes were readily available to children, and there were no warning labels on cigarette packages, Dad was heavily addicted when he died at age sixty-eight. World No Tobacco Day began eleven years later, in 1989. It would be at least that long, and more, before the tobacco industry was confronted, a few lawsuits were filed and settled, and it would be declared official: Cigarettes kill.

During the summer of 1978, Sister Veronica wrote to Father Duane, "In June Dad was diagnosed with inoperable lung cancer. It does not sound like surgery is even an option. I feel the doctor is aloof, evasive, and not telling Dad much. Or maybe Dad is the one who is not saying. I told him I just might call the doctor myself and he blurted out, 'Won't do you any good.'"

She did call. The doctor told her the cancer was in both lungs, but had not spread to the lymph glands. "They hoped to reduce mass size and ease the pain — to palliate — for one to two years. I am not inclined to habitually ask for healing of one who has already enjoyed so much of life, and has already lived it fruitfully. I tend to let things be much as they are. But, I do feel for Dad's suffering."

She was realistic. "According to statistics, cancer of the lung occurs in twenty-two percent of male cancer patients, but thirty-three percent of patients die. I look for the worse — that it is more widespread then the doctors indicate, since Dad had too many other problems before. He was admitted to the hospital in June with stomach pains, his sciatic nerve bothered him, and his appetite has been poor. He's had emphysema, and a chronic cough for several years. Still, the doctor told him there was no reason he couldn't go home, and eat and drink, just as well as he was doing at the hospital.

"I told Dad that Medicare covers ninety days; Blue Cross covers thirty; and he has almost used those up. If he would go home, or to a nursing facility for two months, he would be eligible to start over on the 90+30 days for insurance coverage. Then Mr. Hollern from the [Solomon Valley] nursing home stopped by. Dad must have shocked Hollern when he asked, 'Have you got any extra rooms?'

Hospice programs were later introduced in the United States, but these were not available in Rooks County at this time.

"Later I asked Dad what the nursing home would offer that he couldn't do at home. He confessed that at home he sees things that need to be done, and in the hospital bed he doesn't think about any of that. What bothered him most was wheat is still only $2.85 a bushel and he hasn't yet collected on the milo, or pasture rent. I said, 'Let me send a bill for the pasture.' He told me what to write, and seemed relieved to have that done. I don't pray for very many special things, but this time I really prayed that wheat prices jump fast so he can sell it, and settle down in peace.[1]

"Later, after getting Dad home from the hospital at two in the afternoon, he wanted to sell his wheat. I drove him to Palco, then Damar, where he sold three truckloads for $2.98. Up 13 cents per bushel since I prayed! What we each set out to accomplish is not exactly what is to happen through us. I never dreamed I'd be running around helping him with some secretarial detail. Later, the wheat prices went to $3.00, but I think he was satisfied."

In another letter to Father Duane she added, "Dad has been complaining all week of pain and coldness in both arms. Sounds like poor circulation. He is too weak even to turn doorknobs. He has been in and out of the house trying to warm up. He wanted to drive out to look at the watermelon patch, and the milo crop, which he is waiting to sell at $2.70 a bushel."

"I got talked into helping Mother make pressed dried flower greeting cards. This is no place to write letters, read, pray, or study without pretending to be asleep. Afterward Mother went into town. Dad and I sat and rocked for an hour, mostly in silence and 'Mickey Mouse' talk, until I finally shared with him that, as a child, I was afraid of having to let go, someday, of this beautiful world, and how this summer has really helped put things in place for me, and appreciate people more, too. I talked of why we like to sit, just appreciating beauty, and knowing it will go on even if we don't move a finger."

During this time she found solace in the book, *St. John of the Cross: Living Flame of Love*: "With respect to the spirit, there are two kinds of life; one is beatific, which consists in seeing God, and this will be attained by means of the natural death of the body."[2]

Dad expressed an interest in knowing more about laetrile, an alternative medicine offered at treatment centers in Mexico. He read a book on the topic, although did not pursue it further.

While not the wealthiest man in the county, Dad amassed property, having risen from humble beginnings, like the honest and prosperous, yet dying farmer, Wang Lung, in Pearl Buck's *The Good Earth*. "Of his land he thought no more what harvest it would bring or what seed would be planted or of anything except of the land itself, and he stooped sometimes and gathered some of the earth up in his hand and he sat thus and held it in his hand, and it seemed full of life between his fingers."[3]

At home from the hospital, Dad spent each crisp, fall day looking out the large south-facing "picture" window and napping on the carpeted living room floor, bathed in the warm afternoon sun. Other times he sat outside on the front steps, pensively gazing over some of the 400 acres accumulated over their years together. Looking toward Sand Creek, the cottonwoods were turning golden-yellow, orange and red, and Mother wondered if he knew this was the last autumn of his life. He knew.

Sister Veronica was the one to keep Father Duane informed in faraway Brazil. "It will be a difficult responsibility to let you know when you should come to his side," she wrote after a terminal diagnosis was made. He came to stay for the month of October. Coincidentally, after his return, all airmail was suspended going into Brazil, due to a postal strike, and her mail to him was returned twice.

"I have no idea how effective laser radiotherapy is," Sister Veronica continued in another letter. "His cancer doctor comes from Wichita only occasionally. They expected side effects of nausea, fatigue, loss of appetite, and difficulty swallowing during the six weeks of radiation, but not so soon in the third week. Apparently, technicians administering the treatments badly burned his esophagus."

In fact, his esophagus was raw and damaged and she could see that it caused him great pain to swallow. These were before the days of slow-release morphine patches for the terminally ill. Consequently, Dad lost all appetite. His primary cause of death was malnutrition, secondary to cancer.

She told Dad that proper nutrition was important for keeping up the body's defense in fighting cancer cells, but it was too late. "Malnutrition is of significant concern, so I urged him to be concerned if his doctor wants to hospitalize him for intravenous feedings," she wrote beforehand. He did return to the hospital.

Throughout medical school, doctors have only one-hour focused on nutrition. With Sister Veronica's professional background, it took special diligence on her part to refrain from saying, "If he would eat something, he would feel better." His doctor did just that and asked Mother to prepare his favorite food. The next day Mother brought homemade navy bean soup into his hospital room. Eating only a few spoonfuls became a burden, making it even more difficult for him to breath. The body needs very little food for the brain, heart and lungs when it begins to shut down.

Earlier, when Dad was at home between several hospital visits, his pastor, Father Joseph Weimer, who had been in Stockton for three years, routinely drove out to the farm to give Dad communion. Father Weimer also went to the hospital to give Dad communion, as the Eucharist serves as the *viaticum* for passing over to eternal life. He administered the Anointing of the Sick, too, just days before Dad's death, just as Father Duane did during his month-long stay.

Currently only a Priest can administer the sacrament, (once called the Last Rites.) Will that change with the outcome of a proposed Vatican III? Will Sisters, or even laypersons, in the near or distant future, be allowed to anoint the dying? This would have been a natural extension for Sister Veronica in the scope of her hospice services throughout her rural ministry in later years.

Pope Paul VI, and Pope John Paul I both died that same year, and Pope John Paul II was elected six weeks before Dad's death.

"I am afraid it won't be much longer that we have dear Dad, and this letter will be out of place by time you receive it," she wrote to Father Duane before the ease of faxes and e-mail. "When I called Mother today to tell her to pick me up, at the bus station in Hays, it took me three minutes of talking before I could choke out, 'I'm coming.'"

The loss of hand strength distressed Dad. He resisted IVs, which disrupted his peace and serenity. Suddenly less tolerant of conversation when the large family gathered in his hospital room, he turned his back, which was confusing and a cause of anguish to his loved ones. He seemed to become detached. However, this behavior is normal, as the dying move from the physical world, into the spiritual realm. Sister Veronica knew this. Once death was eminent, she ministered to his soul.

In their mind the dying seemingly go through a state of confusion as they go about their chores, or regress to their childhood where they do not recognize their own children, because at their stage of regression, children have not yet been born. Dad did not experience this although, on occasion in his final days his mind regressed at times when he prayed aloud, in fluent French, a language not spoken since childhood.

Sister Veronica's last visit with Dad was three weeks before he died. "He was sleeping with his eyes open, which I understand is a sign of great weakness. I called Doctor Votapka's office, in Stockton, and he said it seemed Dad had given up. He said Dad talked at great length with Mother that morning."

She regretted not living closer to our parents, although she took as much time, and as many long weekends, as she possibly dared from her hospital dietetic work. During each visit she could only stay a few days due to her schedule. The twelve-hour drive, each way, was tiring. On occasion, she took the long twenty-three-hour bus ride from Rockford, Illinois. Family members living in Kansas gathered, too, as well as those from Colorado and Idaho, to spend with Dad at home, at St. Anthony's in Hays, and later at Plainville Rural Hospital where he died.

On the last day of November 1978, Sister Veronica made the somber and long journey to bury Dad, braving the treacherous and icy driving conditions, heading west on Interstate 80, across northern Illinois and Nebraska, before turning south into Kansas.

Back at work, she wrote in her Christmas letter, "This year will be touched with missing Dad. Let us recognize that we have come into a tremendous inheritance of his love for life. Each of us must live out in our own life the gifts we have received from him. For some of us we find we have his gifts of listening, contentment, and friendship, gentleness, perseverance, and patience." The qualities she described in Dad suited her, as well.

She said seven months later, "I think of him so much these June days with lots of sentimental dates — Father's Day, [often falling on] his birthday [the summer solstice], the first of his hospitalizations, and of course harvest time, too, being such a part of his life."

Even years later she said, "Dad continues to be a strong presence to me." Several family members also continued to feel his spiritual presence, and especially at her twenty-fifth Silver Jubilee. Sister Veronica fully adhered to the belief that even though a family member has died that does not mean they are no longer a part of your life. She felt close to many ancestors who passed on long before she was born, especially in her genealogy writings.

"I asked Father John Walsh to say Mass at seven p.m. when we meet at Roger's house in Stockton for Thanksgiving week, as it is Dad's seventh anniversary of death." When this writer composed a poem on the tenth anniversary of Dad's death, Sister Veronica wrote to me, "Your poem was a real tear-jerker." Subtlety, the loss and remembrance came to the surface repeatedly. "By tomorrow, I wanted all siblings to get the enclosed prayer, 'On the Anniversary of Losing a Parent.'"

"Each time an old person dies, a library burns down," goes the saying. Dad carried many stories to the grave, and left few written documents. After he died, Mother was encouraged to pour out her memories, many of which are included here.

Within a month of Dad's death, Sister Veronica said, "I tend to think of Mother as rather strong, but dependent. She does not hesitate to call for help, which could get rather old. During Roger and Rodney's visits she seems to ask them to do things. I've noticed in her conversations, with friends, she seems to switch back to her memories, experiences, and feelings, particularly as related to Dad's illness. I pray for her that she will trust herself, her own judgments, and capabilities. And that she, as we all need the facility, may listen more deeply to what others say, and share what they experience, and outwardly comfort others, as we have been comforted."

✝

Chapter Twenty-two

"I often regretted not accepting an eight-hour-a-month consulting position with the [Belvidere Manor] nursing home. It would have afforded me contact with the pioneers in the nation's consulting dietetic field," Sister Veronica said. She declined the offer due to Dad's illness, making the long drive to Kansas as often as she could.

The year before, in 1977 she co-chaired the two-day state dietetic assembly of Illinois Dietitians, in Rockford. "We had 850 attendees, and it was quite a success. Perhaps now I can return to the gentler lifestyle, if that's what He wants of me."

The spring after Dad died she was asked to accept the nomination to ballot for incoming president of the Illinois Dietetic Association. "I declined. I couldn't even keep on top of my own work. Furthermore, I felt I had peaked as a professional and felt certain that I would be leaving the area within a year or so, which I did. Professionally, I was visible at the state level, serving [within 1968-79] as district president, treasurer, program chair, state convention co-chair and committeewoman for bylaws and diet therapy."

Among her varied extra-curricular activities was helping form the Diocesan Sisters Council of Rockford. This council set up educational programs, the whys of reporting and receiving information from the Bishop, the Constitution and area salary surveys. She also worked on the second draft of the CSJ position paper on "Life and Ministry of Religious" for the Diocesan Synod.

While the Meals on Wheels Association of America was not formed until 1974, Sister Veronica was on the cutting edge of the local program in 1972.[1] "Under the Area Agency of Aging, which was just beginning, I took the Mobile Meals project and made it work well between the two local hospitals and community church volunteers." The guiding principle of this program was to help the elderly, homebound, disabled, frail or those at risk.

She developed early in life a fondness and respect for the elderly. During a single month in 1979 she traveled to Chicago six times, as well as attended seven funerals. "I also took Sister Midreda CaVallo to Chicago to visit her three invalid sisters. I have been trying to get some ministerial visiting in to sick and dear, old friends."

Over the years she wrote of her employment. "I have been working on a new budget of $263,000 for dietary, plus have to budget capital expenditures for equipment. Next year, I am supposed to keep below nine percent increases, but have been working to increase the pay levels of three of my employees who had more responsibility, the past year, without proper recompense."

Following one blizzard she said, "For three days I had seven employees who couldn't get into work, so many activities got canceled, but hospital life goes on. The maintenance crew is putting new synthetic walls and ceilings in our three walk-in refrigerators and freezers, so they have to be emptied.

"I have been busy, mostly with purchasing and implementing new menus. For heart month, in February, each day I posted the recommended cafeteria menu from which employees could select, along with some educational blurbs on heart-healthy eating.

"Last month we started serving steak and champagne candlelight dinners to the new mothers and fathers the night before they take the baby home. We really don't need any gimmicks to promote our place, but there is nothing wrong with celebrating.

"I got a new diet manual edited and implemented, as well as more-sophisticated adult and pediatric nutritional education, since this is the International Year of the Child.

"Seems like everything I've worked for here at St. Joseph's, these ten and a half years, is coming to a head. I think administration thinks some of my projects are good ideas. Although, sometimes I feel insubordinate in persistence, but if [the hospital administrator] wants ideas and well-written position papers, I'll keep throwing him more. He has commented so much about free food to Medicare recipients, students and doctors that I gave him a paper ending with six alternatives. But I've heard no response."

A few months later she wrote, "The Administrator [a lay person] really exploded at me for starting an evaluation and recommendation process. He seems threatened and seems to think I want to do the deciding, and has told me he runs this place! I never had anyone talk to me so rough, letting me know, 'I just work here to carry out the policies he makes, and that he does not have to discuss any policies with me before he makes them, and he says, furthermore, what I learned at Leadership Workshops in Kansas do not pertain here.' But of course they do! It is the whole power cycle of Evaluate, Recommend, Decide and Act. I very well understand my role, as a department head, is to put policies into action, evaluate conditions, and make recommendations.

"It seems he is threatened by the department heads, particularity me and the Chaplain, when we make recommendations. Both of us really "got it" several days apart without knowing that the other also did. I really thought he was going to fire me, but I would have taken it to Arbitration/Reconciliation Board of the Diocese. I learn a lot from getting older. Is it true that wisdom comes only with experience?

"The Administrator has built up a distrust of the Chaplin and forbids him to handle the collection of money. It is absolutely groundless, and reflective of the doubt he has of what the Chaplain does during his hours on duty. The Administrator questions the number of his visits to patients, and anointings. It is really dumb, and I am sure very embarrassing to the Chaplain."

She was away for a few weeks and upon her return she found the Chaplain was leaving that weekend and transferring to a neighboring parish because of impossible relations with the Administrator.

"Things are just cold now. It is very likely that a big part of the issue is declining morale in this place. [The administrator] believes the issue is second-rate bad food and poor cafeteria service for the evening shift. It is ironic because patients, medical students, visitors, and half of the Sisters compliment us on dietary service.

"I know from my position and longevity that I am biased and half-blind, but I still feel the issue is not food. Nevertheless, I have worked on visible changes this past week with quality and quantity of food, plus in-services on personal attitudes, with those involved, and especially that as a service department we are here to serve others, not ourselves."

She continued to struggle. "I have been rather depressed about my employment here, as I am trying to discern the whole Belvidere hospital picture, and the Gospel message of knowing when it is time to shake the dust from my shoes and move on." And shortly after she repeated, "I have felt some unrest about work, and the [stability of the] CSJ Community here, these past several months. It is rather unsettling because there are not a lot of choices — where to, Lord — as far as dietary work for the Community. I am considering a change. Nothing serious, just praying to listen to the Lord's Will. I am most desirous of knowing how, and where best to serve Him, without concern for my own need for support."

A year or so earlier she said, "Our hospital-patient census remains at 30 to 35 percent," which may help explain some of the pressure the hospital administrator was under, having been hired the beginning of 1977. Later she added, "We are not doing well here this summer. Census continues to decline since May, right when it gets crucial for either being in the black, or the red. Some of this is due to doctors taking vacation, but I think the real reason is the shortened length of hospital stays. Medicare indicates how many days a patient may stay, so we have almost complete turnover of patients within five days."

And then she commented, "We have been very busy this winter. The medical and surgical wings have stayed full, but no babies since last month. The other hospital in town beat us in purchasing a new piece of fetal monitor equipment, so doctors are taking all their patients there. It appears, across the nation, that Catholic hospitals may be giving up obstetric services rather than refusing people what they want. I am trying so hard to know what does make a

Catholic hospital."

What she suspected came true. "Administration announced the closing of our maternity/obstetrics department in August, so that has lowered the morale of almost everyone, especially the Sisters. It means we will lose potential family units as patients. For once I am afraid we may be folding up before much longer, unless we change something drastically, like reaching out to where the real needs are. For example, start an alcoholic detoxify unit, or one for the terminally ill. Both of which were rejected by administration.

"In September [1979] he fired our sixty-seven-year-old Sister, head of OB, in a fiery rage, in a hot temper, which everyone knows he has. I feel I should try to correct some of this. I have reflected so much on this in my own unpleasant encounters this winter and spring. We are gifted. We have to speak up, and contribute what we can in any situation, although I am very intimidated about it now. It is just not worth the uncomfortable feeling,

"This action has left the employees and others angry. He is changing the story now that employees have heard of it. I submitted a news release titled 'A Legend Leaves Belvidere.'"

According to Sister Diane Brin, the head of obstetrics, Sister Agnes Marie L'Allier, was one of Sister Veronica's best friends. "Sister Veronica knew the details and how to get stories published in the newspaper about her friend, who had been there thirty-six years. Sister Agnes Marie was truly a living legend in the lives of families. They kept her memory alive by telling each new generation that she was with them during each of their births."

Sister Agnes Marie had given her life to the hospital. While the department was being closed for financial reasons, this treatment didn't seem fair to Sister Veronica. Since the Sister was not paid much, money could hardly have been the issue. What could have been treated as a retirement, or layoff, became known internally as a "firing." She felt the injustice and painful hurt for her friend. Surely she thought, "If a compassionate and dedicated Sister could be dumped by this administration, they could do it to me just as easily."

"I drove Sister Agnes Marie to Concordia last weekend to await her new assignment. At that time, I talked with House Superiors about the situation. They leave it up to me with the exhortation that 'one Sister cannot take upon herself a whole Community commitment to an institution.'"

Sister Christine Doman remarked, "It seems Veronica did act out of her own conviction and conscience in this matter. Her actions express the love she had toward those involved, and the conviction with which she chose to move out of the situation. There were hardships endured."

It was not unusual for Sister Veronica to spend the weekend with Aunt Jeannette and Uncle Bill, as she was welcome anytime to stay in their lovely home not far from Belvidere. She often went with the excuse of using our aunt's sewing machine. On one occasion Sister Veronica was on her knees using the floor as a spacious workspace. With her back bent, she took time to pin and cut the fabric to perfection, matching the plaids just right, as she had been taught in 4-H twenty-five years earlier. All the while animated and almost in a joking manner, she expressed her dismay at the injustice of the firing of her friend. Aunt Jeannette said, "I could tell she felt intensely about this issue, and she was quite disgusted. This seemed to add to her reason to resign, perhaps in protest."

The combination of the firing of her dear friend, Dad's death ten months earlier, a busy schedule and exhaustion took its toll. "My very first hospitalization — for twenty-four hours. I was not responding to medication for a dry cough. I've been sleeping a lot. I think my resistance was lowered due to a depressed and intimidated spirit. I have just gotten over a nine-week bout of bronchitis. It felt more like whooping cough, mono and asthma."

Over the years Sister Veronica had become more vocal and open with newfound purpose and vigor. Her letters were filled with truer feelings. "Some of my moments of deepest revelation and insight have come from the hard times — the mistakes. I have also begun to see more clearly my anxiety and relative lack of trust [in myself]. If I were ever to develop an ulcer, or hypertension, it should have been by now.

"It isn't quite so embarrassing anymore to admit I don't have reports ready or schedules not posted on time. It was hard for a while to let a day close, knowing so much was yet undone, especially when I didn't even have the energy to pray. I preferred just to romanticize about falling asleep in the Lord's loving arms. So I pray the dear Lord to grace me with the sense to hang looser, to allow Him to do His work through me, to enjoy waiting time now.

She gave the future more thought and came to discern about moving elsewhere. "I appreciate the article on hospitals in Inner Cities. That sort of confirmed my feeling. I look for the CSJ Motherhouse to pull out of their commitment to this hospital, and let Sisters work and live where they can, with our other Sisters." This is indeed what later happened.

Adhering to the belief that everyone deserves the right to basic health care, the mission of Catholic hospitals is to provide treatment at the appropriate place, and at the lowest possible cost, all the while to be responsible to Catholicity, rather than to the shareholders. The situation for St. Joseph's, and other Catholic hospitals over the nation, forced them to cut costs and reduce duplication of services. Catholic hospitals, then and today, began to form partnerships with other hospitals so they would not be excluded from managed-care contracts.

More than twenty years later, in 2002 with the 29th anniversary of Roe v. Wade, the ACLU and MergerWatch are targeting the more than 600 Catholic hospitals and those dozens of mergers linking Catholic and non-Catholic hospitals. Their issue is that by receiving Medicaid and Medicare payments Catholic hospitals must, in turn, provide women with every service, including reproductive health services of their choice — a way of saying abortion and sterilizations must be made available.

According to *Footprints on the Frontier*, written in 1948, St. Joseph's Hospital, Belvidere, has always had a difficult existence.[2] Nevertheless, a new hospital was completed in 1961. Changes in policy and problems continued to loom in the horizon. After she left, the hospital did change sponsorship, in the late 1980s, under the direction of CSJ President Sister Mary Savoie from her office at the Motherhouse in Concordia.[3] The hospital ultimately closed in September 1999.

Sister Christine Doman offered, "It was a very emotional time for us. These were trying times for the Sisters who were in hospital ministry, because we didn't have the personnel or finances to keep them. Divesting ourselves of these dear ministries took a toll on our patience, and letting go of them was most difficult. [These years were] a time of great stress, change, and decision-making for Veronica, and this occurrence reflects the strength she had to hold fast to her vocation through difficult times."

Sister Veronica lamented extensively over the issue and could see the handwriting on the wall. Financial considerations began to create a reduction in staff hospital-wide, including her own department.

Another deciding factor for her may have been that her friend, Sister Frances Alma Royer, was going to be named House Superior at the hospital, but moved to another convent location instead. With each new letter Sister Veronica grew closer to a resolution about moving on. She had no definite plans, but in anticipation of a long-awaited trip to Brazil to visit our brother, she had a passport photo taken at Dale's Studio in Belvidere.

Finally in November she said, "Tomorrow night I am announcing to the Sisters my intention to resign, as of January 11, 1980, then announce to Administration the next day. This place will be shaky with me gone. Of only eight of us still here, five are more than sixty-two years old."

Her replacement was a laywoman. "The new dietitian starts tomorrow, following me around all week, so that will be the hardest part of all, talking constantly and explaining things. Although we are not that busy with patients, and I have all my administrative work done."

She said with a tone of poignancy, "This has been a lovely place these eleven years. These experiences affirmed me richly, and I felt capable. The Sisters of St. Joseph were quite loved in the Belvidere community. We felt supported even when there were serious studies about closing, or merging with the other hospital in town."

During this time she developed strong friendships and reclaimed her voice.

"I felt strong enough to venture out into the Lord's plan, of which I knew not where." She resigned as head of dietetics with her eyes wide open. "It will be hard getting a job like the one I have, where I can be my own boss in the department. I could work at Highlands, the other local hospital, but I am considering moving to another city where our other Sisters live. I need to live with some younger Sisters awhile.

"It would be nice to be closer to Motherhouse activities at Concordia, and of course, closer to my family. I hoped for a job in Manhattan, Kansas, so I could do some studies at K-State, but just last week it was announced the Sisters were ready to sell that hospital and pull out of town."

"I am hoping to get into St. Mary's [Hospital] in Kansas City, or St. Joseph's or St. Francis Hospital in Wichita, (which has 400+ beds) so I can get specialized experience in clinical dietetics. If nothing opens, I'll try the 200+ bed places in Kansas City, Topeka, Salina, Great Bend, or Omaha.

"I think I will leave job-hunting until after my trip to Brazil," Sister Veronica said. "It is so hard to know what to do. I feel some peace about it, but it will be difficult to leave here. It just seems if I could be more faithful to prayer, the answer would be clearer, but God seems to give me answers when I am least expecting them."

✝

Chapter Twenty-three

Ten days after resigning her position as hospital dietitian, and at Mother's longtime insistence, Sister Veronica flew to Brazil in January 1980, for a month-long vacation. There was no job to come home to. "I knew not where I was going, but my time had come to move on. It was part of transferring to the unknown — my faith journey."

Our parents had traveled to Brazil in 1974, and soon after they wanted Sister Veronica to experience the foreign land where our brother had been living since 1971. She planned to take up our parents offer for her 20th anniversary.

She wrote to Father Duane in early 1978: "There is so much awareness that I have to gain in meeting other people, and participating in another lifestyle. I reiterate that I am not much for going to see things, but I do appreciate soaking in an experience, which affects my whole lifestyle and vision."

She wanted this to be a slow-paced trip, "making part of it into a retreat during a long bus ride, perhaps going part way on a freighter." She especially wanted it to be "a pilgrimage to be in touch with the needy, and experience the humbling effect of being so helpless and not even understanding, and the gift to be able to live with the shock upon returning to the States and its luxury." Being exposed to the home economics of Brazilian life was important for her, too. "The food, the ways of preparing and home life."

Of highest priority was to meet the people who supported our brother, Father Duane Roy in his lifestyle and community. There he was called Dom Rui, pronounced *Who-ee* in Portuguese.

"I know I couldn't master enough language to travel a great deal by myself, although I am trying to learn a few phrases. I was never confident with languages, so I do fear traveling alone." She had struggled with the verbal part of college French and was realistic about learning a foreign language due to poor hearing, and inability to distinguish many sounds.

She postponed the scheduled trip in 1978, due to the diagnosis of Dad's cancer. That summer she wrote to Father Duane, "I cannot make plans to visit. It has been delightful in planning, but I can let it go with no regrets. Perhaps there will be another time, and we will know when it should be. I want it to be when it would profit both of us, and so have not set a new date."

After Dad died the farm equipment was sold, and Mother generously shared the profits with her children. Sister Veronica said, "I hope Mother understands I get all I need and want from the proceeds, even though the donated gift is to the CSJ Community [as my patrimony]. The Motherhouse has assured me that when I am ready to travel, the money is there.

"I could put the trip off another year or so, in case Mother changes her mind and decides to come with me. She says 'No,' but I suspect she doesn't want to try duplicating a wonderful experience she had with Dad." Bravely, Mother did take a second trip by herself, in 1982, two years after Sister Veronica's return.

Sister Veronica's travel to Brazil in 1980 was all, and then some, of what she expected. The words of Marcel Proust echoed this stage: "The real voyage of discovery consists not in seeing new landscapes, but in having 'new eyes.'" Her new eyes acted as a catalyst for what lay ahead in her remaining years.

She visited Carlos Eduardo De Queiroz Bezerra, a Brazilian foreign exchange student who lived with our parents six years earlier. "Carlos' parents showed enormous hospitality, with their Latin affection, and could not do enough to make Veronica feel welcome into their home in Recife, Pernambuco," said Father Duane. "Her travel coincided with the world-famous Carnival of Rio de Janeiro. Dancing the Samba, and rubbing shoulders in the streets, she took in the warm and intimate culture of the Brazilians.

"The trip was a workshop in new attitudes and methods of working with people. During her years of service in a hospital environment she was a stickler for strict sterile guidelines. Here, she was appalled to see the unsanitary conditions where people ate and slept, and was aghast to see the way they washed dishes. She saw real poverty and destitution — people grappling with the bare necessities of life. What she saw changed her future forever."

Some have claimed that the pre-Vatican II church was for the rich; the emphasis was on faith, worship and right behavior. Yet Pope Pius XII (in office 1939-1958) called for the Leadership Conference of Women Religious to be engaged in social action, advocating disinvestments in South Africa, and forcible land reform and redistribution in Latin America.

From 1963 to 1978, spanning the same years Sister Veronica spent in hospital dietetic work in Cincinnati, Concordia, and Belvidere, Pope Paul VI's greatest achievement was to put the Catholic Church, and the papacy itself, in the center of the world stage. His visit to New York and address at the United Nations were landmark events. He abolished the Index of Forbidden Books, introduced a retiring age for Bishops, inaugurated the Synod of Bishops, and did away with some of the flamboyant features of clerical attire. Perhaps two important aspects of his papacy that spoke to Sister Veronica, was his commitment to work for justice throughout the entire world and his awareness of mankind's struggle.

All Church members, as disciples and servants, are called to holiness and to spread the gospel of Christ. The Church has had a developing social doctrine since the late 1900s, and began to see itself as, "the people of God." As a result of the Second Vatican Council, the mission of the Catholic Church became even more concerned with the social justice needs of the poor and oppressed. The Pastoral Constitution of Vatican II declared that the church shares "the joy and hope, the grief and anguish of contemporary humanity, particularly of the poor and afflicted." It also included building an international understanding, assuming a clearer responsibility for the fate of the world opening before its eyes.

To this end, the Sisters of St. Joseph of Concordia took up a mission in Teresina, Piauí, Brazil beginning the year after Vatican II convened. Sister Donna Otter, one of Sister Veronica's fellow "Sixteen Prophets," moved there.

In 1994 Sister Donna took an indefinite sabbatical from her mission work in Teresina, having been there since its inception thirty years earlier. Sister Veronica spoke highly of her friend. "Sister Donna has numerous relatives in New Almelo so I am happy to await some time visiting with her." Her brother was one of Sister Veronica's neighbors there, and she was pleased to keep in touch. "We entered the convent together, and I always thought the world of her." Sister Veronica was sympathetic to her friend's plight upon returning to the States. "She went there when she was about twenty-six years old, before she even finished college, so I am sure she will feel inadequate in the U.S. trying to job hunt."

After her return, Sister Donna learned the therapeutic art of foot massage, and practiced for a time at Junction City, Kansas. Sister Veronica wrote, "She wanted to learn something concrete. I can understand there is little satisfaction in women's pastoral ministry, unless one is actually doing something."

Irmã (translates as Sister) Verlene de Freitas Leal, a native CSJ from Brazil, visited Concordia on her trip to the U.S. Within several months Sister Veronica noted, "Already she has learned English very well. Sister Pat Neihouse, who lives in Brazil, came for the Senate meeting. A third Sister, Pat Vaughan is finishing coursework at Notre Dame so she can return to Brazil to be a school superintendent in the state of Piauí.

During her travels, Sister Veronica did arrange a major side trip to the northern part of Brazil, seeing the Sisters of St. Joseph at the convent in Teresina happily doing their work with a sense of purpose, real results and effective returns. In the capital city of Goiânia she saw the dedicated work of the Franciscan Sisters of Joliet, Illinois. She visited a group of CSJs from Rochester, New York working in the small interior town of Caçu, Goiás.

She also visited Benedictine Sisters from Atchison, Kansas who had taken up a mission in Mineiros, Goiás. One of them, Sister Elaine Gregory, OSB, spoke in later years of a heart-wrenching episode, after being on mission in Brazil only a short time and having not yet mastered the Portuguese language: "I saw a grieving, new mother carrying her dead infant through the streets, and I had no words to comfort her. All I could do was embrace her to extend my deep sorrow."

Mother Teresa earned sainthood for her work in Calcutta. There are many other

Sisters and laywomen, too, who also sacrifice personal comfort, and sometimes their lives, for others. These women give their all to take up the earthly work of Christ, at home and abroad. There are numerous tales, including those from a former Sister, our cousin Juanita Morin Wald, of the harrowing, yet rewarding experiences of living in extreme primitive conditions, forgoing an easier life as she took in their culture while living with the natives of Chad, Africa.

The Second Vatican Council aimed, among many other things, to end cultural isolation, or stated positively, to promote the appreciation of all cultures. The term, *inculturation*, began to creep into the Church's vocabulary. Evangelization can take place only when the Church first inculturates itself in each culture, respecting it and blending local spiritual riches.

Eight years after her Brazil trip, three Sisters from the Brazil missions stayed with Sister Veronica at her WaKeeney, Kansas convent-home. "This is the first U.S. visit for Nair and Antônia, both professed twenty years. Only two other Brazilian Sisters have been to the States," she wrote. "They were delighted with all the souvenirs and photos I have around the house from Brazil, and noticed the keepsake box that Linda brought back for me from her visit last month." Her visitors, Sisters Patricia Neihouse, Irmã Antônia Pierote and Irmã Nair, thanked her for the hospitality: "God bless you and accompany your steps in Christ's reign and Kingdom."

After Sister Veronica returned home she wrote to Father Duane, "I wonder how your preparations are coming along for the new seminary. Have you talked the Brazilian Sisters into helping with some courses? That's the thing nowadays — Women [Religious influence] in the seminary."

Through his writings, Thomas Merton (1915-1968), the Trappist Monk of Gethsemani Abbey in Kentucky, voiced the concerns of many Religious. He told of his own spiritual journey, which gave confidence and inspiration to others. In his writings, he covered issues of contemplative prayer, political struggle and social justice as integral aspects of religious commitment.

After Vatican II, Sister Veronica, and others, began reading Merton's writings, the works of Dorothy Day, Mother Teresa, the Polish solidarity founder and 1983 Nobel winner, Lech Walesa, and "brother of the poor," Brazilian Archbishop Dom Hélder Câmara, among others. She learned from the writings.

Following the Latin America Episcopal Conferences at Medillin, Columbia (1968) and at Puebla, Mexico (1979), the Latin Church became strongly committed to the total liberation of the poor. Sister Veronica began to appreciate the efforts of many Priests and Nuns to become actively involved in the organization of the poor to defend their rights and denounce social and economic injustices. The new wave of Liberation Theology in Latin America gave a theological base to support the struggle of the impoverished and the oppressed.

Several years after Father Duane moved there, some Brazilian theologians were in trouble with the Vatican for disseminating Liberation Theology. Still today, theologians gather from Brazil, Peru, Costa Rica, Bolivia, Panama, Columbia, Ecuador, Haiti, Mexico, Chile, El Salvador, and more to discuss liberation spirituality, political models and the preferential option for the poor — a central axis of liberation theology. Some conservatives, including Pope John Paul II, criticize the mixture of evangelism and Marxism.

Currently, there is a strong renewal of social concern and social doctrine among many Catholics and Evangelicals. Biblical studies began to take on new understanding, once read through the eyes of the oppressed. Empowered by awareness, organization and dignity, the poor classes can become a decisive factor in social and economic change in these Third World Countries. They are the majority of the population. Liberation Theology legitimizes this conviction showing God on the side of the oppressed.

The words of farm-labor organizer and spokesperson for the downtrodden, Cesar Chavez succinctly attests, "I am convinced that the truest act of courage, the strongest act of humanity, is to sacrifice ourselves for others in a totally nonviolent struggle for justice. To be human means to suffer for others. God helps us to be human."

Father Duane had already worked nine years in Brazil when Sister Veronica visited him. He had absorbed the culture of the people in the interior of the vast country. He was sympathetic with liberation spiritually of Central and South America.

During her visit Sister Veronica witnessed first hand how the positive effects of his practical and grass roots political actions took hold in less than his ten years there. She came to understand that work with the poor is more than giving aid and assistance. Perhaps like St. Francis of Assisi another champion of the poor, Father Duane didn't go to convert the Brazilians — he went to be with them as friend and brother. Sister Veronica wrote during this trip, "Each home is so proud to have Duane and I stop in. They treat me as a queen, being a sister of their *Padre*. One can surely tell they love him."

This sentiment was echoed twenty years later when five members of our family visited Brazil. Nearly 2,000 of his supporters gathered to welcome and embrace the family of their beloved spiritual leader, in an unprecedented reception with food, gifts and cultural talent.

The author Patricia Hampl writes, "This 'suffering while being with' creates a ground of equality missing from other missionary motives with their inevitable one-up/one-down benevolence. Perhaps this is why St. Francis of Assisi has been an attractive model for the liberation theology in the Third World."[1]

Sister Veronica recognized the validity of "being with the other" as mission. She would later speak of the "ministry of presence." More than miles measured the distance she traveled on that trip in 1980. Indeed, she experienced culture shock, but she also witnessed profound love and came home a changed person. "I remain grateful for this Third World experience."

Heeding the call to blend faith with the basics of life — food, shelter and human dignity — Father Duane became involved in social populist movements. He helped the poor become more aware of their rights and dignity, and organize in a manner to defend themselves through legitimate channels as opposed to relying on handouts. The former promotes human freedom and personal dignity; the latter promotes dependency though paternalism.

Gandhi-like, but never jailed — although detained — he saw grinding, abject poverty, and economic injustices firsthand. He also saw the need for land reform issues, writing in local newspapers and supporting the National Land Reform Movement. "To avoid [political involvement] is to take a very strong stance in favor of the 'status quo,'" he remarked twenty-five years after first arriving in 1971.

Our brother lived there for nearly thirty years, as a highly respected religious and civic leader, well known throughout the huge interior state of Goiás. As an esteemed leader in the community Father Duane was awarded recognition, in 1999, as one of the six most influential people in the city of Mineiros. It was not uncommon for him to be asked to be involved in civic action, such as mediator regarding teachers' pay raises, or as a peacemaker settling business disputes.

There is a national program of the Catholic Church in Brazil, known internationally as *Pastoral da Criança* (Child Pastoral Program). Established in 1985, this program addresses the nutritional needs of Brazilian women and children to combat infant mortality. Father Duane was adviser to this program in Mineiros during the years 1993 to 2000.

After Sister Veronica's death, Father Duane conceived a way to combine his work with the poor, with her personal interest in nutrition. He projected the construction of "the Sister Veronica Memorial Center" in Mineiros, Goiás. This facility became the administrative center of Pastoral da Criança. The building was dedicated in March 2000 in Sister Veronica's memory.[2]

Among the authorities present for its inauguration was First Lady of Mineiros, Naiba Maria Barcelos, the mayor's wife. She was also the Secretary of Social Services in the county. She and subsequent administrators support this service to women and children. In 2001, this Brazil-wide program was nominated as a candidate for the Nobel Peace Prize. (See the Epilogue at the end of this book for more details.)

Father Duane was not shy in asking for what was needed, whether in asking the First Lady of Goiás, the governor's wife, to provide funds for a car for the *Pastoral da Criança*, or asking locals to support a non-political public service radio station.

Exceedingly active in the ministries of several communities in Mineiros, as well as the humble villages of Santa Rita and Portelândia, he taught Sociology at the local college for ten years, as well as serving on the Board of Directors at the college, and on other civil and church commissions. He trained rural families in advanced agricultural and dairying methods. He was successful in writing grant proposals for the ecology of the nutritional and medicinal use of native plants of the *cerrado*, the high savannahs.

Having looked starvation in the face caused not only by poverty, but also by poor skills and lack of education, Sister Veronica couldn't return to what she left behind. She couldn't go back to just patching up people. She felt called to teach preventive nutrition. "Since I terminated my hospital work as a dietary manager, I don't know that I can ever return to work for people whose real problem is too much food, when I have lived for a month with people struggling to survive. I have to do something to help people not get sick."

Her disdain for waste also prompted creative acts of charity. For example, after our mother's death she sent a dozen or more of Mother's newer brassieres to the sixteen native Sisters in northern Brazil. She also collected more than a hundred tee shirts in various sizes for this writer to take to Brazil during my trip the following year.

At this point, she made a decision to reach out to alternative ministries. The CSJ community is supportive of their Sisters searching out paths to serve health care in non-institutional ways. She began to look for other choices in the medical field, and how she could best use her talents.

The same year as her trip, three Nuns and one layworker were slain in San Salvador. Undaunted, she explored the possibility of working in foreign health care. Sending a formal application to the Catholic Relief Services (CRS) team for mission work in Cambodia, she knew it was, if not dangerous, certainly not without discomfort. Her visit to Brazil drove home the realization of the need for trained professionals in foreign lands.

"I've been waiting to hear if I was accepted for the three-month medical team assignment to assist the refuges in a Thailand camp. That team leaves in May, and another in July. As a RD [registered dietician] I feel I have a chance to serve among the starving people."

A letter notified her that CRS was unable to accept her skills at that time, as they were only accepting the positions of MD, RN, and EMT. "I learned last week that the Thai government still had their guidelines, and I was not accepted." She took the disappointment in stride. "There are other ways to serve," she said. "Love inspires ways of participation (Puebla 1979)."

Sister Veronica could have been an enormous asset in foreign service. Long before the popularity and easy availability of lactose-free products, she was aware that more than one-half the world population, and the majority of people in Third World Countries, are lactose intolerant. When powdered milk was sent to these countries, the result was rampant flatulence, bloating and diarrhea. The recipients of the milk products thought the United States was trying to poison them. Had dietitians, like her, been consulted, these episodes, which resulted in future mistrust, may have been avoided.

While disheartened, she understood it wasn't a personal rejection. Although, had that CRS opportunity opened up, her life would have taken on a whole new path. Still, the seed had been planted. If she would not be assisting with health care in a foreign country the next best option was turning her energies toward the less fortunate, which included those living in rural areas not having access to metropolitan hospitals, the latest technology and highly skilled professionals.

She briefly considered ministering to the needs in Appalachia, and pondered how she might help the poverty-stricken rural mountain folks living in the hills and hollows of southeastern Tennessee, where she would be nearer our cousin Sister Diane Brin, who lived not far away in Rome, Georgia, outside of Atlanta.

Six years later the CSJ Senate theme was, "Walk Around the World," she wrote. "So that we will be ready to address problems beyond the vision of most of us. The opening day will have displays of show and tell, to put us in a frame of mind of worldwide needs. We may be called to serve before we realize it. I am working on displays of the Subcontinents, especially Sri Lanka (old Ceylon). Most of our social analysis reveals that their problems [of violence and its many ramifications] are rooted in religion."

During the prayers of the faithful at Sister Veronica's funeral Mass Sister Beth Stover read, "As an apostolic woman, Veronica had the heart and passion for worldwide service and ministry. May all missionaries be so graced to walk humbly, to listen sensitively, and to work for justice and peace to alleviate the cause of oppression in our world."

Sister Veronica had much to ponder after her travels. One thing she fully understood: there is no other country like the United States that bows so low to economic wealth. She didn't accept being engulfed in materialism. She never did. She never would.

Sister Vera Meis added, "I'm sure the visit to Brazil touched her heart with more compassion for the poor. She had a strong desire to speak for those who were underprivileged, and strived to live a simple life style."

At age forty, Sister Veronica described her ongoing Spiritual Journey: "On leaving a routine life in 1980, I enjoy the leisure of a reflective morning and quiet time at the end of the day, for whatever is there for me. Yet as I measure, generally nothing happens. Occasionally I break out with strong feelings, with tears about something. Sometimes I doodle a prayer. Mostly I am content now, and patient for a new way of praying to emerge when I unfold into a new ministry."

✝

Chapter Twenty-four

After the trip to Brazil, which was sandwiched between her resignation from nearly twelve years as hospital dietitian, and a retreat at the Motherhouse, Sister Veronica applied to twelve larger Catholic hospitals in, and around the perimeter of Kansas for work as a clinical dietitian, "so that I could work with someone else awhile, instead of always being number one."

There were two offers; one in Administrative Dietetics, at Archbishop Brogan Hospital in Omaha, and the other as Dietitian in Great Bend, Kansas, at Central Kansas Medical Center, a Catholic Health Initiatives Hospital, founded by the Dominican Sisters.

"During retreat I prayed, reflected and discerned whether to continue institutional work or be open to something else. It would be much easier and secure just to be back working in the hospital.

"Obtaining a Master's degree was never appealing to me before, but apparently my time had come. It became clearer; I wanted to return to school fulltime. The opportunity seemed quite appealing, and I called universities for pursuing a degree in nutrition. I was interested in doing course work at Columbus, or Iowa City. Not a lot of places offer much in Advanced Clinical Dietetics.

"I was accepted at Kansas State University, moved to Manhattan and began reviewing alone." The college town, nicknamed the "Little Apple," is located in the Flint Hills, 130 miles west of Kansas City. The graduate school office, in Fairchild Hall, boosts more than 3,000 graduate students. The total enrollment was over 21,000.

For two months, she lived at Seven Dolors school convent and received mail at 731 Pierre Street, the next block over from where Mother attended the Sacred Heart Academy in 1929-1930 at Pierre Street and Juliette Avenue. Incredibly, Sister Veronica never mentioned this proximity to the original Academy school, and it is most likely she did not make the connection because it was no longer referred to as the Academy.

The other Sisters at the convent, where she was temporarily staying, reminded her to "back off from studying all the time." Nevertheless, she found it to be productive. "This time may do more for me than the formal program. I lined up correspondence courses and did some private refresher classes until summer school started. I went to the library about six hours, four to five days a week, studying textbooks and current literature on nutrition.

"I found a college French book. I hope reading [and writing capability from Marymount days] will be sufficient to meet requirements for a second language." This ability served her well while corresponding with distant relatives, and researching records of French Canadian churches throughout Quebec for the two genealogy books she compiled ten years later.

In June 1980 she matriculated at KSU. Home Economics is located in Justin Hall. She attended summer, fall and spring semesters, completing 117 credit hours with a grade point average of 3.727. At age forty-one, she received a Masters of Science degree in Foods and Nutrition. During this time she became a member of Kansas Dietetic Association (KDA), and Western Kansas District Dietetic Association (WKDDA).

"My first two-week, two-hour summer credit course was 'Concepts of Holistic Health and Human Development.'" She later presented an overview of this course for "key" Sisters in Concordia. She jumped right in with the realization, "I will miss working for a while, but if I'm ever moving on, now is the time. I've worked sixteen years on what I learned sixteen to twenty years ago. Dietetics is a science, and always changing. With more than twenty-five work years ahead, I need some recharging. I think it will do me more good than just working in larger institutions."

For the remaining semesters, she rented at 2617 Marion, from Velma Osborn, a house that she shared with Sister Betty Suther CSJ, who was working with St. Isidore's Catholic Student Center, at Anderson and Dennison streets.

"It is so good to be unpacked after eight weeks of living from a suitcase. This transition has been a pleasant experience. After twenty-one years of [hospital convent] institutional living, I had some insightful, but difficult adjustments. For example, my disillusionment about 'how wonderful aloneness would be' has been straightened out. How dead if aloneness is just the absence of others, rather than the presence of God, knowing how much richness comes full circle from His presence to enjoy in others.

"All of life's activities are so much more enjoyable when shared with someone. I am looking forward to a delightful and intimate year, as both Sister Betty and I are committed to respecting time and space for each other, and yet being vulnerable to whatever can be shared."

She settled in for the long haul. "Every minute has been spent studying. I have an eight-week/three-hour class on Social Work with Aging using four textbooks, and a twenty-page paper is due. Later I'll take Family Education, then Nutrient/Drug Interaction, which I've heard is super hard." She took classes in Statistics, Bio-Nutrition, Community Nutrition, Diet Therapy, Biochemistry, Nutrition in Life Cycles, and Food Science Systems, "a required colloquium for no credit," and audited Child Development and Intro to Clinical Dietetics, "for review of what's new."

Even as busy as she was, she helped at the Catholic Student Center with SEARCH, a religious Renew program on the college campus for youth, involving an intense Weekend Encounter. There she ran into Father Bob Reif, whom she had known as a seminary classmate of Father Duane. Reif, who retired a few years later from active ministry and left the Priesthood, was associate chaplain. She also met Father Daniel Scheetz, who was chaplain. "She was very supportive of our efforts to bring relevant liturgies and homilies to the faculty and students," he said.

Coincidentally, the pastor at her parish church in Manhattan was Father John Moeder. "He gave the baccalaureate sermon for my high school graduation. He said at the time he wondered what good would come from the small Webster school." No doubt she gloated for a moment, recalling the successful and productive lives of most of the graduates.

The year before she reflected, "This has been a special fortieth year for me. It's only the second Christmas I've spent with family in twenty-two years. I can't believe I let it go like that." But the following year, just before Thanksgiving, she wrote, "I really hoped I'd be closer to family this year, now that I am in Kansas, but it seems as far away as ever, with my nose to the books.

"It is really hard this semester. There are so many papers to write, and little time left to study. I have considered dropping one or more classes before my grades get any worse, but I would just have to take the class over."

She pushed herself and began to show early signs of burnout. But she was still young. "The last three courses have been extremely difficult. I experienced roller coaster, up and down emotions, but through it all the mood has certainly been one of trust, because I have learned that things do work out despite me. I don't think next semester will be quite so difficult, except everyone says Biochemistry is a headache. Then I'll have my Master's Report to finish, present, and defend."

She had little time for correspondence, but in a rare letter during this hectic time she started on a philosophical note, "How can we measure relative time? Is a week better than a minute?

"For eight days straight, I put in seven to nine hours of solid writing on my Master's Report. I borrowed a typewriter from the Motherhouse. I did all the typing myself, and saved $300. Most people, and my advisor, tried to tell me I should have a professional do the final one hundred pages. I figured I was too picky for someone else to do it." She drove herself hard, feeling guilty about taking time, energy, space and available resources for herself. Her frugal nature would not let someone else lighten her burden.

In her finished Master's Report entitled, *Anthropometry in the Nutritional Assessment of Preschool Children*, she acknowledged Dr. Beth Fryer for guidance and support and Dr. Kathleen Newell and Dr. Marjorie Stith for serving on the committee and reviewing the manuscript. (This is currently available in the Kansas Public Library System.)

Sister Veronica prayed about her choice to return to college, just as she discerned all major decisions. Surely it was a large step, not just because of the eighteen years since undergraduate school, but also considering the financial expense.

The CSJ Congregation was paying for her privilege of earning a Master's degree. She hardly needed to be reminded of the cost and of who was footing the bill. In her early years the Mother Superior and Novice Mistress advised her that as long as she continued to get good grades, she would make it. Surely, those words came back to haunt and remind. Earning good grades was not just desirable; it was necessary and expected.

"The first few months I had nightmares of the amount of money I was not producing for the Community, by not working. One of my greatest joys was earning an 'A' in my first graduate course, at age forty. I kept this up for all but three classes, so was once again affirmed personally, and felt eager and ready to serve when I graduated."

At the end of the final semester she wrote, "Three more tests and I'll be out of here. The hardest thing is studying when I'd rather be packing up, cleaning house and learning the things I'd really like to study before leaving all these tremendous resources. When I get my diploma on May 15 another dummy will march off. I tell you, I feel so much dumber than when I came here."

✝

Chapter Twenty-five

"Don't feel badly about still being in school," Sister Veronica corresponded in her big sister role, encouraging her two late-starter siblings, who were also in college. In my mid-thirties, this writer was finishing up course work at the University of Colorado.

A week after his May graduation from Fort Hays (Kansas) State University, our youngest brother, Rodney Roy, and Christi Karlin were married in Great Bend. Among the many guests were his godparents, Father Duane and Sister Veronica, who just graduated from KSU/ Kansas State University the previous week.

Immediately she made arrangements to stay with three CSJ Sisters of the Wichita Province. There she gained hands-on experience, at Wesley Hospital, in nutritional assessment and tube feedings with cancer patients, working for two weeks with a KSU program. "I haven't worked for one and a half years, so I am rather uptight about it," she said, even though well-credentialed to land a good job. It became typical for her to be over prepared and overqualified. "I'll get credit, which I don't need. I just wanted some specialized experience before returning to work."

The next two weeks she worked with the cardiac rehabilitation unit at St. Francis Hospital. She spent another two weeks at St. Joseph's learning about aggressive feeding for alcoholism rehab and hypersegmentation. Following that, she worked with a public health department learning about WIC, a federal nutrition program for women, infants and children, experience that would come in handy twelve years later.

Under the direction of CSJ president Sister Bette Moslander, Sister Veronica wrote her own personal Commitment to Mission Statement the previous September: "As a full-time student, I respond with hope to the prompting of alleviating hunger and malnutrition, and will use this study year to ponder how." In her Life Review she added, "At some point in my studies at KSU, I heard about the scarcity of professional dietitians in western Kansas, and I looked around for some community-type nutrition work."

During spring break 1981, she drove from Manhattan to Stockton to visit Mother, and together they traveled to WaKeeney for Easter dinner with our brother, Kenneth, and his wife Ruth.

The local hospital learned of her availability and invited her to come back the next day for an interview. She accepted the job offer, and after graduation found a place to rent, within a large older house at 310 North Sixth.

The small, sparsely furnished, drab two-bedroom apartment showed its age with brown shag carpet, brown paneling, a radiator wall heater and a bathtub, but no shower. The compact galley kitchen had no dishwasher, and the dining nook was so tight there was no room to walk behind the chairs. But the detached, one-car garage was a more important feature for Sister Veronica, considering Kansas' continental winters. The humble "convent for one" fit her modest needs and way of life, conformed to her vow of poverty, and suited her just fine.

"The hospital offered me full-time employment, just to get someone who would stay and take hold of the department. I took only a half-time position, to be free for other pastoral ministry." Her intention had always been to work, not only in the secular world, but have a presence in the parish, as well.

With a degree in Foods and Nutrition and a member of Omicron, Nu, National Honor Home Economics Society, she continued to maintain professional memberships with ADA and Kansas Consultant Dietitians Health Care Facilities (CD-HCF) and (KDA-HCF) for the rest of her life.

Qualified to serve as a Masters of Science Registered Dietitian (M.S.R.D.), it was her goal to extend this post, in western Kansas, into an outreach consulting position to serve other surrounding rural health care facilities, and small nursing homes. "The law only requires, of consultants, a minimum of eight hours a month, so this allows me time for freelance community nutrition work. My CSJ Community is supportive of searching out ways to serve in non-institutional ways."

She said, after returning from a CSJ retreat in Concordia, "The past week most of the Sisters I talked with thought I was making a very good move, specifically in trying to provide consultation for rural health. It is well known that western Kansas is 'bad off' for nutritional care. There is a big need in rural communities, since dieticians want to work in the cities.

"I think Mother is probably disappointed, in a way, that I am not going to some big place of importance. There are plenty of people to do that, and besides, it would just be an eight-to-five job, and I would not function creatively in a large community as either a nutritionist, or a Nun."

There was an announcement of her KSU graduation in the CSJ Motherhouse newspaper, along with a photo taken thirteen years earlier. "I was so mad I went out and had another more recent one taken," she joked. The next month both Stockton and WaKeeney newspapers carried a similar announcement with the new photo: "Sister Veronica Roy has been hired as a dietitian...She has long anticipated being able to serve rural health care needs with an emphasis on wellness, and is happy to be a part of the WaKeeney community."

She privately admitted to wanting emphasized the underlying message that a local rural girl made it in the fast-paced working world and chose to return to rural life for a while.

The article continued, "She is available for counseling and lectures on nutrition and various religious subjects. Her interests include: physical fitness, jogging, tennis, swimming, and all kinds of handiwork, oil painting and creative writing."

In mid-summer she began working at the non-Catholic Trego County-Lemke Memorial Hospital and Long Term Care Facility, which she referred to as the WaKeeney Hospital, in a town with a population of 2,300. In contrast, she had just come from a college where the graduate school enrollment alone was over 3,000.

WaKeeney is not an Indian name, as many people think. The town was founded, in 1879, as a professional prairie town designed by two Chicago land companies, Warren and Keeney. According to the Kansas commerce webpage, "WaKeeney has earned the reputation of 'Christmas City of the High Plains' for its forty-foot handmade Christmas tree adorned with handmade ornaments and more than six thousand lights." Moreover, it is proudly known as "the town that time forgot." It is like other small towns along Interstate 70 — Grinnell, Grainfield, Park, Quinter, Collyer, Ogallah and Ellis — midway between Denver and Kansas City.

According to the *Catechism of the Catholic Church*, the word charism refers to graces and gifts of the Holy Spirit. These are to be accepted, with gratitude, by the person who receives them, and used with charity. Among Sister Veronica's charisms were patience, tolerance and forgiveness. She was called up to live by these graces, and was well aware that obedience to God's way requires effort. While her scholarly coursework during college was taxing, in hindsight, it seemed a mere respite before the real work began.

In her book *Dakota: A Spiritual Geography*, Kathleen Norris mentions a study titled, "Vision 2000." It suggests that small-town people often look upon professionals, who move to the plains, with suspicion. "If they were any good, they would be working in a bigger place," is how the reasoning goes. Unfortunately Sister Veronica, as an outsider, became an easy target, as are many excellent teachers, doctors, lawyers and ministers from cities, who choose to move into, and serve rural areas.

"The hospital had a record of noncompliance with [previous employees.] The physicians welcomed me, and gave me much encouragement. I also established credibility with the nurses in that I could handle part-time education and nutritional assessment, drawing on newly acquired knowledge." In the small hospital setting, Sister Veronica began to question the way things had always been done because, as a qualified and licensed expert, she had an obligation to comply with State Health Standards and the American Dietetic Association code of ethics, which she would not compromise.

It wasn't long before she showed signs of frustration. "Opening a 'Convent of one,' and living in it alone was traumatic, but totally unanticipated was the resistance I encountered with the kitchen department employees who resisted me coldly. I was powerless with them. By the first month there, I knew I had met my challenge to my professional life…Nevertheless, I felt committed to help solve some of these problems, since administration backed me up."

At age forty-one, health conscious, and recently earning a master's degree, Sister Veronica demanded much of her staff, but no more than she demanded of herself. Good at organization and having high principles, she inherited a staff, some of whom had been previously permitted to perform at a less-than-satisfactory level. Never one to accept mediocrity, she would not give into the phenomena, not uncommon in small towns, where professionalism is sometimes allowed to slip. Even the town's website touts, "Escape from the pressures of city life. Kick back, relax."

Possibly some of the kitchen staff thought she would be with them only a short time. However, she was unlike some professionals who move on for more money, or to advance their careers. That was not her agenda. Her goal was to serve the people in this rural community in the best way she knew how.

Before she knew it, she became a threat to the workers who "always did it this way." Sister Veronica knew that to make progress she would be challenging some fundamental assumptions and established habits. "Those women are the hardest I have ever worked with," she wrote. "So I have stepped lightly, verbalizing a lot of 'what ifs' without saying that we were changing anything. 'They are not about to be pushed harder,' they have told me. They make about five and a half hours of work last an eight-hour day."

Experienced and well-educated, she tried sharing what she knew. She suggested different approaches, and that alone was enough to provoke anxiety with some of her staff. Coping with change is difficult for most people. Routine often makes a person rigid, since there is a general desire to stick to one's own level of competence. Getting out of the comfort zone takes a little push. Most psychologists agree that, typically, people have a lot of inertia.

Granted the kitchen staff was small and the budget was tight. But, in the meantime, she was not going to tolerate faulty work. "The main goal in the kitchen is to get their attitude refined. Now they just get the food out, no matter whether it is served hot, or attractive. This is a service department, and we are going to be proud of our product. There have also been reports, in the past, that this department refused to allow other employees to eat in the cafeteria, simply because they forgot to sign up on time."

Dedicated to helping her employees be a part of a professional hospital team, she was determined to treat patients and staff alike, as customers. These were before the days of defining the customer, assessing customer satisfaction, and the total quality procedure in organizations. She was ahead of her time, and correct to demand service, support and accountability from her employees.

Intimidated by her credentials, her businesslike tempo did not sit well with some employees. A sense of light-hearted humor and an ability to chitchat with their everyday gossip might have helped, but unfortunately, these were not her strengths. While Sister Veronica was intelligent and competent, assertiveness was not one of her strengths, either. Instead, as a gentle soul, she depended much on her example, and the Holy Spirit, to move and motivate people. No doubt, she longed for a kitchen crew, like in Belvidere, who loved and respected her.

In her Life Review she wrote, "In the early weeks I knew I would endure only by the faith that this was my calling, and that things would take time. My leitmotif motto [a recurring and often dominant theme] quickly became my kitchen hanging. [New York Senator] Padavan says, 'Never despair of the community one serves; it will resurrect me when I have died to myself.'"

The situation had still not changed the next month. She said, with pain in her heart, "Home from a very disgusting day. Today two employees steamed all over me. They said they were short of help, and all I did was sit on my 'can.' It was really crude language, and they just threw it all at me because, 'It was all my fault.' It is very nauseating to hear people talk like that. I have visions that they will end up coming around, unless I break first. So I just kept repeating what they were saying, and what I was hearing."

Not much later she added, "[One employee] really blasted me again. She did the same thing a month ago when she said, 'I didn't do anything while they worked their tails off, and I always make more work for them, and there never was anybody like me before as their dietitian.'"

She would let neither their first impression of her, nor their bully techniques, get in the way. Nevertheless, she was severely stung by the abuse of those who worked under her direction. Perhaps they thought if they continued to be stubborn, she would loosen her standards. Unprepared for the attacks, she reeled at their aggression: "This is an unreal life for a Nun."

Evidently she was not the only department head having trouble with morale. At the end of the year, she said, "The hospital scene is so depressing that the Board asked the Area Director to give an all-employee pep talk."

There was little to be tranquil about during those years. "My blood pressure has been up all summer and fall, despite diet and exercise. Stress was the only factor not controlled." Experiencing other health problems as well, she was scheduled for medical tests. "All this was enough to make my [menstrual] cycle go wacky."

She was fortified with the scriptural passage, "You armed me with strength for battle; you made my adversaries bow at my feet."[1] All the while she kept in mind the vows by which she lived, and the Holy Rule, committed to memory years ago. Maxim 66 (1975 version) speaks to the danger of losing heart: "Be courageous to undertake what God wants of you, and constant to preserve in what you undertake, never giving up, whatever difficulties occur and whatever obstacles may be placed in your path unless you become totally powerless against them."[2]

The 1978 version of the Maxim of Hope 12:2 states: "In the difficulties and contradictions met in carrying out your laudable undertakings, strengthen yourself against the dread of human fear and do not permit your heart to be overcome. When it seems that everything should throw you into total despair, hope for everything from the divine goodness, and in order to enliven your confidence, believe, as indeed you should, that, if your plans are of God, confirm or perfect them…" [3]

"It takes time and patience to manage the dietary departments, and so I swing back and forth between disgust and impatience and hope and joy. My life must speak for itself. She found strength in another biblical passage: "God endures with much patience."[4]

There were several more encounters of verbal abuse before making any noticeable headway. "Three, of the kitchen employees, are outright vicious at times. Three others will not budge in their ways, but the other six are at least speaking and sharing. I have come to identify two key people as the trouble. They have a problem with modern Nuns."

Later she noted, "[One employee] must have been converted. Now she goes out of her way to ask me questions and even speaks to me first. Sometimes." Another time she said, "The kitchen crew is noticeably warmer these days, but I suspect a lot of it is the anticipation and uncertainty of who, if anybody, will get an end-of-the-year pay increase.

"I may put the raises on hold for several months — if any are approved. It's likely that only two or three have earned a raise, and technically if the others haven't earned one, they should be [written up and first put on notice, before being] fired. I have grounds to fire six of them. However, I did not come here to destroy and tear down and do it myself, but to try to build and improve."

She likened this experience to a biblical lesson. "'Like clay in the hand of the potter, so are you in my hand.' My model has been the potter working gently and timely with clay. The clay and the environment have to be right, or in pulling at the wrong time a fine crack will develop which, when fired, will destroy the creation."[5]

Soon after she said, "Things are going a little better at work." After falling backward off a chair while hanging a chart, she fractured the elbow on her right arm and was in a cast for two weeks. "Not bad typing with one left finger. It's given me the time to practice the management techniques of explaining to people instead of doing things myself. I missed only one day of work, since I still couldn't slow down."

Later yet, "I think we are on our way out of the depths finally after a year and a half, and I've done nothing but be patient and show love, in return for snobbery." Sister Veronica followed the Maxim of charity, and guarded to keep signs of coldness, bitterness and animosity in check. Careful not to show gestures, or use words in the least way offensive, she was mindful to "do unto others what you would have others do unto you."

Later on she wrote, "I really felt things are starting to give a little, and they are trusting me because I have only been loving and gentle, believe me." She admitted when she did win supporters, it was by sheer determination. "I figured one thing I did that impressed the kitchen people. I went around taking photos of them in action. 'Nobody ever did that before,' I heard. So I will make a 'Health Careers Day' poster for the local high school."

Undoubtedly, she was pleased with the slightest progress. "Gossip around town is that things (food) are much better since Sister (I) started at the Hospital. Actually, sad to say, things haven't changed. It's just that I visit all patients and nursing home residents regularly, and listen, and they think all is better. Number one lesson in public relations is listening. This Advent keeps reminding me that Jesus is the One. He not only brings answers, He is Answer."

There were many other passages, such as 11:6, the Maxim of zeal that she heeded and which lent her strength: "Clearly yet energetically continue to the end what you have determined and prudently judged to be in accordance with the greater glory of God."

Peter Hebbblethwaite says in his book, *In the Vatican*, "The saint is an everyday Christian who tries to take seriously the demands of the Gospel in his or her life." She also tried to live up to Maxim 6:4, "People are more profoundly moved by a saintly example than by words."

✝

Chapter Twenty-six

Two months after Sister Veronica's arrival in WaKeeney, she accepted a supplementary dietitian consultant position for the Grisell Memorial Hospital, in Ness County, with its thirty-four long-term-care beds. Located in Ransom, it is a neighboring town to the south having a population of fewer than four hundred.[1]

That winter she said, "Work goes very well there. The eight- to twenty-four hours, two days a month are really pleasant." This second job required a fifty-mile roundtrip drive over county roads. She needed a reliable car. "My tires are threadbare. I finally ordered four new ones, and have an appointment tomorrow to have them put on. Four to six inches of snow is forecasted for today, so it is unsafe to leave town. I will write loved ones, clean house just a little, then some dues mailing for three Kansas consultant Dietetics groups, of which I am secretary-treasurer. It doesn't sound like much, but I secretly desired an excuse to stay home just for these three projects."

Perhaps later on that same winter she wrote, "We had twelve inches of blizzardy snow. I walked the seven blocks to the hospital to cook breakfast, as one cook said she could not get through until midmorning."

Since Sisters have to earn their own keep, the following year she took on a third dietetic consultant position. In the county seat of Graham, Hill City has a declining population of under two thousand. In fulfilling her commitment to rural ministry, Sister Veronica accepted a one-day-a-week position at Dawson Place, a long-term care facility for fifty-three patients, which is affiliated with the Hill City Hospital. "The pay is $10 to $14 an hour," she noted.

She headed due north on Highway 283 for the sixty-mile round trip drive. Many relatives and family friends, who lived in Graham County along the east-west Highway 24, chose this hospital and long-term care facility. This opportunity, to minister to countless people she knew, was very special to her after being away from the area for nearly twenty years.

Back at the WaKeeney Hospital, she continued to feel bogged down with the shortage of space. "We assumed all along, the past four years, we would be included in the kitchen remodeling, but now we find we are not. There is too little money budgeted. I am working on a plan, anyway, that only requires several new pieces of equipment. I also want to knock out the outside wall and install a walk-in freezer, but that would eliminate some precious storage space." Finally she made her point with management and the partial remodeling began. "I have the go-ahead with a system to keep the food hot for LTC residents. I also plan to move equipment around to serve employees from a kitchen serving line instead of the tacky way we do now." She also purchased some badly needed dishes.

"The three combined hospitals represent forty paid hours, so that is all I can handle for now, plus ten hours as pastoral minister, except I've been putting in more like fifteen to twenty-five hours per week. Seems like all my free time is spent making plans, so I have to check my calendar each day to see which way to go." The parish and volunteer charity activities, professional organizations, as well as regular CSJ meetings kept her stretched. Her ministry knew no bounds, and she was pulled in many directions. She was also involved with the preparation and delivery of food to the Trego County Senior Center.

Never holding an outside job herself, sometimes it was difficult for Mother to understand Sister Veronica's job responsibilities. Mother, who by now was a senior citizen herself, did not like to drive. But, she found she had to make the 100-mile round trip herself, once in a while, if she wanted to see her beloved eldest daughter every other week, or so. Typically, our brother Kenneth and his wife took them to a local Chinese restaurant, one of their favorite eating-places in town. During these visits, after church, Mother accompanied Sister Veronica on her rounds to the nursing home, the hospital and private homes to administer communion.

"She came over today and gave me a home permanent, but she had to get back to WaKeeney tonight," Mother said. Sister Veronica spent most holidays on the farm with Mother, but often found it necessary to drive back to help with the hospital holiday evening meals.

Even though she could have pulled rank on the employees, she did not. Many times throughout the years her holidays, Sundays, or other days off were spent serving others, and Sister Veronica often offered relief to her kitchen staff. "I have a terribly soft heart when too many employees want time off. But as long as our Roy family is going to be together Sunday, December 23, I guess I won't be missing a thing." Another year Sister Veronica worked on Christmas Eve, "since I am going to be home anyway." And another time she said, "I was a hostess at the Long Term Care, on Christmas Day. I fixed a nice table with white tablecloths, and arranged so they could eat more family style instead of on the 'never-ending' trays. It was lovely, and all seemed to appreciate it." Another holiday she said, "Our little hospital has been filled to overflowing with lots of pneumonia. The Long Term Care part is always full. I always have someone to eat with, if necessary, with my fingers in food services. I sat down for a dinner there, then came home."

For the next nine years, in addition to her other jobs, she was the regional consultant dietitian for the Homestead Nutrition Project of the Area Agency on Aging. She did the work from home. "It feels more relaxing than being around so many people all day. I get paid [a flat fee of] $177 a month. It used to take me fifteen hours to plan these, then eight. Now I am really efficient and can get done in four hours." She felt guilty for her resourcefulness. "It comes up to $44 per hour. Each month I plan and certify Meal Site menus for senior citizens in twenty-one Northwest Kansas counties. As a government subsidized program, they get their meals for whatever they want to pay." When she went to check on the program in Damar, she took the opportunity to visit our elderly Uncle Dona Roy and Aunt Irene Morin.

The Homestead Nutrition Project now has a website providing nutrition education to seniors. Today, Sister Veronica would have been a viable resource for the Agency and eager to blend her skill on the computer with her knowledge of dietetics.

She accepted an additional consulting dietitian position for the Development Services of Northwest Kansas (DSNWK) servicing eighteen counties. She provided menus and assessments of nutritional status, a position she continued for another three years after her move to New Almelo. The administrative office in Hays serves the Reed Developmental Center there, and Kid-Link in Stockton, among many other various locations.

When the Norton State Mental Hospital was converted to a minimum-security prison, mentally disabled patients were placed with caregivers in group homes of six, under the auspices of the Frontier Developmental Center. "I spend six hours a month consulting in Norton and Hays for the four neighborhood group homes for the very handicapped adults and severely retarded, who have less than two years of age mental and social abilities."

Not long after she added, "The work for the group homes has been much more than I imagined. I've already used thirty of my allowed [seventy-two] hours for the year in the past two months. Now that we are organized, hopefully three hours per month may keep me on top of things." Undoubtedly, she put in more work hours, for which she did not charge, chalking it up to charity.

Her work was varied and ongoing. At the WaKeeney Hospital she wrote a column, called "WELL DONE," for the employees' monthly newsletter. "I capitalize each time I use the word well in the column, connecting nutrition and wellness. Light reading."

Although shy, she firmly believed in adult education and felt obligated to teach what she had been given the opportunity to learn along the way. Better educated than most rural schoolteachers, her professional background in nutrition was a tremendous asset to these small communities, which otherwise would not have had this caliber and ready source of information. Making herself available throughout neighboring counties, she spoke on topics of her expertise, however, she was frustrated at the general lack of interest. She complained, "Parents will do headstands for their children. They drive forty miles just to see their child do a somersault, but when an opportunity comes along to improve their own mind, health, or lifestyle, they do nothing."

"The Hospital Board also wants a Heart Smart program, so you can guess who the professional is to present most of it. I balked at only one aspect, and want them to get someone else to do weight control and exercise sessions. The PR person has done nil to advertise it, so I'm secretly hoping we don't have the five-person minimum I set for it to go. This is really stretching me to get current, and to apply myself."

She was also concerned for her own health, since our paternal grandfather, P.H. Roy, died of arteriosclerosis heart disease, and a high percentage of relatives, on both sides of the family died of heart ailments.

Changing an individual's lifestyle requires exercising, eating less, partaking of a low-fat diet for weight control, and watching carbohydrates. In short it means giving up bad habits, and that is very difficult for many people — herself included. "I can hardly wait until I get my own cholesterol values to see if trying an aggressive approach makes a difference."

In 1999 a study confirmed that a high fiber diet of cereals, fruits and vegetables, of 22 grams per day, can significantly decrease the risk of heart attacks in women by 47 percent, can lower blood sugar, boost sensitivity to insulin and lower the risk of blood clotting. Fiber contributes to cardiovascular health by reducing levels of blood cholesterol, especially artery-clogging LDL cholesterol. She knew of this information long before, as she conducted six two-hour Cholesterol Countdown workshops in WaKeeney and Ransom.

She also developed and presented a five-hour workshop on Sodium Controlled Diets to fourteen kitchen supervisors, and repeated it later to another seven. "They gave me an excellent rating of 5.5 on a scale of 1 to 7," she beamed.

Additionally, she spoke to the northwest Kansas Chapter of the American Diabetes Association on the topic of high fiber diet and calorie intake, and again when two new diabetic units formed in Plainville and Russell. "A local three-hour workshop on diabetics also resulted in excellent ratings"

She taught that obesity, age and sedentary lifestyle are risk factors, and that diabetes is deadly serious and a cause of blindness, amputations and nervous system damage. Knowing that eating correctly should be part of everyone's overall health plan, controlling adult-onset diabetes is an example of the impact of a balanced diet. For those patients, who after twenty or thirty years found it difficult to change their own diets, as a nutritionist, she was a diet coach to help them develop new menu ideas.

She helped people outside the community, too, with her knowledge of nutrition, blended with a compassionate nature. For example, she advised a Brazilian Monk: "Tell Father José to keep on his nutrition and not give in to 'no appetite.' That is cyclic. The worse one feels, the less one eats, the worse one feels. It is amazing how much the body can take when it goes to the extremes, as shown by Father José, in welcoming death, then wanting to get [back to teaching in] the classroom, all in the same week."

It was her job to know about foods that help break links to disease. She enjoyed sharing the knowledge. During family gatherings, with her sisters and sisters-in-law in the kitchen, she instructed, in a casual manner while washing dishes, or sitting around the dining table, that beans cut cholesterol; oatmeal and celery help control blood pressure; broccoli, Brussels sprouts, citrus fruits and peppers are cancer protectors; garlic and onions fight stomach cancer; ginger is a stomach settler; fish in one's diet helps prevent heart attacks; cinnamon helps blood sugar levels; and she confirmed the folklore that cranberries ease bladder infection.

She also knew all about kitchen-borne germs. However, contrary to her biblical Martha role, it was evident that housework and kitchen duty weren't priorities in her own home. Living alone, and during one especially busy week, she admitted to leaving dirty dishes in the sink the entire time — not having a dishwasher. She confessed to later washing these with a Clorox solution, knowing that by dowsing the area, sponges, and washcloths with household bleach, the bacteria count would drop by ninety-nine percent. Mind you, she was sanitary and would never subject her visitors to such conditions. However, when she was alone, her personal housekeeping standards gave way to other concerns and creative endeavors.

A public servant, she was eager to be active in both her religious and secular community. She passed the American Red Cross Cardiopulmonary Resuscitation Modular System (CPR) instruction, in 1984, and often donated her "A positive" type blood during local drives, aware of the need for untainted blood.

In 1985 the Kansas district dietitians hosted the state convention at Hays with the theme of Wellness. It was rare for her to not be involved in the planning of these conventions, but it was during this time that Mother was diagnosed with cancer, and Sister Veronica was her active caregiver.

As if she needed to take on more, "For extra involvement in the community, I go to the *LaLeche* league meetings for nursing mothers." Even through breast-feeding was not advocated in Mother's era, Sister Veronica was educated in its benefits, which aided her involvement in the local WIC program several years later.

By the spring of 1986 she eased up on herself somewhat, or perhaps she simply had a good day: "The WaKeeney hospital is becoming more agreeable. The other hospitals are quite pleasant, but still a little too much, especially for this quiet reflective season upon us. Although, I will be taking a little more time off from the WaKeeney hospital by cutting down to two ten-hours days instead of three days. I hope I don't spend the freed-up time just running around for the parish. Or I will get burnt [out].

"In the meantime, dietetics and parish work is a delightful blend of a ministry. Always trying to plan something for the hospital, or the parish, which is a source of more joy, in service and peace."

Throughout the ten years she lived in WaKeeney, she struggled with her resolve to keep a slower pace. In 1988 she took on the added responsibility of consultant dietitian for a fourth facility — the Gove County Hospital in Quinter.

In the spring of 1989 the Colby Citizens Medical Center hospital asked her to work one day a month. "So I am praying about that. The hardest thing would be the three hours on the road, unless I get used to listening to cassettes in the car." Wisely, she declined.

Idleness and complacency were not a part of her personality. She kept her chin up, and struggled to keep the rural hospitals in compliance. While only paid for part-time work at each hospital, the hours totaled to well more than full time, not even adding in the countless hours on the road. Simultaneously, she was deeply involved with parish ministry. It was like working eighty hours a week.

Determined to turn that corner of her life on a positive note, she said, "I have truly appreciated all the associations and benefits of employment in local health care." She was worn thin from too many commitments. After ten years in WaKeeney she let go of the hospital contracts. It was time to move on. This is the path of a pioneer. She had paved the way for others.

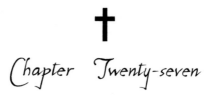

Chapter Twenty-seven

Is any among you sick? Let him call for the elders of the church, and let them pray over him, anointing him with oil in the name of the Lord. The prayer of faith will save the sick man, and the Lord will raise him up, and if he has committed sins, he will be forgiven."

— James 5:14-15

During her year and a half studying at KSU there was no income. And tuition, room and board had been costly. Upon receiving a master's degree, Sister Veronica's first priority was a paying job, which she quickly found.

"I anticipated this move, not only for the professional dietetic work within a sixty-mile radius, but also the challenge of being the first resident Nun in the community. I had a secret, unvoiced desire of a pastoral ministry of some type, developing into a 'ministry of presence.'"

Like other Sisters, she was eager to take up the work of pastoral ministry in its varied forms to build, mend, repair and instruct in her attempt to bring the world back to Jesus — when she wasn't attending to the nutritional needs of the community, although the work was not mutually exclusive.

While in years past, ministries in the Catholic Church were male dominated, the role of service is a natural outpouring of nurturing energy, and is often explained through female images. She, like many of the other Sisters of Concordia, fit the picture of one who gently forges ahead — one who is strong, reliable, compassionate, decisive and intelligent.[1]

The Vatican II agenda was threefold: renewal, modernization and ecumenism. While the mission of the Sisters of St. Joseph was previously that of teaching and nursing, now it had expanded to serve all levels of education, parish ministry, health care and social work in urban, and especially rural areas. The Sisters have always identified with the needs of people on the frontier, since first locating in Concordia, in 1883. They realized there is now a new frontier, one they could no longer neglect.

Inspired to live according to the principles of the Second Vatican Council in her daily life, Sister Veronica yearned to meet the needs of the people in their own cultural setting. After nearly twelve years of living in Belvidere, Illinois, not far from metropolitan Chicago, and spending another year in the bustling college town of Manhattan, Kansas, the thought of sparsely populated, wide-open spaces was appealing. So was being nearer her childhood homestead, where our aging mother still lived.

Here she could feel the closeness of nature found in a farming community, and all it stands for. The town of WaKeeney's website touts, "Discover rural America, where community values are still important and neighbors continue to help their neighbors." She was ready for a change, and eager to take on the role of a modern pioneer when she moved to western Kansas.

In *Footprints of the Frontier*, Sister M. Evangeline Thomas wrote, "The first Reverend Mother Stanislaus Leary was encouraged to go on with her noble work. Undoubtedly, as the pioneer of your community...you will have many heavy labors and many trials to bear."

Almost one hundred years later, as pioneers in their own right, Sister Veronica and her colleagues bore their own heavy labors and trials, and faced new challenges of the twentieth (and twenty-first) century. "We realize the importance of building a support group with each other, and I am very excited about that," she said.

"If I do get the WaKeeney hospital job," she speculated ahead of time, "I would be right in the middle of this group of five now considered, by the CSJ Community, as pioneers on the western front." The five other Religious Women already in place in surrounding counties were Sisters Doris Marie Flax, Ransom; Vera Meis, Norton; Clarice Richmeier and Adeline Marie Wasinger, St. Peter; and Barbara Ellen Apaceller, Oberlin.

A month after the Blessed Virgin Mary allegedly first appeared to visionaries in Medjugorje, Bosnia-Herzegovina (the former Yugoslavia) Sister Veronica moved to the small town of WaKeeney, in June 1981, to begin her work as dietetic consultant. She lived amid meager surroundings in the unassuming apartment — what she called a "Convent for one." Even after Vatican II, when the strictness of the vow of poverty eased somewhat, she continued to live humbly.

She quickly became aware of being out of touch with current events. "I have no TV, and can't stand the radio. I am terribly lacking in international news, or any news for that matter." A farm girl at heart, she was most interested in Statewide and rural issues. "I try to glance over [the Hays daily paper] at work." Although she did say, "I absolutely must check which weekly news magazine has the best coverage of the world Church."

Local news spreads fast here, and the townspeople quickly became aware of her presence upon reading an announcement in the Trego County *Western Kansas World*, and Mother's hometown weekly newspaper, the *Rooks County Record*.[2]

"When I first arrived I can honestly say that not more than two or three people made the effort to say, 'Hi.' And I am talking about after Mass." Her sudden appearance, in the predominately Catholic community, should have come as no surprise, since it was also announced in the church bulletin.

"By the first month in WaKeeney I knew I had met my challenge to my professional life, my religious life and my womanhood all at once. I was losing my Sister-friends by distance. I felt so terribly alone, having to initiate all the house calls to people in the community. Somehow, breaking through the ice is letting people know that we, Religious, are purely human, not some supernatural [being] to talk about."

The cool response from those she came to serve caused her great disappointment at first. It was a rude awakening, and not at all what she expected. Disheartened and disillusioned, in a letter to Father Duane she wrote, "I can just imagine you thinking, 'Good grief, if she wants some appreciation, let her come to South America.'"

She persevered, and each week tried to become acquainted with more in the parish community. "After daily Mass this morning I tagged about five of the parishioners to come over for a get-acquainted coffee after Mass on Thursday. I will probably tag a couple more tomorrow. Later she mused, "Five ladies showed up, but then I don't have much trouble with the 'oldsters.'

"Meanwhile the new pastor, Father Dennis Schaab, arrived the same week I did. He appeared to be warmly received. He told the people, from the pulpit, that he wanted to be invited for a meal." Local farmers, Elaine and Duane Newcomer were among the first to invite Sister Veronica and Father Dennis into their home, a kind gesture that continued.

"I invited him over to bless the house, my first weekend, when Mother was here. Then I had him over for supper, another night, to get acquainted. Father Dennis is very easy to visit with, but appears shyer than I have ever been. I think he'll be okay.

"I received encouragement, from some parishioners, at the time I asked for recognition as a parish minister." The ice had been broken. She was commissioned at Christ the King Parish on September 27. To show their ecumenical support various non-Catholic members of the local Ministerial Alliance attended the event, as did numerous Sisters, Priests and several family members who lived nearby in Kansas.[3] In their representative roles, parishioners and community leaders, alike took part in the ceremony. "Just something Father Dennis and I worked up to impress the people. And I admit it did, without being too much."

Later that evening, Mrs. Julius Bollig and the September work group supervised a potluck supper, at the VFW, officially welcoming the two into the community.

Following the event, an article appeared in the local newspaper. "Simplicity was the keynote. More than 250 people from this small rural community packed the church service. The Very Reverend Basil Torres, of Grinnell, served as installing official at the afternoon ceremony, and asked that all present pray to

Christ the Healer to be with Sister Veronica in her mission to the sick of the community. Sister Doris Marie Flax, of Ransom, representing the Sisters of St. Joseph of Concordia, presented the profession cross to Sister Veronica, charging her to become an apostolic religious in service to the people of WaKeeney."[4]

An accompanying news photo showed Mother in a ceremonial "laying of hands" on Sister Veronica. The act is a simple blessing, an ancient biblical symbol of strength. However, the sign and the source are not to be confused. It does not bestow spiritual authority like ordination, as some parishioners were glad to know.

With the public recognition of Sister Veronica's role as parish minister, the parishioners were forced to internally assess their own views on power relationships, specifically with Sisters and laywomen becoming active in the Church. Needless to say, not everyone in the parish was pleased with a woman receiving a transfer of power.

"Today I went on rounds with Father Dennis and he announced, to the residents of the nursing home, that I would now be bringing them communion from the Sunday Masses. I had already been visiting with twelve of them, plus the hospital patients, so I foresee no particular problem." Although, becoming a Eucharistic Minister, in WaKeeney, created some tension. Perhaps a few parishioners feared, "What will come next?"

Sister Veronica was first appointed as Eucharistic Minister in the diocese of Rockford, Illinois six years earlier. The meetings of Vatican II (1962-1965) urged women and men to share tasks and authority, including that of Eucharistic Minister, in order to reflect God's full image. But the resulting changes did not come easy.

Here she stepped back in time as a pioneer doing basic grass roots work. In 1981, active and vocal Sisters and laywomen were not a popular concept in this rural community, or even in some metropolitan parishes for that matter. It was with a spirit of optimism that she moved to WaKeeney. However, the challenge of being the first resident Sister may have been more than she bargained for.

In her conversations with Mother she painted a safe picture, describing only her day-to-day work. But to a few of her siblings, she revealed her frustration over what she sometimes perceived as an uphill battle. She would walk in Jesus' footsteps many times over, as he, too, met with resistance in his public ministry. Nevertheless, as a pioneer, a role model and change-maker, she was pleased with the slightest breakthrough, albeit slower then envisioned.

Even though the new liturgical provision allowed for receiving the Eucharistic communion wafer in the hand, Sister Veronica respected the conservative Catholics who believe the sacred wafer should be placed on the tongue, and only by a Priest.

Then, as well as today, churchgoers (not to mention a handful of Priests) fear the power of a humble woman taking over sacred functions. Nuns were urged to be meek and compliant in their religious formation during the Postulancy and Novitiate, before the Second Vatican Council. That was how some parishioners expected Sister Veronica, and other laywomen, to continue.

She was very much part of the society in which she served and did not shelter herself. Religious Women, as a whole, are not pursuing personal power — only the right to better minister in the Catholic Church. Yet they constantly had to prove themselves, breaking through prejudices and carving niches, as others tried to figure them out. Furthermore, these same women had been reflecting on their own identity for a long time. "Who are we?" they asked themselves privately and in meetings. "How do we fit into the fabric and structure of the Church? Are we clerical, lay or some special hybrid of our own?"

Father Duane, working in the Brazilian Church where clergy is sparse and the base communities are many, once told of a survey, which revealed that over 65% of Sunday Catholic liturgies there have women presiders. In the American Church, apart from the male clergy, the majority of parish staff, pastoral agents and volunteer service personnel are women.

In many of the 174 Religious Orders in the United States, a common complaint, though a silent one, is "the Sisters make the bread, the Priests only consecrate it." The image is poignant. Pastoral action, like bread making, is a meticulous work with a variety of ingredients. Only with measured quantities, experienced expertise, and patient waiting will results be beautiful and palatable.

During the Second Vatican Council, all the Bishops met in Rome to scrutinize the state of the Church. On the agenda was the issue of the role of Sisters, since they outnumbered Priests three to one. The Council clearly spoke in favor of a greater role of women in the Church, but the male vote continues to dominate. It was a male hierarchy that refused these Religious Women a choice or a voice in most matters conceived in Canon Law regulations.

Surely Sister Veronica wondered how Christ would feel about the way the power of the Church remains firmly grasped by men. In married life and in the business world, generally, women are expected to take a subordinate role. Discrimination occurs not only in the secular world. Surprisingly, the religious world is guilty, too.

A few months after her arrival in WaKeeney she wrote, "Things are rather quiet, so I stir up my own goings-on. I was sitting here this morning, after Sunday Mass, moping that no one says 'Boo' around here, much less invites me in, or over. Not that I am excited about going out a lot, but the whole business about a ministry, of any kind, is interpersonal relations. I ended up calling the Sisters [Clarice and Adeline Marie] from St. Peter, Kansas, to go for a picnic at the Castle Rock formation, about fifteen miles southwest of here."

She was especially sensitive to the importance of developing friendships in a new community. "Our welcoming committee of three people is doing quite well. I get a list of newcomers to town, from the electric power company, and call them to introduce myself on behalf of our committee. I ask if anyone in the household is Catholic, and if we can come over to meet them. We average ten newcomers a month, making visits to three homes."

In her Life Review she wrote, "Building relationships is a type of ministry." She admittedly sought, "to heal old notions of ruler-wielding and crabby Nuns, who are now being so disobedient as to not even dress like Nuns. But I won't admit that reason for my preoccupation with relationships." Sister Veronica took to heart the task of trying to erase the stigma of stern Nuns, and she found it one of her toughest challenges in life. She tried her best to help others overcome their angry feelings and old ideas.

On the other hand, there are still a few people left today who praise these demanding task-master disciplinarians of yester-year, who taught them about consequences.

Just a few months after Sister Veronica's death, thirteen congregations from the Greater Cincinnati region gathered, in February 1996, and formed *Sisters United News*. It was an effort to promote a positive, up-to-date representation to help change the varying images of the ruler-wielding figures of days gone by, as well as the laughable singing Nuns of the Whoopi Goldberg movie, *Sister Act*. Instead, the *Sisters United News* rightly promotes themselves as "hidden treasures in society." They felt the true stories of today's dedicated Sisters were not getting out, and their mission was often misunderstood. Oftentimes, Sisters initiate and do work in areas where society and governments fail.

Sister Veronica encountered a few who asked, "Why aren't you Nuns dressed in black...and in church on your knees praying?" There was at least one parishioner who voiced his desire for all Sisters to return to wearing the head-to-toe garb. He wanted to see the visible outward symbol, as if faith in action was not enough.

"He asked me if I still had my Nun's Habit," Sister Veronica said. "He thought that it would be nice for me to wear it to give communion. I said, 'No, I made a suit with it.'" Sister Ginger Pearl verified that retort. "All of us woman, who opted into street clothes, recycled our Habits into beautiful wool suits. They were stunning."

Before Religious Women began wearing secular clothes, they were easily identifiable in their voluminous black Habits. It was a uniform as such, an easily recognizable symbol of Catholic identity, and still used by the Hollywood film industry today. The long Habit was an outward expression of the Sisterhood in Christ, but was also an obvious barrier to building relationships, which was one of the many reasons the majority of Sisters chose to do away with it. "It gets in the way — the wrong way," said one.

Remembering the days of the Habit, there was a formality, or stiffness, associated with the title Sister, Nun or Woman Religious. "I can't talk about that subject with her because she's a Nun," is an often-heard comment. Imagine how difficult communication was in the days when even today many people pull the imaginary curtain on conversations when they discover they are talking to a Sister. Suddenly no longer spontaneous, each word becomes guarded. Rarely will this woman be thought of as just "one of the girls," once she steps into the room. Many people still think of these women as different. Sometimes Sister Veronica's family was as guilty of this as others.

She continued, "The older nursing home residents understand that I am a Nun much easier than grade school students do." For many of these rural children, it was their first encounter with a Religious Woman. "Some of the students thought I was Father Dennis' sister because he kept calling me, 'Sister.' One student said, 'But you don't wear a Nun-suit.' I replied, 'That's because I am not a TV Nun.' They understand the word Nun better than Sister. So I am still learning."

Quoting one newspaper account highlighting the 350th anniversary of the founding of the Sisters of St. Joseph, "Today, the Sisters are almost unrecognizable. No longer dressed in the Habit, they blend in with society, although many of the Sisters glow with the spirit that comes from helping others."[5]

Sister Veronica often wore a cross hanging from her neck, or a small simple one pinned on her clothing, to distinguish herself as a "woman of faith." This outward sign of witness was worn not only during Church functions; the cross was a daily visible display reminding others of the Church's, and her, willingness to be involved in social issues.

She gave the parish community a lot of credit, and worked around what they would, and would not allow. "I realize I have not searched for new ways to serve here, but these people are about seven to fourteen years behind, so I really feel like a pioneer.

"Nuns in parish ministries are a frontier work here. There are still some strong problems with accepting a 'modern Nun.' My life has spoken for itself, and there has never been any cause for anyone to wag their tongues, except maybe for seeing me run around the streets in sloppy clothes at 7 o'clock some mornings," she tried some humor.

In a letter to Father Duane she wrote, "I'll slip in an article on 'Presence.' It's actually a dream, rather than reality. I only want to be a religious presence here, and my presence has given courage to others who try to get this gift of ministry accepted. Still, I am struggling to find a way to be meaningfully present. This weekend after Masses I am going 'Open Forum,' about 'Nuns in parish ministries' for anyone who shows up. I really want to design a day, or evening, of group prayer, and recollection and sharing, or whatever it turns out to be. But each time it seems to be the same people who take part in activities. The challenge is to broaden participation. I also want to plan some mini retreats in women's homes, over a shared noon meal. But with Father Kilian Dreiling in retirement here, the word 'retreat' would not jive with what they know of his terrific ability to give retreats. His occasional homilies are jewels, as is his style of delivery."

After three months of volunteering ten hours each week, she had a meeting with the parish council. "I asked them to consider reimbursing me for one-fourth time on the parish staff at the stipend recommended by the Salina Diocese, which is $1,000 for the entire year, or $2.50 per hour. This hourly rate is less then what teenage babysitters earn.

"The problem is that people here traditionally have done everything as volunteers. Hardly enough money to bother discussing, but they appeared shocked, and could not answer." Father Dennis is supportive, but he wants the people to decide."

In 1981 the grain market was glutted, prices plummeted and government in Washington, D.C. ordered a fifteen-percent cut in crop planting nationwide. Perhaps the local parishioners, who farmed in Trego County, felt this cut and it is possible the church collection basket experienced the pinch. However, in the scheme of things, the salary Sister Veronica asked for amounted to each family contributing a little over three dollars per year to have a Religious Woman at hand.

Historically, Catholic parish communities had no tradition of hiring people in ministries, other than Pastors. Not only were some of the parishioners stunned at seeing her in street clothes, living alone, and active in their community, they were annoyed at her for being there among them. When she asked for the small stipend, they were further flabbergasted, as if the vow of poverty means to starve, or work for free.

"Perhaps, this Catholic rural population wasn't easily convinced that this type of ministry deserved a salary," said Father Duane. "Perhaps the attitude most prevalent at the time was, 'Sister Veronica is doing her thing.'"

A parishioner, Elaine Newcomer, commented, "There was some resistance in the beginning when she first arrived. There were a few who murmured, 'since WaKeeney never had a Sister before, she wasn't really needed.' But before long she won them over."

Another parishioner, Marie Billinger, agreed, "When she first arrived, the Parish was not very receptive of having a Nun living here. But, with her ability to do, and say, the right thing, she was soon accepted. I think of Sister Veronica as a pathfinder. She did many things for our Parish, and our community. If she believed in something very strongly, and there was resistance, she would find a way."

†

Chapter Twenty-eight

It comes as a surprise for many Catholics to realize the Vatican does not financially support Sisters. They have to earn their keep, and find ways of sustaining themselves — all the while keeping the faith that the Lord will provide.

When Sister Veronica first entered the convent, in 1958, economic survival was not a concern. Many years ago the Sister-teachers and nurses, received a stipend of approximately one dollar a day. They worked for Catholic schools and hospitals kept afloat by little salary outlay, aside from low-paid lay teachers. Earned money was not paid directly to the Sisters, who took a vow of poverty, but was handled by the Motherhouse for their support. For these women, social security benefits are almost negligible, if non-existent, because there was so little to report on income tax W-2s.

Following the Second Vatican Council, financial consideration was something the Sisters, in many Orders, now had to contend with. With the onslaught of the 1980s came the theme of entrepreneurialism for the CSJ Sisters and the additional responsibility of doing their part to meet the challenge of dwindling funds and retirement benefits for elderly Sisters. The small salaries of the working Sisters don't cover the skyrocketing costs of retirement health care, housing and everyday living expenses.

Less than one-fourth of the Sisters, these who are young enough to work, face the dilemma of caring for the remaining three-fourths of the elderly population, which is growing much faster than the declining rate of those entering the Order. At one time the CSJ of Concordia, Kansas had over 600 members, which decreased to 250 in the mid-1990s.[1]

"'Bringing home the bacon' is a basic need of anyone who isn't a child," said Father Duane. "The hierarchy of the church has always let those in Religious Orders know they have to foot their own way. The Church — that is the Bishop, the parish, the Vatican — never paid the way for those in Religious Life — the Laity has. Religious life is basically supported by the earning power of its members, portfolios and contributions. A good balance of these three factors is important for financial stability.

"In the past, in the American Church, lay people have always been generous and supportive of religious life. It may be that when the good Sisters maintained the church structure (especially in social works such as hospitals, schools, and orphanages where admirable deeds touched hearts) many people, in turn, opened their pockets to support them," he continued. "With the change of scene, after Vatican II and Renewal, it became more costly for Sisters to live. When the

Sisters moved out of the big convents, there were now individual rents to pay, utilities, food, cars, gas and phones. More clothes were required, as well as getting into diverse activities, meetings to attend and more trips.

"The general psychology of the Sisters was their desire to be treated as professionals, and administer their own financial affairs, such as handling bank accounts, and credit cards in their own name. They competed with, and had a somewhat similar lifestyle to, lay professionals in their field, and were expected to earn money. This different type of Sister now has more of a lay role — professional and independent — and many parishioners were not too sure they wanted to support that type of Sister. Contributions fell off considerably, so the Sisters themselves have to bring in more money to support themselves."

In 1989 the National Conference of Catholic Bishops acknowledged the problem, and intervened in the crisis situation with a nationwide collection. Subsequently, the annual Retirement Fund for Religious Appeal assists, somewhat, in offsetting these living costs. "The collection, brings to light there are many retired and elderly Religious Men and Women, and the Community of religious orders, to which they belong, have not been able to adequately provide for them. Thus the appeal to the Laity," Father Duane concluded.

At the beginning of the next year, Sister Veronica was hired as Pastoral Minister for three hundred families. "The parish council finally agreed last Sunday morning, but only for a six-month period, as if the past six months of unpaid time doesn't count." Later she added, "I should be more relaxed now that my official role was guaranteed at the last parish council meeting. I felt I had to prove myself this spring, so this is the first week since I've been here that, at last, I feel a little more lighthearted, and at home. It may be the initial joy of finally getting one thing that I wanted.

"This is a small triumph, but I recognize it as a large step for me, and truly represents a victory for my personal desires, for the church of WaKeeney, for women in the church, and for Nuns of western Kansas, considering the Church here was seven to fourteen years behind most urban parishes last summer. It becomes an official approval of what I've been doing."

†
Chapter Twenty-nine

Sister Veronica's triumph over her paid ministry position was short lived. What followed, she called, "our parish horror story." An anonymous and disgruntled conservative parishioner placed an unapproved letter in a 1982 parish newsletter. [1]

"We, too, feel we are getting too much entertainment at Mass. Seems everyone wants to get into the act. Soon there will be no room for the Priest in the sanctuary. Why do we need all these changes, all of a sudden? Change is good. We all need that in our lives. But let us not go overboard. Can't we keep any of the old? We older members who helped build, establish and support this wonderful parish, have a right to ask, and demand (if you will), that we keep at least some of the old Liturgy of the Eucharist. We don't need women coming into the parish to tell us what Liturgy to use." Needless to say, the woman in question was Sister Veronica.

A Second Vatican Council website states: "Opposition to changes in the Church's liturgy became a rallying point for those whose discontent with change ran far deeper." This above mentioned letter was a prime example, as it challenged changes taking place within the Catholic Church.

"We also elected a parish council to represent us on parish matters," the caustic letter went on. "They should speak for us at the council meetings. It should not be open to every Tom, Dick and Harry who wants to express their opinion. Express your opinion to council members and let them speak for you." Sister Veronica penciled in, "I go to the council meeting, but never speak up unless asked."

The humiliation continued. "Our lay people have done a beautiful job in CCD, etc. Why do we need to pay someone to do the same things our people have been doing for years? Also, we would like to see only the parish name and phone number on our Sunday bulletin." Sister Veronica noted in the margin, "That's me again! I work twenty-five hours a week in the parish, and get paid for ten, and my name is printed in the bulletin with the rectory phone number."

There was a second anonymous Letter to the Editor. "Yes, we agree with your Newsletter. The church is turning into a show house. Saturday night, when they started to play the guitars, it sounded like we were at a dance instead of a church. A couple behind us asked if we wanted to dance, and the ones in front of us turned around and said, 'What are they doing playing dance music?' People across the aisle looked up to the choir to see what was going on. I called Father Dennis the next morning and told him what I thought about the guitar music. When I go to church, I want to be in church, and not in a dance hall. There are a lot of people who don't want that guitar music. I told Father Dennis that one of these days the people will do like they did at Goodland. Half of them stopped going to Mass. I've seen that myself." To this Sister Veronica commented, "Not true."

"And the women up there giving out communion, that's out in my books," the anonymous letter persisted. "A lot of others think that way, too. Why didn't our Lord appoint women when he picked the twelve apostles? He must have had a reason."

Sister Veronica wrote to Father Duane, "The newsletter editor, and a married couple, crashed an organizational meeting for Liturgical Planning and complained of guitars, women, cantors, music during communion, quiet time and more. The guitarists apologized for the so-called 'bad music' written about in the newsletter, but which was no more than one song the night in question. [In their defense] both the cantors and guitarists have been superb. Very prayerful, and well done.

"I received calls from about fifteen people expressing horror about such printed words. We decided not to make any response. This newsletter got printed, with these two nasty letters, after our pastor, Father Dennis, left for a three-week vacation to the Holy Land.

"A week later I was scheduled to be the Saturday night Eucharistic Minister, with [a visiting Priest] as our celebrant," Sister Veronica continued. "When he came into the sanctuary, I thought he had suffered a slight stroke. He looked awful and fiery. As we were ready to leave the sacristy he sneered at me, 'You are on the outside!' I didn't know what that meant, so I headed for the chair beside him, where all twelve of us Eucharistic Ministers have been sitting — up to today. He motioned for me to get out of the altar area, so I kneeled outside the altar rail, very obediently, but my heart started racing.

"Before Mass even started, he made this twenty-minute announcement that 'when he is celebrant he determines what goes on. He would have no guitars and no cantor up front — only in the balcony.' There was no mention of me, or other women, but he dared that anyone who said he was wrong would cause him to leave town. He said, he had 'prayed all day for God to take him, even on the pulpit, if he was wrong. He said that Father Dennis did not have the courage to tell people they were wrong.

"This Priest was having awfully grandiose psychosis, if you ask me. Sunday Mass was the same, except that the male Eucharistic Minister got to stay in the sanctuary. Meanwhile, at daily Mass, this Priest continues to expound on the glories of himself.

"Today's Lector got an upcoming schedule of Lectors and Eucharistic Ministers, with the women's names crossed off — including mine. Four different women have been over to my place to cry about this form of psychological rape." There were more supporting phone calls. "'Will Father Dennis be home tonight?' everybody is asking me.

"The four people in Music Ministry, who suffered so personally, just skipped Mass and went out to dinner together. That day Father Dennis was back home in time for evening Mass. Everybody pretended nothing happened, except there was no music.

"After a few days, a bulletin announced the other Priest would be leaving town the next day. But the next day this Priest shows up at Mass again, and announced that [supposedly] Father Dennis bugged him to stay awhile. Horrors again.

"I still don't know what Father Dennis even knows, except I think it best if he gets the whole truth after the other Priest leaves town. I hope the other Priest was able to leave without too many hurt feelings on anyone's part. No one can match words with him.

"This has been such a mess since Glorious Easter that I have put off writing until I had something sensible to write. The above is a 'nutshell' of my delayed death and [resurrection]. What God does, God does well! It sounds trite on paper, but it is important to those who were close to the situation at Christ the King parish. Now to pick up the pieces."

Later on she observed, "I imagine Father Dennis must feel like a town pump. The phone is always ringing, and people come and go at ease to the rectory. I can't see how he gets anything else done, except meet people. And it seems he is always invited for meals."

Not much later a Deacon was added to the staff. "This made me wonder if the council would now think I am unnecessary, but luckily the parish is not pushed for money." She was honest in her letters: "I find myself envious of the time the new Deacon and Father Dennis have for each other, and for the community. Envious, too, of how well the people have taken to the Deacon, especially the younger kids, when I struggle so hard to talk with anyone.

"My whole purpose in coming to WaKeeney was to do just what Father Dennis so effectively has done, and gotten all the credit for. But underneath, both of us know I enabled him more than the community will ever know. I've had to struggle with my own feelings of jealousy for wanting a fraction of the attention, and concern, from the people that he gets."

She shook off the self-pity. "It has been encouraging to have weekly planning sessions with Father Dennis. What I expect is to be part of his realization, and spiritual sharing. I let go of that hope when [the visiting Priest] was here. By Thanksgiving, I felt a new trend emerging."

No doubt, Sister Veronica was sympathetic and understanding to those parishioners who were slow to change. She readily admitted that she, too, had to be convinced that something was worth adopting before accepting it herself.

This included the Habit change in 1968, Renewal, Liturgical innovations, and participation in the Catholic Charismatic movement. Nevertheless, she graduated years ago from the simplicity of the doctrines in the *Baltimore Catechism I and II*, and moved into the dense philosophical writings of Father Teilhard de Chardin, and other theological essayists.

She attended periodic lectures at the Motherhouse. In 1982, one was held on the topic of Thomas Merton's pacifist spirituality. At that time, he was considered the most significant American Catholic figure of the twentieth century. She read the autobiographical *Seven Storey Mountain*. The many volumes of spiritual writings by the noted Trappist Monk were popular with Religious Men and Women. Following his accidental death by electrocution, in 1968 in Bangkok while meeting with the Dalai Lama, a collection of Merton's works became even better known.

Addressing the seven deadly sins — pride, covetousness, lust, anger, gluttony, envy, and sloth — Merton describes climbing the mountain on opposite sides and "a coming together at the peak." Sister Veronica could relate this to her own mountaintop experiences. She read of Merton reaching across cultural lines to include East-West thought, and specifically of Buddhist meditations to eliminate anger, which she had a chance to use many times over. She learned that "self-emptying" is at the heart, not only of Christian beliefs, but of Buddhism, as well. "Effective change [comes about] by a refusal to participate in lies or deceptions," is one of Thomas Merton's memorable lines.

The Canadian writer, Alice Munro, also writes about self-deception — more specifically about the lies we tell ourselves about who we really are. In Munro's fictional book, *The Love of a Good Woman*, there is a closeness, yet friction, in her story telling of deception in her analysis of small-town life: "You have no privacy at all. You have a role, a character, but it's one that other people have made up for you."

"At times I've felt a gently humbled scapegoat," Sister Veronica said. "Other times a forerunner of someone greater to come in my place, and generally a weak instrument." She was accused of destroying the very substance she was there to build. More than a few times she bore the blame for the mistakes of others, but she quietly lived the Gospel. She treated the parishioners as if their souls were under her care. Sometimes she feared she had failed. She generated anxiety in the less secure by her sheer presence, but she was sure that people would come around, given enough time. She wanted to be accepted, shortcomings and all, and was willing to review her self-perception and common frailties. Those who really knew her appreciated that she came from a different mold: courageous, invincible, and absolute in her convictions.

Most times, she stood up to, and passed beyond, these difficult situations in her pioneer ministry. Other incidents hardened her heart. Afterward she would pray for forgiveness of not being more Christ-like. The times were tumultuous. As she faced minor surgery, she reached a positive conclusion: "I was all in a tizzy trying to decide whether to have [the surgery done] here, or go back to Concordia where my other records are. Then I faced why I wanted to leave town. I didn't want to go into surgery, not feeling loved around here. While I was trying to decide what to do, some strange man drove by, and waved a big smile. Then I remembered all the people who do love me. So that settled that."

After a while she said, "I think I have remained remarkably sane. Since the first of January, I feel I now finally belong here. The whole parish suffered together, and later I felt us all grow together. Many supportive comments confirmed this was all in God's Plan when I said 'yes' to leaving the security of the hospital in Belvidere, and heading for some unknown.

"This second year has been growth inspiring and finds me full of new resolutions. I am confident I will be happy here. Traditionally, it takes me awhile to settle in. Many of the blessings in disguise were apparent only in retrospect. The biggest thing in my life now seems to be claiming the role as Pastoral Minister. Where there may have been fifteen people vehemently against me earlier, I know not of a single one now. It has been a triumph for women in the church, as well as for me personally. Dear Dad, with his patience and confidence in people, has been a model for me."

Grandparents Stanislas and Rosanna Hebert Morin. Grandmother died in 1917, at age 41, during childbirth after twelve live births.

Left to right, Back row: Dad (John Roy) and his siblings: Dona, Emile
Middle row: Philip, Edmond, Sister Laura Annette (Jeannette), Omer, Oscar
Front row: RoseLee, Grandpa P.H. Roy, Grandmother Laura Saindon Roy, Zella

In 1960 John and Olive Morin Roy were presented the SCCN Kansas Rural Catholic Farm Family of the Year award for their participation in civic and religious groups over a period of years.

Ila Mae lived here, her childhood home, from 1940 until she entered the convent. Homesteader Eli Sherman built this eleven-room stone house of locally quarried limestone around 1885. In 1960 the house was demolished and a four-bedroom ranch style house was constructed. This photo was taken around 1945 before repairs and improvements were made.

Ila Mae, 4, and Ronald, 8, standing in front of the bay window of the stone house on Ronald's First Holy Communion day, May 1944. He most resembled Grandpa Roy with his sturdy frame, red hair and freckles. In later years Sister Veronica recalled that he carried her piggy-back from chair to chair, then hung a picture of the "Assumption of Mary" on the wall. Two months later Ronald drown while wading in Sand Creek, just south of the family home. The tragic loss of this beloved brother may have caused the onset of her life-long anxiety.

Ila Mae, along with her brothers Gary (Father Duane) and Allan, and Dad, shows her 4-H grand prize winning Hereford, 1952. In later years she returned to Kansas as Pastoral Minister, taking part in the Rural Life Commission and was involved in sustainable agriculture issues.

Ila Mae, seated center, holding Cheryl, posed with her siblings while home from Marymount College. Religious articles adorned the walls of the family living room. 1958.

Webster High senior graduation, 1957. Although hearing impaired, Ila Mae was an honor roll student and had a dream of becoming a math teacher. She held leadership offices, excelling both in school and 4-H. Ila Mae won numerous awards in cooking and sewing, gardening, home and grounds beautification, recording keeping and livestock care. She also participated in basketball, softball, track, cheerleading, band and chorus at school.

The magnificent St. Joseph's Catholic Church, in Damar, stands as a spiritual beacon on the Kansas plains. This was the place of Ila Mae's baptism in 1940, and her parent's marriage, in 1932. Grandfathers Roy and Morin, and great-grandfathers Hebert and Saindon helped to construct the church, which began in 1912.

Nazareth Convent – the Sisters of St. Joseph Motherhouse, Concordia, Kansas. Established in 1883. Sister Veronica is buried here at Mount Calvary Cemetery.

The Postulancy. The Sixteen Prophets and Nine Junior Angelicas, 1958 - 1959. Ila Mae Roy, back row, third from the left. Bishop F.W. Freking in center back.

The Sixteen Prophets outside the entrance to the Sacred Heart Chapel just before taking vows to become Brides of Christ.

A Bride of Christ. Ila Mae Roy. March 19, 1959, St. Joseph's Day.

Grandmother Laura Roy, Sister Veronica Mary Roy, after receiving the Habit and a new name and her aunt,Sister Rose Irma Morin, 1959.

1963-1964. Dietetic Internship. Good Samaritan Hospital. Cincinnati.
Sister Veronica, Front row, second from left. Hospital Sisters wore white Habits.

St. Joseph's Hospital, Concordia, Kansas.
September 1964.

Sister Veronica holding her nephew, David Monarchi, Jr. Golden, Colorado, April 1968. After the Second Vatican Council, Sisters were given the option to adopt a new style of dress, as shown by this transitional Habit and modified veil, with front hair showing. She made the complete transition later that year to regular clothes and with no veil. This much discussed transition stage was approached with apprehension by some Sisters and wholly embraced by others, while lay people, as a whole, were even slower to accept the Sisters change.

Sister Veronica returned to college after working as head dietitian for nearly twelve years at St. Joseph's Hospital, Belvidere, Illinois. She earned a Master's degree in nutrition at Kansas State University, Manhattan, in May 1981.

May 1981. The Wedding of her godson and youngest brother, Rodney Roy and Christi Karlin. Left to right: Kenneth, Linda, Father Duane, Joan , Mother, Christi and Rodney, Cheryl, Roger, Sister Veronica, and Allan.

Father Duane Roy, OSB, her younger brother and spiritual advisor, with Pope John Paul II at Montecasino, Italy. September 1980.

Sister Veronica visited Father Duane in Brazil. She was an avid letter-writer and corresponded frequently with him during his thirty years there. He returned to Brazil in 2002 after a one-year sabbatical

Silver Jubilee March 1984. Ten of the remaining Sixteen Prophets.
Sister Veronica, fourth from left.

Sister Veronica served as Pastoral
Minister in the WaKeeney, Logan
and New Almelo parishes. 1981-
1995

As a graduate of the LUMEN
Program. Sister Veronica to the
right of Bishop Geo. Fitzsimons,
1992

November 15, 1995. On the day of her death the CSJ Leadership Team gathered with the elderly Sisters at St. Mary's Convent, Concordia, Kansas. Sister Veronica, back row, left end.

✝

Chapter Thirty

She started off 1984 by saying, "I certainly have all I can manage. The year predicted to put us critically between disaster and peace, the year of Jubilee, the year of Reconciliation, the year of our CSJ Centenary, and now mine." It was as if she was saying to herself, *"I'm either going to become a flop at this pioneer venture, or I'm going to make peace with it all and celebrate it as a giant step, for the people here and for myself. It's my Jubilee Year!"*

Just as married couples celebrate their anniversaries, so do those in Religious Orders. On St. Joseph's Day, March 19, the eleven remaining of the "Sixteen Prophets," came together at the Motherhouse in Concordia, for their Silver Jubilee.[1]

She delayed her individual celebration. "Lent is just not the time." Instead, she waited until the first weekend in May. Christ the King parishioners, CSJ Sisters, and her own immediate family attended the two-day occasion.

"I worked with both choirs to select music. Saturday is a guitar set, and Sunday is a more traditional assembly, which usually sings from the Gregory hymnal for communion. Remarkably, we ended up with similar songs — a work of unity.

"I was the greeter, before the two weekend Masses, in case some people chose not to come to either reception. The family began the procession, with my brothers and sisters bringing in the symbolic offertory gifts (an earthenware vessel, loaf of bread, Brazilian Crucifix, and family photo)." Our late father's spiritual presence was felt that day, too.

"For the profession of faith I gave a brief explanation of my vows, which I then renewed. Father Dennis Schaab blessed my profession ring, and also of the two other CSJ Jubilarians present.[2] Beforehand, I baked the unleavened Eucharistic bread, and helped break it, since the Gospel of the day was the Emmaus story. I was not a Eucharistic Minister, however, since those who serve wear robes. The Altar Society and Knights of Columbus gave me a suit, and I didn't want to cover that up."

At first, the gift of the pastel blue suit made her feel uncomfortable. She was not use to anything new, or "flashy" as she called it, but she was grateful for their generosity. She tried to heed the biblical command, "When women adorn themselves... in expensive apparel, they are not leading silent lives."[3]

"The parish, specifically the Altar Society, wanted to host whatever I wanted and that meant a lot to me, as I could hardly put on my own receptions." She requested one after both Saturday evening and Sunday morning Masses, with simple refreshments of coffee, punch and cake. Ninety-eight guests showed up on Saturday evening, and 114 on Sunday. "This affirmed me, as generally our people don't turn out very well for teas or receptions, except for the usual pillars of the church, and few show up at all for any socials on Saturday night."

She was extremely pleased with the outpouring of support and willingness to help with the occasion, since she had neither time, nor funds. "I know Father Dennis was instrumental in making the people think it was their idea. There were so many ways the parishioners helped with the celebration, but I did a lot, too, and that made it exceptional." She told her story, of the past twenty-five years, by creating a display of scrapbooks, the CSJ Eulogies of four hundred deceased, and publications to advertise vocations.

"A banner was made, and I prepared a bulletin board to match the verse on the prayer card from Micah 6:8. *'You have been told, O man, what is good, and what the Lord requires of you; only to do right and to love goodness, and to walk humbly with your God.'*"

She was especially happy that so many from out of town were there, in western Kansas, to celebrate her special commemoration. Immediately after, she sent nearly one hundred handwritten thank-you notes. "I am so grateful you were able to share the occasion of my Silver Jubilee. Your presence really did add to my joy, and I was so elated with the whole weekend. I do have memories of a lifetime."

Afterward she added, "I am one for memories and treasures, and am trying to relish more of what my Jubilee year says to me. I began to understand why some of the older, wiser CSJs insist that we send greetings to all Jubilarians. Many older Sisters are still around to celebrate their golden years of service to God." There are even a few who have celebrated sixty, seventy, or seventy-five years.[4]

"Our group of sixteen, who entered the convent together in 1958, was exceptional. It was very unusual. We won't see any more large groups like that anymore. I will work on photo publicity for the Hays paper about our Silver Jubilarians from hometowns around western Kansas."

In mid-July, she drove her dear friend, Sister Francis Alma Royer, to Gary, Indiana, where she would serve as Chaplain of an inner-city hospital. After returning from this trip Sister Veronica's hometown parish, St. Thomas, hosted another festive, but smaller reception. She responded to Father Duane who sent a letter to be read at the ceremony. "I read again the loving tribute you sent for my Jubilee celebration at Stockton. I have it hanging, as a gentle prod, to allow these reflections to shine and work, where necessary, to bring them into being."

Following the celebrations in WaKeeney and Stockton, she was astonished at the generosity shown to her. "The family gave me a color television. I received $450 in cash from the parishioners. Father Dennis put in $100 of his own money.

Relatives and friends gave a total of $250, so I have applied for a $595 discounted tour package to the Holy Land." Fifteen years later a similar pilgrimage would cost more than $2,500.

She delayed the trip for ten months. Once home, she issued a press release. "Sister Veronica Roy recently returned from the Bible Lands. She was accepted by Wholesale Tours to make the study tour, in mid-February, on their subsidized rates for Pastors, with ministers and their spouses of six denominations, four from New York, and thirty from Canada. The group was in Israel for nine days, then continued to Athens for another three days. Sister is grateful to the many friends, of Christ the King parish, who made this pilgrimage possible at the closing of her Silver Jubilee year."[5]

"I began a scrapbook three months ahead, typing in Sacred Scripture, and leaving space for photos. This process heightened the anticipation, and it is something I would recommend for other trips." The scrapbook also served as a guide for several slideshows she was asked to present for the parishioners and to the Federated Women's Club Convention upon her return.

"The trip was a living Bible course bringing meaning to the Words of Scripture. An excellent Christian-Arab guide shared the Old Testament history of God's people. Jerusalem was very special. It had been a long time fantasy of mine to sit in the garden of Gethsemane." To her disappointment, it was walled in.

On a postcard she wrote, "It was hard to imagine all this from reading or seeing pictures. It was low season for tourists. Mostly dreary, a little unseasonably chilly and not all the flowers are out." She referred to Bertha Spafford Vester's 1962 book, *Flowers of the Holy Land*, featuring the Garland Chrysanthemum seen in fields and lowlands. The Pomegranate, cultivated since Biblical times, dotted the land, as well as almond trees, which are the first to blossom in winter. She noted the fertility, "Willpower, endurance, irrigation and industrialization have made a desert bloom."

She walked the *Via Dolorosa* (street of sorrows) "alone and thoughtful." In Bethlehem (the house of bread) she kneeled on the steps near the Holy Manger Grotto, and "many others followed to kneel." She was always a leader, in her silent ways.

Accompanying the slides of Bethany (the house of poverty) she narrated, "There were some excavations at what the guide called the House of Lazarus." Sister Veronica was a bit of a mystic, that is, one who searches for truth without reference to reason, the senses, or thought, but only through contemplation and love. Not surprisingly, she said, "This was a home with three rooms, in which I personally sensed hospitality of the time. Extremely small, but meaningful. It was a place to which Christ often resorted, and was the home of his friends, Lazarus, Martha and Mary.

"Another location, maintained by the Anglicans as Golgotha, is an example of multiple places that are revered as true sites, so we are called to remember that the shrine is in the heart. Other sites I found touching were Capernaum, Nazareth, Cana and the Jezreel Valley."

She explained, after wading into the 10-by-50-mile Dead Sea, (so named because no life can exist in its waters due to an abundance of mineral salts), "It felt like I had on tight elastic stockings. Very therapeutic."

The tall, climbing thicket rose, a pure white wild flower, grows abundantly in Galilee. Here she purchased from the street hawkers a souvenir "Loaves and Fishes" plate. Having a premonition of her own death, she made a notation on the back and willed it to Father Duane.

She saw a few ancient olive trees — some dated three thousand years old. This particular tree does not die, but forms new growth from the trunk. How appropriately Mother was named. Sister Veronica purchased another souvenir, a hand carving of the Holy Family, made of the olive wood, and willed it to our brother, Roger and Jacalyn.

In later years she recalled this trip, as well as the one to Brazil, as highlights in her life, and reflected that both were gifts from those who loved her.

Chapter Thirty-one

"...Jesus entered a village where a woman whose name was Martha welcomed him. She had a sister named Mary who sat beside the Lord at his feet."

—Luke 10, 38-39.

Sister Veronica pushed herself to "The More" in living out the Maxims of Perfection of her CSJ Community. Her ministry expressed itself in many ways, and her daily life was an example of the living gospel. When our brother, Father Duane, described her parish work as a "partner-role," she replied, "I've remembered that, and it has served as an inner vision for me these months."

Each year all CSJ Sisters write their own Personal Commitment to Mission statement. This year she wrote, "I will depend more on the local parishioners for input and personal support, as we respond daily to inspirations of serving one another, as we journey together in our worship of our loving God." Sister Veronica clearly understood that while a church is a building, a Church is people.

The elderly in the parish had a variety of reasons for being especially fond of her, but the common denominator was, typically, the no-strings-attached attention she paid them. One explained, "She organized monthly Golden Age Potluck Dinners in our parish, then had a little program planned, or a game of cards or bingo, and ended with a prayer or Benediction in church."

"We all enjoyed her very much," said Rosemary Bollig. "My husband and I are in our eighties. Sister Veronica treated old people very nicely." Another said simply, "She treated the elderly with great respect."

In the early years in WaKeeney, Sister Veronica and the pastor, Father Dennis Schaab, attended a two-and-a-half-day Pastoral Care of the Sick workshop. Later she said, "We had parishioners go to a Pentecost session on Evangelization and Ministry to Aging. Now I want to take the next step. When I first arrived, I felt the parish was behind the times. But now, three of us have been bringing Communion from the Sunday Liturgy to the hospital, two nursing homes and generally to two to six homebound."

"At one time Sister Veronica was the only one taking Communion to the old people, sick and homebound," said Marie Billinger, a parishioner. "After much hesitation, I asked if she would like me to help. She accepted my offer, and after a while encouraged me to do it by myself. I did not feel worthy to administer Communion. She said, 'Pray about it,' and I was soon commissioned."

In later years Elaine Newcomer, a parishioner from nearby Ogallah, was also commissioned as Eucharistic Minister. "Sister Veronica served the parish in many ways, including visiting the sick and sorrowing. Whenever someone had a problem to discuss, or needed support, they went to her."

It was difficult for Sister Veronica when she first moved to the parish. Not everyone knew her purpose, and she wasn't always warmly received. "I felt so helpless after a funeral this week. I feel there must be a problem with my identity. I went to the home of the deceased and after a while they said, 'Do you want something?' 'No,' I said. 'I just came over.'"

She felt strongly about corporal works of mercy, and often attended Christian wake services at the mortuary. "Thanks to our Liturgy committee, we now have a lay bereavement minister," she said. "Except I will be doing the first funeral, as she is with her own critically ill mother."

"It is a rewarding ministry," Rosann Felder added. "We go to the family immediately upon notification, assist in any way needed, and help plan the liturgy for their loved one. Sister Veronica got me started, always giving an example, and invited the rest of us to do likewise. Perhaps it took a little push, and then she offered to go with us, or was there when we needed her to carry on."

Sister Veronica was among the first Hospice volunteers in northwestern Kansas, and spoke to the I CAN COPE (cancer support group) and donated her professional guidance from a dietetic perspective. The year before her own death, she often referred to Kathy Kalina's guide, *Midwife for Souls: for hospice care workers, and all who live with the terminally ill.*

Regretfully when our dad died of lung cancer in 1978, the Hospice concept had not yet spread to the community of Stockton. Therefore, he was not a recipient of this compassionate type of care, unlike Mother who benefited seven years later, as she was able to spend her final months at home.

Sister Veronica learned from these experiences with our parents and afterward brought comfort to many people who came her way. "She helped my husband when he was dying, and brought him such peace," said one parishioner. Another added, "At three o'clock in the morning, she came quickly to be with us when our mother died," added Marion Parke, "When my daughter died, Sister Veronica drove twenty-four miles to our home just to be with us, and pray with our family. She offered a spiritual and comforting presence." Mary Aschenbrenner noted, "Sister Veronica ministered in many ways. She came to visit me often, and was a lot of help when my husband died."

She was involved in activities, some of which might seem mundane, but each was important to the community. "We had a birthday party for twenty-nine children who were baptized in the past eighteen months. We wrote it up for the [Northwestern Kansas] *Register*, with a nice photo. I got one of our creative writing women to be our contact. I have been doing it, but as we know, the greater challenge is to get someone else to do it well."

Another time she said, "The big news of the week was the Ordination of Steve Parke, C.PP.S. at 4 p.m. Friday. His mother is a dear friend of mine. She has been as much in the 'front of the church' as I've tried to be, as one of the three female Eucharistic Ministers, and a Bible Studies leader for several years. She was a C.PP.S. Nun until it came time for her final vows." She left the convent and married. "Steve is the oldest of her six children.

"The Ordination Mass was bad timing for harvesters and merchants, but still that did not excuse so many," said Sister Veronica. "I feel the parish has been apathetic, and noticeably lagging in attendance at many functions. If it weren't for large families and other Religious...About twenty-five Precious Blood Priests have been around this weekend, making me all the more homesick for my own CSJ Community.

"The 6 p.m. ordination dinner was nice. A polka band played from 9 p.m. until midnight — a source of tongue wagging. 'Never heard of an ordination dance,' the gossip started. Few from the parish showed up, but it sure made sense to the people who attended. Might as well be celebrating their joy at a dance, rather than just drinking the night away. Father Parke's First Mass at 1 p.m. on Saturday was appreciably represented by the parish. Our Saturday evening guitar group played at Mass. (They were the ones blasted back in April, and when I was thrown out of the sanctuary.) The C.PP.S. Director of Liturgy [Kansas City Province] came the night before, and polished up the group. All the details were well thought out. The music was outstanding — exceptional."

When the parish celebrated its fiftieth anniversary, Sister Veronica was in the midst of a quilt project designed by more than 170 parish families. The quilt blocks were sewn into three banners for display. We had lots of committees. That was the main thing — getting people involved in telling their own story. I could tell by the way people were coming into church that it would be joyous. Bishop Fitzsimons was principal celebrant. I was the commentator and also wrote the intercessions and offertory explanations."

When the Women's Lenten Breakfasts were having difficultly finding a place to meet, she invited them [to the hospital where she worked]," said one parishioner. Another added, "Sister attended Vicariate Priests and Religious Meeting Days, Lay Vicariate meetings, Council of Catholic Women Meetings, Religious Education meetings, and those for the Altar Society. She was an educator, telling what she had learned, and invited us to attend these meetings, too." Another parishioner said, "Several of us attended a Sunday meeting at nearby Hoxie. Sister Veronica volunteered to have dinner ready, and waiting in the oven at her house, when we all got back so we wouldn't have to worry about cooking. She was thoughtful in so many ways. Another time we did not have time to fix lunch. Sister Veronica just invited us to eat with her."

"I find the many jobs a rewarding combination of the biblical Mary and

Martha, and realistic of both body and soul needs," Sister Veronica said. Indeed a blend of the two.[1]

It was Sister Veronica's desire to empower others by developing their skills and talents. Rosann Felder stated, "Sister Veronica was a great enabler. She shared her vision to live a Christian Life. She was a giving person, which allowed others to be giving, too, by working in many ministries inspired by her religious presence. She was a model of what a Religious [Woman] should be, and because of her example many have offered their talents and abilities making it possible for Christ the King to grow as a faith community." Marie Billinger tagged on, "She was always there for whomever needed her. If she didn't have the answer to something, she would get it."

She was involved in a multitude of charitable causes and activities long before a major and lengthy theological Second Vatican Council analysis on world hunger was prepared addressing obligations to the poor and afflicted. In her Life Review she wrote, "At home, during my childhood, we prayed for vocations, missionary lands and for the Holy Father's intentions. We contributed to Peter's Pence, among other charities, for use in spreading the gospel, which, through the Holy Father's hands, is a universal means of practicing works of mercy. Blood was donated to the Red Cross. Many pounds of used clothing were given through our church to be distributed overseas, especially in the later years, to South America [where Father Duane served on mission].

"Money was also donated to support CRS [Catholic Relief Services]." As the U.S. Bishop's Overseas Relief and Development Agency, it typically funds the systems needed in villages for drinkable water, agricultural improvement and women's training programs. The life-saving essentials, such as high-protein food, sanitation, blankets, clothing and medicine, benefit the poorest of the poor around the world, without regard to race, beliefs or location, but especially children, the sick and elderly and pregnant women.

A Christ the King parishioner said, "If there was anything worthwhile going on, Sister Veronica was involved with it." One way she urged the local community to greater charity and sharing was through CROP, a program of Church World Service/CWS, an inter-congregational effort to solve the root cause of hunger. Her participation in CROP was a living example of the way she reached out, in an ecumenical way, to those of other faiths. This was in keeping with one of the aims of Vatican II: to establish a better relationship with other religious bodies looking ultimately to the healing of division in Christianity.

During youthful years our neighbor, Merle Grover, taught this family about *ecumenism* long before it became a household term for Catholics in the 1970s. This holy Christian woman, a devout Methodist, was a great influence and inspiration in Sister Veronica's life. From Mrs. Grover, she first learned about Christian Relief Overseas Program/CROP, which is the Protestant counterpart to CRS.

Perhaps Sister Veronica recalled how Catholic Relief Services had turned her down in 1980, when she volunteered her services in Thailand. Now, in WaKeeney, she did what she could to serve at the grassroots level.

"Locally CROP has a good reputation, although I extremely dislike the fund-raising aspect." Nevertheless, for five years Sister Veronica was involved in "The Walk," an event used for fund-raising. "More than 85 to 90 percent of every dollar raised goes mainly for self-help in meeting human needs. That is direct assistance versus administration costs." This is in sharp contrast to other agencies that have highly paid administrators. "Those who donate can specify their funds be used for either CRS or CROP. About 30 percent of 57 million dollars, raised last year, came from appeals in local communities such as walks, fasting and other awareness exercises. I only agreed to chair it, for the [non-denominational] Ministerial Alliance, on the basis of consciousness raising.

"I have been spending about two hours in the evenings at the booth that I put up at the Trego County Fair, so that people would say, 'Sure, I know what CROP is. I saw it at the Fair.' The display is attractive, serving as an advertisement with influence, but not popular in the sense that we had no giveaways to attract people. "We usually have about eighty-five participants. I am planning for more this year with a choice of a four- or eight-mile walk. I walked eight miles, in two hours and ten minutes, and felt great." The next year she said, "We had over one hundred walkers. The following year they raised $2,500, which doubled from four years earlier. Ever the volunteer for worthy causes, Sister Veronica was modest about her participation. However, upon her departure, the Pastor, parish and civic community applauded her work with CROP, along with all the other ways she was a public servant in her daily walk with the Lord.

During Pope John Paul II's Papal Visit to the United States, in 1995, he blessed CRS efforts: "Your determined efforts to meet the needs of the countless number of people around the world who turn to you for help bear eloquent testimony to the Christian virtue of charity...I gladly entrust Catholic Relief Services — its benefactors, staff and volunteers — to Mary, the loving Comforter of the Afflicted, and I make my own the prayer of Saint Paul: 'May the Lord increase you and make you overflow with love for one another and for all.'"[2]

Archbishop Cordes said, "For us Catholics, charity activity is a real proving ground for the church's credibility and its message." At the same time, he cautioned that the church's humanitarian activities must be distinguished from evangelization, or the world may see the church as a 'type of Red Cross,' ignoring its Gospel message.[3] In keeping with that plea, Catholic Relief Services has continued to work closely with other international organizations in providing food, shelter, medicine and spiritual aid. In recent years it aided the exodus, in biblical proportions, of the peoples of Kosovo, and in 2001 assisted earthquake victims of El Salvador.

It's difficult to comprehend that in addition to handling parish ministry, during these years, she was also working at several hospitals, writing a family genealogy book, doing volunteer work, as well as taking college classes. "I am doing three Practicums on prior learning experiences in CCD [Confraternity of Christian Doctrine] and parish ministry. I declined pay this month, asking for a nine-month contract, instead of the usual ten. I have ten meetings this month all related to the parish. That does not even count [separate dietetic] contract meetings."

She continued, "I got on an ad hoc committee to design a survey of preferences of parishioners. Religious education was their top priority." She was very concerned with all aspects of rural life including the need for religious education. Since there was no Catholic school in the vicinity, much like her own childhood, CCD religion classes (formerly known as Catechism) are held in this parish, as they are nationwide. She understood the importance of teaching children about their faith, especially in today's world, for without this foundation, their minds are easy prey for cults.

"I'd rather teach than coordinate, but now I've got both. There are phone calls to make for recruiting volunteers, schedule them to come in to get acquainted with the resources in our nice library, then get them to commit to four nights of catechist formation training classes given around the diocese, and encourage them that they are doing just fine. I want to get the year lined up before July. Traditionally I do that during August, but I get so nervous about it, as we have not always had all our books in time."

One year she said, "We start our first CCD classes tonight, then I hope to breathe easier. The staff really did hearten me. A very impressive group of volunteers — nearly forty teachers, aides, musicians, media, library and nursery for children of the staff. A sneaky way of educating the adults, too, by getting them to agree to help the little ones." She also got some of the teachers to take college credit courses.

One year she said, "I am up to my ears. I am getting sour dreading what's ahead. It seems to trap me in administrative work, and not leave time for parish ministry. I am keeping track of where the time goes, and fifty percent of parish ministry is CCD. The actual time last month was 140 hours, and already I am up to 105, for three weeks." All the while, she was only paid $25 each week for her parish ministry position, in contrast to some lay religious education directors in parishes now, some of whom are paid $25,000 to $40,000 annually, and sometimes substantially more.

"People may not go to church, but it seems one hundred percent will send their children to CCD. They really [participate in] preparations for the sacraments of First Penance, First Communion and Confirmation. Entire families come for the half-hour interview, which I see as a real hunger to pass on the faith. I have been helping second-graders prepare for their First Communion. Tomorrow, six of our older students, grade four through eight, are making their First Communion. I was their main teacher, which I enjoyed very much." Another year she said, "I helped two fifth-graders who never made theirs."

Over the years she handled a variety of age groups. One year a volunteer took a paid position as community night school teacher, leaving a vacancy for the eighth grade class. "I'm now teaching them. A lovely group of eleven students, well known among teachers to be the best class of all. Another year started off without a teacher for eleventh and twelfth grade. "So I taught them last week using the U.S. Bishop's *Peace and Pace*.

At the end of the school year she said, "Confirmation was three weeks ago; last classes of CCD were last Wednesday; staff evaluation meeting this Wednesday; and this Sunday night Bible studies are at my home, which means trying to clean it up at the last minute."

She also taught Rite of Christian Initiation of Adults (RCIA) classes to three families. This is the process by which adult converts are received into full communion with the Catholic Church. "I am always home Monday evening at 8:15 p.m., after I finished teaching this class."

One year she served as co-coordinator for the religious education program, with an enrollment varying between 200 and 250. "Our parish is having its first carnival today. The proceeds are earmarked for CCD and CYO. Two women are scheduling children to work in booths for an hour at a time. If children have to be somewhere, generally parents are supportive. That is the only way to get people involved. Parents, grandparents, aunts and uncles will travel for miles to see their children in the spotlight, even for one somersault. Otherwise, many don't want to be bothered."

Both parishioners Elaine Newcomer and Mary Aschenbrenner agreed that Sister Veronica did a lot for the program. "At the parish picnic she organized little skits for the children, and games for us. A real supporter of CYO [Catholic Youth Organization], and youth activities, she attended all possible events."

Nevertheless, Sister Veronica wasn't afraid to speak her mind. "I always thought we overdo Masses. We sent nine young teens to a Junior CYO convention, in Hays. Mass was at 2 p.m. on Saturday. Maybe it was a first time 'big Mass' experience for lots of rural kids, but it seemed more like a time filler, when they were there for a fairly short time." Clearly, she saw that age group could have benefited from hands-on gospel teachings.

In previous years the parish hosted dinners at local restaurants around Christmastime to thank the volunteers. "This year the Pastor wants to invite those who served the parish in other ways, too. I feel this gesture will be a source of reconciliation among the many who do so much. I designed special invitations for nearly 150 diners, including spouses." However, several weeks later she exclaimed, "After the invitations were distributed I found that some volunteers feel this is unfair, since they do more than others. I say the biblical lesson [of generosity] we hear every year about the laborers in the vineyard still needs repeating."[4]

Because of so much prior complaining, and to hold down expenses the next year, a parishioner cooked an evening dinner, in the church basement, for the religious education volunteers. "I usually do a fairly good job of being Master of Ceremonies. For entertainment, we tapped talented high school students who were recipients of speech class, and debate team awards," Sister Veronica explained.

Directly after Vatican II, the Blessed Virgin Mary had been put "on the back burner," so to speak. In general, Mary was not as revered, as during the pre-Vatican II era. On the other hand, Marian devotion continued to be figured in the spirituality of Sister Veronica, as she carried the middle name of Mary for her thirty-six years of religious life.

After Mother's death in 1985, Sister Veronica inherited her ruby red chaplet, a type of rosary, which Mother bought in Canada during her lifelong dream of a pilgrimage to St. Anne de Beaupre shrine. In 1988, Armelia Dreiling, a Christ the King parishioner, gave her two chaplets of the Holy Infant Jesus (one is gold; the other is blue capped with gold metal filigree). "Except where noted, I have all of them listed, with instructions how to recite. There are about fifty, plus the others that are not chaplets. The old ones are even more special. If you ever see any that are different from five-decade rosaries, think of me, even though I probably will have it already."[5]

To celebrate the Marian Year in 1988, she arranged a pilgrimage, for Christ the King parishioners, to visit the churches in the area, named in Mary's honor. For an educational display, she grouped pictures of local grottos and statues of Mary. On bulletin boards different rosaries were labeled. Her hobbies took on a flare of instruction, as she made herself available for speaking engagements. She helped the joyful, sorrowful, and glorious rosary sequence of mysteries come to life in presentations, especially in children's groups.

Another hobby was a small collection of about ten pictures and statues of the Face of the Suffering Christ. At the time of her death Sister Veronica was wearing a Face of Christ medal.[6]

Sacramentals, like these, and relics are signs of God's saving power, but do not have magical properties apart from God. Relics appeal to the material needs, and affirm the human desire in children and adults alike, to touch, hold and see proof of a supernatural reality. According to St. Jerome, the proper attitude toward relics is one of veneration, not worship or adoration. Some of the most famous relics are the Crown of Thorns, the Holy Grail, and the house in Nazareth where Jesus grew up, which Sister Veronica visited in 1985.

An innovative program of the updated Catholic Church was in full swing, during the mid-1980s, following the Second Vatican Council's *Dogmatic Constitution on Divine Revelation*. Sister Veronica enjoyed this evangelical program of renewal (*aggiornamento*), seeing how it well served her ideal of parish unity and salvation. Evangelization 2000 and Lumen 2000 were part of the Catholic Charismatic Renewal, in preparation of the Jubilee celebration in year 2000. It promotes spiritual renewal and worldwide transformation. The concept of Renew, found in the book of Deuteronomy, is a call for loving concern for others, in particular to show proper respect and regard for widows, orphans, foreign aliens and the poor. Some parishes extended the renewal program to blood drives, and other social awareness concerns.

At the end of 1984 she wrote, "Three parishioners [including Barbara Parke] and I attended the Parish Renewal Weekend at Oberlin. Father Larry Grennan spoke on the Shifting Focus in Catechesis. We will be part of the core team, along with our Pastor, for three scheduled Renewal weekends in our parish. It is structured much like SEARCH [for youth groups], and Marriage Encounter, with processes that lead one to a deeper appreciation of 'what it means to be Catholic.'"

Father Grennan, as Director of Religious Education, for the Salina Diocese, bestowed Master Catechist to her on behalf of the Diocesan Certification Committee, a title she earned "...In light of your continuing efforts through the adult education courses at Hays, your involvements with Renew, and the leadership in the catechetical ministry you have given to your parish."

The Bible teaches that the Lord is present when two or more are gathered in His name. The Renew program encourages families to gather in homes for parish-based small group faith-sharing of Scripture reading and reflection, and for reviewing basic doctrine. "We have been working eleven months now getting ready for Renew. We still have a lot of ignorance and ill will about anything 'new.'"

The next month she added, "We had our first Renew. It was a tremendous success. We had the top cream, that is, mostly the older, stable parishioners who already attend daily Mass. Their enthusiasm may spark some curiosity among others." However another year she said, "About forty parishioners made the parish renewal program, but it was rather shallow, with no follow up. Continued socializing, with some occasional faith-sharing, would have been helpful. People need to belong to a group."

She was well aware that gathering and discussion are important to a parish's spiritual growth and development. "Small groups are the heart of the program. We just plant and work the ground, and add a little water, but God gives the growth and the yield. When the next semester comes around, during Lent, there will surely be some increase in numbers to hearten our spirits."

She wrote a related article for the *Northwestern Kansas Register*, the Salina Catholic diocesan newspaper, about working the ground, and of bringing a green plant to her current convent home. "It had two leaves. How long should I put up with something like that? Our lives are like that — signs of growth. A lesson of spring is that each person is involved daily in the miracle of steady growth. What in my life, this Lenten season, needs more time for me to become fruitful? What would be a good environment to be more productive? The gospel message, of the parable Jesus told about the fig tree threatened with extinction unless it bore fruit, is one of reform and renewal.

"Some persons see what happens to others. This becomes the 'hoe' that works them to repent. A return to wholeness affects an entire community of believers. Nothing is more important to a creative response than to shake from the way we have always done things. Do I try to create an environment for my family, or my community, which is a 'holy ground' (Ex. 3:5) and allows persons room to turn around, and freedom to grow, and bloom?"

This writing is analogous to her philosophy of life. Not believing in doing the planting and watering for others, she would "hoe around" to aid and develop. She finished the article, "A fond childhood memory was of forcing a budding branch to bloom for Easter. The barrenness of winter, and the purpleness of the forty days, was too much. The process of the dying seed, then budding, is the very mystery that Christ lives in us as we live Lent."

Later she said, "I'm getting the Lenten 'Ashes to Easter' groups organized. I am extremely pleased after our organizational meeting. Five leaders each want to host a group. One man will do so in his home, and the others in a [church classroom]. I am planning the Seder meal for three to four groups toward the end of Lent, with potluck food.[7] So things are moving right along." One parishioner commented that Sister Veronica did that each year during Holy Week. "At the last one she was called away, but she had trained her help to carry on."

Another year during this time of Renewal, ten committees were trained in Stockton. "We have a fantastic core of leaders. I walked them through a practice session last night so they could see how it goes…the symbol/theme table focus, shared faith questions, and open/closing prayers in total will last fifty minutes to two hours, depending on the group.

"My role is to support them, and tell them it will work. I am not on a team. The parish still doesn't understand why I wouldn't coordinate it." Elaine Newcomer said, "She was very involved. Even though her name was not on the roster of implementers for Parish Renew it should have been at the top of the list, rather than the parish Priest's name. Sister Veronica was the 'wheel' and the rest of us were merely the spokes."

Chapter Thirty-two

"The fruit of the Spirit is love, joy, peace, patience, kindness,
generosity, faithfulness, gentleness, self-control."
—Galatians 5:22-23

The consecrated life, which Sister Veronica embraced in 1958, required detachment from material values, and separation from family. However, it did not release one, in Religious Orders, from the filial obligation of helping parents who experience difficulty because of sickness. In the years before Vatican II, Sisters never had a choice of what job each would take, or where to live. With each new spring their trunks were to be packed and ready to move on mission where needed.

Well after Vatican II, Sister Veronica's move back to Kansas was a well-thought-out decision to be closer to Mother. She sacrificed her "big town" professional position and her newly earned Masters Degree, which went barely recognized in rural communities. She spent four years with Mother, closely monitoring her health, and keeping other family members informed, often spending summer vacations, and many weekends and holidays, with her on the farm.

As a widow, Mother continued over the years to grieve the death of her beloved husband. During the Marriage Encounter, the four years before our dad's death, Mother wrote, "I do want so much to go on living together for many years, until God calls one of us. Without you, life would be so empty and cold, that I wouldn't care about going on. I do love you, and all these years God has given us together."

Mother tried to keep busy with friends, crafts and gardening. She was comfortably well off to suit her modest financial needs, and took trips to Canada, Jerusalem, Rome, Mexico, Brazil, and across the United States to visit her children.

Throughout her life, Mother was sentimental and kept a few special letters, one in particular from Sister Veronica, written in 1961: "House of Studies [Marymount College, Salina]. JMJ. Happy Mother's Day. There is so very much contained in the word, 'Mother.' To me it stands for all that a woman is and can be, as she knows humanity from its depths of sorrow to its heights of love, seeing the potentiality along with reality. That vision of a Mother is realized in you, my very own Mother who, by your very example of selfless dedicated love, has taught others to see, in each person, a member of the Mystical Body of Christ. May our model and mother Mary obtain and bestow blessings as she sees they are needed upon you and your loved ones until all are united in one bond of love in Heaven."

Sister Veronica, more then other siblings, cared for and nurtured Mother in her declining years. While she did not resent this, she expected her siblings to fulfill their obligations in the shared ministry. At one time she said that when the time comes, and she can't be there, she hopes everyone understands and doesn't expect her to be there just because she's a Sister, or because she's the closest. But, that is what happened — although, while the three other daughters lived out of the area, each took extended time from work to spend with Mother in her last few months.

Shortly after moving to WaKeeney, Sister Veronica said, "I don't know if Mother is afraid I am bored, or lonesome. Or maybe she is. She often wonders when I am coming over. Good grief, I've seen her five out of seven weekends since I've moved here." Mother admitted herself that she was a "Leo, who liked plenty of company and attention."

There were few restaurants in the rural area where Mother lived, and it was a long-anticipated treat when Sister Veronica occasionally drove her to nearby Nicodemus for dinner at Ernestine VanDuvall's Diner. Here they tasted the best smoked chicken and ribs in all the surrounding counties. In this African-American community there has always been a history of sharing their talents and culture with those nearby.[1] Each year their famous *June-teenth* celebration brought people of color together from New York, California and many states in between.[2]

Quite often Sister Veronica drove Mother to Colorado for family visits, since three siblings lived there. "I am very impressed with our Heavenly Father's works of beauty in Boulder Canyon," Mother wrote afterward. "It was my first visit in the fall. The beautiful aspen trees were changing colors." Sister Veronica agreed that Colorado was one of her favorite vacation spots, too, and she was there twice during her last five months of life.

Two years before her own death Mother wrote, "I believe in being generous toward our church, and other charitable works. I hope all my children will be very generous, too." She knew her health was failing, but would often say, "All I have to do is look around and see those who are suffering more."

Mother had a kind face and lovely features, although she was left with a slight pull of the mouth, following an operation, at age sixty-two, to remove a non-malignant tumor in the throat area. While she was not vain, this upset her. She was healthy and strong until age forty-eight, when she had surgery to remove a non-malignant tumor and ovary. Gall bladder distress and a chronic cough followed.

"Mother doesn't feel she is able to make the trip to the Holy Land with me next year, being susceptible to coughing spells," Sister Veronica wrote during the Christmas season of 1984. "She's also limping from either a pinched sciatic nerve in the hip, or an arthritic knee."

A few months later, in March, Mother was diagnosed with a malignant cancerous tumor of the ascending colon and liver. An attempt to remove part of her colon was unsuccessful due to the cancer's advanced stage. It is doubtful that a routine colonoscopy was performed on her every five years, as is now highly recommended for those over fifty. An extremely effective diagnonistic procedure, it could have prolonged her life.

She declined chemotherapy, remembering the distress radiation had caused Dad. The next four weeks were spent at St. Anthony's Hospital, in Hays, where "she was beautifully resigned to her fate," said her friends Alma and Simon Davignon.

She wished to remain in her own home during the final months. Sister Veronica saw firsthand the outpouring of love from Mother's many visitors as the pages in her guest book quickly filled. A neighbor, Eleanor Bellerive, said, "Olive would talk with her friends about God, her health and loved ones. Those last days were comforting to all who visited, realizing what deep faith can do." Family and friends celebrated her seventy-first birthday with cake and ice cream.

"Up until a week before her death, when she took to her bed, Mother was reasonably able to care for her own needs, with the help of care givers and her children, who began taking turns. Genny Robben and Sandy Kuhlman, of the neighboring Phillips County Hospice, enabled Mother to make her own choices, allowed her to be in control, and maintain her dignity in the precious weeks that remained.

"Throughout her life Mother prayed for 'a happy and peaceful death.' As the end approached, her family did not overreact, or insist on additional medical intervention, and respected her wishes not to be subjected to any type of treatment to prolong life," said Father Duane.

Even though both parents suffered the debilitating effects of cancer, they strongly opposed suicide, assisted suicide, or any Kevorkian-type method of euthanasia. Mother faithfully believed the purpose of life includes offering up one's suffering and bravely accepting the challenge to suffer with Christ "the cross one must bear" up to the end.

Father Duane came from Brazil to stay at Mother's side during her two final months. "Even still, Mother felt most secure with her eldest daughter nearby," he said. "Three days before Mother's death, Veronica attended a Catechetical Convention, about seventy miles away. Near the end of the day Mother's condition became worse, and almost in a panic, she asked for Veronica. I telephoned the contact at Hoxie. No answer. I called her home in WaKeeney. Still, no answer. Veronica soon appeared on the scene and took over. That evening Mother wanted to talk with all her children. She talked privately with her eldest daughter first. To those who were not there, she weakly spoke by telephone."

For the remaining days Sister Veronica stayed at Mother's side until her death, as did all the siblings, as they arrived from near and far. Surrounded by her family by day, at nightfall each took turns keeping the twenty-four hour bedside vigil, ministering to Mother's needs, praying for and with her. The day before Mother died, she requested a Mass, celebrated bedside by her pastor, Father John Walsh, and Father Duane, to be offered for the intention of religious vocations.

Just minutes before she died — on September 11, 1985 — Grandfather Morin's chime wall clock, which had been set fast, struck midnight — as if calling Mother to her eternal home. Sister Veronica and the other women in the house, symbolically cleansed Mother's body, as in biblical times, and dressed her in a fresh nightgown, before shrouded and taken by the county coroner.

The next day Sister Veronica, together with siblings, selected a silver casket with a rose and wheat motif. Then, with the assistance of Mrs. Smith, the funeral director's wife, the daughters dressed Mother's corpse in a favorite rose-colored dress. This writer styled Mother's hair, as she previously requested.

Sister Rose Irma, who by now was confined to a wheel chair as a double amputee recalled her sister's funeral, "It was a day that can't be forgotten." Mother's longtime neighbor, Leota Probasco, agreed, "The service was beautiful, and the overflowing church showed how much she was loved."

Sister Veronica took charge of arrangements for the funeral mass, flowers, program, prayers and music, and participated fully. Although afterward, she said she had not wanted to carry so much of the burden. Her siblings, who thought a Religious Woman would know just what to do, had a tendency of letting her do the majority of work, in family matters, which was a serious omission in not seeing the task at hand. She was wholeheartedly in agreement, with my unconventional suggestion, that siblings, even the daughters, serve as pallbearers with Father Duane leading the casket.

Bishop George Fitzsimons and together with nine other Priests, including Father Duane, con-celebrated the Funeral Mass of Christian Burial in the packed Stockton church of 225 more or less — with standing room only — a testimony to a kind and generous woman.[3]

During the eulogy, St. Thomas pastor, Father John Walsh, praised Olive Morin Roy as the "Parish's Goodwill Ambassador, leaving evidence not only of her presence in the parish church, rectory and center, but around the world, touching people's lives by her visits, and correspondence."[4]

Sister Veronica was thirty-eight years old when Dad died. Now she was forty-five. Back at work, within several weeks she was stretched to capacity, but yet rose to the occasion when invited by the pastor of the United Methodist Church, in WaKeeney, to speak on, "Women: Professional, A Church Woman, and Person." A few days later she drove a carload of CSJ Sisters to Salina for cluster meetings. The next day she went to Russell for a meeting of regional pastors and pastoral assistants. The day after that she was guest speaker for the

Federated Women's Club Convention on her trip to the Holy Land.

"I sure hoped to keep in touch a little more intimately than this, but I have let myself be scheduled much too tight," she admitted. "The first two months after burying Mother I was so horribly busy at work. I felt cheated in time to process my thoughts, and resented the busyness. I went to the farm to rest and putter. Instead I moved everything in the large basement so I could dust and mop." And later, she added, "I have run out to the farm about four times, and each time I aim to reflect, but was always nonstop moving things from one area to another, or cleaning. I did stop at the Damar Cemetery and attended an outdoors Mass there on All Souls Day."

Mourning is an essential part of letting go, as psychologists suggest. People must re-feel all the emotions, attached to the memory, to free themselves of the hold of the past. While this can be excruciatingly painful and lonely, a future becomes possible through this undoing. She hardly had time to properly grieve. Another difficult part of letting go was for her to emotionally allow someone to move into Mother's spacious home. "The renters moved in, and only pay $250 a month. I pay $195 for my little place," she expressed the seemingly monetary imbalance.

In Dr. Elizabeth Kubler-Ross' writings she lists the emotions of anger, denial, isolation, bargaining, depression and acceptance, and how each affects, not only the terminally ill, but also the surviving families. It is a common misconception to believe that those who take Religious Orders do not grieve. Sister Veronica set her own frantic pace and chose, in part, to overwork, and was even compelled to use her spare time productively. She rarely relaxed, having her own strict standards to live by. Eventually, she acknowledged a variety of emotions and began the normal progression of grief.

She requested a Mass for Mother. "That morning I was reading an account of a man who was incurable and died peacefully at home. It was a real tearjerker. Not so much his story, but the remembrance and celebration of Mother's anniversary of death.

"I was at the cemetery today for two hours transplanting plugs of buffalo grass," she said one day. "There's hardly any grass coming into the area near Mother and Dad's headstone. I have been there two other times in June working, since realizing on Memorial Day the gravesite is a mess. It was full of weeds and sandbur stickers. It's supposed to rain tonight and wet the transplanted grass. I am confident it will be fine now."

Not much later, she added with a sigh of relief, "Things at work let up. I began to relax and think about adding to the quality of community life around here."

Chapter Thirty-three

"...So they went and saw where he was staying, and they stayed with him that day..."
— Jo 1:39

"...They urged him, "Stay with us, for it is nearly evening and the day is almost over." So he went in to stay with them..."
— Lk 24: 29

Upon moving to WaKeeney four years earlier, Sister Veronica reflected, "I will miss companionship [not living] in Community, but my college housemate, Sister Betty Suther, at KSU, had hardly been home, so it won't be much different."

Although once settled it wasn't long before she remarked, "There are times I can hardly stand it anymore. I'm gone most of the time, making many home visits on my own initiative, and generally feeling welcome. But, it's just that no one can take the place of another Religious in Community life."

"Opening a Convent, and living in it alone, was traumatic," she recalled. In the days before Vatican II many Sisters were sent two-by-two into missions. Now Sister Veronica faced the village alone, preparing the way for the sacraments and tending the needs of the poor in spirit, the infirmed and dying.

"If it weren't for a recent development of the new Northwest Kansas team ministry, I would have tried to get a Sister companion here. This summer two Priests and Sister Jean Befort, a band member of mine, will be caring for three parishes in Hill City, Logan and New Almelo. I'm delighted she will be in the area. Although living nearly fifty miles away, I plan to spend time with her, and will arrange socials for the Religious of the area.

"At least monthly I have meaningful visits with neighboring Sisters especially Sister [Doris Flax] in Ransom. There is a remote chance that one or two Sisters might be interested in coming to WaKeeney. One is retiring from teaching in Oakley, and the other I lived with in Belvidere for twelve years. She would be great here to complement my people-approach weakness."

In another letter she said, "I invited another Sister to live here, who has never been away from the Motherhouse all these years, but who finally took a pastoral course last fall. She wanted to know what we have here to offer. I said that we just have people, and she would have to develop her own program. So she wasn't ready for that." The yearning was on going. "I am still interested in someone to live with me, but I don't know what she would do."

And later, "Greetings on Columbus Day! Another day the mail doesn't move. Even the newspaper ads look good when there is no one to greet me, although there is more to Community support than someone at home at the end of the day," she said with lucid foresight.

Again she repeated, "I am getting more restless for another Sister to live here, to the point where I mentioned to Father Dennis that I would be willing to sacrifice my one-fourth time pastoral minister's position, if another Sister could have it in order to bring another one here. I use the word 'sacrifice' choicely, as the parish work is the main reason I persist here alone. It gives meaning to all else, since none of the four dietetic jobs are [in Catholic hospitals.] I don't think I could stand it with just the hospital work. There has to be more than serving the neighbor. I appreciate the 'corporateness' of working together. If I gave the ministry position to someone else, I would continue being a good parishioner, doing much of what I do already, without being the official minister. Although, I worked hard for that and it means a lot.

"Father Dennis doesn't think Sisters should be living alone. I argue, 'that limits those who are able to work in rural areas.'" She offered a solution: "Either find full-time positions for two professionals, or have one, or more, retired.

"The Motherhouse knows I would be delighted to have a companion, especially one retired. I would support her for that matter, if she didn't mind being alone all day. But I'd be miserable if she was terribly dependent for rides everywhere, since I like to walk. And I'm sure I would become envious of her, too, if she was traditional, and loved from the very beginning. I am sure hung up on the words envy and jealousy. I forget which means which."

In mid-1985 she got her wish after a retired Sister moved to WaKeeney at her invitation. Sister Veronica wrote as her annual Commitment to Mission statement: "I anticipate growing in the ministry by my life in Community especially living with [another Sister.]"

The two-bedroom house they shared was very small, and the older Sister preferred polka music and television shows with the volume turned high. Wearing hearing aids, Sister Veronica found loud sounds painfully irritating, and not hearing well over background noise made conversation difficult. Sister Veronica often withdrew into her bedroom to read or work instead. Although she said, "I stretch myself *soooo much* [her emphasis] trying to pull conversation out of her. [My Sister-companion] is even quieter than I am." It wasn't long before she said, "My new Sister-companion seems very unhappy that I am gone all day, and often into the evenings at work."

Once eager to share her convent-apartment, within a short time she wrote, "Without putting the blame on anyone, let me just say that I've felt like I was heading for a divorce since about the first of November. Cramped quarters probably have a lot to do with it." Not helping matters, Mother had been diagnosed with terminal cancer and had died six weeks earlier.

Sister Veronica did not want to be depended upon for rides, and hoped that a car would give her housemate a sense of independence, and more freedom for them both. After Mother's death, Sister Veronica bought Mother's well-cared-for seven-year-old Pontiac to drive and gave the "old faithful" Subaru, which she had been using, to her housemate. A month or so later, just before Christmas, the older Sister rammed the car into a parked pickup, saying it acted like there was dirt in the accelerator. "It was written up as a malfunction. I feel the strings of attachment for it [but need] to let it go. At least, no one was hurt."

The next month the retired Sister asked Sister Veronica to drive her so she could make retreat at the Motherhouse. The next week, upon the return trip to pick her up, Sister Veronica was surprised: "I knew Sister would be praying about her mission, for the coming year, but I was shocked to hear that she was planning to move already. It seemed she is very lonesome for 'her people.'"

"What I mind is the public knowledge, which seems to get around in the religious community, that we couldn't get along, and that I'm not made for living in Community." She was aware that rumors are often more powerful than reality.

"The Community Sister Veronica yearned for was likely based on her experiences in a larger Community. Therefore, she was not prepared for the realities of small quarters and that another person's likes or dislikes could have such an impact on her," said an observer who wished to remain anonymous.

As Religious Orders rediscover their roots, a certain clarity of vision and renewed stability begins to emerge. Within circles of Religious Women and Men the question arises whether there is a need in the future for developing a greater quality of communal life, which is life-giving both for the members and the cause. Some believe that is the trend for men religious, but at the same time leaders of women's congregations are finding it increasingly difficult to encourage women to live with other members within their congregation.

The concept of living in Community is an interesting study in human dynamics. A recent news article featured men who became Priests after they were already in an existing career path. The upper-age limit for acceptance is thirty-five to forty years old for those who wish to enter the Religious Orders of those who live together in Community, such as the Franciscans, Carmelites, Dominicans or Benedictines. The reason given is that it is difficult for a man over forty years of age to blend into a Community group because he has already developed a personal style of spirituality, and lifestyle, different from the Community's older candidates. In addition, he may have trouble bonding as a new member.[1]

The same rationale goes for Women Religious, who also have differing needs. A person doesn't just decide to live in Community and make a success of it. Much depends on the personalities involved, as many failed marriages can attest.

Sister Christine Doman offered her opinion, "Living in small Community situations is a hardship on most of us, as we all have our particular ways of doings things, but this is the challenge of charity, and Community living to which we have given ourselves over to the 'dear neighbor' who are, most of the time, our own Sisters."

One Priest's view on living in community was well stated in a Tucson, Arizona weekly parish bulletin. Father Todd O'Leary said, "If the perfect Associate Pastor for St. Thomas the Apostle parish became available today, I would have to pass on him. The house that I occupy was never intended to be a two- or three-Priest residence. We would be falling over each other. Priests need privacy for prayer, reflection and study. Forced Community would be counterproductive. Many Priests have little in common other than their Priesthood. This is usually healthy for the parish family, but makes living in too-close proximity a constant irritant for the ill-matched clergymen. This is not healthy for a parish. Happy Priests make a happy parish!"

Much of Sister Veronica's sense of self-worth and identity depended on her professional life and specialist role. Whether she was altruistic, ultra-dedicated or had mixed motives, we may never know, but she showed signs of a workaholic, which is a self-serving defensive mechanism, as well as a desire to serve others. No doubt, total immersion in work protected her. She was aware of her own problems. Following the failed housemate situation, she said, "I know that I work too hard, and even more importantly, I don't relax when not working.

"I have never had such a depressing experience for such a long time." After getting it off her chest she continued: "Well, [this is the] reason for the depressing purple paper. I knew that would come out even if not wanting it to, so we will see what happens now. I really hope I can use these two weeks of solitude to work out my own feelings of blame and whether it is all my fault about the quality of life on our mission."

If the Second Vatican Council did nothing else, it was significant that it evolved into recognizing that those who take vows of chastity need to have friendships. The new attitude is that friendships are a healthy gift from God and should lead to God. Nevertheless, it wasn't easy for her, or for other Sisters, to begin discussing feelings immediately after Vatican II when the need for personal relationships began to be voiced. It is especially difficult, after many early years of denying one's emotional side, to suddenly start sharing private thoughts.

Ordinarily women reach out to other women for celebration, for feeling fully alive and for reclaiming their true selves, but Sister Veronica learned during childhood and religious formation not to be overly familiar or emotional. One might question whether it was drummed out of her, or even had a chance to develop when limitations were lifted.

Perhaps she was fearful of intimacy: understanding the values of another, being present to another, sharing affection, love, fondness and tenderness.

Crying on the shoulder of, or telling shared secrets with, your best friend in the convent was not allowed. It is hard to engage in small talk without letting real feelings, and one's weaker side come out. Even though she began developing lasting friendships with a few Sisters, beginning at the hospital in Belvidere, conversations expressing heart-wrenching concerns were often avoided.

The more these Religious Women-pioneers in Kansas, as well as throughout the nation, continue to stretch, grow and reach out to the small rural parishes, they need a network to provide the chance to learn from each other and to gain a sympathetic ear.[2]

A forum was needed for sharing joys and pains of what it is like to walk in the shoes of another Religious Woman. "Intentional bonding" and "building relationships," where each could understand other's unique experiences were talked about among the CSJ. The other pioneer-Sisters in western Kansas became part of her support group, although they lived in communities too far away for a drop-in gab session. However, that was neither her style, nor was talking on the telephone for great lengths of time. If fact, she shunned making many long-distance calls due to the expense.

After suffering humiliation over the implied gossip she said, "I've come to some resolution [about the failed housemate ordeal] and that will probably push me to spend more time with neighboring Sisters. I will go to Norton tomorrow evening to visit Sister Vera Meis, if I can get someone to handle the Communion service Tuesday morning."

Several months later she attended a meeting, on "Spiritual Direction," during what she called "clergy day." "I was there with Sisters Jean Befort and Helen Hake, and Father Ken Lohrmeyer. I've been hunting for someone to share with, and taking more time to have something to share, as in this workshop.

"Then I am going to Salina next Saturday, for a meeting on 'Intimacy in Community.'" This was one of many in-service workshops for the Sisters and Priests in the diocese. Others felt the hardship of community life, too, especially in small missions, and the focus of the 1991-1995 Senate was, "How We Are With One Another."

Sister Helen Hake said, "I was pastoral minister in Oberlin and Herndon, Sister Jean Befort was at New Almelo and Sister Rita Swartz from the Wichita CSJs, was also in the area. Since each of us lived alone, we four Sisters agreed to get together once a month as a way in which we 'shared Community.' Each of us took our turn at hosting the group. We'd arrive around four or five in the afternoon. First we took a long walk, sharing what was happening in our Ministry and personal life. We each brought something for a meal, and then we spent the evening playing cards and sharing conversation. Sometimes the hour was late when we went to bed [in our sleeping bags on the floor.] Our meal, in the morning, was at 10 a.m. leaving each of us free to sleep late if we wished

— depending upon each person's need to get back to her own parish. We departed sometime before noon."

Sister Helen admired the goodness in her friend. "I was always so impressed that Veronica was doing parish ministry as I was, and also worked her regular job as a dietitian. Obviously she was good at planning ahead."

Sister Veronica said in later years: "About eighteen of the Sisters in pastoral ministry from the diocese meet [at Wilson Lake, 80 miles east of WaKeeney on I-70] at Father Olmstead's cabin about three to four times a year. We used to work hard to plan structural strategies in the diocese regarding collaboration with pastors and parish administrators. But if anything, it made things worse, so now we just gather to gab."

In the late 1980s an emphasis on sharing a spiritual connection became popular in the secular women's movement. This paralleled what Sister Veronica and her fellow professed Religious Women were doing at the time. During these gatherings women encouraged and guided each other through their most intimate thoughts of God and spirituality. They discussed those great questions of time, along with the funny moments in life. Sister Doris Marie Flax illustrates: "During a discussion, after I told her of something spiritual I had just read, she often picked my brain, 'How did that phrase or article strike you?' or 'How can you apply that to your ministry, or your own life?'"

She rejoiced in the gathering of small intimate groups and began to feel connected in ways she had seldom felt before. From time to time Sisters from New Almelo, Oberlin, Plainville, Victoria and Hays gathered, including Sisters Mary Reiter, Sister Mary Jo Thummel, and Sister Marilyn Wall. "Plainville had a Mass and parish potluck for Sister Renilda [Keller's] 70th."

In February 1987 she wrote, "Three of the areas Sisters, and Sister Rose Moos, whom I get together with once a month for support, will be spending Sunday afternoon and most of Monday at my place." This support group meant a lot to her. Sister Veronica's hospitality was well known, and gave her great joy. "My regional coordinator was here for supper and then overnight. The area Sisters had meetings in Plainville last Saturday on Finances." Another time she added, "Sister Jean [Befort] called a little while ago. She will stop here for dinner tomorrow noon, then we will be on our way to a movie in Hays."

She took delight in houseguests and marveled at the way some people, like our mother, made it look effortless. After six months went by without a get-together she commented, "I will probably declare Ascension Thursday as gathering date, if no one else does. Meanwhile, three or four of us area Pastoral Ministers gather as a support group every four to eight weeks; next time is at my home. We are the group that spent considerable energy working for Rural Lay Pastoral Administrators."

Sister Veronica often spent holidays alone and she had to create her own excitement. "Since I get my birthday off work, [December 28] I am planning to visit the Motherhouse." Historically, the Sisters spend St Joseph's Day together. As their profession day, it is held in high regard for all CSJ. In 1989 Sister Veronica wrote, "We celebrated with 'the greatest possible solemnity' as we always do on the Saturday nearest March 19. I joined our thirteen Jubilarians at the Motherhouse. Sister Rose [Moos] from here went with me for a fast trip, leaving at 6:30 a.m. and returned by 6:30 p.m. Another year St. Joseph's Day was celebrated at Plainville with the Sisters living in western Kansas. "We have been meeting at Plainville and Russell mostly since I left WaKeeney [and moved to New Almelo] otherwise they went there quite a lot, since I was usually the one to get it organized."

Sister Doris Marie Flax agreed that Sister Veronica enjoyed inviting neighboring Sisters for parties and get-togethers. "Often, she was the one to host them, making the tables festive with decorations. Sister Veronica acquired a four-shelf food dehydrator and delighted in making dried apricots, apples, pears and pineapples for these parties. "I might dry the grapes somebody picked for me because they are too many to eat now and I get allergic [from eating too many] and lose my voice," Sister Veronica said.

Sister Doris Marie was amused: "Veronica loved grapes. On several occasions as she traveled from WaKeeney to Ransom she stopped at a store to buy some to eat in the car on the way. I always knew when this happened because her lips would be blistered by time she arrived. It didn't help to tell her that perhaps a dietitian should know better than to eat unwashed fruit. She'd just laugh."

When our cousin, Sister Diane Brin, took a Sabbatical, she traveled to see her siblings in Damar, then on further west to WaKeeney to spend time with Sister Veronica. "Our lives intertwined in the Postulancy, Novitiate and five years in Belvidere, and I will always be grateful for those times in addition to the annual encounters with letters and CSJ meetings. I got to know her better during this trip. We had a good time talking."

In the early part of 1989 Sister Veronica thought about visiting Sister Diane at her ministry in Rome, Georgia — "just to soak things in and sideline around Appalachia, which I have always thought I wanted to do." In a ten-year prediction letter, written just for fun, alongside her siblings, she wrote on January 1, 1990. "Did I get [hired as pastoral minister at] either Damar or the Appalachians? Why/Why not?" Perhaps this trip was another of her unfulfilled dreams. Was she planning to check out the Appalachians as a destination for her next rural ministry? Instead she got deeply involved in writing two genealogy books, her life took another path, and she never made the trip.

✝

Chapter Thirty-four

"Take care and be earnestly on your guard not to forget the things which your own eyes have seen, nor let them slip from your memory as long as you live, but teach them to your children and to your children's children..."

— Dt 4, 9

The seeds for Sister Veronica's first genealogy book, *Our Saindon Cousins*, germinated in her youth, long before it became trendy to trace ancestry. She had always known that friends come and go, but families last forever.

In the fall of 1949, September to be exact, when Ila Mae/Sister Veronica was impressionable, and nearly ten years old, Grandfather Roy's French-speaking sister came from Canada for a rare visit to Kansas. Our grand-aunt's strange-looking words in Mother's autograph book intrigued the young Ila Mae. "*Mr/Mme John Roy. Le temps passe tres vite a Stockton avec les neveux et nieces. Nous esperons vous voir au Canada prochainement.*" "The time flies very fast in Stockton with the nephews and nieces. We hope to see you soon in Canada. de Wilfred Bruis, Louisa Roy."

Genealogy, the study of ancestry, is an ancient, honored tradition in nearly every culture. The Egyptians and Chinese first tracked records for purposes of power and wealth. Similarly, Europeans tracked royalty for reasons of inheritance, ascension to the throne, and bloodlines. In the early days of North America ancestry was a way to gain entry into exclusive patriotic societies, like the Daughters of the American Revolution. However, this practice of tracking was not usual for the common man.

Interest soared around the bicentennial of the U.S. in 1976. Adding to the popularity was Alex Haley's best-selling classic novel, *Roots*, and subsequent televised mini-series, in 1977, tracing his seven generations from Africa through slavery, as preserved through oral history. It would be another ten years before Sister Veronica began to research and fully uncover her own roots when she traced the Saindon line to the eleventh generation, and to the seventh generation for the Heberts.

Currently some teachers include a family-history unit, in humanities classes, to put a face on the past. Parents typically don't take time to show young people how history relates to today. Consequently, many students complain of a lack of interest in times gone by.

Our parents did not discuss important historical events with us either, although we heard them reminisce with relatives about the way things were. Even though we thought them "old-fashioned" in many aspects, we were curious and enjoyed listening in on their conversations and storytelling. Additionally, Mother kept scrapbooks of mementos and photographs — all of which we were allowed to peruse repeatedly — as well as her before mentioned autograph book.

Dad left few life stories when he died in 1978. We felt as many families do: "We should have asked more questions." Subsequently, in 1980, as a gift to Mother, this writer encouraged siblings to piece together childhood memories. "I wouldn't take a million dollars for [the fifty-six-page booklet]," she said. In turn, Mother was inspired to recall her own life stories, for this writer to document, over the next two years.[1]

Our newly widowed mother took a chartered bus tour, and photographed sights along the shore of the St. Lawrence River on winding roads from Quebec City. It was a childhood dream come true as she visited St. Anne de Beaupre shrine, of which her long-deceased father often spoke. This area proclaims Catholic and French origins of people who grew up under the guardianship of St. Anne, grandmother of our Lord.[2]

To visit the land of our ancestors was one of Sister Veronica's lifelong dreams, too. She and Sister Francis Alma Royer, her longtime friend from the late 1960s, planned a trip to Canada in 1994. "But she can't take that much time off now. It would be six days driving. I think next year we'll go with more planning." They never made the trip.

When Mother died in 1985, it was natural for Sister Veronica to become our sociological matriarch. Family members were scattered, and she felt it up to her to see that siblings came together regularly and continue the storytelling.

Nationwide, family reunions have become increasingly popular, say some studies, but the Roys and Morins had a long history of periodic gatherings years before the trend started, as black-and-white photographs from the 1940s confirm. Similar features, mannerisms and vocalizations are reflected throughout reunions. Regardless of achieved economic status, or in which part the country a family settles, there seems to be an instant connection during these times, with topics in common.

In our family a noticeable characteristic over the years is the generally well-behaved and happily noisy children freely running throughout. Although, it is normal for there to be stressful times, too, when siblings discipline their children in different ways, or after a death or divorce, the new "significant other" juggles to fit into tight-knit families. Our reunions were typical in these aspects.

Sister Veronica eagerly looked forward to reunions of any size. She would often help with massive mailings to announce large reunions involving hundreds of cousins. On gathering day, she arrived early to help set up. People often commented that she made them feel especially welcome. "Sister Veronica always took time to speak with me," said Rita Brin Newell, one of our oldest cousins, who cared for Ila Mae as a four-week-old infant. "She had a way of making you feel special."

It was part of Sister Veronica's nature to like a structured environment, with an agenda and introductions. However, she learned the hard way that people prefer to chitchat, catching up on family news and gossip. Paradoxically, she found those times to be when she harvested valuable stories that breathed life into her two highly researched family history books, *Our Saindon Cousins* and *Ma Famille*.

Just as many monumental projects begin, *Saindon Cousins* started small two years earlier, in anticipation of upcoming Roy and Morin family reunions in 1987. Furthermore, during Father Duane's visit from Brazil to the U.S. the next year, he and Sister Veronica drove to Boise, Idaho to visit this writer's family after we were transferred there, in one of our many professional moves.

The two of them stopped at Salt Lake City on their return home, had a tour of Temple Square, and explored the extensive records at the Family History Library, which is open to non-Mormons.[3] This trip fueled the sleuth in her. "We found the 1871 and 1881 census of St. Sebastien Parish, Iberville County, Providence of Quebec. I got the names of the fifteen brothers and sisters of P.H. Roy. [Later she discovered the names of another six half-siblings.] It also confirmed our great-grandparent's names.

"I've got an update on names, but not dates, so all this week I have been delving deeper into Roy history," she said. "I'm on vacation from two of my five jobs this month, so the past weeks I have papers of both Morin and Roy ancestry all over the house, with library references on genealogy, but no 'how-to' it should be written. I am interested in updating and standardizing both histories. However after August 1, and back to full-time duties, I will probably lose interest."

She did not lose interest. Instead, she plowed full speed ahead. "I don't know why I always go for the big stuff, 'the More' of our CSJ spiritually," she said. "I've been typing non-stop since July 1st, or at least running in circles deciding what to do next. Last night I had a case of exhaustion, or more like craziness. Last week was like the week before 4-H Fair week. That is, getting it all together for show. I'm proofreading now. Cheryl will photocopy these. I never appreciated the work she did, in 1984, before now.

"At the reunion I posted an eight-foot circle with six generations. There was always someone standing around it. And it was quite an attraction. Everyone was studying it, and I was, too. It thrilled me to see teenagers fascinated with it, so that was reward enough in how we all fit together. It must have been confusing for those fourth and fifth generations and their spouses, but it makes more sense than numerous pages." She did not pursue researching the Roy family line beyond several generations. However, had she lived she would have. "Hopefully, the Roy genealogy can be researched [more in depth] in another five years," she said.

At another Roy reunion, attended by well more than one hundred relatives, spouses and children, she conducted a brief memorial service for the twenty cousins who died during the previous forty years — a list of names not previously gathered.

One of Mother's passions in later years was quilting. She sewed many heirlooms, with each of her children owning several. Sister Veronica appreciated their lasting quality, and the loving stitches that went into each one. Feeling the need of her own legacy after Mother died, Sister Veronica also began quilting. "Someone from WaKeeney loaned me a quilt book. I went through it and picked out twenty patterns. I may decide to make a variety of quilt blocks, of different crosses, to force me to sit down at night to relax and pray again." She realized the importance of a pastime, and the need to have other interests besides work.

In the 1990s, when this writer was rushing to make a doll quilt for great-nieces Nicole, Brianna and Maggie Lawson, and after Sister Veronica saw my long and careless stitches, ever the big sister and a perfectionist at that, she cautioned me to take my time: "Even doll quilts are around for a long time."

While paying respects at the adjoining gravesites of Mother, Dad, and our young brother, Ronald, which Sister Veronica often visited, she began to take note of dates and names of other countless relatives buried there. The intriguing thought of a family history book, an interest she carried from youth, again began tugging at her soul.

Serendipitously, as it happens in life, quilts, cemetery markers, and a renewed interest in genealogy began to weave a spell and pulled a bit more at her heartstrings. She put the quilting aside. Instead of stitches, she would create with words. In place of needle and thread, computer and paper would be her tools, as she began to cut, shape, and join the web of genealogy. Like a "crazy piece" quilt, she found the written fabric of life, stitched and mended, endures and becomes more valuable throughout generations.

As genealogists agree, there is a lot of plain hard work that goes into research, but it feels good as it comes together. Sister Veronica acknowledged this, and in September 1988 she said, "I am getting hooked on genealogy again. It is my only hobby these days, and I need some diversion. I've really been up to my neck in paper work this fall with three additional jobs. Ideally, a hobby should be the opposite of what I already do. I have been communicating with people about the possibility of writing [grandmother Roy's] Saindon family history."

Sister Veronica submitted various photos and stories for the 420-page

Damar Centennial History (1888-1988) edited by cousin Barbara Brin Balthazor and Pat Newell Belisle. She also attended the centennial celebration, in October of that year, and provided various items for the Time Capsule. These included a pre-Vatican II Missal prayer book, and Dad's initial "J" (for John) tie clasp, with a note that these items were to be returned to nephews John Calvin and Jason Roy, two young children most likely to be alive in the year 2038, when the fifty-year Time Capsule will be opened.

"By Divine Province I met five Saindon cousins, from Colorado, at the Damar centennial celebration," Sister Veronica said. This chance meeting was a major turning point, and her project propelled into more then a casual hobby when the cousins told her about Alverize Brin's writings. He was a cousin, by marriage to Exzlina Saindon, and had a vast collection of photos, a windfall that she acknowledged in *Our Saindon Cousins*. He had died the previous year.

Sister Veronica drove to Denver and was excited to take possession of the priceless antique assortment. She poured over these for hours connecting with faces amidst her newly found treasures.

Once the project was underway, she said, "Three times I panicked when tornadoes headed to town, knowing these photos could have been scattered. The computer pages could be run off again. I've felt all year that something strange could happen to keep this from coming off."

In the introduction of *Our Saindon Cousins*, in her mystical way, she wrote, "I have felt close to their spirits during this year. Three relatives [Alverize Brin, Alphonse Saindon and Alphonse Desmarteau] were really deep into the family history, and each died before publishing anything."[4]

She acknowledged another distant cousin. "Rita Roberts was a help, in the beginning, by providing initial information. Imagine finding ninety-six first cousins of Dad's, most of them still living, when I didn't know he had more than three or four." In the book, she also acknowledged the work of distant cousins Marlene Newell, Nelda Desbien Jones, Robert Saindon and Carol Manley.

She wrote to ask for at least one photo from each family, and names, dates and places to fill the pedigree charts. She invited them to include education, military service, work history, location of burial plots, street address or directions to their farm, and other pertinent information they wished to share.

"About fifty percent of the forms have come in. There are about thirty-five more I am hoping for before moving onto the next phase." She began weaving anecdotes into a living family history savoring each morsel. "February 14 seems to be a favorite wedding day for Saindon cousins," she observed. "Also, Sister Wilfred Desmarteau, who recruited Sister Laura Annette (Aunt Jeannette) in the 1940s, is the only other Religious Woman in the Saindon family. And I've investigated eight generations. It would be fun if someone wanted to go through the book and glean the trivia."

Each tidbit became more intriguing, drawing her deeper. Once Sister Veronica was smack in the middle of research, she referred to this work as "a big jigsaw puzzle." She was fond of puzzles. Like others who become interested in genealogy she found the intrigue like a virus that she could not shake. Other genealogists agree it is more than a hobby; "It possesses me," they concur. Her project, a treasure hunt, was a liberal education in itself, complete with history, geography, religion and politics, including sources.

In the middle of June she wrote, "I worked six days in a row on this history, just now completing another eight hours, and wonder if I will hold up typing at least ten pages a day. That alone is five hours work." By September 1989, she continued to put in an incredible number of hours, and began a habit of staying on to use the computer and "burn the midnight oil" after her full workday of parish ministries and hospital dietetics.

"I worked from 5 p.m. to two in the morning, just getting one family record on the computer." Two more nights she worked twelve hours from 5 p.m. to 5 a.m. "Last Saturday I worked from 5 p.m. until 8:30 a.m. knowing that I wouldn't be caught still in the office when the hospital staff came back to work. I'm holding my breath that the WaKeeney hospital administrator doesn't say, 'Enough!' before I get done with this book. He knows I'm working on something personal."

She appreciated the large chunks of time available to her, not having to answer to anyone, not having a family to cook for, or pick up after. "I have no idea how a person with a family gets along while writing a book.

"What was to be a two-month summer hobby is now three months old, and will go into the winter. Imagine attempting all this on a small kitchen table, a card table in front of the window fan, and the spare bedroom bed."

Sister Doris Marie Flax, a fellow CSJ parish ministry pioneer, said, "While working on family history her apartment living area was strewn with piles of papers. When I dropped in to see her, I'd have to step over these. She'd apologize for the clutter and offered to pick up the pages. I told her if she could 'high step,' so could I. Then we'd have a good laugh about the mess."

While Sister Veronica was a perfectionist, she was only selectively so. Her kitchen, and especially her car, could be untidy, and it was only when these were so bad that she paid attention to them. She didn't have time for what was not important to her. On the other hand, she treated her presentations, her lasting legacies, with dignity, and these were handled with utmost care. If she deemed it so, she'd work nonstop, forgo sleep until she had it done right. And only then would she stop and collapse from exhaustion.

Early on she said, "I tried to teach myself how to operate the computer for dietary work at the hospital." The next month she signed up for a class through

Colby Community College at the local high school. "Before I get bad habits."

Few people in the modern age write a book without the aid of a computer, but the antiquated one she rented had its limitations. "I've set up a daily quota to meet the deadline of when I need to return this Wheel Write IBM computer. This machine wastes a lot of space. I can't even put this into memory. Last week I tried to copy a diskette. Since I don't know how to format floppy disks, I put one in the disk drive that I already used, thinking that if there were no room it would tell me so. But no! I wiped out one hundred pages of Saindon history. Let's see. That's 100 pages times 20 to 30 minutes each. How many days' work have I just lost? I have not released that discouragement yet. I am still too shocked to know how much this will set me back." Even though she was accurate, and typed 60 words per minute, this caused a delay.

"Meanwhile to get this book going, I rented the Xerox Memory Writer 6025, for thirty dollars a month. It has sixteen pages of memory, but with an extra twenty pages memory added via a cassette. It is full now with my first forty pages."

No matter how furiously she worked, there were outside influences that continued to slow her down. "I am waiting for a 15-pitch printwheel and italicized printwheel. So I am at a standstill. I have three days to finish up. That is, if the printwheel comes in. I've broken the 'N' on two $50 printwheels and they take ten days to arrive. I've gone through eleven rolls of $8.00 ribbons, partially because I chose to print in bold — that, and large photos, should please the older cousins."

Her project was a decade too early to take advantage of the helpful Internet sites that have revolutionized genealogical research. In addition, a software program, with fancier printouts and Web publishing options, would have allowed her to incorporate scanned-in photos. Nevertheless, she enjoyed the work immensely even without the most up-to-date methods.

Several months after moving to New Almelo, in December 1990 she said, "For my birthday I went back to the WaKeeney Hospital to use their office computer. I did three hours work, and then found there was no room to save what I did on the disk. So I had to do it over again. The Hospital Administrator agreed to let me stay into the night again, like old times. The high school was going to let me use their computer, but it ended up being a non-compatible Apple."

The mechanics of the project were frustrating. If something could go wrong, it did. She ran into many brick walls, and it is a wonder she did not give up. To a less-determined person the several times she lost work "down the drain," could have been the final blow, but she was single-minded and kept at it. She could have used the help of St. Isidore of Seville, named in 1999 by the Vatican's Observation Service, as the patron saint of computer and cyberspace pioneers.

In taking vows thirty-some years earlier, Sister Veronica surrendered her life to Christ. She knew to put her trust in the Holy Spirit, and let that power guide her. Often she did stop to pray for guidance, then drew on her unselfish determination, and followed the advice Mother often gave, "God helps those who help themselves."

By now she recognized the importance of having an editor. "Collecting is fun, but committing it to perpetual print is intimidating," she readily admitted. "I feel I've run it by a family rep often enough to catch big or obvious errors, such as having a name omitted, but it is the nuance of how something is said, that will probably bother someone."

Letting go of a project is hard for many people, but for a perfectionist, like Sister Veronica, it was doubly so. "Last Monday was scary as I mailed the paste-up dummy and Mac 3 1/4" disk, along with the first chapter, to my editor, a third cousin, who is a magazine publisher. I had a really tight schedule that I made back in February, to get the books mailed at the end of June.

"My editor suggests letting it set a couple months, but knowing me, I want to stay on schedule to mail the books on time." She did not make the deadline and on August 15 she had another setback. "Received bad news today from my editor. He is resigning from his company, moving to accept another job in Montana, and no longer has access to the Macintosh desktop publishing equipment. Not a lot of people I know have access to the PageMaker program. I was hoping the new date for mailing to be in time for Thanksgiving. That would be another one of my miracles."

Soon after, she located a new layout editor, another distant cousin. "She assures me she can get it done in six weeks, once started. Then the printing will need another six to eight weeks."

At the beginning of the next year, Sister Veronica received a note from the new editor, "The book will not be of professional quality, but if you are willing to accept less than perfect results..." Here Sister Veronica penciled in the margins, *"Me [accept less than perfect]?"* The letter continued, "I'm sure I can finish the job. By less than perfect, I am referring to the little extra touches that are beyond me, such as the decorative letters and indentions and such." Sister Veronica noted further, *"This is crucial. It must be indented for the generations."* The editor went on, "I could work on it in February and March." Surely this drove Sister Veronica up the wall as she was in a hurry for completion. *"I expect to mail books in the spring, or at least by June 1."* Early on in the project, she set deadlines — a self-imposed pressure — that she could only admit afterward as "unrealistic."

At the bottom of the photocopied letter Sister Veronica noted to me, "I thought you would appreciate the update. After praying over it a couple more days, I may do it myself." She gave credit in *Our Saindon Cousins* for assistance in editing Chapters I, II and III.

"I could cut and paste some of Jacalyn Roy's interesting heavier fonts. Basically what I really wanted all this time was to have complete control of the layout myself. Although, since I am so independent and particular, I prided myself with the concept of having others help me."

Among Sister Veronica's possessions were several travel books on Canada, which she used as resource material. "After reading six books on ancestors I added about eight pages. I'm proud of myself for finding that section [of the Saindon relatives who traveled to Kansas. This] will make the book more expensive, but I will ask [hint] for extra [money] when I mail the books."

In early December, she mailed 150 form letters explaining the unexpected large size of the project, and the reason for delay, although she did not ask for additional money. "Every book sold helps, as it looks like I'm donating fifteen percent [thirty-one] of the books, but I am confident of recovering all expenses in sales."

When this writer requested information from family members for a project and told Sister Veronica of my frustration of receiving information from only a few, she replied, "Then you must understand my frustration in waiting for those who said, 'they would work on it' instead of just saying, 'Bug off!' I've called about twelve cousins this week, and written to at least twenty-five more, with follow-up requests for information and photos. That's not too bad a percentage, but I had already called or written to them before."

When Sister Veronica was asked to do something, she did it thoroughly and promptly. But she understood the adage about "her needing them more than they needed her." "You never know, the next one may want to buy a book, and I really need to sell at least thirty more, if I leave in all the pages.

"I had hopes of submitting my first pages to the newspaper by the end of March, to begin making plates. It would be worth typing the entire 400 pages over again, if I could make my deadline. So undoubtedly, I'll be antisocial the next six weeks."

By April she wrote, "I've finished ninety pages. At this rate, it looks like I could have all pages submitted to the printer by May 15. Again I work until two a.m., and then up and at it two hours before facing the parish day. I'm praying I don't get carpal tunnel syndrome with this furious typing."

Sister Veronica still had the rented Xerox Memory Writer. "I need to return it today. I've had it four months and will really miss it. One last act was to update a Perpetual Calendar of family birthdays, anniversaries, and deaths in our family that Linda first created."

Sister Rosalyn Jueneman said, "A marvelous gift Veronica had was putting together the wonderful family history books. I personally know she burned the light very late many hours. It almost seemed as if there was an urgency inside her to get that done. She would lose track of time, when working on the history, and found the clock pointing to two or three in the morning many times before she would stop."

When Father Duane gently reminded her to take it easy, she replied, "Yes, I remember this is a hobby, but my word is precious, too. Three times I foolishly set a delivery date, so now to preserve face, I'd like to keep this deadline." Sister Veronica upheld the Victorian principle, "A promise made is a promise to be kept." When our brother placed his pre-paid book order she volunteered, "You, and 135 people, put enough faith in me to get this finished.

"It seems my project took a breather this month, but I stewed about it every day, even though I haven't been home to work on it lately. I can't believe I worked day and night on this project, from May 1989 to June 1990, and have hardly touched it since. It will be good to get it finished. The whole project is delayed due to the broken promises of some people. I'll wait some more, and give them a chance. I need not blame them, as I could have just said, 'Too late.'"

Later she vented, "I'm ready to start throwing things at the phone. This has been a real lesson in human nature. I am so determined to get this book one hundred percent complete without missing information." She naively expected full cooperation, if not enthusiasm. Instead, she got apathy and excuses from a few who delayed. But at the end, through her patience and perseverance, she had ninety-five percent participation.

"It's really hard to let go, meaning that is the way I want it. I dropped the final layout pages in the mail today to the WaKeeney newspaper [for offset printing.]. That will take six weeks." In August 1991 the printing of *Our Saindon Cousins* began.[5]

She scheduled a collating party earlier that year. But when the project was held up she rescheduled, with a realistic date, seven months later. Although, in mid-September, the printer assured her of only fifty percent of the pages ready for collation. "So, I am praying for more by October 4th, when we gather."

She calculated, with the help of seven adults, it would take a solid three hours of work. She invited family members for a home-cooked prime rib dinner at the Logan rectory where she lived at the time. (The book was started in WaKeeney, but finished in Logan.) Later that day, they worked, in production-line fashion, around tables set up in the basement.

She wasted no time delivering stacks of collated pages to Koerperich Bindery, in nearby Selden, which assured her earlier they would move her project to the head of the line. Three weeks later, she picked up 210 hardbound copies. The next day she started delivering, in person, books to nearby relatives, and mailing out-of-town orders.

Afterward she said, "I just discovered some books have our own family page misplaced, as well as all of Grandma Roy's collage page reversed. I suppose someone got distracted and tried reading pages while collating. If I had noticed, I would have sent correct books at least to our family. I have no idea how widespread the error is. It shows up in six of the nine books I still have."

She deliberately involved family members in the collating to share ownership of the project. Her letter does not convey her extreme disappointment over this permanent flaw to be passed on in history. While she believed in delegating, she also had the view of a perfectionist, "If you want something done right, do it yourself."

On November 1st she reported, "It's been really low keyed these three days. New Almelo had its first storm of the year with twelve inches of fresh snow. Today I looked for misplaced items, going through records to made sure all book orders were indeed mailed."

She was a meticulous record keeper and followed up with a general letter to all who ordered. "Do you find your ancestors in the table of contents for *Our Saindon Cousins*, the 439-page hardbound family history? On this form I have penciled the number of books delivered, between October 25-30, within your family unit. A limited number of extra books are available for forty dollars, which includes tax and handling. Remember information cut off date was June 30 of last year."

She found she should have charged five dollars more per book; prepaid orders were only $30, and some only $25. "I initially budgeted fifty books, at 150 pages, with 350 photos for $30. She printed three times that number of books, doubled the photo count, nearly tripled the page count, and kept the price the same.

Soon after the books were shipped she received accolades. "Everyone says the book is far beyond what they expected, 'Hypnotizing and magnetic.' They can't put it down or leave it alone. 'Absolutely wonderful.' I was floored with the number of long distance phone calls from those wanting to get a copy of the few remaining."

The copies sold out quickly. She was disappointed for not having more printed. "If I had ordered 250 to start, the last fifty could have been profit. Although, I felt some apathy among those ordering, so I did not trust in the extra sales. I sent a flyer to approximately fifteen families who did not order. I have a hunch they may wish to, sooner or later."

Having taken the vow of poverty, she only had a meager bank account to draw from, and it was necessary to collect money in advance. She was trusting when fifty people wanted to see the book before paying for it. "I sent them second billing notices this week." She had to send third notices to fifteen people. "This bill would be a nightmare, if I didn't already have the money [from the majority]."

There was another predicament. "One package of four books that I mailed to Denver was lost. The UPS driver said he left it on an unattended porch. The company offered to pay the cost. Even if I have the reimbursed money for them, it's not the same. That sets me back four copies."

About fifteen requests for additional books come through. "I will probably wait through the summer of '92 to see how many orders come in to decide. Kinko's, in Wichita, has acid free paper. They can collate, and possibly ship them UPS to me for binding. It will cost from $2,000 to $3,000 for up to one hundred copies, but I need to sell seventy-five to eighty to break even on the second printing. Each one will be money on the shelf until sold, which I don't feel like undertaking since I barely broke even on actual expenses with the first printing."

At the end of the year she was sold out again. "I'm holding two for public library copies, one will be a gift for my godson Rodney and family, and three more just in case someone has to have one for a Christmas gift."

Following the first printing she said, "After paying my taxes, I may have $800 if I don't reprint anymore." Instead, after completing the financial statement for *Our Saindon Cousins*, she was in debt by nearly that amount because of all the donated copies. The income received was $7,250. Her bill of $7,992 was for expenses only. She did not pay herself for the more than 1,500 hours she personally worked on the project.

"Why would someone do that?" some ask. It was a work of love, a gift, and a legacy.

Father Raphael Gauthier, a distance relative in New Iberia, Louisiana, wrote, "I am sure the younger generation will devour this, and thank you for it. May you live many years to add to this family history, and find someone to keep it going." This was her wish, too.

Another distant cousin, Laurent Saindon, wrote a book in French, *Histoire et Genealogies de la Famille Saindon d'Amerique du Nord*, which Sister Veronica ordered from French Canadian cousin, Marc Saindon. This sparked her curiosity. "I look forward to learning more about the Saindon Association and gathering in Cacouna some day," she corresponded with him in French no less, drawing on her college days and textbooks.

She was particularly pleased to receive a letter from Fernand Saindon of Beauport, Québec requesting a copy of her book. "You must have a great knowledge of the history. You have made many Saindons very happy in revealing to them a part of their history and origin," he wrote. Of the 800 names he wished to contact, regarding a gathering in Cacouna, she provided addresses to him for the one-half who were English speaking.

Sister Veronica was especially interested in learning more about our first North American ancestor, Michel Saindon. In *Our Saindon Cousins*, she credits distant cousin, Nelda Desbien-Jones for contributions, giving hope that someday the stories of all the descendents of the first ancestor be connected. It is most likely Sister Veronica would have become involved in blending these histories, too.

She released one of the last books to Margaret Eichman, a descendent of the Michel Saindon line. "It boggles my mind to think of the work that had to go into it," Eichman wrote. "I really like your idea of an album with all the pictures. I don't aspire to anything nearly as ambitious. Isn't it frustrating to think of all the good stories we missed along the years? I repeatedly asked my relatives if they had any family material. Nothing. And no interest."

It was evident Eichman and Sister Veronica were kindred spirits. Both felt it a pity there was so little concern, in some families, to know their ancestry. Letters like this validated Sister Veronica's unlimited hours spent on this valuable document.

There was, however, a blistering letter from a distant cousin she had never met. It stunned her, and serves as a reminder that a few unkind words can undo a multitude of compliments.

It reads, with errors intact: "I'll write again about book. Boy, I can't thank it take this long. I don't know what going on there but I would like that book or my money back. And [L.T.] and her daughter to its been over 2 years now or longer now sure it don't take that long. I go to mail ever day thanking I'll get the book. No. No book each day I get upset over it. And more upset I can't believe you could do this to us. So now I would like the book. Or my money. Didn't thank you be that way. Going to mail now. Today if the book not there I'll send this letter. Signed, [P.T.]"

Sister Veronica was in a state of disbelief. As a woman of faith she turned her cheek, but was hurt and humiliated. "Her letter was postmarked October 29, 1991. I mailed her book four days earlier. I'll bet she died the next day. Only I nearly died myself."

A lack of appreciation prevailed even several years later from a few complaints that the price was too high, or when they did not get free copies. Nevertheless, she shook off the ingratitude for her tireless work.

She knew the book was longer lasting than her life itself, as she wrote in *Our Saindon Cousins*, "This is not only a compilation of a family's interesting history and honorable legacy. My prayer is that all who read it will realize the importance of living today so the legacy each one leaves will be positive and honorable for the generations who follow us. Christian love and faith is the greatest inheritance one can receive."

✝

Chapter Thirty-five

"There was a slight blemish to my Jubilee celebration elation," Sister Veronica remarked after the event. Father Dennis Schaab, a member of the Society of the Precious Blood, announced his transfer to Park Falls, in northern Wisconsin, the following week. "His C.PP.S. Community is having a hard time finding men who can work together in larger parishes, so he will be working with another Priest. Our parish has been so downhearted. In a way, I guess the timing is appropriate. People were using the term 'adore,' in describing him. I think he feels he hasn't done a thing here, but I've tried to let him know that he met our needs, and more."

"I have enjoyed my years as a Priest, especially these past three here at Christ the King, and you have been an important part of this happiness," wrote Father Dennis to Sister Veronica a month before he left WaKeeney. "Your offer to help on Tuesday is very welcome, and eating together even more attractive. There are a number of things you might be interested in — perhaps working on the constitutions for the parish council and committees would be most helpful for the future of the parish."

After the Pastor moved away she missed him and his work style, "and how he made it his business to be where everybody was, especially during anything 'churchy' going on. It was always spooky to me of his most mysterious way of knowing when I was working around the church, or CCD building."

While they had a few minor differences in the early months, the two ended up working well together. Sister Veronica discovered that Father Dennis was not one of the "women-hating Priests" that she was told about upon arriving.

In July 1984 the replacement Pastor arrived. The contrast between the two Priests was sharp. The former was young, open, energetic and sociable. For Sister Veronica the new Pastor was both a plus and a minus. New areas of ministry opened for her. There would also be new challenges and deceptions. She soon manifested apprehension: "Our new Priest is only fifty-five years old, but looks rather sickly. I hope the parishioners do not drop him in sharp contrast with [Father] Dennis, whose absence has made a difference in my own approach. I already feel my satisfaction in ministry is lowered by the differences of these two guys. So like everyone else, I'll probably give in, and back down to a lesser degree of involvement." Although, she did like the new liberty to move around the parish at will, assuming new responsibilities. "He is very accepting of my role here, even anxious to give me more, and wants to take Thursdays off. So I am free to take phone and door duty at the rectory, if I choose, and handle whatever else comes up. I am determined to spend time there, even to do my laundry and written professional or personal work, just to train the parish that they don't have to ask the Priest everything. There are decisions that we all can make, and there are answers around. So I keep telling myself not to be apologetic that the Priest isn't here. Rather I ask, 'May I help you?'" However, she admitted, "I have found it hard to handle requests from transients.[1]

"He was gone 3 1/2 days this month, as well as ten days at the end of September, so I got to feel really important. I took care of daily communion services at church with a shared reflection. It couldn't be a homily, since lay presiders cannot consecrate. Thank heavens, a funeral was over with before the Pastor left," she noted.

Rosemary Bollig explained, "When the Priest was away much of the time, it was Sister Veronica, and some of the other lay women, who assisted. Sister was the one to train the presiders, in case of emergency, and we have had to use them."

Sister Veronica traveled to Kansas City, with the Pastor, for a three-day, four-state Team Ministry convention. "We were among 800 participants. The topics were mostly about men and women getting along on teams, so we had some good visits on the way home. This Priest prefers to play it by ear. I do, too, but it doesn't help with the team approach. I miss formal, regular, and organized team meetings that Father Dennis and I had. I miss being able to talk about what is going on, and knowing who is accountable. I miss not being able to make future plans."

Not a lot has changed, in general terms, between Priests and Sisters in the fourteen years since that remark. At a 2001 national gathering for religious leaders, in Chicago, these same issues were rehashed. "Improved collaboration, among women and men in the Church, must start with moving the site of decision-making out of the rectory, or other locations closed to women," was one of the mandates by Women Religious. Sexist decisions, attitudes and comments within the Church were also discussed at these three-day meetings.

Among the many written recommendations at the 2001 National Conference of Catholic Bishops was one to study Canon Law to determine precisely what roles are open, or closed, to the non-ordained. Another was a plea for more honest education of parishioners about the realities of the Priest shortage so that they will be more supportive of lay ministers and the sharing of parish resources."[2]

As the months rolled on, Sister Veronica internalized an increasing concern and felt the pressure of having to tend to her own Pastor. "The Priest from [a neighboring parish] told me the new Pastor drinks a lot, so that puts a load on me, forcing me to minister. I need to work harder on bringing some Gospel values to my feelings, which people expect me to share with them. One parishioner remarked, 'I can't figure that man out. I can't talk to him.' I probably cover up an awful lot for our Pastor."

Among the many Maxims of Perfection was one that reminded, "Always speak favorably of others, and value highly the good in the other, excusing and covering up, in the best way you can, the deficiencies they might have." After she moved to another parish, she returned for the day to participate in a celebration in his honor, when he moved on, out of respect for his position.

The increasing ministry, the demands of her various professional jobs in health care, and the emotional strain caused her to say, "Something has to give. I need to let up on something, and parish work is what is making my Type A personality worse. I know my cholesterol is high. I feel like a candidate for a stroke. It really shook me on Thursday when a fifty-year-old CSJ had quadruple-bypass surgery."

After completing a graduate level course in Pastoral Administration, she admitted, "I usually work 130 hours a month [in the parish], which is like three-fourths time. I am only paid for one-fourth." When she compared notes with the other CSJ Sisters, the consenus was, "Most half-time parish workers say they end up working full-time. It seems more attractive just to be present. But I don't feel my 'presence only' is effective. I found an Edna St Vincent Millay poem that expresses my comings and goings.

> *"my candle burns at both ends*
> *it will not last the night*
> *but ah, my foes, and oh, my friends,*
> *it gives a lovely light.*

Since she held consulting jobs at outlying hospitals, the only free time she had were early morning hours. "I still walk all over town, going to 8 a.m. Mass, then on the go for the day. I am just not healthy, especially personality wise these days. I'm really negative and burnt out with the parish. My first motto here was, 'When I've died to self, the community will resurrect me.' So much for dying [to the world]. I don't know what that means now. I am in worse shape than ever, physically, mentally, and even in my prayer life. I don't know how much longer until I get settled into a prayer routine again. I've heard it said that a change of mission alters ones relationship with God and prayer, and it may take some time to work that out again." The *Catechism of the Catholic Church* states that prayer is both a gift of grace, and a determined response on our part. In short, "Prayer is a battle."

"I had been at the education building five hours last night, and four hours already today, on 'work galore' for religious education. I am typing and trying to clean up the office and getting ready for a new CCD year. "I really enjoy not doing anything, although I pretend this is prayer time, but I am terribly lazy at it. I can waste more time just sitting and looking out the window — not even praying." She was not wasting time looking out the window; the Holy Spirit recharges in the quietness. Incidentally, there is a saying among the Benedictines: "to work is to pray, but work will be prayer only if there is also prayer that is not work."

Another time she wrote, "I had what I call a free day — not having to do anything — but typically I get up to my elbows in something. I experience guilt in just sitting too long." Even though she detested impersonal conversation about the weather, once in a while she made it sound almost poetic. "We had gorgeous icy trees, the past three days, until the sun finally broke at noon to chase the lace away. It truly was glorious."

Another time she said, "This summer I have been doing more light reading than usual, so maybe something good is happening. I am resolved not to be so busy, but relaxing personal work is okay by me."

Her role as pastoral minister, she thought, obligated her to shepherd and protect around the clock, as the name implies. By keeping herself overloaded, she neglected to look at a deeper anxiety. "I think what I am so depressed about is always being the one who reaches out to others, stopping at people's porches, calling them, trying to make a lot of meaningful contacts. I guess I want something in return. It goes against my introversion preferences to be pushing out so much. Our new Deacon says his [master's] thesis was about, 'the Spirit being unfree in introverted people.'"

In 1987, after gathering with other Sisters, in the area, to work on the Rural Lay Pastoral Administration Committee, she weighed the pros and cons, and strongly debated whether to stay another year at Christ the King. "I have been feeling incapable of renewing my parish contract. It should be revised if I renew it. I am just plain tired."

No doubt it was during one of the many overextended times that she said, "Holy Week starts tonight, and I am not at peace about undertaking this Lenten season. I'm so much on the go. I don't have time for myself. I'm in perpetual motion, and I don't like that. I need to talk with the Pastor badly. I am doing a lot, and [dismayed] by his lack of leadership. I feel I am really dominating things with him, but without communicating.

"I was all set to invite the Pastor for coffee last night, then backed down. I was afraid I'd be pushed to take a stand about whether I still belong as pastoral Minister, and I am not finished discerning that. I argue with myself. I know I would continue being involved, as a parishioner, but at least it would be a choice and the pressure, hopefully, would lift."

She asked the parish council to make the final decision about renewing the contract. "This is something we have never done here. It has always been between the Pastor and me."

Ultimately, she came to realize she had to renew the parish contract for the sake of all future honor to the position. "Otherwise, I would be jeopardizing my credibility and making it difficult to justify giving salary in the future to official lay ministers."

✝

Chapter Thirty-six

The good news, coming out of a twenty-eight-year study, between 1966 and 1994, was that the U.S. Catholic population increased from one million to sixty million. The bad news was a major decline in the number of parish Priests, according to a report from Georgetown University.

A more recent study, in 1999, conducted by the National Conference of Catholic Bishops, concurs with those earlier findings. "A worsening shortage of Roman Catholic Priests will result in fewer Masses, more Priestless parishes and Deacons leading worship services. Fewer than sixty percent of Priests are active in parish work, and more than a quarter of Catholic parishes lack a full-time Priest."[1]

For many years Father Robert Brown was the pastor of St John Newman church in the large and affluent community of Reston, Virginia, not far from Washington, D.C. In 1999 he said that he imagined a future time when even large parishes, like his, would have only one Priest.

About this same time, on the occasion of his Jubilee, Father Todd O'Leary, of Tucson, said, "Much has changed in the Priesthood in the past forty years, not the least being the critical shortage of Priests. There are many reasons for this. I can't help thinking that part of the problem is looking at the Priesthood as 'giving up' something. My generation of Priests never thought in these terms. We were convinced, and still are, that we were the recipients of the greatest gift a human being could receive — that of making Christ present in the Eucharist. This mystery is at the core of my being, and always will be."[2]

As long as the Priesthood is viewed as a "giving up" it is unlikely that vocations to the religious life will germinate in today's culture of wanting it all, and wanting it now. Among Mother's many favorite sayings was, "God never takes away without giving something greater in return."

With its severe drop in vocations — a legitimate concern and serious problem — the Catholic Church faces great challenges. There were even discussions as to whether a third Vatican Council should be held sometime in the year 2000, which did not happen. While the Second Vatican Council opened the windows to fresh expression, it also produced a range of dilemmas. There are exceptions in each diocese, but the delicate issue of the role of women up to, and including, their ordination will need to be papally revisited.

Referring to Pope John Paul II's October 1979 visit to Chicago, Sister Veronica observed, "I was fifteen feet from him." It is unknown whether her presence in the city was a political statement of dispute during his American

Tour. However, it is clear that some other Sisters were there keeping a silent vigil outside the Cathedral, protesting the Pontiff's attitude over limiting the role of women in religious life. The Pope also made a trip to Washington, D.C., that same year, and met a gathering of Sisters at the Immaculate Conception Cathedral. There was a call for women to be allowed to share in all the ministries of the Church, which was a thinly veiled reference to the ordination of females as Priests. However, Pope John Paul II still stands firm as of 2002: "The ordination of women is not possible."[3]

The main reason, apparently, is based on the reluctance to break with tradition. Biblists and theologians continue this disagreement. One argument is that Jesus, the true mediator of God's salvific presence, is historically a man. Therefore, it is logical that only a man in ministerial Priesthood can be the true "icon" of the historical and glorious Jesus Christ. Another argument is that Jesus historically called and commissioned only men, the Twelve, to be His apostles.

Among scholars there are many other interesting debates as to whether biblical interpretation weeded out references to women in leadership positions. It is not only in the business world where women move slowly into the traditional male domain: in the Catholic Church, women have hit the figurative "glass ceiling" as well.

In 1989, Reverend Barbara Clement became the first female Bishop in the Episcopal Church. The Berlin Wall fell that year, too. Surely Sister Veronica saw both events as positive signs of things to come. Perhaps she thought the Catholic Church might soon be ready for more female involvement — perhaps not — yet the Catholic Church is not the only church that shuns feminine authority.

In May 2000, the Southern Baptists — America's largest Protestant denomination — stated that ordained women should no longer be allowed to serve as Pastors. The Reverend Molly Marshall, a Southern Baptist, said the proposal "signals a long, repressive period." The Reverend Anne Thomas Neil, of the same denomination, added, "The proposal would leave the denomination a crippled body. Women have never had opportunities for full expression of their gifts." Two years earlier, that church declared that a woman should submit to the leadership of her husband. About a dozen congregations cut their ties over that remark.[4]

On the other hand, in mid-2000, the African Methodist Episcopal Church elected Reverend Vashti McKenzie, the first female Bishop in that denomination's history. "Because of God's favor, the stained-glass ceiling has been pierced and broken," she was quoted as saying. In her acceptance speech, McKenzie praised the pioneer work of women who had been trying to become Bishops for several decades, saying, "They had sacrificed, cried, died and gave their very best."[7]

It is interesting to note that in non-Catholic churches, which have female leaders, female attendance is up, while male attendance is down. Undoubtedly, the Catholic Church has taken note.

The Diocese of Arlington, Virginia is across the bridge from the Nation's Capitol. It was among one of the most traditional and anti-feminist in the country, as recent as the 1990s. Because of an ultra-conservative Bishop, female altar servers were not allowed. In many of the parishes there also were no women Eucharistic ministers in that diocese, up until 1999 — a good thirty years beyond the Second Vatican Council.

Following Vatican II, male versus female issues have been addressed. "Forms of social or cultural discrimination in basic personal rights on the grounds of sex, race, color, social conditions, language, or religion must be curbed and eradicated as incompatible with God's design."[8]

The movement to incorporate inclusive language in the liturgy became strong. It was a refreshing and freeing experience, for Sisters and other women, to hear God referred to in feminine, or at least non-gender, pronouns. Theology and spiritual writings began to incorporate the feminine metaphors to express God's presence and action. Sister Ginger Pearl remarked that the sole male image, the reference to "He," offends some of the Sisters. "If it can be stated, and not sound awkward, we prefer to say 'One.'" It is the feminine, in all its aspects, which mirrors the process of growing into maturity.

Closer to home, in the mid-1980s, Sister Veronica felt personally defeated each time one of her own was set back. "A Sister applied for full-time parish ministry in Hill City. She was going to live with me and commute, since Father Labbe favored that she live [in Community] with someone. I thought twenty-three miles was rather far to travel, but she may have been more structured during the day, than I, with only occasional evening meetings. The Pastor was in favor of the position; however he let the parish council decide.

"They said they could not afford her at $4,000 a year, as they had just built a new church. They would not even try her for six months. I can't believe it is a money thing, rather [another example of] the struggle all of us Nuns have in trying to wiggle into non-institutional work."

There is a fundamental Catholic population, both in metropolitan and rural areas, desiring to live in the shadows of the pre-Vatican II Church. Change does not come easy, neither in the workplace, nor for churchgoers. But this inflexibility hits sparsely populated areas very hard. Shortsighted actions are a blow to all Religious Women, where people are fearful of what change might bring, especially empowering Nuns to take on the role of Priests.

A pioneer, Sister Veronica clearly saw these as solvable challenges requiring forward thinking. Dealing first hand with difficult change herself she knew a transforming Church, and modernization, are not incompatible with faith.

"We are challenging the 'Plan' to close small parishes," she said when the Densmore church closed in the mid 1980s. "It seems to me they could still gather, as a faith community, to pray during the week, and carry out Christian projects in the name of the church. Certainly, to bury their dead from that parish, if desired."

She feared many rural parishes, such as those in Kansas, would revert to mission status, as they were a century ago. She was especially worried that Stockton would someday fall victim. When Father James Grennan retired, in July 2001, and was replaced with Father Joseph Thalananyd (a Priest from India, who is a Vincentian Father of the Congregation of the Mission) our hometown parish had been staved off mission status for a while longer.

"No changes announced in the diocese yet, but I'd guess in about three years, the Bishop may be to the point of agreeing to appoint Sisters to administer a parish, rather than closing it, or expecting a Priest to handle two big ones. I'd look for Damar to be among those changes before 1990."

Sometime in the 1980s the predominantly Catholic village of Damar, with its dwindling census of 115 active family units, lost its resident pastor, although one Priest began living in retirement there in 2000, and the Hill City pastor ministers to the church. The once vital parish school and CSJ convent had been closed years earlier.

Sister Veronica had tremendous compassion for those families, with whom she shared a French Canadian heritage. She had strong ties to the 100-year-old parish of her roots, her baptism, and marriage of her parents. The church, itself, held a strong pull having been constructed in part by both grandfathers and great-grandfathers. As she noted in her genealogy book, *Ma Famille*, "This was a place of strong Catholic devotion, large traditional families, and birth place of several vocations to the religious and Priestly life."

"It takes a long time for me to fit into my role and find my identity, and for the people to know what it is, too," she reflected in a letter. "So I look forward to many more years here in WaKeeney." She had planned to stay there another five to ten years. "Then possibly be able to minister in Damar, Stockton, or Zurich into my retirement years. I imagine the next fifteen years to come very quickly."

She planned to patiently wait until the Bishop appointed her to a parish. However, coinciding with her fiftieth birthday, she resumed thinking about a pastoral position the next summer in Damar. She was bubbly, and excited about the possibility: "If it worked out, I'd probably change my name to Sister Ila Mae — especially Sister Mae — and do it in the same church I was baptized in.

"Another Sister also wants the Damar parish, but on a full-time basis. She is good at gabbing, and I am good at adult education and general planning." Sister Veronica hoped they could co-share the ministry. At the end of February 1990, she made an appointment to speak with Father Labbe, the Hill City pastor-in-charge. "He is of the opinion Damar can't afford full-time." A few months later she wrote, "I would settle for one-fourth, or one-half time, since that's all it seems they can afford."

God gives each of us special gifts to share, and talents to develop, which we must not bury. Sister Veronica offered her individual abilities, seeing this need in Damar. Surely she yearned for the reflection of our Lord's words: "Well done, good and faithful servant! You have been faithful with a few things; I will put you in charge of many things."[9]

She wrote directly to the Bishop expressing her interest. "He said he would take it to the Priest's personnel meeting at the end of the month." She followed up with a telephone call. "The Zurich parish council will be meeting with him next week." A few days later she heard from the Hill City pastor, "The Damar parish council want to try it alone."

Occasionally Sister Veronica wrote articles for the *Northwestern Kansas Catholic Register*, the Salina Diocesan newspaper. One in particular was a gospel meditation titled, "Nearing The Answer." In it she said, "A children's game of hiding an object bring squeals of, 'You are warm, or hot, or cold.' We like to know where we stand in relationship to something, or someone else. Other games, children and adults play — picture puzzles and crosswords — center on the goals of finding the answer until everything falls into place. Likely the people of Jesus' time wanted to know where they stood."[10]

Sister Veronica wanted to know where she stood, too, but things did not fall into place as she wished. She felt more rejected than she let on and tried not to brood about it, although her letter ended, "p.s. Neither Damar, nor Zurich want any help. I was so shocked!" It was another dream shattered. But she managed to save face: "They want to do it themselves. And perhaps my name was not mentioned when the topic came up."

Her words do not express her disappointment. She dearly wanted to return to her roots, the community of her birth, or even to nearby Zurich, for that matter — the place of marriage of both Morin and Roy grandparents and burial place of Saindon great-grandparents. This seemed a low point in her life. This unfulfilled vision was a big heartache. Letting go of this dream was a painful part of moving into her fifties.

Unfortunately for her, and the people of Damar and Zurich, their respective parish councils did not have the sensitivity, foresight and financial wisdom to hire her, or any other dedicated Religious Women for that matter. It would have only been a few dollars outlay per family to have a Religious presence on hand, especially one like Sister Veronica, who excelled at ministering to an elderly population.

In a pioneering spirit, she pulled herself together and forged ahead. Her central purpose in life was to serve as a holy woman where she was needed and wanted. She was determined to make the best of it.

Currently, in parishes throughout the United States that have no resident Priests, it is not unusual for Sisters to be named Pastoral Administrators. But, in the late 1980s in Kansas, there was no mention of Sister Veronica being appointed to such a position. Nevertheless, she did not give up hope.

Shortly thereafter she heard of an opening as Pastoral Associate. She wrote a letter of inquiry to the Logan and New Almelo pastors. "Over the past four years they had several Sisters between those two places — both in full-time position."

She received a phone call in return. "Both Father Mark [Berland] and Father Darryl [Olmstead] are excited with my application. New Almelo, thirty miles west of Logan, lost its gas station and grocery store three years ago, and lost its post office this year. So, I'll prefer to live in Logan." She went on to divide her time between two parishes. It was just like her to try replacing two people.

She resigned from the various hospital dietetic positions, and pastoral ministry, after giving more than a month's notice. A going away party and potluck dinner was held in her honor, beginning with a Mass.

"It was a great pleasure working with Sister Veronica for nine years," Elaine Newcomer was quoted in the local newspaper. "She was instrumental in helping revamp guidelines as the new directives came out of the diocese." In the same news article the Pastor noted that Sister Veronica extended herself beyond the parish limits. "She was a blessing, not only to the parish, but to the community and surrounding area. She was an inspiration to all, and will be missed greatly. Her religious presence and friendship will remain in our hearts and minds for many years to come."

Sister Veronica first went to the rural town of WaKeeney with uplifted spirits, a sense of hope, and high expectations. In a press release she wrote, "A goal of my ministry has been to unfold, with others, the reality of Jesus and our relationship. The people here have a strong tradition of serving the Community. They are living reminders of what it means to love unselfishly, hope boldly and call others to responsibility for one another. I hope that my presence models with them creative ways of living our faith in the unity of all people as we model ministry one to another." During the nearly ten years there, her statement of ministry was consistent: "To be present in loving, caring, praying, sharing and working with, and for them."

"She empowered others," said Verna Flax, a parishioner. "She worked herself out of a job, teaching others how to do for themselves." She felt a sense of achievement with the WaKeeney parish, programs were in place, and lay people were well trained. In prior years she had encountered challenges and faced some struggles, but by time she left, she was well loved and respected.

While she felt somewhat defeated in the resistant-to-change hospital environment, she left feeling she had learned a great deal about human nature. She tried to cope with the slower pace. She wasn't one to overly push, rather she suggested, gave hints, and exhibited enormous patience. She moved on, trusting the momentum would build into "The More" of her Community's spirituality.

She tackled the 1990 move with renewed optimism. "Yesterday was my last day at WaKeeney. I'm definitely in transition and ready to let go, shake the dust, and get charged up with great ambition to start afresh for God's people."

A new Priest, Father Joe Scheetz, heard of her good works from his WaKeeney parishioners. He eulogized her in late 1995 in a memorial service: "The good name and zealous pastoral ministry of Sister Veronica Roy, in the 1980s at Christ the King, is very much alive still. In her sudden exit and call to gloryland, I anticipate even further fond memory and inspiration. Sister, you were both a Martha and Mary for us. We thank God for the gift of your nine years with us. You were a shepherd leading the flock to the mountain of God. We will miss you deeply. We will all be expecting you to continue to gently touch our hearts and minds with our shared visions from the mountain top."

Indeed Christ the King parish miss her, and her memory lingers on. In 2000, ten years after she left that community, they sponsored a "Sister Veronica Walkathon," with the proceeds designated to the *Pastoral da Criança* Sister Veronica Roy Memorial Center in Brazil.

It came as no surprise when a parishioner, Marion Parke, remarked, "When we were having some special event, in the parish hall, and everyone was busy doing the 'important things,' it was Sister Veronica who checked out the bathrooms. Then when Mary Jo Kluvenger and I prepared lunch for the senior citizens, it was Sister Veronica who was in the kitchen cleaning, giving it that last-minute scrubbing herself, never thinking she was too good to do these tasks. Many in the parish would never consider doing this themselves, but nothing was beneath her. She was a humble servant and content to serve behind the scenes."

She was most remembered for her humbling pioneer work, as she valiantly lived by rules of the Sisters of St. Joseph. Maxim 47 states: "When there is question of many things to be done at the same time in the community, and the choice is given to you, choose what is more lowly and difficult, and leave to others what is easier and brings more honor."

Chapter Thirty-seven

I heard the voice of the Lord saying, "Whom shall I send? Who will go for us?" "Here I am," I said; "send me!"

— Is 6, 8

Just before she took on the challenge of serving two new parishes, Sister Veronica wrote from the Manna House of Prayer in Concordia, "A brief note before retreat starts after supper.[1] The next seven days will be based on Sister Joyce Rupp's book, *Praying Our Goodbyes* and directed by her, too. It's called a transition, or letting go retreat. How appropriate that I selected it six months ago."

She was eager to live and work in both Logan and New Almelo in mid-1990. "Neither church has a resident Priest. Both of my Pastor-bosses will be okay to work with. They seem appreciative and willing for me to do as much as I can handle."

Indeed, the Priests welcomed her, since they had their hands full with two parishes each. "Father Darryl Olmstead will travel from Phillipsburg to Logan, which has 130 family units. Father Mark Berland [a second cousin] travels from Norton to New Almelo."

She jumped right into activities. During the first three weeks, there were two weddings and the annual bazaar in New Almelo. "It was a wonderful initiation into parish life. I took before and after photos, of the bazaar, to document how everyone really works together to make this traditional event a big success. It lasted from 5 p.m. to midnight. They have been doing this since the 1930s, otherwise they probably would not have such widespread participation." She noted that even those who did not go to church, on a regular basis, worked on the bazaar to make it a hit. "Ladies in the parish made ten quilts, which were auctioned off for $525 apiece. A pit barbeque supper was open to the community. We raised $16,000.

"Imagine a parish with eighty-five families, but with only eighteen Catholic families in the actual town of New Almelo, so you can guess how the parish extends into the countryside thirty miles each direction." Logan extended equally far. "My ministry covers six counties, so I carry maps constantly. I think of Father Duane a lot, in rural Brazil, when I travel dirt roads trying to find people at home."

These communities fit the definition of a frontier, as do many other Midwest rural counties in Kansas, Nebraska, Iowa, and Minnesota, by having two or fewer people per square mile. A reliable automobile is a necessity for rural ministry. She had been driving a twelve-year-old Pontiac Grand Prix that she purchased from the family estate after Mother's death. In 1990, due to extensive road travel, the Motherhouse gave her permission to purchase a replacement car with the stipulation, "that it cost less than $11,000, and have less than 11,000 miles on the odometer. I got a white car, which does not show road dirt too badly."[2]

At the time of her death in 1995, the Chevy Corsica she had purchased five years earlier was still in good running condition, even though the fatal accident report indicated it had over 100,000 miles on it. She was actively looking for another car the same week of the head-on collision. Even still it would not have had airbags, which reduce the risk of death by thirty percent, as these were only required in the 1998 and newer models.

Traveling throughout the spread-out parishes, she knew full well that the central and northwestern plains are blizzard country. She used caution when winds blew snow horizontally, reducing visibility to near zero. There was also the danger of black ice and gusts. And wet, driving snow can clog the engine leaving drivers stranded. She never owned a cell phone.

Drifts are typical around Kansas. Sister Veronica grew up playing in mounds of snow and remembered when rural schools were shut down during seasonal storms, like the one that halted construction of the Webster Dam the winter of 1953-1954, with a repeat the winter of 1955-56.

County roads, like the ones she maneuvered, were sometimes impassable for a few days, until the overburdened snowplow operators could get to them. It was also not unusual for the 115-mile-long stretch of Interstate 70, from Hays west to the Colorado border, to be closed from blowing snow or high winds, which often forced hundreds of travelers to spend the night jammed into small-town motels and community shelters set up by the Red Cross and National Guard.

Unpredictable snowstorms can be deadly for animals, too. A farm girl at heart, Sister Veronica sympathized with the farmers tending cattle during severe winters. She could hear the helicopters from Fort Riley hovering overhead to drop bales of hay when farmers could not get to their cattle, as they did in 1990.

While never a Girl Scout, she was prepared, nevertheless, with coats and blankets in her car when occasional temperatures dropped dramatically, after hitting highs of 70s and 80s, to overnight lows in the 20s, typical of a spring storm. She also kept holy water in the car, and was known to use it.

Like other locals, she tuned in regularly to news flashes of severe thunderstorm and tornado watches and warnings, knowing that summers in the Midwest can be equally dangerous. She knew to take cover immediately when seeing violently rotating columns of black dirt and debris-filled tornados, extending from a cloud to the ground, covering a two to six mile area.

On more than one occasion family members dropped to their knees, in prayers of thanksgiving, when Mother's home was saved, due to an unpredictable change in direction of these deadly wind funnels. Some of Mother's Rooks County, Belmont Township neighbors were not as fortunate.

Mobile homes, or manufactured homes as these are sometimes referred to, are especially unsafe during tornadoes. It is not unusual for them to be torn from their foundation and crumbled like tin cans. The one that served as the New Almelo rectory shook and rattled, but Sister Veronica was never one to complain of the safety factor, or the noise, even when brutal hailstorms plummeted her modest housing with golf ball-size stones. Although, she was especially pleased to live at the Logan rectory made of brick. It was solid and spacious, a ranch style, similar to our parents' home.

After being there a few years she said, "Ten years earlier, in 1983, there were ninety-one family units in New Almelo. Now there are eighty-one, which is considered constant, although population has dropped in half. We have buried many members, and have lots of widows/widowers, for such a small parish. Many of our high school graduates are staying here and becoming their own family unit, although with fewer children. Some of the inactive parishioners are becoming active again. I am training thirteen new Special Ministers of Communion since none have been trained in ten years and we have lost a number of the older ones."

At first her schedule of living in two places was confusing. She preferred a more organized and structured calendar, but was capable of "going with the flow." "I live at Logan on Monday and Tuesday, at New Almelo on Thursday and Friday, alternate Sundays and Wednesdays, and Saturday is 'free' so can be either, or neither. I will still have a little running back and forth to do, if meetings get switched.

"I plan to keep detailed accounts of how my time is spent. My two parishes are enough work, since I value knowing what is going on, getting to know people with some frequency, and not just crisis intervention. I'm expected to be out among the people, yet available for consultation and meetings. I leave the house by 7:50 a.m. for rosary and communion service.

"I hope to appear equally at home in either rectory, as both places wanted a full-time religious presence. Both communities are quite active in social concerns, religious education, lay ministry and diocesan-wide participation. The parishioners have always done all this themselves, and both parish councils said they want to continue. So, they must want me here for a variety of reasons.

"I'm trying to keep my life orderly by keeping all dietetics, sewing and crafts at New Almelo. All CSJ correspondence, Senate and Executive Board, family projects and the Saindon book project I'll keep at Logan. I'll still receive mail at either place. I hope my letter sounds positive, like I feel I belong here with enough challenge to keep me on the go."

"A Religious has to have a well-structured spirituality to hack opting to live among the poor, and organize them," she wrote to Father Duane. While she was not working with the impoverished, as our brother was, many of these rural families were far from affluent, so she could have been speaking of her own work, as well. Yet, she found they donated generously to their church.

However, after a short while she discovered, at an Open Forum meeting, the New Almelo parish council was unaware of their financial responsibility, and had failed to pay their share of the mission-pastors' benefits, such as insurance and vacation — with the exception of round trip mileage twice a week.

"The Norton parish agreed to take on poor New Almelo as their mission and continued to pay the pastor in full. However, I doubt that would set very well with a new pastor. If they ever have to pay their fair share of 25 to 33 percent of what Norton pays in benefits and salary, as suggested by the Salina Diocese, they [may not want] to support me."

Soon after, she found a similar error in Logan. "Perhaps if I was not here, the Pastor's benefits should be thirty to forty percent. Previously, Sisters at St. John's parish exchanged a day of work with the Pastor, at Phillipsburg, so there was no exchange of salary or benefits, other then mileage. We went through the hassle of straightening that out, too.

"The brand new church in Phillipsburg gets dedicated Palm Sunday. This is a thorn in the side of the 'Loganites,' who are jealous that this new church, twenty miles away, possibly means they will be deprived of any [pastoral] services in the future. Their way of thinking is, 'If Phillipsburg has money for a new church, let them pay the Pastor in full.' Father Darryl asked for twenty-five percent of his benefits to be paid by Logan. The parish council offered twenty percent, plus mileage."

Sometime later she added, "The Logan parish had to cash in a certificate of deposit to pay bills. Our primary supporters are dying, or moving onto retirement areas." Her understanding of their financial picture was accurate, and after two years her contract in Logan was not renewed.

Upon arrival, she tried creating a nest in both homes, making them comfortable and welcoming. "I've received a lot of compliments on my [Flying Geese quilt pattern table] runner. I enjoy adding some personal touches, and look forward to the space for sewing again, as I will need a time filler after the [genealogy] book is finished."

After getting settled she said, "I enjoy both homes, and the variety my work routine brings, which makes the weeks go by too fast, since they are only three days long at each house." Her home and office were one and the same, and there was often something going on. It was typical for her to say, "We have a meeting or CCD staff party here at the rectory, so I need to clean up."

But, it wasn't long before she realized that at Logan she had no privacy. The same thing happened in New Almelo. "Both parishes pay two-day-a-week secretaries, who are in and out of the rectory, as is the director of religious education, as well as the housekeeper. Having to share office space with others at both of my homes, is almost too much. I started on a positive attitude knowing this would happen." Later she added, "The secretary, who also handles finances, worked here today for five hours and roped me into doing way too much work with her, considering my vacation status."

These were awkward living arrangements, even though she was the sole resident at both homes. There were times when parishioners were underfoot and she felt compelled to leave, for several hours or even days at a time, so as to not make it awkward for those who said they needed to use the rectory for a while.

During one summer, in Logan, Sister Veronica was visibly embarrassed to have to ask a weekend guest, after she traveled nearly a thousand miles to visit her, if she would mind sleeping in a damp basement bedroom. The main guest bedroom, on the main floor, was taken over by an enormous wedding dress for an upcoming ceremony. She wanted to avoid coming under criticism for moving the dress.

In the days gone by, when there was a full-time Priest living in each parish, the rectory was a place where the faithful would make appointments with him, and there was respect and consideration shown for his time and space. St. Paul wrote that one needs a quiet and silent life, in all ways godly and respectable.

Most people need a calm place, free from intrusion, from time to time, not only for the mind and body, but more importantly, for the soul. In the book, *Care of the Soul*, Thomas Moore suggests that it is possible to see in a house "signs of the soul that lie hidden in the everyday and commonplace…and fundamental to the feeling we have of being at home…home spirits that are so important in sustaining our lives."[3]

It was difficult to be at home where others had the run of the place, and consequently she often felt displaced. She did not have the privacy others assumed she had, and which she especially needed, given her introverted personality.

In her day-to-day work, she tried to assess the real needs of the people. She thought her role was "to uncover requests they may have, and assist them by networking, inviting or planning programs to meet those requirements." She advised, instructed and talked of how to make things better. She listened and consoled. After a short time she said, "I have to reread the accounts of Evangelization. I thought it implied getting warmed up to people on their level. That is, getting to know their interests, especially their families and doings, which I am trying like a tornado to do these past ten weeks at both parishes."

The first several months she visited twenty-three homes — over one-third of the parish — in the spread-out, rural New Almelo community. "That is the best way to get to know people and ask how I can be of service to them. Now that I know who most of the people are, for my eyes only, I am beginning to chart, in column form, whether [I had] phone or written contact, visits at home or yard, social greetings and other significant meetings. There are others I meet weekly at Bible Studies or community services. There are some persons I would never meet otherwise and would dread to ask who they are in the future."

She did this for the Logan community, too. She learned from prior experience that when she didn't receive invitations, she invited herself, in a friendly way. She wanted to be there for the parishioners on a daily bases, and not just on Sundays only.

Ten years earlier, in 1982, while still in WaKeeney she said, "Mary Lou Goetz and I are co-chairing a Trego County-wide census for determining Catholic population. The Bishop [Daniel W. Kucera, OSB, 1980-1984] has ordered this diocese wide. So we have started marking out districts and finding ten leaders and one hundred workers. Another energy getter."

Before the Second Vatican Council, census taking was one means of contact, between a Priest and his parishioners. It was also a way to stimulate lax Catholics and add enthusiasm to the spiritual lives of active parishioners.[4] Aside from that 1980s mandate from Bishop Kucera, the recent custom of visiting homes in rural communities became a social call, a friendly contact and a way of introducing services provided by the church. Nevertheless, she was coldly greeted in some cases. "Some people fear 'the business' when they see a religious presence coming to the door."

She understood as Father Andrew Greeley explains in his book, *Furthermore! Memories of a Parish Priest*, that rules and regulations rigorously enforced by overzealous lay people can drive away practicing Catholics and keep away those who wish to be reunited with their Church.

In metropolitan parishes, there is a program called Alienated Catholics Anonymous, a series designed to address the needs of those who have fallen away from the Church. This explores reconciliation and return to active participation in one's faith. Sister Veronica tried to tackle this single-handedly. One parishioner noted, "Not only did she regularly visit shut-ins, the sick and hospitalized, but even those who stopped coming to church." Another parishioner, Geneva Long observed, "In homes where there were 'fallen always,' she had them returning to the Sacraments before long."

She even turned to letter writing in her ministry of the salvation of souls, praying, "If I could get even one back a year, of the fifteen inactive and fallen away Catholic families in our parish, or rather the Lord through me." It was her prayer to bring back, into the fold, those who left for myriad reasons, and who now were ready to accept redemption and love through the community of Church.

"I see some progress. We try to keep 'the door open,' to be approachable to the locals who quit the church. A family lived here for fifteen years. Upon leaving here, they quit going to church, and were away for an equal number of years. In the next state where they moved, they were too embarrassed to ask for a Catholic funeral for a family member. Or maybe here in New Almelo is the only place where they felt at home, in all their frequent moves in the oil well drilling business."

She ministered to converts to Catholicism, too. "On most Wednesday evenings, since Advent, I am working with eight converts at the Logan parish. The three children have been in CCD all their grade school years."

She reached out in a variety of ways. "I plan to go to New Almelo for 9:30 Christmas Eve Mass. I'll then drive thirty miles, to Logan, for carols at 11:30, then midnight mass, followed by breakfast with the choir, then 8:00 a.m. Mass again. I'll meander around Logan, looking for parishioners who have company. I'll stop in and meet them, unless I get an invitation."

One year she reported, "I stayed with a ninety-year-old parishioner, who has no one but a friend. I sat with her all Christmas morning, and ended up cleaning her house. I took her to the doctor the day after. She only had cracked ribs, but I was sure it was more than that." Sister Veronica ministered in subtle ways, in ways a Priest would not have thought to do.

A group she called "the oldsters" cherished her. "I served twenty-three senior citizens a potluck turkey dinner, at Logan, just after Thanksgiving. Yesterday, I had twenty-two guests after communion service at New Almelo for St. Nick's feast. They are all so appreciative." One sang her praises, "Many mornings Sister Veronica would get up at four or five, bake some quick breads, and have people over to the rectory/house for coffee and snack after communion service. Other times, after communal Penance, she organized Robber Bingo, or a film, such as one on World Hunger, then we all went over and had cookies and beverages at the school. We also celebrated birthdays, anniversaries, or 'It's a great day' day."

In 1996, 91-year-old parishioner, Gertrude McNeive, and her 93-year-old sister, Loene O'Connor, from the village of Edmond both said, "We attended St. Mary's from the time we were born. But the Bishop closed the beautiful church, in Densmore, and since 1985 we have had to drive thirty-six miles round trip to attend Mass in New Almelo. We loved her from the very first day. She had so many ideas to share."

"For World Marriage Day, February 14, our Family Life Commission made homemade chocolates for all fifty couples," Sister Veronica said. "We tied pieces in red net and ribbon, and passed them out at Sunday Mass before the final blessing. Also the local fire department had a Sweetheart Ball benefit on Saturday. Very country."

One parishioner noted, "Sister Veronica touched the lives of many people in our community. She was a good friend, as well as a spiritual advisor." Another added, "My father-in-law fell and ended up in the hospital. She visited each week and put a small cross on the wall for him. When she left the parish, and moved to Concordia, he worried about her cross. He said, 'You better take it. These kids won't know what to do with it.' She told him to keep the cross, as she had many. It still hangs on the wall. He talks about it often, remembering Sister, and instructs us to get the cross back to her family when he dies."

Betty Otter related another story: "A local bachelor, in his late fifties, went to the hospital in Hays to get his medicine readjusted. His house was in terrible shape. A group of us, including Sister Veronica, completely refurbished it. We worked nights and weekends, and some people during the day. For two weeks, we painted walls, recovered a sofa and couple of chairs, scrubbed floors, put up curtains, and replaced the mattress and box springs, some carpet in his bedroom, new towels, sheets and curtains. The Knights of Columbus and St. Anne's Sodality paid for materials.

"Sister Veronica took on the task of fixing a filing system for his papers that we knew he felt were important. She got a metal trunk, like the ones the Sisters used years ago to ship their clothing when going a distance, and tried to make order of it. She put current papers in a large popcorn can. After he came home, she had to show him where things were filed. If that wasn't enough, she loaned him the television her brothers and sisters gave for her twenty-fifth Jubilee Anniversary. She took him food, and made special trips just to check on him."

More modest of her involvement, Sister Veronica merely said. "So many took it to heart and are doing something of service this afternoon. To the ones who asked about working on the Sabbath I said, 'It doesn't count when doing good for another person.'"[5]

Trying to live out the Gospel's great ideals in a contemporary world, she strived to make Catholicism a living faith — one that speaks to the moment, as well as to eternity. She ministered to the sick and dying, continuing the Hospice-type work she did in WaKeeney. She was one of the first contacted by anyone in dire personal need.

In New Amelo, when Father Mark was not able to come from his Norton parish, she organized and presided over wakes and led prayer services in the school gym, as it was the custom in this community, since there was no funeral home in the area. The Mass of Christian Burial, of course, was in the church.

Helping grieving families work through decisions, she assisted in planning liturgical details and made herself available for bereavement counseling. "I assisted with four funerals this week," she said in one letter. She was never paid a stipend, for funeral planning, as Priests are. Many Sisters continue to face the struggle with these financial oversights and other power issues, too.

Currently, only ordained Priests are allowed to administer the sacrament of anointing the sick. However, a canon lawyer, Father John Lyons of Tucson, Arizona, who at mid-life gave up his law practice to become a Priest, describes the anointing: "It's not magic, but a deeper miracle of comfort and grace." Sister Veronica did what the Church allowed her to do, as she brought comfort, to the seriously ill, and grace through the Lord's word.

✝

Chapter Thirty-eight

Due to her hectic schedule, she was unable to attend the funeral of longtime family friend, Franklin Veverka, although she did attend his vigil service in Plainville. "Very few [parishioners] there," she complained. "I often recall how Mother would get so annoyed when people 'don't bury their dead.'" Both mother and daughter firmly believed that corporal works of mercy are a responsibility of the entire parish community.

Another time she said, "There was a pathetic funeral in New Almelo yesterday for an eighty-three-year-old bachelor who was raised here, left in the 1930s, then came back to be buried next to his parents. He had five first cousins in this parish, and two in Logan. Only three, of eight relatives, came for the service. The sad thing was that only ten attended the vigil, and five other people from the parish even showed up for the funeral.

"I honestly tried contacting twelve different organists, and each had a reason not to, and it was looking icy, so I ended up acting as the organist, which was actually a tape recorder. I was able to manage enough recorded funeral music, except the 'Song of Farewell,' which the soloist did acapello. The out-of-town folks were on the opposite side of the church, so I don't think they realized I was not actually playing. It was quite nice, I thought.

"Four years ago the parish bought a $3,000 piano, with recording capabilities, and stops that sounds just like an organ, so they would always have music. They rationalized that once we have 'dead liturgies,' we will be closed as a parish. We hardly have an organist in our parish now that a high school student, who played, has moved. We have a seventh grader, who plays the piano, and is learning one or two pieces a year. I sit with her so she can learn to manage the recorder for additional music. Last March the Parish Council was talking of replacing me with someone who could play music. That is still not out of the picture," she said with lucid foresight since she had little musical ability.

"Having religious education coordinators in both Logan and New Almelo parishes is a true blessing, knowing how hard I worked on those positions in WaKeeney," Sister Veronica said. She was relieved that her job descriptions did not include that of Director of Religious Education — a relief that was short lived.

Qualified as a Master Catechist within the diocese, she went on to teach religious education a total of fifteen years in Kansas alone. She said, her first fall there as co-director of weekly classes during the school year, "I don't expect very many children." She was surprised. "About seventy-six percent of our four- to ten-year-olds came, so it is a happy time for teachers and kids, since they want to be there. I just bombard them with a lot of different activities to see and do."

A parishioner remarked, "When the CCD Coordinator job was dumped on Sister Veronica's lap, she organized the program so the parents and children did the lesson together, read next week's gospel, and served drinks as a family unit."

"There were a number of parents involved in her program, and it was well accepted, with only a few exceptions," another parishioner added. "Her talent for creativeness shone through. She could take those words and work them into a theme people could use in their daily lives. She did so many things right." Gertrude McNeive added, "Many parents were thankful for her contributions."

"I worked with Sister Veronica, both on the Education Committee and the Liturgy Committee," said parishioner Betty Otter. "When I stopped teaching CCD, after twenty years, she told me maybe my calling was to take over the Chairmanship of the Liturgy. She tried to make our meetings as educational as she could about spiritual matters. In our hurry up world, we tend to put God on the back burner.

"Often she included the children, even the very youngest, in the liturgy. Children's masses were worked into the schedule. The students loved to read, usher, and be song leader — all those grownup jobs. Sister Veronica always had some neat project for the students to do, like making homemade Valentines for the older members of the parish. And programs for each Holy Day. Sister Veronica helped plant the seeds of faith and religious history, teaching children about Christ's journey to Calvary. The kids loved reenacting the fourteen Stations of the Cross. A few scraps of cloth, and makeshift costumes, gave meaning to the actions. For Lent the students acted out the glorious, sorrowful and joyous mysteries of the Rosary before Mass," Mrs. Otter concluded.

"The children started the season off grandly by decorating our Jesse Tree, the Family Tree of Jesus, one of my favorite Advent things," Sister Veronica recalled. Perhaps it would not be until adulthood that some of these youngsters would call to mind their own childhood events. She understood that ritual is an integral part of developing one's personal faith.

Eight years after Pope John Paul II instituted World Youth Day in 1985, Sister Veronica and several parishioners attended area meetings in Stockton to plan for the special event scheduled for Denver that year. Every other year, World Youth Day is held in a different country. However, it was held in Denver a second time, in 1993, then in Manila, Paris, Rome, and in Toronto in 2002. Many young people, from more than one hundred countries, spend the night in sleeping bags, on bare dirt, to be ready to hear the Pope's message, one year, urging the resistance to pursue prosperity, which increasingly draws young Catholics away from religious vocations. In the year 2000, banners strung about the gathering of two million urged, "Don't be afraid to be the saints of the new millennium."

She did not plan to attend the 1993 World Youth Day event herself, having seen the Pope in 1979 in Chicago. "I was there for two masses. So I was satisfied." Furthermore, she was hesitant to get on the bandwagon. "I just can't get motivated to encourage a youth group, with the probability of them having to walk three miles [in the hot sun, from the parking lot to the site for Mass]. Some will only do what is easy for their faith." However, she was in the midst of things, once the two groups of high school youths and four adults were committed to going to Denver. When the parish was ready to raise money for gas, food and lodging, she was eager: "With a little help, I am putting on a sausage, gravy and biscuit breakfast after Mass this Sunday for an extra fundraiser.

"We are very conscientious about our youth." By now the parish had grown to nearly one hundred families. "About one-third are young families, or singles," she explained. "They are a large group and could make the difference whether we have a parish here in fifty years. The active ones are really good about coming to church, but I'm sure they expect more from the parish. I want to find out what that is, and hopefully sponsor some activities for them."

In 1993, she took a night classes on Marriage and Family at Selden, twenty-five miles away. "I am just taking it for clock hours, to gain some insight into what young families around here expect of the church." She also attended numerous lectures including one titled, "Dealing with Teens in the Classroom," presented by Father Mike Scully.

"I invited four young adult parish council members to meet with me after Mass, to plan something for the sixty-five parishioners in this age group. They are sort of stuck to help me. I asked them to survey their group and come up with some suggestions of how we could help. 'Nothing!' they said.

"Ironically, at our open General Assembly last fall an identified need was for the young adults who chronically complain, 'Nothing to do around here.' Several of them pointed out, 'Don't plan anything for us, because you don't know what we want.' The Family Life Commission scheduled volleyball, videos and discussion, but generally only the planners came."

She wrote of "missing the boat with the youth." She readily admitted this was a difficult set for her to relate to, especially young materialistic women, because she was so austere in her own youth. "This is the age group I am least comfortable with, perhaps because my own years from 18 to 35 were so ascetic."

Reflecting on her own strict and rigorous youth, she sensed they were not comfortable with her either. Having always followed rules in her youth, she was clearly frustrated with the younger population in their lack of goals, respect, or initiative, talking back, talking out of turn, raised voices and inattention. Failure to complete homework or strive for higher education was incomprehensible to Sister Veronica, who sought nothing less than excellence in all her academic endeavors, and everything she undertook thereafter.

"I used china cups for that Assembly, and asked the young adults to wash dishes, but they refused." No doubt, she was surprised at their reaction, remembering youthful days at the kitchen sink as one of the few times when spontaneous conversation emerged for her. She hoped to recapture and share that camaraderie with this group. But it backfired. Her ministry took tenacity and stamina, but she persisted, in the name of faith, with what lay ahead.

✝

Chapter Thirty-nine

One day, while tending the graves of our parents, Sister Veronica was overcome with emotion. "Perhaps I was crying that my own family history stops with me." Maybe this realization sparked a streak of creativity. She had a deep sense of eternity, found her life rich in heritage, and felt indebted to her family. She came to appreciate the uniqueness of what only past generations can offer.

After moving to New Almelo and completing her first genealogy book, *Our Saindon Cousins*, Sister Veronica took a few months to relax, then pushed onward. On August 12, 1992, three days before the Feast of the Assumption, she sounded almost apologetic in her letter. "I feel like I've avoided writing, knowing that I need to say something about my next project. So here it is. Since I had such good participation with my last book, I have been thinking about collecting information from Mother's maternal cousins — the Heberts."

This name is pronounced "He-bert" in Kansas because, upon homesteading, land grant offices required anglicized names. In other parts of the country it remains "A-bare," the French pronunciation.

Before the book had a name, she gave it the working title of "Project dit Larose," since research showed the Canadian Heberts carried the surname "Larose" in the old country. "I've decided on the name, *Ma Famille*, a last-minute choice. A Desmarteau distant cousin, a historian, suggested it last month. I know I'm not suppose to use a French title, if it's not written in French, but I thought about it a long time and that's what I did anyway."

She began gathering addresses with the intention of publishing something on a smaller scale than the previous 439-page book. "With some success under my belt, putting together a second book sounds easier to me. Am I crazy or what?" She hoped the second book would be cheaper, too, than the $30 to $40 she charged for the first. She found it was neither easier, nor cheaper, and to answer her own rhetorical question, yes, she must have been possessed to undertake this project. However, her countless relatives are indebted to her for pushing ahead and producing the 510-page volume.

"During my summer vacation I worked hard toward the Hebert-Frigon-St. Peter-Morin-Senesac family history, but it's not generating enough interest," she said. By mid 1993, she received only eight replies from the 250 inquiries she mailed. Four of those sent money. "I have been up and down daily as to whether I should continue. If I don't get more cooperation, I'll just bind about six private copies [for the siblings] with very few photos. What I'd really want to write would be better unpublished anyway." She followed the advice Mother heeded: "Leave the door open. It's too hard to open once it's shut."[1]

Much to her relief, momentum began to build. "I really have a lot collected, including prolific photos." In *Ma Famille* Sister Veronica credits Rita Roberts, a second cousin and Damar historian, "for the use of much of her information and photos, which gave me the burst of enthusiasm to begin the project."

Sister Veronica also received many photos from Uncle Ed Morin. "He had so many old pictures to go through that Mother and I said we would come back another time. The next month, in 1980, he came to Mother's house and brought photos to give us. I didn't know he was not well, yet I could detect he seemed to have an urgency to make the days count." He died from throat cancer the next month.

While still a high school student Ila Mae learned that after grandfather Stanislas Morin died, in 1929, his youngest child (our uncle Levi) inherited a 22-page ancestry booklet. A second cousin, Oliver Gosselin, translated the French writings. Ila Mae typed a copy of this family history. Uncle Levi updated the basic history in 1970, "with the hopes it would be perpetuated." For a high school project our sister, Cheryl Roy Calvin, updated this record again the next year in 1971, and subsequently in 1984.

Laura Morin Knipp and Sister Veronica collaborated their interest in genealogy in 1987, by mailing data forms to cousins, requesting a prompt return. Later, along with Easter greetings, Sister Veronica sent a notice to each cousin about an upcoming Labor Day family reunion, in Damar, and included a second reminder copy of the form to those families who had not yet responded. She wrote to Laura, "They are not sending them back. I don't want to bug them too much, but we still need lots of information."

Collecting this data seemed overwhelming. "I keep thinking I am not doing this again." But, relatives were important to her, and she went the extra mile to preserve memories and relationships. "I spent the rest of my vacation polishing up the family history."

After Cheryl photocopied the newly-completed 67-page booklets, these were offered for a few dollars, for the cost of printing only, during the family reunion in 1988. The contents show the Morin Coat of Arms, meaning "Equally strong and faithful."

"This project was a dream fulfilled," Sister Veronica said. Yet, it was a mere springboard for a more tedious, time-consuming project culminating in *Ma Famille*, in which she credited Cheryl Calvin and Laura Knipp with "maintaining the Morin book through the Thirteenth Generation."

By researching the Salt Lake City genealogical library, Sister Veronica found a missing generation omitted in Uncle Levi's document. "Our great-grandmother, Olive Morin, [after whom our mother was named] was actually the ninth generation, instead of the eighth." This error most likely was undetected because she married a Morin cousin, and her last name remained unchanged.

She also discovered a little-known fact that, due to false accusation of immoral conduct, around 1688 the second-generation family of Pierre and Françoise Chiasson Morin was banished from Beaubassin, in Acadia — the territory between and east of Montreal and Philadelphia. This was before the French were deported in 1755, as depicted in 1847 with Henry Wadsworth Longfellow's *Evangeline* when many families were scattered — many to Louisiana — and were never reunited. She summarized, "Thanks be to God for this [prior] eviction, that the family has been preserved." This family went to live at the head of the Chaleur Bay, then to Restigouche, before settling in Montmagny County, Province of Quebec, where the scandal was cleared.

While visiting at this writer's new home in Florida, she noticed my office space set up in an unused walk-in closet. She liked the idea of a workspace out of sight, to keep the room tidy, since her home served as the parish office. Upon her return home she set up the computer in her guest room closet.

After Gabe Deeming, a parishioner from WaKeeney, graciously volunteered to videotape the 1988 family reunion that summer in Damar, Sister Veronica asked him to go with her to the nearby cemetery to film the grave markers of the many relatives buried there. Fighting the constant Kansas wind, she narrated, referring to her ancestors as "a grand family," and asked those who lost a loved one to send the eulogy to add to the family history, "that we might be warmed in knowing more about this person." As she rushed around the cemetery, in her typical manner, the elderly Deeming commented, "Getting in a hurry at my age could be fatal." She replied, "I have yet to learn that lesson."

She was in a hurry about many things, which irritated some people. Her friend and CSJ councilor, Sister Rosalyn Juenemann, confirmed that she seemed to have a sense of urgency to finish *Ma Famille*. In retrospect, her relatives would be poorer by far for lack of family history had she not acted quickly on her dream.

The project began to take shape, although she was surprised when encountering some hostility. "[A distant cousin] wrote to say leave her family out of the historical research, or I might have a legal case on my hands, as did two other families. One of their nieces, a Sorrowful Mother Sister, wrote a similar note that I better be prepared to document what I print and I had errors in their information,' but she wouldn't say what the errors are."

Sister Veronica quickly met with an attorney in nearby Hill City, specifically about printing what is already public record from newspaper articles and other sources. "'Could I publish and add photos without specific permission from folks?' The lawyer told me, 'The First Amendment rights are stronger than rights of privacy. Anyone can write anything, as long as there is no intent to slander or libel, and for sake of good journalism, the facts are reasonably correct. History would never have been written if writers had to ask permission of those involved.'

"The attorney made it sound so fundamental. I was relieved. It sure shows my ignorance. I've been around hospitals and health-care facilities too long, [and sensitive to their] rights of privacy." Later she responded, "Antagonism? No, just those few who scared me, which prompted me to seek counsel fast. The rest [of the comments were based on] laziness, poor social skills, lack of communication, disinterest and apathy."

In the introduction of *Ma Famille*, Sister Veronica acknowledged, "Some families requested certain information be eliminated; in many more cases, information was simply not contributed, and not all marriages are listed."

While never trained as a journalist, Sister Veronica understood a truism from the Hutchins Report, "It is no longer enough to report the fact truthfully: it is now necessary to report the truth about the fact." In contrast, Jennifer Crichton says in her book, *Family Reunion*, "Family lore has its own truth, which may not be factual."[2]

In her research she began to find all the elements of a good novel — love, hate, jealousy, sex, religion, tragedy. "There seems to be a little resistance to poking around in the Hebert ancestry story. It will be a challenge to tell it respectfully, but with some honesty." She especially became intrigued with the tragic story of Fred and Anita Frigon Hebert, and their family, briefly covered in the next short chapter.

Their daughter, Rosalie Hebert, became a benefactor for *Ma Famille*, when she donated some minor pieces of jewelry for Sister Veronica to sell. However, living up to her vow of poverty, she could neither own, nor handle the small transaction. Designated as her Power of Attorney, this writer handled the sales. "These checks assure that I will purchase a printer," Sister Veronica said.

Later she said, "I regret I didn't get a color printer for $100 more." Instead she got an HP DeskJet 520. "It's so much quieter and faster than the Commodore. Since my word processor is primitive (Better Working Word Processor) the recommended setting for my new printer is limited to Courier or Elite (plain old typewriter look). I comfort myself knowing that most folks just look at the pictures anyway."

Our sister, Cheryl, and her husband David Calvin, donated their IBM compatible computer to Sister Veronica, who was especially pleased if not for the storage capacity alone. "I was trying to decide to buy other software, and retype the whole thing, when I discovered its potential to act as an expensive PageMaker for layouts. I still have about seventy pages to retype from the Commodore 64 software."

By the end of the year, she said, "I still have received only sixty percent of the information. I will write the other 40 percent of the cousins personalized letters.

Her own immediate family was the last to send photos and information. "Now multiply that frustration by 260 cousins, and what do you have? No wonder I'm so appreciative for any contributions. This has been quite an experience in human relations, as most of the second and third cousins don't know me 'from Adam.'"

"She was proud of the two publications," said Sister Vera Meis. "One of her favorite things to do was spend time in the library working on family history." Each time she was called out of town on business she tried to extend her stay. In Manhattan, she spent the day at the library and genealogical society. She had a membership, with research privileges, with the Kansas State Historical Society, in Topeka. While in Wichita, she visited the Mormon Library, as well as making the trip to Salt Lake City for the extensive library there.

"I worked nonstop on the book during my two-week vacation, except for the 48 hours with family and going to church three times. I'd get up at 5:30 a.m. and work until 9 p.m. Many times I didn't answer the telephone, until I first checked the answering machine. For the most part, locals thought I was gone on vacation. I'd even sneak out the back door to get the mail, and basically just grazed on junk food."

"This project is much harder than *Our Saindon Cousins* because of the large volume of photographs, which really transform the book. With hindsight she said, "My biggest error was in choosing to make the photographs too large. I was determined that all faces be one centimeter high. Nine hundred photos take quite a lot of space, but they transform the book.

"I have to lay out pages all over again. Some I might need to cut and paste. I'm really disappointed the style will be rather plain when there are so many nice capabilities on computers."

She set a price. "Those who support the project immediately have a chance to get one for twenty-five dollars. Those who indicate they might want one will get it for thirty dollars. The rest will be at forty or fifty, depending on the actual cost to me."

She took layout pages to the *Ellis County Star* newspaper in Hays, to be printed on a photo quality copier. "It will not be offset this time," she said later on. "If I had known I would order 260 books, with more than 500 pages, I would have had it done offset, at probably the same price."

When she picked up the finished copies from the Koerperich Bookbinders in Selden, she was exhilarated to have a second published book to hold in her hands and hug like a newborn baby. She had prepared address labels and shipping boxes the month before. "I mailed 120 copies [to arrive in time for Christmas]. The book will be outdated the day it is printed," she realistically said.

A week later she noted, "I'm happy to be done, but of course I see some errors. I didn't correspond much this summer, with all my free time going into this project." Although normally a faithful letter writer, once it was finished she said, "My first act of celebration is to send letters and start walking again, even in the cold weather. I am determined to get on a routine."

Just three weeks after her book was completed our brother, Allan, died from cancer.

While on a business trip in Illinois, just months before her own death, Sister Veronica had the opportunity to visit places of ancestral significance where maternal great-great-grandmother Mathilda Frigon is buried and where great-grandparents, Leon and Louise Hebert, were married. "I spent an afternoon at St. Anne, and the research library at Watseka, as well as the towns where the Heberts and Frigons lived — Martinton, Papineau and Beaverville. The towns were smaller in size and proximity of Zurich, Palco and Damar. It was Columbus Day, so not much activity around."

A distant cousin wrote, "It warms my heart to see the town of Beaverville, and its past occupants, in *Ma Famille*. Having grown up in that small town, in the cornfields of Illinois, I never would have thought it was so important to the history of French Canadians in this country."

She was especially pleased to receive, from a professional genealogist, confirmation of Frigon information. "My queries among some genealogists are catching up with me. In *Ma Famille* I gave them a free advertisement for their 'Frigon Association of Families in North America' newsletter printed in both English and French."

When one picks up *Ma Famille*, it is hard to imagine not having all this information in one place, prior to 1994. The book includes many detailed stories of the nine children,[3] 62 grandchildren, and 225 grandchildren of Jean Leon and Louise Frigon Hebert.

Sister Veronica was gratified and knew the more than two years it took was worthwhile when letters of thanks poured in. She was pleased with the acknowledgement from the Graham County, Kansas Historical Society: "We are quite impressed with the book and feel it will be used often." She kept this, and other letters, in her small box of treasures.

Many cousins wrote to say they appreciated the storytelling, rather then merely a book of names, dates, and places. "I like all the personal stories...The pictures of my father, when he was growing up, brought sunshine to my life...if I'm not too late, I'd like to have three more. I'm crazy about the book...It was so sweet of you to send it before you received my money...Now I'm so sorry I didn't send pictures.

"Thank you for such a unique and beautiful gift... I was expecting to just receive pages in a folder. When I saw the book I was very surprised... I can tell it took a long time to accumulate information ... I have read it twice, page by page, and scanned through it several more times...I found it so interesting I couldn't put it down... It ties up many loose ends... Most of the reading was fun and interesting, and a small amount was sad. My son and daughter are thankful they received a copy, and told me they will cherish it forever, because it is packed with much history about our family."

Other letters included more words of praise "To gather so much information and photos, from so many people, had to be a tremendous and time-consuming job... Thanks for the beautiful keepsakes for my family... It has brought enlightenment, smiles and tears. I will treasure your book forever... Thank you for your time, expenses and dedication...You have put in numerous hours...Thanks for all you have done on the family book. I am so proud of it. Are you planning any more projects? I'm sure you will think of something...It's well worth the money for the time you spent working on it... I wish to extend my gratitude for your undertaking. I have spent hours pouring over the pages recollecting memories and learning new things. This book I will cherish always."

Following Sister Veronica's death, inquiries and orders for the remaining books continue to come in, even six years later. A distant cousin in California, who was barely mentioned in the book, found it a helpful research tool: "It's absolutely beautiful. I never dreamed it would be so complete and thorough. It has everything in it I spent a lot of time working on. And I never did get into it as deeply as Sister." Another distant cousin wrote, "I always enjoyed her enthusiasm and clear thinking."

It distressed Sister Veronica to know some families do not appreciate ancestral history. "I don't understand why folks won't order lasting gifts for Christmas presents, anniversaries or birthdays. People appreciate something that will last a long time: something to pass on to their children and grandchildren.

"It's not selling as quickly as I'd hoped," she hesitated at one point. "I have more than $3,000 worth of books just sitting on the shelf, not counting the time."

Of the nearly forty books left over, Sister Veronica kept most of them in her car trunk, ready to sell and deliver. At the scene of her death many copies of *Ma Famille*, which she lovingly completed not even a year earlier, were thrown onto the dark narrow highway.[4] These copies were cut from broken glass and splattered with blood, from an unverified source — but most likely it was from Sister Veronica. These, and other contents from the car, could not be released until after her burial. The two automobiles were inspected, and weighed, as part of the fatality investigation.

When the tattered books were finally returned to the Motherhouse, Sister Christine Doman, as president of the Congregation, had to make a tough decision. "There is a danger associated with blood contamination. The damaged books were buried in the grave a few feet away from Sister Veronica [with the elderly Sister Zephyrine Letourneau, who died about the time the books were released]."

Sister Beth Stover, CSJ, petitioned during the Prayers of the Faithful at the funeral mass, "For all members of Veronica's family — that the heritage of their deep Catholic faith and family life, so beautifully expressed in her recorded words, [*Our Saindon Cousins* and *Ma Famille*] will continue to flourish for God's greater honor and glory. Amen."

In a deeply personal questionnaire, Sister Veronica states that completing the two family history books were among her proudest accomplishments. Surely, at the moment her lifeblood spilled to consecrate these books, her soul was reunited with cherished ancestors who had gone before. No doubt a host of spiritual beings greeted her in crossing the bridge to the other side.

Distant cousin Rosalie Hebert was notified of Sister Veronica's sudden and tragic death. "I wish we could have started corresponding twenty-five years earlier," she wrote. And, as if she had nothing more to live for, the lonely ninety-year-old spinster died two months later.

Chapter Forty

While working on *Ma Famille*, Sister Veronica became interested in Joseph Hebert, Mother's maternal uncle, from whom Mother inherited, after her marriage, a sum equal to a year's earnings. It is reported this bachelor accidentally shot off his toes. This was the same method not infrequently used by soldiers to get out of serving during the First World War (1914-1918) and written about in *A Very Long Engagement*, by the French writer Sébastien Japrisot.

Known to be an extreme introvert, perhaps great-uncle Joseph was a pacifist, even though reportedly he held a draft card dated 1918. He died of a heart attack at age 65, the year of Sister Veronica's birth. It was Sister Veronica's wish to continue her work in genealogy and, had she lived longer, she would have undoubtedly continued to investigate and piece together his story.

But more importantly, she wished to look into the interesting, if not wretched story, of his brother, Fred, and Anita Frigon Hebert, first cousins, who married. Sometimes there is an outcast who brings shame on a family. Unfortunately, great-grandmother Hebert protected her son, "pretty boy" Fred.

Anita and Fred Hebert, a mean-spirited man, produced seven children; only three lived to adulthood. While there are current Kansas domestic abuse laws in effect as of 1979, these two were married much earlier, in 1904. It is a sad and pathetic story of dysfunctional people, most of whom came to a tragic end. This was a peculiar family; two of the girls died as teenagers, one from a sudden and suspicious abscess to the head from an unknown cause (perhaps from a head trauma); several of the other children died young. None of them married, leaving no dependents — no issue to carry on the curse. Perhaps it was a genetic weakness that affected childbearing, as well as mental instability.

Sister Veronica uncovered the address of one of Mother's sixty-five maternal first cousins — Fred's eldest child, Rosalie. "During the past year, I have been writing to Rosalie Hebert, trying to get more information, of any kind, on that family." As a teenager, Rosalie ran away from home to escape Fred, an abusive father. She refused to return to rural Damar, and was taken out of his Will. Since 1932 she had lived alone and isolated in San Francisco. In 1960 she moved to 523 33rd Avenue, where she lived out her life in the city.

Rosalie Hebert was a recluse, yet she became a benefactor for the genealogy book, *Ma Famille*, after Sister Veronica earned her trust. They exchanged dozens of letters during more than three years of correspondence. An avid reader and self-educated, Rosalie was eighty-seven when they started writing, and she spoke of a "tired old body having lived too long." The spinster often used the phrases "bad luck" and "life had been for nothing."

She alleged her siblings also suffered abuse from their father, "bully boy Fred," as well did her mother, Anita. "If my sister, Agnes, and I told you the things we saw done to Mother, you would not believe us. Mother gave herself a bad life by marrying Fred Hebert." Their mother, Anita, died in childbirth in 1919; Rosalie ran away from home in 1923. Agnes was placed in the mental institution at Larned, after another sister, Anyse, died in 1931. (Records from Larned were reportedly destroyed after fifty years.)

Around 1991 Rosalie expressed her concern to Sister Veronica about Agnes, her only remaining sibling. Agnes lived alone southeast of Hill City, on a farm once belonging to her grandparents Leon and Louise Hebert. Bachelor-great uncle Joseph continued to live there and took great care of the house and outbuildings until his death in 1939. Then Fred moved in. Phillip, Rosalie's brother, killed himself, in 1943, when the sheriff's department came to arrest him on charges of treason for failure to appear for the WWII draft. However, it was this father Fred who destroyed the draft notices that arrived in the mail. Shortly thereafter, Fred went to claim Agnes from the mental institution, after she had been there for over ten years. Fred moved off the farm, and into Damar, that same year.[1]

It is reported that Agnes drove a horse-drawn wagon into nearby Palco and waited outside a tavern throughout the day and into the night, while her father, Fred, spent this time inside. She was threatened not to speak to anyone. Her sister, Rosalie remarked, "You know how strict he was." Fred Hebert died six years later in 1949 as a result of an accident with his team-drawn wagon.

At the old homestead outside of Hill City, Agnes had no telephone, running water, electricity or heat even into the 1990s. This woman did not own a car, and walked four miles into town for groceries — mostly cartons of oatmeal — hauling them back in a child's red wagon to what was by now a ramshackle house.

Sister Veronica was ill equipped to fathom what she heard of the substantiated story, having little familiarity with such anger and an abusive family life for that matter. At least four of the times Sister Veronica visited Agnes, at Rosalie's request, Agnes confronted her outside with a rifle in hand. Sister Veronica was never invited inside the filthy, cluttered and inhabitable stench-filled house (which the county eventually condemned and burned).[2] She was unable to determine whether Agnes was a danger to herself, or others, but she concluded, "Agnes Hebert is very antisocial and strange."

Any cherished possessions in the house belonging to great-grandmother Hebert had most likely been easily stolen away from the deranged Agnes.

Valerie VanLoenen, a kind-spirited woman, looked after the odd woman, and given time, Agnes went to live with her for a while in the nearby village of Bogue.

With a suspected diagnosis of dementia, not able to read or write, compounded with her other peculiarities, Agnes by now in her 90s, was moved by a state-appointed guardian into Dawson Place, a long-term care facility in Hill City, coincidently where Sister Veronica once worked as dietetic consultant. Moreover, this move took place on November 15, 2000, exactly five years after Sister Veronica's death.

Some may quarrel that such social ills in a family are better left uncovered. Nevertheless, Sister Veronica befriended Rosalie, who believed she had nothing to live for. Rosalie finally had a chance to tell a portion of her life story through dozens of letters. "Squeeze all the goodies from life," Rosalie told her, after losing her eyesight, and only able to read and write with the aid of a magnifying glass.

"Rosalie Hebert gave me an appreciation for stories and books. They were her life," Sister Veronica said. Up until her retirement, Rosalie supported herself throughout those lonely and bitter years by working in a large second-hand bookstore near Market Street. Undoubtedly, she felt as Erasmus, the Dutch Priest and humanist, "When I get a little money I buy books; and if any is left I buy food and clothes."

After they had been corresponding for some time, a package arrived in the mail containing a "Miracle Crucifix," a gift from great-grandmother Hebert to then ten-year-old granddaughter, Rosalie. "I had to kiss it," Sister Veronica said after opening the little box. "I told Rosalie in previous letters that as a newlywed Mother wished for something from this woman, even a small dish, but never got a thing. Rosalie acknowledged, 'Grandmother Hebert had beautiful crystal dishes in a cabinet with glass doors.'"

Sister Veronica wrote, "I asked Rosalie if she would like to make a contribution to the genealogy book I was writing, since she told me dogs and books were her life." While Rosalie was living on a pension and had no extra savings to donate, she sent some amethyst colored rings, what she called her "beauties," which she could no longer wear due to swollen fingers from arthritis. "I had seriously thought of going on a ferry boat ride on the Bay and pouring the jewels into the water," said Rosalie. "So glad I sent them to you. No use sending them to Agnes. Would have been taken away from her."

✝

Chapter Forty-one

Fearing she sometimes failed with relationships, after attending one especially meaningful CSJ retreat, "How We Are With People," Sister Veronica grew to be more comfortable giving voice to emotions long buried. She drew even closer to the memory of ancestors and became comfortable with her own place in history.

Not wanting to be on a pedestal, she was content being an ordinary woman. While not a notable such as Mother Teresa, Sister Veronica was a role model, and touched the lives of countless people in doing the common place. Even after death, Sister Veronica Mary is a legend among family and friends. Undoubtedly, she would be honored that two great-nieces, Veronica Jill, and Mary Marie, were named in her memory.[1]

She understood and shared the need for giving thanks and breaking bread, preserving memories and telling stories. Myths and folklore are powerful to explain the inexplicable. Larger-than-life characters abound in the themes of birth, death and resurrection — the belief in eternal life.

"Sister Veronica embodied the true meaning of what the Sisters of St. Joseph are about," said Sister Margaret Schreck, tour director of the Motherhouse at the time of this writing. "Continuing to strive for excellence in the spirit of gentleness, peace and joy — that best describes her."

A fellow band member, Sister Ellen Divel, agreed and said simply, "Veronica was an example, to me, of all that a CSJ should be."

Many intellectual models inspired her in daily life. Some were teachers, retreat directors and colleagues. Yet it was our aunt, this simple woman, having entered the convent in 1920, long before Sister Veronica was born, who was for her the epitome of all that a CSJ should be. Rosie, as Sister Veronica came to call her, set a fine example and held a powerful influence.[2]

After moving to WaKeeney in 1981, Sister Veronica oftentimes took Mother to visit her sister at Stafford Hall in the convent, which opened for elderly Sisters in 1970. "Sister Rose Irma had her right leg amputated above the knee last week, due to a pseudomonas infection that would not heal on an ulcerated bunion," Sister Veronica said. "She was in such good spirits that it did me good just to be with her."

This tender woman bravely faced her trials in life, including the subsequent surgical loss of both legs due to circulatory problems. "She wanted to talk constantly, which seemed to distract from the pain. I am sure her suffering is a powerful prayer. She wanted to look as soon as she came back from surgery.

There is no denial or seeming angry about it. I know she has been in misery the past eighteen months."

It was not unusual on a holiday, after having noontime dinner with a retired Priest's housekeeper, for Sister Veronica to drive forty miles to visit aunts Lucille and Irene Morin in Damar, then continue to drive another 130 miles to be with Sister Rose Irma by nightfall. Each time Sister Veronica was in Concordia to attend meetings or retreats, even after Mother died, she stopped in to visit, and especially when Sister Rose Irma was moved to St. Mary's Convent and Health Center for the Infirmed, at 830 West 11th Street.

Over the years, this elderly woman, with the angelic face, also became a role model for Sister Veronica in how to live and die with grace. Sister Rose Irma breathed firsthand the Maxim, "How to live...an interior gentleness...suffering peacefully in perfect repose of spirit in God and in loving acceptance of all the plans of his divine will." She was also the maxim of patience. "Endure without murmuring, without complaining so as not to make your suffering too noticeable."

Sister Kevin Walker complimented the niece and the aunt. "They both were naturals in the kitchen, and great seamstresses, too."

Grandmother Rosanna Morin was an excellent seamstress, and several in the family carry on this talent. "After her first amputation, Sister Rose Irma would spend hours on the sewing machine, making objects that would be sold at the annual festival of the Motherhouse. She would not allow herself to become useless. She wanted to continue her contributed services to the Community," Father Duane recalled from his visits with her.

"[After the second amputation] Sister Rose Irma became weakened to the point of not being able to use the sewing machine, something that had provided many decades of joy," Sister Veronica said.

Sister Veronica wrote Sister Rose Irma's memoir, *As Grains of Wheat*, in August 1987. "Then I inserted general information taken from Mother's biography, *A Kansas Woman*, of their early family life that Rosie didn't seem to know. Each Sister was asked to submit her life story for our CSJ of Concordia one hundredth Anniversary [in 1988]. A Life Review is meant to be written by the individual Sister, but I thought it ideal for me to write Sister Rose Irma's, from her many hours of storytelling. A copy goes into our CSJ community archives. I also wrote my own, which I will probably update whenever I make a transition to the next journey — wherever that is."

Sister Liberata Pellerin, affectionately known as Liebe, is in charge of Motherhouse archives, at the time of this writing. Many Sisters are not aware of what is stored inside their own individual small cardboard file box. Although this is not out of the ordinary, since Sisters live the "hidden life," meaning they are not focused on themselves, or their personal history.

This is one explanation as to why there are few full biographies of Religious

Women. Although when there is an autobiography, such as *A Story of the Land: The Autobiography of Sister Scholastic Schuster, OSB*,[3] it typically reflects that life is good and full of blessings, and the author does not dwell on her own suffering and burdens.

"Every time we visited with Sister Rose Irma, or Sister Veronica, we could feel the specialness of their being," said cousins Melvin and Marguerite Desmarteau. "It was such a spiritual uplift to be in Sister Veronica's company and wonderful feelings of respect and love flowed between us. We always continued on our journey feeling all would be right with the world. She spent the night at our house one time, and very shortly we received a thank you letter, and postage funds for return of her rosary that she forgot on the bedside table."

Shortly before Sister Rose Irma's death, her two nieces, Sisters Veronica and Diane, visited their aunt in the infirmary. "She was confused about who different nieces and nephews were, although she mentioned Melvin by name," they both agreed.[4]

Few family members were able to attend Sister Rose Irma's vigil the night before her funeral. Since Sister Veronica was the homilist she repeated the eulogy the next day for thirty relatives and Sisters who attended.[5] "All were noticeably moved, so I am sending copies of my reflections to those relatives not present. The Sisters expressed that surely the large number who did attend, was a testimony to what a great woman Rosie was. She corresponded promptly encouraging her family to accept God's Will in their lives.[6]

"Following her funeral I discovered all of Sister Rose Irma's letters and papers were destroyed. The house superior threw all these away the day after. I was horrified," Sister Veronica said. With all those records gone, the historian in her was greatly upset. Marguerite Desmarteau agreed, "A great insight into her daily life was lost."

Having attended their aunt's funeral, the Desmarteau relatives hoped for a sacred reminder. "Unknown to them, I had the undertaker remove her crucifix before closing the casket and it will go to them," said Sister Veronica. "Melvin has teased about wanting my crucifix someday, so he will be delighted with hers."

The crucifix Sisters wear is a daily reminder of Christ's resurrection. Understandably, not one of the cousins, or siblings, received Sister Veronica's pendant crucifix. It was a decision of the current superior, Sister Christine Doman, to leave it in the casket at the time of burial, no doubt symbolic of Sister Veronica's own eternal resurrection after a sudden and tragic death, as bones were crushed and her body required extrication from the wreckage.[7]

Like Mother, material goods never meant much to Sister Veronica unless they held sentimental value, such as photos, letters and papers. She understood that it doesn't take much to make a person happy. She avoided the superfluous and was content with only bare necessities.[8] The vow of poverty required Sister

Veronica to become detached from temporal objects, which helps explain the way she lived.

With the onset of the 1973 oil embargo, the price of oil and gas skyrocketed. Americans worked together to conserve resources by reducing speed on the highways, forming car pools, and lowering thermostats. The CSJ Sisters readily adopted these practices. Ten years later, Sister Veronica continued to be conscientious about these issues. "Trying to keep warm tonight, typing on a short stand, while sitting on the floor in front of the wall furnace. Actually the place has been rather cozy, except the spare bedroom is ice cold, as I keep the door closed to reduce the gas bill.

"I've always felt like a miser — no, frugal is the word — about water and paper. I appreciate, very much, the pattern of living-with-less, leaving more for others, from the Living More With Less worldwide experiences of Mennonites. It is part of a challenge to use renewable resources wisely, and non-renewable ones hardly at all. Foil is the worst." She lived simply, making do or doing without, except of course, for gasoline for her car, her lifeline to the outside world.[9]

Finding a way to rejoice in poverty, she sought out garage sale items, and was satisfied with products of inferior quality in her home. Long before owning a computer she wrote, "THIS IS NOT THE GREATEST TYPEWRITER, SO BEAR WITH ME. IT ONLY TYPES IN CAPS. I SAW IT AT OUR CSJ HOUSE IN SALINA, AS IT WAS READY TO GO TO THE THRIFT SHOP, SO I TOOK IT. I TEND TO WRITE MUCH MORE STUFF ON A TYPEWRITER THAN BY HAND, SO JUST READ BETWEEN THE LINES."

"For Christmas decoration, I used a tumbleweed decorated with advent candles." There are many examples of her frugality and dislike of waste, especially food. Leftovers provided several more meals.

After sleeping in her cold house, and seeing that her nightgown was ready for the rag bin, this writer gave her one in pale blue, long, soft and warm. Most likely, she thought it too beautiful and passed that on to someone more needy, knowing I would forgive her for that. A parishioner gave her a second-hand, yet expensive, leather coat. That, too, was passed on. Often times her clothing was bought at second-hand and thrift stores. By contrast, when she sewed her own clothing she was a perfectionist, even though she searched fabric stores for sales.

When the first jumbo jet entered service, in January 1970, the enormous planes revolutionized commercial flight. But Sister Veronica did not feel free to travel by airplane, since the high cost seemed wasteful. Instead, she adhered to a more austere vow of poverty than required, since the Second Vatican Council liberalized the interpretation. She continued to drive everywhere, into the 1990s, in part to save money, but also because many rural places where she traveled to see relatives were a great distance from the nearest airport.

Furthermore, she did not want to burden them to pick her up. She also appreciated the freedom that one's own car provides.

When I asked her if she would like to take a trip with me to Manchu Pichu, Peru, she replied, "Our vacations are to be in keeping with a simpler lifestyle, but of course there are exceptions and interpretations to this. Ordinarily we are not allowed such extensive vacations, but I do hope to plan for another out of the country visit to either Israel or Brazil, both very dear to me. However, this summer is too soon to consider it, from the financial side. I feel my two trips abroad were very special and treasured. But then each were gifts."

During the early years as a young Sister, she made her own collage greeting cards, adhering to the three R's of managing waste — reduce, reuse, and recycle. She believed that recycling is a Christian spiritual expression of solidarity with creation and the rest of the world, and is a simple solution to consumption of household waste.[10]

Recycling also provided a creative outlet. "I look at things and ask, 'Why not?' I was ready to throw way the dozens of photos that Rodney took of trucks, cars and motorcycles, while he still lived at home, and I used them as 'on the move' change of address notices after being hired for the Logan and New Almelo parishes. Now, I have to write lots of letters to get rid of the old return address labels."

She continued to recycle cards in later years, too, as an artistic expression and often cut out messages from old ones: "A sister is a special part of all that's precious to the heart." "This card really fits you. You grow more beautiful…with each passing year." "Know that my love for you is added to all the others ways that you know love in your lives." "Just a note to let you know I think of you often — not all the time — but a lot. (From a favorite Peanuts caption — a Charles Schultz cartoon.)" Typical of her style, another handmade card reads, "Peace, love and joy as you begin another new year. May it be one that really touches to the heart of who you are. You have been a big comfort and delight to me."

After Mother died, Sister Veronica gathered her birthday, get-well, and sympathy cards. "Generally I use the front as a postcard, or cut the inside out and get by with a glue job. I am quite notorious [sic] about salvaging cards. It's thrifty, and I don't like to dispose of lovely things. I went 'shopping' for your card among the one hundred that I received, for my own Jubilee," she wrote to honor Father Duane on his 25th Jubilee. "Hope you don't mind. I remember Mother saying you thought cards are a waste."

Combining creativity and her dislike of waste, she also began collecting cancelled stamps, which she called, "mini works of art." One of her favorites was a twenty-nine-cent Madonna and Christ Child Christmas stamp featuring the art of Elisabetta Siran, (circa 1663) an artist she especially liked. It was thought that a painting of cherubs, in the Founder's Room at the Motherhouse was a Sirani.[11]

Sister Veronica embodied the words of Georgia O'Keefe, another artist who was featured on a postage stamp: "Nobody sees a flower, really — it is so small — we haven't time, and to see takes time, like to have a friend takes time."

Although she was introverted she was attentive to the needs of others in times of happiness and pure sorrow, and in the everyday, too. Even though Sister Veronica kept up a whirlwind pace, she kept in touch with people she loved, and who loved her in return. "I used to think I lost my friends due to distance. Now, I know it is from neglect. Your letters at hand frequently remind me of this truth," she once remarked. In reality Sister Veronica did not neglect friends. In her writings, she expressed her feelings and concerns about keeping in touch — truly a sacred and precious connection.

In pre-Vatican II years, Sisters were subjected to restrictive observances. In her younger days of being a new Sister, letter writing was seen as a mission to instruct, which limited the expression of feelings and reflected the outer persona only. After the Second Vatican Council rules were relaxed, she continued to find it difficult to express her inner feelings. However, a good ten years after Vatican II, one letter showed the beginning of self-expression: "Often in writing we are able to know what we think, to clarify it a little more." Sister Rosalyn Juenemann said, "When Veronica wrote, she could say so well what she wanted to communicate. She was gifted in letter writing. I always appreciated her letters."

Like Hemingway, she wrote to relax as a form of occupational therapy. While some of her writing seems steeped in misery, it is important to remember that she did not express herself well verbally. Through the safe distance of letters, she had a safety value for sharing feelings. There were very few times when her mask slipped, her eyes filled with tears or her voice quivered, and hardly any people saw her this way. "I try to journal once a month, and draw much strength from expressing myself. Things don't seem quite so bad when laid out to read."[12]

Letter writing was therapeutic, cathartic and provided a safe place to vent. Her innermost thoughts often started off heavy in tone, but seemed lighter, more upbeat at the end. Although in hindsight, one can see a loneliness creeping in. She ended one letter, "I knew that would come out even if not wanting it to, so we will see what happens now. I really hope I can use these two weeks of solitude to work out my own feelings."

She offered insight into her own periodic despondency when trying to comfort a relative in the depths of despair. "My letters to you were based on my feelings over the years, which I have mistrusted. I flunked my personality tests," she joked. "Seriously, my personality testing shows I should operate on my feelings. I have to get things factually and mentally right, so I was just checking if I was correct."

In her roles as Sister, daughter, big sister, sister-in-law, aunt, niece, neighbor, boss and friend, she was always there, to listen and lean on. She was not judgmental. Rather she was consoling and kind when one was down. To one family member she wrote, "These must be difficult days for you. But I trust that you experience moments of peace, and that peace becomes the predominant mood. Know that we all love you. May you find strength in that knowledge."

Father Duane understood how important her outreach was: "Thanks for the fine ministry you do of letter writing." She wrote back, "[Another family member] is real good at covering up, but I know that I can, too, knowing that folks don't understand religious life, and probably still put us on a pedestal."

Her spirituality shone through, especially in those letters to Father Duane, in far-away Brazil. "I hope these days before the Ascension are filled with awakenings of the Lord walking right into your life, making you more and more open to the unexpected." In early 1977, when he was asked to serve as Prior of his monastery, she wrote, "My prayerful congratulations of your new role in the [Benedictine] community. It is one thing to be asked to do something, and another to allow it to be accomplished in, and through you, and with confidence in yourself because your [Monk] Brothers place confidence in you, and in yielding to the work of the Spirit through you."

She understood the importance of having a trusted friend, albeit her brother, to speak with about matters that were disturbing. In 1978 she wrote, "I thank you for being a special brother to me. It seems I have only come to know what I believe, and what I feel, by having shared that with someone."

Some might wonder why Sister Veronica spent so much time on her correspondence. In short, she cared about people, and it was a way of staying connected. Letter writing, as an extension of her ministry, provided contact, something she found hard to do in person. Although neither a poet, nor a recluse as Emily Dickinson, there are some similarities. Here, in the written word, she could joyfully nurture relationships, convey the essence, the thing itself, love, concern, the joy of life, the fun of cheerful exchange with none of the distractions, such as time, space, and matter, illness, fatigue or embarrassment.

In a treasured letter she said, "So many things I could think of to write as I was out walking this afternoon. Paper never quite does much for my thoughts, but neither do my spoken words. I do want for you a peaceful happiness, and that happiness we have to find for ourselves, mostly alone — like facing the morning sun and the dark wind alone, even in the presence of others. The presence of peace, in a decision, is a confirmation of the whole discernment process, and no one can tell us whether we have this peace. We have to find it alone. You certainly have all my love and support, and I hope you will be true to the vision of your life before you now."

She was a holy woman supportive of her siblings in their business endeavors, too. "Congratulations on the honors you brought to your job. There is growth in the darkness of waiting. Just look at the winter wheat seeds, and how photographs are developed in the dark. Don't forget the power of the Lenten season to transform us like cocoons into butterflies."

When a particularly suitable clipping, like the following passage from former Priest and psychologist, Eugene Kennedy, crossed her path, she enclosed it: "One of the marvelous things we learn in scripture is that God always makes room for us to begin again. It all depends on whether we are prepared to face truth — good or bad — and continue life with a new slant in God's presence."

After leaving Christ the King, she sent fifty notes thanking the parishioners for the many ways they showed their support. It was typical on her part, a gesture she practiced throughout life. During an ice storm when she could not get out to drive, she personalized 220 Christmas cards to parishioners in New Almelo and Logan.

In subtle ways her faith-filled missives guided and influenced: "When the cards and wrappings are put away, then the real work of Christmas begins, to heal the broken, to bring peace to all nations."

Her holiday notes were like divine epistles: "I find, more and more, life is not so much what we get done day in and out, but living the present moment to the fullest that what we feel called to from deep within — His actions in us. This also relates to time for prayer — not making it so much what we are doing about prayer, but think of it as doing nothing for Him — till we gradually learn, He is the one who does things. Sometimes it takes me a long time to learn, and relearn."

Her 1992 letter read, "Greetings for a Blessed Christmas. Aren't we surrounded by so many beautiful traditions during this Advent and Christmas season? Cards, loved ones and dinners — together with the traditions of Christmas music, giving gifts, decorating the tree and homes, partaking of festive gatherings and especially our concern for others — these are an important warp of our Celebration of the birth of the Lord, Jesus Christ. The sending of cards and letters with prayerful wishes is one of my favorite parts of the holy season. In some small way, we try to reach our loved ones, especially those we will not be able to savor with our great family dinner.

"The wisdom of the Church has given us a period to prepare ourselves. Like Bethlehem, we are too tiny to imagine the greatness within us. Like Elizabeth, we say, 'Who am I that the Lord should come to me.' And come, Jesus has and continues His presence. Immanuel means God With Us. Thank you for all the ways you help make God's presence felt."

Another time she said, "Today we have a beautiful, heavy, but dry snowfall. Good excuse to stay put." That year she said in her annual letter to parishioners,

"Christmas is not over on December 25th. The work of Jesus continues all year, that of instructing, healing, consoling, building bridges, and making peace. A homecoming is a special part of this Christmas season. I know that you will experience a warmth among our parish family, who believe that once Church family — always family."

This letter to parishioners included the missive: "We all hope we will keep Christ in Christmas. This Christmas let us ponder that in our Baptism we became another Christ. If we recognize Christ in one another, then giving gifts makes sense. We better understand what His coming to us at Christmas means, when we recognize His presence in one another. So this year, will we not only keep Christ in Christmas, but more importantly recognize Him in one another. Let's not be too busy to see Christ."

Another year she wrote, "Christmas is a homecoming. It can also be a return to the home of our spiritual ideals, with illumination of something that we have always known. May this Christmas be a time of feeling your closeness with people everywhere, because of the spirit of Jesus who quickens new life."

Her last Christmas letter to me reads, "Christmas is a time of nostalgia, a time of memories. We may remember the first time we became aware of the Christmas story, the first Midnight Mass, we remember the smells of home that wonderful season. We may remember the numerous relatives because most lived close by. Other memories crowd around, too — perhaps the years we were not with loved ones that Christmas Day, or when the sparkle and joy was temporarily gone that year. Yet for all of our memories of the past, we also look to the future with hope in our greatest gifts of Love, Peace, and Good Will to all."[13]

When one of her sisters was going through a divorce, and Sister Veronica spent the Christmas holiday at the family farm, she said, "I don't expect to bring our parents much cheer these days, but it is important for them to have their loved ones home." It was in 1980 when she started being at home for the holidays after leaving so long ago in 1958. Much later, in the early 1990s, she wrote, "Although I was invited to Christmas Eve dinner and exchanged gifts with a young parish family, spent Christmas day with another family, then spent the day after with other parishioners, by Saturday night I was nostalgic for my own family. This will be the first New Year's I have been at home in eighteen years."

Whereas siblings had their own families, each were all Sister Veronica had. While recognizing that everyone has a busy life, hers was equally demanding, and she never took her beloved family for granted. In a deeply personal questionnaire, she counted her siblings among her closest relationships. She was upbeat and willing to be there any way she could. Saddled with the burden of being the family communicator, she stayed connected by frequent visits, or brief phone calls to those who did not write, just to keep up with family news. She was let down when late-breaking news within the family was not shared, or not spread quickly. "I was disappointed that not everyone knew of our news. I assumed everyone else knew after I had been told. I'm really sorry, as I don't think people need be spared disappointment."

Receiving letters was important to her, and sometimes she was let down by the indifference and apathy that sometimes occurred. "The round-robin letter, which Father Duane started, our sister-in-law, Jacalyn, got organized, and I got on its way, is held up after seven months. I can hardly wait. Some folks may just feel like changing the date if nothing more is happening with their loved ones." The concept of this kind of letter, to get the non-letter writers in the family involved, seemed like a good idea to her. She was prompt in replying, even though she wrote, "I don't know when I will learn to mail things right away instead of waiting until 'finished' with everything I know."

The round-robin letter wasn't anymore prompt the second year. "It has been ten months since I last saw the package with photos." The third year still had not changed. "I miss the family letter not coming around faster than five to six months." In the fourth year she said, "It always seems so long before it gets around, and I miss it." Her last letter to family, written ten days before her death, prophetically began, "Anyone out there! Do you need my address? Where is the round-robin letter? Did I miss a turn? Where has everybody been?"

One year she enrolled in an eight-week class. "Calligraphy means beautiful writing. The first thing the instructor did was say I had very nice writing, then picked it apart." Her handwriting was lovely. Still she enjoyed using the computer for its various features, including spell check. As a well-educated woman, her grammar and spelling were excellent, even though she threw in folksy phrases now and then.

Over the years she became more computer literate, although her equipment did not yet have a modem and E-mail access. We will never know for certain how she would have responded to this seemingly impersonal way of communicating, but it's a safe guess she would have eagerly embraced the technology, as Father Duane does. She probably would have used it heavily, as it has the capability of bringing loved ones, in other states or foreign countries, within daily contact.

Nevertheless, it is certain she would have continued to use the U.S. mail. "The giving and receiving of cards still give me a thrill," she said. A study by Pitney-Bowles, in 2000, showed that receiving personal mail is one of the most eagerly awaited daily events, among receiving phone calls, watching television and reading the newspaper.

She reminisced how important it is to keep in touch, and to have things to pass on down the years. "Perhaps I tend to accumulate rather than to let go, but the desire is there to share. Thanks for sharing the set of great photos."

While some parishioners and family members took letters, greeting cards, or thank you notes for granted, Sister Veronica kept up the effort and continued to be generous. "When I write to loved ones, I try to help reflect the good that is in them — and being free with them, letting go of them, not expecting a response. It's just the gift of a letter or remembrance."

She never forgot a birthday, even if it was a short post card. "I want to get Jason's 6th B-day card in the mail." She was gracious and thoughtful, remembering anniversaries, too. "Today is Roger and Jacalyn's twentieth. I am sending my own card. I appreciate several, rather than one group signed card. We need all the excuses to reach out in our own correspondence with one another." Following an overnight visit it was typical for her to write, "Thanks so much for the restful hospitality. I enjoyed your family very much."

Trading books, or sending them as gifts, was another way of connecting, as it provided common ground for discussion, since what one reads is an indication of what is valued. Sister Veronica enjoyed reading, especially books her friends or family recommended. When I sent her the fictionalized account of the Ebola virus (a Sister Veronica was a character in this 1990s novel) she was eager to find out what else I was reading.[14] Years earlier I sent to her Reverend Robert Schuller's, *When All You've Ever Wanted*. She replied, "I appreciated his other book, *Bad Things Happen to Good People*, so I know your choice was excellent."

A friend loaned her Ann Beattie's book, *Where You'll Find Me*, which touched an emotional chord and she instantly felt the "presence of community." She knew there was truth in the passage, "Any life will seem dramatic if you omit mention of most of it." Another passage validated her day-to-day activities, "People forget years and remember moments." An elderly cousin, Rosalie Hebert, echoed those words, "Enjoy the moments. The years take care of themselves."

†

Chapter Forty-two

Sister Veronica helped Father Duane plan his U.S. travel schedule each time he visited from Brazil, at which time he was often called upon to perform marriages and baptisms. It was common for family members to inform Sister Veronica, rather than writing him directly, assuming she would take the responsibility for communicating the request. She questioned him, "Doesn't anyone else write?" Before the days of fax, she arranged for him to visit a ham radio operator, in WaKeeney, who allowed her to send messages this way.

After planning her own Silver Jubilee in 1984, and after Dad and Mother died, in her big-sister role and duty bound to responsibility, she was eager to help Father Duane plan his own twenty-fifth anniversary in 1992, knowing it would be difficult for him to manage so far away. "I have his Jubilee celebration on Bishop Fitzsimons' calendar [a year early], as it fills quickly."

She began gathering ideas two years ahead and, like a nervous, yet proud Mother-of-the-Bride, gave every detail great thought. Three months before the celebration Sister Veronica, Cheryl, and Joan gathered at this writer's home in the Florida Panhandle to vacation at the beach, take in the opera, *Tosca*, and dine *alfresco* on a Gulf of Mexico pier. "It's among my touchstones of markers in life," she graciously thanked me.

At her best in planning, she guided us in reviewing more than one hundred choices for the Jubilee program cover, and then went on alone to price 300 to 400 invitations. "The invitation has the same cross as your Ordination invitation — in silver," she wrote to Father Duane. No aspect was too mundane. Working on a draft for a memento/holy card she told him, "I want the reflection by Archbishop Romero on it." Indeed, it was a beautiful keepsake.

Later, she worked on a mock newspaper page for display at the event. The masthead was US TODAY, with photos and a variety of creative headlines like, "Fr. Duane meets with mentor" including a photo of him with Pope John Paul II taken in 1980.

Having experienced an awkward situation, when helping Mother and Dad plan their forty-fifth anniversary celebration, she was careful to not slight anyone. "The more I think of sending invitations to area friends, the scarier it gets of leaving people out. So a general invitation will go in the Stockton paper the same week the invitations get mailed." Afterward she summarized the event in a news article.

Her role was undisputed as organizer, greeter and kitchen coordinator for Father Duane's long-awaited jubilee weekend. She also delivered the benediction before the barbecue dinner. It was also her idea to "throw in the two-hour dance, as a mixer, to get people to linger longer."

An estimated three hundred attended the two-day gathering, which came off without a hitch, thanks in large part to her planning. Most people assume those events just happen. Having invested a great deal of time, she wanted the commemoration to go smoothly. She did not relax easily when there was so much at stake. As she rushed about, on the day of the celebration, her feelings were hurt when a family member told her to "chill out."

Sister Veronica used every opportunity to spend time with family, which she dearly loved, and any disappointments were seldom and minor. A part of her vacation each year was spent visiting others, and often she was one of the few who showed up with a camera.

With her nudging, there was a Thanksgiving get-together two months after Mother's death. It is unknown whether she was consoling herself, or someone else, when she wrote that Christmas, "Remember the kingdom is right here, although we wait patiently, we are part of the kingdom and in the time before, we celebrate God-with-us. Meanwhile, we improve our relationship with all others in the kingdom, so we know in a new way how God is with us." She drove to Colorado that Christmas Eve. "Seems all Joan, Linda, and I talked about was Mother, now that she is gone, and which of her belongings we each have."

It was not until a few years before her own death that Sister Veronica stopped trying so hard, and others were forced to take up the responsibility of planning a gathering. "I would be excited to think of a mini-vacation. If anyone gets together I will be there, but I'm not too creative right now to think of how, or when."

"The three other apartments are empty now," she said another time speaking of the house in WaKeeney, where she rented a small two-bedroom apartment. "But I am hesitant about organizing parties and guests. I try too hard and all seems to fall for me. Just sour, I guess, about so much work to do this month, and missing vacation." She often rebounded. "I think I'll work with [so and so] to get us together for a holiday."

She was not domineering and so it was discouraging when she was criticized for trying to take charge, when those criticizing would not take charge themselves.

Family gathered at her home in WaKeeney, after Christmas of 1989, to celebrate her fiftieth birthday for an end-of-the-year weekend. It was especially meaningful for her that several traveled from out of state, and Father Duane came from Brazil for a rare winter vacation. "Your reflections on turning fifty were quite a lift," she later replied to him.

Our sister, Joan, and this writer brought all the fixings for a festive party, all the way from Denver and Boise, along with a decorated cake. A cheerful tablecloth was laid with an array of colorful ribbons, balloons and candles. An assortment of hot and hearty appetizers were brought in to serve. She was especially overjoyed to be treated as a guest in her own home, as she beamed with childlike delight. The Pastor, Father Paul, stopped by, as did many parishioners, who filled up her meager living room sharing stories and swapping jokes like old friends.

The memorable weekend concluded with a New Year's Eve party of card games and Charades, followed by New Year's Day, 1990, spent with siblings writing predictions and goals for 2000. The thought of a Millennium family gathering excited her. "It sounds great to me. We will have our ten-year time capsule letters to read."

Her letter tucked away under lock and key, was opened after her death ten years later: "Dear Mother and Dad, As I remember, you each mellowed so beautifully around your fiftieth years, and became so close to friends. Help me to grow into that awareness of others' needs more.

"Today is the beginning of a New Year [1990] a new decade, my golden 50th year. Will [2000] be a 'year of Jubilee' of forgiving debts and starting anew, as in the Biblical tradition?

"In the midst of my constant work, I anticipate [the completion] this spring of the Saindon book. Will the books be mailed by June 30, 1990, as I predict? Will I have traveled the St. Lawrence River, during May 1990, or will it no longer be important? Will I still have time for my other works done properly — and time for family?

"Up to the year 2000 AD, what changes have happened to Pastoral Ministers, and to rural parishes? Did I get to [work at] either Damar, or the Appalachians? Why/why not? Are we really down to less then thirty [Salina] diocesan Priests as predicted?

"I suppose our elections for CSJ leadership's will have gone through more revisions to simplify things. And I trust all my dear family will be together again on January 1, 2000 to enjoy life to the fullest. (Signed) Sister Veronica Roy, or will it be Sister Ila Mae Roy."

She regretted not having the gift of gab like our youngest sister. Cheryl's lively conversations seem to flow like a faucet. When the sisters got together a spirited exchange was certain to follow. Sister Veronica saw these gatherings as slumber parties and was the last one in bed, not wanting the evening to end. "We girls seem to have a mini-tradition of getting together for spring break," she said.

A few years later she was there, along with her three sisters, in the mountains of Colorado, at Keystone, to celebrate Joan's fiftieth birthday. A few years after that she had planned a surprise trip to the Washington D.C. area, where my husband, Randy, had been transferred, to make my mid-century celebration even grander. Instead, her life was taken two weeks short of the day.

Watching old family videos, which our brother, Roger, converted from reel-to-reel, eight-millimeter tapes, was always a hit. Stories and spontaneous laughter accompanied potluck gatherings and board games, while little nieces and nephews ran through the house shouting with glee.

Watching television was wasted precious time, as far as she was concerned. Although occasionally after a full day of visiting, and too much noise from the beloved, yet rambunctious children, she enjoyed sitting and relaxing with her host family, watching a rented video, such as *Fried Green Tomatoes*, or *On Golden Pond*, a story of family reconciliation.

She took delight in stomping around the farmland when family members gathered, with their children in tow, to dig millions-of-year-old Cretaceous fossils from native limestone. Afterward the family gathered to view more fossils at the Sternberg Museum of Natural History, a department of Fort Hays State University, and even later, at the Museum of Natural History, in Denver.

"I would be interested to see what kind of documentary Linda comes up with. Sounds rather dry to me," she confided to Father Duane, after I told her I would be taking slides instead of videotaping the chalk hills. She was willing to participate in any project a family member dreamed up. Later, for Father Duane's twenty-fifth Jubilee, she openly praised the slide presentation of wildflowers and pastoral scenes, accompanied by the taped music of Louis Armstrong's "It's a Beautiful World," and two versions of "Ave Maria," by Aaron Neville and Luciano Pavarotti.

Anticipating each family reunion, her letters were sprinkled with a variation of, "Looking forward to seeing all, especially the little nieces and nephews." They never failed to lift her spirits. "Did you notice Laurie called me 'Gramma' at our 4th of July? She did on Easter, too; in November; and again last week. I was amazed she makes this association being only two years old when her Grandmother died. I did not correct her. I just said, 'Come talk to Aunt Sister.' Big shoes to fill to be her Gramma."

Her friend, Verna Flax of WaKeeney, recalled how she often pulled out of her purse photos of nieces and nephews to show and brag about. She took great delight in organizing younger ones to perform skits and found great joy in the little things they did.

At a Christmas gathering she coached the youngest cousins (Jason, John and Laurie) in a short reenactment of Balthasor, Melchior and Gasper — the three Wise Men — presenting gifts to the Christ Child: a gold foil box (kinship), a stick of frankincense (divinity), and a wrapped box symbolizing myrrh (humanity). Another time she organized the children in art projects to mail to those not present.

Going through Stockton or Hays, she broke up the long drive with short visits to see Roger or Rodney's family. When in Salina for meetings, she often planned to drive further on for an overnight stay with Cheryl's family. It was not unusual for her to leave from work around 4 p.m., and drive to Wichita to spend a holiday." I really miss [Cheryl's] kids. There are some food baskets for the poor to deliver from the church before I leave." Other times she said, "I am going home shortly to bake pumpkin and pecan pies, and hope to be there by 10 p.m."

During a July 4th gathering, a tornado watch was alerted near WaKeeney. Our brother, Kenneth, in his service role as Chief of Police, took his post along Interstate 70, while his wife Ruth, Joan, Allan, and Sister Veronica were in his family basement as she led them in prayer for his safety, as well as for their community.

"How I wish I were down a more-beaten track, so folks could stay over," she wrote when living in the large, well-built brick rectory at St. John's parish in Logan. When Kenneth commented that this rectory reminded him of our parent's 1960s ranch style home, she felt especially comfortable.

Living and eating alone, she found great joy in entertaining and hosting weekend family gatherings. "Pre-holiday dinner. Come after 3 p.m. for 6:30 dinner. It will be like Christmas for me. I'll be at the Motherhouse till noon, so just go in the side door, in case I'm not there yet. I'll ask one of the women from church to put the roast in the oven after 11:30 Mass." When she arrived, home from her meeting in Concordia, everything was ready. And perfect. She prepared meals for loved ones with special attention — even baking homemade yeast rolls, like Mother used to make.

For the New Year's weekend of 1991, she cooked an eight-pound prime rib roast, packed in kosher salt, and so memorable the family is still talking about it a decade later. Often simple acts of graciousness are unforgettable. The rectory table was set with a "Flying Geese" pattern quilted table runner that she had hand stitched with care.

After dinner she took guests to the Dane Hanson Museum, in Logan. Aviation art was exhibit at the time. In this small town, it is surprising to find both permanent and rotating Smithsonian collections of high caliber. Another time she took family members to view a major quilt exhibition at the museum. Mother's work was not included, but earlier, in June 1986, as part of the Kansas Quilt Project, Sister Veronica registered one of Mother's quilts documented as: Olive Roy, ID. Bb71, pattern, Attic Windows, or Crows Nest.[1]

Sister Veronica was thrilled to be invited to celebrate life's joys, as she saw people at their brightest, happiest moments by attending weddings, birthdays and anniversary celebrations. Chances to gather with family were a priority, even when she had to make a sacrifice. "I am skipping a big meeting at Concordia [to attend nephew Duane John and Nena Roy's wedding at Our Lady of the Plains, in Byers, Colorado]." She was often called upon to be the scriptural reader for many weddings, including for this writer, Linda, and

Randy Cross, at St. Catherine of Siena, known as the Chapel on the Rock, near Allenspark, Colorado. She also served as reader for niece, Denise Rader and Mike Mooney, at St. Jude's in Lakewood, and Susan Mitchum, whom she said, "Is a lot like family." She attended Jason's First Communion (her Godson's first-born) at St. Mary's Church, in Hays. She tried to be at all the baptisms, too. She was most unhappy when she had to miss a special event. "Sorry I can't be with [nephew] John to share the joy of his special First Holy Communion Day."

Mother's final request to Sister Veronica was to not let the family drift apart. In the months and years that followed, she took up the burden of struggling to keep the family bonded over the miles, while yearning for a shared responsibility. She had a big heart and sacrificed without complaint, trying her best to carry out Mother's last wishes: "I pray that my children and my grandchildren will continue the family tradition of helping to make this a better world, and to always keep in touch, although miles apart."

✝

Chapter Forty-three

"It wasn't just family occasions she frequented. Oftentimes, she spent holidays cheering up elderly parishioners," said Geneva Long from New Almelo. "Sister Veronica went beyond the call of duty and visited hospitals, and the shut-ins regularly." Sister Vera Meis added, "Veronica did a lot of behind-the-scenes type work. She wrote personal cards to those in her parish who were sick, celebrating anniversaries, or other special events."

As a pastoral minister, she showed random kindnesses in many ways, and even stayed in touch with Mother's friends. "Gerri Miner wrote a huge letter. She is quite a writer and one of a kind."

Sister Veronica lived alone, awoke to an empty house, and often ate alone, including holidays. Alone she unwrapped those few Christmas and birthday presents that arrived in the mail. She often spent her birthday home alone, writing Convent House Annals. "Traditionally, I do this on my birthday/holiday, but last year with you, I never did make up the day, so I had two years to write. It is healing, so I can start the New Year reconciled, and ready for surprises."

In the spirit of hospitality, learned from our parents, she often invited parishioners into her various convent homes, when she did not receive holiday invitations herself. "I'll cook up a whole dinner on Thanksgiving Day, and hope a couple widow-ladies can join me." Instead, she said the holiday was a quiet one. One year, she shared a holiday dinner with a single older neighbor-lady.

The following year she announced, through the parish bulletin, "Anyone is welcome to come for Thanksgiving dinner," but only one couple came. "I roasted a turkey received as a gift last Christmas, and made both [traditional and French-potato] dressings that Mother always made, and had about six kinds of vegetables that local folks had given me over the summer. It was fun putting a whole meal together. I haven't done that since I quit cooking on Monday nights for Father Darryl at Logan."

Another time she remarked, "Two families rented a hall [over Thanksgiving] and invited me to join them. Gertrude McNeive said, "My sister, Loene O'Connor and I became close to Sister Veronica, and she spent several Thanksgivings and Christmas celebrations with us. We felt she was part of our family." Another Christmas morning she spent at a neighbor's house. If she was not spending the entire day with friends or family, it was typical for her to share the rest of her holiday weekend at the Long Term Nursing Care Center as hostess.

One parishioner emphasized, "Sister Veronica was one of us, sharing our happy, and sad, times, too. She was at our forty-fifth wedding anniversary celebration, and at the weddings of two of my children. Before I visited the Mother Cabrini Shrine at Denver, she gave me some literature and films to watch."

Sister Veronica knew that most people are emotionally open during life-cycle events. Being present with someone during moments of sheer joy brings out so much that is genuinely beautiful. These times can be electric. When invitations were not extended for baptisms, she explained church protocol, "Anything held in the church is open for celebration by anyone." Another parishioner offered, "When the parish Priest had a Baptism or anything special, she had things set up to make it extraordinary. She believed in festivities and was the one to put on that final touch."

She went to Damar, for Sister Rose Alma Newell's sixtieth Jubilee, and attended the twenty-fifth jubilee of Father Larry Grennen, in Salina. She drove to Atchison, for the Ordination of Bishop Herbert Hermes, as well as attending countless celebrations of other religious men and woman throughout Kansas.

She was there during the saddest occasions, too. When Father Stephen Letourneau died as the result of an auto accident, she attended his funeral. The list goes on.

Mother and Dad made it a point to attend funerals of friends and relatives. Sister Veronica followed in their footsteps and adhered to corporal works of mercy, oftentimes driving hundreds of miles to attend a funeral. It is understandable that the churches were filled to overflowing at the funerals of Dad, Mother and Sister Veronica.

Perhaps Sister Veronica learned early in life, when she was only eleven years old, how important the outreach of families can be. In 1950, on Christmas Day, Aunt Alma Newell Roy died of cancer at the age of forty-three, and barely a year later her husband, Uncle Edmond, also died a premature death of viral pneumonia. Their orphaned children went to live with various family members. The third child, teenage cousin Germaine, was the same age as Mother when she was orphaned, and it was a painful reminder. There was always a special place in Mother's heart for these children who, in turn, kept in close contact with our parents.

Thirteen months after Mother died, Sister Veronica attended Uncle Levi Morin's funeral in Omaha. "I brought a plant, from the family, and a 'Kansas Monks in Brazil mass card.'" Another time instead of roaming around Damar on New Year's Day, as she typically did, the next day she attended the funeral of our cousin, Omer Morin. "He was sixty-seven years old and probably died of heart problems." She was especially distressed to have missed Uncle Omer Roy's funeral, just the month before her own.

She represented the family when cousin Clarence Brin died, as she did for many other funerals, weddings and gatherings. She attended a funeral to represent a sister-in-law, who was vacationing in Toronto. "Ruth is his only niece, so I [thought my presence] might be helpful."

After the death of a loved one, it is not unusual to seek deeper spiritual understanding, and return to one's faith at mid-life. In her outreach to grieving parishioners, Sister Veronica often tapped her own experiences, and felt the rare privilege of being close to people at such sacred moments; closer sometimes than to their own relatives. One parishioner remarked, "When my husband was on oxygen for five years she drove every Friday, to where we lived out of town, with communion and prayers for him, and later saw us through his wake-vigil service."

Sister Veronica, like our mother, never forgot a friendship and both had some that lasted a lifetime. Lucille Desmarteau Morin, mother's sister-in-law, was also her childhood friend. Aunt Lucille was with Mother the day before she died. Many of Mother's elderly neighbors were widows by then, like Marjorie Biery, who outlived Mother. Sister Veronica attended funerals of those around Belmont Township. Josie McEwen, a neighbor, who died at age 102, even in her later years provided fresh cream, when we each came home for reunions begging Mother to make homemade ice cream and caramelized popcorn.

As newlyweds, our parents lived with, and worked for, the Gosselin family. Sister Veronica made a special trip to Garden City to help Lillie Balthazor Gosselin, a second cousin, celebrate her one-hundredth birthday.

Another friend of the family, Jean Grover Lindsey recalled, "Getting reacquainted with Sister Veronica was a joy, and seeing the beautiful person she became in her walk with Christ. It meant so much to my mother, Merle, that she kept in touch with her over the years."

"I attended the funeral of Merle Grover, our lifelong childhood neighbor and friend," Sister Veronica said. "I had to, for myself, for Mother, and for the entire family. The service was beautifully simple, and just like Merle. The Methodist preacher said something about us being there was like sitting around a table, sipping lemonade, while the hostess is elsewhere. Instead of a hundred dollars worth of casket flowers, her huge Bible was opened, on the casket, with some homegrown spring flowers sticking out. That left a big message for me."

To some people Sister Veronica may have seemed outwardly stoic and without feeling. Yet in her letters, and to very few others, she revealed her deep sadness about a loss through death, or other normal emotions laid bare, that made her all the more human.

"The Lord help us when Mark [Beckman] leaves us," Sister Veronica said of a New Almelo parishioner. "He's been doing so much for the church, and the cemetery, since he came to live with Monsignor Vornholt at about age six. When Mark dies, I'm sure Joe will become our next sexton [caretaker/bell-ringer/grave-digger.]

"Joe [Mindrup] was the altar server for Father Duane's visit. He attended St.

Benedict's Abbey for a semester, hoping to become a Priest, and then had to return home so his brother could go to war, who was then killed overseas during WWII. I will cry another seventy-two hours when Joe dies. He is giving some clues of 'wrapping things up' though only seventy years old."

Works of mercy take on a variety of forms. When it became evident, in 1979, that proper finance records for cemetery funds had not been maintained in the Damar parish, Sister Veronica wanted to be certain that our family obligation was fulfilled for upkeep around the three spaces taken by Mother, Dad, and brother Ronald's graves. "Does anyone know, besides our three buried there, is there a fourth burial plot, or an eighth?"

Even though the fee covered the cost of employing a caretaker, and the maintenance of the cemetery, Sister Veronica stopped by on regular bases to check on things. "I spent many evenings at the Damar cemetery, since Mother's burial, trying to beautify the folk's lot, and also of both Roy and Morin grandparents, and Hebert great-grandparents."[1]

Gatherings, especially those including aged relatives, were special to her. "Kenneth sent me about twenty-five photos of our Roy reunion. It was a historical moment, having all the surviving aunts and uncles present. The photo of them must go into the *Stockton Sentinel*, which I will work on."

While visiting Uncle Ed Morin the month before he died, he blessed her with an abundance of photos for her genealogy book. On regular intervals she continued to visit Aunt Irene, whose own children lived far away. After Sister Veronica's death, our elderly aunt deeply missed these visits.

Compiling the family history books gave Sister Veronica even more of an excuse to reach out. She was a preserver of memories. Anytime in the vicinity of an older relative, she made certain to stop in for a visit, and gather information too, knowing each took delight in re-telling stories.

She drove to Kansas City to celebrate Aunt Zella and Uncle Paul Rickard's fiftieth wedding anniversary. Then while in Terre Haute, Indiana for summer classes, she made it a point to stop along the way to visit relatives. There were many others times, too, that she visited those in Colorado, Nebraska, Iowa, Minnesota and Illinois.

Her godparents celebrated their sixtieth wedding anniversary, and she was there. A few years later, after Aunt Nathalie's death, she continued to visit Uncle Dona Roy, in Damar. "Joan and I borrowed a spade from him, after he gave us some sidewalk runners of grass. We went to the cemetery to plant these at Mother and Dad's grave site." She was there when it was Uncle Dona's eighty-seventh birthday, and visited him at the Hill City Hospital during illnesses. After he died at St. John's Hospital in Salina, and was brought back to Damar, for the funeral Mass and burial, she was there, too.

The next spring she painfully watched the sale of her godparent's household goods, and empathized with her cousin's loss. "Nearly the only ones bidding were family members, although the rest of Damar showed up for Saturday morning coffee and entertainment. I did buy a few things — ice cream freezer, box camera and kitchen stuff. If someone started the bid at one dollar, they might have gotten it for that. If the family was bidding, folks stopped, and let them have it. Don't they see the family wants people to drive up the bidding?"

For many consecutive years she placed flowers at the Damar Cemetery and attended Mass there on Memorial Monday.

"The past few years Ila Mae took part in the annual Memorial Day Webster Alumni reunion dinner and meeting, held at the Stockton school. She conducted the service of memory for those gone before us," said Jean Grover Lindsey. "She had such a kind and gentle spirit, and was still the quiet, pleasant person I knew as a child. She was a blessing to everyone she met."

"She did an admirable job," said Lorabell and Dale Arbogast, a classmate. We saw Ila at many of the Webster reunions. The class of '57 always laughed at the fact that theirs was the only class that was one hundred percent there, since they were a graduating class of only three. During one of these times, after seeing three of our children, she made the innocent remark, 'Are you sure they have the same father? All the kids have different color hair.' I just laughed. It was obvious she liked kids."

"Usually Dale Arbogast, John Fetteroff, and I are the youngest ones there," Sister Veronica said of the school reunions. No longer wearing the voluminous black Habit of earlier years it was easy, for those who knew her from school days, to fall into the custom of calling her "Ila" or "Mae." The Webster Alumni Secretary-Treasurer at the time, Mrs. Clark added, "We really loved Ila Mae. I knew her best [of the entire family] and miss her terribly."

One of the topics that often came up at these annual meetings was storage of the trophies, once belonging to the closed Webster school. These were now displayed at the Stockton grade school. "There was rumbling in the group, as they were tired of fighting with Stockton, about displaying the trophies. Some suggested we sell them. So, I volunteered to serve on the committee for several years," Sister Veronica said.

Through corresponding, comforting and caring she believed in celebrating all of life's mysteries and occasions. Her handwritten message, in Christmas cards one year, makes it clear where her heart was and would always be, "God's gifts to us — family, faith and friends. May you be surrounded with them across the miles and throughout the new year."

✝

Chapter Forty-four

Years before, Sister Veronica had become increasingly troubled about the rising number of Priestless parishes. She began discussing it while in WaKeeney, but the topic came up in New Almelo, too. She was willing to do her part to fill the void of Priestless parishes, as were many Religious Women. She pondered privately whether she would ever be accepted as Pastor. But in her heart she knew it would not happen soon.

"Sometimes she joined our hour and a half long Bible study group," said parishioner Bernadine Diederich. "Afterward, we played Canasta, followed by lunch. In the casual setting of the card game Sister Veronica said that if the Catholic Church would approve of women being ordained, she would like to be a Priest."

"Sister Veronica had dreams of improving the parish, and did her share to make it a better worshiping community. When officiating at a Psalm or Communion service her ability was well demonstrated," agreed Gertrude McNeive.

By circumstances, Sister Veronica became a presider and a preacher, and felt comfortable doing it. Although introverted, she secretly looked forward to those times when the mission Priests could not make it for weekend Mass due to icy roads. Weather, on the Kansas Plains, can be treacherous, and the week before Christmas 1992 she wrote, "Since yesterday, we had twelve inches of snow. Our Sunday replacement Priest did not come from Ellis." This would have been well over a ninety-minute drive, in the best of weather.

Another time when the Priest was not able to make the trip due to weather she said, "We had a communion service and about twenty-five families attended, with all Eucharistic ministers present. I always thought folks showed up, with even more determination, when weather is bad, perhaps to see who else came. Maybe they want to show they could get though, or perhaps there was nowhere else to go. Seriously, though, these folks in New Almelo really are committed to handing down faith values. It is an act of faith and love for the Eucharistic Lord."

The next time that happened she said, "I presided at the communion service, in lieu of Mass. I preached to a pleasantly packed congregation, more formally than usual. "The topic of my homily was, 'At Baptism, we became grafted into Christ (as used to produce fruit) not simply to receive the blessings of God, but also to become an instrument of the purpose of God. All are empowered with God's Spirit, and held in God's hand. I also preached on the methods prophesized by Isaiah that 'the servants be quiet, not loud; respectful, not judgmental; flexible, not rigid; peaceful, not violent.'"

New hope arrived when some Bishops around the country began to appoint Sisters to Priestless parishes as Pastoral Administrators. Sister Veronica's aspiration was renewed when, in a groundbreaking move, Bishop Fitzsimons announced two Sisters as Pastoral Administrators. "Sister Janis Wagner will replace Father Larry Grennan, who went to Belgium for six months. Sister Carolyn Juenemann was appointed at Oberlin, to work alongside Father Lutgen, beginning July 1994. I plan to visit her frequently, and to chat about what is going on. I hope to be as good for her, as I know she is for me."

Other Sisters began serving as Pastoral Associates in the towns of Oakley, Salina, Goodland, Beloit and Manhattan. "It was announced last week that Laywomen were selected for Leoville and Selden."

Father Duane explains this turn of events, "The Code of Canon Law, in its 1983 revision, speaks of three types of parish leadership: Pastor, Parochial Administrator and Parochial Vicar, this latter more popularly known as Assistant or Associate Pastor. The code does not permit a non-ordained person to be at the head of a parish. Only an ordained Priest can hold all three offices. All are appointed by the diocesan Bishop, and can be removed only by him, or by the diocesan administrator.

"Salina Diocese, as in many other dioceses, with the shortage of Priests began to develop lay ministries and began using the terms Pastoral Associate and Pastoral Administrator. The Pastoral Administrator is usually a lay people or a Sister who is designated as responsible for the parish communities where there were no resident Priests. On the other hand, "The Pastoral Associate is normally a layperson, a religious or a deacon, who works together with a Pastor or Parochial Administrator. This Pastoral Associate was the position Sister Veronica held in New Almelo. These communities rely on what is sometimes called, 'Sacramental Priest' to visit them occasionally to celebrate mass, attend confessions and anoint the infirmed," said Father Duane.

"A diocesan-wide survey showed sixty-six percent of our parishes are rural, and twenty-five percent of people responded in the survey," Sister Veronica reported. "It showed that fifty-five percent of the total surveyed said they would accept a trained layperson as a Pastoral Administrator. Truthfully, I guess I am holding out for that to come. If small faith communities have validity, then there should be other forms of Priestless parishes."

Sister Veronica and two other CSJ Sisters served on the new twelve-member Salina Diocese Planning Commission. "This will have a lot to do with what rural parishes look like, and how they are served in the coming years, so it is a scary task." She was also among many other Sisters and diocesan Priests who traveled to Hays for a "Listening Session" to discuss the identity, mission and qualification of Women Religious, and if and when they would become Pastoral Administrators in the growing number of Priestless parishes.

"Four of us worked on a proposal system for appointments to parishes." As a member of the Rural Support Team she noted, "We were invited to the Diocesan Priests Personnel Board to talk about blending Religious Women's process of discernment for their ministries, and Priests assignments. Priests are just appointed, but Sisters discern where to be appointed. So we ask for dialogue. As more parishes are ripe to hire Sisters, we need to be [ready]."

In the meantime, she began to qualify herself more intensely for a Pastoral Administrator role, knowing she was dependent on Bishop Fitzsimons and his Council of Priests for the appointment. She had developed a working relationship with him over the years, in CSJ meetings and other diocesan functions.

In the late 1980s, the Bishop praised her guidance for one of the many activities she handled at the grassroots level: "I want to thank you for your participation in the Salina Diocese Centennial Committee for all the work that was accomplished through your leadership. In conversation with many of the people who attended the event, all seemed to be in praise of the booths, the wonderful Liturgy, the community of faith, and the presence of so many people. The celebration at Colby, in the month of August, was well attended by the people of the west," he recognized her in the letter.

In 1986, she took vacation time to attend a graduate-level Pastoral Administrator class at St. Mary-of-the-Woods, Indiana, the home of the Sisters of Providence. All but five of the 125 students were Sisters. From this college near Terre Haute, she received three continuing education units, toward Pastoral Ministry, "to gain credibility, and back up my five years of pastoral minister experience when the time comes to leave here and try to get in somewhere else," she said, "I don't see myself as Pastoral Administrator for a long time, but feel inclined to be on the team with someone else who would fill up the gap of my deficiencies," she said while still in WaKeeney.

She also attended a summer institute for Rural Pastors and Parish Workers, at Aquinas Institute of Theology in St. Louis, Missouri, a Dominican graduate school, with three other CSJ pastoral ministers. "I stayed an extra day and a half for one graduate credit."

As an outcome of the Second Vatican Council, the Dogmatic Constitution on the Church (*Lumen gentium* /Light of the Nations) looks at the universal call to holiness. It shows how the People of God share in Christ's Priestly and prophetic office.

Since 1986, the Diocese of Salina had this program. Soon after, while still in WaKeeney, she wrote to the advisor from Marymount College, Father Frank Coady, asking to become accredited in Lumen. In the fall of 1987 he replied, "Since most of your [undergraduate] course work was done before Vatican II, I originally thought that you should take all the courses in the Lumen program. Since your current pastoral work requires considerable reading and updating, that would leave you with the other four required courses, plus the electives. I have decided to waive Fundamental Theology, Old Testament, New Testament and Christian Spirituality.

"The Moral Theology course, you are currently taking at Hays, leaves you with three required courses over the next three semesters: Ecclesiology, Sacraments and Liturgy, and Theology of Ministry. After that, all you will need are the two electives."

The assigned book for Moral Theology was *Principles for a Catholic Morality*. As she underlined many passages of the weighty material, it became clear she had the organized mind it took to follow Timothy O'Connell's textbook for intellectuals demanding that Christians be grounded in God's love to be moral people in a moral world.

She said in early January, "I never did get a degree in Ministry or Spiritually, from Marymount College. The last [classes] I had on Sacraments were pre-Vatican II, in the 1960s, so I have a chance to finish up some requirements. This would look better on future job applications." She drove to Hays for the three-hour, nine-credit college class on Ecclesiology.

Later she said, "I've continued to work every free moment all summer on the genealogy book, but finally stopped two weeks ago to study for my last class, Theology of Ministry, to write three papers and read three books. I got an A. It was a fifteen-week class."

Her Lumen advisor, Father Coady, continued, "I would need to know the name of someone who could act as a supervisor of the project. If there is no one above you, then we could use a co-worker who could testify to the amount, and quality, of your work on the project. The practicums are available whenever we agree on a suitable ministry, or catechetical experience."

She replied, "I feel that both practicums, in Pastoral Ministry and Catechetics, should be waived, on the word of three co-workers. Rosann Felder, for one, has thirty years experience as a catechist at Christ the King parish, and plans to be credited for the Practicum." Mrs. Felder commented, "She got me started on an equivalent, and I received certification for Major I Religious studies. Then I took others with me, and now a half dozen people are taking college credit courses."

Sister Veronica continued with her advisor, "Something else that could indicate that I have indeed practiced here would be to compose a calendar for future Religious Education Coordinators universal enough for any rural parish." Otherwise, as an elective, she suggested crediting a course she had taken on Family Life in Religious Institutions, from KSU.

"A second choice would be a reflection on these past seven years titled, 'Part Time Ministry in the Fast Lane,' to complete the requirement for a practicum in Catechetics." These were not waived and she proceeded to write up her lived experiences. "I have piles of papers all over the house."

In mid-1991 a news article in the *Northwestern Kansas Catholic Register* announced, "Sister Veronica Roy is one of the first two graduates of the *Lumen* program, receiving a B.A. degree in Pastoral Ministry from St. Mary of the Plains College, Dodge City, Kansas."[1] She began the Lumen classes in WaKeeney, but finished while in New Almelo.

Father Daniel Scheetz, one of her instructors in Hays recalled, "She was endearing and lovable, and a very good student — perceptive, loyal, mature and always her own person. She was fully cooperative, a co-equal partner in ministry, and always able to interact with others without dominance or superiority. She was a self-affirming person, trusting of self and others and independent, yet committed, and loyal to those with whom she had identified. Family and friends were important."

She eagerly attended conventions and lectures on various topics, knowing full well that study opens both the eyes and heart to truth. She was well qualified to provide personal guidance in a Priestless parish.

The author, Kathleen Norris, sees it another way and suggests, in *The Cloister Walk*, there is a current mania for accumulating credentials to measure what can be quantified. Sister Veronica fell into this trap. She felt the need to prove she was qualified to be of service of others. The credentials stacked up to secure her worth and acceptance. In the end, she was paid less and less.

✝

Chapter Forty-five

"All who had people sick with various diseases brought them to Him. He laid hands on each of them and cured them."

— Lk 4, 40.

She stayed close to home in New Almelo covering the parish during the mission Priest's extended absence while he recovered from surgery. After his return, and no longer having the Logan parish contract, she said, "I can't believe it has been three months that I have been working only three days a week in parish ministries. The days go so quickly. I have not started any second job search. I am not feeling right about only working half time."

At the March 1993 Western Kansas District Dietetics association meeting in Garden City, she planned to inquire of dietetic consultation positions that might be opening up. "Otherwise, I will start submitting resumes to nursing facilities, and actively looking for one or two dietetic consultation contracts, even if I need to go into Colorado, or Nebraska and stay overnight."

In the meantime she had worked for several years with Developmental Services of Northwestern Kansas, (DSNWK), continued from the time in WaKeeney, "with lots of paperwork that comes due quarterly for my only dietetic job of handling four homes for mentally retarded adults in Hays and Norton." She continued to keep active her professional affiliations through the Kansas Department of Health and Environment (KDHE) and Health Occupations Credentialing Kansas Dietitian License (LD).

By now, she had either lost or voluntarily given up one or more of her contracts. She was well aware of her discomfort with young adults and even those her own age and felt her dislike of small talk was a barrier to ministry. It was during this time she sought professional therapeutic counseling because she dreaded searching for further employment because of her introversion, as discussed in a later chapter. "If I just worked three days a month, it would pay the same as another part-time job in parish ministry."

After fifteen months of searching she seemed especially thrilled to land a job, even though it was a 130-mile round trip. "I finally have something that I never dreamed I'd be wanting two months ago. I work one day a month as the High-Risk Nutrition Consultant with the Rooks County [Stockton] Health Department. WIC is a special supplemental nutrition program for women, infants and children, and the MI program is for mothers with infants. The difference in the two programs is income levels.

"The job pays $20. I asked for $25.50, but that's all they had budgeted. Phillips County [Phillipsburg] called me for the same position. There is a possibility I may do something for Norton County also. Both counties had consulting dietitians driving from Salina and Goodland every three months. The Salina dietitian backed out because of mileage.

"I surrounded myself with a pile of resources on women and children's nutrition to refresh myself, since I have not done much of it in hospitals," she downplayed her credentials. Along with her 1981 Master's degree in nutrition, a two-week internship with WIC, and her 94-page thesis, *Anthropometry in the Nutritional Assessment of Preschool Children*, proved a strong and suitable background.

The programs are administered at each county seat, in rural areas, and provide services to income-eligible pregnant, breastfeeding and postpartum women, infants, and children up to age five who are determined to be at medical and/or nutritional risk.

Sister Veronica was an asset to WIC, and did not have to be sold on the benefits of breast-feeding, knowing it is more than nutrition. Studies show it promotes a positive interaction between antibodies of the immune systems of mother and child. Previously she attended LaLeche League meetings and understood the positives, even before studies came out showing that formula-fed babies tend to have more illnesses. She also knew that breast-feeding was a part of maternal bonding. Many mothers have the intention of breast-feeding, but stop after the first few weeks because they encounter difficulty and have no support. Through the WIC program she offered that information and support.

Our mother, and many women Mother's age, did not breast feed due to a variety of reasons as discussed earlier. "The science to show the benefits of breast-feeding was not around during the post World-War II years, a period characterized as 'medicine's period of ignorance,'" said Father Duane.[1]

According to the WIC Internet website, this health and nutrition program is one of the most cost effective and preventative plans of its time. WIC contributes to reduce infant mortality and morbidity, improve participant health outcomes, and produce savings in health care costs.

The program also collects and reviews the immunization status of these infants and children, and makes referrals to keep them up to date on their shots. The way Sister Veronica explained it, "President Clinton marked WIC as a priority, as one of his favorite programs. Funds and caseloads will be expanded ten percent by January 1994. I am amazed at the nearly 200 clients for Rooks County, and 170 for Phillips County."

WIC is basically a threefold process: assessment, one-on-one nutrition education, and a free food coupon package valued at $40 to $50 per month. In collaboration, with the Department of Food and Agriculture, it provides participants with coupons, redeemable for nutritious foods such as fresh fruits, fruit juice, vegetables, milk, cheese, iron-fortified cereals, peanut butter, eggs, and dried beans. "The trick is to encourage mothers to use the coupons for purchasing food for her children, rather than for pets, and discourage them from giving away the beans to a cousin, or neighbor.

"I enjoy the work. Even though I talk to people all day, the difference is they come to me for help, and I don't get so tired," Sister Veronica explained. This was in sharp contrast to parish ministry, where she found initiating contact exhausting.

Before long she began to realize the County Health Department was shortsighted, and behind the times in many areas, not unlike many rural health departments around the country. Attuned to the possible failure-to-thrive diagnosis of an adopted great-nephew, Sister Veronica found an article on zinc status in relation to growth failure, along with a bibliography on short stature. Recognizing one of the many flaws in the system, she said, "Unfortunately the failure-to-thrive diagnosis is an area where WIC has not developed a state-wide protocol of actions." Most likely, as detail-oriented as she was, she began to systematically document for emerging patterns with this high-risk population.

"The first day, in Stockton, I had to stay two hours overtime to do the paper work, even though I only scheduled three clients an hour, and several did not show up. A very scary part is that clients are scheduled fifteen minutes apart, and within that time a professional must warm up to the client to get subjective data, look at nurses' objective data, make an assessment, and do some teaching." She began to understand she was asked to do the impossible, much less in a slip-shod manner, which was not her style. "Believe me, I am taking out professional liability for this private practice."

The limited appointment time, she was allocated for each client is much like the current HMO medical practice. "An HMO gives you fifteen minutes. You can't find out what's wrong in fifteen minutes," said the 101-year-old, Dr. Leila Denmark, noted as the nation's oldest practicing physician. "Doctors need to take time to find out what makes our children sick, instead of just giving a prescription."[2]

Furthermore, Sister Veronica became aware of a vicious cycle within the system. Incomes are typically lower throughout rural counties, resulting in a lower tax base to draw from, which in turn, limits funds available for social services. Then federal monies are sought that have stringent, and oftentimes nonsensical administration guidelines.

A while later she confessed with angst in her heart, "I've been too embarrassed to tell anyone the WIC office in Stockton, in my own hometown, fired me in July. They said the grounds were that clients were not keeping their appointments." She saw through this defect early on, and offered a solution that fell on deaf ears. "This is typical all around the country. Let's change the appointment date to the day they have to come to town to get their food vouchers."

She was smack in the middle of "catch-22." From the beginning she sensed the locally administered program was flawed in demanding client turnover each fifteen minutes. She suspected that allowing clients more than their allocated time was a factor in her own demise. Although she came to realize it was a federal restriction, not local. She continued working with the Phillips County WIC program for a while longer.

Her friend, Sister Ginger, summarized, "Veronica called these 'Holy Ground years.' She spoke of her biblical Martha and Mary experience, and of the new blend of service, which encompassed feeding the hungry and giving proper nourishment to infants, along with sacramental pastoral ministry."

Chapter Forty-six

While it was humiliating to lose the one-day-a-month WIC contract, a job Sister Veronica enjoyed, she was not bitter. She found throughout life, "there are other ways to serve."

The computer bug bit this modern-day "woman of the cloth," who became hooked on its benefits. Her skills were a tremendous asset to the parishes. Often letters were peppered with tidbits of her fast-growing, self-taught knowledge. It was not unusual for her to end a letter by saying, "Well, there is more to my life than PCs."

When she first arrived in New Almelo, and without much of a computer to work on, she felt edged back to the dark ages. But the next year, in 1991, $2,000 was donated to the parish to buy a new computer. In the fall of 1992, the council gave her permission to investigate the computer market. "I have spent a lot of energy learning about different computers and printers during my free time. I'll probably recommend using our Swintec typewriter, which is an IBM printer, so that we can buy a great system. I'll use a personal printer for some nicer work."

When the council delayed the purchase, pending interviews with the parish secretary, she was frustrated and put on hold a second time. Then the Pastor had surgery, and council meetings were postponed for several more months.

"You no longer allow yourself deliberately to wish for anything except that God's holy will always be done in you and through you," emphasizes Maxim 10:8. So, when the Motherhouse gave her permission to buy a replacement car she said, "I have been given the go-ahead to get any accessory, as long as the total cost of the car is less than $11,000." Chidingly she added, "I'm wondering if a portable computer in the back seat would be okay?"

By the spring of 1993, the parish council finally approved "to get a used PC for as cheap as I can. I had fun learning this program, and now there's no reason for messy letters with uncorrected spelling. I hope I don't get stuck on just a few options."

She got the parish secretary set up to use the IBM computer for word processing and financial reports. "I hope she, and the parish council, will appreciate it and see the need for a laser or DeskJet type printer, and maybe even a full-page scanner."

In the meantime, Sister Veronica, who lived at the rectory-parish office and the one most affected, was not made aware the secretary changed her daytime hours to 4-7 p.m. after starting a full-time job elsewhere. "I don't mind so much the change, as the not knowing. The secretary said she talked it over with the

Pastor last month, but neither one saw the need to inform me. That was the theme of my last retreat. It seems I have to be the one to initiate communication, and I still never know anything. It has been awkward the past two years having to make appointments, with both the parish secretary and the Pastor, just to chat or go over things." Aware of her reaction to secretaries in general, she said, "I've really tired hard to be congenial, and this was probably my biggest success of the past three years."

Later on, after the secretary quit as she felt she did not have enough time to do a good job, Sister Veronica picked up the responsibility, in addition to her other duties, since the secretarial position was only budgeted for six hours a week. "I would rather do it myself. I get energized from paper work." Furthermore, she often laid out the paperwork for the secretary, who then got credit for it. "Bad case of envy," she confessed.

It was almost startling to hear her speak of envy, one of the seven capital sins, along with pride, covetousness, lust, anger, gluttony and sloth. One of the maxims of her CSJ Community warns to be hidden, not looking for credit. Still, she was human and admitted her faults.

"My first interest was to start out with 'clean books,' so I audited all of our accounts (checking, certificates of deposit, memorials, stipends, and cemetery fund), and got quite a lesson in bookkeeping. Thank heavens, I found we have more money then we thought, and not the other way around."

A stickler for details, Sister Veronica believed emphatically that parishioners should know how church funds are distributed. "I set up the New Almelo parish financial expense sheet on PC-CALC (using Alpha4 database). Our Finance Committee meets every two months, and will get the first report in May. I expect them to be very pleased. My [CSJ] Community ledgers are set up similar to this. I just write a code on the check, and a company does the rest.

"Next, I made a flyer of our ten-year finance picture, along with capital improvements. It is very flat. For example, utilities are the same. Sunday collections are the same. It is amazing, considering all the improvements that have been done on our buildings and grounds. The theory is that we'll be dead, as a parish, fifty years from the date we stop the upkeep.

"Our primary supporters are dying, or moving to retirement areas, although the parish is generous. On a typical Sunday the collection basket is $500 for the eighty family units. [If the Priest] mentions a need outside the parish, for example, the Diocesan-wide drives for international concerns, parishioners will throw in another $500. Our parish sent a $900 check [to the Salina Diocese] for the aborted infants' memorial weekend.

"One of our parishioners, an older bachelor [Mark Beckman] who died in October 1993, left about $200,000, from the sale of his land. We are 'counting our chickens,' since someone seems to be contesting his Will. He was an only child and had no one, except distant cousins.

"The bachelor's mother was [Mrs. Beckman] the Priest's housekeeper.[1] When she moved to New Almelo from Damar, the parish Priest [Monsignor John Bernard Vornholt] helped the housekeeper raise her son. This Priest had served the Diocese from the 1910s until retiring in 1946. [He died here on August 24, 1951.] His housekeeper died in 1978. The bachelor son, Mark, inherited his mother's estate, as well as that of the Priest. Mark, who was also a sacristan in our church continued living in the house until his death." Since he was knowledgeable of liturgical work in the sacristy, the people popularly called him their Deacon.[2]

"Only the interest, from this Last Will [and Testament], is to be used for parish upkeep, improvements, and the cemetery, but not for monthly bills. Maybe we can interpret propane as a legitimate upkeep. Very interesting, the week the land sold, our checkbook balance was zero for the first time since I've been here. A few months earlier we had to cash in a certificate of deposit to pay bills." Once again, she had faith that the Lord will provide.

The year before Mark Beckman died, she returned home from a CSJ summer retreat in 1992, and said with clarity of vision, "I'm going through stuff, trying to place it meaningfully, or dispose of it gracefully. This is always a nag with me — getting material things simplified and what our parish will be glad to have, if we ever establish something like a Historical Site. This dream of mine would be housed at our 'Deacon's' home, our first rectory built after the 'soddy type.' From what I've seen inside, I suspect nothing has changed since his mother, the housekeeper died."

Circumstances prevented Sister Veronica's dream of establishing a historical site from becoming a reality. This is unfortunate, because she had the persistence and patience to see goals like this completed. Had she continued to live in this area, a historical site would not have been outside the realm of possibility.[3]

St. Joseph's parish marked their 115th anniversary in 1993. "The Mass was set up nostalgic-like. Our Pastor wore a twenty-pound gold chasuble [tunic], borrowed from St. John's in Logan, on top of a white lace alb. He also wore a biretta [beret], while greeting the parishioners before and after Mass and the final prayer was in Latin. The altar boys were good sports to wear the old pre-Vatican II style black cassocks and ring the bells. We pleated altar cloths, used the huge ornamental ciborium and oldest chalice we have, put our tall candlesticks on the back altar and lit incense an hour ahead. It was very tastefully done, but folks did not comment or thank me."

In *Care of the Soul*, Thomas Moore suggests that the soul requires ongoing attention in every aspect of life. "The conditions of work have...much to do with disturbances of soul." Sister Veronica did not need a lot of recognition in living the maxim of "Hiddenness." Still, she was human and a simple few kinds words, such as, "Thanks for helping to make it a special occasion," would have gone a long way when she went the extra mile. A dedicated servant, she didn't take her jobs lightly. She nurtured others, but few returned the attention, or consideration.

After one Good Friday service she said, "I don't look for anybody to stop over in church for a visit this afternoon, so I have no qualms about getting it decorated this early. I dressed up the sanctuary, somewhat. With the dark paneling, behind the tabernacle, things can look so drab. Two other ladies stayed to help me decorate for Easter Vigil Saturday night and Sunday morning Mass."

Like Mother, Sister Veronica was interested in handicrafts. She was a wiz with a hot glue gun and draping fabric, or adding a little candlelight for that unique finish. Dried thistles and yucca from a pasture, took on a new, yet symbolic and appropriate touch. While city dwellers pay florists a premium for sunflowers to add to their décor of expensive furnishings, country folks only see these as ordinary weeds. But not Sister Veronica. Armed with a sharp knife she walked along roadsides to cut armloads full.

Geneva Long agreed, "She walked through the streets, in our small town, to pick flowers to decorate the altars. We looked forward to seeing how pretty it was. She went beyond the call of duty. When the Priest had a Baptism, or anything special, she was the one who had things set up to make it extraordinary."

Only a few noticed. One was long-time parishioner Betty Otter. "She had a creative talent. It was always a joy to go into church and see what she had done with a few flowers. If none were available, candles took on a new role. She saved glass containers the sanctuary lights came in. Then every Christmas Eve she put vigil lights around the platform of the church, out to the highway, and around the levels of the parking lot. Many enjoyed the splendid sight, but some complained she was wasting her time."

Sister Veronica understood, intuitively, that "God is in the details," and these subtleties act on the subconscious to elevate the spirit. It was hurtful when an insensitive few complained about her bothering with that "little stuff." Some parishioners took for granted the special touches, and those who made these happen. There are people who cannot see beauty even when it is laid out before them.

Pope John Paul II came to understand the need for beauty in one's spiritual life, even a decade before. "The church needs the arts, especially for its liturgy, which is meant to be a work of art inspired by faith, drawing upon all the creative forces of architecture, sculpture and painting, music and poetry." In short, the arts enhance the worship life of the community.

During her tenure at St. Joseph's, she left a considerable legacy. Inspired by the Holy Spirit, she went on to tackle "The More" of her CSJ spiritually. After the parish council gave their approval, she applied for a grant.

"One for $3,000 was awarded by the Kansas Humanities Council of the Historical Society, for the purpose of preserving and cataloging the many documents we have in our parish. A population index will be compiled of everyone who has lived within the 100 square miles area around New Almelo, within the past 116 years, beginning in 1878. We have to match the funds, but I have done that much work already."[4]

The grant reimbursed locals for the rental of cameras to videotape families, and a smaller amount paid for Sister Veronica's "secretarial type work," as she put it, serving as Project Manager for the next eighteen months, "during her free time," she quipped.

Following the grant application, and before the year was up, she felt Christ's hidden mystery stirring once more. Again, she approached the council, this time about collecting written and oral history, from the community, in preparation for their 125th anniversary. "In remembering who we are, these stories might penetrate our hearts with sentiments of what is important. I hope all of us can find a way to be part of the storytelling, as we move through the memories toward new life," she told them.

Gertrude McNeive nodded. "Not only was she instrumental in collecting the early history of the parish and parish families, she was concerned with everything and everybody."

Sister Veronica uncovered the names of families who moved away from the area and wrote their stories so that they would be included. She gleaned reliable information from newspaper clippings, including obituaries. "Quite a story can be concocted from these facts," she admitted. Betty Otter added, "I had the pleasure of working with Sister Veronica on the survey. She used land records, cemetery records, and agricultural census. Then, she and Joe Streit put it on the computer. She even wrote biographies of many families still in the parish who had nobody to write for them. She downplayed her role, saying she merely polished up the stories, but it was she who actually wrote them."

In the church bulletin, she listed about thirty videos reflecting family values, which families could view in their own homes, or invite someone in to discuss. This was a modern tool she used for faith-sharing, feeling it was the remembering and storytelling that would bring the parish together. Only three families responded for video requests. One was Rosalia Stephens, "She showed us a film on 'why and how,' and then encouraged us to write our own stories. Because of this I have written my own."

"The grant was important because it will be the base for parish history." Sister Veronica had the foresight to see as the database project neared completion. "If time is left, I will add notations of which early homesteads are still lived on, or livable, along with oral history. [I will also include] local photographs of the St. Joseph's school [started in 1922] which was consolidated with the [public] Lenora School around 1970. "By the way, we have nine foreign exchange students. Otherwise, we would have been in danger of losing our school at Lenora having less than one hundred students [a fate that closed the consolidated Webster schools in the 1960s]."

After endless hours of research and typing, Sister Veronica made several trips to Topeka to consult with the Historical Society. Daniel Fitzgerald then made the trip, from the state capital to summarize the findings of the Population Index grant, which was basically: "The reason why western Kansas lost its population."

"The more I worked on it, I wondered why the Historical Society would have approved the grant for such a small area of Kansas," Sister Veronica said. Living a modest and humble lifestyle, it is not unusual for many rural Midwesterners to feel they do not have a story to tell. But the Mexican-American writer, Preciado Martin, emphasizes, "Storytelling is an act of love because it connects people and generations. Left to others, our stories can be distorted or trivialized. Or not told at all. When we don't write down our stories or document our history, we abdicate that power to others. It's our rich oral tradition that makes us laugh, cry or just remember ourselves. It passes down lessons of life and values. It's significant that we do it for our families and ourselves."[5]

Furthermore, the psychiatrist, author and lecturer, Carl Hammerschlag, suggests the message is important, "But no more then simply the telling. Native Americans believe in handing down stories for seven generations, yet that is lost in contemporary life." Hammerschlag, with a web page called Healing.Doc, sees storytelling as healing. "The role that old stories have, in connecting the past with the future, has a direct bearing on health," he believes. "A healthy spirit generates a healthy mind and body. People want a connection with their healers. They want them to touch their hearts and souls and the spirit within."

Even the Hospice Foundation of America found the process of story telling to be therapeutic as they produced, *A Guide for Recalling and Telling Your Life Story*, to assist the terminally ill in writing their autobiographies.

Sister Veronica was concerned about all aspects of her faith, including blending family and community with the historical and celebratory. Years earlier she pleaded with Father Duane, "The pastor in Stockton, Father Metro, knows of nobody writing about our hometown parish. Please, can we make it a joint story? An important part of ministry is reflection on what has happened." Not much later, her article, "Growing up Catholic," appeared in the *Northwestern Kansas Catholic Register* newspaper.

The act of digging into research seemed to be symbolic for uncovering deeper meaning in her own life. Perhaps, as a premonition, Sister Veronica had a sense of urgency about this project, too. "We have always used 1878 as the beginning of our parish. Now, I am trying to use 1874, since Masses were first said in homes that year. We have a historical marker one-half mile east of one of these. Using 1874 moves our 125th anniversary to the year 1999, instead of 2003, which is an incentive to hurry up and get this book done in our lifetime. I'd especially like to be a part of the ongoing compilation and completion before I turn sixty-four years old, and before all the history-makers are gone."

In 1993, when Father James Grennan was the new pastor at her hometown in Stockton, she reminded him that parish also had their 125th anniversary coming up in 2003, and wondered if St. Thomas Church was planning to celebrate in ten years. She expressed her eagerness to have a hand in that historical event, too.

That same year she began a smaller project. "I researched and wrote an article about the leaded glass windows, in St Joseph's Church, which were installed in 1980. The eighteen windows then cost $564."

Research projects were not in Sister Veronica's defined job description, although these were a part of the many ways she lived "The More," of the CSJ Maxims. "All I have to show is a full calendar of more meetings and social life around here, and pages accumulated on the word processor for the Parish and Community History, which will probably be the only thing I will be remembered for on leaving here someday," she lamented.

Like many writers, who are observers and sometime outsiders, she preferred to lead a quiet life and work from home. Perhaps she was not aware that being an introvert can sometimes be a gift. She was at her happiest and found great comfort doing what came natural to her — collecting, organizing, and writing.

Through her talents, initiative and willingness to do the solitary work of research, she left a spiritual inheritance to this community. "Hopefully, over the next five to ten years, we will collect more family stories [on video], especially in the ways they have touched the life of St. Joseph's Church. Then someone can use updated technology to splice these, along with a narrative, to create our own documentary. This would be a gigantic work, a Jubilee Book, of oral history translated into the written word."

She downplayed this contribution to her spiritual life, but the unglamorous side of research, paperwork and secretarial duties are also doing the work of the Lord. St. Thomas Aquinas' writings remind, "It is possible to regard scholarly work as a service to God."

During the Prayers of the Faithful, at her Funeral Mass, Sister Beth Stover implored, "In her statement of strengths for community leadership, Veronica wrote, 'I reach out in attentive, intensive and caring presence, desiring to keep in mind the big picture, the historical connectedness, seeking after "The More." May the fruits of her leadership gifts continue to live in the community."

Sister Veronica's gifts continue to live on in a variety of ways. In 1985, when rising production costs, falling lands values and low prices for farm products forced many families off their land, world-famous musicians Willie Nelson, Neil Young and John Mellencamp founded FarmAid, a concert benefit. Likewise, Sister Veronica was not one to sit still. Desiring to help farmers succeed and stay on their land, she did her own "FarmAid thing" eight years later, and helped area farmers one way she knew how. "I wrote up a grant application for $1,000 to educate ourselves."

What she called her "ministry of presence" expressed itself, especially at the grassroots level. She knew that education does not solve all the problems of the world, but she understood that it helps one make more informed decisions, and education is something that can never be taken away.

In the rural area where she lived, there were twenty-three locals involved with organic farming and sustainable agriculture. "Part of the funds was for a case study of ones' progress toward becoming an organic farmer," Sister Veronica said. "The rest was spent on a panel discussion/presentation on sustainable agriculture to a four-county-wide area [Rawlins, Decatur, Norton, Phillips], which we are right in the heart of. I was really nervous, and feared that only the twelve speakers would be there, along with all of Mrs. Stephen's children. In fact, only about twenty percent were locals. But behold, 90 to 100 folks, came as far away as Nebraska.

"I asked Leo Olivia [a local historian, who specializes in areas around northwest Kansas] if he would consider being our consultant. He agreed, and hopes to make some analysis of trends in the area with a comparison of tenant farmers to owners."

The National Catholic Rural Life Conference expresses a nationwide concern over the past and future economic losses and hardships that farmers endure. In Nebraska, three Bishops, Curtiss of Omaha, Bruskewitz of Lincoln, and McNamara of Grand Island, issued a joint statement: "Rural communities, and the communities of faith within them, are challenged by the social consequences of these economic hardships and stresses. The loss of family farms and ranches is not the fading of a nostalgic past, as some claim, but occasions of real loss for businesses, schools, churches, community services and a sense of shared responsibility for the community's well-being."[6]

Today, Internet websites give voice to farmer's positions: "Farmers, affiliated with NCRLC, demand a suspension of further releases of genetically engineered seeds and agricultural products; demand a ban on patenting of seeds, plants, animals, genes and cell lines; demand that corporate agribusiness be held accountable, and their monopoly practices end through enforcement of anti-trust laws; demand that consumers have the right to know if their food is genetically engineered; and demand an end to check-off programs using farmers' money to support genetic engineering and corporate control."[7]

Yet despite the growing controversy over the use of biotechnology in agriculture, American farmers are not significantly scaling back their planting of genetically altered crops, which the world's largest seed companies have invested billions of dollars to create, a recent government survey shows. Mega-corporations, like Monsanto, make certain they sway media reports, like an Op-Ed headline that touts, "Bio-tech foods helping U.S. farmers."[8]

Rosalia Stephens from nearby Jennings quipped, "You can take a person off the farm, but not the farmer out of the person. We are a farming community, and Sister Veronica was a farmer, too. She was very concerned with the decline of rural life, and studied organic farming and sustainable agriculture. She rode the bus with the farmers to their fields, and listened to speakers."

Betty Otter added, "She attended the farmer's area meetings, was involved in a group working on alterative farming and helped cook large meals for those gatherings. She was the secretary-treasurer; Joe Mindrup was the shepherd for the group."

A news article in 2001 points out, "The struggle over the agriculture bill turned bitter, with Democrats accusing the White House of abandoning farmers who have been hard hit by a drop in commodities prices."[9] She would have been sorely disappointed.

In 1992 she wrote to 12th district representative Fred Gatlin on rural Kansas issues of solid waste disposal and agriculture. Even after moving away from this agricultural community, and taking a leadership position within her CSJ community, Sister Veronica continued to pay attention to the endeavors of rural life. With her educated yet practical background, she understood that health care, including all kinds of nutrition components, education and social security, severely impact rural people and places. Due to the lack of employment alternatives, in this depressed rural area, she knew that strong ethical leadership would be needed to help rural residents realize their potential. From her firsthand experience, she could see that adult education, including a literacy component to WIC, was needed, too.

"The day of her fatal accident, she wrote a Letter to the Editor offering her views of the [1995-1996] Farm Bill, and we were scheduled to participate in a Rural Life Commission meeting, in Hutchinson, two days later," said Sister Roslyn Juenemann. "One of the overnight accommodation options was to sleep on the floor of the Presbyterian Church where the conference was being held." They planned to do that. Her sleeping bag was found among the wreckage, along with a new pair of twenty-dollar navy pumps she had purchased at Payless earlier that day.

Chapter Forty-seven

The year 1994 started off badly with the illness of Allan, who was two years older than Sister Veronica. Following the funeral of someone he once worked with at Union Power — a man who had been electrocuted on the job — Allan suffered a heart attack.

Allan made televised news, as it was sweeps month, and a local television station had been camped out all week at Aurora Presbyterian Hospital waiting for an emergency heart patient to come along who would require TPA, a clot-busting drug.

He had done electrical work steadily for months on end at the Denver International Airport, which was due to open the month of his heart attack. But there were several postponements. "Allan said that caused him a lot of stress, which does horrors to a body. He knew he was due for an attack, just from other symptoms," Sister Veronica said.

She drove to Strasburg, Colorado to visit with him after his hospital release, and kept the other siblings informed of his condition. "His coloring was not a gray as I remembered it last July 4th."

Allan died only a few months later, ironically, not from a heart condition, but from advanced Lymphoma-Sarcoma. Having served in the U.S. Army at New Mexico's White Sands Missile Range and Proving Grounds, he suspected the cancer months earlier; even telling doctors he felt it was located in the spleen area.[1] He could not persuade the professionals, however, until it was much too late.

It is uncertain why he did not receive proper palliative care (that which only eases the pain) to relieve his suffering, which is offered for patients with life-threatening illnesses. One guess it that he was fearful of becoming addicted to the pain medicine. This is not uncommon in today's society. Furthermore, it is doubtful that he reported to the doctor and nursing staff the full extent of how much he hurt, what the pain felt like and how much the pain affected his life.

It was only in 1995 — the year after Allan's death — that the American Board of Hospice and Palliative Medicine was established. And only now are hospitals establishing specialist palliative-care consultation teams encouraging patients to talk about the care they want. Allan died as much from the pain as from the effects of cancer itself. The year after his death, the medication for severe cancer pain, OxyContin, was approved by the FDA and rapidly became widely prescribed for a consistent level of relief.

It became evident to his family that Allan was terminal, even when the doctor appeared to remain certain he could recover. Having worked in hospitals for over twenty-five years, Sister Veronica knew a good health care provider when she saw one. She was not pleased about the care Allan received, and was vocal about the insensitivity shown to the patient and his immediate family.

"Tell me how bad your pain is, on a scale of one to ten," is a common practice most cancer doctors used for pain management even in the 1990s. His doctor did not use this simple technique. Instead a psychologist was brought in, during Allan's last week of life, to help him relax and meditate his pain away thinking of green pastures and ocean beaches. Our brother was a simple man, and this technique only further distressed him. Instead what gave him comfort was to be surrounded with family, and a few close friends — among them the Fellins, Unreins and Elpers.

While Mother remained chatty, except for her last several days, Allan was in considerable discomfort throughout his terminal illness. He closely identified with the suffering and withdrawal that Dad experienced toward the end. They both were the strong, silent type.

Years earlier, it was a painful loss when Dad died. Then after the death of Mother, we could only seek comfort from each other. As Miquela Rivera suggests in a newspaper article titled "Despite loss of last parent, ties can remain, 'Keeping in touch across time or distance closes the gap that would otherwise widen.'"[2] Sometimes a death brings one family together, while tearing another apart. Nothing remains the same. This family shared their grief, as well as the financial inheritance.

"I believe, now with Mother gone, we are still searching our family roles to play," Sister Veronica said. "Who does what? And what to do if such and such is not done?" That did not come to full realization, for her siblings, as much as it did when Sister Veronica's own life tragically ended. She was a rock, and our glue.

The strong emotional bonds were kept in tact heeding Mother's words from our childhood, "Be nice to your brother and sister!" There is a powerful and complex bond between siblings. These relationships can be among the most important in life, becoming even more so as one ages. Research shows that the way one got along with siblings while young can influence the choice of friends and marriage partners later on. Our family relationship is harmonious, and harmony is what each sought in marriage.

Traditions in our family include annual gatherings honoring relationships in marriage, baptisms, anniversaries and birthdays. Memorable occasions mean spending time with family members during sickness, too. As marriages crumble, and friendships fade, the sibling relationship becomes, for many people, the only intimate connection that seems to endure and has the potential to last from the cradle to the grave. A brother, or sister, is the most likely of all relatives to be at your side when you die.[3]

Mother saw this first hand. As the youngest daughter, she attended many funerals of her older siblings and their spouses. Our aunt, Sister Rose Irma, was the third oldest of thirteen, yet when she saw her siblings dying off, she had a fear of being the last to die, which she was.[4] Our youngest brother, Rodney, especially understands this somber truth, after his godmother, Sister Veronica, and Allan died within eleven months of each other.

The psychological and the spiritual came together in the form of visions for Allan. A man of few words, he spoke to his only daughter, Teresa, of a peaceful angel, who often reappeared and waited with him during his final days, even before the highly rated family show, "Touched By an Angel," a Sunday night television series showed this phenomenon.

During Allan's hospitalization in the Denver suburb, Sister Veronica was a great comfort to him. Knowing that he was dying, he privately asked her if it would be considered suicide if he simply gave up the fight to live. Sister Veronica assured him it would not be suicide. "It would be okay. Rest comfortably. Say your goodbyes." He did this.

As a family man, Christmas was important for him, which became even more evident as he waited until the first signs of dawn the day after, before he let himself be carried away by his serene "angel of death."[5]

Once more, Sister Veronica took on the responsibility of telephoning most of the relatives from near and far to let them know of Allan's funeral arrangements at Our Lady of the Plains Church, in Byers, Colorado. She participated in the Christian wake-vigil service, as did Father Duane, who traveled from Brazil several weeks earlier to stay at our brother's side in the hospital.

Allan's wake was on December 28, the evening of Sister Veronica's fifty-fifth birthday. The family solemnly celebrated her special occasion later that night, with a cake in her honor — her last birthday — as her own funeral was, paradoxically, on Allan's birthday — November 18.

Ten years earlier, in 1984, the U.S. Bishops issued critiques of capitalism stating that inequality is immoral. This subject was forcefully revisited in the homily, during Allan's funeral Mass. Sister Veronica was aghast. She was dismayed at the judgment of the local parish Priest who chose to preach on this topic, knowing that funerals and weddings are the few times non-Catholics are in a Catholic Church. While she wholeheartedly agreed with the injustice of capitalism and had taken, and lived out her life keeping the vow of poverty, she believed this harshly delivered message was ill-timed and inappropriate for the grieving family and friends, who could have used well-chosen words of comfort and grace.

Most likely she would have further disagreed with, and have wanted modified, a directive issued in mid-2000 by the Archbishop of Northern Ireland, who called for strict enforcement of the Church rule against eulogies at funeral Masses, saying they sometimes seriously distract from the sacred nature of the liturgy, and can occasionally be offensive to the congregation.

Sister Veronica was often reserved and restrained in her comments. Although, as she aged, she became more vocal, more wise and practical. Having taken the vow of obedience, she firmly believed in upholding church doctrine. Although she understood firsthand that the poor in spirit need gentle loving words and ministering to, as well.

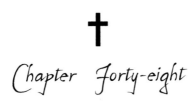

Chapter Forty-eight

"In the suffering and pain that come to us, we are not alone.
We are in the hands of our Almighty loving God."
— Providence 104:27

In 1990, when Father Mark invited Sister Veronica to serve as Pastoral Associate in New Almelo, she eagerly came on board, wanting to be part of the team. The offer and acceptance were made in good faith when she moved there. Yet for those next five years she was required to go before the parish council, defend her position and request an annual contract renewal — unlike her WaKeeney experience. This defensive posturing was humiliating, given her introverted personality.

Many times, throughout parish ministry, Sister Veronica was frustrated and had a sense of failure. There is an old Korean proverb: "After the mountain, more mountains." And so, she trekked on in determination. She knew that, oftentimes, one is motivated, not by results, but by love. This evangelical sense of mission, and spirit of gratuity — giving oneself without expecting returns over the years — was an ideal for her.

She said in March 1993, "Last night I asked the parish council to either offer me a contract, or not — whatever their wishes. They promptly asked me to leave the room, while they conducted an 'executive session.' I was feeling faint by the time they called me back — twenty-eight minutes later.

"I know there were some rumblings by two thirty-ish-year old guys. I felt I had to pull out of them why the conversation went on so long. When I asked what the lengthy discussion pointed out they said they want me to attend the children's CCD classes twice a month, be more visible, and make more home visits. One woman on the council said 'maybe I should be there for special friends.' That really turned me inside out. But I did not respond. She asked if I had enough to keep me busy, or if I wanted full-time. I'm sorry now that I didn't respond. Instead I only said, 'Extroversion drains me. I need other types of work to get recharged. I will be even less visible this year, and will stick to working half-time, and not bump my other commitments, like funeral ministry.'"

At one time her CSJ Leadership Team councilor, Sister Rosalyn Juenemann, told her, "You are too young not to be working full-time." Although her ministry in New Almelo was only part-time, she continued dietetic consulting with DSWK, writing grants, researching and writing parish history and compiling family genealogy. But she also updated her resume.

"I want to spend my golden years here, until I'm seventy-five. Like fine ivory and old lace, to appreciate, and be appreciated. I am still trembling about their offer, a contract on the same terms, with a budgeted pay raise of only $90 per year," Sister Veronica said after the meeting. "I accepted. Although, they did not want to sign the contract until the [bi-monthly] meeting in May. The next month, in April, I may consider an Open Forum at the next regular parish coffee. There was no affirmation at all. Nothing like, 'We want you.' There was just Jane trying to smooth things out." She would have liked the council members to recognize her contributions.

The following year after the Pastor had surgery, the parish council meetings were canceled for three months. After his recuperation, Sister Veronica asked what he thought about again asking the parish council to either offer her a contract, or let her move on to a full-time position somewhere else.

When she approached the parish council to renew her annual contract that year in 1994, she was told they would be looking for her replacement. "I asked if they could give me a clue as to why. Nobody wanted to say anything. Finally the one who teaches the confirmation class with me barked at the three young women on the newly formed search committee, 'Well, now is your chance to get it out of your craw. Tell her!'

"They want somebody to work with a children's choir. [They want to find a Sister] who is musical." This was never brought up as a requirement when she was first hired, since she made no claim to being musically talented. However, she tried her best to fill this void and readily admitted, "A parish will die in ten years without music.

"The second issue was they want somebody to plan activities for young adults." The ongoing complaint from teens and young adults, "there is nothing to do around here" is as old as man, and one middle-aged Nun was not going to be able to satisfy normal teenagers in either metropolitan or rural areas.

"And third, they want me to visit peoples' homes. Gosh, I initiate never-ending phone calls, and have been in eighty-five percent of the homes." She privately wondered, "If this was not enough, how much would be?" It was an invalid complaint.

"I said very little. I could tell there were sides in the room. 'We'll never get another like her. She's already working more than half-time. You don't know what she does,' pleaded one council member." In this light, it is puzzling how, in some areas, a few parishioners ignore the sobering reality of the dwindling number of Priests and Sisters, and the resulting ramifications.

"Meanwhile, the Priest closed the meeting and left [while I was waiting outside for the closed door discussion]. When I was invited back in, the gist of the conversation was that he was being transferred. I was mad at him all the next day for not telling me, or bothering to put it on the agenda.

"The next evening I called one of the members to thank her for her support, and I asked what the Pastor said about transferring. 'Just that this is his tenth year, which is the maximum for a Priest being in one parish. He said he couldn't do it without me, because of his illness, and they would never get another trained part-time minister here, and especially would not get another Sister.' So, I repented of being mad at him. I was glad I didn't call him to spout off. I resolved, again and again, to keep communications open." For the remainder of the year she felt appreciated by the Pastor, heard no more rumblings about the council replacing her, and was lulled into thinking all was okay.

In the meantime our brother, Allan, was diagnosed with cancer the fall of 1994, and died six weeks later. The year 1995 began on a sad note, and her final eleven months started off dismally.

In March 1995 she went to Concordia for a scheduled retreat. "Several Sisters informed me their convent houses received letters seeking my replacement." Sister Veronica had neither been given a chance to resign, nor had been directly asked for it by a certain date. She had been left hanging, and had no other job lined up. Justifiably, she felt used, and embarrassed in front of her CSJ Community.

"The search committee was appointed, over a year ago, to find replacements for all our parish jobs, and had not done their work. I took on the job as Director of Religious Education by default [when no one else would take it]."

The few members on the search committee failed to inform the parish council of their recent action. "I suspect they did not dream I would find out about the numerous phone calls and letters to more than a dozen parishes in the diocese."

A few days later, after returning home from Concordia, she said, "Only half the members were present at the parish council meeting. I asked for a report, and only one woman from the search committee was present. She was having a hard time saying that fourteen letters had been sent out. The parish council members were upset, too. The sad thing is the instigator announced in January she was moving from the parish in May. Her argument was to first see if there was anyone else was out there willing to take the job, then let me go."

All along she thought she would be informed how the search was going, and perhaps she would be consulted. And then she could plan accordingly. The episode, and the way it was handled, was degrading. "Even when I was Director of Religious Education, the first conference was held without me knowing about it."

In the cut-throat business world it is not altogether unusual for replacements to be found before an employee is let go, but in a proper setting of church ministry, this behind-the-back scenario, orchestrated by a vigilante committee, bothered her deeply. Furthermore, there were strong hints that a few powerful townspeople, who did not care for modern Nuns, used their considerable influence.

"I felt this committee member was the scapegoat, having no idea of the implication of advertising for a position that was still filled. I said something I learned at our family gathering at Rodney's house this January, when we were thinking of selling the family farm. 'When land is advertised for sale, and does not sell, its value goes down.'"

This was not a money issue, and while not wanting to focus on the economic aspect, she finally had to admit, "There is no one as stupid as me for taking less-paying jobs. Talk about being counter-cultural. I am happy to serve, at increasingly less pay, but not in the sense of being rejected for it." She learned the unkind lesson that many people place little or no value on what is done free of charge, or at a lower rate of pay than their own.

"It is ironic. I left Belvidere, in 1980, when I was making about $18,000 working at the hospital. Then I went back to school, got a Masters degree and afterward took seven jobs totaling about $15,000. Next, I took two ministry jobs totaling about $15,000. Later I earned an additional Bachelors degree in Ministry, and now get paid less than $10,000, counting the housing," she said when she still had both New Almelo and Logan parishes. In reality, she was living well below the national poverty level.

Other Sisters like her, who were young enough to work, were expected to earn their keep, and many were engaged in "grassroots" ministry throughout the country paving the way as pioneers. Throughout her career, Sister Veronica was overworked and underpaid, which is one of the major dilemmas of the vow of poverty. Many Sisters continue to face the harsh reality of their vows, yet the loss of "a living wage" is secondary in concern to a thankless ministry.

She suffered a most understandable time of weakness, in her resentment, at the rejection from those whom she wished to serve. Sister Veronica was a competent professional woman, exhibiting much initiative. She wanted some measure of gratitude, which she, like many other Sisters rarely received, since there is no longer the distinctive Habit to remind others of their benevolent positions.

She debated, in depth, the reasons for staying, or moving on. It was more like an examination of conscience. "While my vision of life is of pure service, I was rejected personally, professionally, and religiously as a gentle and trained woman. This fuzzy awareness of somebody's discontent with my service has pretty well cooked my desire to serve in parish life again, although I am good at many aspects of it. I could easily go back to dietetic work, but I will wait and look around first."

All too often little recognition is given to those who work hard using their talents trying to make life more pleasant, or more meaningful for others. She did not toot her own horn. If parishioners could not see the good work she did, day in and day out, she didn't think it was her place to shake them up, and ask for credit. Instead, she would endure by her example of living the life of a holy woman, in her ministry of presence.

Like the scriptural woman at the well, when she met people, she met them with humility and in service. A humble servant, as her vows demanded, she lived the "hidden life." It took a lot of humility and genuine love when results were repeatedly not attributed to her. Still, she lived by the maxims of her order. One of which was, "Follow through on good works that you undertake until they are almost completed and then, if it can be done conveniently, have someone else complete them and get the glory before others, and you will have greater glory before God."[1]

Father Duane said, "This aspect is essential in understanding Sister Veronica, and what was going on in her life. She made the option to treat people this way, as is very ingrained in the CSJ charisms."

She may have even been considered weak, ineffective, or even slow in getting things done by a few parishioners. There were times when she wrote along the lines, "We do a lot of things by committees — the arms by which we get things done — with some ownership. But the parish does not see me out front, and assume they can do without me. A few, that is. I realize it is my own style of ministry, to set up something, then let others get all the credit, but it is really starting to cost me the trust of those who welcome my presence."

"Catholics are used to being told what is right and wrong, of taking orders from the hierarchy," Father Duane continued. "As a modern woman, in the post Vatican II church, she developed a different manner of working with people. In her sensitivity to personal gifts and mannerisms of others, she was not one to tell people what to do. Instead she would invite others to work something through.

"Her style was to work herself out of a job — teaching others how to do the job so they would be more fulfilled in their personal journey. Instead of doing projects herself, and being acclaimed, she provided opportunity, and space for others to do things, and say their opinions. In rural pastoral ministries this approach is new to most people. The changing image of Sisters will be further enhanced as the natural God-given individual talents continue to emerge among the religious communities."

Upon her arrival, nearly five years earlier, the parishioners were jubilant and excited, and Sister Veronica felt embraced by them. The lesson of Jesus' arrival, when he miraculously feeds the multitudes, was not lost on her. Within a short time, the crowds turned away from Him. She, too, suffered at the hands of a few.

She admitted to being momentarily angry. However, righteous anger that promotes justice is not a sin. Nevertheless, she was careful not to put her anger onto another person. Most of all she felt misunderstood, which is not uncommon for a pioneering woman, much less a holy one.

Service was her calling, but pastoral ministry was dragging her down physically and emotionally. It is easy to blame a combination of trying too hard, expecting too much, and dealing with an unappreciative few who made this an uphill battle. But Sister Veronica was the first to admit that she brought on some of the conflict herself in her growing need for quietness, and lacking the desire to initiate conversation. She readily admitted her hearing loss increasingly aggravated relationships and her dislike of small talk was a distinct barrier to her ministry profession.

Sister Veronica came to those in need of spiritual aid; she instructed, advised, consoled, and comforted. There are those in life who do not appreciate gifts laid before them. As a Pastoral Associate, not everyone drank in her works with loving docility. When a supporter asked her why she did not reapply for the position she said, "This has been going on since I got here."

In the book, *Dakota*, Kathleen Norris writes, "Outsiders who leave such a town do so under a cloud…often they are turned into scapegoats by a group that can't face [their] own internal differences."[2] In reality, many unresolved conflicts have been festering for years — not just in this town, but many others like it. These conflicting occurrences weaken, rather than strengthen communal bonds, and it is the community that suffers the most.

She was especially pleased and fulfilled after she realized that, except for a very few, this parish did care and were appreciative of her presence. Family, friends and community were very important to her. She would not worry about a few who strong-armed their views on others. She was not going to track down those who wished to see her ousted.

"My expectations, of a parish growing spiritually, were in question." She jotted some recommendations for mutual healing, as she experienced the parish pulling apart. These included a preface of Reconciliation, "…that the parish have a night of community penance to bring its healing salve." Celebrated in the atmosphere of warmth and kindness, scriptural readings, homilies, psalms, hymns, and prayers constitute the ritual of community penance, and offer deliverance from emotional sicknesses, which hampers and weakens.

In 1996 Pope John Paul II said that while penance may seem like an outdated religious practice it is as necessary as ever. The penitential practice carries not only an individual, but also a communal obligation, and because sin has a social dimension, it is right that the remedy does as well. But the renewal of the community and reparation for its sins must begin with an individual examination of conscience and individual repentance.

This bickering within a church setting was not the first, nor would it be the last. The late Cardinal Bernardin, of Chicago, once wrote of how all Catholics should get along, and complained there was too much fragmentation among the laity. He recommended the faithful not spend so much time arguing about the particulars of the faith. "Unless we forgive, we will not be forgiven. Therefore, it is our Christian duty to forgive each other, and be charitable even when we disagree completely."[3]

Sister Veronica was tested to forgive, and bear wrongs patiently. She lived the gospel showing mercy that allowed her to forgive seventy-seven times and even seven times in the same day.[4] To a search committee member she gave the benefit of the doubt. "I gave her a formal announcement [of resignation]. I said something to her about being the scapegoat, with her name on the letter. She said she never wanted her name on it. She seemed aloof."

Rosalia Stephens, one of Sister Veronica's faithful supporters said, "I don't think life was always easy for Sister Veronica. She was very human in that aspect. She took a lot of knocks, but as a servant of God, she always carried on." Parishioner Betty Otter agreed, "I'm sure she had frustrations, but even when she was 'ousted' as she was, the hurt was in her eyes and not in her speech."

Another friend, Bernadine Diederich, confirmed the suspicion there were only three or four persons in the parish who resisted her work, and created difficulties. "We never did find out what [the issues] were. She had many friends throughout the community."

On the other hand Gertrude McNeive wrote, "We are not aware of any parish resistance. She didn't let it be known if there were any problems. I never saw her frustrated, even though I am sure she had many occasions to feel this emotion. I feel she was giving her very best."

In the days ahead she received acknowledgments, from her supporters, of what they called "a pink elephant — a badly handled mistake." She confided to at least ten parishioners, who were not on the grapevine, and asked them, in their view, "What happened?" They disapproved of the action taken. "We do not like this."

Given encouragement Sister Veronica jotted some shorthand notes to herself: "Clarify with the candidate whether they want to be either a social worker, or Pastoral Minister. Be accountable to the Pastor, rather than the parish council." In no particular order the list continued, of conditions on which she would stay, or which would help with her replacement hiring: "Reimburse for excess mileage. Provide a food allowance, and do not charge for food functions. Provide stipend for funeral planning. Give back pay for continuing education units not used. Continue to offer gratis tickets to visiting parish ministers. Acknowledge the person as a human, and invite to teas and card games, too. Suggest they belong to the Minister Alliance. Recognize that full-time status is five days a week. Assign the next Pastor with the new Pastoral Associate's knowledge. Allow an occasional Sunday homily. Hire a Director of Religious Education [aside from the Pastoral Associate]. Set aside one day a month to plan with the Pastor. Be made aware of CYO activities. Celebrate May 1st as St. Joseph the Worker Day."

After giving it much thought, she declined the offer to remain as the Pastoral Associate, even though a replacement had not been found after the clandestine search. Instead she drafted conditions of reinstatement as the parish secretary/bookkeeper, a job she enjoyed, and which had measurable results. "The secretary's calendar dictates working a predictable schedule of days and hours." But she stopped short, and never submitted her name for candidacy.

"During the week I was able to come to some peace about submitting my resignation as the Pastoral Associate. I was certain of letting go of the parish, so went through my closet and trimmed it in half."

She wrote her resignation to the parish council, effective the end of May. "Are you sure this is the right decision?" one parishioner telephoned her to say. He really felt bad and was not a part of the ousting, and wondered if there was any chance she would reconsider. He wanted to get a petition signed. There were other parishioners who wanted a petition to keep her, too. She declined. "No. I need to hear from people, not just a signature."

She considered the prior action improper and ungrateful. She was human. There was private complaint, but never rude and public railing. She occasionally got hung up in disappointment, and then she'd shake it off. Each time the demon of frustration returned.

As the French author Father Pierre Teilhard de Chardin experienced, "There were bitter tears, frequent bouts of depression, and obsessive worries that obeying orders do violence to truth and conscience." Like Teilhard de Chardin, she had her shadows; like him, at times, her spirits bordered on despair. And perhaps like him, she prayed not to die embittered. Like him, she stayed God's child of obedience.

Her CSJ Community took a stance on not letting violence, in any form, be a part of their lives, after "Violence to Self" was a topic of discussion at a Senate meeting in a prior year. She reported, "Most significant was our nearly unanimous corporate stand of our Community, and personal lives, as a Violence-Free-Zone."

After this experience she said, "Something is going on with interactions that is doing violence to who I am." In agreement with the CSJ Community stand on non-violence, Sister Veronica's decision to leave that position, in good conscience, was validated. Violence to the body is easier to see, but violence to the soul is even more damaging and lingering.

Many times over the years she felt lost and alone, but that is the way it is with pioneers. There is no standing still in holiness. Holiness does not mean one seldom fails, or never falls. Holiness is to allow God's grace to fill us with strength to get to our feet, knowing full well we will be knocked down again with injustices. Sister Veronica never stayed down for long, and never gave up hope. Christianity, after all, revolves around hope.

She knew where the truth lay; to serve others one must get up from the table. She knew that one doesn't change by feeling bad; one changes because one wants to grow. She recognized and converted the demon state of self-pity into a gift of the willingness to give and get help. "I am sure I will want to go back into counseling as part of getting stabilized again."

She followed in Christ's' footsteps during her trip to the Holy Land ten years earlier, when she walked the *Via Dolorosa*, the street of sorrows, retracing the Stations of the Cross. She continued to walk in His footsteps daily knowing that the devil (self will) tempts with power, pleasure and possessions. She rejected each one. Yet, she increasingly found parish ministry rejecting, oppressive and tiresome. Sister Doris Marie Flax said that it caused Sister Veronica great sorrow when her ministry was not accepted.

Knowing that demons hang on the shirttails of gifts and talents, she also knew it is sinful to bury one's talents, or to keep them unused. While she occasionally gave vent to bottled up frustration, she quickly rose above these human weaknesses and refused to dwell on them.

Sister Veronica lived by the creed, "Thy will be done." With her decision to move on, she turned the corner without bitterness, or anger. While staying true to her vows she found her voice, "I guess I am too hard on myself."

Her friend Rosalia Stephens confirmed this feeling, "I saw her very hurt when she decided to leave, but before she actually left she seemed at peace and ready to go. She was here at the right time."

✝

Chapter Forty-nine

As a professional nutritionist, Sister Veronica expected herself to eat better than she actually did, in consuming junk food occasionally. She delighted in eating favorite treats from childhood — popcorn and ice cream, especially the homemade variety. "I have sweets at the monthly Friendship Club, and on the road driving past an ice cream store, stopping twice a month."

Her Class C Kansas drivers license shows her weight at 130 pounds, in proportion to five feet, six inches, was within the normal range. However, she put on a few unwanted pounds after turning fifty years old. She knew that health comes from all things in moderation: rest, exercise and diet.

Father Duane recommended a self-purification diet. "I decided to do it this Holy Week. It is one-half cup lemon juice first thing in the morning. One-half cup water every half hour all of waking day. Nothing until noon, then only vegetable roots and leaves. A light supper. No snacking. My legs felt rubbery from lack of food, but it all passed quickly, and I felt fine until morning. Legs rubbery again. Sadly, I've only lost two pounds that I doubt will stay off."

The diet also suggested to cut back on meat, eliminate fats, sweets, soft drinks and caffeine. "I drink a whole pot of coffee throughout the day, but make it with one-half measure. I was interested to see if I was addicted. By 3 p.m. my head was in a vise for about five minutes, but not sure if it was from caffeine withdrawal, or lack of food. I use very little fat, except the best and more expensive canola and olive oils." Her cholesterol was often around 240 with elevated triglycerides, so she tried to maintain, "a very prudent, low-level cholesterol diet."

She wasn't neurotic about her health, although being in the health care field she visited her physician on a regular schedule. "I've been having my blood pressure checked and, strangely, half of the time it runs high." The doctor wanted her to take medication. Instead she told him she first wanted to "lose five pounds in six weeks, double my walking time, and relax more at home in the mornings, by not going to daily Mass one to two times a week."

She jogged regularly in her thirties, and at age forty-two ran a five-mile race, competing with about twenty others. She found it amusing to receive a medal as the first female over age thirty-five to complete the race, coming in third from last place. During that time she ran one and a half miles, three times a week. "My heart rate is still too high for so much running, but no problem."

As she aged into her fifties, she stopped jogging and was satisfied to walk, knowing the recommendation for that age group is at least twenty minutes, three times a week. "I've started walking fifteen minutes after our 8 a.m. Communion service."

Sister Veronica began to listen to her body's message, and only then did she seek answers to help her lead a more fulfilled and contented life. She learned that she had to care for her personal needs, although she was known to fall off the regime many times and procrastinated even more. She was conscious of staying in shape and admonished herself, "Now if I would only start walking again! But I am too tight to give up any free time away from writing [the genealogy book.]" She fought with the demon of time and, like many people, felt pressured to produce.

Over the years, taking walks didn't seem productive to her, even though she knew exercise is a powerful way to reduce stress. As a noted poet and essayist Kathleen Norris wrote, in *The Cloister Walk*, spiritual direction and walking are good for lifting despondency.

A difficult work environment in the 1980s led to despondency, which is known to bring on toxins to the body, and was at the core of her health problems. The long hours Sister Veronica put in her various parish ministries became a source of stress, too, and a detrimental health factor. "I will be taking a little more time off. I hope I don't spend the freed time just running around for the parish." In the winter of 1981 she wrote, "I feel fine, except for depressive type feelings related to popped ideals, and overextending my energy."

It became clear long after Vatican II, when discussions and readings were beginning to be encouraged, that she began to understand the connection between mind and body, and felt freer to write about how pressure affects both. As most women know, anxiety plays a big part in the regularity of the body. "I had sixty-seven points on a stress level questionnaire with sixty-plus being a candidate for heart attack. I am a sure candidate," she said, even though both parents and a brother died from cancer. "All this stress was enough to cause my [menstrual] cycle to go wacky, so I wouldn't be surprised if results of the biopsy are negative. But it could be caused by tumors, so we will see."

By then she was forty years old, and since Mother was still bearing children at this age, Sister Veronica thought herself a little too young for the "change of life." Later she wrote, "I made it through the biopsy just fine. No misery at all. Probably just an imbalance. I'll probably refuse any hormone medication for now, since it is not much of a problem."

Perhaps some people still regard Sisters as sexless and androgynous. Possibly it stems from the old days when they wore the shapeless Habits. Although even today, without the flowing black garb, few people acknowledge that Sisters have female bodies and emotions until they are shocked into reality when they hear on the news that a few Sisters get pregnant, have addictions, or are brutally raped in Africa, Central America, or even in the USA.

Celibate women have feminine bodies experiencing menstrual cycles and menopause. Many die of breast or uterine cancer. In general, human sexuality was neither discussed in convents, nor in homes across America, during the 1950s and early 60s. No doubt Sister Veronica was ignorant of her body then, as were her younger sisters, which was standard for that era.

So it was a huge step forward, within religious communities in the decades after Vatican II, when Sisters were beginning to hear lectures on sexuality, following the writings of Jung, and of how psychic energy can be transformed creatively. Kathleen Norris gives an excellent description of how celibate sexual energy is channeled into hospitality in the chapter, "Learning to Love: Benedictine Women on Celibacy and Relationship," in *The Cloister Walk*.

Years ago there was no forum for understanding sexual dynamics for any woman. Sisters, especially, had to figure it out for themselves, which usually manifested into intense prayer, plain hard work and long hours. In trying to understand the whirlwind pace Sister Veronica set up for herself, it is helpful to understand that the vow of chastity not only obliged her to renounce marriage and avoid everything forbidden by the sixth and ninth commandments,[1] this vow also required her to avoid idleness.

The Fourteenth *Maxim* focuses on the good use of time. "Take care to use time fruitfully; it is precious and its loss irreparable." Using time well not only forbade wasting time, it also required that actions be performed with faithful care. Being a pre-Vatican II Sister-in-Christ was to strive for perfection not only when others depended on her, but for her own work, as well. In short, avoid imperfection and give yourself over seriously and wholeheartedly.

Perfectionism, in the psychological sense, is a form of self-protection, and a way of trying to evade shortcomings by limiting attention to narrow areas of existence. In joining the religious life, Sister Veronica was no longer open to criticism. She constantly tried to meet and exceed her own expectations and high standards, by which she subconsciously perceived the world around her. Highly driven, she thought she was losing control if falling short of her own ideals. She lived with the day-to-day search for quality and carried an almost Victorian standard for adhering to self-imposed deadlines. She rarely took anything lightly.

She combined the maxims of zeal and good use of time. She was energetic, and began projects with enthusiasm and vigor. In contrast, interactions with people sapped her psychic energy. Many of her letters are peppered with examples: "I'm just plain tired from the busyness of the day...I get so drained in six days of people ministry...It tires me to be around lots of people for a long time. More so than the work itself...By 6 p.m. I'm exhausted from socializing." Referring to a letter from Father Duane she said, "Sure makes me tired to hear of all his doings, especially meetings.

"It seems I go about half the year, then collapse for several days...I slept for

36 hours — exhausted. Maybe a touch of flu, headache and achy legs. Felt privileged just to sleep...Had a severe cold the past week. Couldn't get the house warmed up the first day of below-zero degrees, so put sofa pillows on the floor in front of the furnace to sleep...Friday night I had a case of exhaustion, or more like craziness."

There were more instances: "I crashed this week, after going too much. I finally gave myself a permit to stop, and had a bad cold and fatigue. I slept three days and have some renewed energy again. The funny thing about all those things I had to get done hanging over me that were making me so tired — one by one they all got taken care of in between naps and it wasn't so bad after all. It all got done without any sweat. Felt like cheap therapy, whatever that is... Today is a lazy sort of day, mostly since my car is in the garage. So I am somewhat confined. Also, because I feel another collapse coming on from overwork. Every waking moment is loaded with things to be concerned about and mostly to do."

These times were just the permission she needed to take the rare time for herself. She had an inner drive of what she called, "non-stop running in circles," deciding what to do next. "I am keeping much too busy. As usual I have been burning the candle at both ends, and probably will collapse in several more weeks at this rate, but at least I recognize it." Women especially have difficultly doing one thing at a time and feel more in control and less anxious if more is done in less time.

Unfortunately, this cycle occurred numerous times, but in one particular letter she said, "I am working on the inner journey to renewal these days. I found a 14-day, self-guided book, *Burnout*, and cassettes to renew my energy." After short rests, she bounced back refreshed and ready to tackle the challenges ahead with renewed gusto. She showed amazing resilience.

Intellectually, she knew the danger and poisonous emotions brought on by overwork and under appreciation. The way she privately dealt with this made her all the more human. Her dark side was purged through letters, which were peppered with the negative, but these were her release — her outlet, and it becomes even clearer how therapeutic writing was for her. One can look at what she chose to write about in her everyday life, and it is obvious that her faith and both her CSJ and biological families were foremost on her list. Here her safety was guaranteed. There was no defensiveness. No distrust. No tiredness.

She was loving and very forgiving to family in their transgressions. Although when she was told at a celebration to "chill out," she was especially embarrassed and humiliated that even a family member found her stiff. Ethical and precise, she embodied integrity, politeness and formality. Taken to the extreme these honorable attributes can take the joy out of life.

Sister Veronica rarely relaxed, and it is well known that chronic leisure deprivation is damaging. It is clear she took on more work than her share. Rather than politely, calmly and respectfully saying "No," she took on "The More" of the CSJ charisms. Impelled with the words of St. Thomas Aquinas, "the more deeply a soul is drawn to God, the more it must go out into the world to carry the Divine Life into it." She pushed ahead, leaving precious little time for herself.

In CSJ Community Living one has to make time for others, and give other Sisters priority over tasks. Perhaps living alone, and not accountable to the routine of others, which would limit spending of herself, was the only way she could maintain a heavy workload. She repeatedly went into new situations with a sense of openness, but often burned out in the face of long, grueling hours. She lived a life of being busy to the point of discomfort.

She was also unable to laugh off conflict in the work or parish environment before it became resentment. Then she would repent and blame herself for her all-too-human pettiness when she found herself in annoying or offensive situations. "I am in perpetual motion and I don't like that. I think I am coming across as bossy, too harsh among parishioners and much too productivity oriented. I intend to take Fridays off, as well as the usual Saturdays. I already put in too much work for the parish."

Sister Veronica considered hard work a virtue. As Father Duane explained, "She embodied the American work ethic of her age, and the missionary spirit of the Roman Catholic Church of the 19th and 20th century. In her traditional spirituality she preferred to spend herself in work and service to others. However, rather than a virtue, this extreme became her 'sin,' with its negative consequences. It sometimes happens that those in religious life not comfortable with intimacy issues turn to an intense spiritual life. One doesn't substitute the other, however. True spirituality grows on the bases of human intimacy, social interaction and physical well-being."

The management consultant and columnist Bill Repp suggests that to release internal pressures from one's job, one must not suffer in silence.[2] This is something Sister Veronica did habitually in living the "hidden life." Repp's advice is applicable in one's personal life, too. Although, talking back was never tolerated during her childhood, or religious formation, either, for that matter. In taking the vow of obedience, one does not complain. At times she became emotionally rigid, not understanding how to redirect her feelings. Yet, she always came around, in her devotion to Christ, as she followed the advice of our aunt, Sister Rose Irma: "Offer your sufferings up to the Lord."

If there was one thing missing in Sister Veronica's life it was balance, the cornerstone of health. She repeatedly fell into temporary states of burn out. The columnist, Repp, also offers ways of managing personal and job stress to put one's life in better balance through redirecting and releasing pressure, and delegating. Sister Veronica found this difficult to implement.

Her CSJ Community held a two-part Wellness Retreat, in 1989, focusing on managing stress, so she knew intellectually what to do. Putting it into practice was another matter. Injured at work when she fell backward standing on a chair she admitted, "It's given me time to practice the management techniques of explaining to people instead of doing things myself. I missed one day of work and still couldn't slow down."

While she was gifted with high energy, which enabled her to accomplish so much, she could have used periodic breaks. Currently, there is a trend toward the energizing five-minute power nap, which helps one to relax and refocus. Perhaps this is how she was able to work for months on end with little sleep. It was not unusual for her to work until 2 a.m. and be up again at 5 a.m. when writing the genealogy books. She never complained about lack of sleep, although she could have benefited by slowing down, and relaxing with a massage, some form of exercise or with meditation and prayer. It is important to spend at least fifteen minutes alone each day in quiet and relaxation for well-being.

Her position did not allow the amount of quietude she sought. She enjoyed being alone, but sometimes spoke of being lonely. "I get energized being alone and having time for myself, but that has been very shallow. So I think I will take up walking again and maybe I can get some praying done then."

She admitted to going through spells when she did not take the time to pray and confessed to being "dried up." "I am in worse shape physically, mentally and in my prayer life than ever." It can also be a habit for some people to be just too busy to spend time to connect with other people. A 1,500-year-old doctrine of the Benedictine Monks is: "When one is too busy to pray, one is too busy."

Formation in the religious life was a lonely road before the Second Vatican Council. Deep personal friendships were not permitted in convents or, at best, discouraged. During that era, Sisters also faced detachment from their families. Aside from the absence of physical intimacy, tenderness and understanding also were missing in her life. And, no doubt, in the lives of countless other Sisters.

In 1975, when Sister Veronica made a directed retreat, she admitted to one again having a "loving relationship with Christ." Perhaps then she first understood it was also a sin against celibacy to not have affections at all, and that it was possible to love God, oneself and others, while keeping her vows intact.

In the 1980s, the pioneering CSJ Sisters of northwestern Kansas did attempt a stab at intimacy issues through support group meetings, at each other's homes, several times each year. Sister Veronica eagerly looked forward to these gatherings, and to each time it was her turn as hostess. While she was introverted and disliked small talk, this group of fellow Sisters were like family, as they shared common bonds and experiences. These were potluck gatherings, which many times went late into the night. Like teen-age slumber parties, these brought out the much-loved child in her. The women camped out in their sleeping bags stretched across the floor and conversations lasted until the last weary Sister faded — most likely Sister Veronica. While these gatherings were joyfully welcomed undoubtedly they were too infrequent, and not sufficiently in depth to drag up, and out, and unpeel layers from years past.

As a side note, a recent study based on the hormone, oxytocin, released during stress, shows that women react to stress differently than men, who tend to become aggressive. In contrast women respond by caring for children, or leaning on friends, which keep them calmer. However, since Sisters are seen to be "above it all" by others, typically they lack the outlet of "girl talk" and are not prone to pick up the telephone and chat when they have a bad day. Furthermore, sharing can be a painful process often bringing tears, just as unwrapping an onion, layer by layer, can bring an unwelcome sting to the eyes. But sharing has a healing component, too, like onions, and people with social networks tend to live longer and are healthier than those who are isolated.

On a rare occasion she pampered herself. "I've shared all the other candy and cookies but [kept your gift of the] toffees here for me. So special. Really trying to space them out as a reward for a day well done, and for being me. Thanks for your love in felt ways. Today is a gift, since I have been so stressed desiring some time for myself."

She began the solitary hobbies of collecting stamps and quilting for a while. But once she started writing two genealogy books, it was more like a second full-time job.

Another time she said, "I am still intent on modifying my activity to allow time just to appreciate the sitting." Hopeful that her schedule would calm down she said, "I hope to quit making such U-turns with most people, always having to be somewhere else more important. In that anticipated free time I trust I may grow more graceful like old ivory and old lace."

In Ann Beattie's book, *Where You'll Find Me*, is a paragraph perhaps Sister Veronica could have written about herself: "She was tired. It was as simple as that. This life, she loved so much, had been lived all along with the greatest effort." No doubt there was a rush of truth as she also read, "I was getting depressed this afternoon. When the light starts to sink so early, I never can figure out what I'm responding to. I gray over, like the afternoon, you know."

After Vatican II, Sister Veronica tried very hard, as well did many other Sisters, to listen to and share experiences with others, become softer, more human, and less austere and ascetic. Only in the last few years did she begin to scratch the surface, find her inner voice and articulate feelings.

Chapter Fifty

There are many assessment tools available for in-depth analysis including interviews, observations, personality tests, dream interpretations, free associations, creative products and self-reports. In 1983 Sister Veronica was eager to use some of these instruments to figure out what made her tick.

Among the various tests is the Guildford-Zimmerman Temperament Survey.[1] In this highly accurate profile Sister Veronica depicted her restraint level as quite high, and not at all spontaneous, yet she was not a compulsive, 'picture straightener' type personality, either. She liked to know what was going on, preferred a schedule to work around and enjoyed the planning process.

Having a higher than average energy level, she liked to keep busy, a trait the rest of her siblings also have. At her funeral vigil this writer eulogized her as, "a dynamo. Grass didn't grow under her feet." In a family situation she often assumed responsibility. Another epitaph that night was, "She was the family glue."

During childhood Sister Veronica's siblings saw her as a little bossy, as big sisters are prone to be. But later in life she seemed to have a fear of dominating, perhaps drummed out during religious formation. She was involved and seen as a leader, yet on the G-Z profile she described herself as "hesitant and, depending on the circumstances, satisfied to let others take the lead." She led by example. This was verified when she, among the group of six women elected to the CSJ Leadership Team in 1995, all considered themselves "gentle" leaders.

Adhering to her vows, Sister Veronica rarely challenged others out of respect for their opinion. She was especially fascinated with City Council debates that she attended for "extra involvement" in WaKeeney. "I like to watch how adults argue and discuss without getting upset." In a retail situation she was hesitant to demand an exchange, or a refund. She would not argue over prices, although she was a careful and frugal shopper.

Continuing on with the paper-and-pencil G-Z profile, she described her mood as prone to uncertainty and often in a state of anxiety. She did not make acquaintances easily and rarely chatted about things in general.

At about the same time, Sister Veronica completed the Strong-Campbell Interest Inventory, a career-counseling instrument that offered even more insight into her strengths and skills.[2] Not surprisingly, the results indicate she had a very high interest in religious activities, domestic arts and visual art. She also showed a very high interest in office practices, a strength she only came to honor in her last year of life.

Her high interest in writing was given wholehearted expression through letter writing to friends and family, press releases, and letters to the editor, as well as successfully compiling two family genealogy histories.

A farm girl at heart, her high interest in agriculture was applied by acquiring sustainable agriculture grants to assist local farmers around New Almelo.

It is curious to note her high interest in music and dramatics, two areas she did not fully develop, although in which she had a measure of success during high school years. Most surprisingly, she showed only an average interest in teaching and mathematics, which at one time were of great interest to her.

She also rated an average interest in mechanical activities, science, nature, social service, business management, athletics, sales and public speaking. Not surprising was the low interest shown in military activities, law and politics. She expressed the lowest interest in adventure. While she enjoyed hiking with her Sister-friends in the mountains of Colorado, adventure by this test's definition indicates she was not comfortable with dangerous or hazardous activity, and was not one to act sporadically or casually.

In the 1980s Religious Life began to explore the Enneagram to improve Community living and spiritual enrichment. At one time, church leaders considered this testing tool no more than witchcraft.[3] However, today it is used in retreats, workshop and renewal programs as a tool for self-understanding and personal growth. This ancient system of typing personalities into nine categories became widely used in the business world to improve human relations. Sister Veronica was exposed to the Enneagram in Catholic workshops. It is unknown what her type was.

Her CSJ Community made available to all Sisters, that same year, a six-day summer retreat called, "Personhood," based on the Meyers-Briggs test and its combination of sixteen Jungian personality types: Introversion vs. Extroversion, Sensing vs. Intuition, Thinking vs. Feeling, and Perceiving vs. Judging. Not surprisingly, Sister Veronica came away with a label of "Idealistic," and a profile of INFP — Introverted, Intuitive, Feeling and Perceiving. "I am a rare creature. One percent of the population." Simply by being in this atypical category distanced her from others.

"A large percentage of folks get their information from their sixth sense — intuition. The 'P' prefers to perceive more information instead of wanting to make a judgment, with the facts or data one has," she shared in a letter. "I can see where my 'T' [thinking] shadow is getting stretched and used more. Although my strongest function is 'F' [feeling]. People don't know that because I keep my favorite [strength] to run my favorite world — my inner world. So I usually appear to the outer world as unfeeling. A large number of people also process their information with feelings rather than their heads (like I do, also.) So what is going on can still be detected, somewhat, but of course only we know our own motives and desires. Are you still there?" she joked.

"Extroverts prefer to function in an outer world of people and things. Introverts, like me, have a preference for the inner world of concepts and ideas," she said.

Some introverts are timid, reserved and find it hard to overcome self-consciousness and initiate personal relations with others. There were many times when Sister Veronica felt alienated, different from others and not widely accepted. Not a good mixer, she realized that she was often not "with it." She wanted relationships, but admitted to not knowing how to develop them.

The writings of Jung describe the introvert attitude in *Basic Writings in the History of Psychology*: "Aloof, the introvert does not join in and has a distinct dislike of being among too many people. Crowds, majority views, public opinion or popular enthusiasm never convinced them of anything."

As a well-educated woman, she wanted to legitimize actions with the right way to do things. She ended up second-guessing herself rather than following her intuition, another one of her untapped strengths, which would have helped her to relax and go with the flow. Furthermore, she was an intellectual introvert. It was harder for her to relax and have a casual lunch with new acquaintances, for example, than to follow the lofty theological writings in Timothy E. O'Connell's, *Principles for a Catholic Morality*.

She found the retreat helpful and went on to offer the Meyers-Briggs test to individuals and couples as part of her pastoral ministry. "I really enjoy working with the [Jungian types of the test] because these are an indicator of preferences, which shows up very much in meetings. It sure helps understand people and their problems in life, after which comes accepting, and then loving them.

"By time a person is fifty years old they have automatically developed more skill in using all the functions, with the forties being the time when the shadow side is emerging. This is why [most] older people are mellow," she said.

An interpretation of the INFP type can be found on the Meyers-Briggs Internet website, and in the description general fit her: "Some have a gift for taking technical information and putting it into laymen's terms. They never seem to lose their sense of wonder. One might say they see life through rose-colored glasses...Of course, not all of life is rosy, and the INFP type is not exempt from the same disappointments, and frustrations common to humanity. INFPs struggle with the issue of their own ethical perfection, e.g., performance of duty for the greater cause. The inner conflict is not as good versus bad, but on a grander scale, good versus evil. Although the dark side must be reckoned with, the INFP type believes that good ultimately triumphs. This type has the ability to see the good in almost anyone or anything. Even for the most unlovable the INFP is wont to have pity. Their extreme depth of feeling is often hidden, even from themselves, until circumstances evoke an impassioned response."[4]

Appearing awkward and inhibited at times, introverts are often misunderstood because they keep their better qualities to themselves, as even she admitted. They also keep difficulties and conflicts to themselves, too. It was only in her letters that these were disclosed. She did admit to being envious when a Priest was routinely invited to Sunday dinners, and she was not. Introversion oftentimes manifests itself in feelings of inferiority, which can lead to resentment. She was first and foremost a Sister-in-Christ and although trying to temper her weaknesses, such as envy, she was only human.

✝

Chapter Fifty-one

In 1993 Sister Veronica took a hard look at herself, admitted to being physically and emotionally fatigued and recognized that other issues needed to be faced, too. She was especially frightened when a Sister who had recently left a different convent took a fatal overdose of pills. Perhaps it was because Sister Veronica tried to reach out beforehand to this woman in despair, but could not locate her in time that she, herself, realized she needed help, too, and began looking for answers.

In the years prior, psychological writings caught her attention. She began taking classes and reading works of Rogers, May, Kelly, Skinner, Freud and especially Jung, which blended the psychological and spiritual, such as in Jean Gill's *Images of My Self: Meditation and Self Exploration Through the Jungian Imagery of the Gospels*.

Sisters have their public persona to protect, just as laypersons do. Yet, in her maturity, Sister Veronica realized the need for professional therapeutic counseling to overcome the painful discrepancy between how she would like to feel about herself, and how she actually felt.

Psychological counseling, when used well, offers greater self understanding, removes obstacles to spiritual growth, facilitates responsible decisions and leads to a fuller Christian maturity. From the Greek root *psuch_*, (soul) + logos (discourse), psychology is defined as the study of the soul.[1] Psychoanalysis, as most commonly taught and practiced in the pre-Vatican II era, especially the pansexualism of Freudian (Sigmund Freud) psychoanalyses, was incompatible with Catholic teaching, since it is based on a philosophy of materialism and hedonism. After the Second Vatican Council psychological counseling became more acceptable to Catholics. Most still follow Jungian (Carl Gustave Jung) writings, which are not as much in conflict.

Seeking professional assistance is not an admission of weakness. Rather, it is a demonstration of self-love, strength and wanting to move forward with a feeling of wholeness. Sister Veronica was at a developmental stage in life ready to search the deeply ingrained part of her Self. It was a major step for her to seek mental health therapy to determine, "Why do I choke up at times? What hinders my freedom of expression?

"I began counseling at the [branch office of the Midland] Mental Health Clinic regarding my own quietness problem. I feel it is getting worse. I chose the clinic at Colby [located on Interstate 70] as an excuse to also do some shopping in the 'big' town. My counselor, Louise, about fifty years old, ended the session by saying, 'Oh, you are just above everyone else.' I guess she meant that I am a Nun. I deliberately left off any reference of being a Religious, on my personal history form, so she would treat me as a human being."[2]

Sister Veronica's first appointment, earlier that year, was postponed. The county sheriff's department reported drifting snow, which closed highways. "Louise called my office to reschedule and I answered the telephone, 'Sister Veronica,' so she keeps bringing up how we are not like we used to be."

Sisters are not like they used to be; that is true. Nevertheless, images of typical Sisters are still idealized, and held to a high standard. Rejecting any nonsense of being a saint, she was annoyed at those who wanted to put all Religious Women on a pedestal. She rightfully complained, "Most folks don't know what we are about."

She also repeatedly felt it a personal challenge to help middle-age adults overcome the nagging image of ruler-wielding mean-spirited Nuns of yester-year. Those intimidating, strict enforcers were no less confused, thinking they were doing the right thing by closing down their feelings.

Sister Veronica was never mean-spirited, nor did she ever want to be stigmatized this way. A negative description often linked with Sisters calls to mind one who is dowdy, submissive, meek and docile. While Sister Veronica presented herself as professionally dressed and groomed, on occasion she surprised her family by wearing stylish bright colors, of red and orange, that she once found garish. She was finding her style of dress as an outward expression

It is not unusual to hear whispers behind Sisters' backs, as they are seen about town in everyday clothes and conducting business as professionals, "She doesn't look like a Nun," which pleased her. Sister Veronica lived a dichotomy that few people can grasp, in wanting to be fully accepted as one who gave her full and undivided attention to living "The More" of the CSJ charism. All the while she wanted to be valued as a solid citizen and leader in the parish and community. She strictly adhered to her vows of poverty, obedience, and chastity, a life few people understood, and which never allowed for material rewards, emotional selfishness or assertiveness. Many knew her to be an introvert, intuitive and reflective. Some called her a mystic. Clearly, she was intense and intelligent. She was also an over-achieving perfectionist, which intensified her proneness to anxiety. She just wanted to project herself as a normal woman.

Surely the counselor in Colby was well meaning. Nevertheless, she failed to see Sister Veronica as an ordinary woman in need. Furthermore, the counselor was probably not equipped to deal with the lonely journey and unique complexities required of a Woman Religious, especially one living alone.

Full of hope and not yet aware of predictable life cycles, she attended a district dietetic meeting fourteen years earlier, in 1979, where a colleague asked her how things were going. "I sincerely said, 'Great! I really feel on top of the world. Everything is under control.' I was enthusiastic, having faith and courage to change things, and eager for challenges. The colleague laughed and said, 'You must be forty years old.' Sure enough, I had just turned forty. How did she know?

"After my 'Mid-life' retreat, I could see a pattern of letting go of youth and dreams, and readjusting values, all the while appreciating the tugs of male versus female, creativity versus tension. I felt noncommittal and wishy-washy in areas I was headstrong at forty-one, when arriving at the WaKeeney hospital and parish in 1981. There is not too much really important anymore," she admitted. "Today, I wouldn't even honestly answer, 'How are things going?' to most people, as things are heavy. I am out of control. I have hardly been able to measure success anywhere. Sure sign of burnout."

Not unlike most people, Sister Veronica had many crosses to bear, including a disrespectful superior at one job, and rude employees at another. There were offensive comments from parishioners, too, which made her feel unwelcome. One hostile parishioner went so far as to ask her whether she knew a Sister, in the news, who got pregnant. She quietly confided in another letter, "I heard last week from a mother that I am to blame because her daughter, and another topnotch girl of the parish, did not get last year's parish scholarships, even though I was only one among seven on the committee."

One time Sister Veronica was directly insulted, at the beginning of Mass, by an insensitive Priest, formed in the pre-Vatican II era and who did not like self-assured Sisters out of their Habits and claiming their rightful space in the Church. She worked with another who made life more difficult because of his poor communication skills and exclusionary attitude.

She wrote after her second counseling session, "I don't feel Louise is using skills I thought were needed." She questioned whether the therapist was Freudian and was informed of an eclectic approach. The third session was also less than satisfying. "I need to take hold and tell my counselor her approach is not what I want from these visits, which is to get in touch with what hinders my freedom of expression and why I don't enjoy small talk. My counselor does not pick up on past history, or anything I think is important to talk about, especially when I choke up. She keeps saying, 'Get out of the work you are doing so you don't have to talk to people so much.' I keep saying, 'I had this problem in high school and before having a job. I cannot run from problems.'"

One might argue that her busy youthful schedule, with school, church and 4-H activities, kept her connected to people. Although as a simple farm girl, she related only superficially during activities and was intimate with no one. Even as a teenager, she felt uneasy with other youth her age, "What would we talk about? What would I say?" Later she admitted that being in the kitchen with our mother, or washing and drying dishes with her sisters, was a time when she had the most relaxing and fulfilling conversations. A desire to return to this scenario continued throughout her life. Here she could be herself, not tense or rehearsed. Long car rides with one other person prompted conversation, too.

On the other hand when a niece, in her twenties, chose to ride with her boyfriend, instead of her mother, when they were both going to the same destination three hundred miles away Sister Veronica could not understand why her niece would want to do this. The excitement of the dating stage escaped her. She never experienced what it was like to be "boy crazy." She grew up in a world of innocence. Having a sheltered youth, she did not date in high school or wear make-up. Obedient, when most teens were rebellious, she was a model of good behavior looking up to our parents for direction. She was every parent's dream-daughter, truly living the adolescence of a virgin saint.

While she was a bright girl in high school, Ila Mae felt tongue-tied and slow, and did not relate well to others. "I prayed as a teenager for lockjaw so I'd be spared small talk, which continues to come rather labored and veneered. I stutter in my haste to get something out before others cut me off. My speech continues to be icy and choppy, yet drawn out with incomplete sentences because I expect others will finish the sentence. I try so hard at communication, although I do yield to the niceties of social conversation in my mature years. There are a few persons with whom I delight to chitchat, so it is not impossible," she shared in her Life Review. However, she especially detested talk of the weather, as a substitute for genuine conversation.

She could have used the help of books with titles like, *How To Talk With Practically Anybody About Practically Anything*, or *The Art of Conversation*.[3] The fear of meeting new people, and not knowing what to say, is very common. Even Katharine Graham, the late icon of the Washington Post, was known to say of black-tie Washington dinners, "I hate those things. I never know what to say to anyone."[4] This is why letter writing was so important to Sister Veronica. One Christmas season she said," I used up 410 postage stamps. This is my way of extroverting."

The counselor pointed to symptoms of social phobia/social anxiety, the third most common psychological problem in the United States today. However, a retired psychiatric nurse offered her own opinion that it was unlikely Sister Veronica's diagnosis was completely accurate: "I don't see strong evidence of a social phobia. Those I've seen could not have had her accomplishments without much more treatment."[5] It is the opinion of this writer that the diagnosis was partially correct, but to a mild degree because, in extreme cases, some people have not left the safety of their home in years.

In all fairness to the small town counselor, who held a professional degree of M.A. R.M.L.P.,[6] identifying social phobia may have been a breakthrough into Sister Veronica's lifelong anxiety. Yet this "social phobia" may be a catch-all and trendy phrase, since it is misdiagnosed almost ninety percent of the time. The first book specifically dealing with this issue was published in the early 1990s, just before the diagnosis.

Shyness, anxiety and social phobia are all distinct diagnoses. It is most likely Sister Veronica had threads of them woven together. Self admittedly she was shy, but this condition is a personality trait often mistaken for social phobia. On one occasion she remarked that she thought a Pastor was "much more shy then she ever was."

One co-worker believed Sister Veronica was, "a little shy and did not seem relaxed when speaking to an audience." This is normal. Public speaking is the number one fear of most people. Nevertheless, she forced herself to meet the challenge, coped very well in this area and served on CSJ Community committees. A therapeutic forced exposure, a type of desensitizing, is highly successful in bringing about a comfort level in public. She found a margin of success in presenting workshops during 1980-1990, and giving slide presentations following her Holy Land trip. She looked forward to delivering occasional homilies at Mass and was competent in organizing presentations for groups. In general, her profession helped her. As a consultant, people had to come to her. There was not the need to take the initiative in reaching out to others, except in her pastoral work.

A study in 1998 suggests that the stress hormone, cortisol, can hinder memory. It is assumed that Sister Veronica was not a stressed test taker, as a student, but admittedly she overly prepared for college exams and later in life for meetings. However, it was not unusual for her to return home from business meetings in a frustrated state. She was trained from childhood, and in religious formation, to not interrupt when others were speaking and she was rarely able to "jump in" at the right time.

She could have benefited from anxiety management training, relaxation and deep breathing techniques and social rehearsing/social skills training. Sufferers of social phobia are easily overwhelmed, and often keep their eyes away from anyone else's gaze. Likewise, Sister Veronica withheld eye contact, finding it uncomfortable if held too steady by herself or the other. It is uncanny how she took in as much as she did because, "she did not look at people directly when speaking," as Louise pointed out to her.

"My Counselor offered one piece of advice, 'Look at people all the time while communicating with them.' I said, 'I thought that was abnormal — more like staring at people. Being an introvert, I need to glance down to think. I already work hard at that. I get recharged by looking away and within.' Louise said she could tell it did not come natural."

Our sister, Cheryl, noted, "She did look away. I do, too," attributing it to hearing loss and as a way to process thoughts. Father Duane added, "Looking at people is not staring; it is a type of intimacy. I think Veronica did not feel comfortable with this intimacy, and avoided it. Eye contact is openness, and looking is communication — entering into communion with others. In my opinion this is not so much cultural, as psychological."

Furthermore, those with social phobia have racing thoughts, their face turns red, facial muscles freeze and they are unable to fully smile, they get a lump in the throat, they stammer and hesitate, and their voices quiver and sound scared. Sister Veronica did not appear to sound scared or tentative when she spoke with family members, although she did have a habit of yawning before speaking, which helps voice resonance, but this may have seemed like an odd behavior to others.

In her younger days throughout college and early convent years, Sister Veronica admitted to being anxious about failure, incompetence or giving herself away by not knowing answers. The feeling from childhood, of having nothing to contribute to a conversation, continued into adulthood. She persisted in writing lists of topics to talk about, a technique she admitted to in the early convent days. Unlike Mother, who was spontaneous and had a gift of gab in social situations, Sister Veronica felt artificial when engaged in small talk.[7] She felt an increasing discomfort, which she feared was a barrier to ministry.

"My counselor recommended the book, *Too Good For Her Own Good*.[8] I tried to journal some thoughts while reading it," as was requested of her. "The book is helpful, but emphasizes too much that only little girls are expected to be nice. I felt the boys in our family were also taught not to talk back, not to argue, not to be loud and not to fight or be pushy. Be nice. All the siblings were good and very quiet. I told my counselor, 'Our family had the same rules for both boys and girls.'" Sister Veronica, and her siblings, grew up with the adage, "Don't cause trouble. Don't make waves."

She described her early family life as very happy. Nevertheless, like many little girls of that era she learned to deny anger, and certainly not express it. Furthermore, the book suggests when females take too much pride in being good, they are deeply offended by feedback of being less than perfect, and want others to maintain the image they see of themselves. Women, who deprive themselves of knowing and accepting their true feelings, are incapable of being a 'little bit bad.' For years Sister Veronica repressed frustrations and had difficulty expressing long-hidden emotions.

Even if Sister Veronica was aware that, at times, it is healthy to express anger, it is doubtful that she would, fearing she would not only be labeled selfish, but that she would actually become self-centered, which is contrary to all that a Sister-in-Christ stands for. Religious women, especially, are sensitive to how they are perceived and what is said about them.

It tends to be most problematic for women raised in the 1950s to be assertive. She confided that she even drank her coffee black so as not to pose a problem in requesting the need for cream or sugar. She did not want to inconvenience others.[9]

According to the above referenced book, when girls are ruled by the Goodness Code (be attractive, be a lady, be unselfish, be of service, make relationships work, be competent without complaint) they lose the capacity to choose. They become driven by the need for approval and by fear of being powerless to get it. "Our life is taken over by basic female shame and we become too good for our own good," say the authors Bepko and Krestan.

Specifically the book is recommended to improve self-esteem and assertiveness. The contents also discuss anger, guilt, anxiety, humiliation and depression. These feelings occur when one fails to meet other people's demands or one's own unrealistic expectations. Perhaps she was looking inward when she wrote, "Depression…and we know that comes from repressed anger…It is not easy to be so far away from family, from support systems, even for the sake of the Kingdom."

One of the ways to make a distinction between conflicting boundaries and the way people define and assert who they are is by expressing anger. This right to assert boundaries is conventionally denied to women, in general. Molded into kindness and tolerance, and as a good and responsible person, Sister Veronica felt she must maintain control at all times, and at all costs. However, confrontation is inevitable; otherwise, conflicts cannot be resolved. Even the Bible speaks of righteous anger, fraternal confrontation and correction.

During 1979 Sister Veronica said to Father Duane, "Linda and I talked about why three daughters in our family married [the first time around to men unlike our father] when it is said that girls tend to marry men like their father. Even myself, I have two rather aggressive friends, but I can surely see from my perch that I wouldn't be happy with either one of them for long, either. So you can use that statistic in your marriage counseling."

Businesswomen were beginning to apply assertive techniques outlined in the 1970 book, *Stand Up, Speak out, Talk Back!* by Alberti and Emmons, and in Robert Ringer's trendy 1977s book, *Looking out for Number One*. The Sisters made an attempt with transactional analysis (TA) in the 1970s. But it wasn't until the 1980s when CSJ Sisters began to receive training in healthy conflict resolution techniques themselves, and began to accept that it is self-destructive not to assert oneself in legitimate ways. On the agenda for discussion during at least one CSJ Senate meeting was the issue that not speaking up for oneself permits violence to self-esteem. The Sisters took a CSJ corporate stand that violence, of any type, is unacceptable especially any form of abuse that causes one to suffer emotionally. Nevertheless, Sisters feel the push and pull of the dilemma of conflicting ideals. Knowing what one should do, and doing it, are two different things.

Sister Elizabeth A. Johnson, CSJ, Fordham professor and former president of Catholic Theological Society of America, wrote the 1993 prize-winning book, *She Who Is: The Mystery of God in Feminist Theological Discourse*. Sister Elizabeth suggests we invite the Blessed Virgin Mary to come down from the pedestal, where she has been honored in the past, and rejoin us on the ground in the community of grace in history. Sister Elizabeth says that viewing Mary in her actual historical setting, likewise our foremother Miriam as a Jewish village woman of faith, makes them both sisters to the unchronicled lives of marginalized women in oppressive situations everywhere.

In contrast, Pope John Paul II, as the most widely heard proponent of the view of Mary as the model of the feminine ideal for all women, emphasizes gentleness and a nonassertive attitude, which Sister Elizabeth believes blocks the personal development of women, and can even be dangerous by inculcating passivity in abusive and violent situations.[10]

"What is going on in me? I don't have it," wrote Sister Veronica. "Needless to say, I have tapes playing in my head about my inadequacies, which were the cause of seeking mental health counseling a year ago over this nebulous rejection in Logan, but which I quit because the counselor said, 'Get out of the type of work you are in.' Then, I was angry with the retreat director last June who told me nine directives, one of which was also to get out of New Almelo."

Within the *Maxims of Perfection* chapter titled, "Charity toward the Neighbor," an excerpt states: "Loving the neighbor as yourself with a pure and constant love; patient, beneficent and totally obliging, bearing no trace of bitterness or animosity, of unfavorable or rash judgments, of detraction or the least sign of coldness and of words or gestures in the least way offensive; forgive all injuries; gladly please as far as possible those who offend you and who displease you the most; interpret all things kindly; always prefer the contentment of others to your own; if you have difficulty submitting to the will of others and overcoming your reasonable wishes to follow their whims, in no way let your difficulty become apparent…"[11]

Sister Veronica wasn't getting the answers she needed and came to her own conclusion for her quietness problem. "I told my counselor that Mother said she feared my birth from the time of conception and having another cranky crybaby, like Allan, born two years earlier. I am convinced I knew this from the womb. So I set out in life to be good, to entertain myself. I was no bother to anyone. I was a good baby. This was such a relief to Mother, although I was not affectionate to Mother, and I didn't need anybody else either.

"I said to my counselor, 'Don't infants pick up those feelings? I am convinced they do, even in the womb,'" she repeated. "Louise did not even acknowledge I said that." According to Evelyn Bassoff, a Boulder, Colorado clinical psychologist and regular columnist for *Parents* Magazine, "Even before birth a mother's voice has extraordinary power and her words are set forever in a child's heart."

Allan weighed only nineteen pounds at age two, when an average weight is twenty-seven pounds. Mother did not breast-feed any of her babies, and Mother suspected Allan suffered intolerance to cow's milk. In addition, Allan may have had other childhood food allergies. It is probable that neither mother, nor the rural doctor, had ever heard about food allergies in the late 1930s. Allan was a picky eater and it is also possible he was hypersensitive to his surroundings, which is a relatively new study in children. In a family of docile and passive children, his irritable moods were hard to understand. He had nagging headaches from childhood, some hearing loss and did not do well in school. Mother indicated he was the most challenging. Yet as an adult, he expressed his wish that life were as simple as his childhood growing up on the farm.

Even five years before seeking counseling Sister Veronica wrote, "I always ache so much for [a sibling, divorced and alone]. It kind of goes back to when we were kids. My sister was always getting the scolding and I was always the perfect child. I hated myself for that." Typically, siblings have their own way of coping with the presence of a difficult child. Stanley Turecki, M.D. shows in *The Difficult Child*, that such a perfect child, like Ila Mae was, needs to be released from the position of family saint. If the child gets too involved in that role there can be trouble later on.

In contrast to her own perfect childhood behavior, one great-nephew, who was in a constant state of irritability since infancy, had daily outbursts of rage from an early-onset rapid-cycling bi-polar disorder, which was not diagnosed until age nine.[12] Sister Veronica was compassionate about raising a troubled and difficult child, and she was more accepting and insightful than most about the long and trying path of this adopted toddler's journey. She was well read, sensitive to the issue and non-judgmentally listened to what the parents had to say.

When Sister Veronica was a child, sixty years ago in the 1940s, not much thought was given to a child's psychological make-up. Yet, both she and this young boy experienced significant losses — her loss of a beloved brother when she was three and a half, and his from leaving his birthmother and being adopted at age fourteen months. Initially, thinking the boy's diagnosis was Attachment Disorder, she said, "Now that it has a name, I can see a lot of the problems in myself, especially my first thirty-three years. The whole element, in most of us, of being out of control is mystifying. Some of the socially unacceptable [behaviors, like anger] we are aware of, we try to keep under control. So I pay $78 a visit to talk to a counselor about that. Being conscious of something is the first step in control, we counsel adults in the spiritual life. So what is the connection for a child? No doubt, [the by now three-year-old great-nephew] has his way of trying to communicate some of what is going on within him."

Identities are strongly developed during childhood years, according to the generational values author Dr. Morris Massey. He claims that individuals are programmed from birth to approximately twenty years of age.[13] Unless a significant emotional event comes along, one will most likely continue on with the same attitudes developed while still living within the family.

Dipping into Sister Veronica's earliest childhood recollection, the loss of her beloved eight-year-old brother by accidental drowning was her first experience with the mystery of death. As a young child, this significant event was beyond her comprehension. In a state of helplessness, she witnessed pain all around her, something that would not go away. Such a childhood trauma can trigger fear-terror emotions, as intense as an infant's abandonment anxiety.[14]

It is probably out of genuine concern that our parents sheltered the children from their own grief for many reasons; among which was that death was a topic to be avoided in the 1940s. In addition to the lack of honest answers, there was most likely little physical contact, in the way of hand-holding and hugging, from our grief-stricken Mother because, in addition to Ila Mae, she had a two-year-old, and a toddler to care for, as well as a six-year-old and ten-year-old, who needed her, also. There were too many to comfort. Furthermore, social norms of the day did not encourage this.

Rabbi Earl Grollman says that when he was still writing the book, *Explaining Death to Children*, in the late 1950s, it was taboo to talk about death, as if it would magically disappear if not discussed. Now he says that silence and secrecy heightens the sense of isolation, and deprives children of an important opportunity to share grief. "Good mental health is not the denial of tragedy, but the frank acknowledgement of painful separation."[15] Each time the child talks about the death, the loss becomes a little more bearable, but this did not happen in our family.

When a child gets to be eight, nine or ten years old, and abstract thinking sets in, he or she can look toward the future. With each physical, emotional and spiritual developmental stage, children go back and review that loss. Most who are in the seven-year-old age group think death is a temporary state, and that the dead have feelings and biological functions, according to Dr. Alan Wolfelt, in his book *Helping Children Cope with Grief*.[16] When they finally do understand, a feeling of loss of control sets in as they realize that nothing one says or does can undo the loss. It is typical for children in the three-to-five-year-old age group to think death is reversible. They associate death with sleep or a journey. It is reasonable to assume Ila Mae and her siblings were told, "Ronald has gone to Heaven to be with God."

According to Allen Cunningham, director of *Tu Nidito* — "Your Little Nest," which joined forces in 2000 with Children-to-Children, a grief counseling program in Tucson, Arizona,[17] "A four-year-old is self-centered, has guilt associations and magical thinking, too. It is typical for people to think four-year-olds don't have feelings, and will forget or get over a loss. On the contrary, it is very common that the loss young children experience, like the death of someone very chose to them, can change their life forever. This loss is analogous to having an elephant in the room. The family may never talk about it, but it takes a lot of energy to ignore its presence. The child then imagines the worst, and insecurity issues arise. A drowning, itself, also has a trauma to it. Since these feelings were never dealt with, and the loss was never discussed for fear that it would stir up feelings that were too painful, that added to the anxiety, too." said Cunningham. [18]

The worst pain for any parent is the loss of a child. It is also an immense trauma for siblings. Due to the sudden nature of Ronald's death, there was a great deal of general upheaval in the home, and there were many saddened visitors filing in and out, which added undue distress.

Boys typically express grief through anger and rage, while girls turn the primary feelings inward, and depression is a result. Unfortunately, some children are taught that "to be good" means one never expresses anger regardless of circumstances.[19] Crying and talking are natural releases, but Ila Mae believed she was already programmed not to be a crybaby from birth. This frightening and explosive dimension of Ila Mae's grief was not given an outlet. It is apparent she suppressed feelings, and on an emotional level never fully reconciled with her brother's death.

There is a phenomenon where surviving children are afraid to smile and have fun. Furthermore, the "empty space" occurrence written about in the book, *Children Mourning, Mourning Children*, was most likely a very real occurrence in our family, even though four more children were later born. When a significantly loved person and playmate creates this empty space, the way Ronald's death affected the adoring Ila Mae, the loss intensifies to an even deeper level.

It is typical for children to feel the deceased has abandoned them. This kind of thinking often leads children to reject others for fear of being abandoned again themselves. Sister Veronica admitted that as a child she unconsciously isolated herself, not needing others and cut herself off from the possibility of affection from others who might leave her. On the other hand, in her insecurity, she wanted to be with Mother more, rather then playing alongside siblings or friends, which continued throughout her teenage years.

Experiencing a traumatic event may lead to recurring feelings of anxiety, and a sense of threat and alertness based on insecurity which makes one feel the worst is about to occur.[20] Based in fear, this condition of anxiety is possibly a part of our *primordial soup*, a dread that cannot be explained, and a signal that harmony is missing. It was that mysterious condition whose ancient origins are as old as man, which seemed to cause Sister Veronica the most aggravation in adulthood.

Yet this was a farm family that had to get on with life for survival, and this was a place where children frequently saw death in chickens and livestock, cats and dogs. Moreover, the family held a strong faith and belief in the full circle of life, which includes death.

Mother experienced significant loss, too, in the death of her own mother, when she was little more than three years old. She was fifteen when she lost her father, and the accidental death of her beloved older brother when she was sixteen was especially difficult. Not to diminish her sorrow, Mother was an extrovert, who feely interacted with others.

After Sister Veronica summoned up the courage to find a counselor — a guide like Virgil in Dante's *Divine Comedy*, someone who would help her find her way out of her own version of hell — she was dissatisfied with the results. "At my fourth visit next month, I plan to ask Louise about our different styles of communication and that I want, and need, some acknowledgment of what I am saying. I want to give my counselor a chance, but I am disappointed. She just ends abruptly, takes me to the receptionist and says, 'Schedule her in two to three weeks' without even asking if I want to come back. I want to tell her I'm not here to see her like it is a workshop to study [the handout I was given on 'Communicating More Effectively,' and read a book about] my problem, but to talk it out. I hope to be clear about my expectations, and ask for someone else, if necessary. Or just quit.

"I took a credited class on Pastoral Counseling last fall from Father Bill Surmeier in Phillipsburg. I learned I have a right to what I expect from counseling sessions and, of course, I don't have to stick with it if it is not working for me."

She was given an opportunity to switch therapists, but when she was introduced to a male counselor, who said he would be taking the same approach, she felt it a waste of time. She last sought counseling thirty-five years ago. It was a less than satisfying experience, as well. After four or five visits, around 1966 during her first management job, the counselor could only offer, "you know what your problem is," and left it at that.[21]

Sister Veronica was complex, however, probably not any more so then the average person with their own unresolved issues, although, she did have the stringent guidelines of religious life to contend with. Still her prognosis was good with her strong commitment to search within. She felt confident that if she could uncover the source of the problem, the solution would be close behind, and well it might have with more in-depth probing.

Furthermore, if a topnotch counselor had been available, in the small western-Kansas town, in 1993, perhaps there would have been a more insightful resolution to "her quietness problem." Dealing with issues unique to the religious life require highly specialized professionals, like psychotherapist Dr. Vincent Bilotta, who work with both Priests and Sisters, and their distinct concerns. These specialists are usually found only in large metropolitan cities. It is unlikely she, or others living in rural communities, would find a psychologist trained to deal with the requirements of those adhering to religious vows. And so, she and her counselor limped along, neither of them getting much satisfaction. Still, she was wise to first realize the need for professional help and began to understand she must consider some lifestyle changes, which she made two years later.

Sister Veronica terminated the appointments when the counselor suggested long-term therapy. Instead, she said she would, "try to appear to be more interested in others," hoping that would be the solution. Moreover, it was a financial burden without immediate results in sight, especially for one living in poverty.

The role of a therapist is as facilitator or catalyst. Perhaps had Sister Veronica stuck with the sessions, she might have also discussed the dimension her hearing loss held, and delved into the void created with Ronald's death. There were other issues she did not tackle head on, either, such as stress, overwork and burnout.

Additionally, the nationally known psychotherapist Dr. Bilotta explains a restlessness showing up in religious communities that focus on the completion of tasks. One's value is not dependent on how much work one can finish in a day, but many people act as if it does. The quietness issue was only the tip of the iceberg.

"My problem really seems a teeny concern compared to others. I know I am good at what I do." Perhaps consoling herself she added, "My trouble is I set things up for others, make them look good and they get all the credit." But she never got around to discussing this bothersome issue with her counselor, either.

She was guided on by *The Maxims of Perfection*, one of which states: "When you work for others, have a very unselfish love which expects no reward for its service; presume rather that you will receive only ingratitude, which happens often enough."[22]

In keeping their vows, Religious Women do not set themselves up for distinction. Rather, they live the "hidden life." Sister Veronica did not take credit, receive recognition, or acknowledgement for what she did. She lived the Gospel as a humble woman. She learned as a child to be truthful, loyal, honest and exemplary in all her actions. She was generous, doing good deeds from the heart, not expecting just compensation in return. This was one of her most noble and endearing qualities. But at a high price.

Bilotta suggests that being a slave to constant service leads to exhaustion and disillusionment. Never-ending and unselfish service to others, without reward, is demoralizing. She fell into this trap of busyness. Holistic writers emphasize that when one derives self worth from anything outside of oneself a feeling of out-of-control ensues.

Her self-esteem came from the soul, although a little ego slipped in now and then, adding to her human dimension. When a basic emotional need, especially that of being recognized and appreciated, is not met the predictable result is sadness and depression. Sister Veronica possessed some saintly qualities but she also experienced some unsaintly feelings, too, such as frustration, jealously and feeling unappreciated. This is expected, according to generalized psychological findings among those in religious life.

"I'm sure she had many frustrations, but I never heard any except, 'How can we get people involved?' She tried very hard and seemed to know where a person could fit [and grow with] that job," echoed several parishioners. Her looming sense of responsibility haunted and bogged her down. "Who is going to carry on?" she worried. Throughout the years, she was especially thankful to be able to count on the support of a few in each of the WaKeeney, Logan and New Almelo parishes, her biological and CSJ family.

Taking the road less traveled, as a new nineteen-year-old Sister, she moved into an unknown world, often misconstrued by the general public. She redefined herself in the way she believed God wanted her.

During her first years in the convent, life began taking a different course than anticipated. Because of her hearing disability diagnosed in the convent, she experienced the loss of a childhood dream of becoming a teacher. The vow of obedience and her aptitude pointed toward a career not to her choosing. At twenty-three, after earning a bachelor's degree in dietetics, she was put in charge of a hospital dietary/kitchen department.

Later, in 1970, when leadership training became a business world buzzword, convents also got on the bandwagon, believing these skills could be taught. Sister Veronica continually took courses, and read books on her own, to strengthen skills. In the field of dietetics she was obliged to keep up to date. She heaped credential upon credential in pastoral ministry, too.

In 1980, at nearly forty-one years old, she returned to the idealized rural life of her youth and began serving in pastoral ministry. After more than twenty years of being away, by the time she returned to Kansas she had worked in various jobs, was well read and well educated with a master's degree, and had traveled to a Third-World country. Perhaps, unwittingly, her experiences distanced her from the people she wished to serve, many of whom never lived any place else, more than a few had never finished high school, much less earned a college degree, or never traveled outside the United States. With her technical knowledge she became overqualified for rural hospitals and parishes, but she never held it above those she served.

While she had hopes of living and ministering at the Damar Parish among her many French Canadian relatives, no job was offered. Perhaps in using a relationship term, "on the rebound," she accepted a challenge of serving two other parishes simultaneously. She was an underpaid professional, and the small church communities was unable to offer more than $3,000 a year.

More complicated still was mingling with people, as needed for parish ministry and hospital dietetic consulting, which did not come easy for her. Following techniques learned in books, workshops and seminars, she managed others, but this responsibility was a struggle. No amount of reading could change her introverted and shy personality.

She was not a quitter and did not like suggestions that she should give up. Advised to get out of parish ministry, at first she resented and resisted. Perhaps she thought the solution was to take on even more obligations, accept impossible situations, and fight to make them work. But gradually, she came to honor her inherent talents and interests.

Along the way she came to realize that not only seclusion and shyness, but hearing loss also kept her out of conversations. Often viewed by society to be a shortcoming, a hearing disability has a tremendous impact on social exchanges, which distanced her even further from meaningful relationships. Like most people, she had a basic need to be understood and appreciated for herself — flaws, foibles and all. Good mental health depends on a combination of factors, such as the ability to cope with stress, job satisfaction, and a strong support system. These were all being tested.

It wasn't until the night of her funeral vigil, listening to Sister Ginger's eulogy that even those especially close to Sister Veronica discovered her pain of isolation.

In hindsight, it is easy to see her strength was in technical support, or research, rather than supervising others — a torturous task for her. She sought counseling for better understanding. Instead, what she got was a book she found simplistic. Furthermore, some of the remedies in the text were in conflict with the Maxims, or gentle rules, by which her CSJ Community adhere.

In actuality Sister Veronica's counselor's advice, and the book she recommended, *Too Good for your Own Good*, offers a lot of insight. "Be comfortable, direct, responsive, nurturing and firm. Being too responsible is another name for being too good. Replace goodness with balance." It was balance that was missing in her life.

After a total of fifteen years at the WaKeeney, Logan and New Almelo parishes, she reviewed past challenges and looked forward to new opportunities. She was on her way, and the counseling did help. She took the suggestion from other sources, too, and got out of the work she was in.

She struggled for years to find her niche, and toward the end of her life, she discovered her talents. She began to focus on successes and identified what enhanced her energy, rather then worrying about weaknesses. She was able to admit to herself that her gifts were secretarial duties, research, office organization, in short, providing support to others. Among her strengths was her tenacious dedication and gentle leadership. Her soul was rejuvenated when she used her energy in positive ways.

Chapter Fifty-two

Here I Am Lord
    — Isaiah 6
I know that you can do all things, and that no purpose of yours can be hindered.
    — Job 42,2

One might not think of Sister Veronica as a child at heart, yet at many gatherings she encouraged fun and high spirits. Wanting to maximize every moment, she rarely took a casual approach to anything. Her favorite entertainment was "just hanging out" with family and friends. She was freer at small intimate gatherings over card games, in the kitchen, or when she could get on the floor to play with the little ones, who devoured her attention. It is typical for Sisters and Priests who come from large, close-knit families to view their nieces and nephews as "alter-ego" children.[1]

At our last reunion, to the delight of their parents, she took her interest in dramatics to their level, and organized the youngest (Laurie, Kellie, Amanda, Nicole, Brianna, Maggie, Cole, Jonathan, Christopher and Joshua) to perform a skit with each child acting as a color of the rainbow. As Erasmus is quoted, "We only truly know one another, and joined in friendship, through foolishness." Most of her older nieces and nephews where there too: Joyce, Duane John, Teresa, Denise, Jackie, Jason and John. [2]

Typical of reunions, there were photos, old family videos, and plenty of good food, too. Drawing on her dietetic background, she concocted what she called a "Snow Mountain" appetizer of refried beans forming peaked mountains. Green onions and chilies made trees; and sour cream was the snow, in keeping with the theme of the YMCA Snow Mountain Ranch family center on 5,000 acres of mountainous beauty, between Winter Park and Grand Lake, Colorado.

The morning of departure, Sister Veronica put baked beans on the table, among other leftovers from the night before. Nephews, Jason and John, howled with laughter to think cold beans could be eaten for breakfast. The older ones understood their frugal aunt didn't like to throw food away.

"I have beautiful memories of our times in the mountains," she wrote. Afterward, she made time for another family gathering and she encouraged siblings to gather for our brother, Roger, and Jacalyn's Silver wedding anniversary. Aunt Irene Morin's 90th Birthday party was held the same day in mid-July. "I plan to be at both celebrations." And she was.

In her last few years a new spark emerged, eagerly keeping step with the modern-Sister image. Not known for radical changes, she surprised her family that June reunion weekend, with a reddish tint to her normally drab gray-brown hair. "Just to try it. All the other Sisters are coloring their hair these days. They say it invigorates them. It's time to get with it," she smiled.

Times had changed, from thirty-six years ago, when she first took vows. Hair cutting then symbolized dying to the world. Sister Veronica considered her naturally curly and unmanageable hair a nuisance, and often complained all she got were "Nun haircuts." Little things made her happy, and when this writer gave her a "non-Nun" haircut that weekend, she was grateful and filled with joy.

It may seem a contradiction — not wanting to be identified as a Nun/Sister — but it pleased her when she overheard in whispered tones, "She doesn't look like a Nun." The label of "Sister" did seem to block communication. Casual conversation was never easy for her, and she tried hard to remove barriers, be it a haircut, color, or style of dress.

As a modern Religious Woman, Sister Veronica had the freedom of choice to move to various parts of the country. Four days after the family reunion in the mountains, she lifted her chin, packed her few belongings in her Chevrolet Corsica, and left the mobile home-rectory that shook and rattled, when the Kansas winds blew.

The previous challenging time had provided an opportunity for her to look within. The one key element she was missing was balance and she would have to work constantly on that. Many times, in the past, she grew weary. At times, there was a voice screaming inside for privacy. Difficult situations are often growth opportunities. "A smooth sea does not make a skillful sailor." She knew this to be true, holding up the options to God: "Which one, when you embrace in your heart, gives you the most joy, peace and comfort?" When she broke from the desert, to climb the mountaintops, she came away refreshed, and ready to tackle "The More."

Sister Christine Doman said, "Veronica left many signs of spiritual sparks in the lives of the people where she ministered. Our lives are the fruits of our contemplation. The gifts shared with the Church, and in-community, grace the ordinary simple life as open, as our hearts and hands are in the giving. We seek the reign of God everywhere in gentleness, joy and peace. In many ways, we live our lives day to day in the simple ways of loving our 'dear neighbor' striving for 'The More' as [our founder] Father Médaille invites us. We are to be hidden in our spirituality with the charism of unity and reconciliation.

"While the energy of the Holy Spirit invites us, and calls us, to challenge the injustices in our society for the most part it is recognizing the quiet breath of that Spirit in our daily journey. But the passion with which we live it is burning deeply in our community mission in communion with the needs of the church. The result of wins are signs of God's presence in our ministry," Sister Christine concluded

Throughout her ministry, Sister Veronica experienced a laboring, like during childbirth. During the time of intensity many women have wondered, "Why did I put myself through this? Never again." They are momentarily exhausted, as this is a time of great pain and distress. Like the universal mother, Sister Veronica endured at the expense of her own comfort, in the building, nurturing, and feeding of others. She aided in the growth and development of the parishes she loved. She showed them how; she applauded, and was proud when they did it themselves — an apt metaphor for ministry. A spiritual ambassador, she carried God's concern for the rearing of the faithful of the parish. She suffered pangs "until Christ be formed."

Sister Veronica had a genuine appreciation for those with whom she served. She loved, and was loved, by the "oldsters," as she called them. And families with children knew she loved them, too. Her strength of encouraging the talents of others, prompted several poems written in her honor. Perhaps like Father Andrew Greeley in *Furthermore! Memories of a Parish Priest*, she was a bit surprised at how much she was loved. Many parishioners showered her with cards and letters of thanks and praise for her work, as they lovingly bid her farewell. Sorrowfully, five months later many parishioners traveled to Concordia to bid her farewell once more in her eternal journey.

There was a common theme of admiration, which ran through her stacks of mail before and after departing. She was grateful for their support, keeping the letters in her small box of treasures. "Thank you for your special way of presence to, and among us…for serving in our parish…I enjoyed everything we shared together…You have done so much…God will give you a better place." These were not mere empty platitudes; the love and support was heart-felt.

"You do a lot that others aren't aware of…Everyone should be thankful for all you have done." She was praised for her home visits and Bible study classes, and being attentive to the elderly and sick. "I have seen your interest in helping in all areas of Parish Life." She was commended for working with the young childrens' singing pageants, and with confirmation classes.

There were letters that expressed their shock, or sadness over her departure. "I am devastated…In the past we heard, through the grapevine, of some things not getting along, and now see what the talk is about…We love you…You done great…You have my support…I'm behind you one hundred percent…Thank you for the friendship…We get wrapped up in own affairs and we forget to tell how we feel…You are so unselfish…I'm at a loss for words…You will be missed."

"Our Sisters at each CSJ convent house at Kansas City, Las Cruces, [New

Mexico] and Grand Junction, [Colorado] have personally invited me there. I am considering moving to Grand Island, [Nebraska] this summer, where we have a convent of twelve women. I have lived alone [with the exception of a few months] for fifteen years," she reflected.

Sister Rosalyn Juenemann added, "In the last two years of her life, she deeply felt the need to go someplace where she could live in Community. Veronica felt that living alone was not helpful to her own inner spirit. She planned to move to Grand Island for that very reason."

She prepared her resume with the objective of promoting individual, family and community health through nutrition. Her work had always helped define her identity, but she finally realized it was time to slow down, and she allowed herself to look around for fresh options. "I don't know if I want to get back into dietetics, although I visited four nursing homes for dietary consultation positions, and met the hospital dietitian. I lost a lot of information by not using it these past five years." Nevertheless, she kept up her license with the American Dietetic Association.

"Tucky, a parishioner, recommended I get into the paralegal field, but Grand Island attorneys only use legal assistants. I am leaning toward a secretarial pool 'to put food on the table.' I also left resumes for a secretarial service at a hospital for the hospice and mental health clinics. I visited the local community college and a business school two blocks from the convent.

"My first preference is as parish secretary, which is literally the heart of the parish life, the focal point and place of first impression by all visitors and folks with needs." She had a trial run at New Almelo and knew she was well suited for it.

"My second choice is assistant-in-training at a library, or anything that does not put me in a position of dealing with lots of people." Still feeling the effects of burn-out, she emphasized, "For this year, I think I'd like to just do the work and go home — being free for other interesting aspects, and volunteer ministry."

There is an adage, "Put yourself on the track of life you ought to be living, and doors will open for you." She began to tap the spring of eternal joy and listen to her intuitive voice, which allowed the hidden hand of the Holy Spirit to guide her. During her few remaining months of life, Sister Veronica quickly put aside mundane anxieties, rising above hurts and petty indifferences.

Like Dante, in the *Divine Comedy* — who looked at his own sins, then the sins of others, and finally looking above, transcends himself and the rest of creation — she, too, began awakening to full consciousness. Reborn from a figurative death, she attained peace of mind. Like a resurrection, she was about to come back "in all her glory," receiving intense satisfaction and the opportunity to use her special talents. By the grace of the Holy Spirit, she began to see the gorgeous days ahead and began to reevaluate her gifts: honesty and integrity, consistency, energy, strong faith, empathy, acceptance and generosity.

She discovered a beautiful person within.

The first week of June she headed north with a partial carload of her belongings to drop off at the convent in Grand Island. She briefly looked for a job to begin, in July, after a one-week family vacation in Colorado, followed by a three-week retreat and Senate Elections.

After a few days she headed east to the Motherhouse in Concordia, at a time when she most needed the support of her other family — the CSJ Sisters. After fifteen years, a seven-day-a-week parish ministry had taken its toll. She was "tired of being tired," as she put it. She had sought professional counseling to talk about her fears and hurts. She was ready to move on.

Rather than the implied detachment of pre-Vatican days, Sisters now want more meaningful relationships in their Community life. Many of the CSJ women are highly intelligent, well educated, active, and have considerable drive, zeal and personality. Of special interest to them, in their continuing commitment of service to others, is searching out meaningful work and a way of life that will make a healing difference.

Some of Sister Veronica's friends were still in teaching or nursing, but more had gone into prison ministry, operating shelters for homeless or battered women, directing camps for the blind, hospital chaplainry or alternative healing methods such as massage therapy or reflexology, the healing science of touch. Some train dogs to assist with special needs. Another is a founder of a Native American tribal college. Others are poets or artists. Some even gave shelter to immigrants. The list is varied and as interesting as the Sisters themselves.

Issues of social concern, oppression, peace and justice spilled over into conversations. After the Latin hymns were laid aside, sacred music like "We Are Called," "Let Justice Roll Like a River," and "Here I am Lord," was composed and grounded in scripture to address the needs of mission and ministry.

Sister Veronica's life in ministry had changed in recent years by embracing humanitarian causes and promoting enlightened voting. She addressed social issues through Letters to the Editor.

It was a fitting tribute to her that after a twenty-year struggle, the sixteen-mile, two-lane section of road where she was hit head-on and killed was finally identified as unsafe. A newspaper clipping headline reads: "Nun killed in wreck served as leader: Sisters to fill heavens with prayers for U.S. 81 project."[3] Offices of both Governor Bill Graves and Secretary of Transportation Dean Carlson were stormed with petitions and letters from fellow Sisters, family and friends, to finish widening U.S. 81 to four-lanes all the way to the Nebraska border. It was finished by the first anniversary of her death.

Seventeen years earlier she wrote, "Sister Bette Moslander, our CSJ president, invited forty of us younger Sisters, along with the Executive Board, to a series of four Leadership Training Workshops, to develop future guidance."[4] This CSJ Community understood the need for younger blood and fresh ideas, just as most corporations do. As a result, the next year Sister Veronica was active in facilitating small group discussions at Senate meetings. "We are concentrating on our new Constitutions, so I feel like I understand why every phrase is in it."

In 1987, she attended a forty-eight-hour workshop to discern whether to leave her name on the ballot for a leadership role. "I was happy to be a part of the process and was really affirmed, but I withdrew my name."

In their four-year report, ending June 1995, speculation about Vatican III came up. The outgoing CSJ Leadership Team issued an account of the dwindling number of Sisters. Another topic was what to do when other women wished to join with the Sisters in some capacity, other than vowed life. Six years later, that became a reality when, in December 2001, five women made a formal non-vowed commitment as CSJ Associates.[5] Perhaps this formation program of a spiritual program will be the wave of the future, rather than perpetual vows, as they share with the CSJ community and incorporate the charisms of unity and reconciliation.

Sister Rene Stevens CSJ, and Marge Denis from Ontario, facilitated a three-week-long encounter in June 1995. They also assisted with the first phase earlier that spring in March. Before each Sister arrived, they read the short book, *Open Space Technology*, which set the retreat theme.

"We arrived with a burning passion, ready to work hard on topics of interest and knowing the next month all members were to endorse at least seven Sisters for leadership positions," Sister Veronica said. When they gathered the second time, in May, twenty-three CSJs came forward to discern future Community leadership. "Anyone who received endorsements could make the retreat. I have until next week to declare my intent. It would be easier to get out of the process, but something continues to hold me. I argued with the Holy Spirit to remove my name, but I got the jitters, so left it in. I will fax you this so you can PRAY for me!" she wrote Father Duane.

Maxim of Perfection number 15 reads, "Be very faithful to the grace of the Holy Spirit, listening to Him attentively, obeying Him promptly and entirely, attributing to Him, as is indeed just, the honor resulting from the success of your good actions." [6]

Sister Rene Stevens, CSJ, and Marge Denis, returned in June to facilitate the final stage whereby a team of four-year term leaders would be elected. "Those of us who made ourselves available for leadership were officially nominated and commissioned by the Senate to begin discernment, among ourselves, with the guidance of the facilitators. In a blaze of festivity, eight candidates were sent to the nearby Manna House of Prayer."

At the discernment retreat she said, "I came in readiness to be of service, if necessary, but with no aspirations." Like the others, she had to constantly rearrange her views on power relationships, and saw first hand how power and privilege oftentimes corrupt the soul. She fully understood any leadership position she might undertake would be in the spirit of helping, and not of status. She wished to return the past support from councilors through shared experiences and a sympathetic ear.

She wrote a gospel meditation twelve years earlier for the *Northwestern Kansas Catholic Register* titled "Nearing The Answer." "We are good about hiding the talents and strengths that make us unique, often so good at hiding, even from ourselves. To put our wholeness into a response may bring an insight, like that gained by the student of Jesus. Imagine the energy released, in allowing the unique combination of ourselves, with the sacrifice of Christ, once and for all. Each person's need to be reminded to let the individual way of loving come through, is evident in the moments of 'Hear, O Israel...Listen, you!'"

Each of the candidates submitted a page of self-analysis, a vision for Community and its relation to the Church. "When communication skill is a big need, we ask of ourselves and our leaders, why do I think I can do it now when the parish communication broke down?" She reflected on her past. She finally accepted her gifts and talents, and herself as valuable.

"In small groups we shared our strengths and limitations, then mirrored back the same to each other, in light of the qualifications set by the Senate in March, which was, 'To be most effective, what I need from those on the Leadership Team is: An atmosphere of open, honest, and respectful communication; Knowledge of the needs of the Community, Church and the world; Ability to collaborate and delegate; and Openness to the inspiration of the Holy Spirit.'"

Over several days, the voting members engaged in dialogue to question and clarify differing positions of those endorsed to determine those who would be selected for the Leadership Team.

Sister Carm Thibault noted, "During our discernment, Veronica was open and candid about her life. At one point, she expressed great sadness about the lack of appreciation from the people at her last job. She seemed to have given her best, and few noticed."

Sister Veronica was indeed humiliated. Nevertheless, knowing that pain can be a time for growth, she found love and wholeness in the days ahead. She took to heart a passage from the Book of Proverbs: "It is good sense in a man to be slow to anger, and it is his glory to overlook an offense." The years before were trying ones. Like the biblical Job, she recovered her trust in God, which was deepened and strengthened by her suffering.

Chapter *Fifty-three*

"Come to me all you who are weary and find life burdensome and I will refresh you."
— Matthew. 11:28

In the spring before her death, Sister Veronica was apprehensive about the decision to throw her name into the hat for election to the Leadership Team.

"We shared our strengths and weaknesses, and listened to others share theirs. She shared the depth of her struggle at prior community assembly days," said Sister Anna Marie Broxterman. "One of Veronica's limitations was her hearing disability and her own felt sense of others' reactions to it. I told her, 'Veronica, what concerns me is not another's reaction, but your own self acceptance.' She recognized that as Truth. Later on when it was more obvious that Veronica was being asked to be on the Leadership Team, we returned to that point."

No doubt, Sister Veronica prayed for open hearts to understand and embrace her disability, which made life so burdensome. She prayed for her own receptiveness, too. Perhaps Sister Anna Marie's statement struck a chord. Acceptance? Perhaps not. But she adapted (meaning to make fit) to the cross that fit her. She knew that no one is unfettered in this life. The list of trials is as unique as the individuals who bear them. It is little wonder that our aunt, Sister Rose Irma, was her inspiring role model, having been plagued with medical circulation problems for years and suffered the amputation of both legs. In the eulogy for our aunt, Sister Veronica spoke of the "yoke of burden, and how it fit Sister Rose Irma's strength."[1]

There are scriptural writings that describe fleeing to, and wandering in the desert. The biblical desert experience, which Sister Ginger Pearl described in Sister Veronica's eulogy, is one of isolation. It is a lonely place, and even though one is not abandoned during this time, one feels alone. Although it is here, in the thick of spiritual battle, where one is called to, cared for, and led through, that the glory of the Crucified One is found.

The late Claude Pepper, Congressman from Florida, was one of thousands of people with a hearing problem. He remarked, "Hearing impairment is one of the impediments that come along in life…We should accept it with equanimity when it comes. Not lose our poise, nor lose our high purpose. We should make the effort to alleviate it, or diminish it, and keep on with our face towards the east, marching into the sun. We should not be discouraged. Make the best of what the Lord allows us, and keep going and doing."

Perhaps for the first time Sister Veronica had a forum, during this discernment process, to express herself fully and truthfully about this condition, and how at one time, or another, she felt isolated and left out, irritable and annoyed, frustrated, confused and resentful, and all kinds of other emotions — upset, discouraged and depressed.

Sister Vera Meis knew her well. "Veronica did share the pain of hearing loss, which I believe caused some of her loneliness." Sister Ginger Pearl added, "One of Veronica's greatest pains was she could not express her depth of feeling, especially of her mystical experience."

Sister Anna Marie continued, "Veronica shared how she prepared herself prior to these days [and other assembly days in years past] to be present to others in affirming ways. But because of not hearing well, or not being able to connect quickly enough, she would inevitably return home in frustration and loneliness because she had not connected at the depth that she longed for.

"I will never forget her tears and the depth of her anguish. Her sobs remain almost audible to me, and I can visualize her facial expression during this time when she revealed her 'shadow' and what she was most afraid of. Her expression of grief continues to be a most profound experience to me, and a reminder, as e.e. cummings says, 'To be a little more careful of love, than of anything.'"

It is not that Sister Veronica felt sorry for herself. She understood that no one else was supposed to hold her hand, take care of her, and make her feel good. She had always stood on her own two feet, but all these years she had repressed the toll that hearing loss had taken. She kept this sadness, and all other emotions, just under the surface. It came spilling forth, during the Leadership discernment, as she bared her soul. At age fifty-five, she was forced to come face to face with her burden.

As her peers looked on and listened in quiet, Veronica recalled past wounds, and wept openly in front of them baring the depth of her struggles. Her fellow Sisters saw her with new understanding and insight. They looked and judged, as to whether this was a weakness or a strength. They saw her for all that she was, and all that she had to offer.

Perhaps for one of the first times in her life, others did not interrupt. They gave her the attention and the time it took to answer. Being present to each other, in genuine sharing, was a tremendous accomplishment that week. Here, love was found in those simple moments, and they looked at each other with grateful hearts. To feel such love from her fellow Sisters that she could face her "shadow," to be listened to, really listened to, and be heard…The emotion was overpowering. Her humanness shone though. She was loved and accepted just the way she was. The support she received during the weeklong discernment dissolved her fears.

Father Duane summarized, "Veronica blossomed after she shared her burden, found acceptance and affirmed that it is okay to be deaf and still be a wonderful, useful person. Unfortunately, it took her too long to experience this."

Faith must be rooted in unpretentious and innocent trust, not in complicated theories and incomprehensible doctrines. A great load had been lifted once Sister Veronica brought the menace into light. Jung indicates that growth only comes from facing one's "shadow."

Using the words of Teilhard de Chardin, "...Changing the darkest shadows of the world into light," six short months before her death, she came to know that after the dark of night, "the living flame of love does shine forth." Sister Veronica put away her grief, was ready to change gears, to be of service, and to do what she knew she could do. She would turn her yoke into a gift.

The question Sister Anna Marie asked her, about whether she accepted her disability, was a pivotal one, and freed her from the depths. Once she spoke freely of her burden, she was able to move forward and keep "going and doing," as Congressman Pepper challenged. She was ready to accept that while she was alone, that is different from being lonely, and that looming aspect diminished. She came face to face with the demon. It no longer haunted her, and it no longer held its power.

Sister Anna Marie realized during that week, "How much of the mystery lies in living together, and seeing each other afresh." The other Sisters saw in Sister Veronica the strength it took to be a good candidate. She gained the trust of her community as they elected her to the governing body of their congregation. She was in charge of ministering to the growing population of older Sisters. She was a nurturing "oven" to them, and they loved her. She was perfect.

✝

Chapter Fifty-four

"An image I see are footsteps wading through deep sand in the desert. They are plodding along," said Sister Ginger Pearl as she eulogized her friend. "Veronica gives an indication of why the desert experience is so deep. It was her perception of how people accepted her because of her hearing loss. For whatever reason she said she felt alienated from many persons."

"My relationships are marked by my hearing difficulty," Sister Veronica told her therapeutic counselor. "Responses are slow since I need to decipher what is said. I am annoyed at the hard work involved." She did appear tense in public, as she tightly held her hands together. And her speech was not spontaneous, either, as a function of her hearing loss. But when she did hear the topic, she speech was well intact, logical and goal-directed.[1]

Father Duane pondered whether she didn't accept, or was ashamed of her hearing loss. "For me it's a disability not to be hidden, because it can't be," he said. "Once people know one is deaf they normally are willing to help. Perhaps Veronica did not want that kind of help."

The hearing-impaired population typically have generalized feelings of isolation and perceived rejection. An emotional pain accompanied Sister Veronica's hearing loss, which affected interactions with friends, co-workers, parishioners, strangers, and to a much lesser extent her family. Five other siblings also suffer the burden of hearing loss, but none as severely as hers. Kenneth, the oldest; Rodney, the youngest; and Linda, this writer, are the only three spared of hearing loss.

Father Duane also questioned whether being a loner at an early age was based on her hearing deficiency. Many factors develop a personality, and being hard of hearing held a significant impact for her, but she never mentioned the problem. Nothing was made of it when she was young. It wasn't corrected or challenged. Her siblings got used to her tone, inflection and mood, and she to ours. Not a lot of communication was required to complete routine household chores, either. And even as a youngster, Ila Mae/Sister Veronica was a tremendous help to Mother. If not every word was grasped, she was attentive and knew the gist of what was expected. A quick response was more than adequate.

While her hearing worsened with age, she said that she first became aware of deafness at the age of seven in the private confessional enclosure during the sacrament of Penance. "I watched for the Priest's hand making the shadowy closing Sign of the Cross through the screen. Then, I assigned my own penance." Our sister, Cheryl, agreed that going to confession was difficult during childhood, especially after learning to read lips. In the 1950s, before the changes of the Second Vatican Council, there was no face-to-face reconciliation.

In later years, Sister Veronica claimed to have coped so well, in childhood, because she drew strength from the family's devout Catholic faith. Mother deliberately placed our family in about the fifth pew from the front, in the long, narrow pre-Vatican II church, so the children would pay attention to Father Dickman's sermons. Still, the young Ila Mae could not hear. Much later she owned up: "As a child I confronted the Lord at Sunday Mass, 'Look, if I am supposed to learn anything, you better teach me. Or let me know what it is!'"

When she was nine years old, her baby brother, Roger, was occasionally left in her care. For the first time she realized she was unable to hear his cry from another room. Other than that, she didn't know how to explain her hearing problem. As the other younger siblings were also her responsibility, there were fearful episodes, too — in particular, when she was walking with them in the chalk hills out of eyesight from the house. "What if someone called out to me? I wouldn't be able to help because I won't hear them."

As a youngster, it probably never occurred to Ila Mae to ask for a hearing aid, believing Mother and Dad knew what was best. She noticed, when visiting Aunt Irene and Uncle Ed Morin that he had to speak loudly, even though our aunt had a hearing aid. Ila Mae probably thought, "Why bother having one of those if it doesn't help?" Furthermore, during that era, the thinking was that those devices were only for old people.

Ila Mae appeared dreamy, or faraway, at times — a distinct manifestation of hearing loss. "The aloofness is something one recognizes first before realizing a person has a hearing problem," said Cheryl, who first noticed her own hearing loss in high school. "As a teenager I was referred to as, 'the girl the boys would whistle at twice.' Apparently I appeared either stupid or stuck up, and neither was true."

Father Duane remembers Mother calling attention to Cheryl's hearing ability in her teen years. "You say 'yes' too easily. Some day you are going to say 'yes' to the wrong thing." Unfortunately, there were many laughs, at Cheryl's expense, at home and school, when she was mistaken about a phrase and replied to a question incorrectly.

Even as a child, Ila Mae was quiet and retiring, and preferred smaller groups. One might wonder whether this was due to her hearing deficiency, or to shyness. Nevertheless, from the time she was twelve, and throughout high school, Ila Mae had acquaintances in the 4-H club who shared common interests: cooking, sewing, livestock, gardening and square dancing. Interestingly, these activities allowed her to assume leadership positions, not by charisma, but due to her organizational ability. Someone had to take charge. Why not her? Not only did others admire her, she learned to believe in herself, too.

Interestingly, her hearing loss did not interfere with functioning during 4-H, at home or school. Admittedly, she was shy at the larger Stockton High, but felt comfortable in the smaller rural Webster school. It's unclear whether she wanted anyone to know she was hard-of-hearing. The subject never came up with her teachers either, because of her attentiveness and good grades, which boosted her confidence and self-esteem. She was smart and could usually figure things out.

As she grew older, Ila Mae intuitively positioned herself to be in the right place. She could figure out what was going on by watching those around her. Intuition was one of her strengths. She instinctively learned to read a face and body language. She sensed things that others might not have picked up.

She learned "speech-reading," which used to be called, "lip-reading." Unfortunately, it is impossible to speech-read a bird song; this exquisite part of nature was not part of her experience.

Ila Mae excelled in mathematics. The course work is solitary. The answer is either right or wrong. Little discussion is needed. It was an ideal school subject for her. As a studious person, one way she found to escape the limitation of hearing impairment was to excel in her studies, learning primarily from books. But, being a bookworm was not a popular concept at home. Cheryl said, "[For those with a hearing loss] reading often becomes a favorite pastime."

For the most part when a sibling, or a classmate, responded to a question with "Huh?" or "What?" they were told, "Pay attention!" Since Ila Mae was very observant, she grew up rarely asking someone to repeat. Verna Flax, a parishioner from WaKeeney, knew her in the 1980s, during the ten years in that parish, and agreed, "When she wanted you to repeat something she would question, 'Please?' rather than 'What?'"

Father Duane further added, "Mother taught us this. It was one of the rules we siblings grew up with. It's not nice to make people repeat. And don't interrupt." Not wanting to ask others to repeat, Sister Veronica pieced together conversations and guessed at the best possible meaning. "We were good at guessing, as we were taught not to impose on another. This sums up a lot about us with hearing impairments. To pretend isn't the solution," he offers from an adult perspective.

Overhearing laughter in a conversation, Sister Veronica often missed the point. But, one would have never known. Our sister, Joan, admits she will smile and laugh, too, although often not hearing the entire joke. In a crowd Joan is a good sport, but unfortunately large noisy parties provide little enjoyment for her.

In 1993 Sister Veronica's hearing loss registered at 50-75 decibels. Even with hearing aids in both ears, spontaneous and idle chatter was frustrating for her.

"Veronica didn't like small talk, and said she wasn't good at it," relayed Father Duane. "This is probably ninety percent of socializing. It is most likely this was due to not being able to hear. Although, it is also possible she lacked general interests, strong convictions, or general knowledge and thus compensated by conversing about her specific professional field. In this area she was vocal and assertive."

Another key reason she probably did not enjoy small talk is that conversational topics often jump from subject to subject. She would still be on one subject, when the topic had already skipped to another, then quickly on to another.

Six weeks after entering college, Ila Mae wrote to Mother and Dad about a three-day Retreat she attended. "We had five lectures a day. I don't know what the first three were about. I didn't have enough sense to sit closer." It was during this time in college that she heard herself on a tape recorder, and first realized she mumbled. Quickly she understood how the voice plays a pivotal role in perception. Immediately she began to correct the problem by putting pebbles in her mouth to force clear diction. She learned to pause on vowels. After that, one of her pet peeves was listening to people who mumbled and did not enunciate clearly. Later on, she developed the habit of taking a modified yawn before speaking. This seems a peculiar trait, but is a recommended tip to relax the throat and increase resonance.

"I hear, but I don't always distinguish. There is a difference," Father Duane explained his own problem. "Pronunciation is hampered by not distinguishing sounds. I don't pronounce well the stops. Bull shit comes off as *bu shi*. Veronica said *helm* instead of him." Another sibling says *sloup* instead of soup, and *samwich* for sandwich. Our parents did not correct mispronounced words like *aluminum* and *cinnamon*, or mild speech impediments where the *w* sound is substituted for words beginning with *r*. The distinction between *pen* and *pin* is especially difficult for several to hear.

"[In college] my parents took me to several physicians," Sister Veronica said. "One of them tired nicotinic acid to open the vessels in my ears. I was told I had an inherited nerve loss." It is possible she was born with genetically damaged auditory nerves, as the doctor of more than forty years ago claimed. According to medical guides, nerve deafness varies according to the location and extent of damage. Often there can be quite good partial hearing. Fibers concerned with the highest pitched sounds tend to be first affected so that good hearing remains in the lower-pitched regions.

There are many contributors to hearing loss including birth complications, high fevers, blows to the head, cleaning fluids, as well as, prolonged deafening noise pollution. Sometimes over-the-counter drugs, prescribed drugs, or the absence of medication are contributing factors. Trips to the doctor, for routine childhood illnesses, were seldom made in our family. Not until recently have doctors paid attention to the consequences of ear infections in infants and young children.

There are other circumstances that may have worsened Sister Veronica's condition. Both she and Father Duane had serious bouts of childhood measles, and other siblings were exposed, as well. "I was told a 'frying' of the nerves at one time in life damaged them," he offered perhaps referring to a high fever. "As with Veronica, the doctor first tried the unsuccessful process of dilating the nerves." She was told a surgical operation could not correct her loss to the certain degree it did for Joan, who had surgery on the stirrup, anvil and hammer of the inner ear. "It was discovered that I have nerve deafness, too, and not conductive deafness. Hearing aids were recommended as the only solution," Father Duane said.

"To tell you the truth I don't know how I was accepted for the religious life as a Priesthood candidate, at the end of the 1950s when this type of impairment was seen as a hindrance," Father Duane reflected. "Apparently mine wasn't as noticeable. I became more aware of my hearing loss at college, and even more so living the Monastic life in Community, when others told me I didn't hear well. [At age nineteen] during my Novitiate training, at St. Benedict's Abbey during 1960-1961, I requested a hearing aid."

Mother Superior Helena Robben was the first to acknowledge the potentially severe impact of Sister Veronica's hearing loss after she took religious vows in 1958, and was cloistered in the Motherhouse convent during the next year.

As a Novice at age twenty, the headpiece of the Habit, worn by the Sisters, fit tightly around the ears, muffled sounds and further diminished her hearing ability. "With my acceptance into religious life Mother Superior assured me it would not be a deterrent as long as I got good grades at college." Sister Veronica wrote in her Life Review, "We were sixteen Postulants, then when nine more joined us for the last six months of Novitiate I was noticeably the quietest of the twenty-five. She appeared hesitant, even frightened, to speak at times. "I worked hard at having something to say. I wrote a booklet of stories, jokes, and daily happenings. I practiced repeating them, but somehow never got the opportunity to jump in. I felt scared in the presence of the other younger [close-knit band of the nine Junior Angelicas] Sisters, most of who tried so hard to help me. I felt as a non-person during my early convent years."

Our cousin, Sister Diane Brin, who was in the younger band, offered, "Veronica seemed at the height of introversion. It was painful just watching her. You could tell she was trying to think of something to say, to give voice to her thoughts, but she couldn't get it out. I was as uncomfortable as she was just watching her."

Even later on in life Sister Veronica said, "I stumble over words. I stutter in my haste to get something out before others cut me off." The general population has a difficult time tolerating silence — Americans in particular. When there is a lull in conversation, which last for more than five seconds, someone usually speaks up again.

It may seem peculiar that as an intelligent woman, she did not have words to express her thoughts, however, it is more complex. It's typical for someone with a hearing loss to pause before replying to process information for accuracy of perception. She also had more trouble when nervous and could not synthesize as rapidly. She even considered herself slow; when in reality she was intellectually very bright.

Our younger brother, Roger, spoke of a similar experience when he was in elementary school. It became self-apparent that he wasn't responding as quickly as other students, and as a result of his hearing loss, it took him a few seconds longer to process what he heard. He generally figured out questions, based on answers. Our parents were not aware of his hearing impairment either, until shown the results of a screening administered to all elementary students. He did not begin wearing a hearing aid on a regular basis until he was forty-five years old.

After observing her during the Postulancy and Novitiate, Mother Superior and committee concluded that Sister Veronica's disability was great enough that it prevented her from becoming a successful teacher. Unable to hear questions and answers from the back of the room, she might have found it difficult handling noisy students, and maintaining control. She would expect no disruption or talking in class, unless called upon. That's the way it was when she was a student.

"Then I understood one day what was happening," she wrote in her Life Review. "I wasn't going to be a teacher. I had to sever the thin thread of my childhood dream." She did not fall apart, but it was heart wrenching and a considerable regret. Instead she was told she "would be best suited in a job one-on-one."

Her friends stood by her as Sister Ellen Divel explained, "Veronica shared with me how very painful it was when told she could not be a teacher. Her hearing loss was very frustrating, but she never complained."

Sister Ginger added, "She spoke as though everyone has a cross to bear, and Jesus loaned this cross to her. She was deeply affected, and so conscious of not being able to hear. [In the early days], I do not think Veronica thought she would ever be able to function normally as a college student, and surely not as a teacher for which had been a deep yearning. [During the Postulancy at the convent] our spiritual teachers were extremely helpful to place her so she could read lips. One of them, Sister Eloise [Johannes] sometimes jotted important points on the blackboard during lectures, talking as she wrote, then faced her class, and explained again. Sister Eloise noted that Veronica was very good at lip-reading, and rarely needed additional notation."

After a total of eighteen months in the Postulancy and Novitiate, she returned to Marymount College to begin her sophomore year. Classroom sizes were larger there, compared to the small classes at rural Webster High. She began sitting toward the front of the room, and achieved good grades due to sheer determination.

In her Life Review Sister Veronica said, "[In college] I know I was labeled with 'still water runs deep.' I blamed much of my early reticence on my hearing loss, but my [quietness] was just a defense for not wanting to appear stupid, and not confident in my own answer to a barely heard discussion." Having her ears covered with the headpiece of the Habit surely compounded the problem.

In 1961, when Sister Veronica was twenty-one and a junior at Marymount, at Mother Superior's suggestion, she was tested at an audiology clinic in Oklahoma City, due south of Salina on Interstate 135. "I was fitted with my first hearing aid, with a cord, which helped tremendously, as long as I was attentive."

Cheryl remembers the early model, "A beige-colored plug and cord went into the ear and the volume control was in a box, which Sister Veronica carried in her pocket." The battery control box was slightly larger then the size of a pack of cigarettes.

As a teenager, and unaware of my sister's hearing loss, this writer thought, "What is she doing wearing that old fashioned hearing aid? It's probably just a gadget to make her look meek, and even more like a humble Nun — to go along with the matronly and unstylish rimless eyeglasses she now wore." This was at a time when everyone else was wearing dark-rimmed glasses.

If today's technology would have been available then, it is very possibly Sister Veronica could have pursued her goal of teaching. Although microchips, loops and electronic devices are rapidly improving, these were unheard of back then. Hearing aids left a lot to be desired more than forty years ago.

During their few months together in the convent, Sister Diane was not aware her cousin wore this bulky hearing aid. "In the days of the Habit and headpiece, it could have easily been concealed. It wasn't until many years later that I knew of her hearing loss. Veronica was wonderful at lip-reading; she never asked you to repeat. That's why many people never knew she had a hearing impairment."

She used this boxy model for fifteen years. On the other hand, Father Duane only used the cord-type hearing aid for about a year. "Then I changed to a binaural type, fitted in the temple bars of eyeglasses, which I used throughout theology school. After ordination, in 1967, I purchased another pair, better quality yet. The earlier types were a bother, or perhaps during the phase of adaptation they appeared to be a nuisance. I adapted well to hearing aids. They were part of my apparel. Each new purchase was an improvement, a relief."

It was not until 1976 that Sister Veronica asked for a cordless model hearing aid from her CSJ community. This coincides with the year she made the request to attend a thirty-day silent religious retreat. She was searching for many answers.

Father Duane offered, "Sometimes the religious life is referred to as the 'silent life.' There is time and space where one has more silence for prayer, study and meditation, but it is also a world where the hearing impaired suffers more. Here people are soft spoken and so much of the richness of communication, in this way of life, can be lost: confessions, homilies, public spiritual readings and meetings."

Her hearing continued to deteriorate over the years. She was first motivated to get a hearing aid for the other ear when she saw herself on videotape, leaning toward a speaker, and straining to hear. She said, in 1989, just short of her fiftieth birthday, "I got a second hearing aid last week, and am now trying to adjust to one in each ear." She ended the letter, perhaps with a deliberate pun, "As usual, I am up to my ears in work."

Until she got used to it, this model was noisy, confusing and stressful. It was a nuisance. The volume on older hearing aids was adjustable, but still these emitted a piercing whistle, if set too high, or when the battery was low. Onlookers would gawk, "What is that strange sound?" Few people realize that even modern hearing aids whistle when touched while still in the ear, which can be a source of embarrassment and physical pain. Consequently, Sister Veronica was cautious about giving and receiving loving embraces, or having someone touch the side of her head, which made her seem even more remote and distant.

Eventually she tried different types of hearing aids with more powerful batteries, as each became too weak for her. "I should have used a second hearing aid a lot sooner," she noted. Father Duane agreed, "She should have used better quality ones, too, although she wasn't one to make a request, even though she was doing professional work and studies." She took the vow of poverty seriously. The major deterrent for not getting the additional unit sooner was the high cost.

It is remarkable that several family members did not know Sister Veronica had hearing aids in both ears — probably because she did not call attention to them. Cheryl said, "I did not even notice her impairment that much until I fully accepted my own loss. Then it makes one more compassionate."

Cheryl was diagnosed with a hearing loss in 1971 and, as a sixteen-year-old, was also fitted with the old fashioned boxy model. When it squealed during class, she felt particularly awkward among her high school friends, and refused to wear it after that. The deaf or dumb labels of yesteryear were hurtful for a teenager, and she rejected the thought of being fitted with another until many years later.

In 1995, Heather Whitestone, a young deaf woman was crowned Miss America, with her hearing aid somewhat visible. As the first disabled woman to hold the title, Whitestone set an example for many hearing-impaired young women everywhere. This was a major breakthrough in bringing this topic to public attention, and ease the shame or awkwardness that often accompanies deafness, in its many degrees, to the younger generation.

Just before her fortieth birthday Cheryl was determined to complete her college degree. She realized she must sit in the front of the classroom, and would need a hearing aid to help her attain good grades. Sister Veronica offered Cheryl this advice, "I hope you adjust to your new hearing aid. Practice with the radio first. Television has too much background noise, gibberish and ringing bells, which make understanding nearly impossible."

Many people claim hearing aids are not perfect instruments and will not restore hearing to near ideal, in contrast to eyeglasses, which can often bring about nearly 20/20 vision. On the other hand, Father Duane disagrees that hearing aids have their limitations due to his own successful outcome. "One can hear almost normally if willing to invest in quality equipment, and train oneself." Because of his insistence on a quality instrument, he found it necessary to periodically schedule visits to a U.S. specialist during his thirty years in Brazil. He has adapted well. "Many times I use them fifteen to eighteen hours a day." However, he is willing to admit, "We who have hearing loss react differently. I see that my reaction is different from that of Veronica, Roger and Cheryl."

While most television sets on the market today have a closed caption feature for the hearing impaired, the one Sister Veronica received from the family, as a Jubilee gift, in 1984, was not so equipped. Consequently, television held little entertainment value for her. Father Duane commented, "It is more enjoyable for me while wearing a head set. I appreciate the dialog more."

In general, background sound is better controlled now with modern hearing devices that filter unwanted commotion. Father Duane's new digital aids, purchased in 2000, automatically lower background noises, while amplifying the vocal. However, there is a down side with this better and snugger-fitting model. Moisture can accumulate in the ear, which may lead to a fungus. A hairdryer is recommended to first dry the ear before insertion.

"With constant use, hearing-aid users adapt to their surroundings," Father Duane says. "The brain has a capacity to filter and regulate intake." Sister Veronica had greater difficulty with surrounding noises than Father Duane. However he concedes, "Riding in a car with the windows open, and trying to understand what is said, can be stressful. It's easier for me to hear when the windows are shut, which cuts down on road racket."

As an important side note, Sister Veronica's hearing loss did not contribute to the accident that took her life. Statistics show that drivers who are hearing impaired typically have superior driving records because they are especially alert and attentive to clues. A polite and defensive driver, she paid close attention to the scene around her, and habitually used rear view and side mirrors.

Sister Veronica was not an avid moviegoer, either. Older movie sound tracks were often difficult to understand before the days of Surround Sound. Those featuring foreign accents were especially hard to grasp. On the other hand, Cheryl does not have difficulty with movie theaters. "The volume is loud, and the screen so large that it is easy to lip-read and pick up what is said."

Several family members find it especially difficult to hear in restaurants amid raised voices and the din of busboys rattling china, flatware and crystal. It is not usual for the hearing impaired, in general, to turn down invitations and stop socializing altogether, as the condition worsens over the years. Due to her frugal nature and vow of poverty, Sister Veronica never dined alone in restaurants. Yet, she did not decline invitations or pass up opportunities to be with those she cared about.

What was most enjoyable for her was to be invited into one's home. Although, even in a quieter home environment she, like many hearing impaired, had difficulty hearing women and childrens' higher pitch. So as to not miss out on their tiny voices, Sister Veronica was careful to sit close to her young nieces and nephews, and often got down on the floor to be near them.

It may have appeared that Sister Veronica was good at communicating, but nothing comes easy to the hearing impaired. The way she listened affected her ability to understand, but she always tried to listen with an open heart. Her family often thought of her as a good conversationalist because she always had something to offer, but that's different from responding appropriately to questions. More often than not, Sister Veronica talked at others. At times it was as if she was giving a speech, which was her way of offering something to the conversation. Cheryl agreed. "Sometimes I do this, too. I wonder afterward if I've offended someone by dominating the conversation. A person with a loss can do a lot of talking, particularly if they cannot hear when others are also carrying on a conversation."

When Sister Veronica was relaxed with family, she sometimes let the conversation flow around her. However, outside this safe circle, feelings of stress, anxiety and uncertainty were common, creating an endless and frustrating vicious cycle. She learned that straining to hear was fruitless. Leaning closer doesn't always help, either, since many times lips need to be seen. Cheryl added, "Straining creates tension. I get headaches using the hearing aid all day because of background noise. My stomach even gets upset."

Roger commented further, "In the summer months, when the insects are droning, the noise often sets me on edge." One school of thought is to remove the hearing aid, once in a while, as a break from background noise. He agrees.

In a large crowd, one-on-one conversation is troublesome for him. "I can actually hear better during those times by taking the instrument out."

In the public eye, Sister Veronica often felt it her responsibility to carry her part of the conversation. On the whole, she couldn't relax and have a nice easy conversation, living in a world of unheard or misheard words. She often missed out on the subtleties of humor. Every spoken word presented a constant challenge making life more difficult and tiring, straining all day to listen intently to employees and parishioners.

There were times she became so stretched that she needed to rest and be alone. After having her hearing aid on full volume there were times, at the end of the day, when she reached a point of being so irritated that she became short tempered and tense in constantly trying to be alert to what others were saying. "So instead, I just grew quieter," Sister Veronica said. When she was tired, she couldn't decode speech as well. She needed time to grasp the sense of what was being said. Fatigue plays a very important role in a person's ability to understand. The mind does not process the information as efficiently. Father Duane agreed, "It is a strain on energy."

Many people commented on her boundless energy. Although, by day's end many times she was drained — more so then she would have been had she not been hard of hearing — which makes one wonder how much energy she would have had without the impairment.

In general, everyday transactions such as shopping and banking and doctor's visit were a burden. The dentist's protective mask shielded his words, and when she was speaking with a mustached or bearded man, she was at a disadvantage not being able to see his mouth forming words. She dreaded getting haircuts, since she had to remove her hearing aids at beauty salons, and then could not hear what was being asked of her. Furthermore, water and hair dryers can ruin expensive hearing aids.

"A cold, an allergy, sinus or ear infection can also put one at a disadvantage. It can cause great difficulty," Cheryl offered. "And, you have to be very careful not to blow your nose too hard."

Joan, who is hearing impaired in one ear, sleeps on the good side so as to not be disturbed by suburb sounds. Likewise, neither did night time noises disturb Sister Veronica's sleep, but nor could she hear the telephone ring, for emergency calls, after taking out her hearing aids upon retiring.

Living alone had its own set of obstacles. She could barely hear everyday household sounds, such as whistling teapots, pots of boiling water, or kitchen timers. Answering machines were a great aid, since telephones and doorbells often went unanswered. She said she sensed the phone ringing, or felt the vibration of the doorbell, or shadows alerted her to some activity rather than hearing anything outright.

She tried to eliminate interfering noises during outgoing phone calls, making sure the water wasn't running, and the radio, television, washing machine, or fan were turned off, as well as anything else that might break the silence. A person in the same room turning pages of a newspaper, or using a typewriter, made it nearly impossible for her to hear a voice on the line.

Due to recent technology many telephones now have volume controls in the headset, but hers did not. One-syllable responses, like "yes, no, yeah, right, wrong, here," were the most difficult. Understandably her phone calls were often brief. She never used a cellular phone and might have had difficulty with the wireless instrument. A year after her death, the Telecommunications Act of 1996 mandated that telecom companies provide equal access for people with disabilities. However, it wasn't until mid-1999 that a new product became available to help some hearing-aid wearers make clear connections with digital wireless phones.

Often a speaker does not realize they are not fully understood. Calling to Sister Veronica from another room could be frustrating for both parties. Instead, she needed to be addressed directly. Father Duane offered, "Visual observation is very important. I like to see the speaker. The meaning comes across more complete. During meetings I like to sit up front, perhaps not so much to hear better, but to see better." Body language helps to clarify words, tone and emotion.

"I'm deaf, but apparently not as much as Veronica," said Father Duane, "I never had any problem in communicating with her, even though I have a tendency to mumble and stumble on my words." They had a lot in common, never lacking for subjects to ramble on about. "Loving relationships are important because one feels accepted and not only tolerated," he shared.

Many times people avoid being with those who are hearing impaired — not wanting to repeat, having to talk louder or not being properly understood. In her sensitivity, perhaps she felt this and didn't want to burden others. "People around those with a hearing loss need to be patient, too," he admonished. "It's more a burden for others, perhaps than for ourselves. I don't accept being a burden. It's my problem and not theirs. It's not that much of a problem, or I don't allow it to be one. I learned to cope. Many times one suffers the temptation of not paying attention. Perhaps not hearing well makes me a better listener, making me more attentive, hearing with the heart. To my delight, I feel society is now more tolerant of hearing loss," Father Duane continued in his typically generous manner. "People try to be helpful by speaking louder, slower and more distinctly."

This kind of disability was not visible, like being confined to a wheel chair. Yet the business environment is a hearing atmosphere, and still there are prejudices. Sister Veronica never drew attention to her disability, but she never tried to hide the fact that she wore a hearing aid, either. She only spoke about it if asked. Otherwise, it might seem she was asking for special consideration. She did not ask others to adjust their speech for her. Although, it would have helped her greatly if she would have asked co-workers or parishioners to enunciate clearly and look at her when they spoke.

While not always hearing words precisely, Sister Veronica was often able to pick up on the topic and then tried to predict the meaning of the next sentence. That's how the mind works — it builds a picture, captures the topic, then guesses or imagines what the next bit of information might be. She often understood the gist of the conversation, and was attentive enough to pick up the message, knowing there was more to communication than words. The rhythm of the sentence, her knowledge of how language works, and the topic discussed, helped fill in the blanks. Most social conversation is very predictable, but problem solving is not so. And larger meetings held their own complex equation "As a Religious, she was almost constantly in group interactions, which are more difficult than one-on-one conversations," said Father Duane.

Most people did not realize the extent of Sister Veronica's hearing disability — if they knew of it at all. Even many of the other CSJ Sisters never realized the full magnitude of her impairment, assuming the instruments restored her hearing. Each year she planned ahead, going into CSJ senate meetings and assembly days mentally prepared with topics to discuss. Instead, she often sat reticently. Many times her efforts were fruitless, as she tried to understand and be understood. If the speaker was behind her, at these assembly meetings in the convent's large auditorium, it was nearly impossible for her to hear what was said in its entirety, especially if the many Sisters shifted in their seats, and chair legs and shoes aimlessly scraped the floor.

Furthermore, when several CSJ members "talked over" others during meetings — when four or five spoke at once — she would be lost. However, the Sisters make it a point to not cut off someone in mid-sentence.

Occasionally she seemed inattentive by repeating what had just been stated, as she failed to pick up appropriate clues. Sometimes, she focused on an incorrect key word, or changed the subject, mistakenly taking the conversation in another direction. She tried hard not to get the typical odd expression on her face when she didn't understand. The person might back off and say, "It's not important." She was good at masking confusion. She tried to be attentive and enthusiastic when she actually heard about one in three words, at best, and sometimes, only one in ten.

Sister Rosalyn Juenemann recalled, "I felt her hearing difficulty was a real disability because many times she did not understand conversations during meetings. Consequently, there were times when her contributions were few, and sometimes not at all, I am sure that was a real source of frustration for everyone."

Indeed, these were frustrating experiences. On occasion Sister Veronica admitted, "I feel wound as tight as a rubber band," and often left these, and other large gatherings despondent and in a state of tension because she couldn't jump into conversations fast enough. Nevertheless, during these emotionally low times she would take a look around, keep her disability in perspective and say, "My troubles are small compared to others."

Chapter Fifty-five

In Sister Veronica's box of treasures was found a birthday card from four years earlier. On it were the symbols of her birth from the Native American medicine wheel retreat theme, during a 1991 senate at the CSJ Motherhouse. "People born during the Earth Renewal Moon have the potential for great power, both in things of the earth and of the spirit. They are organized people with respect for tradition and authority, and with a deep understanding of religion and ceremony. They see life clearly and have minds that can soar. The great powers of the universe can flow through them if they don't become too stubborn or rigid. Snow Goose people, who have successfully learned about change and renewal, often become great teachers and leaders."[1]

"There was rumbling for me to be eligible as [CSJ] president," Sister Veronica said. "Although I said, 'I am well known in the Diocese — but known as reticent. Our Community deserves, not a stronger figure, but one not so retiring.' Several folks said I was just radiant. This has transformed me. Everyone said I did quite well. I had an answer for everything. For me, it was a double affirmation. The same peace I felt before continued throughout the discernment."

"As we came to some clarity about who would be on the Leadership Team, Veronica was very excited about the idea of serving this way," Sister Carm Thibault offered. "She told how she loved to organize and putter, and find ways of connecting. After elections, she wrote tons of letters, and did a lot of relating and affirming. Veronica was quick to find ways of recognizing each CSJ member and making everyone feel included, which may have come from not always feeling included herself."

Sister Christine Doman added, "When we were at Manna House for discernment, Veronica told me how seemingly unorganized she was because of her many projects. I asked her how she knew where the stuff was to finish a task. Veronica had a great sense of humor, which I loved. She smiled shyly, and said she really wasn't sure herself, but somehow it all got done."

Prior to this they had received training in Open Space Technology.[2] This model engages the full energy of the workforce. It creates an environment for innovation, problem solving, creativity, teamwork and working within rapid change. A coffee break format was used based on the assumption that conversation flows easier during unstructured time, people speak freely what's on their mind, and topics are more varied than at structured meetings.

There were three candidates in each room and a facilitator, who received questions. Voting members could float between rooms asking questions. Afterward, the voting members of the Senate went into their own retreat at the Motherhouse, guided by Rita Patenaude. They prayed for their individual openness and receptiveness, to make a recommendation regarding whom, among those nominated, seemed to be truly called to leadership, for the next four years, under the guidance of the Holy Spirit.

According to the CSJ newspaper, "By [the sixth day] the work of discernment was completed, and the recommendation of the nominees was offered to the Senate body, with the understanding that while it represented the clearest and best recommendation of nominees, as to the movement of the Spirit among them, it was not binding upon the Senate members. Each deliberative member of the Senate was free to vote according to her conscience. The recommendation of the discernment group was: Sister Christine Doman, President; Sister Esther Pineda, Vice President; Sisters Vera Meis, Veronica Roy and Carm Thibault, Counselors/Regional Coordinators."[3]

Sister Veronica continued to describe the CSJ Concordia elections, "I think the entire Senate was absolutely pleased to have a choice, rather than just ratify what was recommended."

Sister Evangelista Kehoe, a young-spirited yet elderly Sister who entered the CSJ Congregation long before Sister Veronica was born, and who formerly held the position of councillor/counselor herself, admitted that when Sister Veronica's name was on the ballot, she thought, "Oh no, not Veronica, she is too gentle and too reticent in her answers." But then she realized, "Why yes, she will be perfect. And she was during her time in office."

In the last six months of her life, in her role on the CSJ Leadership Team she was useful and loved, nurturing and nurtured. It was what her spirit needed all along. When she followed her heart, her spirit took wing.

Sister Frances Alma Royer, one of Sister Veronica's dearest friends, was on hand to watch the Senate proceedings. "Congratulations, on your new Ministry in the service of the Lord," she wrote. "He has chosen you, and I know that you will do a good job. I rejoice with you in this new beginning of your life. You were so peaceful and honest in all your answers. Rest assured that I will keep you in prayers."

Sister Vera was also newly elected. "I believe Veronica felt especially recognized for her gifts. She was happy, full of zeal and knew she had much to give. She received a lot of praise, which gave her more energy and joy."

The temperament of each Congregation's President is vitally important to the happiness and well being of the Sisters. In some convent, not necessarily those of the Sisters of St. Joseph, there are stories told of Mother Superiors, many decades ago, who ruled with an iron fist, like it was an army, an asylum or worse, a prison. Before the Second Vatican Council there was a great lack of understanding, rather than outright lack of sympathy. Some Superiors were autocrats, either by nature, or because they thought they were supposed to be. Later, in the 1960s and beyond, after Vatican II, the qualities desired in a Superior were to be firm, yet motherly. Although, with each new regime, different personalities emerged.

Over the past thirty years, leadership for the Concordia Sisters took a variety of forms and emphasis, each one responding to the needs of the times and the capabilities of those entrusted with the role. The process of selecting these leaders also evolved into seeking a new leadership model. "We have a lot of angry women, who have been concerned with 'strong leadership,'" Sister Veronica wrote. These competent, mature women did not need, or want to be told what to do, or to be governed by overly rigid rules by efficient and impersonal 'CEOs,' following models in the business world. The Congregation of Sisters wanted to be listened to; they wanted their voices heard, and action taken accordingly.

So in 1995, with the election of Sister Christine Doman, a kind yet effective leader, the team took on a dynamic personality. When the least intimidating group of Sisters emerged, that too, was a sign of the times. "Our team statement was 'We need you.' We are all gentle and soft-spoken women. No strong folks," Sister Veronica said. "This is looked upon as a new team. From the group, we are about the most reticent." And also the most compassionate.

After the election, Sister Veronica wrote, "Providentially, I am now on regular annual retreat. A marvelous place to begin my orientation. We are reviewing the spirituality of our founder, J.P. Médaille, S.J. The 1640s original documents of our foundation are laced with the word 'compassion.' The Sisters of St. Joseph were the first Community of Religious Women to be apostolic versus enclosed, that is being contemplative in action."

Drawing on the biblical Martha from within, she said, "Now to meditate on the hidden, humble power of yeast and salt and aprons. I suspect our work is that of Restoration. Mindful, this is not a step up the ladder." Her election to the Leadership Team was a validation and a hopeful sign that even a gentle and quiet woman could come to power, but a power based in humility with only the intention of serving others.

One of the ancient CSJ Maxims written by Father Médaille and by which they continued to live was, "Be completely humble, since whatever you are, whatever you have, and whatever you do for yourself and others, depends on a pure mercy and an infinite condescension of God. If you are not humble in every way, you make yourself unworthy of these and of the assistance of his graces."

Surely she thought, "This is just the beginning." Following elections she wrote, "Oh my. What a week! Our Loving God is full of surprises." Just three weeks earlier, and without a job, she had packed a carload of belongings and headed to the convent in Nebraska. She never had a chance to unpack.

Sister Ellen Divel said, "I was looking forward so very much to having

Veronica live with us in Grand Island, which was her plan. Then God decided she would serve our Community, and was elected to the Leadership Team, and for almost six months she served. Every Sister just loved her."

Under the direction of new president, Sister Christine Doman, Sister Veronica wrote her annual commitment to Mission statement: "…In this new way of serving, I trust to gently touch the hearts and minds of us in our shared vision."

On July 1, she officially began serving on the four-year term. From the time of arrival, the pace quickened. "It was a blessing for you to have trimmed my hair," she told this writer. "I went right into six days of hard discernment and it was great to at least have my hair under control. The enclosed photo, for the newspaper, was taken minutes after the Election."[4]

After quickly getting settled, a week later she mailed a few more photographs. "Do you remember my 'bride [of Christ]' picture in front of the double doors leading to the chapel, and the life size statue, which is now pushed back against the wall?" Another photo showed her in the Founders Room, standing next to a grand piano, with the alleged Sirani oil painting of two cherubs in the background above her shoulder. It was here where her belongings were laid out for distribution to family following her funeral.

One photo was of her office, "which needs greenery. It is just up the hill west of the Dairy Queen on Highway 81 coming into town." No doubt, living within eyesight of the ice cream shop was a daily temptation for her.

Another photo showed their residence, the former Little Flower Home for the Aged, next door to the CSJ administrative offices. On the back of another photo she noted, "The kitchen needs remodeling. But as part of a historic preservation project, the [fabric color and design of] draperies were replaced in the Motherhouse, Manna House, and the television room in our home, to reflect [the Victorian era of] 1904, the building year."

Sister Carm Thibault and Sister Veronica Roy, while not related, had an uncle and aunt in common (Archille Benoit married RoseLee Roy). Sister Carm said, "Veronica and I moved into our house, on Mound Street, the same day. I got there earlier, and she rolled in [from Grand Island] about three in the afternoon with all her possessions in the car. As the only ones there, we began our new venture together, as new kids on the block. Veronica felt that cleaning was the best way to find where everything was. She scrubbed the kitchen floor of wax build up. We cleaned cupboards and reorganized a bit. After the other Sisters returned, from their response, we realized we had moved quite a few things around in the kitchen. 'Where is the paper towel holder? It's gone. Who moved that?' We got scolded and teased at the same time."

No doubt this joint effort, in the spacious house, reminded Sister Veronica of early home life with her sisters. "[In my teen years] I took delight from crawling into cupboards, taking everything out, washing shelves and arranging everything so neatly."

Laughter and joking did not come natural for Sister Veronica, but she loosened up in her new surroundings. Previously not one to celebrate Halloween, she now felt comfortable clowning around wearing a costume for a party with Sister Carm, who was raised in a house full of glee. As her eternal journey drew near, Sister Veronica rejoiced in the camaraderie. She laughed and was lighthearted. It was good for her soul to be around these others Sisters.

Her last letter rang with friendship and joy. "If anyone is looking for a different video to rent, try a Victor Borge Musical Madness series, such as one done in London, in the 1970s. We were hysterical watching his hilarious variations of classical music." Borge was a vividly relatable, antic comedian.

She relished her teammates, yet each provided the other privacy and space in the large house, as needed in any adult household. She was especially pleased at the ease she felt in relating to people her own age — something she had found difficult before. Each member actively worked and traveled extensively. They weren't needy, or dependent on each other. Instead, they had common interests and enjoyed each other's company.

This was in sharp contrast to a failed living arrangement ten years earlier when, for a short time, she felt accused of "not being capable to live in community." In past years she suffered from loneliness. "This is a wonderful group," Sister Veronica wrote. "It will be the first time to live in a house with a few others, having lived alone fifteen years. I lived with Sister Betty Suther, in 1980, when I got my Master's degree, and in [hospital and convent] institutions twenty-two years before that."

Sister Rosalyn Juenemann expressed what others also deeply felt in their hearts, "I am extremely grateful that her last few months were very positive. This was probably due to living in Community with other Sisters."

In the early weeks Sister Veronica said, "I am the only one home for three days, and hoping we don't have a funeral, or disaster. It is hard enough [administering to 250 Sisters] when everyone is home." Later she wrote, "Our team is quickly getting limbered up. Today, this administration had our first funeral. Many Sisters said I did so well in presiding at the Vigil last evening. A big goal for me is to use the talents of many, especially those whom we never see in public. I asked an elderly Sister to carry one of the two candles leading the body out of church at the funeral. Something like this sounds small, but I know it means a lot to them to do it for the first time."

Sister Christine explained, "Each time there is a new Leadership Team the old Sisters, at the Motherhouse, take note of the new persons and how they reflect their personalities into ministry. When Veronica led vigil prayers for Sister Regina Mari Dickman, it was a new observation from those who have lived through several leadership styles. Veronica's contribution to the team was a noteworthy one."

"What I came to realize was that Veronica truly knew our CSJ documents," Sister Carm added. "And she used those words in talking about our lives, the Maxims and Constitutions. It should not have surprised me, but then not everyone takes time to reflect and apply [the Maxims of Perfection to] what we say in our lives."

Sister Veronica's interest and ability with computers continued into her new phase of life. "Our [previous] president took her computer, as she is a doctoral candidate now.[5] So guess who got the new computer — the only one with Windows. Me!"

She donated her old computer to the elderly Sisters living at St. Mary's Convent, at 830 West Eleventh. "Several of them, who write poorly due to Parkinson disease, arthritis or some other illness, are interested in learning enough to write letters. I am trying to get one Sister de-addicted from Sweepstakes entries, and into computering."

Sister Christine added, "She encouraged a couple of the retired Sisters to 'get with the program,' so to speak. She was eager to share her knowledge, and had the patience to hang in there with them. But poor eyesight and swollen fingers slowed down much progress. It was just fun for them to share with her.

"Just a week before Veronica's death there was an in-service meeting, on Windows 95 in nearby Salina. She was elected to attend the meeting, since she had the latest model and she was our computer expert, compared to most of us. There were booths, where she signed up for everything, including a random drawing for a new computer, which she won! When the vendor learned it was a Nun who won the prize, they threw in additional software programs, some of which we thought were very complicated."

After a few months on the job Sister Veronica said, "So far the work is all communication — listening to, and following up on personal health directives, plans and desires. I'm receiving accolades from the eighty Sisters in my region, and invites to their missions during the coming year."

According to the CSJ newspaper the job duties were explained, "In their new positions, the Sisters will serve in the governance and administrations of their congregation. Their responsibilities include, besides the day-to-day administrative task, both the civil and canonical function of leadership in a religious community. They assist all of the members in their personal and ministerial needs. Their work includes long-range planning and representing their congregations in civic and church organizations and meetings. The Sisters are well known throughout the area for their work in education and health-care ministries and a variety of pastoral and social services."[6]

Learning to drive on country roads when she was fourteen, Sister Veronica handled a car very well. She was often selected as the designated driver and this continued throughout life. "I picked up our vice-president [Sister Esther Pineda] at the Wichita Airport, and on the way home we stopped in Salina for ice cream.

"I'll probably read a lot on the road," she added. "For some reason, I started reading mysteries late at night since my new job. There is already so much reading to do at work each day, but I look forward to reading *Ebola*, the book you sent. Sister Esther is an avid reader, too, and will no doubt want it next.

"Work is going well, and at a rather relaxing tempo right now." But after weeklong meetings, in Concordia and Topeka, she began a whirlwind four-week tour driving through New Mexico, Texas, Illinois and Michigan. "I'll be rather busy now till Halloween. The team will be driving to Silver City, El Paso, and Las Cruces the last week in September, and then back up north." They headed south and west on Interstates 135, 40, 25 and 10.

Sister Christine emphasized, "We enjoyed our long trip to the southwest and were taken with the beauty of the [numerous mountain ranges] of New Mexico, and sharing our insights in prayer and recreation. Veronica visited every mission assigned to her before her death. At each convent, Veronica gave particular attention to each Sister individually, since they were her responsibility. Several of these Sisters had lived with her in Belvidere, so that were very special to her [like Sister Frances Alma Royer, in Las Cruces.] Each work of service was done with a personal touch to get to know the needs of the individual Sisters. Veronica blossomed in her new ministry of leadership for our CSJ congregation. She was happy, and beamed with joy, as she worked on each task given to her."

In Silver City, New Mexico, the team visited one of her band members, Sister Rosemary Farrell. Rosie, as she is now affectionately called, lives in the convent that previously housed a large number of Sisters. "We used to have a high school and grade school here," she said. "It has been closed for years. A Montessori school now uses a couple of the buildings." Also located there is El Refugio, which was under the direction of Sister Carmel Garcia. It is a non-profit center, which provides shelter, counseling, advocacy, prevention and education services for families affected by domestic violence. In 2002, a new building was dedicated.

Everyday Sister Rosie lives the gospel as she advocates in the courts for children's rights and uses play therapy to reach their tender souls. Sister Carolyn (Juenemann), Ph.D., began an alcohol and drug counseling transition program on site for women and she later offered workshops and spiritual direction. Sister Rita Plante once served the mentally and physically challenged at Life Quest, and in 2002 gave Faith and Light Retreats for the handicapped.

Sister Marquita Murguia, an artist, in the CSJ El Paso Community, holds art retreats. Sister Christy (Meyer) is in nearby El Paso. Each of the CSJ Sisters has her own unique "hidden story" of dedication and service yet to be told.

Sister Veronica and the Leadership Team were there in Silver City on practical matters to assess the value of pouring money into the old convent, which needed a new boiler, versus selling it and finding smaller quarters. "It was a business trip," said Sister Christine. "But we had a fun side trip [across the border from El Paso] to Juarez, Mexico, visiting sidewalk booths and shopping centers. We laughed at the time Veronica slammed the car door shut with the keys inside, when she stopped for gas. Then all three of us tried to get the door open."

In late September, after completing their travels to the southwest, Sisters Veronica and Vera Meis headed north to visit CSJ Sisters in Marquette, Gladstone, and Escanaba, Michigan, and West Burlington, Iowa. Sisters Veronica and Vera's path had crossed many times over the past thirty-eight years. They were in college together at Marymount, and they attended the same thirty-day Ignatian retreat at Hales Corner, Wisconsin. "We had a great time on our trip, and had several very good conversations. I treasure the times we had together" said Sister Vera.

They stopped in Chicago, Sterling and Belvidere, Illinois. It was as if these were Sister Veronica's "good-bye trips," as she visited many Sisters and lay people, whom she had known over the years. "She was given a surprise party by some of her old staff at St. Joseph's Hospital," Sister Christine said.

Clara Chamberlain, who was eighty-five years old at the time, was one of the six "oldster" retired employees who came to the hospital that morning for coffee and rolls, then stayed on to visit during a noontime dinner. "We surely were so glad to see her, and I think she was glad to see us. We had a tour of the hospital, as it had been remodeled since we left."

Sister Veronica was in Belvidere when Uncle Omer died in early October. "I never got the message until Aunt Vula called after his Vigil." Had she known, Sister Veronica would have found a way to drive back from Illinois to Damar, Kansas in time for the funeral. "From my experience of not getting word that you called, I encourage you to identify yourself, and ask of my whereabouts, since we generally don't give out that information," she urged each family member in her last letter.

Never one to miss an opportunity to visit relatives, Sister Veronica squeezed in a weekend with Aunt Jeannette and Uncle Bill in Bartlett. While in Illinois she was also excited about finally visiting towns she had only read about: Kankakee, St. Anne, Martinton and Watseka, and visiting the research library there. She also made it to Beaverville, "where Mother's maternal great grandmother Mathilda Frigon is buried."

The year before Sister Veronica was born, the question, "Should capital punishment be abolished?" was a hot issue. Over sixty years later, a poll, in February 1999, found 71 percent of Americans favor the death penalty. At one of the CSJ Senate meetings, the Congregation took a corporate stand against this same issue.

Eliminating capital punishment is not only a Catholic issue; the National Prison Ministry Conference of the Episcopal Church is actively involved, too. Sister Veronica sided with the U.S. Catholic Bishops' rejection of capital punishment, and would have approved Pope John Paul II's success in commuting a death penalty to life imprisonment for a death row inmate during the Pope's visit to St. Louis in January 1999. "His Holiness, joined by his fellow Bishops, is pleading for us to recognize that in our era the death penalty can no longer be justified except in the most extraordinary circumstances."[1]

Sister Ginger Pearl's experience with prison fellowship and regeneration, as chaplain, brought the two together in heartfelt conversation. On one of their long drives together, Sister Veronica spoke candidly against capital punishment, and the need to pray for the soul of a father who had killed his own children. In her Christian faith she believed the murderer, guilty of this heinous crime, deserved to be treated with the respect and dignity that is the right of every human being.

The Academy Awarding winning movie, *Dead Man Walking*, based on the 1993 book by the same name, was released the month after Sister Veronica's death.[2] Sister Helen Prejean, another religious woman of French origins, tackled timely questions addressed in the anti-death penalty document adopted by the Bishops in 1980. She has called for a Moratorium on the death penalty, especially for crimes committed by those younger than eighteen years old. She wisely adds that the Church must also offer support for the victim's family. "The Roman Catholic Church has to be on both sides of this issue."[3] Or, as she put it during a speaking engagement in Tucson, pointing to Christ on the cross, "there are two hands at work here."[4]

It is certain that Sister Veronica would have found great courage and compassion in her true story. In 2001, Sister Helen addressed ninety graduates at St. Mary-of-the-Woods College, Indiana, where Sister Veronica once attended a summer session. "It is hypocritical for the government to execute people," referring specifically to Timothy McVeigh's scheduled execution at nearby Terre Haute. Her key question was not whether he deserved the punishment, but who deserved to kill him?[5]

On another issue, Sister Veronica sympathized with Sister Ginger who memorialized her ancestral martyrdom by participating in the Oklahoma Trail of Tears march, or the "Trail of Death," as she calls it. It was a deeply healing experience for Sister Ginger to be among those invited, during the Reconciliation of past hurts Jubilee year 2000, to accept the Church's apology for the atrocities to the Potawatomi Tribe. In addition to the rights of the indigenous peoples, Sister Veronica cared deeply for the oppressed in their spiritual and nutritional needs. She one time considered working in Appalachia.

Closer to home, Sister Veronica took a political stance and adhered to the Sustainable Agriculture belief that crop seeds should not be altered through biotechnology in the name of progress. She felt that Christians have a duty to be politically active, to register and vote, to speak up about the issues that affect the common good. Within weeks after her move to Concordia, she became a registered voter in Ward 3, School district 333, Cloud County. She didn't often speak of social issues with family members but in one letter she wrote, "There is a fine line between 'subduing the earth' and playing God. I am referring to the many ethical decisions that people must make because of so many opportunities presented by findings in Science."

Five years after her death, Pope John Paul II endorsed organ donation and adult stem cell study, but condemned human cloning and embryo experiments, in issuing moral guidelines for medical research in the 21st century. Sister Veronica would have also had a hard time with the Genome project and Dolly, the Scottish lab-cloned sheep, which opens the door to human alteration. She would have been especially appalled with the approval, by Britain, to clone human cells for research, and with the Massachusetts company which accomplished the cloning of six cells in late 2001.

In October 1994, as co-director of the CSJ Mission Development, Sister Veronica flew to Cincinnati with Sister Donna Otter. She arranged the schedule, and enlisted other Sisters to go with her to fundraise for the Brazil Mission. One weekend, the next fall, she drove to Sharon Springs in western Kansas, and helped Sister Ginger spearhead the Brazil Mission talks. Previously given by Sister Margarida Boucher after her return from Brazil where she ministered for twenty years. "I am not the regional coordinator, but there is a vague chance of getting to visit [our CSJ Community] in Piaui [Brazil] during my four-year term. I would arrange a side trip to your state of Goiâs," she wrote to Father Duane.

Continuing the appeal, she and Sister Ginger traveled west to Pueblo, Colorado, for World Mission Sunday. Held in October each year, Catholics are called to pray for all peoples of the world, and to offer generous financial help supporting the Propagation of the Faith, which is distributed in the Pope's name to continue the worldwide mission of Jesus.

On the way back they spent the evening with Sister Marilyn Carpenter,

OSB, at Benet Hill, who was assistant prioress at the Benedictine Monastery, in Colorado Springs. They shared experiences and reminisced about the good people they knew at New Almelo.

Sister Ginger called this Colorado trip a "mountain top experience" for them both. The two friends, Veronica and Ginger, found themselves with Jesus on the top of a high mountain. Mountaintop experiences are few and far between, but they do happen, especially to those whose faith is alive and strong. When they left that lofty peak and returned to their everyday world, it was with renewed faith and hope, much as it was for Sister Ginger five years later on an Alaskan trip to Denali, the local Indian name meaning high one.

In 1963 Martin Luther King delivered his "I Have a Dream" speech, on the steps at the Lincoln Memorial, calling on "the freedom of every hill and mountain...out of the mountains of despair...the prodigious hilltops and mighty mountains...and from every mountainside... and continue to work with the faith that unearned suffering is redemptive."

Sister Vera Meis added, "Veronica let it be known that while over the years she had been wounded and let down by several people in her life, she believed in forgiveness, would want others to know they are forgiven, much as she asked for forgiveness, too. She wouldn't want anyone to feel guilt over past actions, or would never want to harm another's reputation. She shared with me her joy, and peace, and how very close she felt to God and was now free of any past hurt. She worked them out with her God, and let them go."

Sister Veronica also shared with Sister Ginger some of the discouragement and "unearned suffering" she had experienced over the years "Then one day all this changed," she said.

After her death, a parish memorial service was held in WaKenney and Mike Wahlmeier adapted and performed in her memory, "Go Rest High on that Mountain." One CSJ of Carondelet said, "We recall the great stories of mountain peaks, and wonder about what we tend to believe. We strive for heights, pushing ourselves to ever-higher summits of achievement of development. Yet, what if the real adventure of life is to learn to live at the bottom of our mountains and find them beautiful?"[6]

Due to a crisis, Sister Veronica was asked to hurry back from this Colorado trip. She telephoned to postpone a scheduled visit to the Loretto Center in Denver, as well as a planned overnight stay with our sister, Joan. It was a visit not meant to be, just as was her plan to visit me the next month for my 50th birthday — a family tradition among her sibling sisters.

"In a hurry I flew to Chicago, put an ill Sister on the airplane back to Kansas, closed her house, and drove her vehicle back to Concordia. It was quite an experience," Sister Veronica said.

Sister Christine explained, "Veronica was called upon to make this trip to

Chicago two weeks before her own death. This ill and elderly Sister that Veronica went to help had tons of personal belongings inherited from her family. I called Veronica in Chicago to see how she was doing in sorting out all the stuff. She told me she had lots of it packed in the Sister's car, ready to drive home the next day, but had trouble getting the snow blower in the Dodge Colt hatchback. I almost fainted. 'What in the world are you doing bringing back a snow blower? I asked. 'Well, the workmen told me they could use it at the Motherhouse, and besides now that I have it packed in, I don't intend to get it out.'

"I was concerned about Veronica driving in the wind, with such a big load, but she just laughed at my worrisome spirit. Once she got something started, she never turned back. She drove non-stop, after a few roadside rests, and arrived safely with her surprise load. God was certainly on her side that week."

A major problem facing the United States is the lack of respect for human life, including the aged, another topic that bought out strong feelings for Sister Veronica. While there seems to be a growing awareness of the needs of immigrants and the poor, the aged are often poor, as well. On the anniversary of Mother's death she said, "It hardly seems possible it was ten years already. I look at many of our eighty-one-year-old, and older, women here, and ponder how Mother would have been," she said just two months before her own death.

Mother, who died at seventy-one, was especially resistant to the idea of living in an extended care nursing facility, and it was Sister Veronica who provided the majority of care in her declining years and final months of illness.

On the pastoral level, Sister Veronica had an extraordinary capacity for empathy with individuals in need, and this compassion served her well. A niche where she was perfectly suited was caring for the aged. One of her responsibilities, while on the Leadership Team, was to bring elderly Nuns back to the Motherhouse, and administer to those who were not able to care for themselves.[7]

"We assigned to her the huge job of coordinating the moving of the more frail Sisters from St. Mary's [convent for the retired], then helping the Sisters, at the Motherhouse, open their home to them, too. She gave her untiring energy and loved the challenge," said Sister Christine. "Veronica took time to give special attention to the most ill and frail of our Sisters. They loved her for it, and felt very special because of her endearment."

✝

Chapter Fifty-seven

...In your book all are written down; our days were shaped, before one came to be.
— Ps. 139:16

In Sister Veronica's last letter she wrote, "During the last five weeks, I was home about two days. I believe that should take care of my long distance business trips for this year." On the night of Novermber 15 she was returning from nearby Salina tending two elderly Sisters; one was Sister Annuciata Krauchunas.[1] "I was the last person to see her alive," she said.

There is an adage, "We die the way we live." In her case, it was while driving...being of service...helping the aged...yielding to others...even as the reckless oncoming driver took over her space on the darkened highway shoulder.

It was her nature to do good works, but whether she lived a holy and exemplary life due to her premonition of a lifetime interrupted is unknown. There were numerous indications she intuitively felt her life would be cut short. On New Year's Day, 1987, she labeled her few possessions. In October 1989, she again mentioned this omen. "I must have felt a premonition of something as I went around the house all day, in spirit with each family member, marking gift items."

Sister Helen Hake recalled, "When Veronica was hosting a gathering at her home, she showed us how she had marked each personal belonging with the name of a family member whom she wanted it to go to after her death. Little did we realize how soon that time would come."

Sister Veronica had a typed list of possessions to be disposed of, and claimed by family members. Each possession was clearly marked on the bottom or back. Taking the vow of poverty, it seemed she was merely returning what had been given to her, or was handing down items she had accumulated or collected through garage sales, or other such ways.

Sister Christine Doman explained that to be so prepared is not part of their CSJ Community, obligations or vows. It is not a part of what is expected of a Nun. With her orderly and organized mind, it seemed important for Sister Veronica to depart this world in dignity and good standing. This she did. Her papers were in order. Telephone numbers and addresses were at hand. She entrusted to this writer her most valuable possessions — her books, writings and photographs.

Sister Veronica gave another warning, "I am a perfect candidate for a heart attack or asleep on the highway. Sounds fatalistic. The Community disposes of all personal items on death. So family really needs to speak up the day of the funeral, if they want something." The CSJ Leadership Team, under the direction of Sister Christine, had most of Sister Veronica's personal items ready the day of her funeral for distribution to her family, as many had traveled from out of state.

In a telephone conversation with her niece, Teresa Roy, she expressed an overwhelming and urgent need to touch base with her family. Furthermore, she mailed multiple copies of her last letter to six other family members. "November 8, 1995. Anyone out there! Do you need my address? Where is the [family] round-robin letter? Did I miss a turn? Where has everybody been?"

She further expressed her urgency by faxing a copy of this same letter to Father Duane in Brazil, rather than waiting the ten days for "snail mail", which would have been three days too late. She added this note to him: "I fully intended to send a CARE package via Father Kieran last month, but I waited until the last moment and missed the chance. I wanted to send along the book on the Ebola virus that Linda gave me. I will scan the Benedictine newspaper closely for future opportunities to send something along with a carrier." The day of her funeral the book still lay on her office desk.

Sister Vera Meis poignantly added, "It seemed Veronica sensed her time was very close, and did many preparatory things. Only several days before she was cleaning and organizing the trunk of her car. I thought it strange when she said, 'If I die before you, I am sure that Father Duane won't be able to come from Brazil on short notice for my funeral. And I don't expect him to. But if he is able to come for my funeral, I don't expect him to say Mass; it would be too hard on him emotionally.'"

Coincidentally, Father Duane was already enroute to Goiania, the closest city with an airport, when he received the tragic call by cell phone. He took the next flight out to Rio, and onto Miami and landed in Kansas City the next afternoon. After an icy, three-hour drive from that airport, and having traveled for nearly twenty-four hours, Father Duane arrived just minutes before the evening vigil service.

Bishop George Fitzsimons attended the service, along with more than 350 who signed the guest book for both days.[2] The next morning Father Alfred Wasinger, Chaplin of the Motherhouse Convent, along with Father Duane and thirteen other Priests, gathered around the altar to celebrate the Mass of Christian Burial.[3]

In her mystical way, Sister Veronica insisted on a group photograph, just hours before her death. Sister Carm Thibault explained, "We were at St. Mary's Convent for the elderly Sisters for a midday dinner party for the director, Sister Francis Cabrini Wahlmeier's feast day.[4] After the meal, Veronica asked the cook to take a photo with her wide-angle camera. Little did we know…

"That day she was wearing a flowered blouse, (which her sister Joan had given her), a dark blazer, and a straight skirt with a slit in the back. As she kneeled to find the correct position where she wanted the cook/photographer to stand, the other Sisters teased Veronica in a camaraderie fashion that she had 'nice looking legs.'

"No day goes by without sharing Veronica's memory. Especially traveling on Highway 81," Sister Carm said. A week after the fatal accident the camera was found broke open amidst the wreckage. It was evident only a few exposures were taken. But a certain feeling overcame Sister Carm, and she took the roll of film to be developed. The wide-angle exposure clearly shows everyone in attendance — including Sister Veronica, as she had hurriedly squeezed onto the end.[5]

While ministering to the sick and elderly CSJ Sisters that day at both St. Mary's in Concordia, and Médaille Center in Salina, her presence to them is likened to an anointing. She visited Drury Place, took Sister Vianney (Brunette) to a doctor's appointment that afternoon, and dropped by St. John's, the Salina hospital before her return home, planning to arrive back in Concordia to her teammate-Sisters by 7 or 8 p.m.

Father Ronald Rolheiser says in his book, *The Holy Longing*, that just as a Priest does in the sacrament of the sick, the act of touching a sick person's hand by an ordinary person, or speaking kind words of affection or consolation to a dying person, in its own way, anoints them for their own impending death. "Perhaps in the anointing, one is anointed. The incarnation has given us incredible power. Jesus is saying: 'Because of this it will be easier to not give in to bitterness, and easier to die. Knowing that I am so loved, it will be easier to leave this world without anger in my heart.'" [6]

And so, there was surely forgiveness in her heart for the senseless and reckless action of the teenage driver who took her life. As Sister Veronica left this world for the next, it can only be believed there was neither anger nor bitterness in her heart.

One of her earliest childhood memories was of standing on a hill and looking into eternity. Ila Mae had finally come home. She had come to the mountaintop where her spirit lives on with all those who have gone before, and where she continues to radiate love for all mankind.

Epilogue

In the hours, days and years that followed Sister Veronica's death there were many incidents, for lack of a better word.

Within minutes after notification of her death three people, in varying locations, each heard deep within their soul: "It will be all right," along with a physical sensation of a touch to the shoulder, a hug. A friend, who had not yet been notified, had a dream of Sister Veronica that night not speaking, but holding a sign: "It will be all right."

When several others gathered to pray, the next morning, they saw the contrails from two jets intersect, at dawn, to form a cross. Later on, the sound of rustling papers was heard in her empty office.

Another saw, on the evening of her vigil, a life-like image of Sister Veronica smiling, and standing next to her casket.

At the Manna House of Prayer, where the family slept the night before her funeral, a shadowy woman briskly walked along the hall as if for no other reason, it seemed, then to make her presence known.

The night of her funeral a lone female walker was spotted, by a carload, alongside the shoulder of the stretch of U.S. Highway 81 where she died. There was no stranded car in sight.

For another, a sleepless night was calmed after laying on one of Sister Veronica's blankets. A lost aid was found. And a long-awaited diagnosis was made through her intercession.

These few occurrences merely scratch the surface. The list is endless. Sister Veronica's spirit lives on to remind of the timeless one-ness of the eternal.

In homage of Sister Veronica's first anniversary of death, Father Duane Roy, OSB conducted an imaginary interview.

Duane: Veronica, you once told me that one of your favorite Biblical passages is the episode in which Jesus visits Martha and Mary. What is it that you find so significant in this event?

Veronica: First of all, it reveals to me a very important aspect of who Jesus is. The Gospel shows Jesus in this event as one who is friend. He goes out of his way to visit two women, if one can use this manner of speaking. I don't think Jesus really "went out of his way." Everything he does is part of his way! The event shows that friendship is a value Jesus cultivated.

LINDA ROY CROSS

Duane: In a nutshell, who is Jesus, for you?

Veronica: Jesus is a man so capable of loving others he had to be God! The Son of God, with us. Jesus never left his small world of Palestine. But what he did in those few years, and in that small space, left a profound mark on humanity. Jesus is a man who has a project, a proposal, a program to transform the way people live.

Duane: How has Jesus marked your life?

Veronica: I have to admit that over the years, the person of Jesus and his teaching, have constantly called me to be more open to others, to be more compassionate, patient, listening and loving. Never to judge and condemn. To be prayerful and care-full, among other things.

Duane: The Gospel event of Martha and Mary shows two types of women. Which one do you identify yourself?

Veronica: To answer this I would have to tell the story of my life!

Duane: Well, that's all right. I think many would like to know much more about you.

Veronica: There are moments I identify with Martha, other times with Mary. I think many people see me as the Martha figure, the busy one in the kitchen getting everything prepared for a meal or for a celebration. As a nutritionist and administrator I guess I assumed that role. I like to organize things. I'm good at that. While others are setting around waiting, visiting, talking, I'm busy preparing things. I'm a stickler for details. I believe food has to be nutritional, taste good, and look good. Eating is a special moment, a holy moment.

Duane: You once said that a festive celebration, to be an informal and fun-filled moment, has to be well prepared.

Veronica: Perhaps that's something you men don't really understand and appreciate. Things just don't happen when people come together. People like to eat and drink while they socialize. These things have to be prepared well. There has to be ice, clean glasses, and salads. The appetizers have to be well prepared beforehand. Meat has to be selected, cleaned, and tempered well before it's cooked.

Duane: I remember you were one to always look after these things. Looking back did you feel that people took advantage of your willingness to serve, to provide these aspects of our family gathering?

Veronica: Never! Well, there were times. But all in all, I was always glad to do it. I guess I have that knack. That was the way I participated in these gatherings. I think I'm a lot like Mother in this way. For her, the preparations and the eating was the celebration. She always said that as soon as we get all this done we can seat down and visit. That moment, however, would rarely come. By time she was ready to sit down everyone would be scattered.

Duane: Getting back to the Gospel story. You said there were times you would identify with Mary, the one who put all duties aside to sit at the feet of Jesus, just to listen to him.

Veronica: Those times were more that many would believe! I'm a busybody, but I pray and meditate a lot, too. I value the intimacy of friendship, dialog, listening, being together. I think that as I grew older, matured spiritually, being present to the other became more and more important.

Duane: Yes, I remember you writing about the ministry of presence. Talk more about this.

Veronica: You're getting me to do all the talking! Anyway, by ministry of presence I see exactly this in Mary's gesture. Mary put aside her duties upon the arrival of Jesus in her house. I think all of us can understand this very human gesture. She gave him her undivided attention. When friends come to visit us, it's not to see us doing our duties, but to share themselves with us. Mary was the gracious hostess. She could see that Jesus didn't come to her house to be fed, to be entertained or to look at things she was doing, but to be with her, to share life, joys and sorrow, to be present to one another.

Duane: So being present to the other is a type of ministry.

Veronica: Very much so. It took me a while to comprehend this. I was use to the idea that ministry is doing things for others, like Martha. Now I can see that the type of ministry Mary offers is something better.

Duane: But isn't that a manner to justify passivity, a do-nothing attitude?

Veronica: Of course it isn't, and you know that. To be present to the other is long from being passive. It's being hospitable, being open to the other in front of you. It's not doing things for others; it's being for the other. Dialog is possible this way. This creates space where each can be themselves, and not simply function in a task-centered manner.

Duane: The Gospel leads us to believe that Martha was a friend of Jesus also. Friendship, as a form of love, is service to the other, isn't it?

Veronica: Without a doubt! And I think it very important that you bring up friendship. I would guess that 86% of ministry is friendship. At least, that is, when we are at our best! Martha manifested her friendship by her service, administration, etc. I'm sure she was most pleased to have Jesus in her home. She wanted to do her best to receive him and serve him well. She couldn't do enough for him. This mentality is what kept me busy over all these years! Service is a form of love.

Duane: Can you say you cultivated friendship in your ministry?

Veronica: Fortunately, yes. That's probably what held me together. A task-oriented ministry many times treats the other as an object of our good works. Friendship treats the other as an equal. My experience with the bereavement ministry, ministry to the elderly, to sick, even to children, is that most people don't come looking for solutions. They want a presence. Maybe I'm overworking this word. But the notion is there. I'm comfortable to say that yes, I have been friend to many, many people. And I know they cherished me, too.

Duane: Are you timid by nature? How has this influenced your ministry?

Veronica: Timid by nature, but courageous by conviction. How do you like that? Yes, I'm timid and at times insecure. I always felt I had to force myself if I want to get anything done in life. I'm not all that self-assertive, but I learned that there are times one has to be. I think I've done a good job at it.

Duane: We grew up taught to be achievers, but not pushy. Don't be lazy nor a show-off. The job is to be done, do it, do it well, and feel the results. Nothing succeeds as success.

Veronica: Yes, those were some values we grew up with. We are products of a Post-WWII, the great USA, capitalist capital of the world, free enterprise and the works. Even in the Religious Life, our Congregations taught us much of the same. The Gospel however, is a constant challenge to renew perspectives. Jesus taught me a lot, too. I think that is why I many times found myself counterculture.

Duane: Returning to the Biblical narrative of Martha, Mary and Jesus. What do you think they talked about?

Veronica: I'm sure Martha and Mary were very concerned for Jesus' well being. I can believe that Jesus was shaken with the brutal killing of his cousin John the Baptizer. Jesus became a marked man. Their conversations weren't social niceties. They were up against serious options. I think Martha and Mary understood Jesus' position. Venturing further I would conjecture that these two women provided Jesus with a feminine logic.

Duane: That's a good one. What in the world do you mean by feminine logic?

Veronica: I just picked the phrase out of the air. What I mean is that they could perceive that all other logic is meaningless. On one side, there is the logic of revolt and hatred. The powers at large have dominated the people for so long. Jesus was very much aware of this. His own mother was now alone; Joseph had died in a work gang of men conscripted from Galilee to build roads for the Roman soldiers. There were so many other families like them. Things had to change. But the logic of revolt seemed meaningless. Jesus could see that his death also was certain. In what could people place their hope?

Duane: How do you see Jesus offering hope to people in these circumstances?
Veronica: Martha and Mary, two women, friends of Jesus, could see that he had to act according to his convictions. He loved his people; he loved his enemies. Love cannot be snuffed out. Death can't do away with love, nor get in the way of love. People have a memory. As the saying goes, a woman never forgets. People will never let love die.

Duane: Love remembered generates hope. Beautiful! You come up with some real jewels! I never considered Jesus' death and resurrection that way. Then you are saying that Martha and Mary... are you saying that your life has followed this logic?
Veronica: The Lord knows I tried. I hope that I will be remembered mostly for that.

Father Duane Roy, OSB
Mineiros, Goiás, Brazil
October 31, 1996

The Rock House
By Father Duane Roy OSB
Mineiros, Goiás, Brazil
May 6, 1995

Built long ago, when I don't know.
It was my place to be born and grow
Place of family, friends, work, prayer and play
Never to forget the cold winter night,
The hot summer day.

Standing watch over the south forty
And bottoms
Partner to a big red barn and a small brooder house
Wheat fields to the east and to the north
Alfalfa mowed and stacked in mounds of sort.

Scrubbed and occupied in the thirties
Lights and water in the mid forties
Youthful play and work into the fifties
Maturing and home until early sixties

A porch, the second floor, a living room
Pool table from attic to basement, every space used

Hard wood flooring, linoleum marred by the door
Hot gas stove warming walnut ice cream,
Popcorn on the floor.

Ample beds to rest after work, meals and pray
Stairway to maturity climbed every day
Siblings aplenty, guests never wanting
Card table setup, Jack of spades missing.

Birthday, evening prayers,
Wedding dinner for Ruth & Ken
Billy the dog, a lifelong faithful friend
Graduations almost annually, Christmases, company coming
Celebrate life and faith, all of us uniting.

A kitchen table for use daily,
Another with leaves for occasions special
Mashed potatoes and gravy, each in their place
Fried chicken or roast beef, somebody say grace.

Fenced in lawn, leveled and planted, farm and animals, too.
Knights and Daughters, Mom and Dad much to do
Kids growing up, learning, caring, many prizes won
4-H, HDU, FFA, PTA,
Catholic Farm Family of 1961.

Cedar and elm trees, buffalo grass,
Fire & tumble weeds,
Sand burrs, anthills, rusty nails and cockaburr seeds.
Barefooted from spring to fall after class
Anybody remember broken glass?

Swing on the porch, climb a tree,
Many summer evening
Floods, hail, tornadoes, storms a-brewing
Sunburns, cuts, bruises and sores.
Anyone feel hard times? Or bored?

Oil wells around, paraffin smell, salty brine,
Engines humming into the night
Bringing sleep with rhyme

A monthly oil check and hopes. What will we buy?
"A set of silver and plates that match," says Mom with a sigh.

The old rock house served its term, held its time,
Ceding only to modern hopes of something fine.
Transformed into elevated road
and back yard shrine.
Mother's hand painting immortalizes its memory, yours and mine.

Divine Gift Giver
Composed by Sister Veronica Roy, CSJ
New Almelo, Kansas @1993

In this food and drink have been the taste of the heavens.
We acknowledge that this food and drink we have enjoyed
Has been sun soaked and coaxed to life
Through the efforts of many hands
Rural and town together.

Now that the darkness of night is upon us,
We are mindful that the darkness of greed and exploitation
Also lengthens its shadows over our small plant Earth.

May we find hope in the lights
Kindled in this evening's presentations
Hope in one another and in all who form the web-work
Of peace and justice that spans our world.

May we treat with profound reverence
Each blade of grass and the earth beneath our feet,
The food and drink that nourishes,
And every person whose path shall cross ours.

By our lives and service, call forth from each of us
The light that is in every heart.
If you are willing,
May the seed of all our plans and dreams
Be sealed with your providential care.
Then we may in our days, behold your divine face,
Feel your embrace and live in your blessed presence.

Grant this prayer in the name of your Son, who dwells with you
And the Holy Spirit, One God forever and ever. Amen.

The "Sister Veronica Memorial Center" affiliated with Nobel Peace Prize nominee

In March 2000, five members of the Roy family, Ken, Ruth, Joan, Roger, and Linda traveled to Brazil to meet with our brother, Father Duane Roy, OSB, to attend the inauguration of the "Sister Veronica Memorial Center," and to witness where real miracles take place.

This administrative center of Pastoral da Criança, "Pastoral of the Child" in Mineiros, Goiâs, Brazil is a small, but efficient facility built from donations from family and friends in Sister Veronica's memory. Many local businesses in Mineiros, Brazil donated labor and materials, and the local Catholic Church donated the land.

In 2001, the Brazil-wide Pastoral of the Child program was among those nominated for the Nobel Peace Prize. The "Sister Veronica Memorial" affiliate in Mineiros is but one of many strategically placed centers.

In light of the September 11, 2001 terrorist attacks on the World Trade Center in New York, and the Pentagon in Washington, D.C. it was announced on October 12, 2001 that the Nobel award committee selected the United Nations and their General Secretary, Kofi Annan.

Dr. Zilda Arns Neumann, founder and national coordinator of the program said, "Future peace depends on today's children. It is necessary to invest in them and in their families. This is what Pastoral of the Child does, completing eighteen years of uninterrupted work to prevent sickness, to promote health, to better quality of life, to prevent violence by the construction of a culture of peace in our day-to-day life."

She went on to say that the Nobel Peace Prize award would have crowned the work of thousands of poor volunteers who share what they have with their neighbors, struggling for a better quality of life. Nevertheless, to be nominated was reward enough.

Pastoral of the Child is a social action arm of the National Conference of Bishops of Brazil and one of the largest in the world to work with health, nutrition and education of mothers and children from pre-natal to age six. In Brazil, 42 million people are living in a state of poverty, and 16 million are in a state of absolute misery.

Children below the age of six are the first victims of family degeneration, many times caused by unemployment, lack of housing, security, basic health and education services. Actions are aimed at the communities of needy families in the outskirts of big cities and the centers of misery of the small and medium-sized cities throughout Brazil.

Evaluating the past ten years of experience, the Pastoral of the Child program shows that it is possible to get to the root of the problem and reduce child mortality and malnutrition, develop the potential of the child, educate women, reduce criminality and violence in families, and as a consequence, promote Christian fraternity in the communities and streets through continuous education.

A base of 150,000 workers — mostly volunteers — makes Pastoral of the Child possible. Only 10.8% of all receipts is spent on administrative and technical assistance, making it a model for many other Third World countries.

The 12-step action plan is based on support to pregnant women with nutritional guidance for breast-feeding; monthly weight and growth monitoring of the child; advising of foods with great nutritional value; controlling illnesses such as diarrhea with homemade serum; controlling respiratory illnesses; promoting the use of herbal medicines and routine vaccinations; educating parents; preventing accidents in the home; preventing sexually transmitted illness such as AIDS; and natural family planning using the collar method. A final action step is to restore human dignity through developing the spirituality of the child. In short, these actions save lives and sow seeds of peace and hope.

It is a tribute to the life and good works of Sister Veronica Roy, CSJ that her name is associated with this outstanding program.

(Cf. www.rebidia.org.br, Homepage of Pastoral of the Children. "A History of The Pastoral of the Child; Sowing Hope and Peace." Translated by Father Duane Roy OSB, February 3, 2002.)

NOTES

Chapter One

1. In the other car that stuck Sister Veronica's car were three teenagers, who were all seated in the front, however, none were wearing seat belts. One of them died, too.

2. Traffic accidents are the number-one killer for people up to age thirty-seven. From 1982 through 1996, an estimated 85,396 lives were saved by safety belts. They reduce the risk of fatal injury to front-seat occupants in cars by 45 percent. However, a head-on collision is statically the deadliest. The police report indicated Sister Veronica probably died instantly.

The following graphic description is adapted from "Buckle Your Seat Belts," by the Georgia Paramedics Against Drunk Drivers.

During the first tenth of a second of the head-on collision, the front bumper and grill collapsed.

The next tenth of a second found the hood crumbling, rising and striking the windshield as the spinning rear wheels lifted from the ground. Simultaneously, fenders began wrapping themselves around any solid object. Although the car's frame had been halted, the rest of her Chevrolet Corsica was still going 55 miles an hour. Instinct caused Sister Veronica to stiffen her legs against the crash — these snapped at the knee joint like toothpicks. Her hands had gripped the steering wheel and the delicate bones shattered.

During the third tenth of a second, the steering wheel started to disintegrate and the steering column aimed for her chest.

The fourth tenth of the second found twenty-four inches of her cars' front end wrecked, while the rear end still moved at 35 mph. Sister Veronica's body was still traveling at 55 mph.

In the fifth tenth of a second, Sister Veronica was impaled on the steering column and blood rushed into her lungs.

At the sixth tenth of a second, the impact had built up to the point that her feet are ripped out of her shoes. The brake pedal broke off. The car frame buckled in the middle. Sister Veronica's head smashed into the collapsed windshield as the rear wheels, still spinning, fell back to earth.

In the seventh tenth of a second, hinges ripped loose, doors flew open and the backseats broke free, and anything in the trunk struck her from behind. Her firmly buckled seat belt couldn't protect her from this force. In the last three tenths of a second Sister Veronica was already dead.

3. Among the neighboring families were: H.W. McCauley, Joe Griebel, Raymond Biery, Dave Hunter, Fred Reed, Oria Grover, Frank Carpenter, Carl Holsman, Carl Probasco, Reid Baxter, Albert Blauer, W.H. Burton, G.E. Graham, Zack McEwen, P. Probasco, D.C. Grover, and Floyd Blauer.

Chapter Two

1. Later they heard from the pulpit that Pope Pius XI condemned Nazism in his 1937 encyclical. After that Pope died, in February 1939, only six months lapsed between the coronation of Pope Pius XII and the outbreak of the Second World War. In the Jubilee Year of 2000, the Vatican apologized for not taking a stronger stand against Nazism during this war, and asked forgiveness especially from those of the Jewish faith, and others who suffered as a result.

2. This was the equivalent of the current Community Food Banks/First Harvest where government-issue foods are stored, as well as packaged foods donated by local churches and charities through food drives.

3. Currently, a charity called Christ Child Society (whose motto is "We are called to see Christ in every needful, disadvantaged child") has been providing layettes to newborns for families in need for over a century of service, regardless of race or creed.

4. St. Joseph's Church in Damar rivals St. Fidelis Church, in Victoria, Kansas, which was completed in 1911 and is commonly known as "Cathedral of the Plains."

5. Father Duane Roy officiated at the baptism.

6. The boundaries of Rooks County defined by the Legislature in 1867, were organized in 1872, and established its first post office that same year. The county took its name from John C.

Rooks, a soldier of the 11th Kansas Cavalry. The first settlers arrived in 1871. The first newspaper was dated 1876. The tide of immigration really started for Rooks County in 1878 when the advantages of the broad open prairies became known. The first reliable census taken in 1875 totaled 567, while five years later, the population jumped to 8,112. In 1996 the population was nearly 1,500; currently, it hovers between that number and 2,500.

7. http://www.kansascommerce.com/0107/funfacts.

8. After WWI the anti-Catholicism Ku Klux Klan flourished nationwide. While it died out somewhat in the 1930s, its fundamental sentiments and mentality continued to linger among some groups of people. On a related note, in 1925 the Denver Catholic Register listed more than 2,400 names of the KKK "hooded ones." During Prohibition — before 1933 — altar wine required a permit, and the KKK specifically attacked its use.

Chapter Three

1. The children of Stanislas and Rosanna Hebert Morin: Anna, Alphonse, Angela (Sister Rose Irma), Emile, Mary, Rosa, Joseph, Edward, Phillip, Joseph, Olive, Levi, unnamed daughter died at birth.

2. As reported by neighboring cousin, Vitilane Senesac Plante, and retold by Marieda Brin Newell.

3. See the 23-page booklet, "The Roots of Seven Dolors," Sacred Heart Academy, by Sister Susan Kongs, CSJ, 1982-1983, for a history of the school. CSJ Motherhouse archives, Concordia, Kansas.

4. After the Academy was no longer a boarding school and changed its name to Seven Dolors, Sister Rose Irma was placed in charge of the dietary department at St. Mary's Hospital in Manhattan, Kansas from 1936 until her retirement in 1970, while the Sisters of St. Joseph ran it.

5. Doka, Kenneth, Editor, *Children Mourning, Mourning Children,* pp. 64-65.

6. In 1992 Sister Veronica became fascinated by this accident. Researching library records, and interviewing relatives, she found the scene and reenacted how it might have happened.

7. While biblical studies are encouraged today, in pre-Vatican II days Bible reading was not encouraged for Catholics. This was a throw back to the Protestant Reformation.

8. In 1993 an heirloom came into the family. Rosalie Hebert, who inherited a four-inch Miracle Cross from her grandmother Louise Hebert, bestowed it on Sister Veronica with the stipulation that it was never to be sold, and was to always remain in the family.

9. *A guide for hospice care workers and all who live with the terminally ill.* Saint Paul Books & Media.

10. Interview with Ron Campbell, a senior at Plainville, Kansas in 1963.

11. At some point his sister, RoseLee, lived and worked for Doctor Peterson in Palco, taking care of the house and children.

12. Linda Roy Cross, *A Kansas Woman: Biography of Olive Morin Roy.* 1980-1982 manuscript.

13. Mother later returned to Marymount for a retreat in 1963, thirty-two years later, after six of her nine children left home.

14. Marriage banns, a pre-Vatican II church law, required pastors to publicly announce the names of those who intend to wed, during divine services on three successive Sundays or holy days, for the purpose of discovering any existing impediments to the marriage. The announcement was to mention the obligation of the faithful to reveal any knowledge of such impediments.

15. In the pre-Vatican II days the four types of Masses were pontifical, solemn, sung Mass or *Missa Cantata* (a high Mass) and low Mass. Low Mass was celebrated without music, the entire Mass being said by the Priest instead of being sung. Altar server boys were the only assistants.

16. At one time there were three towns in Kansas named Kenneth, including one in Rooks County, which became extinct sometime before the 1911-1912, as did the Sheridon County town, which was located in 1877 and abandoned in 1886. Currently there is a town in Johnson County, by that name with a population of under 1,000.

17. Sister Veronica compiled *Our Saindon Cousins* in 1989-1991 and *Ma Famille* in 1992-1994. This writer collected stories from my siblings in 1980 as a gift for our mother. The 56-page booklet is called, "I Remember, I Remember."

Chapter Four

1. Classmates were: Gary Burton, Gerald Lindsey, Billy Harman, Wayne Lowry, Darrel Bedore, Johnnie Fetteroff, Leigh Arbogast, Leonard Folsom, Juanita Northup, Rea Burton, Phyllis O'Connor, Connie Larson and Claudia Anderson. Source: 1952 *Eagle School Annual*, Webster, Kansas.

2. Our brother, Allan, was hired to drive a 13-cubic yard Euclid bottom-dump truck to haul earth, during construction near the Kirwin, Kansas Reservoir. During an accident, he lost up to the first joint of his finger.

3. *Hays Daily News*, March 22, 1990, p.16.

4. *Hays Daily News*, October 9, 1955, p.8.

5. In the 1963 graduating class of Webster High were John Hance, this writer Linda Roy, and Shannon Veverka.

6. *Hays Daily News*, October 9, 1955, p.8

7. Ibid.

8. Source: www.gp.usbr.gov/ks/WEBPC.HTM, Webster Unit, Kansas Project Construction.

Chapter Five

1. Oria Grover, Floyd Blauer, Frank Lindsey, Dale Kellogg and Harold Riffe.

2. John 12.24.

Chapter Six

1. Massey, Morris E., *The People Puzzle: What You Are Is Where You Were When*, c.1979.

2. There were other farm-related accidents. Dad's brother, Philip Roy died in 1999, as a result of being thrown from a wagon while training horses.

Chapter Seven

1. During 1998, more than 91 percent of the land in Kansas was devoted to agricultural use with about 45 percent used as cropland. Each year, Kansas wheat farmers harvest about 20 percent of the U.S. total. www.kansascommerce.com.

Chapter Eight

1. As Jesus and his disciples were on their way, he came to a village where a woman named Martha opened her home to him. She had a sister, named Mary, who sat at the Lord's feet, listening to what he said. But Martha was distracted by all the preparations that had to be made. She came to him and asked, 'Lord, don't you care that my sister has left me to do the work by myself? Tell her to help me! Luke 10:38-42.

Chapter Nine

1. The Nova movie theatre was renovated for live performances. Donations were accepted for sponsorships. Some family members sponsored chairs, while our brother, Roger and his wife, Jackie, fittingly sponsored the popcorn machine.

Chapter Ten

1. One of Da Vinci's best known masterpieces, a mural of Jesus telling his twelve disciples that one of them will betray him. In mid-1999 "The Last Supper" (1494-1498) emerged again after a twenty-one year restoration, and draws crowds, by reservation only, to view the religious art of which surprisingly the faces, of Jesus and the apostles, show an intensity in their expression."

2. The Marian Outdoor Shrine Guild of Conception, Missouri gives these advantages for having an outdoor shrine: 'It beautifies your grounds and home; enriches your family life; widens

Mary's influence; inspires spiritual thoughts; reminds non-Catholics of devotion to Mary; prods the conscience of fallen-away Catholics; provides a primer of love and faith for children; is an open door to prospective converts; is a source of prayer and meditation; is a center of prayer for your family, and an inspiration to others to build their shrines to Mary." Source, John and Olive Roy application for Farm Family Award, which Sister Veronica compiled in 1960.

Chapter Eleven

1. Sister M. Evangeline Thomas, PhD, *Footprints on the Frontier: A History of the Sisters of Saint Joseph Concordia, Kansas*, The Newman Press. Maryland, 1948, p.354.

2. Sister Cortona Dome taught grades 1-3 at Sacred Heart Academy from 1934-1939, where Mother, herself, attended in 1929-1930. Or this may have been Sister Cortona Marie Robben.

3. As a member of the CSJ Leadership team, Sister Veronica officiated at Sister Regina Marie Dickman's Bible vigil and funeral Mass, in August 1995, just three months before her own death.

4. It is claimed that these mulberry trees had such a huge canopy that these would provide shade for 100 people.

5. Venial sins are less serious offenses and do not annihilate the friendship of the soul with God, as do Mortal sins which are grievous sins with full knowledge and consent. Examples of Mortal sins are; murder, grave theft, and blasphemy.

6. When Father Duane Roy baptized Mitchell Jack Roy Davis at Mass for the family at St. Joseph's Church in Damar, September 2001, three fourth-grade-cousins (Christopher Cross, Jonathan Roy and Joshua Roy) were altar servers.

7. *Footprints*, p. 264.

8. May 24, Ascension of Our Lord; August 15, Assumption of the Virgin Mary; November 1, All Souls Day; December 7, Immaculate Conception; and December 25, Christmas Day.

9. Webster Schools competed in basketball with the neighboring rural communities of Edmond, Densmore, Prairie View, Clayton, Bogue, Damar, Palco, Codell and Zurich.

10. "The Lord be with you". The response is: "And may His spirit be also with you".

11. Sister Bernard Marie Schruben CSJ, received her habit 1944. Sister Marie de Guzman, entered the Dominican Order in 1903.

12. Isaiah 6:1-8. The Dan Schutte song, "Here I Am Lord," was sung at her funeral Mass.

13. Ingrid Bergman and Alan Burgess, *My Story*, Dell Publishing, 1980.

14. In 1954, about the time Ila Mae was memorizing the prayer from the ad, the Maryknoll congregation was placed under the direct jurisdiction of the Sacred Congregation for the Propagation of the Faith, and designated as the Maryknoll Sisters of St. Dominic.

15. Tatyana Bobrova. Email correspondence. Jan 10, 2001.

16. *Footprints*.

17. The Congregation of the Sisters of St. Joseph was founded in the village of LePuy, France, in 1650 when Father Jean-Pierre Médaille, S.J., a Jesuit priest called together six women of varied backgrounds to live a communal life and to minister to orphans, prisoners, the sick and the destitute. Disbanded at the time of the French Revolution, it was later reorganized at Etienne, France in 1808 by Sister St. John Fontbonne, who escaped death in the Reign of Terror of 1794. In 1836, at the request of the first Bishop of St. Louis, Missouri, Mother St. John Fontbonne sent six Sisters, from France, to establish a school for the deaf in Carondelet, Missouri, the first CSJ foundation in the United States.

18. cf Lc 23, 49; 24, 10.

19. One of the Brazilian programs of *Pastoral da Criança*, dedicated in Sister Veronica's memory, is teaching prostitutes a trade in sewing, as an alternate means of survival.

20. An additional and interesting historical perspective of Religious Women can be found by reading *Sisters in Arms* by Jo Ann Kay McNamara.

21. Sue Evans, professor with the University of Arizona South, is a student of Advaita Vedantic from an Indian mystic tradition.

Chapter Twelve

1. Edited by Reverend John P. O'Connell, *The Holy Family Catholic Bible, A Practical Dictionary of Biblical and General Catholic Information*, The Catholic Press, Inc. Chicago, 1961.

2. Sister M. Evangeline Thomas, PhD. *Footprints on the Frontier*, Newman Press, Westminster, Maryland, 1948, p.264.

3. *Sisters of St. Joseph of Concordia, Kansas newspaper*, Centenary issue, June 1983.

4. Mary Beth Marklein, "Going back to school," *USA Today*, www.usatoday.com, June 8, 2000.

5. *CSJ newspaper*, Centenary Issue.

6. www.csjkansas.org

7. Sister Patricia McLennon was elected President of the Sisters of St. Joseph of Concordia for the 2000-2004 term.

8. The Immaculate Heart Chapel at the college where Ila Mae "prayed her heart out" was financed by the lifetime private savings of Bishop Cunningham and erected in his memory.

Chapter Thirteen

1. Of the Sixteen Prophets and Nine Junior Angelicas two dropped out before making first vows. The remaining twenty-three women were: Marcia Allen, Jean Befort, Polegia Bloomerader, Diane Brin, Anna Marie Broxterman, Mary Lou Demay, Bernadine Divel, Rosemary Farrell, Bernita Heier, Donna Faye Huelsmann, Patricia McLennon, Nancy Meade, Margaret Mary Miller, Shirley Muir, Donna Otter, Virginia Pearl, Madonna Ready, Barbara Reiland, Ila Mae Roy, Marilyn Stahl, Mary Louise Stroneitus, Betty Suther, Mary Jo Thummel.

2. Within the Bible are deeds and prophecies in a series of sixteen books. They are divided into the four Major Prophets: Isaiah, Jeremiah, Ezekiel, and Daniel and the twelve Minor Prophets: Hosea, Joel, Amos, Obadiah, Johah, Micah, Nahum, Habakkuk, Zephaniah, Haggai, Zechariah and Malachi.

3. The Mistress of Postulants, the much-loved Sister Therese Marie Stafford later became Mother Superior/President. She later died in office of cancer in 1969. Stafford Hall, a nursing facility at the Motherhouse is named in her memory, in 1970.

4. www.csjkansas.org

5. It is unknown who influenced Sister Norbertine's talent. Some say she admired the works of Sickle (or Sickel) and copied many of his paintings. It is possible instead, or in addition, she was influenced by Sully, an American artist who was trained by a French artist, Or perhaps it was Sisley, the French landscape painter known for bringing out underlying emotions in his art.

6. The referenced Father Matthias later become a Bishop in Brazil and after his death a 221-page book was compiled of his significant writings. First written in Portuguese, Father Duane Roy translated the book into English in 2001 on the 10th anniversary of Matthias' death.

7. The biblical masterpiece of the Canticles/Song of Songs is sometimes interpreted as a parable on the true meaning of mutual love — the union between Christ and the individual soul. According to the Bible (Catholic parish 1994-1995 edition) the prophet Hosea began the tradition of describing the relation between Yahweh and Israel in terms of marriage. The Lord is the Lover and his people are the Beloved. The Lord led the chosen people, by degrees, to an exalted spiritual union with himself in the bond of perfect love.

8. St. Paul uses an exalted image in his theology of marriage. Man and woman, in their union, image Christ, who loves and gives Himself to His Church (cf. Eph 5, 21-33). St. Paul also exhorts those not married, like him (widowed) to live the celibate life, as a particular gift from God (cf 1Cor 7, 7; 25-40).

Chapter Fourteen

1. Flower girls were:Deborah Predmore, Christine Tyler, Christine Tieking, Susan Cailteux, Cynthia Chaput, Kathleen Ann Foster, Janice Tracy and Mary Frances Stangel.

2. This is not to be confused with the all-encompassing burqua, the body and face-shielding garment with only a three inch mesh-covered opening for eyes that woman from Afghanistan were required to wear, as dictated by Taliban rule prior to 2002.

3. "The Veronica," also known as the vernicle, or the sudarium (meaning a cloth for wiping sweat), was the cloth offered to Christ by Saint Veronica on the road to Calvary so he could wipe his face. "The Veronica" became the most reproduced image in Christendom and perhaps the most famous relic in Rome. The Italian poet, Dante (1265-1321) wrote about Croatian pilgrims flocking to Rome to see the Veronica in Paradiso, canto XXXI lines 103-108. The Veronica came to stand for Christ's continuing presence as a miraculous image, an exact replica.

4. According to Sister M. Evangeline Thomas, *Footprints on the Frontier*.

5. A Litany is a prayer recited or sung alternately by a Priest or other leader and the people. The Priest or leader recites or sings the invocations, and then people respond after each invocation with the petition, for example: "Have mercy on us" or "Pray for us." Ejaculations are a recited were short, fervent prayers consisting of only a few words, which can be repeated easily and frequently, for example: "Most Sacred Heart of Jesus, have mercy on us," "My Lord and my God," "O Mary, conceived without sin, pray for us who have recourse to thee."

6. Proverbs 12:25.

Chapter Fifteen

1. In 1962, Cesar Chavez, influenced by Gandhi and King Jr., founded the National Farm Worker's Association.

2. *New York Times*. August 7, 2000, p.A22.

3. Doug Kreutz, "Speaking of God: Renewed interest in public prayers raises questions of sensitivity and balance," *Arizona Daily Star*, September 25, 2001, p.E1.

Chapter Sixteen

1. Among the twelve laywomen are five identified as: Mrs Joan Spang, Burnita Bressanrd, Mrs. Norma Richardson, Florita Mascasaet, and Ada Negron. Among the Sisters are Wilma Ann, Willam Mertens, Roseann and Myra.

2. According to the *CSJ quarterly newspaper*, June 1983,

3. Currently St. Josephs Hospital is called the Cloud County Health Center, wholly owned subsidiary of the Salina Regional Health Center.

4. Dobson, Dr. James. *The Strong Willed Child*, Tyndale House Publishing, Wheaton, Il. 1978.

5. Thirty years later, Madelyn Murray O'Hair, her son and granddaughter, all who disappeared in 1995, were found murdered by a business associate. He was charged in 2001.

Chapter Seventeen

1. June 1983

2. Sister Veronica Roy, CSJ, *Ma Famille*, 1994, p.282.

3. As told to Cheryl Calvin in 1999.

4. Sister Diane earned a Master's degree in Nursing and Hospital Administration at St. Louis, Missouri. She became acting administrator at St. John's Hospital in Salina, from 1975-1977, and then moved to Rome, Georgia where she remains in health ministry, as the first neuromuscular therapist-Sister in the CSJ community.

5. The five other Americans were Fathers Matthias Schmidt, Herbert Hermes, Eric Deitchman, Ralph Koehler, and Brother Robert Heiman, who went along with Father Duane in 1971. Schmidt and Hermes were later appointed Bishops in Brazil.

Chapter Nineteen

1. *Cursillo* meaning, "little course" refers to the Renewal movement, which seeks to restore the world to Christ. The program is divided into three sections of three days each. The key to the movement is to change one's own mind according to the mind of Christ, and then to gather with, and support others who have committed themselves to Christ, in order that the world might be transformed.

Chapter Twenty

1. Father Joseph Vann, O.F. M., editorial supervision, *Lives of Saints*, John J. Crawley & Co., Inc., New York, 1953, pp.353-357.

2. The directors of the 30-day retreat were Sisters Carolyn Weethorn, Paula Dross, Marge Pakulski, Janet Mock and Marie Kerwin, and four Jesuits, [Father Mike Rush, John Nande—, Patrick J. Lee, S.J. and Edwardo del Loysey,

3. Jer, 10

4. Ibid, *Lives of Saints*.

Chapter Twenty-one

1. At the time of this writing, twenty-two years later, the price per bushel of wheat is even slightly less then $2.85, and prices have not escalated with inflation.

2. Image Book paperbook edition, 1962. p.200.

3. Pearl S. Buck, *The Good Earth*, Pocket Books, New York, published 1931, Pulitzer prize 1932, 1966 printing, p.342.

Chapter Twenty-two

1. Meals on Wheels originated in Great Britain, during the Blitz in 1939 (the year of Sister Veronica's birth) when many people, who lost their homes, had no place to prepare meals. Later, the U.S. home-delivered program started in Philadelphia in 1954 but was not formed officially as Meals on Wheels Association of America (MWAA) until 1974.

2. P.214.

3. The Sisters of St. Joseph gave the hospital (under the auspices of the St. Joseph Sisters in Wichita, Kansas) to the Franciscan Sisters of Peoria, Illinois, who also managed St. Anthony's Hospital, in Rockford. Rather than a financial exchange, funds were added to the Sisters' retirement account over the next twenty years.

Chapter Twenty-three

1. Patricia Hampl. *Virgin Time: In Search of the Contemplative Life*, Farrar, Straus and Giroux, New York, 1992.

2. The Concordia, Kansas Sisters of St. Joseph Foundation, created in 1981, contributed $5,000 to the *Pastoral da Criança* fund. Other substantial contributors were Sister Veronica's immediate family, especially Father Duane, relatives, friends, and two Brazilian Buffet fundraisers, in 1999 and 2001, hosted by this writer in Tucson, Arizona. Among those present at the March 2001 dedication of the Sister Veronica Memorial Center in Brazil were Roger, Ken and Ruth Roy, Joan Rader and this writer, Linda Cross.

Chapter Twenty-five

1. 2 Samuel 22:40.
2. 1976 edition,
3. 1979 edition
4. Romans 9:21
5. Jeremiah 18:6.

Chapter Twenty-six

1. This is one of two hospitals within Ness County. Grisell was built in 1928. In the 1940s when Ness County wanted its own hospital, the county was divided into two district: Grisell being in district one. Ness County in district 2, was built in 1947. Source: Ness City Chamber of Commerce.

Chapter Twenty-seven

1. Ministry entails education, growth and development, care and challenges, the giving of self, love, and purposefulness. In this fast-paced world, Sisters are racing to keep up with the changing needs of parishes and the Catholic Church. With the Priest shortage, it is becoming feasible and necessary for some small rural ministries to be administered by lay or religious women.

2. In 1989 another newspaper was started, the *Stockton Sentinel*, and the *Rooks County Record* closed within the year.

3. Among the Ministerial Alliance in attendance were the Reverends Exie Barber, Assembly of God; Dwite Brown, Church of God; Glen Sandquist, Bethlehem Lutheran; Robert Dealey, Zion Lutheran; and Floyd Starr, Presbyterian. Among the Priests were Monsignor Armaud Girard, and Fathers Emil Labbe, Alex Leiker, Bob Reif, Basil Torres, Paulinus Karlin, and Mark Linenberger. The Sisters in attendance were: Sisters Doris Marie Flax, Clarice Richmeier, Adeline Marie Wasinger, Vera Meis, and Barbara Ellen Apaceller.

4. *Trego County Western Kansas World* newspaper, 1981, date unknown

5. Sandra Valdez Gerdes, "Goal of local Sisters has been to fulfill Tucson's needs," *Arizona Citizen*, February 23, 2001, pp. 1,2D.

Chapter Twenty-eight

1. A period-end report, prepared by the CSJ of Concordia leadership team of 1991-1995, showed the median age of membership was seventy-one years old. During these four years, there were thirty-eight deaths. Two more Sisters were lost through dispensation (a formal application to sever membership with the congregation).

Chapter Twenty-nine

1. Christ the King parish newsletter, March 1982.

Chapter Thirty

1. Of the original Sixteen Prophets, one died and four left the religious life. The remaining eleven CSJ band members as of 1984:

Current name	Professed name	Convent location at that time:
Sister Anna Marie Broxterman	Sister Mary Jeannette	Silver City, New Mexico
Sister Nancy Meade	Sister Marie Cecile	Boonville, Missouri
Sister Pat McLennon	Sister John Michael	Berkley, California
Sister Joseph Ellen Divel	unchanged	Grand Island, Nebraska
Sister Jean Befort	Sister Margaret Jean	New Almelo, Kansas
Sister Rosemary Farrell	Sister Rose Gabriel	Silver City, New Mexico
Sister Virginia "Ginger" Pearl	Sister Thomas Ann	Pawnee Rock, Kansas
Sister Faye Huelsmann	Sister Jonita	Grand Junction, Colorado
Sister Donna Otter	Sister Frances de Chantel	Junction City, Kansas
Sister Marcia Allen	Sister Elizabeth Marie	Concordia, Kansas
Sister Veronica Mary Roy	unchanged	WaKeeney, Kansas

2. Sister Jean Befort was there, and the most likely the other was Sister Ginger Pearl.

3. St. Paul 2:9

4. In 2002 Sister Rose Grennan celebrated her 75th jubilee. Four celebrated their 70th jubilee: Sisters Evangelista Kehoe, Laureta Dinkel, Mary Kevin Walker, and Edna Louise Kohn.

5. *Rooks County Record*, and the *Trego County Western Kansas World* newspaper.

Chapter Thirty-one

1. It is the biblical Mary who represents the role as a woman seeking education. She was contemplative, learning spiritual truths, and choosing to be educated as a male would learn. Her sister, Martha, was anxious, unduly concerned, overburdened, and distracted by the many chores she had to do around the house. She was confused and driven in many directions. In her frustration, Martha turned her anger toward the Lord. Jesus instead expressed his love for her in showing her what she is feeling and in the way he repeats her name, "Martha, Martha, you are anxious and troubled concerning many things." Jesus tells Martha that what Mary has chosen will not be removed from her. Luke 10:38-42.

2. 1 Thess 3:12

3. *Arlington Catholic Herald*. Oct. 3, 1996, p 12.

4. In the Bible (Mt. 20:14-15) when all the workers in the vineyard receive the same wage, it is due to the owner's generosity to the latest arrivals. The earlier workers are resentful and envious. Yet the fact that the laborers in the parable, who were sent to the vineyard early, while others came along later, were paid the same, it is an encouraging reminder that no matter how great or how small our efforts on behalf of the Gospel may seem to be, if we devote ourselves wholeheartedly and generously to what the Lord calls us to do, those efforts will one day bear fruit." Father Paul deLadurantaye, "Laborers For the Harvest," *Arlington Catholic Herald*, September 19, 1996, p. 6.

5. Joyce Roy Lawson inherited this collection.

6. Father Duane inherited this collection, which has been donated to St. Benedict's Abbey. As our own family relic, the Face of Christ medal, which Sister Veronica was wearing at the hour of her death, has passed throughout the family to share its richness.

7. A Seder Meal includes unleavened bread — like hard crackers — parsley in salted water, roasted egg, shank bones, bitter herbs — like horseradish — and haroseth, a mixture of apple, walnut, cinnamon and wine.

Chapter Thirty-two

1. The Osage Indian nation helped the community of Nicodemus to survive its first winter in 1880, by sharing their wild game with the pioneers. The black pioneer town of Nicodemus, founded by newly freed Kentucky slaves following the Civil War a century earlier, became a national historic site, attracting tourist from around the country. *Wichita Eagle*, Oct. 13, 1996, p.24A.

2. This celebration was actually held at the end of July in this community, coinciding with Mother's birthday, and our parents often joined in the celebration, as Anglos often did.

3. The other Priests were Abbot Ralph Koehler, OSB, Fathers Regis Hickey, OSB and Jude Burbach, OSB, of St. Benedict's Abbey, Atchison, Ks.; Father Bob Reif, Park; Father Ernest Gallagher, Zurich; Father Paul Becquet, CPPS, WaKeeney; Father John Lahey, Osborne; and Father Roger Meitl, Beloit.

4. *Salina Diocese Catholic Register*, October 1985.

Chapter Thirty-three

1. *Arizona Daily Star*, date and page unknown

2. There are some performing arts, such as *Quilters*, a musical that celebrates the spirit of America's frontier women, but none celebrate the work pioneer Religious Women have done for this country. Although the book, *Footprints on the Frontier: A History of the Sisters of Saint Joseph, Concordia, Kansas*, written in 1948 by Sister M. Evangeline Thomas, Ph.D. does serve as a valuable documentary of their earlier accomplishments. Another author, Catherine Whitney, researched and recorded the life of the Dominican Community in, *The Calling: A Year in the Life of an Order of Nuns* (Brilliance).

Chapter Thirty-four

1. Olive Morin Roy's biography, in manuscript form by this writer, is called, *A Kansas Woman*. A novel, *Prairie Rose*, loosely based on Mother's life, is also in manuscript form and is currently being revised by this writer.

2. A third generation of siblings plan to visit the St. Anne de Beaupre shrine in 2002.

3. The largest genealogical library in the world is located in Salt Lake City, Utah. The Church of Jesus Christ of Latter-Day Saints has been involved in genealogy since its founding nearly 170 years ago and it encourages searches and makes its world renowned genealogical library readily accessible. There are more than two million rolls of microfilm copies of census, thousands of books, and other records from more than 100 countries.

4. Alphonse Saindon died in 1961;Alverize Brin died in 1987; and Alphonse Desmarteau died in 1988.

5. She credits August 15, the Feast of the Assumption, with the date of printing.

Chapter Thirty-five

1. In a number of cities Priests have been mugged, assaulted or killed when their assailants arrive at the rectory asking for money. On a related note, WaKeeney is located on the heavily traveled road between Denver and Kansas City. Numerous large drug busts have taken place in Trego County, along Interstate 70, as transients passing through this small town underestimate strong law enforcement, especially under our brother, Ken Roy, who was chief of police for twenty-nine years until his retirement in 1996.

2. Nancy Frazier O'Brien, *Catholic Vision*, April 2001, p.16.

Chapter Thirty-six

1. *Arizona Daily Star.* June 16, 2000. p. A19

2. Father Todd O'Leary is pastor of St. Thomas the Apostle, in Tucson, Arizona.

3. Vatican II, No. 1577

4. *Arizona Daily Star.* May 19, 2000 p. A7

5. *Arizona Daily Star.* July 12, 2000. p. A8.

6. Vatican II, No. 29

7. Matthew. 25:23

8. clipping on file without date.

Chapter Thirty-seven

1. The Manna House of Prayer and Spirituality Center was opened in 1978 for retreats and workshops for spiritual growth. It has 30 sleeping rooms. This is where the Roy family stayed at the time of Sister Veronica's funeral. It once served as a hospital, then as a home for the aged and infirmed until 1977.

2. Sister Veronica called the color of the car "white," although on the fatality report the color is stated as "silver."

3. Thomas Moore. *Care of the Soul. A Guide for Cultivating Depth and Sacredness in Everyday Life.* Harper Perennial, 1992.

4. *The Holy Family Catholic Bible.* The Catholic Press. Chicago, Illinois. 1961. A Practical Dictionary. p. 46.

5. Sister Veronica recalled the biblical passage of Christ taunted by the Pharisees not to heal because it is the Sabbath. Christ didn't cower and say, "Oh you're right, I had better not heal because it is the Sabbath and that is work." Rather, Jesus defended himself, "Which of you, if it was the Sabbath, would leave your cattle drowning in the well?"

Chapter Thirty-nine

1. Luke 13:25

2. Workman Publishing.

3. In the Hebert family one son remained single. One married daughter had no issue.

4. The cause of Sister Veronica's death was a blunt force trauma to the head and chest. It was not only from the steering wheel impact, but also when her car was abruptly stopped by the near-direct head-on collision, with the 1980 Pontiac Catalina, that the books in the trunk propelled forward, rushed against her head, and moved at the same velocity at which the car was traveling just seconds before.

On a related note, this was undoubtedly the same roadway Frigon great-grandparents traveled 110 years earlier, in 1885, during the winter they lived in Cloud County.

Chapter Forty

1. *Ma Famille*, pp.403-411.

2. Telephone interview with Valerie VanLoenen, 2001.

Chapter Forty-one

1. Veronica Jill was born to James and Teresa Roy Davis in 1999. Mary Marie — twin of Chloe Marie, and daughter of Duane and Nena Roy — died at birth in 2000.

2. Mother had another sister, Rosa Balthazor, called "Rosie," who died in 1982.

3. Prepared by Sister Faith Schuster, OSB, *A Story from the Land: The Autobiography of Sister Scholastica Schuster OSB*, Scholastic Printery, Atchison, Kansas, 1996.

4. Melvin Desmarteau is one of Sister Rose Irma Morin's oldest nephews, and the son of Emile and Anna Morin Desmarteau. On a related note, research shows that a significant number of Nuns, who never retire from their work, and lifelong devotion to God, are notable for an absence of Alzheimer's disease. See David Snowden, Ph.D. *Aging with Grace: What the Nun Study Teaches Us About Leading Longer, Healthier and More Meaningful Lives*, Bantam, May 2001.

5. Typically eulogies, a formal speech praising a person who has died, are not given at Catholic funerals because the focus is suppose to be on the liturgical readings at the celebration of the Mass. Liturgists contacted by Catholic News Service said a provision in the Order of Christian Funerals states that after communion a family member, or friend, "may speak in remembrance of the deceased. It should be understood as permitting brief, simple remarks, not a full eulogy." *Catholic Vision*, June 2000.

6. *Ma Famille*, 1994, pp.251-253.

7. The mortuary suggested ahead of time to the CSJ Motherhouse that there would be no viewing of the body. Instead, on the evening of the vigil-wake, and through the professionalism of Chaput-Buoy Mortuary, viewers were cautioned to not touch Sister Veronica's body due to extensive reconstruction required for the open casket viewing.

8. "With regard to religious poverty it is not enough to use goods in a way subject to the superior's will, but members must be poor both in fact and in spirit, their treasures being in heaven." (Matt. 6:25) Proclaimed by His Holiness, Pope Paul VI, Vatican II Adaptation and Renewal of Religious Life *Perfectae Caritatis*, October 28, 1965.

9. A slew of books have been published for the layperson such as, *Living the Simple Life: A Guide to Scaling Down and Enjoying More*, Elaine St. James, Hyperion, 1996.

10. The National Catholic Rural Life Conference has taken a stand on the "Spirituality of Recycling," which the CSJ Sisters of Concordia also addressed at one of their Senate meetings in the 1980s.

11. One of the 1994 commemorative Christmas stamps features a Madonna & Child by the artist, Elisabetta Sirani. "The large gold-framed Madonna & child hanging near the piano in the Founder's Room at the CSJ Nazareth Motherhouse in Concordia, Kansas is by Sirani. We have papers stating that our painting, purchased by Mother Antoinette Cuff on one of her trips to Europe (around 1920), is an original; however the New York branch of Sotheby's of London, when contacted, indicated that we could not possibly have an original Sirani painting! Who knows?" Source is unknown, although Sister Veronica is possibly the provider of information, as this came with her letter dated December 6, 1994.

12. These private journals were not located and only her letters are used in this biography.

13. Letter dated Christmas Eve, 1994.

14. This all too real haemorrhagic fever reappeared in Uganda in mid-2000 to claim lives within days of contact.

Chapter Forty-two

1. Sister Veronica willed the quilt to this writer, and it is currently on loan.

Chapter Forty-three

1. The Saindon great-grandparents are buried in Zurich, Kansas.

Chapter Forty-four

1. St. Mary of the Plains College, in Dodge City, Kansas closed in 1992.

Chapter Forty-five

1. Thomas Stauffer. *Arizona Daily Star*, June 1, 1999. p. B1.

2. *Arizona Daily Star*. July 18, 1999, p. A4.

Chapter Forty-six

1. Mrs. Beckman was the housekeeper for Father Mattingly, in Damar, during 1932 when our parents were married there. Mrs. Beckman followed Mattingly to Chapman, Kansas. Then, she began working for the New Almelo parish and is buried there.

2. As told to Father Duane Roy by Sister Veronica Roy.

3. Due to the tenacity of a handful of people of color, among them the Switzer, Van Duvall and Sayers families, who settled in Graham County in the 1800s, nine sites in the small rural African-American colony of Nicodemus, Kansas were declared National Historic Sites through the National Parks department on August 1, 1998.

4. On their Web page, this is officially listed as a grant from the Kansas State Historical Society Heritage Program-Recipient: St. Joseph's Church. New Almelo, Kansas, Community Population Index, 1878-1995, $2,996 grant.

5. Ernesto Portillo Jr. "Stories for the generations," *Arizona Daily Star*, May 30, 2001, p. B1.

6. In 1982, the Bishops of Nebraska applied the social teaching of the Catholic Church by endorsing and actively supporting Initiative 300, the Family Farm Preservation Act, now Article XII, Section 8 of the Nebraska Constitution. Source: www.ncrlrc.com.

7. Idem.

8. Jim Zimmer, "Bio-tech foods helping U.S. farmers," *Arizona Daily Star*, May 23, 2001, p. B7.

9. Phillip Shenon, "Senate Democrats cut back farm-aid bill by $2 billion," New York Times wire, *Arizona Daily Star*, August 4, 2001, p. A11.

Chapter Forty-seven

1. It is this writer's suspicion that Allan had been exposed to radiation while stationed at White Sands Missile Range and Proving Grounds, N.M. However, ironically, he said during his last weeks of life that his U.S. military service there was among his happiest times in life.

2. Miquela Rivera, "Despite loss of last parent, ties can remain." *Tucson Citizen*. Northeast edition. July 18, 2001, p.1NE.

3. "The ties that bind," *Pensacola News Journal*, Feb. 4, 1991, p. D1.

4. *Ma Famille*, p.253.

5. Bill Moyers points out in *Healing and The Mind* that when death is imminent around Christmas, for Christians it is not unusual for the patient to wait to die until the following day.

Chapter Forty-eight

1. Maxims of Perfection. Printing 1979. Chapter III. No. 15. p.5

2. Kathleen Norris, *Dakota: a Spiritual Geography*, Mariner Books, p.59.

3. Fran Cannon Smith, *Arlington* (Virginia) *Catholic Herald*. Letter to editor, October 1996.

4. Mt 18:22; Luke 17:4.

Chapter Forty-nine

1. The sixth commandment: Thou shalt not commit adultery. The ninth commandment: Thou shalt not covet they neighbor's spouse.

2. Bill Repp, "Working Smart," *Arizona Daily Star*, May 11, 2000. Business Section.

Chapter Fifty

1. As a human resources director in the mid-1980s, this writer analyzed the Guildford-Zimmerman Temperament Survey, a paper and pencil profile for Sister Veronica.

2. In the mid-1980s this writer administered the Strong-Campbell Interest Inventory to Sister Veronica and the results were computer analyzed.

3. Rick Kephart, "The Enneagram versus The Catholic Church," rmk@netaxs.com, 1994.

4. Joe Butt webpage

Chapter Fifty-one

1. Edited by Reverend John P. O'Connell, *The Holy Bible* (located in the back). A Practical Dictionary of Biblical and General Catholic Information, The Catholic Press, Chicago, Illinois, 1961, p. 204.

2. It is most likely Sister Veronica deliberately chose a female counselor. There are some controversial claims that it is virtually impossible for a man to treat a woman client effectively. Many women feel another female therapist can reach into her own experiences, and lend a safe and sympathetic ear to deep anxieties. In the safety of another female, a client can admit her fears. This may also be the reason, in part, she resisted the offer later on to be treated by a male therapist.

3. Walters, Barbara, *How to Talk With Practically Anybody About Practically Anything*, Doubleday, 1970. Morris, James, A. Jr., *The Art of Conversation*, Parker Publishing, 1976.

4. Maureen Dowd, "Kay's amazing grace," *Arizona Daily Star*. July 20, 2001, p. B7.

5. Letter in possession of this writer.

6. Master of Arts, Registered Masters Level Psychologist

7. High Plains Clinic main office is in Hays, with branch offices in Colby, Goodland, Norton, Osborne and Phillipsburg.

8. Claudia Bepko and Jo-Ann Krestan, *Too Good For Her Own Good: Breaking Free from the Burden of Female Responsibility*, Harper Collins, 1991.

9. Source in possession of this writer.

10. Tracy Early, "New theology of Mary urged to see her as friend, prophet," *Catholic Vision*, Catholic News Service, June 2000, p.18.

11. Chapter VIII: 1-10.

12. Bi-polar disorder, which typically had not shown up until adolescence, or adulthood, is now showing up ten years to a generation earlier. For an in-depth study see *The Bi-Polar Child: The Definitive and Reassuring Guide to Childhood's Most Misunderstood Disorder*, Demitri F. Papolos, M.D., and Janice Papolos, Broadway Books, New York, 1999.

13. Morris Massey, *The People Puzzle: What You Are Is Where You Were When*, 1979, out of print.

14. Evidence has shown that babies even as young as six months manifest early signs of separation anxiety when they find themselves without their primary caregiver for any length of time. Kenneth J. Doka, Ph.D. editor, *Children Mourning, Mourning Children*, Hospice Foundation of America, 1995, p. 69.

15. Rabbi Earl Grollman, Essay: "Grieving Children: Can We Answer Their Questions?" Ibid., p.18.

16. Alan Wolfelt, Ph.D. *Helping Children Cope with Grief*, Accelerated Development, Inc. 1990.

17. In approximately 1988, Marianna Cacciatore formed Children-to-Children, a grief support agency for children. This was an outcome of her own grief, at age thirteen, following the abduction and murder of Susan Brady, her closest childhood friend. This took place in Rockford, Illinois in approximately 1969. Ms. Cacciatore is currently writing a book.

18. Interview, September 3, 2001.

19. Wolfelt, p.40.

20. Wolfelt, p.64.

21. Source in possession of this writer.

22. VII.9.

Chapter Fifty-two

1. "Judge: Iran owes [Father Lawrence Jenko's] family $315M for priest's kidnapping," New York Times wire, *Arizona Daily Star*, August 4, 2001, p. A17.

2. Among those absent were Michelle Rader, Michael Roy, and David Monarchi, jr.

3. Carol Lichti, *Salina, (Ks.) Journal*. Approximate date Dec. 20, 1995.

4. During her tenure Sister Bette Moslander, CSJ president (1975-1983) opened the Manna

House of Prayer. (Manna means, "What is this?" as in bread from Heaven.) It is an off-site building, which allowed for expanded retreat work. Sister Bette increased the team membership and moved the administrative offices out of the Motherhouse Convent into a remodeled home located eight blocks up the hill. During this time, she also served as president of the Leadership Conference of Women Religious.

5. *Sisters of St. Joseph, Concordia, Kansas* newspaper. Jan./Feb. 2002 p.14.

6. The 1975 edition.

Chapter Fifty-three

1. Christ extends an invitation to those who are overburdened, as He invites each to Himself. Jesus calls us to take His yoke upon our shoulders because it is easy. While the word "easy" can be misunderstood, in this context it means, "well fitted." The message Jesus conveys is that problems and difficulties in life are fitted to one's own strength through God's grace.

Chapter Fifty-four

1. Source in possession of this writer.

Chapter Fifty-five

1. Medicine wheel card to Sister Veronica dated July 14, 1993. Amber Lotus, A Division of Dharma Enterprises, Oakland, California.

2. This was probably based on Harrison Owen's work from 1992.

3. *Sisters of St. Joseph of Concordia*, Kansas newspaper Vol. XVI, No. 3, June 1995, p.2. Five at-large members were elected to serve on the Executive Board: Sisters Clarene Kennedy, Janice Koelzer, Christina Meyer, Jeanne McKenna and Elizabeth Stover.

4. *Northwestern Kansas Catholic Register*, Salina, Kansas diocese. June 29, 1995.

5. In partial fulfillment for the Doctor of Ministry degree, Sister Marcia Allen, CSJ a fellow band member and president (1991-1995) reviewed the book of one hundred Maxims of Perfection in 1997 to reflect the CSJ identity and mission upon the advent of a new millennium.

6. *Stockton Sentinel*, June 1995, p.18.

Chapter Fifty-six

1. Father Charles Miller, C.M., "The death penalty needs a patroness: Maria Goretti," *Catholic Vision*, June 2001, p.19.

2. First published in 1993 in hardcover by Random House, Inc. New York. First Vintage Books Edition, June 1994.

3. Bruce Nolan, "In the Shadow of Death: Nun Shares Agony of Condemned Prisoners While Offering Support to Victims' Families, *The Washington Post*, January 27, 1996, p. C7.

4. October 9, 2001.

5. Rex W. Huppke, " Spare McVeigh: Dead Man Walking author," *Arizona Daily Star*, May 6, 2001, p. A12.

6. Kate Harrison, "Carondelet women retrace steps of 'Seven Sisters,' *Catholic Vision*, August 2001, p.10.

7. St. Mary's is now closed and currently there are 17 Sisters living at the CSJ Médaille Center in Salina, Kansas where her dear friend Sister Frances Alma Royer moved to in July 2001, at age 75.

Chapter Fifty-seven

1. It is believed that Sister Marie Vianney Brunette was the other person.

2. The Sisters of St. Joseph held a Receiving of the Body Service at two p.m. before the family arrived. Sister Esther Pineda presided with the closing hymn of Ubi Caritas, "Where True Love and Charity are Found."

3. Abbot Barnabas Senecal, OSB, Father Regis Hickey, OSB and Father Jude Burbach, OSB, St. Benedicts Abbey, Atchison; Rt. Rev. Monsignor Raymond Menard, Sacred Heart, Salina; Father Paul Becquet CPPS, St. Augustine, Washington; Father Mark Berland, St Francis of Assisi, Norton; Father Kenneth Lohrmeyer, St. Theresa, Manhattan; Father James Grennan, St.

474

Thomas, Stockton; Father John Wolesky, St. Patrick's, Gypsum; Rt. Rev. Monsignor Armand Girard, St. Isidore's Student Center, Manhattan; Father Larry Grennan, Seven Dolors, Manhattan; Father Curtis Carlson OFM, Cap., St. Joseph's, Hays; and Monsignor John George Weber, Salina.

4. Since Vatican II, Sisters were given a choice whether to celebrate their birthday or their feast day, the aniversary of their namesake's death. Sister Francis Walhmeier's was actually two days before.

5. Those in attendance from left to right, back row: Sisters Veronica Roy, Vera Meis, Christine Doman, Francis Cabrini Wahlmeier, Josephine Young, Henrita Deneke, Bernadette Marie Bruggeman, Emerita Scheetz, Mary Clare Sweeney, Rose Moos, Virginia Marie, Donata Bissett, Seated front row: Sisters Leo Francis Winbinger, Eucharista Lewis, Cyrilla Richmeier, Mary Jane Pfeifer, Carm Thibault, Laurentine Reel, Myra Joseph McConn, Rose Estelle Vering, Rose Margaret Stegeman, and Helena Marie Robben.

6. Rolheiser, Ronald, *The Holy Longing: The Search for a Christian Spirituality*, Doubleday, New York, 1999.

INDEX